ADVANCE PRAISE FOR
The Great American University

"I can think of no one better than Jonathan Cole to lead the crucial discussion on the role of the American university as the preeminent seat of intellectual and technological innovation. In the face of alarming trends in legislation and government intervention, he offers a precise and extremely well-written prescription for how the American university can once again prevail."

—HENRY LOUIS GATES, JR., professor, Harvard University

"A passionate and intelligent defense of the university's role in creating knowledge, not just disseminating it. Every university has its own story; this book steps back to tell the history of American universities as a whole. Cole describes the logic, people, and context that drove the universities to pair teaching with research and discovery. He provides an irresistible tour of advances in science and culture that grew in the universities, from artificial hips to Google to eyewitness unreliability, and a clear-eyed view of their failings, from red scares to groupthink. Cole is a compelling advocate, and his book is a resource for academics, students, and all friends of the university."

—CORI BARGMANN, professor, the Rockefeller University;
member of the National Academy of Science

"The story of American universities has been one of great success. Now, at a time when American higher education in general—and American public higher education in particular—is in crisis, Jonathan Cole's *The Great American University* is a timely analysis of higher education's current problems and prospects. I hope that policymakers will heed the author's cogent arguments about the centrality of American universities in the panoply of our national life, as well as their vital contribution to the economic, political, and social advancement of the United States."

—VARTAN GREGORIAN, president, Carnegie Corporation
of New York; former president, Brown University

"Many think that the principal mission of universities is to transmit knowledge; they miss the key point that teaching and research are inseparable. Jonathan Cole, a pioneer in the sociology of science and a visionary leader and spokesman for the academic community in the United States, emphasizes that to produce the best students, American universities must continue to discover new kinds of knowledge and new ways of thinking. If we are to move successfully to maintain American economic and research leadership in the twenty-first century, this academic mission needs to be better recognized, supported, and enhanced. This brilliant book is a must-read."

ERIC R. KANDEL, professor, Columbia University;
Nobel Laureate in Physiology or Medicine

The Great American University

THE GREAT AMERICAN UNIVERSITY

Its Rise to Preeminence

Its Indispensable National Role

Why It Must Be Protected

JONATHAN R. COLE

PUBLICAFFAIRS
New York

PublicAffairs books are available at special discounts for bulk purchases in the U.S.
by corporations, institutions, and other organizations. For more information,
please contact the Special Markets Department at the Perseus Books Group, 2300
Chestnut Street, Suite 200, Philadelphia, PA 19103, call (800) 810-4145, ext.
5000, or e-mail special.markets@perseusbooks.com.

Designed by Brent Wilcox
Text set in 11.5 point Adobe Caslon

Library of Congress Cataloging-in-Publication Data
Cole, Jonathan R.
  The great American university : its rise to preeminence, its indispensable
national role, and why it must be protected / Jonathan R. Cole. — 1st ed.
     p.   cm.
  Includes bibliographical references and index.
  ISBN 978-1-58648-408-8 (hardcover)
  ISBN 978-1-61039-097-2 (paperback)
  ISBN 978-0-78674-619-4 (e-book)
  1. Universities and colleges—United States.   2. Research and
development projects—United States.   I. Title.
  LA227.4.C64 2009
  378.73—dc22
                                                            2009030874

10 9 8 7 6 5 4 3 2 1

For Joanna, Dan, Nick, Nonnie, Gabe, and Lydia

Contents

Preface

I have spent nearly fifty years at Columbia University, first as a student and then as professor and provost. I arrived as a freshman in 1960, earned a degree in history in 1964, and then turned my attention to sociology, receiving my Ph.D. in 1969. A few years later, I became a sociology professor at Columbia, and from 1989 until 2003 I served as provost and dean of faculties (its chief academic officer) before returning to teaching. Some say I bleed Columbia blue. I am, in fact, what they warn universities against: someone who could never cut the umbilical cord and move away from his mother university. It is generally not a healthy thing for either the individual or the university. There are always exceptions to the rule, however, and I would like to think that I am one of them. In any case, over the course of these years at Columbia I have come to appreciate the spirit of innovation and discovery that characterizes American research universities and the contributions the universities have made to science, technology, and our daily lives. Many of the advances that have taken place over the past century in a host of fields, including medical research, genetics, physics, engineering, and even the social sciences and humanities, are due to the pioneering work that has been done at these institutions and the spirit of academic freedom and free inquiry they embody.

During my years at Columbia, I have had the privilege of getting to know many talented faculty members who have been engaged in groundbreaking research. As provost, I also became acquainted with the presidents and provosts of most of America's other great research universities. Observing firsthand how these men and women spent their time, I couldn't help but notice, again and again, their incredible commitment to their work. On campuses from coast to coast, both in the North and in the South, it is their commitment to excellence that has caused our universities

to thrive, particularly over the past fifty or sixty years as the role of the research university has become so firmly established.

Presidents and provosts of universities are an especially hardworking
lot. They often put in seventeen-hour days, six days a week, to improve
the relative standing and quality of their schools. They strive to increase the
resources available to them, to foster relationships between their institutions and their local communities, and to find new ways to improve access
and financial aid, and sometimes they even manage to persuade members
of Congress to adopt legislation favorable to universities and to reject
harmful bills. Then there are the continual capital campaigns to increase
giving by alumni and friends of the university that they must attend to,
and the many hours needed to adequately defend the cost structures of
their schools and to show why additional investments in them are not only
warranted but necessary.

In part as a result of their leadership, our country is blessed with an
abundance of first-rate research universities, institutions that are envied
around the world. Yet, most Americans seem to take their quality for
granted, unaware of what makes them so distinguished. Most Americans
do care about the relative prestige and standing of our universities, especially during those few years when they are faced with the question of
where to send their children as they leave the nest. Magazines and book
publishers have made a fortune producing rankings and assessments of
colleges and universities as a new crop of parents and children seek information every year. But the focus in those contexts is on undergraduate education. This perspective is understandable. In an attempt to keep parents
and fledgling students informed about the opportunities at various schools
and the relative costs, however, we have overlooked some of the reasons
why universities are so important to our society, reasons that go hand in
hand with their ability to educate our youth.

I remember a conversation I had during my tenure as provost when I
met with a group of illustrious Columbia alumni to talk about the quality
of the university. From their extremely intelligent questions I could see
that their knowledge of Columbia was limited largely to their experience
as students. They were interested, appropriately enough, in the quality of
undergraduate teaching. Had we maintained our commitment to Columbia's famous "core curriculum" of studying great works of literature, philosophy, and social science? However, not one person asked, "What are

some of the most important discoveries that Columbia faculty members have produced in the past few years?"

After attending thousands of lectures at which our leading scientists, engineers, humanists, and social and behavioral scientists described their research and discoveries, some driven by pure curiosity and some by an interest in solving practical problems, I presumed that research discoveries would at least be part of our conversation. I was wrong. The research mission of Columbia, the idea that it was as important that Columbia transform the world through the discoveries made by its faculty as it was to educate undergraduate and graduate students, did not enter the conversation. In fact, many in that audience presumed that commitments to both world-class research and teaching at a great university reflected antagonistic goals. I realized at that moment that most people do not fully appreciate what our world-class research universities have been designed to do. There is little sense, even among well-educated segments of the population, of how the transmission of knowledge and its creation are interwoven and highly compatible. Nor is there a clear understanding of how these universities have helped to shape American society, beyond their effects on social mobility. In subsequent conversations with many fellow provosts and presidents, it became evident that we were all frustrated by the incomplete picture that we had painted for the public of our most distinguished universities.

Realizing these shortcomings, I set out to write a book that tells the story of our great American research universities and why they are national treasures, the jewels in our nation's crown, and worthy of our continued and expanded support. I wanted to provide this critically important audience— the general public—with a sense of the origins of the idea of the American research university and of the values that have shaped its structure. It has taken only half a century or so for these universities to establish their international preeminence. I wanted to describe what it took to achieve this, and to provide evidence that these towers of excellence are not just "ivory towers." Instead, they are transforming our lives: There are exceptionally talented scientists and scholars inside those towers making discoveries that are important to all of us.

Given their world distinction and renown, it is perhaps ironic that forces both outside and inside our most distinguished universities are threatening their continued dominant position in the world of higher education. These institutions are more fragile than most people believe, and their contributions to the health and social welfare of the United States could be undermined if we do not recognize their importance, find out what makes them tick, and continue to nourish and guard them. If we are to continue to benefit from the kinds of contributions they are currently making, and allow them to realize their large untapped potential in the decades to come, we must do what it takes to ensure their welfare and growth.

Introduction

She stepped onto the stage before 150 of the nation's leading scholars and scientists to describe her biological research and discoveries. Moving with controlled animation, Bonnie Bassler, a statuesque woman in a stylish black pants suit, with curly black hair and a Cheshire cat–like smile, began describing her path-breaking work. The subject was "Small Talk: Cell-to-Cell Communication in Bacteria." Over the next twenty minutes, Professor Bassler entranced this diverse and acutely analytical audience of the prestigious American Philosophical Society with stories of the molecular mechanisms that bacteria use for intercellular communication.

Standing under a portrait of Benjamin Franklin, the founder of the Philosophical Society, she recounted her quest to understand the chemical mechanism that allows these tiny bacteria, which would be impotent acting alone, to detect multiple environmental cues and to use a process called "quorum sensing" that allows them to function as multicellular organisms. Acting together, the bacteria gain the power and potency to organize collective activity, possibly to strategize, and to assault the body and cause disease. Using quorum sensing, the bacteria are able to count themselves, and after reaching a sufficiently high number, they all launch their attack simultaneously. That way, the bacteria have a better chance of overpowering the immune system. Bassler has demonstrated that this form of chemical communication can be found in some of the world's most virulent microbes, including those that cause cholera and plague.[1]

Working with her students from around the world, Bassler is doing fundamental science at an extremely high level in her laboratory at Princeton University as well as collaborating with others at America's great universities. But she has also embraced the idea held by Benjamin Franklin of doing science in order to create useful knowledge. The bacterial diseases

1

that Bassler studies have special relevance for biological defense against bioterrorism, since many of the pathogens she studies are among those that experts believe bioterrorists would try to use. She works with a goal of developing molecules that will have potential use as antimicrobial drugs aimed at bacteria that can cause lethal diseases, such as anthrax. She wants to find a way to stop the bacteria from "talking." Although Bassler is only in her mid-forties, her work has hardly gone unnoticed. As testimony to her brilliance and creativity, she has already been elected to the prestigious National Academy of Sciences. She was the recipient of a MacArthur Foundation "genius fellowship" in 2002 and in 2004 became a Howard Hughes Medical Institute investigator, a researcher deemed to "have the potential to make significant contributions to science" whose research is supported by HHMI on an ongoing basis.[2]

Bassler is just one of many extraordinarily gifted people found in the laboratories and classrooms of America's great universities. Like them, she is the product of the greatest system of higher learning that the world has ever known, and her work builds on the past achievements of these academies to advance our understanding and well-being even more. What she and others are doing is transforming American society—developing knowledge that helps to generate new industries, to improve public health, and to create higher standards of living for Americans and people throughout the world. These kinds of people exist, of course, in other countries, but they seem to exist in abundance today in America's best universities.

Now I transport you to southeastern China. In 2006 I went there with two former presidents of major American research universities to advise the leaders of a very wealthy province about how to create a world-class university that could compete effectively with Princeton and the other top universities in the United States and Europe within twenty-five years. The assignment was to "start from scratch," unencumbered by any forms of existing mediocrity, and to create a blueprint for greatness. There could be little doubt about the commitment of our hosts. The Chinese we met had a thirst for counting themselves among "the very best" in higher learning. They held the achievements of America's best universities in great esteem, and they viewed the knowledge produced by such institutions as critically important for building China's future. They have a huge population that covets excellence in education and values educational achievement by their youngsters. Getting into the best Chinese universities makes our college entrance process seem easy. And the province had the financial resources and the workforce needed to build greatness.

The Chinese leaders aspire to the excellence that wins Nobel Prizes, just as they aspired to gold medals at the 2008 Olympic Games in Beijing. They understood fully the value of knowledge and intellectual property in creating a modern, technologically sophisticated economy. Many of the fundamental conditions necessary for building a world-class university exist in China today. As we went about interviewing people and assessing the possibilities, we could see that China was intent upon competing with America for preeminence in research universities. Is it possible to imagine that the great American university could lose its dominant position in the world of higher learning to the Chinese over the next half-century? The Chinese, like the Koreans, the Indians, and the Japanese, among others, want to be contenders for the great prizes produced from new knowledge. They are willing to organize their societies with a sharp focus on achieving these goals and, in fact, have already begun to do so.

On one site for university expansion that I visited, a Chinese province had taken over 3,000 acres of farmland and in four years had built more than 50 academic buildings, libraries, laboratories, residence halls, and houses, leaving 1,000 acres for more buildings linked to a world-class university. They were able to accomplish this in a short time because they were willing to simply appropriate the land, assigning about 50,000 workers to the construction projects. In the United States, it would take more than four years to move from start to finish in creating one or two major research facilities on a university campus. Yet despite their ambition and focus, the Chinese, as of 2008, did not have a research university that ranks within the top 200 in the world.

In fact, a 2008 study conducted at Shanghai Jiao Tong University in China evaluating 500 of the world's universities based largely on their research performance found that 17 of the 20 most distinguished research universities were in the United States, as were 40 of the top 50, and 54 of the top 100.[3] Other efforts at ranking universities over the past several decades have reached much the same conclusion. There are many other great universities throughout the world, such as Oxford and Cambridge, Tokyo and Kyoto universities, and the University of Toronto, but American research universities hold a dominant position among the top 100. Other indicators of American preeminence exist. The number of Nobel

Prizes received by our scientists and scholars is one of them. Since the 1930s, roughly 60 percent of all Nobel Prizes awarded have gone to Americans. Before then, a majority went to the Germans, French, and British. In fact, until Hitler came to power in January 1933, German universities were the best in the world. Today, not one German university is ranked among the world's top 50. And as one further indicator of the impact of the American university today, note that a very high proportion of the leading new industries in the United States, perhaps as many as 80 percent, are derived from discoveries at American universities.

Although certain key players in our history have had the vision and energy to lay the foundation for our great universities—sometimes through policymaking at the federal level—it is the thousands of scientists, scholars, and administrators who have been dedicated to their work on a daily basis that have truly put our universities at the top. Their ambition to excel and their fierce competitiveness to be "the best" have led American research universities to become the engine of our prosperity. The laser, magnetic resonance imaging, FM radio, the algorithm for Google searches, Global Positioning Systems, DNA fingerprinting, fetal monitoring, scientific cattle breeding, advanced methods of surveying public opinion, and even Viagra all had their origins in America's research universities, as did tens of thousands of other inventions, devices, medical miracles, and ideas that have transformed the world. In the future, virtually every new industry will depend on research conducted at America's universities. American higher education represents one of the few sectors of the U.S. economy with a favorable international balance of trade. These universities have evolved into creative machines unlike any other that we have known in our history—cranking out information and discoveries in a society increasingly dependent on knowledge as the source for its growth. Thus, a threat to the American research university is a threat to the health and well-being of our nation.

What has made our great universities so distinguished is *not* the quality of our undergraduate education. Other systems of higher learning, including our own liberal arts colleges, compete well against our great universities in transmitting knowledge to undergraduates. At its best, undergraduate education in the United States is exceptionally good, and at its worst it is very poor, but this is simply not what distinguishes great universities from lesser ones. Nor is it our training of graduate professional students that makes our universities the greatest in the world, although we do that very well in comparison with many other nations. In short, although the transmission of knowledge is a core mission of our universities, it is not what makes them the best institutions of higher learning in the world.

We are the greatest because our finest universities are able to produce a very high proportion of the most important fundamental knowledge and practical research discoveries in the world. It is the quality of the research produced, and the system that invests in and trains young people to be leading scientists and scholars, that distinguishes them and makes them the envy of the world. This is true across the board, from the sciences and engineering to the social and behavioral sciences to the humanities. In fact, almost all truly distinguished universities create a seamless web of cognitive influence among the individual disciplines that affects the quality of the whole. That is one reason I believe you cannot build great universities without representation of the humanities as well as the sciences.

The universe of universities that I attend to here is not limited to the elite Ivy League schools and places like Stanford and MIT but also extends deeply into the other distinguished public and private universities in the nation that contribute mightily to this advancement of knowledge through discovery. It is the properties of the *system* of higher learning that fosters creativity and discovery, and that allows knowledge to be transferred and developed by new industries, which have led to their preeminence. These properties attract extraordinarily talented young people from around the world who seek opportunities at American universities as students, scholars, and scientists. And a very high percentage of these intellectual migrants stay here and populate our advanced industries as well as our universities.

If discoveries and the production of new knowledge are the *sine qua non* for greatness, how did American research universities become the best in the world? Why are these universities superior to almost all of those that exist in Europe, Asia, Latin America, and Africa? We needed the right values and social structures, exceptionally talented people, enlightened and bold leadership, a commitment to the ideal of free inquiry and institutional autonomy from the state, a strong belief in competition among universities for talent, and unprecedented, vast resources directed at building excellence to create an unparalleled system of higher learning. These elements, which were necessary for the rise to preeminence, came together at a particular historical moment in the United States. Without them it would have been difficult, if not impossible, to create research universities that are leading sources of innovation and discovery.[4] Thus far, the systems of higher learning in other nations have not been able to put these elements together in a way that rivals what has been achieved in the United States.[5]

When we look back at the history of higher education in the United States, we tend to frame our thoughts in modern terms. Overlooking the dramatic transformation that has taken place over the past hundred years, we fail to recognize how young American universities are and how little time it took for the best of them to become the greatest in the world. Before 1876, for example, there were no advanced research degree programs and no graduate schools devoted largely to research and the training of scientists, engineers, social scientists, humanities scholars, and other professionals.[6]

Today, the United States has a smorgasbord of colleges and universities of vastly different quality. In 2007, roughly 4,300 institutions of higher learning offered one kind of degree or another. Most offer undergraduate degrees only. Perhaps 600 or so offer master's degrees, and about 260 can be classified as research universities. Within this group of 260, only about 125 contribute in meaningful ways to the growth of knowledge.[7] So, even today, perhaps 6 percent of the colleges and universities are classified as research universities. Of these, in 2006, the last year for which we have data, the 87 leading producers of doctoral degrees accounted for almost 60 percent of the more than 56,000 degrees earned in the United States. The members of this small, select group of universities have ambitions to be "full-service" institutions devoted to the transmission and creation of knowledge; to training students for the professions; and to educating, as well, thousands of undergraduates. Though they are small in number, their influence and impact on American society and the world of higher learning has been huge.

My focus here is primarily on the very top tier of educational institutions in our country. These are deeply committed to the production of knowledge and innovation. Even within this elite group, the quality is uneven. Perhaps only 100 are responsible for the lion's share of the most important scientific and technological discoveries, new medical breakthroughs, and new concepts and ideas in the social sciences and humanities.[8] These same elite schools, which are dedicated in many ways to not being elitist, dominate the ranks of the best professional schools of law, medicine, business, architecture, public health, engineering, and social work. They have student populations that vary from less than 5,000 to more than 50,000. Their economic impact on their local communities and on the national and international economies is measured in billions of dollars annually. These exceptional seats of higher learning not only vary in size but also can be found in all parts of the nation. They have vastly different endowments, they have somewhat different missions, and they have very different histories. (A list of these institutions can be found in Appendix A.)

My concentration on the apex of our system of higher education is not intended to diminish the critical value and importance of other parts of our system of higher learning. The thousands of local community colleges, state universities, other large universities, and small liberal arts colleges are essential to flesh out the opportunity structure that exists in the United States like nowhere else. The transmission of knowledge, the teaching of essential critical reasoning skills and curricular content, and the training in skills needed for a society whose economy will increasingly depend on those skills are essential elements in fostering a vibrant system of social mobility in our society. And that mission, while not the principal focus of my book, is under threat as well. These colleges and universities are expected to educate hundreds of thousands of additional students over the next several decades, increasingly a student body coming from diverse backgrounds, and they are being financially squeezed in 2009 to the point that the quality of what they can offer these students will surely suffer. Other books and authors are attending to these problems within these tiers of America's system of higher education. My lens is focused at the top of the hierarchy, on institutions that drive change in our society and that are dynamic forces for the production of knowledge.

This book is divided into three parts. The first tells the story of how our universities were transformed from sleepy colleges to powerful, complex engines of change. I discuss the origins of the idea of these universities and describe the influences on their evolution from a respectable system of higher learning into the world's finest. The values and structures that were necessary for this transformation, and the people who were instrumental in it, are part of this story. My argument for the exceptional stature that American research universities hold today is predicated on their role as the principal source of discovery and innovation in the United States—indeed, in the world. That assertion requires evidence. Therefore, in the next part of the book I discuss in some detail a number of the discoveries made at American research universities that continue to enhance our standard of living and our quality of life. I also attend to those discoveries that are driven by our imaginations and curiosity for which there seem to be no immediate payoffs—

noting that in the past, such discoveries have nevertheless often had enormous practical application in due time. Finally, in the third part of the book I consider the threats faced by these universities today, some of which result from government intrusion into the freedom of academic inquiry.

Efforts by the government to censor science and scholarship have taken several forms in different periods of our history, from excessive monitoring of researchers' activities, due to fears about national security, to attempts to undermine or halt research out of political or moral certitude; from efforts to muzzle the voices of faculty members who hold positions in opposition to current government policies to strategies such as blacklisting and exclusion. Other threats have come from growing competition for distinction emerging in other nations. But still others, including growing intolerance for radically different ideas that challenge orthodoxy or that run counter to the dominant fashion of the day, have grown in the bellies of our great universities themselves. On a different plane, there are now also threats to core university values from the growing commercialization of discoveries made at our great universities as well as from the growing inequalities of wealth among even the strongest and most distinguished of the nation's institutions of higher learning.

Barack Obama's election in November 2008 has produced hope on our great university campuses that the damage done over the past decade may be quickly reversed. There is a sense that a new political enlightenment that nurtures knowledge production and innovation through universities is at hand. But repair work needs to be done, and there is a large gap between understanding the value of university discoveries in the twenty-first century and creating and implementing sound policy. There is much that the Obama administration will need to do, and much that it cannot do independently of other actors, such as state governments. Moreover, these policy changes, some of which are costly, will have to be introduced in the context of the greatest financial crisis since the Great Depression. That financial tsunami has had profound consequences, at least in the short run, on our universities, threatening the quality of some of our most distinguished public institutions of higher education.

This, then, is the story of how the American university came to its state of preeminence, how it could become still greater, and how it is at risk of losing its dominant status.

PART I

THE RISE TO PREEMINENCE

CHAPTER 1

The Idea of a University

A university, like all other human institutions—like the church, like governments, like philanthropic organizations—is not outside, but inside the general social fabric of a given era. . . . It is . . . an expression of an age, as well as an influence operating upon both present and future.

—Abraham Flexner

The modern American university . . . is not Oxford nor is it Berlin; it is a new type of institution in the world. As a new type of institution, it is not really private and it is not really public; it is neither entirely of the world nor entirely apart from it. It is unique. . . . The university is so many things to so many different people that it must, of necessity, be partially at war with itself.

—Clark Kerr

Think about creating an institution of higher learning from scratch. How would you go about it? How would it be organized? And what would its core values be? You would need to establish admissions principles and figure out how to evaluate the progress of the students. You would have to select a faculty, determine how to measure the quality of their work, and mobilize the finances and resources necessary to design and construct a campus.

What should the curricular content emphasize? Who should determine this? How much emphasis should be placed on undergraduate, graduate, and professional education, and what balance should be struck between teaching and research? It would not be possible to accomplish all this alone, so from the outset you would have to enlist others to become leaders of the university in different capacities. But what criteria would you use to choose these leaders? Clearly, you would need people who could relate well to students and faculty, to overseers and trustees, and to the public. But what other qualities should the leaders possess?

Fortunately, you would not have to create your university out of nothing. Americans have been building schools of higher learning since the colonial period, drawing upon European models of higher education but adapting them to reflect their own experiences, values, and ideas of what the new nation needed. The system of higher education that exists in the United States today hardly resembles the colleges of the colonial period created by our founding fathers—people like Benjamin Franklin and Thomas Jefferson—or for that matter the colleges that existed before the Civil War. The idea and the reality of the university have evolved, adapting to changing needs and changing times. The university of today is not wholly new, but it has come a long, long way from the colleges created for an earlier age.

A glance backward at our own history and the linkages between our first universities and the universities of England, France, and Germany shows just how much the idea of the university has changed over time. The evolving idea of the university mirrors shifting values and trends in American society, including our attitudes toward science and engineering, industrialization, social reform, social mobility and opportunity, health care, and national security. It also reflects the American belief in the important role that new knowledge and discoveries play in creating social and economic progress.

The path from our early conceptions of a university to its current form has not been a straight one. Its architects and engineers have had conflicting notions of what the perfect university would be. Some longed for an insulated, ecclesiastical institution behind ivy walls, largely removed from concerns of the larger society. Others saw the university's mission as serving the practical needs of a rapidly growing republic. Some wanted to divorce teaching from research; others wanted research to dominate the university's activities. Those favoring an ecclesiastical model focusing principally on undergraduate education advocated smaller, insulated communities or units governed by rules and values similar to those of families or monastic orders, where town hall–type governance predominated. Others believed that universities were becoming too complex and needed the rules of governance and the structures usually found in large bureaucratic organizations.

Some founders believed that universities should foster curiosity-driven research aimed at solving the most fundamental problems of nature and science, without concern for an immediate, practical payoff in terms of meeting the needs of industry and the public. Others favored an emphasis on the production of applied knowledge. And still others believed that it was impossible to make a sharp distinction between fundamental and applied knowledge, that both forms reinforced each other, and that our universities must support both. Another conflict pitted those who wanted to develop a full-service university—with a host of graduate and professional schools that would train just about anyone—against those who wanted the focus to be almost entirely on teaching and research that would improve critical thinking grounded in a liberal arts tradition.

As the idea of the research university evolved, critics from inside and outside the academy emerged to question nearly every stage of development. Some of these critics were presidents of universities or other leaders in education, such as deans or provosts. Some were scholars. And some were social commentators who argued that universities were overly insulated, defensive about an arcane curriculum, and unresponsive to larger social needs. The result—what we have today—is the product of these clashing perspectives and ideas.

A number of external forces also influenced the evolution of the university: the expanding U.S. population, with its patterns of internal migration and immigration; the needs of war and how we responded to them; the pressures for educational attainment and social mobility within subgroups of the population; the growing role of science in society; the growing importance of professions and professors; and various pressures from state and federal governments. No single person, or set of persons, controlled the destiny of the idea. What resulted was, for all its deficiencies, the greatest system of knowledge production and higher learning that the world has ever known.

THE BEGINNING

In 1636, only sixteen years after the Pilgrims arrived at Plymouth, Harvard College opened its doors to nine students. Although Harvard was not the first college in the colonies—that distinction belonged to the ill-fated university at Henrico in Virginia—it was the first to succeed. It offered a classical course of study modeled on England's Oxford and Cambridge universities. Although Harvard was never officially linked to any religious denomination, the Puritans designed the college "to advance Learning and perpetuate it to Posterity; dreading to leave an illiterate Ministry to the Churches."[1]

It wasn't until sixty to a hundred years later that other private colleges got off the ground. The College of William and Mary in Virginia, chartered in 1693 by King William III and Queen Mary II, was the second oldest in the American colonies. Yale was founded less than a decade later as the Collegiate School in 1701 and was renamed Yale College in 1718, after receiving a generous gift from Elihu Yale "of nine bale of goods, 417 books, and a portrait of King George I."[2] Princeton, which was chartered as the College of New Jersey in 1746, was the fourth college founded in the American colonies and became known as Princeton after it moved to the New Jersey town in 1756. In 1749, Benjamin Franklin outlined a course of education in a pamphlet entitled *Proposals for the Education of Youth in Pensilvania*. Students would be prepared for public service and business, quite a different mission from the ecclesiastical purposes outlined by Harvard and Yale. In keeping with Franklin's interest in science and in promoting useful knowledge, the University of Pennsylvania was designed to produce men of practical affairs rather than scholars or ministers. About one-third of the three-year curriculum was devoted to science and practical studies.[3] Based on Franklin's vision, the College of Philadelphia, later the University of Pennsylvania, was opened to students in 1751.

Next in line was King's College, now Columbia, which occupied a small schoolhouse next to Trinity Church in lower Manhattan in 1754. The University of Virginia opened in 1825 with 123 students. Its extraordinary architecture embodied Thomas Jefferson's vision of an educational village where learning would become integrated with daily life. It had ten pavilions, each the home of a professor and a group of students who were studying a particular subject.

These fledgling colleges were few in number and rarely enrolled students from outside their geographic area. At first, they did not offer a particularly distinguished education. They sought students—they needed them financially if they were to continue to exist—and on occasion they competed for them. Princeton and Columbia competed for Alexander Hamilton, who became one of Columbia College's most distinguished graduates. He might have chosen Princeton had its president and trustees acceded to his demand that he be permitted to move through the curriculum requirements at his own speedy pace. When Hamilton decided on entering King's College, he was seventeen—significantly older than the average student at the college at that time. Most students entered college at the age of thirteen or fourteen. It's no wonder that he wanted to proceed at his own pace, as he was ambitious and almost alarmingly bright.

But Hamilton was an exception to the rule, as this kind of competition for students was rare. In those early days, individual board members would sponsor students, and the admissions process often consisted only of an interview with the college's president. In fact, there were only 9 colleges in the colonies for Hamilton to choose from. These varied somewhat in size and fiscal well-being, but most had similar goals. By 1800, there were 25 American colleges, by 1830 another 24 were added, and by the Civil War in 1861, 133 more had been established, bringing the total to 182. There were, according to Donald G. Tewksbury of Columbia's Teachers College, fully 516 colleges started in the United States prior to the Civil War, but only 104 survived.[4]

Although some colleges were expanding their liberal arts offerings, the principal function of most of these institutions was to educate future ministers. As the colonies grew, local communities created new colleges as a matter of civic pride. Many of these failed, and among those that survived, many offered inferior educations. According to the social historian Richard Hofstadter, "The name 'college' was given to a multitude of institutions ranging from those that respectfully upheld the name of college to some that would not quite honor the title of high school."[5]

European universities had existed for many centuries, and places such as Oxford and Cambridge, founded in the eleventh and early thirteenth centuries, respectively, became models for the early colonial experiments in higher learning. But they prepared the way only through the growth of a small set of undergraduate colleges that by the mid–nineteenth century had added limited programs in medicine, divinity, and law. In 1767, Columbia became the first American institution to grant an MD, and by 1834 Harvard had thirty theological students, eighty students attending medical lectures, and thirty-two law students.

Each of these schools educated elites. The idea of meritocracy—of colleges and universities admitting students on the basis of their talent and academic potential rather than because of their social background—was totally absent. Impersonal criteria such as standardized examinations were unheard of. Caste and class trumped talent in those who had the "wrong" social origins. Your family lineage, where you "prepped," and whom you knew made all the difference in admissions to these places, although there surely were examples of extraordinarily talented young men from less distinguished backgrounds who could be found at the elite colleges (Alexander Hamilton is a case in point). A list of the prominent graduates of the early elite colleges would include most of the founding fathers of the nation, and virtually all of the major voices in the early days of the republic. But until the middle of the twentieth century, these colleges were, with few exceptions, bastions of privilege. Even to the extent that they offered courses of study in the professions and in the classical traditions found in their undergraduate curricula, they had limited numbers of faculty and students, admitted no women, and were, even in the best places, strikingly uneven in quality.

THE GREAT TRANSFORMATION

The contemporary debate over the idea of a university can be traced to a set of nine lectures by the English-born John Henry Newman. Brought up in an Anglican family, Newman converted to Catholicism in 1845 at the age of forty-four and was made a cardinal in 1879. He died in 1890, having produced several highly regarded books. In the lectures he spoke of "the idea of a university" and talked about his efforts to establish a Roman Catholic university in Ireland. He envisioned it as a "training ground for gentlemen."[6] Drawing heavily on his own experiences as an undergraduate at Trinity College, Oxford, he focused on the teaching mission of the university—the transmission and preservation of knowledge rather than the production of knowledge. He provided a blueprint for what he thought a university ought to do and, perhaps of equal importance, what it ought not do.[7]

Newman argued that the university should be divorced from the research enterprise. "If its object," said Newman, "were scientific and philosophical discovery, I do not see why a University should have students; if religious training, I do not see how it can be the seat of literature and science." The creation of new knowledge and its practical application should be left to the great independent societies, such as the British Royal Society, or to research institutes that remained unaffiliated with universities. Though Newman's idea of a university's purpose and structure framed the debate for educators in the ensuing decades, it did not, fortunately, influence the actual evolution of universities—at least in the United States. Some American educators nevertheless referred back to him with some nostalgia in the twentieth century as universities grew to encompass an ever larger set of roles and functions; it was as if they were looking upon an expanding creature with too many organs for their taste, and Newman's simple conception of the university as a place where teaching would prevail held some appeal. But there was no going back—the creature had a life of its own.

Although Newman's idea of the university never gained real traction in the United States, U.S. educators did draw on European models. Many early leaders of American research universities had traveled to universities abroad, where they sought out scholars and scientists in their effort to understand how higher learning was organized in Germany, England, and France. In fact, many studied in Europe and returned to the United States intent upon bringing their experiences to American students. In the early days of the research university, the flow of intellectual migration for students was toward Europe. Those who studied in Germany and in England could do so relatively inexpensively.

During much of the nineteenth century German universities emphasized pure research, and their work was self-consciously divorced from practical application. But by the beginning of the twentieth century the fruits of German research, especially in the sciences—chemistry, for example—would be used for a great many practical purposes, including industrial and military applications. The combination of teaching and research became the distinguishing feature of the system. German universities had four ways of training scholars and scientists. Lectures were used to transmit the results of new research and the reservoir of background materials. The seminar and the laboratory became the structure for advancing new knowledge. And perhaps most importantly, professors taught their students fundamental methods and techniques. These were masters working with apprentices in a defined hierarchy; the faculty was ordered hierarchically as well.

In nineteenth-century Germany technological training, which had a prominent place in German society, was performed at separate institutes, and the Gymnasium offered basic courses and tool courses (equivalent to many of our undergraduate courses). The university was largely indifferent to vocational interests.[8] American visitors were taken with the quality of the professors and their lectures and the way learning was organized in seminars and laboratories, and they relished the freedom of easy intercourse with other students during their time abroad. They did not, however, embrace the German tendency toward the hierarchical and comparatively authoritarian structure they found at otherwise exceptional places like the universities at Berlin and Göttingen.

If the Germans provided us with a blueprint for advanced research, the British provided us with an outline for organizing undergraduate collegiate education. The British model was built around the idea of a college of undergraduates within the larger university—the residential pattern that was most conspicuous at older Oxford and Cambridge colleges. The oldest university in the English-speaking world, Oxford had developed as a federation of loosely affiliated colleges. Undergraduate instruction was, and is still is, organized around small group or individual weekly tutorials between students and faculty on areas of concentration such as philosophy or political science. The colleges had their own facilities and libraries as well as separate and highly variable endowments. The early New England colleges, such as Harvard and Yale, adopted the Oxford and Cambridge organizational pattern.

Throughout much of the nineteenth century Americans interested in higher learning and the university were simply envious of what they saw in Germany. Perhaps this was part of a more general sense of cultural inferiority among many of these observers.[9] But in fact, the German universities were better than those in America. The quality of the scientists and scholars who worked at places like Berlin or Göttingen was reflected in the Nobel Prizes that were awarded in the early decades of the twentieth century. The Nobel was often given for work done at an earlier time; German scientists, along with the French, dominated the prizes in the first three decades of the twentieth century. Most of the future university presidents, those who would transform the idea of the university, admired German universities and had spent time at one. Andrew Dickson White, Cornell's first president, saw "his ideal of a university not only realized, but extended and glorified"[10] when he studied at the University of Berlin. After his experience there, he was determined to do something for American education. His work found its expression with the creation of Cornell.

In his 1878 book on German universities, James Morgan Hart, Cornell's German-trained philologist, wrote that the German ideal was "the ardent, methodical, independent search after truth in any and all its forms, but wholly irrespective of utilitarian applications."[11] Research was what created real life in a university, and this interest in matters of the mind and original discovery attracted superior people to the university—both faculty members and students.

The first American university to emphasize research rather than undergraduate teaching was Johns Hopkins, which opened its gates in 1876, one hundred years after the American Revolution. Johns Hopkins, who had earned his fortune from banking, real estate, and investments in the Baltimore and Ohio railroad, gave his name and his estate of $7 million to build a hospital and a new type of university. The intellectual architects were a group of enlightened trustees along with Daniel Coit Gilman, the first president of Hopkins. In his third annual report, Gilman explained what he and the trustees had in mind for the new university:

> [The Trustees] soon perceived that there was no obvious call for another 'college.' . . . There was no call for another technological or scientific school. . . . On the other hand, there seemed to be a demand for scientific laboratories and professorships, the directors of which should be free to pursue their own researches, stimulating their students to prosecute study with a truly scientific spirit and aim. . . . A continuance of their inquiries led the Trustees to believe that there was a strong demand, among younger men of this country, for opportunities to study beyond the ordinary courses of a college or scientific school; particularly in those branches of learning not included in the schools of law, medicine, and theology.[12]

Gilman, along with fellow students Timothy Dwight and Andrew D. White, who later became presidents of Yale and Cornell, respectively, had received his undergraduate education at Yale. After graduating in 1852, he served for two years as attaché of the American legation at St. Petersburg; while abroad, he visited various German universities, which deeply impressed him.

After rejoining Yale in 1855, he was employed first as a fundraiser for the Sheffield Scientific School, a project that was resisted by those at Yale with a more traditional orientation. Gilman's job was, in effect, to become a promoter of science at Yale.[13] But after just a year, he became a Yale librarian. Gilman remained in this position for a decade. Hardly challenged by his duties, full of intellectual energy, and unsure of his prospects at that institution, he finally began to look for an opportunity to advance in his career. At age forty-one, he became the president of the recently formed University of California, where he began to build what would become one of the greatest state university systems in the country. Gilman was intent on creating a new kind of university in California—not a replica of the old elite colleges of the Northeast.

He didn't remain in California very long. By 1872, after some early, unanticipated struggles with the California legislature and local interest groups over his vision for the university, Gilman was recruited to help create the new Johns Hopkins University. His commitment to promote research and a higher level of advanced instruction, comparable in quality to what he had found in German universities, differentiated him from previous American university leaders.[14] One who was not prone to hyperbole, Edward Shils, a renowned intellectual at the University of Chicago and a perceptive commentator on intellectuals and higher learning, may have nonetheless gone a bit far in calling the founding of Hopkins "perhaps the single, most decisive event in the history of learning in the Western hemisphere."[15] Nevertheless, Gilman's molding of Hopkins' mission represented the beginning of the great transformation in American higher learning. Although Hopkins put a new emphasis on research, it was not about to abandon the teaching mission. For Gilman, a university must have the "freedom" to conduct research, but it had an "obligation" to teach.[16]

Over the next twenty-five years Gilman revolutionized the idea of the American university. In an attempt to clone important features of the German system, he recruited a small but distinguished faculty, and he gave them a great deal of freedom to pursue their research ideas. He believed that recruiting exceptionally able students was equally important. Among the students who studied at Hopkins in those early years were James J. Sylvester, who founded the *American Journal of Mathematics*; Henry A. Rowland, a physicist who helped found the American Physical Society; Herbert B. Adams, the well-known historian; Henry C. Adams, the renowned public finance economist; Josiah Royce, the idealist philosopher; Thorstein Veblen, author of *Theory of the Leisure Class;* John Ely, a major figure in economics; and Thomas Hunt Morgan, John Dewey, and Woodrow Wilson.[17] By 1884, Hopkins had over fifty professors. Almost all of them had studied at German universities (thirteen had received doctorates from them). In short order, Hopkins was being referred to as "Göttingen at Baltimore." Graduate students and faculty formed a community of scholars, attended lectures and seminars, and worked together in laboratories.[18]

When Gilman retired in 1901, Hopkins organized a celebration of his achievements, a major gathering in the winter of 1902. Perhaps the person to best capture Gilman's accomplishments was Woodrow Wilson, who had earned a Hopkins Ph.D. in 1886 and spoke on behalf of alumni. Then a professor but soon to be president of Princeton, Wilson praised Gilman in the grandest of terms, addressing him directly:

> If it be true that Thomas Jefferson first laid the broad foundation for American universities in his plans for the University of Virginia, it is no less true that you were the first to create and organize in America a university in which the discovery and dissemination of new truths were conceded a rank superior to mere instruction, and in which the efficiency and value of research as an educational instrument were exemplified in the training of many investigators. In this, your greatest achievement, you established in America a new and higher university ideal, whose essential feature was not stately edifices, nor yet the mere association of pupils with learned and eminent teachers, but rather the education of trained and vigorous young minds through the search for truth under the guidance and with the co-operation of master investigators.[19]

Another speaker, William Rainey Harper, president of the University of Chicago, emphasized what both he and Gilman valued in the transformation of the university: The spirit of research, once barely recognized, had become within only thirty years the controlling spirit of the university, ripe for further elaboration.

The new American model, with Hopkins leading the way, forced the older elite colleges and their leaders, such as Harvard's Charles William

Eliot, to rethink the idea of the university and its optimal structure. Con-templating the German system of higher learning, Eliot initially said that it would fit Harvard freshmen "about as well as a barnyard would suit a whale."[20] Only after Hopkins demonstrated that graduate research could become the focus of a university—and after it tried to recruit four Harvard professors—did Eliot embrace a model different from Harvard's tradi-tional focus on undergraduate education. It was not that Eliot feared in-novation or competition, or was hostile toward research; he was in fact one of the most innovative presidents in Harvard's history. But he was not an early convert to the new model.

Hopkins emphasized the creation of new knowledge through research. For most of the older American universities, the boundaries between grad-uate research, undergraduate education, and technical training were blurred. But the hybrid American model that emerged by 1900 at places like Harvard, Columbia, Chicago, Cornell, Stanford, and the large state universities, such as the University of Michigan and the University of Wis-consin, included all of these activities—as it still does today.

THE GROWING BELIEF IN SCIENCE AND TECHNOLOGY

The vogue of scientism—the idea of a scientific basis for knowledge, inde-pendent of theological arguments—had a substantial impact on American higher education in the latter half of the nineteenth century. Originating in Europe, Social Darwinism became acceptable ideology, in part because it was particularly congenial to leaders in industry and higher education. For followers of some of the early European sociologists, particularly Herbert Spencer, who coined the phrase "survival of the fittest," science became the means and the rationale behind social progress and perfectibility. Many rob-ber barons found justification for their extreme laissez-faire business prac-tices in the ideas of evolution applied to the social world. Speaking to a Sunday school class, John D. Rockefeller likened his competitive practices to competition in nature: "The growth of a large business is merely a sur-vival of the fittest. . . . This is not an evil tendency in business. It is merely the working-out of a law of nature and a law of God."[21]

Andrew Carnegie responded effusively to the writings of Darwin and Spencer: "Not only had I got rid of theology and the supernatural, but I had found the truth in evolution," he wrote.[22] Gilman persuaded Carnegie to endow an institution in Washington to support independent scientific research through a program of scholarships, fellowships, and permanent appointments.[23] The mission of the Carnegie Institution, established in 1902 with an endowment of $10 million—equal at the time to Harvard's endowment—was to "encourage investigation, research, and discovery." Gilman and Carnegie hoped to reverse "our national poverty in science" and place the United States in the pantheon of great nations associated with scientific discovery.[24]

The giants of American capitalism were some of the early benefactors of the research university. Rockefeller considered his support for the creation of the University of Chicago in 1892—despite his frustration over how much money was involved in building a great university—and for the Rockefeller Medical Institute (later Rockefeller University) to be his greatest philanthropic achievements. The views of Rockefeller, Carnegie, and other captains of industry were profoundly influential. While today's university presidents have to keep their eyes trained on multiple constituencies that might lend support to their schools, in these early days Chicago's first president, William Rainey Harper, had to keep Rockefeller in his line of sight at all times—to the exclusion of almost any other external source of funding or criticism.

Even if the United States in the mid- to late nineteenth century did not lead the world in higher learning, it was as interested as any other nation in importing scientific and technological ideas. Against substantial resistance at Yale, for example, Theodore Dwight Woolsey began to push for advancing the quality of scientific training. Yale could point to a few great mathematicians and scientists who had studied or taught there, such as J. Willard Gibbs, who was widely recognized for his work in thermodynamics and who was undoubtedly one of the best scientific minds of the nineteenth century. But the ethos at Yale was classical, and until the later part of the century the school resisted efforts to provide advanced scientific training.

As American industrialization became increasingly dependent on invention and innovation, industrialists as well as leading educators became interested in upgrading the quality of the science produced at our best universities. Even if parity between science and classical studies remained a future project, by mid-century Harvard had developed plans for scientific education with a gift of $50,000 from the prominent businessman and philanthropist Abbott Lawrence, an early advocate of constructing railroads to promote economic development. Under the strong hand of Louis Agassiz, the distinguished Swiss naturalist who emigrated to the United States in 1845, Harvard started the Lawrence School, which was originally intended to emphasize engineering but in the end fostered the study of natural sciences. Meanwhile, Yale created a School of Applied Chemistry in 1847 and five years later a department of civil engineering. These two structures came together as the Yale Scientific School in 1854 and then morphed (with a gift of $100,000 from Joseph Sheffield) into the Sheffield Scientific School.

The early push to include science in the formal curriculum led Harvard to offer a bachelor of science degree in 1851; Yale added a new degree for science students at roughly the same time. But the science students tended to be "outsiders" at Yale and Harvard. Their degree took three rather than four years to complete, the admissions standards for science degrees were lower, and, at least at Yale, Sheffield students were "not permitted to sit with regular academic students in chapel."[25] Despite the resistance, the idea of scientific schools caught on and led to the creation of science departments in many public and private colleges. Within a few decades, the state-supported land-grant universities would push forward the scientific agenda in higher education, with an emphasis on research to improve agricultural production.

Eliot, who became Harvard's president at age thirty-five in 1869 and would transform the university over the next forty years, held his first teaching appointment at Sheffield; Gilman's first appointment was at the Lawrence school.[26] After the Civil War, a new breed of educational leaders, including Eliot, Gilman, and White, "seized the initiative in American higher education," according to historian Frederick Rudolph, "the way John D. Rockefeller seized it in oil, Andrew Carnegie in steel, Washington Duke in tobacco."[27] The educational reformers were frustrated by the classical curriculum. Reform meant getting more in step with the values and needs of the post–Civil War society, which was becoming increasingly wealthy, industrial, and urban.[28]

As a result of these changes, the number of American scientists began to rise. Some had migrated from Europe, while others were homegrown. Others, such as Samuel George Morton, whose work on classification and taxonomy captured the imagination and interest of Americans outside of the academy, had attended both American and European universities (in Morton's case, the University of Pennsylvania and the University of Edinburgh). Following in the British and French traditions of the great nineteenth-century geologists Charles Lyell and Georges Cuvier, these scientists used extensive data collection to test hypotheses.

Morton is a good example of this new breed of empirically oriented scientists. He published his findings on some six hundred skulls, most of them from American Indians, in 1839. He had tested a hypothesis that had great currency in his day: that one could hierarchically order the races in terms of their average cranial capacity by measuring the size of their brains. As the Harvard paleontologist Stephen Jay Gould has pointed out, "Morton . . . provided the 'facts' that won worldwide respect for the 'American school' of polygeny. . . . [He] won his reputation as the great data-gatherer and objectivist of American science, the man who would raise an immature enterprise from mires of fanciful speculation."[29] Morton's inaccurate reading of his data on cranial capacity supported the idea that Caucasians were blessed with higher native intelligence than the other races. Prominent Americans such as Oliver Wendell Holmes, Jr., as well as Europeans such as Alexander von Humboldt, the statesman and popularizer of nineteenth-century science, greatly admired his work. Morton's research set the stage for the movement to measure human intelligence, which gained widespread acceptance in the first decade of the new century.

The research on IQ did not diffuse into American culture without its early and harsh critics. The preeminent journalist of his time, Walter Lippmann, wrote several essays in *The New Republic* criticizing and questioning the social class biases and presuppositions in IQ tests. In 1922 Lippmann predicted that if the tests really took hold, those in charge of creating them, who controlled the content and classification scheme, would "occupy a position which no intellectual has held since the collapse of theocracy."[30] In fact, IQ testing became the prototype for the Army Alpha test, first administered under the supervision of Harvard psychologist Robert Yerkes in 1917–1918, and eventually taken by 1.75 million American military recruits during World War I.[31] IQ-type tests increasingly shaped the American civil service system, which began hiring by examination in 1883. Similar efforts by American colleges and universities to find standardized measures of aptitude resulted in the Scholastic Aptitude Test, or SAT.

As Lippmann foresaw, test scores ultimately became the keys to positions of power and prestige in the United States. The testing movement,

which drew from ongoing research by psychologists at the newly transformed American research universities, was not inherently conservative.
For all of the flaws in the conception and application of the tests, reformers interested in increasing opportunity and upward social mobility for new
immigrant groups found that testing offered a relatively impersonal way of
assessing ability. Relying on test results could produce a new, more meritocratic system for making admissions and employment decisions. Nevertheless, there is ample evidence that the tests were also used to exclude
certain religious and ethnic groups from elite private universities.[32] "Scientific" measures to sort, classify, and objectify people—as smart or dull,
able or disabled—and to offer "the elect" opportunities that were denied to
others, represented a triumph for those embracing scientific methods at
America's blossoming research universities.

Although the universities in America lagged far behind those in Germany and other parts of Europe, especially in fields such as physics and
chemistry, to say nothing of the social sciences and humanities, American
researchers did make an impact in one area—the field of genetics. European advances in the study of evolution and biological development, and
Gregor Mendel's discovery of the basic rules of inheritance, were impressive, but at the end of the nineteenth century scientists still lacked "an over-
arching sense of how these bold advances were related to one another,"
observed neuroscientist Eric Kandel, winner of a Nobel Prize in 2000.
Genes and chromosomes had yet to be discovered, and it was an American
who finally made that breakthrough.[33]

The work that brought Mendelian heredity, Darwinian evolution, and
developmental biology together was done by Thomas Hunt Morgan at
Columbia University.[34] Trained at Johns Hopkins, where he received his
Ph.D. in developmental biology in 1890, Morgan joined the Columbia
faculty in 1904 and began to conduct experimental research with the fruit
fly *Drosophila melanogaster* in 1907. Working in the famous Fly Room in
Schermerhorn Hall, in 1910 Morgan demonstrated the role that chromosomes play in heredity. He won a Nobel Prize for this monumental scientific achievement in 1933.

Morgan and his students had worked collaboratively, and this was a
profound departure from the German university model. They thus initiated, consciously or not, a different way of organizing American university
science—and in fact advanced training in all disciplines. Morgan produced

a new organizational structure in his lab, altering the nature of the relationship between professors and advanced students: Instead of relating as master and apprentices, they were a team. As Kandel remarked,

> Until the start of the twentieth century, the leading American research universities—Harvard, Johns Hopkins, Columbia, and Chicago—had all been inspired by the model of the German research university, in which the *Geheimrat,* the great scientific leader, ordered the hierarchy of his subordinates. Morgan, however, based laboratory governance on democratic principles of merit rather than seniority. If one were to ask scientists around the world what is unique about America, they point to the university, and to this day foreign scientists are amazed that students working in a laboratory call professors by their first name.[35]

Morgan was interested in coaxing brilliant young scientists into the lab, and he found them at Columbia College and among the graduate students. Once recruited, they worked with Morgan in a free and open atmosphere— perhaps a bit claustrophobically in the Fly Room, which measured all of sixteen by twenty-three feet (it still exists at Columbia). The quality of one's ideas, in Morgan's lab, trumped age, seniority, and rank. Several of his students and "grand-students" (that is, students of students) went on to win Nobel Prizes.

Alfred Sturtevant, whose work as a Columbia undergraduate produced the first chromosome map, reflected on his experience in the Morgan lab: "The group worked as a unit. Each carried on his own experiments, but each knew exactly what the others were doing, and each new result was freely discussed. There was little attention paid to priority or to the source of new ideas or interpretations. What mattered was to get ahead with the work."[36] Herman Muller, who also worked in Morgan's lab, recalled Morgan's resistance to the more modern views of his students, as well as battles over priority and credit.[37] The memories of both men show how different Morgan's lab was from other university labs of the time. And as the norms and values associated with doing science changed, these new practices were gradually assimilated into the very idea of how an ideal research university ought to be organized. The close working relationship between faculty members and their graduate students would become the new standard in most academic disciplines.

FEDERAL GOVERNMENT INVOLVEMENT

To appreciate fully the evolving idea of the university, we must place it in the social and intellectual context of the times. While Congress and President Abraham Lincoln were consumed by the Civil War, they managed nonetheless to produce landmark legislation that had a lasting effect on higher education, the Morrill Act of 1862, which created the seeds of a system of public higher education and produced financial incentives for expansion and research. The legislation would open up unprecedented opportunities for students who could not have previously afforded higher education and supported science and technological training. And when President Lincoln signed a bill creating the National Academy of Sciences on March 3, 1863, he was not only honoring America's great scientific achievements but also establishing a mechanism whereby the government could obtain expert advice on increasingly important technical questions.

During the Civil War, the U.S. Congress boldly produced incentives for expanding the national system of education and innovation and for increasing the quality of higher learning and research. The Morrill Act (1862) and the Hatch Act (1887) were perhaps the most influential of these bills, achieving more for higher education than any other act of Congress until the G.I. Bill of Rights (1944), the expansion of the National Institutes of Health (NIH) in 1947, and the creation of the National Science Foundation (NSF) in 1950. The Morrill Act, signed into law by Abraham Lincoln, provided federal land for states to establish public universities and colleges. The land-grant colleges that emerged were designed for "the liberal and practical education of the industrial classes in the several professions of life."[38] They were to teach mechanical arts, home economics, military tactics, and agriculture, but not to the exclusion of the other liberal arts. The act provided economic incentives for states to initiate academic colleges and university programs of training and research that would meet state needs, have a clear utility, and develop branches of learning related to agriculture and mechanical arts.[39] The first newly created land-grant school under the Morrill Act was Kansas State University, which opened its doors in 1863.

In short order, schools such as Michigan State University and Pennsylvania State University, which had earlier incarnations as agricultural schools, expanded, and flagship state schools like Rutgers, the University of Michigan, and the University of Wisconsin applied for and obtained land-grant status. Even hybrid forms came into being. Cornell is perhaps the best example of the blended approach to university funding. Ezra Cornell and Andrew Dickson White were elected to the New York State Senate in 1863, and both became interested in extending the idea of the land-grant colleges. Cornell provided the seed money for the school. Both he and White wanted to create a university where "'any person,' whether rich or poor, whether male or female, whether black or white, can find instruction in any study."[40] Under White's leadership, Cornell supported instruction and research in a set of privately endowed colleges and at land-grant public colleges, offering a wide range of studies in law, languages, agriculture, architecture, and engineering as well as in more classical subjects.[41] As Frank H. T. Rhodes, Cornell's ninth president (1977–1995), observed, "with the founding of Cornell, a new kind of university came into existence."

The Hatch Act provided federal support for agricultural research at experiment stations that were affiliated with colleges and universities, and in 1914 the Smith-Lever Act used federal funds to support the diffusion of practical information that would lead, in principle, to increased use of knowledge related to agriculture, home economics, and rural energy generated at universities and experiment stations.[42] The great revolutions in agricultural production and scientific breeding can be traced back to the research stations and agricultural programs resulting from the Morrill Act and its successor incentives for state university research, many of which continue to thrive today.

THE COMPETITIVE SPIRIT

The introduction of Ph.D. programs that emphasized the link between graduate students and their faculty mentors attracted scholars at the forefront of their fields and had a significant ripple effect in American higher education. Although the older, elite, undergraduate colleges were small and circumscribed, their leaders had to take note that the future distinction of their institutions might rest on excellence in producing knowledge. Transmitting knowledge to younger students would not be sufficient to match what the European universities were accomplishing. The major American research universities expanded, setting their sights on being the equal of their German counterparts, and by the turn of the twentieth century Harvard, Columbia, Chicago, Hopkins, Michigan, Wisconsin, and Yale were being transformed into research institutions. Some great colleges, like Princeton and Dartmouth, never fully embraced the new model. Princeton, for example, did not create a law school or medical school, and its graduate programs, while exceptionally good, were always small in size compared with those at the other elite, private universities. Nonetheless, university leaders were creating a blueprint for their schools to become American society's principal producers of new knowledge. The new American model had two main goals: producing cutting-edge discoveries and using that knowledge to serve the needs of American society.

Although Yale conferred the first American doctoral degree in 1861, with Cornell (1872) and Harvard (1873) following a decade later, Johns Hopkins became both the largest and the most prestigious producer of Ph.D.s in the early years.[43] (At that time state universities offered fewer Ph.D.s than private institutions, and they began to offer the degree somewhat later; Wisconsin created its first Ph.D. program in 1892, for example.) Columbia and the new University of Chicago focused their efforts and development on advanced learning and in the 1890s rapidly became leading producers of Ph.D.s. In fact, the younger American universities had an easier time reorganizing their focus on graduate Ph.D. education than places like Yale and Princeton, which had far stronger collegiate traditions than newcomers like Cornell, Hopkins, Clark (1889), Chicago, and Stanford (1891). Columbia had less difficulty transforming itself because its leaders were committed to Ph.D. education and its undergraduate alumni were not as vocal as alumni from other Ivy schools in defending the status quo. With no active resistance to change, the transformation of Columbia—under Frederick Barnard, who reorganized the university into graduate faculties that embraced the goals of graduate Ph.D. education, and later under Seth Low and Nicholas Murray Butler—was relatively simple. The new research universities began to produce a sufficient number of doctorates to staff their growing faculties, and many of the leading scientists and scholars had received training in Europe. Freshly minted American Ph.D.s numbered only about three hundred in 1900.

At this time there emerged many features of the American research university that would later become crucial to its growth and excellence, including competition for the best scholars and scientists. At the end of the nineteenth century, new universities with great expectations tried to coax and cajole faculty from other American institutions, or simply outbid the older, prestigious New England and Mid-Atlantic schools for talent. Only two of Hopkins's initial faculty members, Ira Remsen of Williams and Basil Gildesleeve of Virginia, were recruited from other American universities. But that changed. President Eliot of Harvard competed with Hopkins to retain the best of his faculty; although he won only some of these battles, he recognized that an environment emphasizing research and graduate education would appeal to genuine scholars. Gilman also understood this, and it showed when he launched the University of California. Stanford followed the same pattern.

The University of Chicago is perhaps the quintessential example of how a new research university could achieve high standards in very little time. Its founding president, William Rainey Harper, was a wunderkind. He had entered college at age ten, had a bachelor's degree by fourteen, and earned a Ph.D. at eighteen. A spectacled, pudgy man with a round face, he exuded energy and optimism and, as biographer Ron Chernow noted, "captivated people with his visionary ardor."[44] John D. Rockefeller, Sr., enjoined Harper to seek out, recruit, and pay for the best faculty he could find. Taking this command literally, Harper began to recruit top scholars from established universities. Although Rockefeller, always alert to the cost of doing business, was perturbed by Harper's apparent lack of control on spending, he tolerated the president's efforts at building greatness.

Harper had a taste for recruitment, and the combination of his canny sense for quality, effective competitiveness, and deep pockets produced golden results that quickly lifted Chicago into the ranks of America's leading research universities. The school opened with 120 faculty members, with 5 recruited from Yale and 15 from Clark, virtually decimating that young and aspiring university.[45] Harper's organization became a well-oiled, competitive machine, leading to resentment and criticism from some of his academic brethren. Thorstein Veblen reacted to the new-style university leader and his link to Rockefeller by labeling Harper a "captain of erudition."[46]

Harper's competitive zeal and acknowledged accomplishments at recruiting created a precedent that has continued ever since at Chicago, and in fact has become more intense. The other new research universities gained prestige from the announcement effect of these appointments. They also began to realize that faculty talent was a commodity translatable into rapid increases in financial and other resources needed to seed further growth and development. And of course, quality bred quality. Investments in higher quality scientific laboratories or better library collections enabled universities to compete more successfully for talent and to improve the conditions for new discoveries and scholarly achievements. The presence of talented and productive scholars and scientists became a magnet for attracting others in the American academy, foreign scholars, and superior graduate students.

Those were hardly the heady days of academic free agency that we know today. Nevertheless, competition for talent and the flow of talent from one university to another had already become a hallmark of the American system. Later in the twentieth century, as the competition for talent continued to intensify in the United States, competitiveness in Germany, which had been strong in the nineteenth and early twentieth centuries, began to sharply abate.[47]

The changing idea of a university that took hold at the turn of the twentieth century had two other significant effects. It wiped out, on the one hand, many of the old historical advantages that the colleges of the seventeenth and eighteenth centuries possessed. The competitive race for prestige and distinction would be run from a new starting line. Harvard was, in effect, no older than Hopkins, Columbia, Chicago, Cornell, Stanford, or the universities of California, Michigan, and Wisconsin. On the other hand, those older universities that continued to at least nominally place their elite undergraduate colleges at the heart of their mission built a group of deeply loyal and well-heeled alumni who donated regularly to their alma maters. With wise investing, these schools grew formidable endowments, producing what today are vast inequalities of wealth among the same group of elite research universities. Ultimately, dedication to one's undergraduate population provided a significant portion of the resources needed to create and sustain great graduate and professional programs of study.

Public as well as professional curiosity in the comparative prestige and quality of American research universities began to grow in the first decade of the twentieth century, long before it reached its current level of obsession with rankings by everyone from the National Research Council to *U.S. News & World Report*. Even in 1910, those wanting to rank universities confronted questions of what criteria to use. James McKeen Cattell, a Columbia psychologist, classified 1,000 men of science, including most of the academic stars of the day, in terms of their university affiliations. When Cattell collected his information in 1903, Harvard led the top 10 list with 66, and Columbia was next with 60. Next, in order, were the University of Chicago (39.0), Cornell (33.5), the Geographical Survey (32), the U.S. Department of Agriculture (32), Hopkins (30.5), Yale (26.5), the Smithsonian Institution (22), and the University of Michigan (20).[48] Three of these institutions were not universities, of course, but still strong contributors to scientific advancement. The number of legitimate contenders was limited in those days. And Cattell focused on men of science (there were virtually no women of science)—the rankings might have been somewhat different had he looked for eminent social scientists and humanists.

The Carnegie Foundation for the Advancement of Teaching, which was founded by Andrew Carnegie in 1905 and chartered by an act of Congress in 1906, produced an alternative method of rankings. Using data collected in 1908, it evaluated universities by their total income, allocation of resources to instruction, total number of students, size of the instructional staff, student-faculty ratios, average expenditures for instruction per student, and expenditures for instruction per student in excess of tuition. Columbia led the list, followed by Harvard, Chicago, Michigan, Yale, Cornell, Illinois, Wisconsin, Pennsylvania, California, Stanford, Princeton, Minnesota, and Johns Hopkins (which was included in the rankings because "it would be impossible to discuss American universities without including Johns Hopkins, which, though now inadequately financed, has always laid the greatest emphasis upon the distinguishing feature of a university—that is, graduate work").[49]

Perhaps what is most striking about these efforts to evaluate research universities is how little the relative rankings changed over the next 100 years. Whatever the basis for the rankings, the same small group of elite public and private universities would be designated as "distinguished." The top 10 or 15 in 1903 are still rated among the top 20 or so in most studies of university quality. Why has there been such stability in the relative rankings of American research universities?

One explanation is that once these universities gained renown, a "halo effect" enveloped them, and regardless of their subsequent quality they continued to be regarded as prestigious. But this explanation is simplistic; moreover, there is no evidence to support it. A better answer lies in the process of accumulation of advantage. The oldest private and public universities used their early advantage—better faculty attracted stronger students, stronger students meant greater alumni contributions, greater alumni contributions led to better research facilities, better research facilities drew better faculty, and so on. Advantages such as these allowed the top universities to accumulate even more resources from individuals and institutional backers in order to create still greater advantages in competing for talent.[50] There were some exceptions: Clark University, for example, started out as a prestigious school but eventually could not compete successfully with wealthier institutions. Over time, however, small differences in resources and talent, when properly invested and nurtured, produced greater and greater returns—much like the effect of compound interest. In this sense, after 1890, these institutions had a first-mover advantage.

Roger L. Geiger, a historian of education, collected statistics on the changing endowments of sixteen leading American research universities between 1879 and 1939. In 1899, Harvard's endowment was roughly $12.6 million. Columbia actually had a larger endowment at the time, $13 million. At the same time the University of California (all campuses) had $2.8 million, while Michigan had $542,000 and Wisconsin $530,000.[51] By 1939, the value of the endowments of the privates was remarkably varied. Harvard's endowment was far larger than the others, having reached $135 million, while Columbia's had risen to only $70 million. Chicago, which started with $5.7 million at the turn of the century, had caught up with Columbia by 1939, but both great institutions already lagged far behind Harvard and Yale.

A look at today's figures will place the earlier ones in perspective. In June 2007, Harvard's endowment was $34.9 billion, Yale's $22.5 billion, Stanford's $17.2 billion, and Princeton's $15.8 billion. Columbia, in seventh place, had an endowment of $7.2 billion .[52] Public universities were competitive at this level, with the University of Texas's endowment reaching $14 billion, the University of Michigan's totaling $7.1 billion, and the University of California coming in at $6.7 billion. Followers of private universities' endowments continue to ask how such relative endowment equality had morphed into such inequality by the end of the century. The stronger universities had an advantage over their rivals—and the private ones, in particular, had an advantage over the public ones, which depended largely on public financing of their efforts. The relative advantage of the private schools was substantial and would translate into even greater competitive advantages over the course of the twentieth century.

These resources made a difference in the race for academic glory and in the creation of graduate, research-oriented institutions. The top schools were able to translate the loyalty and wealth of their elite undergraduate alumni into gifts for endowments and for buildings that could be used for undergraduate education as well as for graduate study and advanced research. Thus the conditions for accumulation of advantage were put into place. Of course, good investment strategies also paid off. Most people believe that a university's endowment is largely a product of the number and size of the gifts it has received. True, large and generous gifts (roughly 5 percent of gifts to universities account for about 80 percent of the total amount given) set the process of accumulation in motion. But about 80 percent of the current value of major universities' endowments results from appreciation on investments and sophisticated financial management.

THE EXPANSION OF THE IDEA OF A UNIVERSITY

Over the years, research universities have undergone significant "program creep," often despite substantial resistance. American colleges had long had small programs in law, theology, and medicine, but other professional schools were something new. By the beginning of the twentieth century, universities had begun to form schools to cover a broad range of activities removed from the liberal arts and sciences (for example, engineering or business administration). Those that embraced the idea of a full-service university (places like Harvard and Columbia) were sharply criticized by prominent educators such as Abraham Flexner.

A graduate of Hopkins and Harvard who also studied in Berlin, Flexner joined the research staff of the Carnegie Foundation in 1908. He would eventually be instrumental in founding the Institute for Advanced Study (a private, independent institution near Princeton but not formally affiliated with the university). As its first director, he attracted a number of top scientists, such as, most famously, Albert Einstein, as well as noted scholars in other fields. But he is also known for his scathing criticism of American and Canadian medical schools and his role in the development of research universities.

Flexner championed the German model, admired Gilman, and opposed the expansionary tendencies of the new research universities. For Flexner, who worked from 1913 to 1928 for the General Education Board (established as an educational foundation by Rockefeller in 1902), research universities were clearly straying from their essential mission of advanced teaching and research, particularly in the sciences. By 1930, Flexner opined that American universities were insufficiently focused on "the pursuit of knowledge, the solution of problems, the critical appreciation of achievement, and the training of men at a really high level." Instead, they were becoming an incoherent hodgepodge of "teacher-training schools, research centers, 'uplift' agencies, businesses—these and other things simultaneously."[53] He wrote critically of Harvard itself: "It is clear that of Harvard's total expenditures not more than one-eighth is devoted to the *central* university disciplines at the level at which a university ought to be conducted. Who has forced Harvard into this false path? No one. It does as it pleases, and this sort of thing pleases."[54]

Flexner was convinced that universities were trying to do too much: If he had had his way, Harvard would have closed its school of business, and other universities would have rid themselves of journalism schools and other new professional training sites or service activities, which for Flexner had become "incredible absurdities" and "a host of inconsequential things."[55] He was not a snob about what disciplines ought to be represented at a great university, but he was concerned about resources and thought the universities should focus on the arts and sciences and limit the number of cognate disciplines and professional schools to those, like law and medicine, which had long-standing attachments to American colleges.

In the early twentieth century American medical education was in particular disarray. Nationally, it varied enormously in quality, with no standard curriculum, few licensing examinations, and a host of old and outmoded therapeutic philosophies—some that bordered on quackery.[56] The American Medical Association (AMA) had lobbied for decades for standardization in medical education, but nothing had been done. In 1908 the AMA, through its Council on Medical Education (CME), proposed to undertake a survey of medical education through the Carnegie Foundation for the Advancement of Teaching, in the hope that the results would promote standardization. Henry Pritchett, the president of the foundation and a firm believer in reform, chose Abraham Flexner to lead the effort.

At the time there were 155 medical schools in the United States. Flexner, in a whirlwind tour, visited all of them in the following eighteen months. His report, published in 1910, was a devastating critique of the state of American medical education. Perhaps to this day the most famous single report of its kind, the Flexner Report argued that the financial resources, laboratory and hospital facilities, and level of training among medical faculty was insufficient at a significant number of medical schools. As a result, he said, the quality of education suffered. Flexner did not mince words when he concluded: "We have indeed in America medical practitioners not inferior to the best elsewhere; but there is probably no other country in the world in which there is so great a distance and so fatal a difference between the best, the average, and the worst. . . . The point now to aim at is the development of the requisite number of properly supported institutions and the speedy demise of the others."[57]

After the report was published, state governments began to regulate medical education more closely, and their licensing boards required medical schools to strengthen their admissions standards and produce a far more exacting curriculum. By current standards, the requirements for admission to medical school were hardly demanding. Flexner proposed that the minimal requirements be a high school diploma and at least two years of college-level science. His curricular reforms were based on a four-year program, with the first two years concentrating on the study of basic sciences and the last two on clinical training. By 1912, the Council on Medical Education had begun to set accreditation standards that were later adopted by the newly created Federation of State Medical Boards.

Within two decades of the report's publication, profound changes had taken place. Perhaps to no one's surprise, the number of American medical schools dropped to sixty-six by 1935. Flexner's commitment to university-affiliated medical schools led in great part to the decline in the number of unaffiliated, proprietary schools: Fifty-seven of the surviving schools were part of a university. The report represented a watershed moment for medical education in the United States. It produced such transformative reforms that once they were institutionalized, they settled the issue. In fact, it became difficult over the following decades to consider how they might be improved upon.

However, the kind of university that Flexner and others envisioned in the first several decades of the twentieth century never materialized in the United States. By 1930, the American university had evolved into a new form: It was a hybrid of English and German university systems, but an entirely new set of activities had been grafted in, multiplying the foci of higher learning. As Clark Kerr, the innovative president of the University of California in the 1960s, observed, Flexner's ideal university "was as nearly dead in 1930 when Flexner wrote about it as the old Oxford was in 1852 when Newman idealized it."[58] The "multiversity" had been born, and Kerr observed that it was a hydra of a place, a far cry from Flexner's organism.

In Flexner's ideal university, the parts were "inextricably bound together," Kerr said, whereas in the large modern university many parts could be "added and subtracted with little effect on the whole." In reflecting on the emergence of the American research university and what it owed to other traditions in higher learning, Kerr concluded, in 1963, that "a university anywhere can aim no higher than to be as British as possible for the sake of the undergraduates, as German as possible for the sake of the graduates and the research personnel, as American as possible for the sake of the public at large—and as confused as possible for the sake of the preservation of the whole uneasy balance."[59]

Why did these universities want to grow? At the time, there was a widespread belief that size mattered. The number of undergraduates, Ph.D. students, degrees conferred, professional school students, and faculty members all contributed to a university's reputation. The size of the overall budget, the size of the endowment, and the number of volumes in the library collections also were taken as indicators of quality. Though the emphasis on quantity may seem excessive, to some extent these same indicators are used today to measure the quality of universities. Equating the biggest with the best led to expansion, which in turn meant increased revenues. Tuition dollars were the major source of revenue for these universities. In an era when entry requirements and standards were less rigorous than those required in today's highly competitive world of admissions to the top schools, the revenue from admitting students could fuel investments in additional faculty members and university buildings.

The pressure to expand the number of schools and programs at major research universities has persisted for more than a hundred years. Some of the pressure came from the economic needs of the universities, some of it from professional and alumni groups, and some of it simply from the idea that bigger was better. Many of the leaders of the early research universities were highly skeptical about this expansion, seeing it as undermining their fundamental mission. Critics resisted the "full-service" model because they believed that the universities were increasingly controlled by plutocrats who simply did not understand the true mission of a university.

Thorstein Veblen, the distinguished economist, sociologist, and critic of American society (who coined the term "conspicuous consumption" to describe economic behavior that was intended to purchase prestige), defined what he thought should be a university's priorities:

> The conservation and advancement of the higher learning involves two lines of work, distinct but closely bound together: (a) scientific and scholarly inquiry, and (b) the instruction of students. The former of these is primary and indispensable. It is this work of intellectual enterprise that gives its character to the university and marks it off from the lower schools. The work of teaching properly belongs in the university only because and in so far as it incites and facilitates the university man's work of inquiry. . . . The instruction necessarily involved in the university work, therefore, is only such as can readily be combined with the work of inquiry at the same time that it goes directly to further the higher learning in that it trains the incoming generation of scholars and scientists for the further pursuit of knowledge.[60]

Writing in 1918, Veblen criticized the governance structure of the new universities. His "captains of erudition" were too closely tied to "captains of industry." He had contempt for the "bootless conventional race for funds and increased enrollments."[61] For Veblen, the university should be characterized by "highness and definiteness of aim, unity of spirit and purpose." "But it is quite obvious," he said, "that the institutions which we have used for purposes of illustration [Columbia, Harvard, Johns Hopkins, and Chicago]—the best we possess—are ... merely administrative aggregations, so varied, so manifold, so complex that administration itself is reduced to budgeting, student accounting, advertising, etc."[62] Recognizing the need for some type of bureaucratic organization for the university, he lamented what he saw as the endless search for prestige for the institution and power for its president. Thus the president of a university, the "putative director of the pursuit of learning," annexes vocational schools, creates "summer sessions," and hires schoolmasters rather than scholars.[63] Veblen did not believe that American universities could develop as complex, multipurpose institutions within a structure that was markedly different from the German universities he admired.

Other critics of the Progressive era, such as the socialist muckraker Upton Sinclair, were even more caustic and skeptical about the state of higher learning at these new research universities. Sinclair attended Columbia at the turn of the century, after it moved from its midtown Manhattan campus to its new home in Morningside Heights. In his critique he linked higher education with the American "plutocracy," a system in which three major banks controlled more than 100 major American corporations:

> The headquarters of the American plutocracy is, of course, New York City. . . . It is inevitable that this headquarters of our plutocratic empire should be also the headquarters of our plutocratic education. The interlocking directors could not discommode themselves by taking long journeys; therefore they selected themselves a spacious site on Morningside Heights, and there stands the political University of the House of Morgan, which sets the standard for the higher education in America.[64]

Sinclair singled out Nicholas Murray Butler, or "Nicholas Miraculous," as subordinates called the Columbia president. He was, according to Sinclair, "a man with a first-class brain, a driving executive worker, capable of anything he puts his mind to, but utterly overpowered by the presence of great wealth."[65] His hyperbole notwithstanding, Sinclair made it clear that at least some observers of higher learning in America thought the new universities were too closely linked with superrich power brokers, who were not only benefactors of the universities but members of the boards that formulated educational policy. And the presidents of these universities were, if you listened to the critics, becoming ambitious servants of the wealthy and powerful.

University Leaders in Politics

As educational programs increased in size and universities began to influence a broader spectrum of American life, university presidents gained visibility and influence. In the first decades of the twentieth century, they became major players in politics and in the development of social and economic policies for the nation.

Woodrow Wilson, who in 1902 moved from the ranks of a highly popular teacher at Princeton to its presidency, exemplifies this trend. During
his eight years as university president, he tightened academic standards
and created a unified curriculum for freshmen and sophomores; students
would pursue a concentrated study in a specific subject area only as juniors
and seniors. He altered the power structure at Princeton by creating departments whose leaders reported directly to him, and he took hiring decisions out of the hands of trustees and put them into the hands of the
president and department chairs. But despite his success in hiring new faculty members and expanding Princeton's residential, teaching, and research
facilities, he was unable to place Princeton on the same path that Harvard,
Chicago, and Columbia had followed. Though Princeton never added
many graduate schools, it did build a small and highly distinguished group
of doctoral programs in the arts and sciences—still among the best in the
world. Some alumni who wanted Princeton's focus to remain principally on
undergraduate education considered the failure to expand to be a blessing
in disguise.

Wilson decided to leave the Princeton presidency in 1910 to run for
governor of New Jersey; that campaign was successful, and he went on to
win the U.S. presidential election of 1912.[66] That same election year, Butler ran for vice president with William Howard Taft on the Republican
ticket. The web of affiliations among business, government, and university leaders was much more tightly woven than it is today. It seems almost
inconceivable now that a president of a major research university could re-
tire from his post, enter politics, and within two years be elected president
of the United States. Yet in the late nineteenth and first half of the twentieth century, the "interlocking directorates" making up what sociologist
C. Wright Mills called "the power elite" (leaders of academia, politics, and
industry) were much more likely to include university presidents.

Andrew Carnegie was, for example, a great admirer and friend of Butler's, and when the great steel magnate committed $10 million in 1910 to
establish an Endowment for International Peace, Butler was named a
trustee and a director of one of its three divisions. Harvard's Eliot was influential in getting Butler the presidency at Columbia, and President
Teddy Roosevelt attended Butler's inauguration in 1903. Connections like
these enabled leaders of the new research universities to leverage the
wealth and prominence of the Carnegies or Rockefellers into assets for

the developing reputations of their universities.[67] The university presidents and industrial and political leaders of our era are no less connected, but presidents of distinguished research universities almost never pursue political office. Although under the administration of President Barack Obama the ties between government and academia have become stronger than under President George W. Bush, people from academia over the past half-century have been far more likely to serve as advisers or to be named to cabinet positions than to run for political office. They play the role of experts, using their knowledge to help formulate policies as appointed "insiders."

THE EMERGENCE OF ORGANIZED ACADEMIC DISCIPLINES

In 1665, England's Royal Society founded *Philosophical Transactions*, the first scientific journal.[68] This innovation facilitated the growth of knowledge, supported organized disciplinary work, and contributed to a value system critical to research universities. It created the basis for peer review of works submitted for publication as well as a system for judging merit, quality, and competence, placing the critical role of assessment squarely in the hands of experts in the field. To create incentives for scientists to disclose their discoveries to the broader community, and in an effort to reduce the number of priority disputes over who actually made a discovery, the Royal Society attached the date on which it received a scientific paper or manuscript. All of this provided a mechanism for potential replication of reported scientific discoveries and a means by which members of the community could identify and correct errors, as well as a published record of the way knowledge builds on itself. Thus the ingredients were put in place for a reward system of science—one universities could use to evaluate the quality of scholarship produced by their faculties.

The institutionalization of this reward system took a long time, but by the end of the nineteenth century in the United States these mechanisms for evaluating scholarship and for communicating ideas played a critical role in the development of the research university's disciplinary structure and value system. Once again, Gilman early on recognized the necessity of linking the growth of knowledge at research universities with a mechanism for open communication through disciplinary journals. At

Hopkins, he helped form three learned societies, each with an academic journal to promote research: the Modern Language Association (1883), the American Historical Association (1884), and the American Economic Association (1885). The American Mathematical Society was founded in 1888 to promote mathematical research and its various uses. New journals proliferated rapidly. Clark began publishing the *American Journal of Psychology* in 1887; Chicago established the *American Journal of Sociology* in 1895.

Some of the comparative strength of the universities in this early period is reflected in the journals they published. In 1913, Butler expressed the value of scholarly journals as an outlet for publication, noting that the contributions of faculty to these journals signaled the quality of a university:

> The real test and measure of a university's efficiency are not the number of students enrolled, the size of the endowment, or the magnificence of its physical equipment. The true test and measure can be found in the productive scholarship of the university's teachers and in the quality of the men and women who go out with the stamp of the University's approval on them. Columbia is fortunate in having assembled a truly noteworthy company of productive scholars. Hardly a week passes, certainly not a month, without the issuance from the study or the laboratory of some Columbia scholar of a piece of work that is a genuine addition to the literature, the science or the philosophy of our time.[69]

Who is in the best position to assess the quality of scholarly and scientific work in a host of different fields? Until the growth of professional societies and the creation of an organized peer review system, this job was often left in the hands of university presidents, who began to acknowledge how impossible it was to carry out the task. Charles Eliot said of the early days, "Then none of the societies organized for the development and mutual support of learned and scientific men existed. By 1885 I could get some assistance from the proceedings of the learned and scientific societies. At the beginning there was no such aid."[70] As time went on, the locus of authority to determine academic competence and qualifications for academic appointments and promotion was increasingly vested in faculty members, their academic departments, and their peers at other universities. Today, this is almost entirely true.

THE SUCCESS AND THE CHALLENGES
OF THE HYBRID MODEL

By the end of World War I, the American research university had adopted a hybrid structure, folding together the English undergraduate residential college and the German system's emphasis on centers of research and graduate study along with disciplinary specialization. The American mix provided learning for undergraduates and advanced graduate students, training for an increasing number of professional activities, an infrastructure to carry out laboratory research in the sciences as well as in engineering, and extensive library collections for the humanities.

Tension then grew over what should be at the center and what at the periphery of the university and over how it should be governed. In the 1970s, ruminating on the role of university president, A. Bartlett Giamatti, former president of Yale and commissioner of Major League Baseball, said, "Being president of a university is no way for an adult to make a living. Which is why so few adults actually attempt to do it. It is to hold a mid-nineteenth-century ecclesiastical position on top of a late-twentieth-century corporation."[71]

As the leaders in our system of higher education borrowed from the educational traditions of England and Germany, and mixed them with our own national needs, an idea for a new kind of university—an American model—was born. It reflected American values, aspirations, and energy, and its presence was soon felt on the world stage. The challenge was how to articulate and shape the goals, values, and structures in such a way that the result would preserve the "uni" in the university. Only if the center could hold, reinforcing autonomous free and spirited inquiry while also meeting the need for practical training and discovery in a knowledge-based world, could the system work and prosper. Creating that integrated system of values and structures would prove to be a challenge.

CHAPTER 2

Coming of Age in
Tumultuous Times

*When men have realized that time has upset many fighting faiths,
they may come to believe even more than they believe the very
foundations of their own conduct that the ultimate good desired is
better reached by free trade in ideas—that the best test of truth is
the power of the thought to get itself accepted in the competition of
the market, and that truth is the only ground upon which their
wishes safely can be carried out.*

—Oliver Wendell Holmes, Jr.,
Abrams v. United States, 250 U.S. 616 (1919)

The history of universities in America is inextricably bound up with
the history of America itself. At the end of the Civil War, as the
country began the task of rebuilding itself, universities helped to forge a
path ahead. In the early twentieth century, fear of political dissent threatened to escalate into intolerance and repression of the freedoms guaranteed
by the Bill of Rights. America's universities, still taking shape at that time,
were not immune to intolerance; nor were they untarnished by the preju-
dices of mainstream politics and society. Nevertheless, by fits and starts,
they managed in the end to work against forces of repression through the
principle of academic freedom.

Indeed, the protection of ideas and expression from external political interference or repression became absolutely fundamental to the university.

This ideal and other core values also became fundamental to the production of the kind of new knowledge that drove the advances of the "American century," having effects in industry, government, and other areas of American life. Without these core values, the distinguished American universities could not have been built.

THE UNIVERSITY AND THE AMERICAN CENTURY

As literary and social critic Louis Menand wrote in his extraordinary work on ideas in America during the late nineteenth and early twentieth centuries: "The Civil War swept away the slave civilization of the South, but it swept away almost the whole intellectual culture of the North along with it. It took nearly a half a century for the United States to develop a culture to replace it, to find a set of ideas and a way of thinking that would help people cope with the conditions of modern life."[1] Many of the most important ideas that would replace those of old New England were born and nurtured at the young universities.

Within the first fifty years of the birth of the research university in America, from roughly 1876 to 1925, the United States confronted an unprecedented number of problems and changes: the challenges of Reconstruction; the disjunctions produced by the rapid transformation from an agrarian to an industrial society; the emergence of large corporations and the individual capitalists who led them, which produced glaring inequalities of wealth; the increased adoption of science as a means toward social and economic progress; the social and economic costs of a world war; and the emergence of the Progressive era and its drive for reform.

During this period of developing pragmatism, the culture's reliance on theological leaders declined, and the rise of the academic man or "expert" began. The founders of the research universities were linked to the new ideas of a host of thinkers in different fields. Those in the intellectual limelight included pragmatist philosophers and psychologists John Dewey and William James; legal philosophers such as Oliver Wendell Holmes, Jr.; and the stars of the new discipline of sociology—people like Lester Ward and Charles Sumner. A professional culture in law, medicine, and in many academic disciplines developed, and higher education witnessed enormous economic growth. Between 1883 and 1913, the national income quadrupled, but the income of universities and colleges grew by almost elevenfold.[2]

After the Russian revolutions of 1905 and 1917, there was a growing fear that Bolshevism and anarchism would spread across Europe and reach the United States. By 1904, the Socialist Party, under the leadership of Eugene V. Debs, had become the third-largest political party in the United States. The huge influx of new immigrants propelled the labor movement forward. The leftist Industrial Workers of the World, a socialist union organization, was organized by 1905 in Chicago. Running for president in 1912 against Woodrow Wilson, Teddy Roosevelt, and William Howard Taft, Debs won 6 percent of the popular vote, just short of 1 million supporters.

During the campaign Wilson argued for American impartiality in the affairs of Europe, resisting the idea of entry into the great conflict that became World War I. But as events later drew us closer to involvement, Wilson, using high moral rhetoric, enjoined Americans to fight against autocracy and militarism in an effort to make the world safe for democracy. It was a 180-degree turnaround for him on the issue, and his attitude toward repressing dissent against the war was even more striking. By 1916, he was arguing for new legislation that would limit antiwar speech. There should be no tolerance, Wilson claimed, for those who "inject the poison of disloyalty into our most critical affairs." "Loyalty to . . . [the American] flag is the first test of tolerance."

Wilson fought for the passage of the Espionage Act of 1917, which made it a crime for a person to "make or convey false reports or false statements with the intent to interfere" with military success; "to promote the success of [America's] enemies"; "willfully to cause or attempt to cause insubordination, disloyalty, mutiny, or refusal of duty, in the military or naval forces of the United States"; or willfully to "obstruct the recruitment or enlistment service of the United States." Violators of the act could find themselves in jail for up to twenty years. Congress passed the Espionage Act shortly after the United States entered the war, and it passed the Sedition Act, which was designed to suppress virtually all criticism of the war and the draft, less than a year later.[3]

The effort to silence dissent was swift, powerful, and effective. A massive media campaign, led by the journalist and public relations expert George Creel, took shape to bolster support for the war effort. With Creel at the helm, Wilson established the Committee of Public Information, which enlisted the help of artists, writers, journalists, and professors to develop propaganda that would, in Creel's words, "drive home to the people the causes behind this war."[4] This effort demonized Germans and attempted to persuade the American people that "spies and saboteurs lurked behind every bush; that conscription, bond sales, and 'liberty cabbage' were the greatest national blessings since the Bill of Rights, and that the Russian Bolsheviks were merely German agents."[5]

The government also began to prosecute dissenters, focusing on labor leaders, left-wing socialists and anarchists who opposed the war, and other perceived radicals and subversives. Prominent Americans who spoke out against the war, such as Debs, were indicted, convicted, and sentenced to jail (in his case, for a term of ten years). In fact, most of those arrested and prosecuted for their views were members of fringe political groups with little, if any, political clout. They were hardly threats to the nation's security.

As is often the case in times of political repression in the United States, immigrant groups were targeted first and treated most harshly. In California, the Board of Education banned the teaching of German in the public schools, calling it "a language that disseminates the ideas of autocracy, brutality, and hatred." Universities fired German faculty members. Orchestras fired German musicians. In southern Illinois, a mob lynched a man for no apparent reason other than his German blood; the organizers of the mob were acquitted by a jury, which argued that they had acted out of patriotism.[6]

These immigrants had come from the same German society that had built the great universities that were the envy of American leaders of higher learning. Nevertheless, few American university leaders spoke out against the persecution of Germans, and some, like Nicholas Murray Butler of Columbia, actively supported the repression of speech preceding and during the war. The end of the war in 1918 did not end the political repression, which was now focused on the Bolsheviks more than the Germans. The first great Red Scare in the nation's history had begun.

Whipped up by the executive branch of government into a state bordering on paranoia, and backed by highly repressive legislation passed by Congress, the nation placed national security needs above free expression. The Supreme Court reviewed convictions of Espionage Act violations and in 1919, in three separate cases, adopted the position that speech could be punished if it had the effect, or "bad tendency," to promote action—meaning criticism of the war effort or conscription leading to insubordination or obstruction of army recruiting.[7]

But Justice Oliver Wendell Holmes's dissent in another 1919 case, *Abrams v. United States,* began to develop a theory of free expression that was far less tolerant of government restriction on speech. This theory recognized that those in positions of great power, particularly those in control of the federal government, would naturally resist speech when it conflicted with their ideology and policies. Holmes's view would become wholly consistent with the critically important value of free inquiry and academic freedom that defines truly distinguished universities. In *Abrams,* a case involving the prosecution of Russian socialists and anarchists who distributed a few thousand copies of two pamphlets protesting the deployment of American troops to Vladivostok and Murmansk in 1918, Holmes argued:

> Persecution for the expression of opinions seems to me perfectly logical. If you have no doubt of your premises or your power and want a certain result with all your heart you naturally express your wishes in law and sweep away all opposition. . . . *But when men have realized that time has upset many fighting faiths, they may come to believe even more than they believe the very foundations of their own conduct that the ultimate good desired is better reached by free trade in ideas—that the best test of truth is the power of the thought to get itself accepted in the competition of the market, and that truth is the only ground upon which their wishes safely can be carried out.* That at any rate is the theory of our Constitution. It is an experiment, as all life is an experiment. Every year if not every day we have to wager our salvation upon some prophecy based upon imperfect knowledge. While that experiment is part of our system I think that we should be eternally vigilant against attempts to check the expression of opinions that we loathe and believe to be fraught with death, unless they so imminently threaten immediate interference with the lawful and pressing purposes of the law that an immediate check is required to save the country. (Italics added.)

The Court's opinions in the free speech cases had a predictable effect on the young research universities; they began to embrace the spirit of free inquiry. At the turn of the century, philosopher John Dewey, one of the principal architects of the American Association of University Professors (AAUP), had believed that there was relatively little danger to academic freedom in the United States. There had been only a few cases like that of E. A. Ross, a young economist who was fired by Stanford University for his views, or, perhaps more accurately, for speaking out about them even though they were in conflict with the views of university officialdom.

Ross had joined Stanford University's faculty in 1896 after receiving repeated invitations to do so from Stanford's first president, David Starr Jordon. By age thirty Ross had already attained a lofty scholarly reputation, having trained at the University of Berlin and at Johns Hopkins. He first got into trouble at Stanford when, in the midst of Populist opposition to the gold standard, he published a pamphlet, "Honest Dollars," advocating the idea of free silver, and then made several speeches in support of William Jennings Bryan. Those views offended Mrs. Jane Lothrop Stanford, the recent widow of Leland Stanford, who had created the university with his gift. Mrs. Stanford demanded that Jordon dismiss Ross for his political activism.

With some slick academic maneuvering, Jordon saved Ross from expulsion, but when Ross was again outspoken—about the demise of twentieth-century monopolies, especially railroads, which just happened to be how Stanford had made his fortune—nothing could save him from the exit. Some on the Stanford faculty came to his defense—for example, George Howard of the history department, who likened the ouster to the tyrannies of the ancien régime. A few with less stature than Ross, such as his colleague H. H. Powers, also came to his defense. But Powers, too, was given the boot. When Frank Fetter, another Stanford economist, failed to receive guaranties of free inquiry and freedom of expression, he resigned in protest. So did Stanford's only philosopher, the distinguished Arthur Lovejoy, who, along with Edwin R.A. Seligman, would later draft the fundamental statement of principles for the AAUP.[8]

Professors at universities were earning greater renown, but they remained in a weak position to negotiate the terms of their employment. In 1896, there was no tenure at Stanford. Despite government efforts to impose some regulations on unbridled capitalism, general rules of contract applied to university professors almost as much as to industrial workers. These gave employers wide latitude to fire employees.[9] In 1915 John

Dewey, no longer so sanguine about academic freedom, and Arthur Love-joy founded the AAUP. The purpose of the new organization was to devise and implement new rules of professionalism and to defend faculty members who were dislodged from their jobs because their views offended university administrators, benefactors, and trustees.

Academic freedom was still a novel idea, but it would become one of the fundamental values of the emerging profession. This did not happen immediately. The national hostility toward dissent increased markedly between 1915 and the early 1920s, and liberal faculty members were still vulnerable to the exercise of power by their presidents. Strong tenure rules were not yet in place, and organizations such as the American Education Association, the AAUP, and the professional disciplinary societies had little recourse. One stark example of the chilling effect on free expression and inquiry at the new research universities can be found in the 1917 commencement speech by Nicholas Murray Butler to a group of Columbia alumni: "What had been tolerated before became intolerable now. What had been wrongheaded was now sedition. What had been folly was now treason. In your presence, I speak for the whole University . . . when I say . . . that there will be no place at Columbia University, either on the rolls of its faculty or on the rolls of its students, for any person who opposes or who counsels opposition to the effective enforcement of the laws of the United States, or who acts, speaks or writes treason. The separation of such person from Columbia University will be as speedy as the discovery of his offense."[10]

Butler had the support of the trustees, and it did not take him long to act on his threat. James McKeen Cattell, a highly esteemed psychologist and an abrasive critic of what he saw as excessive concentration of power in the hands of university presidents and trustees (and, I should add, a longstanding thorn in Butler's side), provided the president with an opportunity to exercise his authority later that summer. When in August 1917 Cattell wrote to several members of Congress, on Columbia stationery, asking them to "support a measure against sending conscripts to fight in Europe against their will," Butler acted. The professor was notified that after twenty-six years of distinguished scholarship and teaching, his services were no longer needed at Columbia. So that Cattell would not feel alone, the trustees also approved the dismissal of Henry Wadsworth Longfellow Dana, an assistant professor of comparative literature who had opposed America's participation in the war.

There was little faculty protest of these firings, with two notable exceptions. John Dewey resigned from the Faculty Committee of Nine, an organization that represented faculty interests, and Charles Beard, the renowned historian of American history and author of *An Economic Interpretation of the Constitution*, resigned from the university.[11]

There were other faculty firings at other distinguished universities at about the same time, but neither the AAUP nor the American Civil Liberties Union (ACLU) could do much to blunt the power of those in positions to wield it. The AAUP did not usher in an era of academic freedom in America's new universities; nor was the ACLU capable of thwarting repression during the war or the Red Scare that followed it.[12] Still, the birth of organizations like the AAUP represented the beginning of the codification of principles of academic freedom that would lead to inquiries into cases of its violation within universities.[13]

Despite the often hostile environment for liberals at this time, an increasing share of the ideas that shaped American thought and culture were being produced at the universities. While Holmes and other great jurists worked from the bench to develop theories that protected free speech rights, leading scholars at the universities continued to promote academic freedom. Two important themes emerged during this period of intellectual transition. The first was that ideas were products of social relations, not of individuals: They did not develop by some inner logic divorced from the social life and culture in which they were embedded; rather, they were constantly in flux, themselves part of the process of evolution, and one should develop a healthy level of skepticism toward ideology and ideological assertions.[14] The second was that if we were to learn anything from Holmes's opinion in *Abrams*, it was to be eternally vigilant against the suppression of ideas, especially when they seemed particularly loathsome to our own most cherished beliefs.

As these concepts were taking root, the intellectual landscape in America was changing markedly in another important respect as well. In early America, many of the most influential men of ideas were found among the clergy; by the end of the nineteenth century this was no longer the case. The prestige of the clergy steeply declined, as did their wages relative to those of other professionals—and even relative to the wages of skilled workers. If the clergy no longer shaped public opinion, increasingly academic men did. This was in part a result of the emergence of the research university, as the social historian Richard Hofstadter noted: "The sudden emergence of the modern university . . . transformed American scholarship during the last three decades of the [nineteenth] century. . . . The professoriate . . . was . . . acquiring a measure of influence and prestige in and out of the classroom that their predecessors of the old college era would never have dreamed of."[15]

Professions are marked by three essential properties, each somewhat independent of the others: powerful knowledge, considerable autonomy, and a very high level of fiduciary obligation and responsibility to individual clients and to the public welfare.[16] At this time university professors were making gains in all three. By the 1910s, they were formulating a professional identity. It came from a growing sense of mutual dependence between academia and the larger society. The terms for a compact between these two forces slowly emerged, coming in the form of an exchange. The university would produce the highly trained workforce that the increasingly technological and specialized society needed, as well as discoveries about nature and man that could yield practical benefits for American citizens—if not immediately, then down the road—and in return, society would offer the university a singularly important gift: autonomy from external political interference and the right to police its own activities. Experts within the university community, rather than political leaders, legislators, judges, or even trustees, would evaluate the competence of their fellow professors. Ultimately, the implied compact led to elaborate and critically important university reward protocols—the peer review system.

General professional organizations such as the AAUP may have been one element in this march toward professional identity. Organizations representing scholars in specific disciplines, such as the American Chemical Society or the American Sociological Association, exerted even more influence, as did the many academic journals that proliferated at this time. Scientific journals, for example, disseminated the research results of university work to a growing number of people working in the same areas of science, becoming a focal point for the scientific community.

This development of a professional identity at the university level took place during a period of interest in social reform at the national level. The Progressives of the time were not simply insurgent Republicans who cast their fate with Teddy Roosevelt and the Bull Moose Party in 1912.

Progressives were a mix of many types of people and movements and were shaped by several traditions in American and European thought. They took part in liberal reform movements, many of which had their origins in similar movements in England and Germany, and they tended to favor both free inquiry and academic freedom.

Although the various strands of progressive thinking had no common ideology, the Progressives did share common "social languages," as the historian Daniel T. Rodgers explained: "The first was the rhetoric of antimonopolism, the second was an emphasis on social bonds and the social nature of human beings, and the third was the language of social efficiency."[17] Many Progressives wanted to put the brakes on the ravages of market capitalism. Some were interested in reforming political corruption. But the flaws they focused on had less to do with individual character than with the fabric of social life. A majority of Progressives did generally support the movement toward American involvement in World War I, and they were hardly tolerant of dissent against the draft and the war. Rodgers persuasively argued that the roots of much of the Progressive era could be found in the connections between social and intellectual movements in Europe and the United States, claiming there was "an intense, transnational traffic in reform ideas, policies, and legislative devices." "For a moment," Rodgers wrote, "London's East End and New York City's Lower East Side; the 'black country' of Pittsburgh, Essex, and Birmingham; and university debates and chancery discussions in Paris, Washington, London, and Berlin formed a world of common referents."[18]

Although Rodgers argued against an older idea of "American exceptionalism," which was based upon a form of "geocentricism," he did not deny that in many respects America was different. The development of the idea of the American research university offers, it seems to me, strong evidence to support Rodgers's claim that during the Progressive era we borrowed from Europe, building upon the European experience to craft a set of policies and institutions that incorporated some of the older models with what we found at hand, ultimately creating something uniquely American.

There is another way of looking at this critical era that, while not incompatible with Rodger's view, actually places greater emphasis on the role that the emerging research universities played in the "American century."[19] From this perspective, the American model for the research university led to an increasing appreciation for the role that new knowledge plays in a society that depends on the fruits of scientific and technological research. In such a society the need to inform social and economic policy by new scientific and empirical knowledge is very real, and economic growth depends on the creation of new knowledge. As America became a "knowledge society," a matrix of relationships formed among the new producers of knowledge—the great emerging universities—and the developers of that knowledge in the world of industry, in private foundations, and in government.[20] Industry leaders, learning how best to use the new knowledge produced at universities, began to build their own laboratories staffed by graduates of the universities. They formed relationships with individual faculty members, who became their consultants. As these relationships prospered, the fruits of a knowledge society could begin to be realized.

According to historian Oliver Kunz, these partnerships were well established by the 1920s and only became stronger throughout the rest of the twentieth century: "It is the reorganization of knowledge, not merely the power of capital accumulation, that gave Americans the means both to generate prosperity at home and expand their presence into the world," Kunz wrote. "The new institutional arrangements facilitated the buildup of a large military-industrial complex during World War I, the creation of a technology-based consumer economy, and an enormous expansion of consumption."[21]

Some of this had already taken place in other countries, such as Germany. But America was different from Europe. The United States was able to create technological breakthroughs beyond what most other nations were able to do during the twentieth century, according to Harvard economists Claudia Goldin and Lawrence F. Katz, because Americans embraced earlier than others a societal commitment to mass education right up to and including college education.[22] While proving the causal order between increased human capital and technological advance is a formidable task, it seems abundantly clear that these two phenomena are strongly correlated. The requirements of an increasingly knowledge-driven economy are met by larger amounts of human capital, and our ability to produce that human capital better than other nations until the past thirty years or so put America in an advantageous position in terms of economic growth and improvements in standards of living. In short, high-quality undergraduate education has become an essential means for individual social mobility and a societal mechanism for the advancement of social and economic welfare.

During the same formative period, the leaders and some of the faculty members of the new research universities also played roles as policy and political advisers. They became part of the new academic brain trusts, advising presidents, governors, and political candidates, and were at the forefront of the progressive reform movements. Moreover, the universities began to train scientists, social scientists, and philosophers as well as doctors, lawyers, and engineers who would begin to hold prominent positions in society. Americans began to look to the universities for both experimental and empirical research in the sciences and social sciences, relying on them for the data they hoped would help to solve the problems they faced.

In 1907, for example, a group of reform-minded social scientists, including Paul Underwood Kellogg, John R. Commons, Crystal Eastman, John A. Fitch, and Margaret Byington, took the rather primitive social science tools available at the time, such as social surveys and participant-observation studies, and began to gather data on the industrial workers in America's city of steel, Pittsburgh. Organized by Kellogg, who had been a journalist and later was trained at Columbia, a group of more than fifty social scientists documented the living conditions of Pittsburgh's steel workers. They studied the problem of child labor, examined the challenges faced by women in the workforce, and gathered information on worker accidents, inadequate sanitation, and the like. As their model they looked to the extraordinary descriptions and surveys of life and labor in London conducted by Charles Booth from 1886 to 1903, which in turn drew upon the work of French sociologist Auguste Comte.[23] The Pittsburgh Surveys, as they were called, sponsored by the newly created Russell Sage Foundation, became one of the first large-scale attempts in the United States to use empirical research to generate "facts" that could be used to strengthen the Progressive argument for social and political reform.

The Pittsburgh project was not an isolated effort. A growing number of scholars at American universities became active in promoting reform. John R. Commons, professor of economics at the University of Wisconsin, for example, collaborated with progressive state governor Robert M. La Follette to draft the Wisconsin Civil Service Law of 1905 and the Public Utilities Act of 1907—both elaborations of the "Wisconsin Idea" that

University of Wisconsin president Charles Van Hise conceived of in 1904 to foster a partnership between the state government and the university that would use empirical facts to help formulate legislation to improve people's lives. Wisconsin would become a laboratory for social policy experimentation—using economic data, for instance, to draft the first worker's compensation program in the United States.[24] Although active in the reform movement, Commons and many of his students and colleagues, including some who would turn up later as active participants in New Deal reforms, "sought radical change by conservative means." They were trying to reform capitalism, not overthrow it.

The work being done at universities was brought forth not only in state assemblies and governor's offices but also in the courtroom. When Louis D. Brandeis, who was not yet a Supreme Court justice, represented the State of Oregon in *Muller v. Oregon* (1908),[25] he produced a brief that included statistics drawn from sociological and medical journals to demonstrate the adverse health impact that working long hours could have on women. The case involved female laundry workers, and Brandeis had consulted with Florence Kelley, the social reformer known for her advocacy of children's rights and women's suffrage, as well as Josephine Goldmark, who worked for the National Consumers League. His brief, later called "the Brandeis Brief," was the first brief submitted to the U.S. Supreme Court that used extra-legal data to prove an argument; the data were also used by the Court in its decision. The information not only helped Brandeis win the case but also ushered in a new era in which social scientific and scientific data, produced primarily at research universities, would become significant elements in legal arguments.[26]

A VALUE SYSTEM EMERGES

From 1880 to 1930, the values of science and the values taking shape on university campuses in general increasingly converged. Science and technology began to flower as never before, bringing the achievements of seventeenth-century England and nineteenth-century Germany to new heights. The values of science gave rise to the idea of a community of men and women of ideas, scholars and scientists who, under certain conditions, could produce highly original theories and discoveries—ones that ultimately could change the world.

The great transformation of higher learning in the United States represented nothing short of a revolution. It produced, in terms made familiar to us by philosopher and physicist Thomas Kuhn, a fundamental paradigm shift. When educated Americans thought about universities in 1880, if they thought about them at all, they thought of local colleges that focused almost exclusively on teaching: the transmission of knowledge from a professor to his students. This picture was entirely different from what they were apt to conjure up a half-century later. The local colleges had morphed into internationally oriented research universities—still not the best in the world, but with aspirations to that end.

By the end of the 1930s, most of the key ingredients in the making of the great American research university were in place. It was an amalgam of British, German, and distinctly American structures and practices in higher learning. To be sure, many important evolutionary changes would take place over the ensuing decades—changes that should not be underestimated. There would be variations of the basic model—for example, the extraordinary further development of highly specialized universities such as the Massachusetts Institute of Technology (founded in 1861), the California Institute of Technology (1891), and the Rockefeller Institute for Medical Research (1901). But by 1940 the fundamental structure and core values of the system were basically set. The research university had been cast in a form that would last for the rest of the twentieth century and beyond.

These university structures and values were shaped in part by trends in the larger society. One such trend was the general movement from elitism in the United States toward a greater belief in equality. America as "the land of opportunity" became part of the American ethos. People of all classes and backgrounds came to believe that education, particularly higher education, was a route to social mobility, and that talent should prevail in the distribution of social and economic rewards. This idea became an increasingly strong societal value, even if the nation was slow to translate it into practice.

A corollary of this trend was movement from "exclusion" to "inclusion." This shift began during the first decades of the century, and by the 1930s, the doors of universities were starting to open to young people from various ethnic and religious backgrounds. The process toward inclusion of women as well as a broader range of ethnic and religious minorities would have to wait for some time, and inclusion of racial minorities still longer, but at least the shift toward greater diversity had begun. After World War II, this trend would pick up speed, particularly after passage of the Civil Rights Act of 1964. As a result, the base for academic talent was expanded beyond what would have been imaginable during the neonatal years of the research university.

Research universities grew in size and complexity as the U.S. population increased and became more diverse. Because of the increasing societal interest in the results of science and technology, the university curriculum moved away from classical undergraduate training to include science, engineering, and other subjects relating to technological advancement. At the same time, previously rigid curricula offerings became more open; *at many universities* students were encouraged to explore a variety of subjects before settling on one or two areas of concentration. But as society demanded more specialized knowledge, more students went on to postgraduate studies, pursuing not just medical school and law school but also master's and doctoral degrees in many different fields. These degrees satisfied society's need to assure professional competence through certified training and more uniform and rigorous professional standards.

At the same time, these institutions began to think globally. America's attention had shifted away from the domestic concerns that had dominated the Civil War era, Reconstruction, and the Gilded Age, turning outward to focus on World War I, the League of Nations, and the like; the universities mirrored this change as they gained prominence on the intellectual world stage and sought international prestige. Instead of recruiting exclusively from homegrown talent, they wanted to attract the best scholars, scientists, and students from wherever they might be found. Many universities, particularly state universities that had been born as land-grant schools, continued to place a high value on meeting state agricultural and industrial needs, but the best of America's private and public universities added to their portfolios in ways that have produced a truly international orientation.

While early on these universities embraced the idea that path-breaking discoveries and research were at the core of their mission, they had few ways of generating the resources that would be needed to support such endeavors. Philanthropists and private foundations, such as the Rockefeller Foundation, the Carnegie Foundation, and the Russell Sage Foundation,

funded research, training, and travel in critically important ways for scholars and scientists. Nonetheless, during the early years, the research universities had very limited budgets to support research. There was still much
that could be done—it was an age of "little science," in which most laboratory work took place in small spaces, like Morgan's fly room, that were
occupied by a limited number of scientists and students. This type of science could be done at a world-class level in fields like physics and biology
for far less than it would cost today—even accounting for the effects of
inflation. Had the research universities been limited to private sources—as
they were until 2009, for example, in carrying out stem cell research—they
never could have grown into the creative engines they have become. They
needed new streams of revenue to support basic and applied research, and
eventually that would come from the federal government.

Meanwhile, scientific work intensified despite the funding problem,
and the values of science rippled out to other disciplines, becoming key
elements in the evolving idea of the university itself. The core values of
the university system and the norms attached to them consisted of deeply
held beliefs as well as principles that determined how individuals would
act. They were organizing principles designed to support the institution
in meeting its goals and mission. They influenced the types of social
structures that developed to carry out the activities of the university. They
were binding and constraining, in the sense that the faculty and university leaders embraced these values, believed in them, and internalized
them. For the most part they were also consistent with the values based
in the country's democratic foundations that the majority of Americans
were adopting.

Of course, a core value may exist without being fully internalized or realized. But without core values to shape the norms, attitudes, and behavior of those in the academy, the American system of higher learning could
not have become preeminent in the way that it is today. The importance
placed on different core values may vary from university to university, but
in general the same core values are in place at America's most distinguished
research universities. There are a dozen of these that I have identified as
being the most common. There are others, of course, but these twelve, described below, represent an essential cluster. They are ideals defining the
culture of the research university and the characteristic spirit and prevalent
tone of the academic community. The same values have shaped many of

the top universities around the world, but not all nations, as we shall see later, have put all of them firmly in place.

Universalism. Universalism is the belief that new truth claims and assertions of fact are to be evaluated using established impersonal criteria, not based upon the personal or social attributes of the person making the claim.[27] The extension of this value within the university holds that an individual's contributions should be evaluated and rewarded on the basis of merit and not on the basis of personal characteristics such as religion, class, race, nationality, gender, or political opinions. This principle is essential for the effective functioning of a university, as the growth of knowledge cannot truly flourish within a system that selects ideas and rewards people on the basis of particularistic rather than universalistic standards of evaluation. Without universalism—or, put differently, without the application of meritocratic standards—the research university simply could not develop a fair and trustworthy reward system for its members.

Organized Skepticism. This value enjoins members of the academic community to hold a skeptical view of almost anything proposed as fact or dogma, applying appropriately rigorous methodological criteria to claims of discovery or truth. The university, according to this principle, is a place that holds ideas up to the strongest possible substantive and methodological counterarguments and thus also values tolerance of the most radical ideas that may be proposed.

Students are taught to question the narratives that try to persuade them of the truth of a particular point of view, or about claims to truth in the works of science, social science, and the humanities, and they are asked to formulate arguments that test these ideas. This value often places the academic community at odds with other social institutions that display less of a commitment to skepticism about claims to truth and fact. Nevertheless, the academic community generally agrees that proposed theories and explanations must be scrutinized in this manner so that flawed or false ideas may be weeded out, and the stance of skepticism is an essential core value at the top universities.

Creation of New Knowledge. There are many different measures of quality when it comes to research universities: the scientific and scholarly productivity of faculty members; the impact of their work; the awards and honors they have received for discoveries and scholarship; the research resources awarded to them through competitive grant processes; the library and information resources made available to them by their universities; and their access to facilities needed to conduct path-breaking research. Top research universities value the spirit of discovery. They support the creation of new knowledge and have high ratings on all these counts. The ability of American universities to distinguish themselves along this research dimension has set them apart, producing their preeminence and leading to their critical contributions to the welfare of people around the world.

Free and Open Communication of Ideas. For knowledge to grow it must occupy public space. Within the academic community, knowledge becomes common property, placed freely in the marketplace of ideas for examination, criticism, correction, and further development. It is published in various forms. Discoveries are products of social collaboration: They build on what others have done before, using these bricks to enhance and expand the foundations of knowledge. Sir Isaac Newton aptly said: "If I have seen farther, it is by standing on the shoulders of giants." In the world of universities, the open communication of knowledge transcends national borders.

Secrecy, in contrast, impedes the growth of knowledge. Problems arise for universities and for communities of scholars and scientists when external pressure, particularly political pressure, is applied to withhold or delay publication of ideas and discoveries. One can imagine, of course, scenarios where withholding publication of discoveries might be warranted— when, for example, the disclosure of a method for creating a lethal virus or bacteria is apt to get into the hands of people interested in doing great harm with the knowledge. The vexing problem in such situations is how to define clearly the conditions under which protecting the public welfare requires taking the opposite risk—the risk of impeding the growth of knowledge by withholding ideas from public scrutiny. I'll discuss this problem in Part III of the book when I consider the "dual use" dilemma.

Disinterestedness. The value of disinterestedness prescribes that individuals at universities should not profit from their ideas directly. It should not be equated, however, with altruism or a lack of personal ambition. Scholars and scientists are highly competitive and are concerned, sometimes to great excess, about receiving honorific and other forms of recognition for their contributions. The academy in fact often witnesses battles among its members as rivals jostle to establish who made a crucial breakthrough or discovery. When recognition for one's contributions is the coin of the realm, who got there first matters. And it is often the case that scientists who otherwise profess great humility find themselves embroiled in these kinds of disputes.

In the name of disinterestedness, members of the academy are expected to evaluate the scientific and scholarly contributions of their peers. In addition, they must at all costs avoid plagiarism and fraud in their own work. This principle sharply reduces the general level of corruption in academia, since the sanctions meted out following discovery of transgressions are severe, in most cases ruining careers. In fact, because most fakery and fraud—such as the recent scandal over the use of fabricated data in cloning experiments[28]—is usually uncovered in due time, there is strong reinforcement of conformity with these accepted standards of conduct within the university community.

Disinterestedness has been the value most in flux since the middle of the twentieth century. As the monetary worth of intellectual property has increased in purely economic terms, how it should be handled has become a matter of widespread debate. Intellectual property can be a highly lucrative source of income for both universities and individual professors. But are the core values of science and the university corrupted when ideas and discoveries can be bought and sold? Should professors be permitted to personally profit from their discoveries? Are American research universities selling their souls to the devil? This is a question to which I shall return.

Free Inquiry and Academic Freedom. Truly creative scholarship and science can only take place in an atmosphere in which people with talent are given latitude to consider ideas, to push against orthodoxy, and to explore the unknown. Universities therefore place great value on the freedom to conduct research and pursue one's academic interests—and to speak, write, and publish—without fear of interference by internal or external forces. In this sense, the spirit of free inquiry and academic freedom sets universities apart from most other institutions, where political, religious, or social constraints can more easily restrict the introduction of new ideas.

The two interrelated values are based on the premise that when scholars and scientists are permitted to explore their ideas in an unfettered way, they will be more creative, coming up with better solutions to problems. Societies that create conditions for free inquiry, protecting their scientists and scholars from ideological bullies, are apt to produce more profound and significant discoveries, and they are more likely to have truly distinguished universities producing path-breaking original work.

Societies that have failed to embrace this value, such as Germany in the 1930s and China starting with the Cultural Revolution, have either destroyed the creative spirit of universities that once were great or failed to create internationally renowned universities. As Louis Menand pointed out, "Academic freedom is not simply a kind of bonus enjoyed by workers within the system, a philosophical luxury universities could function just as effectively, and much more efficiently, without." Rather, "it is the key legitimating concept of the entire enterprise." The alternative, said Menand, "is a political free-for-all, in which decisions about curricula, funding, employment, classroom practice, and scholarly merit are arrived at through a process of negotiation among competing interests" in which the power is all on one side—and it is not the side of the professors.[29]

International Communities. The top research universities are part of an international community, with ideas crossing national borders in scholarly exchanges of various types. American universities have sought faculty and students with talent regardless of national origins, and the resulting intellectual firepower—the intellectual capital produced—has been enormous. The quality of student bodies—particularly graduate student bodies—and of faculties derives in large part from this aspect of university recruitment.

Peer Review System. Peer review lies at the heart of the process of evaluation and recognition of new work in the scholarly community and figures prominently in the distribution of resources at universities. Via this process, highly qualified experts in a field (one's peers) are called upon to act as judges of the competence and quality of the work produced and to determine the types of rewards and recognition merited.

The system is based on the logical notion that the only people who are qualified to provide detailed critiques of the work of scholars and scientists are the peers of those scholars and scientists—those with a high level of understanding of the field in general and the relative value of new contributions. What qualifies one to be a "peer" in the evaluation system is sometimes debated in the academic community today; nonetheless, appointments and promotions, grant awards, publication in scholarly journals, and assessments of quality depend on a properly functioning peer review system.

Now that the federal and state governments are major supporters of research, members of the general public, and their representatives, have an interest in keeping this peer review system functioning properly. They have the right to know that tax dollars are going to support the work with the most promise and that the peer review system is without fundamental bias. They must be able to trust that the peers are adhering to basic norms of fairness and universalism. If the peer review system appeared to be biased, people would begin to question whether universities could make impartial judgments, and government entities might begin to intervene, setting up a different system to regulate how those monies were spent. Academic freedom might suffer as a result. Therefore, the peer review system lies at the heart of academic freedom and is essential to its continuance.

In fact, periodically legislators and representatives of organizations critical of university professors do question the fairness of the peer review system. Some have claimed, for example, that it is nothing more than an "old boys' network" where scientists and scholars in elite positions scratch each other's backs and reject the work of other academics—generally with less distinguished backgrounds—who are equally deserving of resources or recognition—or even more deserving. Over the past twenty-five years, independent review panels at the National Academy of Sciences, for example, have responded to numerous attacks on the peer review system from members of Congress and others. Several colleagues and I carried out a comprehensive test of the fairness of the peer review system at the National Science Foundation more than two decades ago for the Committee on Science and Public Policy of the National Academy. We found little evidence of systematic bias or discrimination in the distribution of NSF funds, though there was far less consensus than one might have expected among groups of peers about what work (among highly qualified applicants) should be supported with federal grants.

Working for the "Common" Good. The research university places a very high value on producing knowledge that can benefit the larger society. In 1896, when the College of New Jersey changed its name to Princeton University, it took on the informal motto "Princeton in the nation's service." Since then, this dedication to the public good has become part of the stated mission of many institutions. It is achieved in various ways, including by training graduates for a variety of occupations and producing professionals who will become leaders in business, industry, and government. In addition, as is evident in the Obama administration, many faculty members hold temporary government positions or advise our national and local leaders on policy matters.

Governance by Authority. Over the past century there has been a major shift away from the absolute power wielded by university presidents and trustees toward a "company of equals" model in which the faculty has significant governance responsibilities. Although university presidents and provosts have control over many aspects of university life—from the university's public image, administrative structure, and administrative appointments, to its strategic planning, acquisitions, and allocation of financial resources, among other things—they have far less power in determining who should be hired or promoted among the university's faculty than in the past, and they have little control over the curriculum itself. Presidents rule their universities today through a mixture of authority, power, and persuasion. Authority depends on the consent of the governed, and if the tenured faculty members turn against their academic leaders, it is extremely difficult for those leaders to survive.

Universities are loosely governed organizations. The shift to a company-of-equals model has been an important and positive development, but it has also had a number of unanticipated consequences. When research universities are faced with hard choices between competing goods, for example, they often find it extremely difficult to make decisions. With the ambiguity in the university governance structure, it is often unclear who has the final say on the many matters that demand attention. Universities, unlike traditional business organizations, have by and large failed to successfully assign responsibility for decisions to particular members of the community. This often impedes decision making and can become costly. It creates suspicion among schools and departments about the explicitness and fairness of criteria for dividing up scarce resources, and it reduces the flexibility that is needed for institutions to respond imaginatively and reasonably to new academic needs and priorities.

Of course, research universities should not attempt to imitate corporations in their organizational structure. The hierarchical culture of the corporate world would not further the other important aims of the university. However, universities could take some lessons from the business community (especially in their administrative and business offices). The pace of university life, like that of the off-campus world, has speeded up, requiring more rapid responses, greater initiative, and year-round attention to matters of funding, capital projects, curriculum changes, and so on. This new environment requires a clearer process of decision-making so that universities can make meaningful changes and adaptations in a timely way.

Universities, for example, have a distorted conception of the "life cycle" of academic departments, specialties, institutes, and centers. Academics have a marvelous sense of fertilization; we are experts at gestation and early development; we know about maturation and full expansion; but we refuse to confront death and dying. Once something is in place, it is very difficult to get rid of it: The academic way of death for outdated or redundant programs and entities is traditionally through atrophy at a Darwinian pace. A more pragmatic approach on such matters would permit for orderly governance of choice and the conceptual frameworks to guide those choices.

Intellectual Progeny. Teaching and training the next generation of students is one of the two essential roles of faculty members at research universities. Together with scholarly accomplishment, it is of the greatest importance to the idea of a university. Although honors gained from brilliant science and scholarship are far more visible than the teaching function, it would be a mistake to suggest that faculty members at research universities have not internalized this value. A central mission of the university is to transmit knowledge in a form that challenges students to think more clearly and to begin to formulate sophisticated ideas for themselves.

The transmission of knowledge involves much more than exposing students to a canon of works handed down from the past, to collections of facts, or to descriptions of methods and theoretical models. If that were the case, teaching could be done as effectively on the Internet as in the classroom. What is missing in streaming video is the way professors help students to gain analytic skill. This is achieved through the give and take of classroom discussions, much of which continues in the dormitories and dining halls; through the completion of papers and original research; and through the kind of collaboration and mentoring that takes place in labs, in professors' offices, and so on. One of the ways that teachers at universities measure their own success is in the roles that their former students play after they have studied with them. Nobel Prize winners are not alone in taking great pride in the number of their former students who go on to do exceptional work. Most faculty members think of their intellectual progeny as part of their legacy—as testimony to their success in adhering to the core value of teaching at the research university.

The Vitality of the Community. Since younger scholars and scientists produce a high proportion of the most innovative and revolutionary work, the academic community tries to maintain its vitality and excellence by recruiting the highest-quality new talent in the world. There are strong norms within the community to nurture and promote this younger talent. Those who possess it are given positions of intellectual authority within the university. In short, the future excellence of research universities depends on their ability to attract young people with exceptional minds who are capable of producing novel, sometimes disconcerting, ideas.

This is one of the remarkable features of research universities. Their willingness to entertain new ideas—even those that threaten the relevance of older members of their communities—is a mark of their intellectual vitality. Universities often welcome revolutionary and radical ideas and allow them to supersede the very ideas on which members of the faculty have made their reputations. Why? It is because it is the essential goal of these institutions and their members to make both incremental and revolutionary advances in knowledge. Not every new idea is valid—new ideas must be sifted through the peer review process over time—but out of a large pool of new ideas some will be worthwhile or even path-breaking. Although even the academic community sometimes resists dramatically new ideas, they are in general committed to allowing colleagues to express them so that new and improved theories and explanations of nature and human behavior can emerge.

The culture and organization of the research university are determined by this interrelated set of twelve values. For example, faculty members may define their own research problems and strategies for conducting work. They may determine what they will try to publish, and they may submit their manuscripts to peer review via academic journals and book publishers. All of this takes place in an environment where freedom of inquiry and autonomy from external authority are the prevailing norms. It would be inappropriate for an administrator, even an academic administrator, to influence the publication patterns of members of the faculty. The university, as the formal contractor for grants and contracts for research, mediates the relationship between researchers and external funding agencies, but the work actually carried out has been peer reviewed and approved for funding by the funding agency, not by university officials.

These values distinguish the modern American research university from the traditional universities of Europe, which were based on hierarchical forms of authority and power. The system of higher learning that was built in America, rooted in a more democratic structure, was a dynamic one—always in flux, always seeking ways of becoming a better instrument of teaching and research. The values and the structures that emerged from them have always been under some sort of challenge from either internal or external sources. The university fends off these challenges only by maintaining a sense of what its structures are and why those structures optimize the growth of knowledge. If we fail to understand the role these values play in promoting discovery, we will find it more difficult to defend the university's missions. When the values are undermined, then the structures become weak, and once atrophy sets in and doubt begins to reign about the utility of those structures, the conditions for decline exist. This is what I mean when I say that these universities are fragile institutions: Erosion of consensus on the core values of the university could easily lead to structural changes that would undermine the quality of these institutions as well as the pace of advances in the many different disciplines we depend on for our nation's well-being.

It is in fact striking that the idea of the modern American research university—shaped around the idea of free inquiry and openness to talent and ideas, even radical ideas—emerged and stabilized during such a volatile period in American history. An idea that was derived in part from the research activities of German universities was gaining traction at a time when Americans of German origin were being prosecuted under the Alien and Sedition Acts enacted by a former president of Princeton. That these institutions were being organized at a time when socialists and others who voiced opposition to American foreign or domestic policies were being jailed is even more remarkable.

PASSING THE TORCH:
A NEW GENERATION OF UNIVERSITY LEADERSHIP

The "founding fathers" of the American research university put a system that worked into place. They laid a foundation on which resilient structures could and would be built. In this system, the university was detached from government bureaucratic control, and competition among the universities ensured healthy growth. The basic idea of the modern research university was settled by 1930.

Still, unless a new generation of leaders had emerged to extend the idea and clarify the importance of some of these basic values, it is doubtful that the university would have continued to thrive in the next phase of American history. The nation, along with the rest of the world, sank into the Great Depression and had to confront the enormous challenges of World War II. Fortunately, the torch was passed to new university leaders who came of age in the 1930s and 1940s. They reinforced the core values in ways that had broad institutional implications for the welfare of the research university over the subsequent half-century.

Perhaps the two younger leaders having the most profound impact on how the essential values were viewed were Robert Maynard Hutchins, president of the University of Chicago, and James B. Conant, president of Harvard. Both of these men led their institutions for more than a generation. Both wrote extensively about the idea of the university. Both were critics of some aspects of the university model that had evolved, and both were also reformers who tried to alter certain features of what they had inherited. They made important modifications, enabling the universities to fulfill their multiple missions more effectively, without making radical changes in the university's basic structure or core values. In fact, they reaffirmed and extended the core values, setting the stage for further affirmations of the ideals of the university vocalized by successive leaders of the great American universities on their way to prominence. Although each man's influence is worth extended discussion, here I shall just hint at the ways each contributed to the American university model.

Hutchins and Conant both received their advanced education during the period between 1910 and 1920, and both became university presidents at a relatively young age. Men who could not be labeled easily as either conservative or liberal, they had complex personalities, and though they were not entirely successful in their presidencies, they led their universities during difficult times for the nation. Besides the Depression and World War II, during their tenure they saw the beginning of the Cold War, a period of growing national paranoia about the expansion of communism and the political repression that accompanied it. The issues receiving attention in the larger society were issues that very much affected the values of the university.

Hutchins was only thirty when he was named as the University of Chicago's fifth president in 1929, becoming the youngest president ever to lead a world-renowned university. He served as president and chancellor until 1951. His educational reforms did not always succeed, but he nevertheless became the most articulate defender of the core values of the university in the twentieth century. He was a significant innovator in building structures that allowed new knowledge to grow out of exchanges between faculty and students across disciplines. At the end of the day, he had a huge impact on the tone of free inquiry and the open exchange of ideas in every sector of the university.

Hutchins institutionalized other basic values as well, such as adherence to universalistic principles and the use of meritocratic standards for selecting both students and faculty. While Yale and Harvard were either in the process of purging their undergraduate student bodies of Jewish students or had already purged them by the 1930s, Hutchins embraced the presence of Jewish students. Some 25 to 30 percent of the student body at Chicago was Jewish, many from humble backgrounds, many of them gifted individuals, primarily from New York. They were at Chicago because of their ability, and for Hutchins their religion was irrelevant to the admissions process.

His belief in impersonal criteria of admissions pales, however, in comparison with what he did to defend the value of the search for truth and free inquiry. Hutchins's defense of critical reasoning, and the importance he placed on exchanges between conflicting points of view, had a lasting effect on America's system of higher learning. He believed that "the unifying principle of a university is the pursuit of truth for its own sake." "There is only one justification for universities, as distinguished from trade schools," he once said. "They must be centers of criticism."[30]

His desire to have faculty members who would focus on deep questions, on the pursuit of pure knowledge, while maintaining skepticism toward the prevailing orthodoxies and ideological pressures of the day set a standard for other universities. He courageously defended the idea of the university when it was under attack. In the 1930s, a time when many young people were becoming intrigued with Marxist and socialist ideas, Chicago was accused of being a hotbed of subversive activity. When several students were arrested on charges of distributing radical literature, Hutchins came to their defense. "Americans must decide," he said, "whether they will [any] longer tolerate the search for truth. . . . If they will not, then as a great political scientist has put it, we can blow out the light and fight it out in the dark, for when the voice of reason is silenced, the rattle of machine guns begins."[31]

At the height of the McCarthy terror in 1952, Hutchins, having just retired from the University of Chicago, outlined his idea of the essential ingredients of a great university before the House Select Committee to Investigate Tax-Exempt Foundations and Comparable Organizations:

> Now, a university is a place that is established and will function for the benefit of society, provided it is a center of independent thought. . . . Education is a kind of continuing dialogue, and a dialogue assumes, in the nature of the case, different points of view. In this dialogue . . . you cannot assume that you are going to have everybody thinking the same way or feeling the same way. It would be unprogressive if that happened. . . . A university, then, is a kind of continuing Socratic conversation on the highest level for the very best people you can think of, you can bring together, about the most important questions, and the thing that you must do to the uttermost possible limits is to guarantee those men the freedom to think and to express themselves.[32]

If Hutchins reaffirmed our belief in academic freedom and free inquiry, then James B. Conant did perhaps more than any other American educator to reform the basis on which talented people without wealthy pedigrees could obtain access to the most distinguished American universities. In doing so, Conant helped to institutionalize the ideas of meritocracy and universalism. Conant was not always consistent. Within his presidency he articulated conflicting attitudes toward dissent at universities, for example. But his own upbringing outside of the Boston elite, and his work on the Manhattan Project during World War II, led him to reshape the definition of meritocracy at Harvard, where he had been a professor before becoming president.

Conant admired the democratic ideals of Thomas Jefferson and believed in an "aristocracy of talent," and he was determined to transform Harvard into a place where meritocracy prevailed. While a young professor of physical and organic chemistry at Harvard during the 1920s, he had participated in a faculty committee that assessed the admissions criteria at Harvard. He advocated opening Harvard to children of talent regardless of their families' social origins or economic means. President Abbot Lawrence Lowell, who created the famous Harvard house system while presiding over the university from 1909 to 1933, rejected the idea. However, when Conant became president of Harvard in 1933 at the age of forty, he had his chance, and he proceeded to transform Harvard into a far more meritocratic place.

A deep believer in science and aptitude, Conant embraced the testing movement as a mechanism for changing the composition of Harvard's undergraduate student body. He became the principal advocate in higher education for the expanded use of aptitude tests as a means to sort and judge talent and potential. Conant created a small number of four-year national scholarships that would be awarded solely on the basis of merit for students with unusual talent at public schools throughout the country. This idea would create nothing short of a new opportunity structure in American higher education. It was designed to wash away the aristocracy of privilege and replace it with the Jeffersonian ideal of an aristocracy of talent.

The great universities and colleges, taking their cue from the Harvard program, began to search for accomplished students throughout the United States. They found them in places they had never before dreamed of looking, and they provided need-based financial aid and merit scholarships that increased the life chances of talented youngsters whose parents were not wealthy. None of this did away with the intergenerational advantages of wealth and social position. But Conant took the idea that educational institutions of higher learning were the route to social mobility in the United States and gave it form and substance. Ultimately, this practice greatly enhanced the quality of American research universities, enabling them to draw upon a much more diverse pool of talent—including children of new immigrants, foreigners, women, and students of color, all of whom performed exceptionally well as students—in their efforts to build the best universities in the world.

In the decades following World War II, universities experienced many strains and faced other challenges, and they evolved in ways that none of the great innovators could have fully anticipated. Adaptations followed, but none resulted in any fundamental changes in the role of the American research university or its core values. American universities went on to achieve distinction following this initial period of take-off and growth. Next we will identify some of the key forces that transformed these institutions into universities envied throughout the world.

CHAPTER 3

The Path to Greatness

*Take young researchers, put them together in virtual seclusion, give
them an unprecedented degree of freedom and turn up the pressure
by fostering competitiveness.*

—James D. Watson

I f just one moment in history could be said to mark a decisive turning
point for the rise of the American research university, it would be January 1933. Adolf Hitler came to power that month, having been named
chancellor of Germany, and Franklin D. Roosevelt took the presidential
oath of office in the United States. Although no one could have foretold
the horrors that were to come with World War II, Hitler's preeminence
almost immediately set into motion an intellectual migration that drew
the likes of Albert Einstein, physicist-turned-biologist Max Delbrück, and
sociologist Paul Lazarsfeld to America. Numerous scientists and other
scholars, many of them Jewish, fled fascism, and America welcomed them
with open arms as well as with university appointments, research fellowships, and a level of academic freedom they quickly learned to cherish.[1]
As a result, Germany's great educational institutions began to undergo a
rapid transformation, becoming within a few decades second-rate places in
comparison to what they had achieved over the past century.[2]

American universities reaped incalculable gains from the bitter tragedy
of Europe's fascist regimes. Within a year of his appointment as chancellor, Hitler would dissolve the German Parliament, form the SA and the

SS, complete the construction of Dachau, and persuade the German Reichstag to confer dictatorial powers on his government. He established the Gestapo; Germany withdrew from the League of Nations; and the persecution of Jews took an alarming turn, with the government promoting boycotts of Jewish businesses. That spring he also passed the first of what would eventually become a long list of anti-Jewish laws, including one banning Jews from engaging in the practice of law and another barring them from civil service jobs. "Civil service" did not just mean bureaucratic paper-pushers; it meant any job that was funded by the government, and that included schoolteachers and university professors and administrators.

Hitler moved to rid the civil service of non-Aryans as soon as the Enabling Act, which gave his government full decree powers, was signed into law in March 1933. "The Restoration of the Professional Civil Service" law, passed in April, was designed to purge Jews from powerful positions, particularly from university jobs. Max Planck, one of the great leaders of German science, warned Hitler of the consequences of these perverse actions, but without success. Hitler's contempt for pure science was almost as intense as his anti-Semitism—and because of the abundance of German Jewish scientists of world renown, the two were strongly linked.[3] Einstein, the most revered living scientist of the day, arrived in the United States, a refugee from Nazi Germany, by the end of October.

He and Planck were not the only ones prescient enough to see what was coming. Several other German, Austrian, and Hungarian scientists reacted quickly after the Reichstag fire of February 27, 1933. Leo Szilard, one of a group of brilliant Budapest Jews[4] and a key player later in developing the idea of a nuclear chain reaction, went to his friend Michael Polanyi, director of one of the divisions of the Kaiser Wilhelm Institute for Physical Chemistry, and advised him to get out—to take the offer of a position in Manchester, England, and not wait for the unfolding of a disaster.

Polanyi was incredulous. He believed that "civilized Germans would not stand for anything really rough happening." Szilard was not as optimistic as Polanyi. As he tells the story: "I had no doubt what would happen. . . . I had my suitcases packed."[5] Szilard left Germany on a train for Vienna a few days after the Reichstag fire—only slightly before the firing of Jewish instructors and professors began.

The Impact of Immigrant Scholars

The frightening headline in the May 19, 1933, edition of the *Manchester Guardian Weekly* read, "Nazi 'Purge' of the Universities—a Long List of the Dismissals." The reporter simply listed the names of 196 professors who had been dismissed from their posts at German universities between April 13 and May 4. The list was punctuated by the names of some of the most notable scientists and scholars of that generation, including Max Horkheimer, Karl Mannheim, Paul Tillich, Alfred Weber, Paul Courant, Max Born, and Paul Klee. A handful of those who were named—such as James Franck, the Nobel Prize–winning physicist—had resigned their posts in protest over the firings; a few others, such as Paul Tillich, were not Jewish but had fallen into disfavor on the basis of their ethical or political views. This was only the beginning. Efforts to purge Jewish scholars and scientists continued unabated through the full fury of anti-Semitism following *Kristallnacht* in November 1938. That same year, when Vienna fell into Nazi hands, Sigmund Freud, by then eighty-three, escaped to London. No one—and no discipline—was spared.[6]

In all, more than 100 physicists alone emigrated to the United States between 1933 and 1941.[7] This amounted to about 25 percent of the pre-1933 physics community in Germany, and about half of its theoretical physicists.[8] These scientists were exceptionally talented and were of priceless value to the academic community in America—and ultimately to America itself. They entered a youthful and vibrant physics community in the United States; they did not create modern American physics. But they did cause a burst of scientific collaboration and activity to take place in America that led to an unprecedented level of discovery and to applications that would soon have a tremendous impact on society.

At that time the American research universities were just beginning to show their muscles to the world. The quantity of intellectual exchanges between Europe and America had expanded rapidly, thanks to the many traveling fellowships provided by the Rockefeller and Guggenheim foundations. "Traveling seminars"—conferences held at different universities in Europe and the United States—drew American and European participants, who became more familiar with each other's work. Many of the most promising of the young American scientists still studied at German universities such as Berlin or Göttingen, but there were increasing numbers of "home-grown" products in the United States—physicists and chemists such as Robert A. Millikan, Earnest O. Lawrence, I. I. Rabi, Robert Oppenheimer, and Linus C. Pauling—who were building international reputations and academic departments. The work emerging from American research universities was gaining respect and admiration among some of Europe's top scientists and scholars. By the time Hitler came to power, America's research universities were attracting more European postdoctoral physics fellows than the institutions of any other country.

Rabi, who would later participate in the discovery of radar and train future Nobel laureates, felt he had to go to Germany after earning his doctorate in 1927 to learn "at first hand the new quantum mechanics and experimental skills, above all to acquire the taste and style of doing physics on a grand scale." An upwardly mobile child of New York Jewish parents,[9] he was part of a group of young physicists who would help realize Millikan's prophecy of 1919: "In a few years we shall be in a new place as a scientific nation and shall see men coming from the ends of the earth to catch the inspiration of our leaders and to share in the results [of] our developments."[10] The American research universities had not yet become the most distinguished in the world—either in physics or in any other discipline—by the beginning of the 1930s, and yet they were making rapid progress.

The immigrant scholars and scientists were not disappointed by the academic environment they found here. Victor Weiskopf, who emigrated in 1937 after spending time with Wolfgang Pauli in Zurich and Niels Bohr in Copenhagen, spoke of the general atmosphere at American universities: "Within the shortest time one was in the midst of a society that was extremely appealing and active. . . . You had easier access to everybody. . . . It was an extremely productive period for me."[11]

Both Weiskopf and Hans Bethe, who began teaching at Cornell in 1935, remarked that in America professors and students—particularly graduate students—enjoyed a more collaborative relationship than in Europe. Bethe said, "It was customary in Europe to let the professor address the class and talk and write formally on the blackboard and then leave. The students would listen and try to understand. Occasionally a few came forward at the end of the lecture to ask a question or two; whereas here, whenever a student feels like it, he asks a question. I think it is much better."[12]

Nor was the placement of these refugee physicists altogether haphazard. By this time there were groups in both England and America that mounted efforts to find university homes for displaced scholars and scientists affected by the spreading fascism in Europe. In Britain, the effort had been spearheaded by two men with great skill and political finesse: William Beveridge, who would later become head of the London School of Economics; and Lord Rutherford, the dominant figure in English science at the time. Together they had created the Academic Assistance Council in 1933 "to defend the principle of academic freedom and to help those scholars and scientists of any nationality who, on grounds of religion, race, or political opinion, are prevented from continuing their work in their own country." In America, the first president of The New School in New York City created the "University in Exile" in 1933 to provide safe haven for fleeing scholars and intellectuals. Leo Szilard and others also worked tirelessly to find opportunities for the émigrés.

As a result, scholars found homes at universities that could use their specific abilities. The "placements" did not constrain the new refugees. On the contrary, they opened up new opportunities for them to collaborate and allowed for them to travel in order to share their knowledge freely with others, and vice versa. Bethe, for example, attended theoretical physics meetings in Washington and presented papers at the American Physical Society meetings within weeks of his arrival at Cornell.[13]

Physics was hardly the only field to benefit from the tearing asunder of the German educational system. Another was genetics, which, though typically considered an interest of biologists, actually gained a great deal from the collaboration between biologists and physicists at that time. Max Delbrück, for example, who came to the United States in 1937 to join the faculty at Caltech, was interested in the intersection between physics and biology and given the freedom to explore that interest.[14] By then it was clear that his academic opportunities in Germany no longer existed. Delbrück brought a fresh perspective to the field of genetics that ultimately helped to pave the way for the advances that James Watson and Francis Crick made in understanding the DNA molecule.[15]

Watson and Crick's discoveries in fact built on the work of many other scientists. As Harvard historian of science Donald Fleming put it: "One of the most remarkable by-products of the European diaspora of the 1930s was the profound stimulus given by refugee physicists to the revolution in biology symbolized by the Watson-Crick model of DNA unveiled in 1952."[16] The Watson-Crick discovery of the double-helical structure of the

DNA molecule, which was published in their famous *Nature* paper of April 1953, owed a lot to the work of Oswald Avery and his colleagues at Rockefeller University (which suggested fairly conclusively that DNA was the carrier of heredity material), but Watson and Crick were equally indebted to the new biology introduced to America by Delbrück, Salvador Luria, Leo Szilard, and Erwin Schrödinger. All but Luria were physicists by training who had been instrumental in the development of quantum mechanics.

The physicists were in search of new laws of physics that they hoped would be discovered by studying the gene. Delbrück worked at Caltech, but those who participated in this community, known as the Phage Group, were located throughout the United States and Europe. By viewing biological questions from a different angle of vision, they created a new field, molecular biology. And it was the unusual receptiveness of the American system of higher learning to novel ways of thinking about fundamental scientific problems, and the willingness of the home-grown talent to welcome and learn from these new arrivals, that allowed the discoveries to take place. Many of these scientists were newcomers to biology, which turned out to be an advantage. And like the scientists who were interested in pure physics, they helped to produce the rapid development of the American research universities during the 1940s and 1950s.

The scientists who had the greatest impact on the American scene—especially the nation's World War II effort—were the nuclear physicists, as so many of them participated in the Manhattan Project. But the social sciences, the humanities, and the arts were also beneficiaries of the great intellectual migration.[17] Paul F. Lazarsfeld, for example, born to a Jewish family in Vienna in 1901, collaborated with colleagues Hans Zeisel and Marie Jahoda in 1930 to produce the now-famous study of the working poor in a village south of Vienna, Marienthal, whose population was almost entirely unemployed. The Marienthal study brought Lazarsfeld to the attention of the Rockefeller Foundation, whose Paris representative offered him a traveling fellowship to the United States for the academic year beginning in September 1933. At Columbia, he met sociologist Robert Lynd, who, with Helen Lynd, had already written the first of his two books on Middletown—that is, Muncie, Indiana—which was also destined to become a classic of sociology.[18]

Lazarsfeld was sharply attentive to the growing Nazi movement and the purging of "Jewish science" from German universities. When the fascist Conservative Party came to power in Austria in 1934, his position in Vienna was eliminated and most of his family there was imprisoned. He held posts at several American research universities over the next few years under Rockefeller Foundation fellowships. Eventually, Lynd would prove to be instrumental in bringing Lazarsfeld to Columbia. Austria fell to Hitler in 1938.

Another Austrian who was desperate to leave Europe at that time was Theodor W. Adorno, a key member of the so-called "Frankfurt School," a school of social scientists and philosophers influenced by Marx's early writings as well as by non-Marxists such as Max Weber and by Freudian theory. The members of this group essentially migrated en masse from Germany to New York City during these years. Adorno considered himself a sociologist and philosopher principally interested in culture and music; his self-identity was not that of an empirical social scientist. Yet he took a position in New Jersey working on the radio research projects that Lazarsfeld had initiated. Setting out to discover why people found some radio shows more appealing than others, they were among the first to use social science methods to provide industry officials with marketing information. In time, Adorno and his colleagues would author one of the most influential empirical works of their generation, *The Authoritarian Personality*, which linked certain personality traits to a willingness to accept authority and fascist-type behavior.

The presence of these talented refugee scholars and scientists made a difference for the fields they entered in American universities. They took their fields in new directions and focused attention on different questions, methods, theories, or goals. They were at once "insiders" and "outsiders," shedding light on emerging disciplines with a European perspective, and later with the perspective of newly assimilated American intellectuals who were becoming leaders in their fields. Lazarsfeld, who had been trained as an applied mathematician, became a pioneer in developing modern empirical social science methods. Although these immigrant intellectuals suffered a loss of place, they also experienced a new freedom, and they infused enormous amounts of energy into the new disciplines taking shape in the American research university.

Immigrant scholars often feel that they straddle two worlds without being fully embraced by either. Lazarsfeld perceived himself in this way: no longer part of the Austrian intelligentsia, yet not fully accepted by the

American academy, partly because he was a Jewish foreigner with a noticeable accent, and partly because he studied seemingly low-brow topics,
such as why people bought Maxwell House coffee.[19] Within two decades
of taking up his position at Columbia, however, Lazarsfeld was recognized
as one of America's leading social scientists. He was elected president of
the American Sociological Association and was accepted into the U.S. National Academy of Sciences—a very rare event for a sociologist in those
days. He also maintained a significant following in Europe, especially in
France, and in 1972 became the first American sociologist to receive an
honorary degree from the Sorbonne.

The new intellectual chemistry that was born in the United States
mixed the "horizontally" socially mobile European scholars with "verti-
cally" mobile American scholars who were benefiting from a relatively new
openness to talent, regardless of religious or economic origins, in American society. These encounters often led to extremely fruitful collaborations.
A good example is the relationship that took hold between Paul Lazarsfeld
and Robert K. Merton. Lazarsfeld was from a bourgeois background, despite his family's socialist leanings. Merton came from a Jewish family that
lived in a poor section of Philadelphia. Having received his undergraduate degree in both philosophy and sociology in 1931, Merton was faced
with the dilemma of what to do next. The Great Depression had begun,
jobs were scarce, and Merton's intellectual curiosity was boundless. He was
offered a graduate fellowship at Harvard, where he produced a doctoral
dissertation on science and society in seventeenth-century England. It remains one of the most highly referenced classics in the history and sociology of science. After a brief stay at Tulane, he was hired by Columbia at
almost the same time as Paul Lazarsfeld. It was the beginning of a long
friendship. Merton remained at Columbia for more than forty years—the
rest of his academic career—and became one of the most influential sociologists of the twentieth century.

These two men, from very different worlds, with sharply contrasting
physical appearances (Lazarsfeld was short, thick, and awkward while
Merton was tall, erect, and unusually handsome) and equally divergent
styles of work, became lifelong friends and intellectual companions. Although they rarely published scholarly essays or papers together, they had
enormous influence on each other's thinking, becoming part of that new
chemistry that propelled American universities toward greater distinction.

The fields of sociology, anthropology, economics, and political science were enriched by the combination of the immigrant scholars with the young Jewish intellectuals entering the American professoriate in significant numbers for the first time.[20]

Women scientists fled Hitler's Germany, too. Some, such as the biologist Salome Waelsch, built glorious careers in the United States, earning membership to the National Academy of Sciences and many other honors. But the pathways were unorthodox and they had to bear witness to many forms of differential treatment, if not outright discrimination. This was equally true for American women, such as Nobel geneticist Barbara McClintock, who had to forgo lunch with other faculty members and the important small talk of science and culture that her male colleagues at Cornell enjoyed. Women at the time were not allowed to enter the men's faculty club. The limits placed on their positions, their research, and their opportunities to be full participants in the kind of collaboration that takes place in the universities, including that critically important informal side of life, show how far the scientific community needed to go—and in some respects still needs to go—before the value of meritocracy is fully realized.[21]

Some of the refugee intellectuals suffered from a sense of loss, despite being embraced by their colleagues at American research universities: Having been forced to leave their homelands, they would forever wonder what might have been had the Germans rejected Hitler. How would their futures have been different? These unanswerable questions haunted some of those great refugees of the 1930s and 1940s. The American universities, and American society, were the beneficiaries; the losses for the individuals and for their former societies are hardly calculable. It is ironic, and sad, that the gains of the American university came at the expense of the great universities and research institutes of Germany and Austria, which had made a mockery of the value of universalism. By hiring displaced professors of the first rank and welcoming them immediately into leadership roles, American research universities, within just a few years, multiplied the number of exceptional intellectual leaders and teachers who were actively working on their campuses. In return, the immigrant scholars and scientists helped to jump-start the effort to reach the research frontiers of the academic disciplines.

The legacy of loss for Germany and the other fascist nations has been felt for multiple generations. Those countries did not just lose the scientists and scholars themselves; they lost the children and grandchildren of those scientists and scholars. These later generations have also contributed to the growth of knowledge in America. Gerald Holton, a physicist and historian of science, called the children of the émigrés "the Second Wave." He and his sociologist colleague Gerhard Sonnert have systematically studied the careers of this group of children, noting that, in one sense, they were the lucky ones: This group of some 100,000 children "escaped the fate of 1,500,000 racially or politically targeted children who died in the Holocaust."[22]

Among the notable members of this group were Nobel scientists Eric Kandel, Walter Kohn, and Arno Penzias.[23] Other German and Austrian refugee children included the chemist Carl Djerassi, who was instrumental in developing the first contraceptive pill; the financier Felix Rohatyn; and social scientists and historians Peter Gay, Stanley Hoffman, Herbert Kelman, Henry Kissinger, Lotte Lazarsfeld, Henry Rosovsky, and Fritz Stern.

If we compare the achievements of the Austrian refugees in the Second Wave with American-born men of the same age, we find that some 51 percent of the refugees had attained four years of college education by 1970, compared with 15 percent of the American-born men—and 36 percent of the refugees had advanced education beyond college, which was four times the national average. Women refugees had attained, on average, far more education than their American-born counterparts: 30 percent compared with 8 percent. The average income of male Austrian and German refugee children was almost twice as high as that of American-born men of about the same age, and Austrian and German refugee children were significantly more likely to hold jobs as professionals or managers.[24] It is, in short, a high-achieving group by any standard.

Historians and social scientists have speculated about whether such a large, unprecedented "brain drain" could have taken place in 1933 without the rise of fascism and Hitler's Germany. While it is true that science is an international community and that scientists tend to move to locations with better working conditions, greater opportunities, and superior salaries and benefits, the idea that this level of immigration could have taken place without the wrenching circumstances of the 1930s is almost unthinkable. The scale of the intellectual migration that took place—both in terms of the numbers of distinguished professors and their prominence in their native countries—was unmatched in history.

Today, the United States is the place that many of the most talented young international scholars and scientists want to study and work (although this could be changing), but they do not come here from systems of higher learning that could be rated as equivalent to Germany's in the early decades of the twentieth century. Nor do they occupy prominent positions at many of the better universities, as did the refugee scientists. And it is true that over the past several decades there has been a notable movement of distinguished academic scholars and scientists to the United States from Europe, where the governments have failed to invest heavily in their research universities. The decision of these scholars to emigrate has likely been made easier over the years by the fact that the quality of science, engineering, and social science being produced in American research universities has been the best in the world, and the tangible rewards have been greater than in Europe as well.

So a large migration of scholars is possible during more normal times. Nonetheless, it seems unlikely that the refugee scientists and scholars who came from fascist Europe would have migrated to the United States from privileged positions in Germany and Austria were it not for the reign of terror in Europe. There may well have been some migration toward American institutions of higher learning, but given the economic conditions in both places, it seems implausible that so many of the great scientists and scholars would have chosen to move from excellent positions in their own countries.

Regardless of what might have been, the reality is that, within a few decades of the catastrophe in Europe, American research universities were poised to become the greatest in the world. The talent was plentiful, and the system of higher education was expanding rapidly. But one ingredient to their success was missing: The institutions needed resources that would permit them to attack increasingly complex problems and build upon a knowledge base that was expanding exponentially.

THE BIRTH OF BIG SCIENCE

Science and engineering did not win the war against the Nazis, but it contributed mightily to the Allied victory. The mobilization of the physicists and chemists to create the atomic bomb was an extraordinary scientific, technological, and organizational feat. The dark side of that achievement was as clear to those who produced it as it was to the politicians, military experts, and the larger public. But there were many other products of the wartime research effort that were of critical value as well, such as the discovery of radar, radio-controlled fuses, ballistic missiles, and penicillin. The work of mathematicians as code-breakers; the knowledge gained from humanists who were trained in languages and cultures; and the uses of social-science tools, such as surveys, to better understand the effects of the war experience on soldiers and the public all became essential. Science on a large national scale, well organized and led by a group of academics, engineers, and military leaders, proved feasible—and had captured the imagination of the American public.

Perhaps the nation became overly enamored with what science and technology could do, but for some time people of intellect became national icons. Some, such as J. Robert Oppenheimer, James B. Conant, and Vannevar Bush, appeared on the covers of popular national magazines like *Time* and *Life*. Oppenheimer was the leader of the Manhattan Project; Conant, president of Harvard and a member of the National Defense Research Committee, had helped to recruit some of the nation's top scientists to work on the war effort; and Vannevar Bush was instrumental in mobilizing talented individuals for the war effort. They may not be household names today, but at the time they were instantly recognizable to the general public.[25]

Although Vannevar Bush (no relation to the Bush presidents) is the least well known today of those war heroes, he was no less important to the war effort. A major public figure, vice president and dean of engineering at the Massachusetts Institute of Technology from 1932–1938, and later president of the Carnegie Institution, he convinced President Roosevelt to form the National Defense Research Committee to coordinate scientific research for national defense. He served as committee chairman. By 1941, the NDRC was part of another agency, the Office of Scientific Research and Development, which coordinated the Manhattan Project itself, and Bush was OSRD director. In those two positions, he brought together the nation's best scientists and engineers for national service, including refugee newcomers and individuals who were suspected of disloyalty by some of the more xenophobic members of Congress. Bush also created a blueprint for how basic science and technology should be organized and funded after the war.

The implications for the nation's great universities could not have been more profound. His ideas became the basis for an enlightened science policy that dominated our way of thinking about science and technology for the next half-century. The model for funding science would in fact later be extended to include most of the other disciplines.

We limit stories of the "founding fathers" to those giants who helped create the nation at its birth, but in the twentieth century there were others who were in effect founding fathers—people at our universities, including some who helped to create the research university, who transformed the nation into a modern knowledge society. In this regard, Vannevar Bush was a giant. Like Benjamin Franklin, he combined scientific and technological acuity with a vision of how it could be used in the service of national goals. In fact, parallels have been drawn between Franklin and Bush. At heart Bush was an engineer, but he had very firm ideas about how science should be organized and how it was related to technology. He had enormous intellectual energy, and he was determined to see his roadmap followed. His work during the war demanded access to the highest levels of the scientific, engineering, military, and political communities of the nation. His central role in the war effort not only made him realize the potential value of large-scale scientific efforts, but produced substantial anxiety about whether the effort could be sustained after the war.

Reporting, for example, on a conversation he had with President Roosevelt in late 1944, after it had become clear that the Allies were going to prevail in Europe, Bush said: "Roosevelt called me into his office and said, 'What's going to happen to science after the war?' I said, 'It's going to fall flat on its face.' He said, 'What are we going to do about it?' And I told him, 'We better do something damn quick.'"[26] Questions about the shape that national science policy should take after the war were not new. Congress had been seriously debating them since 1940. But no conclusions had been drawn, and a great deal of what had been done during the war had been on an emergency basis. What came after the war had its roots in OSRD under Bush's leadership and in congressional debates about how to continue to foster scientific research.

What Bush did with the NDRC was legendary. He brought prominent scientists, academic leaders, high-ranking military officials, and leaders in industry together for a common goal.[27] Conant said of his experience on the committee: "Just how Van Bush operated to bring his ideas about organizing science for the defense effort to fruition, I have never known." Nonetheless, Conant viewed Bush's accomplishments with NDRC as revolutionary: "The essence of the revolution was the shift in 1940 from expanding research in government laboratories to private enterprise and the use of federal money to support the work in universities and scientific institutes through contractual arrangements," he wrote. The changes he made were indicative of a long-term plan for science and technology.

Conant went on to describe the point of revelation for him:

> I shall never forget my surprise at hearing about this revolutionary scheme. Scientists were to be mobilized for the defense effort in their own laboratories. A man who we of the committee thought could do a job was going to be asked to be the chief investigator; he would assemble a staff in his own laboratory if possible; he would make progress reports to our committee through a small organization of part-time advisors and full-time staff. . . . Bush's invention insured that a great portion of the research on weapons would be carried out by men who were neither civil servants of the federal government nor soldiers; they would be employees of a contractor.[28]

Bush's committee was designed to fill an institutional void: The scientific problems that had to be solved were beyond the capabilities of existing military and naval laboratories, given all that was already on their plate in attempting to perfect existing weapons systems.[29] As Roger Geiger, writing on the history of American higher education, noted, "Bush was . . . given a free hand to fashion and to direct the type of organization that he and his colleagues believed would be effective—one controlled by scientists and fully independent for purposes of research." "The key element of their approach," he said, "was decentralization, or what Bush called a pyramidal structure."[30]

The organizational framework that Bush developed for the NDRC would anticipate many of the social structures that he felt were essential for creating a vibrant postwar science community. Pure scientific research would be carried out principally at universities as part of a contractual arrangement with the federal government. The government would pay for the research and for the facilities needed to conduct it, but would not create an elaborate apparatus. Scientists would be chosen on the basis of their ability to conduct the research at a very high level as judged by the committee members (thus using the principles of both meritocracy and peer review). However, scientists would not be employees of the state, and they would not be controlled by the military.

In fact, one of the defining features of the OSRD was that, although private scientists had close ties with military leaders, they were granted a great deal of autonomy. This principle demonstrated Bush's conviction that the discoveries of basic, pure research often had more important military applications than work that was specifically designed to meet a need defined by military authorities.[31] The OSRD represented a prototype organization for science policy, and Bush drew heavily from it to create an architecture for policy in the postwar era.

Conant was so taken with Bush's organizational and personal skills that he concluded a chapter of his autobiography with these encomiums: "Bush was a great mobilizer of scientists, a great chairman of NDRC. . . . The reader who understands anything of the ways of men will agree with me when I say the United States was indeed lucky that such an extraordinary man had President Roosevelt's ear in that crucial month, June 1940."[32]

Bush, born in 1890 into a family of limited means, was fascinated by technology even as a young boy.[33] With his slight build and wire-rimmed glasses, he could easily be misjudged as an egghead rather than a fighter.[34] He had many physical problems, both as a child and as a young man. His father was a Universalist minister. Growing up in Chelsea, an industrial city near Boston, Vannevar was far removed from the wealthy Protestant families of Boston and found greater affinity among Catholics and Jews. Though he felt like an outsider, he had enormous ambitions and believed that an entrepreneurial individual with smarts and energy could get "some cash" and close the social distance between himself and the elite in society.

And he would do just that. He was brilliant in science and mathematics, and although he had limited choices for college, because his father had spent much of the family's financial reserves putting his two older sisters through college, he did well at Tufts University. He was a straight A student for all but one semester, when he had to drop out to recover from appendicitis. While in college Bush used his considerable skills to pay most of his college expenses. Voted the top mathematics student by his classmates, he was acting as a substitute instructor and tutor for other Tufts students in physics and mathematics by the time he was a sophomore. He finished both his undergraduate degree and a master's in four years. It was at this time that his skepticism about large corporations, their monopolistic practices, and government bureaucracies took hold; meanwhile, he was becoming interested in the possibilities for engineering society and had a growing belief in the power of individuals as innovators.[35]

Bush believed in the role that knowledge and innovation could play in creating and sustaining a vital economy, but he did not fully understand how factions and interest groups worked in a large democracy. If he was brilliant in science and technology, he was not well versed in political science or the philosophy of democratic society. His students internalized many of his beliefs. One of his most outstanding protégés was Frederick Terman, who, as we shall see, eventually became Stanford University's provost, transforming it from a regional university of moderate quality into one of the great centers of higher learning and innovation in the world.

After holding several jobs outside of the academy, in 1915 Bush entered MIT, the nation's best engineering school, enrolling as a doctoral student in its young electrical engineering department. He finished his degree by 1916 after writing a "contract" with his adviser that specified exactly what he would be required to do. He had job offers from AT&T's research division (later Bell Labs) and from his alma mater, Tufts. Well aware that if he took the industrial laboratory job the company would hold proprietary rights to anything he discovered, Bush decided it would be better to accept the academic offer and supplement his salary by consulting for other companies—helping them to invent new products and introducing them successfully into the market.[36]

The beginning of Bush's career coincided with World War I. There was an increasing likelihood of American involvement in the armed struggle, and Bush wanted to serve the nation. During the latter phase of the war he convinced R. A. Millikan, who was heading an effort to mobilize scientific talent for the war effort at the National Research Council, of the value of his idea for detecting enemy submarines. In typical Bush fashion he convinced Millikan to allow him to privately finance and conduct the research independently of the government. Bush was indefatigable. Although he coveted fame, he was also out to make his fortune. Almost immediately after joining the faculty at Tufts, Bush became involved with the research efforts of the American Radio and Research Corp (AMRAD), which manufactured radio parts and radio sets for amateurs. The enterprise, which was backed by J. P. Morgan's son, needed a research director; Bush was hired to run AMRAD's lab at a salary exceeding the one he received from Tufts. Full of optimism about how to improve radios, he worked on refining the vacuum tubes that were limiting their quality. In reflecting on the relationship between science and technology, Bush wrote: "We have learned that no science worthy of the name is so pure as to be entirely devoid of possibilities of service to the needs of a complex civilization."[37] Nonetheless, AMRAD ran into difficulties after the war, principally because it lost its government contracts.

AMRAD was dead broke by 1922. Ideas for new radio tubes, invented in the Bush laboratory by Charles G. Smith, however, still existed. They had not yet been commercially exploited, but they soon would be. Bush and a college classmate created a company in 1922. It was fortuitous timing, given the exponential increase in the number of radio stations (NBC and CBS networks were formed in 1924) and the great demand for radios. The company, which they named Raytheon, turned out to be a great commercial success, despite efforts by Westinghouse, General Electric, RCA, and AT&T to pool their resources and patents and wipe out this upstart company. The tubes that Raytheon produced lowered the cost of radios and made them easier to use. In response to the challenges posed by its competitors, the company expanded the variety of tubes it made—some clearly based on other company's patents. These experiences led Bush to become even more skeptical about capitalistic monopolies. But with his consulting fees and stock in the company, Bush was on his way to becoming a wealthy man. By this time he had returned to MIT as a member of its electrical engineering department and was actively involved in developing research projects and mentoring students.

Vannevar Bush's time in the sun lasted far longer than the proverbial fifteen minutes, stretching beyond World War II.[38] He not only headed up an important component of the war effort but also crafted a treatise that shaped U.S. science policy after the Allied victory. This document, called *Science—The Endless Frontier*, played a major role in the postwar development of the research university because it outlined the ways in which the federal government could promote and support ongoing research at the university level.

The policy blueprint had its origins in a letter of November 17, 1944, from President Roosevelt to Bush—a letter, almost everyone agrees, that Bush composed for Roosevelt's advisers to review and for Roosevelt to sign. Acknowledging the important role that the OSRD had played during the war, it asked four questions about the role of science in the years to come: (1) How could the United States make its scientific achievements of the war years "known to the world," in order to "stimulate new enterprises, provide jobs . . . and make possible great strides for the improvement of the national well-being"? (2) How could medical research be encouraged? (3) How could the government aid private and public research, and how should the two be interrelated? and (4) How could the government discover and develop the talent for scientific research in America's youth?[39]

Bush formed four star-studded committees with a total of forty distinguished people to address each of these questions in a substantive way.[40] He would play a central role in the entire process, and the result would be greatly influenced by the experiences that many of the committee members brought with them from the war years as well as by the euphoria that came with victory. The "high" following the success of their work during the war was thus tempered by the lessons they had learned, lessons that would guide their policy priorities going forward.

Bush and many others, for example, believed that advances in fundamental science—and in what had been viewed as esoteric specialties, like nuclear physics and microbiology—had paid off spectacularly in truly original technological breakthroughs. The construction of new weapons, or the development of new medicines, were clear examples of this principle. They believed that you had to stockpile basic knowledge that could be called upon ultimately for its practical applications, and that without basic knowledge, truly new technologies were unlikely to emerge.

It may seem ironic that Bush, the consummate engineer, would become the great advocate for pure science as he crafted the national system of innovation. The scientists who had worked under the cloak of extreme secrecy during the war were eager to return to an open society of scientific communication, where results of discoveries would be freely and openly published and widely circulated. They were not blind to the needs of the military and to the requirements of national security, but they strongly believed in the value of open communication for scientific advance. Clearly, both needs had to be accommodated during the postwar period.

Bush's four committees worked hard, and each delivered its report by April 1945. Each committee responded to one of the four questions, but Bush's "Summary of the Report," which runs only a few pages, contained its central messages.[41] The quality of the nation's health—economic, military, physical, and social—required the development and deployment of new scientific knowledge, he said. Science was the principal driver of almost all that we did and experienced, and it was therefore essential that the United States be the world leader in the production of that new knowledge. Furthermore, because of the importance of new knowledge, the federal government had a fundamental responsibility to ensure that scientific progress took place. For this to happen we would need a highly trained labor force and highly trained scientific and technical personnel. Finally, all of this required an organizational structure that would facilitate scientific discovery. Bush called this the National Research Foundation and noted that it would function as an independent agency. The foundation would fund all manner of scientific and technological work, from basic science to military-related research, and would be self-regulating and insulated from normal political processes.

Bush's tone is one of optimism. America had embraced science and technology as a means to victory, looking to its bright future. Scientific knowledge had enabled us to triumph over our enemies, and it would be the chief weapon against disease as well. "No amount of achievement in other directions," wrote Bush, could "insure our health, prosperity, and security as a nation in the modern world." America must not wait to take action:

New products and processes are not born full-grown. They are founded on new principles and new conceptions which in turn result from basic scientific research. Basic scientific research is scientific capital. Moreover, we cannot any longer depend upon Europe as a major source of this scientific capital. Clearly, more and better scientific research is one essential to achievement of our goal of full employment.

How do we increase this scientific capital? First, we must have plenty of men and women trained in science, for upon them depends both the creation of new knowledge and its application to practical purposes. Second, we must strengthen the centers of basic research, which are principally the colleges, universities, and research institutes.[42]

Bush recommended the creation of a permanent science advisory board that would advise both the president and Congress on how science could best be used to further the national welfare. He argued for economic incentives for industries that invested in research and development, and he said that the patent system, which he greatly admired, should be strengthened to support small companies that were innovative but competing against corporate giants. He was deeply concerned with the United States' ability to train a sufficient number of scientists and engineers to bring about the progress he envisioned. Developing scientific talent would require direct support from the federal government, but he embraced the idea of identifying talent purely on the basis of merit.[43]

If the government was going to accept a new set of responsibilities to ensure scientific progress, it would have to create a structure to oversee and implement those responsibilities. As no government structure yet existed to receive funds from Congress for this purpose, he proposed creating the National Research Foundation, which would support "basic research in colleges, universities, and research institutes, both in medicine and the natural sciences." Among other things, it would administer a program of science scholarships and fellowships.[44]

This new foundation would be led by enlightened and knowledgeable scientists—"persons of broad interest and experience, having an understanding of the peculiarities of scientific research and education"[45]—people like those who had been appointed to the NDRC. Funding for the foundation would not be part of the regular federal budget process but would involve an endowment or block funds. In making this suggestion, he was looking for relative autonomy for the foundation so that it would not be subject to the whims of changing politics.

Bush concluded his summary with the following injunction: "Early action on these recommendations is imperative if this Nation is to meet the challenge of science in the crucial years ahead. On the wisdom with which we bring science to bear in the war against disease, in the creation of new industries, and in the strengthening of our Armed Forces depends in large measure our future as a Nation."[46]

Bush was disappointed with the political process that followed the transmittal of the report, which was completed and sent to President Harry S. Truman on July 5, 1945 (Roosevelt had died that April). This means that it was out of Bush's hands before he knew the full effects of the wartime research effort—the atomic bomb was not dropped on Hiroshima until August 6, and the Nagasaki bomb was dropped three days later. Once the public became aware of the results of the Manhattan Project, public opinion shifted, with many leaders convinced that mission-driven research (rather than the pursuit of pure research) should become the norm in the United States—an idea that Bush deeply opposed.

On December 7, a *New York Times* editorial praised the bombing, calling the atomic bomb "the most stupendous military and scientific achievement of our time" and perhaps "the most stupendous ever made in the history of science and technology." It went on to endorse mission-oriented science:

> University professors who are opposed to organizing, planning, and directing research after the manner of industrial laboratories because in their opinion fundamental research is based on "curiosity," because great scientific minds must be left to themselves, have something to think about. A most important piece of research was conducted on behalf of the Army, by precisely the means adopted in industrial laboratories. And the result? An invention was given to the world in three years which it would have taken perhaps half a century to develop if we had to rely on primadonna research scientists who work alone. The internal logical necessities of atomic physics and the war led to the bomb. A problem was stated. It was solved by teamwork, by planning, by competent direction, and *not* by a mere desire to satisfy curiosity.[47]

Bush's ambition was to create a revolutionary national system of innovation, and to do so, paradoxically, he had to both bring the government in and leave it out. Perhaps of first importance, he wanted science to help maintain U.S. military superiority after the war. But he also wanted to create a mechanism for financing innovative science that would be independent of government laboratories and the direct influence of the state. Science on the scale that Bush envisioned would require the use of taxpayer dollars to support research at universities, and nothing short of the government's purse strings could achieve this. Before the war, the idea of federal financing of research was not altogether welcomed by university leaders. Conant, for one, was skeptical of the consequences of such funding. Many others also believed that accepting large amounts of federal support for research would lead to excessive political interference with the universities' autonomy and free inquiry, and most presidents of top-tier universities felt that it would be a mistake for their institutions to carry out secret military research during peacetime.[48]

Bush strongly believed that the American university system should be the principal location for basic scientific research to be conducted and that the federal government should finance it. Basic research should be carried out principally at the nation's universities, he wrote, because they provided "the environment which is most conducive to the creation of new scientific knowledge and least under pressure for immediate, tangible results." Unlike industry and the government, colleges, universities, and research institutes "devote[d] most of their research efforts to expanding the frontiers of knowledge."[49]

The universities would also become incubators for developing talent in the young people who would make up the skilled workforce and scientific leadership of the next generation. Through doctoral and postdoctoral training, the most talented young Americans, regardless of means, would gain knowledge and experience by working in the laboratories of the great scientists and engineers of the day. The National Research Foundation would funnel investments in medical research through the universities as well, particularly the medical schools. Bush's model would transform both the transmission and the production of knowledge in America.

Most of the core principles outlined in *Science—The Endless Frontier* were implemented in the years that followed, but not without modifications. The specific ideas in the blueprint that Bush created and delivered to President Truman were revised during the political process that followed. There were sticking points that slowed down the process of implementation. Although the president and Congress agreed on many of the main ideas, they disagreed sharply over some of the proposed goals of federal science policy and over some of the details concerning the National Research Foundation that Bush wanted to construct. The chief antagonist in Congress was Senator Harley M. Kilgore, a West Virginian and a New Deal Democrat, who had held hearings on wartime mobilization and on peacetime science and technology policy.[50]

Kilgore believed far more than Bush did in social planning—that is, in directing the substance of scientific inquiry to those areas that represented national needs. As Kilgore saw it, members of Congress, rather than the scientific community, might set research priorities. Bush believed in the free market of ideas and found the idea of national planning for scientific outcomes antithetical to his belief in how scientific and technological knowledge grew. He believed that it would be a grave mistake to attempt to socially engineer scientific outcomes—akin to central planning by politicians and military men. The proper goal, according to Bush, and the one that would best assure national well-being and national security, was to build up the stockpile of knowledge and then draw on it for important technological advances. Basic research would yield fruit, often in the form of unanticipated practical applications.

Bush's view of the relationship between science and technology had a great deal of influence after the war. The report contained two aphorisms worthy of Sir Francis Bacon.[51] The first was that "basic science is performed without thought of practical ends," and the second was that "basic research is the pacemaker of technological improvement." In other words, the nation would reap untold technological benefits from its investment in pure science.[52] Bush's formulations, which enjoyed widespread acceptance within the scientific community, helped to promote the idea of academic freedom and made policymakers aware of the dangers of government interference with scientific endeavors; on the negative side, however, they also had the unfortunate consequence of creating a false dichotomy between basic and applied research.

Kilgore, who feared that the lion's share of scientific resources would be allocated to the most distinguished research universities, also insisted that some proportion of the federal funds for science be distributed on a geographic basis. Bush would have none of this, since it violated his principle of merit—the research funds should go to those who were most qualified, who wrote the best science proposals, and who had the best scientific track records, as determined by a panel of peers. Kilgore wanted to fund the social sciences, disciplines that Bush scorned as almost pseudo-science.

Bush also insisted that grantees must be allowed to hold intellectual property rights on discoveries they made with federal funds, and that the federal government be given only royalty-free licenses for their use. He wanted to increase incentives for innovation by ensuring economic returns to those who patented new ideas. Kilgore was less enamored of the idea that the government should give up its rights to intellectual property. The two men also strongly disagreed about how the agency overseeing the federal support for science should be structured. Kilgore proposed that the foundation have a director appointed by the president who would also re-port to the president. Bush favored a quasi-independent body.

President Truman was adamantly opposed to the way Bush had located the new science agency in the federal system. He would be damned if he would allow it to be so far removed from presidential control. He wanted the NSF director to be appointed by the president and reporting to the president even if an oversight board of "elders" existed. He threatened to veto any NSF bill that did not meet his organizational requirements.

During the five years between the submission of the report and the for-mation of the NSF, the political process altered many of Bush's proposals. In the 1945 congressional hearings that considered the Kilgore and Bush models for federal science policy, 98 of the 99 witnesses supported the cre-ation of a single agency to oversee government grants, contracts, and fel-lowships and to support related military research in the physical sciences.[53] There was no consensus on the reporting relationship of the director of the NSF, leaving President Truman unsatisfied. Consequently, no bill was passed in 1945 or 1946. When Congress passed a bill in 1947 that sup-ported Bush's approach to the reporting relationship, Truman vetoed the measure. The 80th Congress was at an impasse on this point and refused to move forward. The 81st Congress yielded to Truman's demands and passed a bill that the president promptly signed, creating the National Sci-ence Foundation.

In the final bill, Congress bought more of Bush's basic ideas about the support of science and its independence from political control than it did his concrete recommendations for creating a structure to implement those ideas. His most fundamental principle—that it was essential to the na-tional interest to have the federal government use taxpayer money to sup-port the long range objectives of science and technology funded through the colleges and universities—was transformative in its implications for the future of science and the American research university. The structural mechanism for implementing this big idea, however—the National Re-search Foundation—was essentially gutted in its transformation into the National Science Foundation—as critically important as the NSF became in subsequent decades.

The emasculation took the following form. The newly organized Atomic Energy Commission took control of nuclear science. Responsibil-ity for biomedical and health sciences research, which had been under the

OSRD during the war, went to the National Institutes of Health, which was reorganized between 1946 and 1949 into a large, complex, in-house set of research programs along with an extensive extramural funding program for research scientists predominantly located at universities and colleges.[54] The Department of Defense, through the Office of Naval Research, also began to sponsor a large number of university-based research projects. Bush's idea of having a group of scientists and technology experts oversee the work of the National Research Foundation led to the National Science Board, which continues to oversee the work of the NSF. The mission of the NSF was narrowed to the support of basic research, mostly in the physical sciences and mathematics.

The NSF grant support system did set up a method of peer review, which became an essential element in the process of distributing funds. Grants would go to the best proposals and the most qualified scientists rather than allocated on a geographical basis. However, given the obvious congressional interest in where NSF funds wound up, there were continual tensions about disproportionate funding going to a relatively small number of universities that were geographically clustered. Because some congressional districts received very few NSF funds, some members of Congress have questioned the fairness of the NSF's peer review system, periodically claiming that it disadvantages the "have-nots" when they compete with the "haves."[55] Because the NSF is financed through the regular budgeting process, members of Congress have sometimes taken aim at specific programs and individual grants that they have felt were not worthy of federal support. The potential for political interference was built into the postwar system for funding science, and the bickering continues today.

Bush was committed to supporting pure science and believed that its link to technological development was linear. Scientific progress was akin to an assembly line that started with basic, curiosity-driven research and led to applied research, which in turn led to development and ultimately to production and operations. Moving from one stage to the next transformed basic science into useful items, such as industrial products.[56] Bush's idea informed the creation of the NSF and in the pattern of funding that became established during the late 1950s and 1960s. The response to the technological challenge presented by the Soviet Union's 1957 launching of *Sputnik*, for example, was not purely technological, as one might have expected. America did not simply invest in building better machines to win the race to the moon. Rather, the country saw this as a challenge to our basic science capacity and responded by investing heavily in the basic sciences, which, eventually, under the Bush model, would lead to technological superiority. The goal was to educate and train a sufficient number of scientists and engineers to compete effectively with the Soviet Union. The size of federal science budgets exploded, as did support to the industries and researchers involved in the race to build better machines that would counter the Soviet threat.

Science—The Endless Frontier produced a broad, ambitious vision for American science after the war. As influential as it turned out to be over the next fifty years, it was a document full of ideas that must be viewed within their historical context. With the value of hindsight, it was easy to see that Bush, the consummate engineer, had produced a system of innovation with some serious design flaws. In fact, criticism of some features of the model began to surface almost immediately, particularly about Bush's determination to fund basic rather than applied research. Several of these design flaws are worth noting because of their implications for funding at American research universities during the period of their ascendancy.

The omission of the social sciences and the humanities from the model seriously damaged the future of both sets of disciplines, slowing down their development and reducing appreciation for interdisciplinary research. The NSF expanded its mission in the early 1960s to include limited support for the social and behavioral sciences in an attempt to correct this error. By then there was greater awareness that highly complex societal problems often require collaboration among the physical, biological, and social sciences. If the National Research Foundation had been created according to Bush's vision, divorced from the influence of political and social goals, it probably would have crumbled from within under its own weight; its reconstruction would probably have entailed the establishment of organizations that would have looked similar to today's NSF, NIH, and the research arms of the Department of Defense and the Department of Energy. It is unlikely that today's level of research funding would have been achieved through the growth of an endowment administered by a National Research Foundation. Moreover, Bush could not have fully anticipated all the consequences of scientific and technological progress after the war. He and his colleagues instantly recognized the horrible potential misuse of nuclear arms, but they were less likely to think about how to deal with other unanticipated negative consequences of scientific triumphs. The impact on the environment of nuclear waste material or the negative consequences of the use of DDT are good examples of the kinds of issues involving science that require the attention of our elected political leaders as well as informed public debate. Bush's idea of separating science from politics completely, though well intended, would not ultimately have been the best option.

In short, Bush believed, incorrectly I think, that science for the public good could be produced without public discourse—to avoid all of the limitations produced by the political process, he wanted to bypass that process entirely. Science cannot be isolated like this from the very society that is on the receiving end of its discoveries and advances. As James S. Coleman, a University of Chicago mathematical and empirical sociologist, argued, behind the façade of every major scientific and technological problem lies a set of social, organizational, and economic relationships that need to be addressed as part of science policy. (Coleman was a member of the President's Science Advisory Committee from 1970 to 1972.)[57]

Bush's blueprint for policy never seriously addressed the question of how the nation's leaders would obtain and evaluate new scientific and technological information. Surely, the president, members of Congress, and federal judges were not equipped to understand, analyze, or question the increasingly complex and esoteric results of scientific inquiry. Consequently, there existed, and still exists, a need for a mechanism by which scientists, engineers, and social scientists can advise members of the three branches of government on scientific matters. Even as early as the creation of the NSF in 1950, President Truman realized the need for sound scientific advice at the top levels of government. But how should the nation best obtain it? This question is not addressed in the Bush report, and, as the National Research Foundation would have been at arm's length from the executive branch, it would not have been well suited for the task. The National Academy of Sciences, crafted during Abraham Lincoln's presidency, was expected to produce advice for government, and it did. But the president needed someone who could distill knowledge, who would be aware of the political aspects of the use of that knowledge, and who could have the ear of the president. Fortunately, William T. Golden, one of the great éminences grises of science policy in this country following World

War II, produced a lengthy report for President Truman recommending the creation of a presidential science adviser, a position that Truman promptly brought into being.[58]

But these omissions in the Bush report were structural. By far the greatest design flaw was the way Bush handled the unresolved tension between "curiosity-driven" and "mission-driven" science, and this reflected an incomplete conceptualization of how science would work in the modern world. The false dichotomy between basic and applied research that his view promoted burrowed its way into the psyche of the scientific community and created an imprecise model of the process of discovery and innovation. Within the historical context, Bush's commitment to pure, curiosity-driven research was perhaps understandable. He and the other great American scientists had just devoted years to mission-oriented projects. They desperately wanted to get back to their university laboratories to pursue their own interests divorced from their military payoff. Some had difficulties with the collaboration that had occurred between scientists and military authorities during the war and were suspicious of any form of military or political influence over their scientific work. They abhorred the idea of "central planning." They feared political outsiders who lacked an understanding of how scientific knowledge and technology advanced, and feared even more the idea of these outsiders controlling their research agendas. As one Bush associate put it, a scientist needed "the intellectual and physical freedom to work on whatever he damn-well pleases."[59] At the time, the nation needed a powerful and articulate advocate for curiosity-driven basic research, especially since it was not apt to find a plethora of such people in Congress, the military, or the media. They found that person, ironically, in the engineer from MIT.

In advocating curiosity-driven work, Bush asserted his belief in a linear relationship between pure research and technological innovation. In fact, however, the history of science is full of critically important examples of exceptions to the linear model. It's not that science progresses without pure research. The history of atomic science in the twentieth century and the Manhattan Project is a sufficient example of how fundamental knowledge can lead to innovation. The model simply fails to represent adequately the complex interplay between basic research and practical use in the history of scientific discovery—a kind of interplay that continues in the work being done at today's great universities. There are many examples demonstrating that mission-driven research works, too.[60]

Donald E. Stokes, a leading political scientist and dean of Princeton's Woodrow Wilson School for eighteen years following his appointment in 1974, created a useful classification of scientists based on their orientation and research goals. Namely, he identified three types of scientists. The first were those whose only goal was the quest for pure understanding, and their tendency would thus be to engage in pure, curiosity-driven research. They were not inspired by any concern with the potential uses of their discoveries, and yet their findings could, at some later time, have practical applications. These were the scientists that Bush thought ought to be funded, and their work ultimately would produce great national benefits. Because the great Danish atomic physicist Niels Bohr, who worked on the structure of atoms, would be in this category, Stokes dubbed it "Bohr's quadrant." The second category was for those who were motivated solely by considerations of practical use. Thomas Edison was Stokes's example, and so he labeled these types as occupants of "Edison's quadrant." But of greatest interest to Stokes were the scientists who were motivated by the quest for fundamental knowledge but also interested in solving problems. Louis Pasteur was the quintessential example, and so Stokes called this orientation "Pasteur's quadrant."

This is where the value of Bush's dichotomy between basic and applied research was compromised. Pasteur is, in fact, a wonderful example of a scientist who achieved path-breaking work in this manner. He conducted basic research, but it was derived from his desire to solve a scientific mystery that would have important practical implications. His case suggests that fundamental research is often informed by an effort to solve practical problems, and that the relationship between pure and use-based research is often not linear but interactive.[61]

In contemporary science, the class of problems belonging to the biological sciences is far and away the most difficult to fit into either a basic or applied framework. Most of the deep fundamental problems are linked to efforts to solve specific practical medical problems. Watson and Crick's discovery of the structure of DNA may have resulted from the passionate pursuit to solve one of the great fundamental scientific puzzles. But since the beginning of the revolution in molecular biology, there has always lingered, just below the surface, an interest in the practical applications that would flow from the basic biology. The discovery of techniques with potential for practical use led to a new set of fundamental research questions, giving rise to further progress.

The effort to find cures and treatments for diseases almost invariably leads to reciprocal interactions between the quest for pure understanding and interest in the use of the discoveries. When Richard Axel discovered the gene that controls our sense of smell, he was interested in fundamental biological questions and in the practical applications for people suffering from anosmia—the loss of the sense of smell—as well as how the sense of smell is linked to the avoidance of predators and to sexuality. In fact, almost all of medical science has this characteristic—it did in Pasteur's time, and it does even more so today. The blurred boundaries between curiosity-driven and use-based research extend to almost all of the physical, biological, and social and behavioral sciences.

Vannevar Bush's own supporters, including James Conant and Alan T. Waterman, the first director of the NSF, and other key science policy advisers to the government, such as Harvey Brooks, began to tinker with the model soon after it was implemented. Waterman recognized that the simple dichotomy failed to capture the way science was often done—and thus failed to justify the funding decisions of the NSF. Mission-oriented basic research, he said, "is distinguished from applied research in that the investigator is not asked or expected to look for a finding of practical importance; he is still exploring the unknown by any route he may choose. But it differs from 'free' basic research in that the supporting agency does have the motive of utility, in the hope that the results will further the agency's practical mission."[62]

Harvey Brooks, a physicist and Harvard administrator who served on science advisory committees during the Eisenhower, Kennedy, and Johnson administrations, elaborated on Waterman's distinction in a 1967 report to the House Committee on Science and Aeronautics: "The terms basic and applied are . . . not opposites. . . . The fact that research is of such a nature that it can be applied does not mean that it is not also basic."[63] The debate was not over mere semantics; it dealt with real differences in the types of research being done, and its outcome would affect the kind of research that the federal government would fund and carry out at universities.

The implementation of the Bush plan, even as the debate continued, ushered in a new era of government-university relations. The social contract that had been crafted earlier in the century between society and the research universities was expanded to include a new element: The government would pay for basic and mission-oriented research, covering, in principle, the cost of administering the research. In return, the nation could expect the research universities to produce new discoveries that would help to maintain U.S. military superiority, that would lead to new industries and a greater number of skilled jobs, and that would solve a variety of biomedical problems. The research universities would educate new generations of young people who would staff industrial laboratories after completing their advanced degrees. In short, the terms of the contract were intended to increase America's chances of holding onto its dominant position in a world where knowledge translated into social and economic welfare as well as power. And to an extraordinary degree, the compact has worked, facilitating half a century of unprecedented scientific and technological growth and achievement. In terms of the diversity of this knowledge, its sheer volume, and its unquestionable quality, the progress is perhaps unmatched in history.

Since World War II government funding of science and engineering as well as of the health sciences has grown at a very rapid, if somewhat uneven, pace. Fields that promised to solve practical military and health problems have received the largest proportion of the funding. That's not surprising, since every member of Congress who votes on science appropriations is acutely aware of national security issues and the desire of the general public for better treatments and cures for diseases and other health-related problems. It has been harder to make the case for funding research on seemingly abstract fundamental problems, such as whether there is an empirical basis for "string theory" in particle physics. And acquiring funding has been even more difficult for the social sciences and humanities, where the problems themselves are often caught up in a web of politics.

Many of the benefits of the compact between the federal government and the research universities that Vannevar Bush envisioned have been realized, but a price has been paid for these gains. The power of the federal government over universities has grown steadily since World War II. The budgets for research and for student financial aid at these universities coming from federal sources run into the hundreds of millions of dollars annually. The best of our universities have come to rely on this public source of funding, and this gives the government tremendous leverage over them. This is one of the outcomes that Bush, Conant, and others feared. On occasion, the government has used its power of the purse to pressure the universities to conform to its political policies at the expense of core university values.[64]

Although the NSF structure that was put into place served the nation well for several decades, government-university relations have not remained static since Vannevar Bush's day, and as a result, some adjustments have been needed. In fact, by the early 1990s there was a sense within the university community that the old compact, which was originally crafted following a major war, would have to be renegotiated. Fundamental terms of the old agreement no longer seemed applicable to the nation's condition—particularly the need for the government to invest so heavily in sustaining military superiority. The Cold War was over; the United States had achieved its military goal; and it seemed unlikely that it would be threatened for the foreseeable future. In addition, a large and expanding federal budget deficit, which had mushroomed under President Reagan and was continuing to increase, caused most science policy experts and active scientists to suspect that Congress would begin to sharply limit the growth of NSF and NIH funding for university-based research. Some experts predicted actual cuts in these allocations. In 1994, science policy experts began to focus on the need to reorient the contract, moving away from supporting military research in favor of meeting public health needs. It was essential, they said, to capitalize on the revolutionary breakthroughs taking place in the biological sciences.

The Clinton administration understood the value of making investments in science and technology through our research universities. As early as 1993, President Bill Clinton and Vice President Al Gore reaffirmed the nation's commitment to leadership in science and technology. This support was made even more explicit in 1994 with the publication of *Science in the National Interest*, a policy document stating the administration's commitment to supporting fundamental science.[65] Consciously echoing much of the rhetoric of Van Bush's report, which had said that it is through scientific and technological innovation that we use the forces of nature to improve the quality of our lives, the president and vice president noted: "Technology—the engine of economic growth—creates jobs, builds new industries, and improves our standard of living. Science fuels technology's engine. It is essential to our children's future that we continue to invest in fundamental research. . . . To reach the goals . . . we must strengthen partnerships with industry, with state and local governments, and with schools, colleges, and universities across the country."[66]

Clinton and Gore had a deep appreciation of the linkages between economic prosperity, the long-term health of the nation, and investments in science and technology. They pursued their policy by making a commitment to doubling the NIH budget within five years and significantly increasing the NSF budget, with an eventual commitment to doubling the latter as well. Under the Clinton administration, the fear of hard times for science and technology that had existed in the early 1990s was dispelled; those at the highest levels of government—in both the executive and legislative branches—understood the partnership between university-based science initiatives and the federal government. Every budget cycle would produce challenges and threats of limited growth, but there emerged within the university community a sense that the president and vice president "got it"—they understood the fundamental principle of the value of the investment in science and technology and the partnership that was necessary in order for the research universities to remain preeminent.

That sense of opportunity evaporated, unfortunately, during the presidency of George W. Bush. Although Bush touted his commitment to making investments in scientific growth, his administration increasingly used ideological criteria to determine its support of scientific work. Important work in the biological and biomedical sciences was stalled, and suspicion of the value and intent of social and behavioral science research returned to the ranks of government officialdom. Although the doubling of the NIH budget was completed in the first years of the Bush administration, by the end of his eight-year presidency the NIH budget in real terms had experienced a decline. The administration placed restraints on certain lines of research, such as stem cell research, made it increasingly difficult for young scientists to obtain research funding, and created an atmosphere of despair in the academic science community. Brilliant researchers—for example, many of those who were working on the problem of climate change or on cures for diseases caused by lethal viruses or bacteria—came to believe that the Bush administration thought that scientific facts were simply up for negotiation.

There are early signs that President Barack Obama understands the linkage between national investments in unfettered research and the national welfare. His choices of Nobel laureate Steven Chu to head the Department of Energy and Harvard physicist John Holdren as science adviser bode well for improved understanding of this crucial relationship. Add to these appointments Obama's selection of Nobelist Harold Varmus, former head of the National Institutes of Health and current president of Memorial Sloan-Kettering Cancer Center, and MIT systems biologist Eric Lander as co-chairs of the President's Council of Advisors on Science and Technology, and you have a powerful cast of people deeply knowledgeable about science, technology, and the process of discovery. These early appointments suggest that we may once again have a president who values the compact between the federal government and our universities, someone who will adopt that peculiarly American metaphor of science as an endless frontier.

CHAPTER 4

Building Steeples of Excellence

The wealth of nations now depends on the performance of higher education as never before, through its contributions to building human capital and accumulated knowledge; and so does the military competition among the great powers—potentially, quite literally, a matter of life and death. The political health of nations also now depends, as never before, on higher education to help create greater opportunities throughout the population, to help break down hereditary class lines.

—Clark Kerr

As America proceeded through the post–World War II period and the Cold War, then through the post-Cold War era into the Internet age, and turned the corner into the twenty-first century, the system of government-university collaboration for pursuing new knowledge set up in Vannevar Bush's day served the nation well. With these structures firmly in place, universities were able to transform themselves into world-class institutions. But why some and not others? Which universities were able to rise to the top ranks, and how did they manage it? In fact, we now have a good idea of the factors that predict greatness for a university. Those predictors of greatness are described below. Number 13 in this baker's dozen is excellent leadership. Following the list I shall describe two extraordinarily innovative and dedicated academic leaders who understood how to use numbers 1 through 12 to achieve international renown for their universities: Frederick Emmons Terman, provost at Stanford; and Clark Kerr, chancellor and then president of the University of California system.

What then is necessary for a research university to achieve greatness? I came up with the following list after years of studying this question. I believe that these are the factors determining whether a research university will be counted among the best in the world. Indeed, I am making a strong claim: We can predict a university's relative academic standing—its prestige and reputation as well as its overall quality and its rank among the world's universities—if we know the mix of these thirteen ingredients.

Creating a university that scores well on each of these components is an exceedingly difficult and costly thing to do, and many forces beyond the control of university leaders may conspire against success. And creating an academic culture and ambience that fosters excellence and creativity goes beyond any set of factors that can be precisely pinned down. What causes greatness and what predicts it are two entirely different things. I acknowledge that a handful of world-class universities are exceptions to my general claim. And some are university "boutiques" that are so specialized in their research focus that their quality is undervalued when we try to predict it by using the aggregate set of factors described here. Nevertheless, on average, these are things that make for a great research university.[1]

1. Faculty Research Productivity. How prolific are the members of the faculty in contributing to the growth of knowledge? How much do faculty members contribute to the most important journals or other scholarly outlets in their respective fields? Is the faculty well represented among those whose books, writings, and original work have had a demonstrable impact on changing the way we think about a variety of subjects? Great universities, almost by definition, require highly productive faculty members.

2. Quality and Impact of Research. Quality is more important than quantity in predicting distinction, but it turns out that quality and quantity of research are highly correlated. Without sheer talent and a critical mass of it, a research university by definition cannot achieve greatness. The citations to the work of the faculty members by peers turn out to be a fairly good measure of the quality or impact of the research being conducted within a university.

3. Grant and Contract Support. The total annual amount of grant and contract support at a university, including dollars from key federal and state agencies, private foundations, and private sources of giving, is a good indicator of the intensity and level of research at a university, especially in the sciences and engineering.[2] Depending on the discipline, funding from specific agencies, such as the NSF or the NIH, may be good predictors of research activity and of success in the peer review process.

4. Honorific Awards. Faculty recognition by peers is an important benchmark for the quality of work that is conducted at a university, and receipt of prestigious awards is an indicator of this recognition. Nobel Prizes, Lasker Awards, and the National Medal of Science; elected membership in honorific societies, such as the National Academy of Sciences, the American Academy of Arts and Sciences, or the American Philosophical Society; and highly prestigious fellowships, such as Guggenheim Fellowships or Sloan Foundation Fellowships, represent organized peer recognition for scholarly achievements. Many other highly prestigious awards are given by professional societies and are further indicators of achievement.

5. Access to Highly Qualified Students. Students contribute mightily to the quality of a research institution. At the graduate level, many of them carry out a great deal of research that is tied directly to the work of the faculty. Great professors attract great younger minds, and then these capable students work with their professors as scholarly or scientific apprentices until they can go out on their own. One cannot underestimate the importance of the close relationship between teaching and research at the advanced levels of learning at American research universities.

This factor represents one of the comparative advantages that private elite universities have over otherwise equally impressive state universities. The smaller size of the undergraduate population, and the ability to establish close working relationships with undergraduates through relatively small classes or seminars, tends to attract some of the best scholars to the private universities. At the same time, it gives research universities an advantage over otherwise excellent small liberal arts colleges that are more devoted to teaching and less insistent about scholarly productivity. From the point of view of undergraduate students, the size

of the faculties at the research universities and the opportunities to study
with professors who are expanding the boundaries of knowledge represent potential advantages.

6. Excellence in Teaching. Excellence in teaching and excellence in research
are compatible and mutually reinforcing. There is a set of myths and half-
truths about this subject. Academic research is often portrayed as the "bad
boy of academia": There is a popular stereotype of the incompetent teacher
who cares only about his or her research. This is unfortunate, because it is
simply not so at most of our great universities.

Of course, there are great researchers who are embarrassingly poor
teachers. But great researchers don't have a monopoly over poor teaching.
There are many poor researchers whom you wouldn't want to place in front
of an eager group of students, either. At the great universities, it is very
often the case, however, that the best researchers are also among the most
brilliant lecturers or mentors of students. These are the producers of fresh
ideas who are truly at the cutting edge of their disciplines and who can
give their students a sense of excitement about scholarship at the research
frontier. Even if the quality of undergraduate education is not what defines the unique character of the most distinguished research universities,
it influences the culture of the institutions and affects their ability to attract
the best scientists and scholars.

7. Physical Facilities and Advanced Information Technologies. Talented academics need facilities in order to reach their research potential. In the sciences and in engineering this need is met in physical facilities—laboratories
and equipment. In the humanities it is met through access to information,
which was previously embodied in great academic library collections.
Today, great collections still matter, but universities must also provide rapid
access to information through the use of digital media and online collections of materials and through the creation of an information infrastructure
that enables students and faculty to exchange ideas almost instantaneously
with others around the globe. Great research universities must now provide
the tools needed for accessing information. They must therefore make investments in both physical facilities and virtual facilities.

Contrary to the growing belief that bricks and mortar at universities
will become obsolete with the development of new digital media, how-

ever, physical space is still necessary. Scientific and engineering labs, classrooms, and offices remain essential ingredients at these institutions. Online video instruction and other forms of digital communication are on the rise, but they cannot replace the in-person communication and instruction that is so essential to dialogue and learning.

Columbia—which is land poor and has less physical space than any other Ivy League university—expanded by about 1 million square feet per decade over the past half-century. Other great universities have experienced the same or more rapid rates of growth. Without room to expand, universities wilt on the vine and begin to lose their competitiveness. Their continued greatness depends perhaps as much on their ability to find physical space as it does on their endowment.

8. Large Endowments and Plentiful Resources. Money talks in higher education, as everywhere else. Universities with large endowments and access to other financial resources have huge advantages that are reflected in the quality of every aspect of the institution. The size of a university's endowment is strongly associated with its perceived quality.

9. Large Academic Departments. The sheer number of faculty members in a program correlates strongly with the reputation of the program. Of course, there are many small programs and departments that are preeminent, but larger programs are generally more visible and highly regarded.

Why should this be so? I believe there are two main reasons. First, the faculty members of large programs who are in charge of hiring decisions are more willing to take risks on people; a poor choice has fewer consequences on the overall quality of the department. Second, large departments simply have more opportunities to hit home runs, even if they are also more likely to strike out on occasion. It is not a department's overall batting average that makes a difference to external judges, it's the absolute number of players with outstanding records of achievement.

Perhaps it is ironic that a department of chemistry with 60 members, of whom 15 are very highly regarded, will have higher standing than one with 20 members, of whom 10 are highly regarded. Despite the fact that the second department has a "higher density" of recognized scientists (10 of 20), the first department is apt to have the better reputation because it has more highly regarded scientists (15 instead of 10).

10. Free Inquiry and Academic Freedom. A research university cannot thrive without a deeply ingrained culture of free inquiry and academic freedom. Without that culture and a tradition of an administration actively supporting it, the other terms in the equation for greatness are not apt to amount to much.

The absence of this tradition in nations such as China and the former Soviet Union has limited the pool of academic talent and stultified imagination and innovation. The best scholars and scientists will refuse to work under such conditions if choices are available to them. This is a difficult characteristic to measure with precision, but estimates of the level of free inquiry permitted at universities will help explain their relative standing—especially across nations.

11. Location. The old adage about the value of real estate, "Location, location, location," holds true for research universities. Universities situated in areas of the country or in cities that are highly attractive to scholars and scientists have a decided advantage in recruiting and retaining the most talented faculty members. They also tend to be places where dual-career couples have an easier time finding two outstanding positions. Places of great cultural interest or of great physical beauty tend to draw people, but the quality of housing and schooling for children also enters the calculations of potential faculty members about where they want to be.

This factor does not necessarily trump the basics: Having the best facilities and resources to get one's work done, and being able to work with colleagues and students of the first rank, can still outweigh geography, especially during the early phases of careers. In short, other things being roughly equal, geographic location matters, providing advantages for universities in locations that are desirable. Columbia's location in the heart of Manhattan, for example, has strengthened the institution's humanities program. For an art historian, New York represents a mecca. Art historians, of course, choose many places other than Columbia, but the best of the art history departments are apt to be located in or near major cultural centers of the United States.

12. Contributions to the Public Good. Research universities that contribute to national and international welfare through their discoveries, that contribute to the training of talented individuals who later gain a high level of recognition for their work, and that have a large social and economic impact on their local communities are apt to be more highly esteemed than those who play lesser roles.

Distinguished alumni garner prestige for the schools that educated them. As graduates head out into the world, becoming successful as professionals and leaders in a variety of areas, whether in the arts or in the sciences, they help to make a name for the universities where they received their training. This principle works at both the domestic and international levels. American research universities are training increasing numbers of young people from other nations who return to those countries and take up leading positions there. International recognition for universities comes not only from the accomplishments of their faculties but also from the accomplishments of their graduates living around the world. Moreover, research universities that are trying to deal with global problems of great magnitude are gaining recognition for their efforts.

13. Excellent Leadership. Bold, decisive, entrepreneurial, and indefatigable leadership is an essential ingredient for a preeminent university. The absence of great leadership may be tolerable for a short time: Some of our greatest and wealthiest universities could run reasonably well for a while on "autopilot," but eventually they would slip in quality. Declines can, however, happen rather rapidly, and it is a fact of academic life that it is far more difficult and expensive to reclaim lost distinction than to hold onto it.

Great leaders not only internalize the ideals of the research university but also articulate a vision for achieving greatness and have the rare talent of being able to turn that vision into reality. They also know how to govern. They must see themselves as the servants or custodians of an institution that has been temporarily entrusted to them, rather than desire to use the prestige of their position for personal glory or rewards. They must want the university to be the best, they must know what excellence truly is, and they must be relentless in their pursuit of quality.

An insistence on measured quality may make them unpopular in some quarters in the university community—especially among those who have become comfortable with mediocrity. The pursuit of innovation and excellence is often resisted by members of an existing academic community when a dynamic new leader comes in. Consequently, the most able leaders must also be politically savvy. The leaders of universities govern by authority rather than power, and they cannot afford to have the faculty turn on them. Some great university leaders have also been able to educate the larger population about the value of education and the contributions that research universities make to American society.

James Lipton and I demonstrated the predictive power of some of these factors in our study of the top medical schools in the late 1970s.[3] By surveying a number of physicians and scientists working at medical schools to evaluate the quality of the schools, we collected a great deal of information about the various characteristics of each school and about the clinical and basic science faculty members they employed. We then attempted to produce equations that would predict the relative rankings of the schools. It turned out that only six factors explained 80 percent of the total variance in the reputations of the schools: aggregate faculty productivity (especially productivity of the basic science faculty); NIH research funding for faculty members, training grants and fellowships for students, the number of graduate and postdoctoral fellows, the size of the full-time faculty, and the eminence of the faculty. Perceived quality is not, of course, the same as quality per se, but subsequent studies have shown that any set of indicators that contains some or all of the factors I've specified above tend to be useful in evaluating the quality of schools and academic departments—and in assessing the overall quality of research universities.

The core values identified in Chapter 2 and the thirteen factors described above must work hand in hand if a university is to realize the scientific and scholarly breakthroughs that will make it a top institution. The same values and predictive factors are, in part, what led to international recognition of American universities. Many universities have at least some of these factors in place, but few have them all. And the one thing that many lack is excellent leadership. Only a handful of leaders, well aware of the opportunities and how to seize them, have built steeples of excellence. We will now look at two case studies showing how a leader of a university can take it into that top tier.

FREDERICK EMMONS TERMAN:
THE ROLE OF GREAT LEADERSHIP AT STANFORD

Federal support of scientific and technological research provided enormous opportunities for a number of quiet, but well-positioned universities to propel themselves into the top echelon. No one took greater advantage of this than the leaders of Stanford. The ascendance of Stanford is a postwar phenomenon of great significance because it shows how an intersection of local and national history with the ambitions of exceptional leaders could create a world-class university within a generation. Although Stanford has had many great leaders, the one leader who stands out the most in this regard is Frederick Emmons Terman, provost from 1955 to 1965.

Stanford had aspirations to high quality almost from its beginnings. Its early leaders wanted it to be competitive with the prestigious private colleges of the East. Stanford had many advantages. Located on the peninsula south of San Francisco, it appealed to those interested in living and working on the West Coast, and it benefited from the flight to the suburbs from deteriorating inner cities in the 1950s. There were few private universities west of the Mississippi at the time it was founded, a time of great expansion into the American West. Stanford was never less than a good university within a few decades of its founding. But for generations it was better known for its undergraduate programs and could not be counted among the world's great centers of higher learning. It did not even rank in the top dozen of the nation in 1925, despite the aspirations of its leaders, and in fact was still significantly behind the great private and public universities in most disciplines. Today, it surely would be listed in the top five universities in the nation, and the Chinese rank it as second in the world.

Much of Stanford's success can be attributed to the brilliant leadership duo of President Wallace "Wally" Sterling and Terman, who served under him as provost.[4] They respected each other enormously, trusted each other, and worked collaboratively. But it was undoubtedly the innovative Terman who had the bolder vision of what Stanford could become, the strategic mind to determine how to move it into a totally new position in the hierarchy of great institutions of learning, and the ability to use his personal history, academic experiences, and social networks to help Stanford realize its potential. One should not minimize the singular importance of Sterling, a Stanford history Ph.D., a former director of the Huntington Library, and an affable and popular network news analyst during World War II, nor the roles played by Stanford's deans and department chairs. Yet it is Terman who deserves greater attention if we are to understand how to produce a preeminent university.[5]

Sterling once said he had "struck it rich" when Terman agreed to become provost. If Terman tended to stay in the shadow of Stanford's presidents, his presence was felt through the power that he wielded and his obsession to create in Stanford a university that could compete successfully with the best of the older eastern elites. The way this pair of administrators worked became a model of effective division of labor between a president and a provost. Their story demonstrates how important social, intellectual, political, and business networks can be to the building process, as well as how a strong provost—the chief academic officer of a university—can complement a superb, active president in governing the rapidly expanding and increasingly complex organization of the modern research university.

Terman was a "lifer"—rare then and rarer today. He was born in 1900 into a famous academic Stanford family—his father was the influential psychologist Lewis Terman. Fred Terman was weaned and raised at Stanford and lived most of his adult life there as well. No one could have been more loyal and devoted to Stanford—or to its football team. By the time he became provost, he had a stockpile of ideas at his disposal about how to build greatness. He would use that knowledge to good effect.

As a boy, Fred Terman was encouraged by his family to pursue his own interests, and, like many youngsters at the time, he was fascinated by the concept of the radio. He majored in chemistry at Stanford, graduating in 1920, but had taken courses in mechanical engineering as well and had continued to pursue his interest in the theoretical and practical aspects of radio technology. He next enrolled in MIT to pursue a Ph.D. in electrical engineering. When it was time for him to choose an area for his thesis and a faculty adviser, he cast his lot with a young and rising MIT star, Vannevar Bush.

Bush, who was not yet the wartime leader he would become, would have a special influence on Terman's career. Terman became a full professor at Stanford and was active in the Institute of Radio Engineers. He admired Bush greatly and nominated him for the presidency of Stanford in 1941. Bush rejected the invitation to be considered for the job, in part because he felt Stanford was drifting without much vision. Bush, in turn, recruited Terman to head an independent Radio Research Lab (RRL) shortly after the bombing of Pearl Harbor. In that position, Terman was involved in countermeasures such as jamming the radio signals of the enemy.[6]

Clearly, in the world of research universities, as elsewhere, there are extensive interlocking networks of associations between the people who become powerful figures within their own organizations and on the larger national scene. Social networks produced opportunities for Terman that would affect the course of his career. Being Bush's student would prove to be of great value—especially since Terman was an excellent student—as would the friendships that he established with other undergraduates who would later become trustees of Stanford. Moreover, Terman's experiences working with these people and observing their habits, values, and methods would have a profound influence on how he conceptualized the growth of Stanford.

Once he completed his doctoral program (and before being recruited for the RRL), Terman weighed offers of positions at both MIT and Stanford (he was recovering from a near-fatal bout with tuberculosis at the same time). MIT was the stronger engineering school, but Terman chose the institution he had always loved. Upon his return to Stanford in 1925, Terman took up his professorship, and, in due course, he assumed the challenge of building a nationally recognized department of electrical engineering. He succeeded both as a researcher and as a teacher and mentor to his students. Among his students would be several young stars, including William Hewlett and David Packard. Some would become the backbone of the new startup companies in Santa Clara County; others would become important actors in building Stanford. Terman's deep commitment to his students, including his abiding interest in seeing them well placed in jobs and well connected with Stanford, would in due time pay huge dividends for his alma mater.

Terman's work at Stanford remains the model for how to go about achieving true distinction for a university. Three features of his work before and during his time as provost are particularly instructive: his experience during World War II at the Radio Research Lab; his success in transforming the Stanford Medical School into a powerhouse of modern biological science and medical research, a feat he accomplished when Sterling moved the medical school to the main Palo Alto campus; and, most importantly, his efforts to build "steeples of excellence" at Stanford—metaphorical towers that would be the equal of any constructed at Berkeley and that would make Stanford the Harvard and MIT of the West.

Terman embraced a dynamic rather than a static model of the university. This meant not becoming stuck in the historical past, but instead being attentive to what a changing society would require from its great research universities in the future. A university's leaders had to position the institution to take full advantage of the new social conditions at hand. They must be open to the dynamics of societal and academic change, constantly looking to the future, and not fall prey to looking backward toward the illusions of a disappearing Golden Age.

Terman's reaction to the federal government's involvement in research funding is a good example of this attitude. In the postwar years when the federal government decided to begin funding science at universities in a big way, some presidents and provosts were depressed. They believed that the government's increased role in university life would lead to a loss of autonomy; that it would distort the curriculum by overemphasizing the sciences at the expense of the humanities; and that it would expand bureaucratic control over the university. These skeptics were committed to an ecclesiastical model of learning, and they were wary of change. Terman, however, recognized the enormous potential of the government's new role and saw that it could be the very thing that could propel universities ahead, making them the engines of national innovation.

Because of his experiences during the war, and perhaps because of innate personality traits, Terman was able to read the national tea leaves properly. He knew Vannevar Bush personally, and he was convinced that the federal government was going to get into the business of research at the nation's best universities and that it would support those places on the basis of peer-reviewed judgments of quality. This would include research that was believed to be in the national interest, including military-related research. Terman saw great potential in the close linkage between the university and new, innovative industrial enterprises.

Terman also believed that the provost should be the ultimate gatekeeper of quality, and by taking the lead in this way at Stanford, he ensured a level of quality there that was unparalleled. He believed that the provost should review every appointment to the faculty, especially tenure appointments, and scrutinize them in terms of research excellence and potential. Recruiting the best, preferably by engaging a group of exceptionally able scholars almost simultaneously, was the path to excellence that he favored. In this recruitment process, the provost, he believed, must not rely solely on the opinions of those who nominated professors for positions; nor should he ever trust just one source. Rather, he should set up a network of trusted advisers to help assess quality. It was also important to evaluate, sometimes brutally, the current quality of the departments and their faculty in order to develop ideas about how they could be improved.

Terman in fact had an obsession with quantification that would become part of his arsenal for dispassionately (some would say ruthlessly) evaluating departments and individual scholars, scientists, and engineers. This reliance on quantification had been handed down from his father, who had been instrumental in disseminating the idea of the IQ test and believed that it was possible to quantify what many people thought were purely qualitative concepts. (Perhaps not surprisingly, this notion of how to conduct faculty evaluations also had its share of critics, and it created some resentment at Stanford among those who did not share Terman's confidence in quantitative evaluations.)

Finally, Terman believed in innovation, and that included innovation in how to lead a university. He was willing to try methods that were not traditional, methods that the older Eastern universities had not yet attempted. His experience at MIT made him much more aggressive about partnering with industry and government than Harvard was in the 1950s, for example. But he wasn't confined by what MIT had done, either: MIT concentrated on specific areas of research, but Terman was not inclined to do this. He encouraged any research that would build on the curiosity and interests of individual faculty members. He was willing to make tough and sometimes unpopular decisions, and he was able to develop thick enough skin to withstand the ensuing criticism from those who had become comfortable with the status quo. In short, he dramatically expanded the power of the provost over all matters of academic planning and appointments.

Terman also was deeply involved with Stanford's budget, deciding how best to use Stanford's resources to build academic greatness and compete with the finest schools in the nation.[7] He knew that to dislodge great faculty from their current positions elsewhere, he would have to provide them with incentives to join Stanford, such as first-rate research facilities and a set of potentially exciting colleagues and collaborators. He and Sterling knew full well that achieving their vision for Stanford would be extremely costly; the resources required to do the job properly would be on a scale previously unknown to the university. To make Stanford one of the greatest schools in the nation, they would have to find new sources of revenue, including government funding, private philanthropic contributions, and alumni pockets.[8]

Because of the huge expense, Terman knew that he could not develop all parts of the university simultaneously; rather, he and the other leaders at Stanford would have to be selective and decide where the university might have strategic advantages over its competitors. They must move first into areas of comparative advantage and create true distinction there before moving on to other areas. Over time, the advantages would accumulate, leading to further research and teaching strength.

Terman was still a Stanford professor when Bush recruited him for the RRL project following Pearl Harbor. He took a leave of absence and spent the next four years with his family in Cambridge (RRL was first located at MIT and then relocated to Harvard). As head of RRL, Terman would build an organization of top-flight professionals drawn from the academy and industry. He recruited engineers, physicists, and others, drawing from both universities and businesses, and maintained strong connections to some of America's leading corporations that were working independently on radio research and communications. When RRL was at its height in 1943, there were about 800 people working there, and the RRL had a budget greater than Stanford's. Although building a large scientific and engineering operation so quickly was not without its difficulties, Terman gained a great deal from his experience at RRL. The program had concrete results for the cause of the war, and Terman discovered that he had a talent for constructing and effectively leading a large, diverse, mission-oriented organization that had a clear set of priorities. Terman would return to Stanford with this experience under his belt, ready to take on larger tasks where his ability would to be put to good use.

As a newly appointed provost, Terman brought his talent for novel, dynamic thinking to the project of helping President Sterling move Stanford Medical School to the Palo Alto campus from its prior home in San Francisco, where it had been located for forty years. Sterling had taken the lead in 1953. He believed that the most distinguished medical schools were integrated in various ways with the other core science and social-science disciplines of the great universities. He had rallied the support of the Stanford trustees and enlisted the backing of powerful members of the medical school faculty, science faculty, and significant alumni. He had successfully navigated the turgid political waters surrounding the move, overcoming substantial resistance from physicians who had built medical practices in the Bay Area, and he had proved equally capable of finding the resources necessary for building the new school. He recommended a fundraising drive of $15 million over three to five years for building a new medical school and teaching hospital, as well as library, classrooms, and laboratory facilities for the faculty and students. Although this figure pales in comparison with today's capital campaigns, which set goals in the billions of dollars, it was viewed as ambitious at the time. The Stanford Medical Center was dedicated in September 1959 after six years of planning and building.[9]

Terman's role is most clearly seen in the way the new science and medical faculties were organically linked to one another and to the core of the university. He would implicate the Provost's Office into the search for talent and would be instrumental in recruiting world-class scientists and students, and he would ensure that the medical school was integrated academically—and to a lesser extent physically—into the essential structure of the arts and sciences. Because of his expertise in engineering and his extensive knowledge of the physical sciences, and his awareness of the impact of Watson and Crick's recent discoveries in genetics, he realized that in the future, medicine would be far more dependent on the basic physical and biological sciences than it had been in the past. He therefore sought to increase interdisciplinary ties.

As Terman saw it, medical researchers and clinicians at the new facility should be able to interact easily with those who were interested in pure science at the main university—the faculty in the biological and chemical sciences, for example. And there were other cross-fertilizations that intrigued him: Accelerator engineers and radiologists might be able to provide new tools for fighting cancer.[10] Terman undertook the painstaking task of recruitment with this commitment to interdisciplinary work in mind, paving the way for the science and medical school faculty to be able to solve large, complex problems through effective collaboration.

Terman sought the best available people when recruiting from other universities and institutions. Using his formidable powers of persuasion, and with the help of medical school dean Robert Alway, he was able to recruit the biochemist Arthur Kornberg from Washington University in St. Louis, as well as the polymath geneticist Joshua Lederberg from Wisconsin, to organize the Department of Genetics (both later became Nobel laureates). Although Stanford already had a nationally recognized program in the biological sciences,[11] Kornberg was also promised that he could make a considerable number of new appointments. He showed his good taste in recruiting Melvin Cohn and Paul Berg, who in 1980 would both win Nobel Prizes for Chemistry for their work at Stanford. Terman, Alway, and others also recruited the research immunologist Halsted Holman from the Rockefeller Institute to become, at age thirty-five, the chairman of the Department of Medicine. Terman thus positioned Stanford to participate in the biomedical revolution that was then taking shape. In 1961, he recruited David Hamburg from the National Institutes of Health to chair the Department of Psychiatry and Behavioral Sciences.[12]

Terman carried out these searches with meticulous care, calling on the opinions of the best people in the country in particular fields and making full-scale assaults on those whom he wanted to bring to Stanford. Throughout the recruitment efforts, he remained flexible and innovative. He considered joint appointments between the arts and sciences and the medical school, amenable to constructing new structures and facilities that would promote research and teaching. He also believed in recruiting en masse, even if it proved expensive.

By 1961, Terman was making deep inroads into the faculties of the great Ivy League institutions. *Newsweek* ran a story that year that featured thirteen new Stanford professors recruited from Harvard, Columbia, Yale, and MIT—with five more on the way. During Terman's tenure as provost, he and Dean Alway doubled the size of the medical school faculty and tripled the medical school's research funding. The bill for all of this was large, and raising the money to pay for it would require an enormous effort. Nevertheless, Stanford's successes at recruiting top scientists and scholars only fueled its ambitions. Renowned author and Stanford writing professor Wallace Stegner called Stanford "a university trembling on the edge of greatness." To push it over the edge, in 1961 Stanford announced a campaign to raise $100 million, encouraged by a three-to-one matching gift of $25 million from the Ford Foundation.[13] For Terman, the campaign provided an opportunity to improve faculty salaries, compete more effectively for the best students by providing better financial aid packages, and build the infrastructure necessary for a rapidly expanding research base.

Terman correctly believed that quality bred quality. Quality in fact also led to cascading resources and renown. The payoff for preeminence was multidimensional. Capital campaigns depend on a group of proud alumni who would like to see their alma mater on the rise, with the value and prestige of their own degrees going up accordingly. Terman was also convinced that there would be substantial federal investment in the health sciences through the National Institutes of Health, and that the lion's share of funding would go to those schools with the greatest scientific talent. Without that potential source of funding, the vision for the medical school would not have been a practical matter for Stanford at the time. Stanford still lagged far behind its eastern rivals in terms of available resources.

Having guided a large-scale science operation during the war, and knowing well the views of Vannevar Bush, Terman was convinced that—like it or not—big science represented the wave of the future. The medical center guaranteed that Stanford was casting its lot with those who were moving from little to big science. The difficult and often contentious effort to construct the government-sponsored Stanford Linear Accelerator (SLAC), which at two miles in length is the longest linear accelerator in the world (it's often called "the world's straightest object"), was also intended to signal this commitment. Construction began in 1962 while Terman was provost and was completed in 1966. Although early on there was a good deal of conflict between some members of the physics faculty and researchers and administrators at SLAC, the facility has largely succeeded in fulfilling its mission to carry out state-of-the-art experiments in physics and making Stanford more competitive in the physical sciences.

The risks taken by Terman and Sterling have been rewarded over time with true preeminence in the biomedical and physical sciences. Today, a half century after the move to Palo Alto, the Stanford Medical Center is one of the best in the world, continually producing medical miracles and novel discoveries, and as of 2007 bringing in about $300 million annually for research and student support from the National Institutes of Health alone.

Terman was not only recruiting in the sciences. He also recruited towering law school figures, such as the great constitutional law professor Gerald Gunther in 1962. The appointment of Gunther and other notable law school faculty around the same time would rapidly propel the Stanford

Law School into the company of the nation's best. Terman also focused his attention on economics and political science (a discipline that had been in dire straits at Stanford in the 1950s) as well as on a number of fields in the humanities. But in keeping with his belief in comparative advantage, Terman focused less on the humanities during his tenure as provost than on many other fields. He was, in truth, more comfortable with his own ability to measure quality in the sciences and engineering and to assess the achievements and potential of people in these fields.

The provost would go to almost any length to establish in his own mind the quality of the candidates he would recruit. His ingenuity at finding appropriate measures of quality could be found in the way he used the opinions of well-established authorities. And he was shrewd. Terman looked at the balloting for membership in the elite National Academy of Sciences—not only for those who were elected, but for those younger people who had just missed the cut. They were apt to be future stars, most likely as good as many who were actually elected—many would in fact be elected in due course—and they were apt not to be nearly so costly to recruit as the more established scientists who were already academy members.

Terman's recruiting efforts didn't stop with Stanford's immediate faculty; he went so far as to help establish independent institutions that would be built on Stanford land and would be loosely affiliated with the university. A superb example of this is his support for housing a new Center for Advanced Study in the Behavioral Sciences that would be initially supported by a grant from the Ford Foundation and would be organized according to the ideas of leading social scientists, including Robert K. Merton and Paul F. Lazarsfeld from Columbia. The idea was to bring young "stars" to the center for a year to allow them to work on new research in areas that would expand their portfolio or to complete projects they had already begun. Between forty and fifty scholars were to be selected each year by a panel of exceptional social scientists. Stanford leased a piece of land it owned overlooking Lake Lagunita, next to its golf course, to the center for $1 a year. The university would help find housing for the scholars and would allow them to use some of its facilities, including its libraries and, later, its computing facilities.

In return, the center would bring the best and brightest of the nation's social scientists (as well as some humanists and law faculty) to Stanford, giving the Stanford departments an opportunity to look these scholars over. In many cases this resulted in recruitment efforts. At the same time, the program gave the scholars, many coming from the Ivy League universities and the best state universities in the Midwest, such as Illinois, Michigan, and Wisconsin, a chance to get a taste of Palo Alto and Stanford and see if it appealed to them. Terman had found a natural form of peer review to help him build the social science departments at the university, and it worked. Since the center's birth about forty of Stanford's tenured social and behavioral science faculty have been recruited from the scholars who spent a year as fellows at the center.

Terman's methods had a huge impact on Stanford, giving it a significant boost in the rankings of U.S. universities. At the time that Terman became provost, Stanford could have been placed somewhere in the range of thirteenth to fifteenth among the top twenty universities in the nation. It was very good, but not among the greatest. That relative ranking rose steadily in the ensuing decades. By 1970, almost all of Stanford's Ph.D. programs, except for those in the humanities, were ranked within the top ten, and most of the science and engineering programs in the top five. This is a remarkable upward trajectory if you realize that, as a rule of thumb, the price for rising arithmetically in the rankings is geometric in cost.

Using imperfect yet widely accepted quantitative assessments, we can measure the rise of Stanford as one of the world's greatest research universities. Fred Terman would have been very pleased with the results. The periodic ratings of the quality of universities and specific departments and programs that began to appear at the beginning of the twentieth century, and appeared with greater frequency as the century progressed, show the trends in Stanford's rise over the decades; the results strongly suggest that Sterling and Terman set the move to preeminence into motion.[14] Stanford was not the only university in America that was improving at this time. In fact, most of the other universities that are now ranked at the top were getting stronger then as well. And there were many up-and-coming research universities that were making progress.[15] But Stanford's relative rise was greater than that of most of the other elite universities, and the speed with which it accomplished its ascendance was greater, too, thanks in large part to Terman.

True to his calling as an engineer, Fred Terman designed and built systems. His conception of the new structures that would enhance Stanford's quality and prestige extended beyond the formal boundaries of the Palo Alto campus. He projected the new research university into the heart of local economic development. The new university would extend its reach to include the needs and aspirations of nearby growing businesses. In fact, Stanford would do what it could to stimulate new forms of technology and businesses in the local area. A new synergy would be created between industry and the university.

Terman had witnessed similar efforts at MIT in the 1920s, and he now used his experience, his own engineering talent, and the postwar explosion of federal and industrial interest in the new electronics industry for Stanford's benefit. The "steeples of excellence" that he had built in engineering and the sciences would extend their influence into the surrounding community. As Terman put it: "Universities are rapidly becoming major economic influences in the nation's industrial life, affecting the location of industry, population growth, and the character of communities. Universities are in brief a natural resource just as are raw materials, transportation, climate, etc. . . . Industry is finding that, for activities involving a high level of scientific and technological creativity, a location in a center of brains is more important than a location near markets, raw materials, transportation, or factory labor."[16]

Silicon Valley would have to wait to be formally named for its high-tech industries; journalists didn't begin using the term for the northern Santa Clara Valley until the early 1970s, after Terman had reached the then mandatory retirement age of sixty-five at Stanford. But it was Terman's vision that had jump-started those industries in the valley to begin with. He was highly successful in attracting money from different sources for advanced electronics research and other high-tech ideas, such as the development of the "klystron," a microwave-generating tube used in particle accelerators.[17] By 1950, when he was an engineering professor (not yet provost), his own research group's support represented almost a fourth of all the federal research dollars spent by Stanford. He envisioned the growth of high technology in the area, and to make his vision a reality, he encouraged his students to begin companies near the university, producing incentives for them and others to do so by using Stanford land to house small start-ups. The Stanford Industrial Park, a highly successful collaboration between industry and the university, was developed on Stanford land by some extraordinary early tenants, including Hewlett-Packard.[18]

The new industrial park was such a success that it became a model to others in the United States and abroad. After General Charles de Gaulle of France visited an exhibit on the park at the 1958 World's Fair in Brussels, he "insisted on making a pilgrimage there himself to uncover its secrets."[19] And while Terman was producing students who would lead these new, highly successful companies, he was enlisting the best scientists he could recruit to explore the basic science behind the technology that was being developed in Stanford laboratories. He was determined to create and support linkages between the basic sciences and the potentially derivative engineering uses.

The success of the industrial-university nexus was emphatically not the work of Terman alone. The historical moment and California's ripeness for industrial growth contributed mightily to the favorable climate necessary for the revolution in electronics and later the development of microchips in Silicon Valley. In a sense, Stanford and Silicon Valley grew up together; both were in the right place at the right time.[20] But in Fred Terman, we see a fiercely competitive visionary leader who was willing to use the advantages at hand to propel Stanford into the front ranks of research universities and devise a win-win strategy for local economic growth and the growth of Stanford.[21]

Terman embraced the ingredients necessary for international distinction that I outlined at the beginning of this chapter. He was obsessed with quality and recruiting productive, highly esteemed faculty members; he was committed to expanding the research base by attracting government financing; and he knew that having the best faculty would enable the university to draw the best students. He looked for the resources necessary to build highly competitive physical facilities. He maximized the value of Stanford's location. In short, he provided the leadership necessary to build a critical mass of academic talent in fields where Stanford had an advantage in recruiting stars or potential stars.

What were the other great universities doing while Stanford was racing ahead with its strategic plan for raising steeples of excellence? Many institutions, such as MIT, were also making good progress, cognizant of the movement of history and changing needs; others were more resistant to change. The University of California, under the leadership of Clark Kerr, was working toward an important adaptation of the American model of higher learning that was designed to meet new national needs (something we'll look at in more depth in the next section). The ones that were slower to see the movement of history fell behind.

Let me use Columbia as an example of a university that was slow to make the necessary adjustments. Columbia did not have leaders who were willing to significantly alter the organization of the university in order to accommodate the rapid expansion that came after the war. Dwight David Eisenhower was an unhappy president of Columbia, and the faculty was equally unhappy with him. Eisenhower did little while there other than prepare for a run for a larger presidency. He had selected Grayson Kirk as his provost, and Kirk had served as acting president while Eisenhower was absent in Europe as supreme commander of the North Atlantic Treaty Organization (NATO).

Kirk became Columbia's president in 1953. He was a "cautious man, less assertive than some of his fellow-administrators in American institutions," according to one of his former students, the historian Fritz Stern. Described also as "shy," "private," even "remote," he was not a person with a bold vision for Columbia in the new age of greater government influence on universities. During the troubled McCarthy years, he was surely a man of greater courage than most of his peers. Devoted to the idea of academic freedom, he weighed in strongly against the forces of repression. In 1950, he said, "It is time for us to stop this witch-hunting and this search for simple explanations." And later, in 1953, when the universities were about to become the focus of the House Un-American Activities Committee (HUAC), Kirk asserted: "Any university worthy of the name must resist at all costs any or all forces, internal or external, which would deflect it from its true course, distort its purpose, and reduce it to an agency dedicated to the propagation of official doctrine . . . fixed by external authority. The voices of the hour and the passions and fashions of the day must never be allowed to move a university from its path. They pass; a university remains."[22]

Columbia's achievements during Kirk's time were at best incremental rather than revolutionary. He did raise funds for some needed buildings, but not enough to delay the overall erosion of the physical campus, which included increasingly shoddy and outmoded facilities for the sciences, social sciences, and humanities. There was no grand plan to enhance Columbia's position in the world of the new American research university.

Kirk, a political scientist who had been a significant figure in formulating ideas for the United Nations and a leading light in the Council on Foreign Relations, began Columbia's foray into the study of different cultures by setting up regional institutes that would be part of a new School of International Affairs. Columbia continued to have an incredibly strong faculty in many fields, but this was due in part to the natural attractions of New York for many leading intellectuals. At the end of his tenure, after becoming more remote from the true challenges that faced the university, Kirk would be known, tragically, more for calling in the police to remove students from university buildings during the campus protests in 1968 than for any of his other accomplishments.

Columbia's provost and dean of faculties from 1958 to 1967, overlapping substantially with Terman's tenure as provost, was the extraordinary cultural historian and public intellectual Jacques Barzun. Although he was a Columbia icon and a superb scholar, Barzun did not have the vision or the will to push Columbia forward the way Terman was advancing Stanford. And Barzun was decidedly ambivalent, if not antagonistic, about the move to "big science" and the move from an ecclesiastical to a bureaucratic form of university organization. Perhaps these attitudes could be tolerated in the short run, because Columbia had already achieved a position as one of the great American research universities, and maybe its leaders did not feel it necessary to make Columbia a dynamic model for a changing university in a new postwar world.

In the 1950s Columbia continued to turn out great physicists and chemists and other distinguished scientists. But it was beginning to run on momentum rather than new fuel. It had built up great humanities programs over the years—perhaps the best in the United States along with Harvard and Yale. It had the advantage of being in New York City. And it was already a powerhouse in most of the social sciences. But its leaders did not see the need for renovating or expanding its rapidly decaying physical facilities for science and engineering or for intensifying the reach and quality of the undergraduate liberal arts school, Columbia College, and bringing it into the center of the university. Nor did they work on raising the resources that would be necessary to compete for the very best.

Although Columbia today has regained its footing and remains among the top ten or so research universities in the United States and the world, and in many fields can count itself among the very best, it had to recover

over the past twenty-five years from a decline that began in the 1950s, and that was dealt a brutal blow by the events surrounding the campus riots of the late 1960s. By 1970, after canceling its first effort at conducting a major capital campaign—the campus was in shock in the wake of the violence, and alumni were not apt to give under those conditions—Columbia was on the verge of not being able to meet its payroll. Few knew this, or that, unable to make competitive offers for new faculty, Columbia would have to make hard choices about what distinguished faculty with offers from other great places it should try to hold on to.

Part of this relative deterioration of the university was also a matter of attitude and belief. In his 1968 book *The American University: How It Runs, Where It Is Going,* Barzun outlined the plethora of new demands on the university from its various constituencies—trustees, faculty, students, alumni, and increasingly, government officials—and the consequences for the bureaucratization of university life. Although he was perfectly clear that government financing of higher education and research had great benefits, it was not clear whether Barzun believed that the benefits outweighed the costs. He pointed to a great number of truly daunting problems that the new American university would have to face, including increased tension between teaching and research as more faculty members received external funding for their work; the expansion of faculty sizes and the number of courses; increased loyalties among faculty members to their disciplines rather than to their university; budgetary pressures resulting from the government's failure to reimburse universities for the full costs of "federally funded" research; the tensions created by the democratization of the university and its increased diversity; the problem of establishing demarcations between what government research should or should not be conducted on university campuses; and the pressures of external social revolutions in race and gender relations on the internal operations of the university and the mounting pressure to change an "old boys' club" into a more open university society.[23]

It is true that these and other problems were having an impact at research universities in the 1960s. Barzun was hardly the only leader of a major university to become concerned about the growing tension between the sciences and humanities and between the needs of a large-scale research enterprise and those of undergraduate education. Many of these tensions continue to exist today. Even the architect of the California university system, Clark Kerr, recognized that the infusion of government funds into research meant that a "university's control over its own destiny" had been "substantially reduced."[24] What differentiates some leaders from others was how they approached these new challenges.

But people like Terman and Kerr saw abundance and new opportunities despite the pressures that came with them. Barzun's inclination was to return with a tone of longing and nostalgia for the cloistered university of Cardinal Newman that concentrated principally on teaching with a more limited research mission. His attitude toward the increased size and complexity of the research university was in fact almost the opposite of Terman's. Where Terman saw great opportunities, both for Stanford and for a growing nation that had new needs, Barzun saw only threats to the integrity of the university he longed to maintain—the university as a sanctuary.[25]

The opportunity costs for Columbia were large. Barzun and Kirk's leadership slowed down Columbia's transformation, and even this slow rate of change was brought to a halt by the debacle of 1968, which led to faculty factions at war with each other, and finally to a mass exodus of first-rate talent. Columbia's financial instability was also exacerbated by the handling of the student protests. Of course, much of what happened at Stanford and Columbia in the 1960s can be accounted for by external forces and events—positive forces for economic growth in northern California and negative forces affecting New York City and Columbia, which was more squarely caught up in the tumultuous political and social struggles of the day. But the quality and cast of mind of the leaders during the 1960s mattered, and Terman took the chance to ride the crest of the wave that was transforming research universities, while Kirk, Barzun, and others at Columbia essentially missed it.

Terman did not formalize his methods for achieving international distinction at Stanford in a way that could be imitated by others. But other leaders of state and private universities independently recognized how they might take advantage of a rapidly changing environment for university research and teaching. Many of the great state universities, such as those in California, Michigan, Wisconsin, and Illinois, recognized what could be gained from the increased resources available for research and innovation. All expanded their scientific research facilities in anticipation of greater government funding, and some, like the University of Michigan at Ann

Arbor, dedicated resources to building core facilities that would enable social scientists to carry out large-scale research efforts that could take advantage of new sources of revenue from both the government and the
private sector.

Michigan's Survey Research Center, established in 1946, would become part of a larger umbrella organization, the Institute for Social Research, formed in 1949. It rapidly became the largest interdisciplinary
social research institute in the world. Meanwhile, Columbia, which
housed the famous Bureau of Applied Social Research at the same time,
put almost no money into expanding its operations in anticipation of
large social science research projects. Michigan and Wisconsin, as well as
Berkeley and UCLA, anticipated this movement in the social and behavioral sciences and recognized that many of the best young faculty
members in these disciplines would gravitate to institutions that could
support more sophisticated research efforts. The competitive advantage
led to a generation in which those state universities rapidly outpaced
many of the privates in building social science quality of the highest rank.
Clark Kerr was one of the most forward-looking of the state university
leaders, someone who could build an entire system of higher education to
press toward excellence.

Clark Kerr: Access and Excellence

While Frederick Terman was helping to create the phenomenon of Stanford, not far away, another Californian, Clark Kerr, was putting into place
the most significant advance in the idea of the American university since
the model had been first formulated in the 1930s. He was developing what
would become the "multiversity," a system of higher education with different schools, colleges, and divisions loosely integrated to fulfill different
functions in complementary ways.

All organisms must adapt to their environments if they are to survive
and prosper. Universities face the same challenge. The American research
university had adapted to meet the expanding needs of American society
in the past, and at the turning point of World War II, it needed to adapt
once again. In every era, there have been skeptics and critics who have
viewed either the expansion of the university mission or the sheer growth
of the university in complexity and size as part of its likely undoing. Many

of the adaptations took place first in the state university systems rather than in the older, private universities, perhaps because the latter were more steeped in tradition. And the university leader who was arguably the most influential innovator in these postwar adaptations was Clark Kerr.

Clark Kerr faced the challenge of building a system of higher education that would not only respond successfully to the needs of California's exploding population but also compete with the best in the world for talented scientists and scholars. In short, he wanted to build a state system that was designed for both access and excellence. This was in many ways a Herculean task, because achieving excellence requires some exclusivity, while providing access for students with vastly different levels of ability requires flexibility and openness.

Clark Kerr's crowning achievement was to produce the Master Plan of 1960 for Higher Education in California, a model for the nation of how both of these basic values could be realized. The plan was simple in concept, yet difficult to implement. It introduced the idea of a three-tiered system for California higher education. At the highest academic level were the major research universities, such as Berkeley and UCLA. This layer would serve the top 12.5 percent of the state's high school graduates and qualified students from out of state. A second tier, enrolling another third of California's high school graduates, consisted of a state college system whose primary mission was the transmission of knowledge, not conducting research. And finally, a third tier, the community colleges, with vocational offerings and two-year programs, were to be open to all the high school graduates who did not qualify for the four-year colleges and universities.

A principal component of the Master Plan was the opportunity for students who succeeded at one of the lower-tier schools to transfer to a higher-tier school. Another principle was that no student should be denied a college education for lack of financial resources. Although Kerr's ambition to create a truly fluid system has never been fully realized, perhaps because he never had complete control over each of the tiers, his ideas were sufficiently approximated to reinforce the belief that the state's system of education offered unusual opportunities for upward social mobility—a chance to realize the American dream.

As the state population grew and the demand for higher learning increased, new campuses in each tier were built to meet the new need. The success of the plan was predicated on the state's willingness to invest handsomely in both access and quality, and for some time, it did just that. Kerr had carved out an ingenious mix of elitism and populism. The result was a dramatic growth in the size of the system and its quality. Under Kerr's careful watch—like Terman, he monitored appointments assiduously, guided by the belief that those hired at top-tier institutions should fit comfortably into the elite group of scientists and scholars who could be found at universities ranked among the top five or six in their field—the University of California rapidly became one of the world's great research universities. Kerr was well aware of the criteria for preeminence: Basically, he needed the best faculty with access to the finest students. He tried to meet the needs of students of varying kinds, and the needs of the state for training young people with varying levels of skills, but he also wanted the University of California to realize research goals so that it could compete successfully with the great private universities in the East.

If there have been few educational leaders to possess both a vision for educational excellence and the ability to successfully implement that vision, Clark Kerr was one of the few. California's success in implementing the tiered Master Plan led the leaders of many other state systems to attempt to produce variations on the core idea. Kerr's ideas did meet with resistance, but that is something that has been true of all bold efforts by educational reformers. Paradoxically, individual university faculty members tend to be liberal, but when they are brought together to discuss educational reform, they become highly conservative. As Kerr observed: "A multiversity is inherently a conservative institution but with radical functions. There are so many groups with an interest in the status quo, so many veto groups; yet the university must serve a knowledge explosion and a population explosion simultaneously. The president becomes the central mediator among the values of the past, the prospects for the future and the realities of the present."[26]

Clark Kerr, born in 1911 and raised on an apple orchard in Pennsylvania, graduated from Swarthmore College in 1932 and then headed west. He received a master's degree in 1933 from Stanford and his doctorate in economics from UC Berkeley in 1939. Coming of age during the Depression, he worked on problems in labor economics before turning to an interest in higher education. He joined the Berkeley faculty in 1945 as a professor of economics and industrial relations, and he directed the newly formed Institute of Industrial Relations. He gained prominence and respect among the faculty when he unwaveringly defended the thirty-two Berkeley faculty members who had been fired during the Red Scare after World War II for refusing to sign a loyalty oath to the U.S. government. Kerr had in fact signed the oath, but he fought against the firings as a basic violation of academic freedom, speaking before the regents on their behalf and arguing in favor of their reappointment.

By 1951 he was clearly "the faculty's choice" when the university was searching for someone to fill the newly created position of chancellor. He served as chancellor until 1958, when he was selected as the twelfth president of the California system. Under his watch, California opened up new campuses at Irvine, San Diego, and Santa Cruz. He was president until 1964, when students were arrested at Berkeley for violating the campus ban on political activity that had followed a thirty-two-hour student sit-in at Berkeley's Sproul Hall. Attacked by the student protesters for his views about the university and its links to government, Kerr also had to endure the wrath of the California Board of Regents, who were frustrated that he had refused to use sufficient force to suppress student unrest on campus.

Students questioned his vision for the university, criticizing the university's ties to federal granting agencies, particularly the Defense Department, because they believed those ties cost the university its autonomy from external control. They also feared the loss of community in the new enlarged "multiversity." Most importantly, they viewed Kerr as deeply opposed to student political advocacy on campus. After all, Kerr did call in the police to quash the free speech demonstrators on the Berkeley campus. Why he came down so hard on the students for expressing political dissent, while earlier defending the faculty who refused to yield to political pressure during the controversy over the loyalty oath, remains a bit of a mystery. But calling in the police to quash student protesters was, if nothing else, a strategic blunder.

A distinct minority of the faculty also questioned Kerr's plan. Some felt that, without proper funding, the multiversity would not amount to much, and that because of the misplaced priorities, the university would be unable to support those students who truly could not afford to pay for their education. And the state, they feared, could not be counted on for proper financing.[27] Furthermore, they believed that Kerr's educational model would produce an unbalanced effort within the university, undermining some of the university's core values: It undervalued teaching, they claimed, and put excessive emphasis on recognition for research productivity. Finally, they worried that it represented a triumph of bureaucratic and administrative management models for the university over the more democratic and participatory faculty governance model that many faculty members saw as necessary for open debate and tolerance of radical ideas.

Some of the California regents thought Kerr had been too tolerant of the student protests. Worried about Kerr's tense relationship with newly elected governor Ronald Reagan, who had made suppression of student demonstrations one of his major campaign issues, the regents abruptly fired Kerr in January 1967. There is now evidence that the FBI was involved in the effort to fire Kerr; after the gubernatorial election, Kerr quickly became a whipping boy for the state's more conservative factions. For all the skepticism of the faculty and others, however, by the time he was fired Kerr had built a system that included at least one of the greatest universities in the world, and that was on its way to producing others. Kerr had created unprecedented educational opportunities for Californians— including second chances for those who had graduated from high school without distinction. Reflecting back on his firing, Kerr once said that he exited the way he had entered—"fired with enthusiasm." Upon learning of Kerr's death in December 2003, sociologist Martin Trow said that "history will simply know him as the most distinguished university president of the 20th century."[28]

Kerr's California model was heavily influenced by two things that took place at the federal level. The first was the passage of the GI Bill, which had a significant impact on colleges and universities following the war. The second was the adoption of Vannevar Bush's science policy and the drive to secure American scientific and technological leadership—and military supremacy.

President Roosevelt signed the "GI Bill of Rights," known officially as the Servicemen's Readjustment Act of 1944, on June 22 of that year. Perhaps the last highly consequential piece of New Deal legislation, it was designed to ease the adjustment of veterans to civilian life and avert massive unemployment. It had multiple provisions, including extended hospital benefits for GIs, special home loans, and educational benefits. The GI Bill offered 15 million veterans of World War II the opportunity to extend their college or vocational education at the government's expense.[29]

Under the bill's provisions, the government subsidized tuition, fees, books, and other educational materials and even contributed to students' living expenses at college. The veterans could choose any college or university they wished, as long as they met the admissions requirements. Because of these incentives, the bill had greater impact than any other government educational program in history—and a much greater impact than, for example, the more targeted effort of the Morrill Act that had been passed under Lincoln. Roughly 8 million veterans received educational benefits over seven years following the passage of the act, and between 1938 and 1948 the number of students enrolled in the nation's colleges and universities nearly doubled.

The consequences for student enrollment at individual universities were enormous—having a huge effect on the economy of these universities. For example, the University of Michigan, with fewer than 10,000 students prior to the war, had more than 30,000 by 1948. Syracuse University's enrollment grew from roughly 6,000 before the war to 19,000 by 1947. Tuition revenues increased dramatically, and much of the increased cost fell on the shoulders of the federal government: Fifty-six percent of the student fees at the private universities, and 67 percent of the fees at the public colleges and universities, came from the Veteran's Administration.[30]

But most significantly, the GI Bill produced a dramatic increase in the demand for higher learning, altering the expectations of young men and women about the possibilities of realizing their dreams through a college education. One of the more enlightened pieces of social policy of the Roosevelt years, the bill would have lasting effects. It promoted the idea that higher learning should be open to anyone who met the qualifications for college or university life. It was no longer an opportunity reserved for the elite class, those with families who could afford it. As with most ideals, this one has never been fully realized. But because of the GI Bill, progress was made in opening up higher learning to a far more diverse group of young people than previously had contemplated a college education. The universities, especially the public universities, now had to prepare for a much larger base of students, who would eventually also seek educational credentials beyond their undergraduate degrees. This was the extension of Conant's ideas of meritocracy and universalism, and Kerr's beliefs about access and excellence, to a majority of the young people of the United States.

The second factor at the national level that influenced Kerr's California model, the changing science policy spearheaded by Vannevar Bush, was grounded in a widespread perception that America's military superiority and economic welfare depended on its ability to develop a highly educated population as well as a smaller elite group of scientists and engineers who would produce ideas that had both social and military value. In anticipation of scaling up research activity, universities had to take a risk; they had to build an infrastructure of science buildings and laboratories so that they could compete successfully in the new peer-review environment. They hoped, of course, to fill the laboratories with researchers who would receive government support for the production of new knowledge. Like Fred Terman, Clark Kerr understood the needs, saw what was coming, and prepared his university for that growth. He set out to accommodate excellence along with access, making the large investments that would be needed to bring in the talented young people who would ensure the nation's continued leadership in science and scholarship.

Kerr believed in a broad system of higher learning. He was comfortable with the idea of the university as a somewhat chaotic and constantly changing place—an institution with many parts and missions that, taken together, comprised a multidimensional "city" where the parts were loosely integrated, rather than a small village or town that was truly coherent. Kerr called this hydra of a place the "multiversity"—a very different kind of place from the one Newman had hoped to see, which would emphasize the "uni" in "university," the unified nature of the institution. For Kerr, the university was a product of external as well as internal dynamic forces—each representing interests and values that were not always in strict harmony. It should be able to accommodate the interests of both humanists, who often sought a more cloistered existence, and scientists, who were very involved at that time in the world off-campus, even advising the nation's presidents. It should be a place where scholars and scientists could freely explore ideas, often without agreement.

Kerr distinguished his multiversity from Abraham Flexner's "organism," in which the "the parts and the whole are inextricably bound together." In the multiversity, according to Kerr, "many parts can be added and subtracted with little effect on the whole or even little notice taken or any blood spilled. It is more of a mechanism—a series of processes producing a series of results—a mechanism held together by administrative rules and powered by money." Robert Maynard Hutchins, he explained, "once described the modern university as a series of separate schools and departments held together by a central heating system. In an area [of the country] where heating is less important and the automobile more, I have sometimes thought of it as a series of individual faculty entrepreneurs held together by a common grievance over parking."[31]

This description of the research university of today is somewhat misleading. The late nineteenth-century German sociologist Ferdinand Toennies distinguished between *Gemeinschaft* (community) and *Gesellschaft* (society)—between communities held together because people—or "locals"—shared a common identity and perspective, and those held together by a sense of interdependence, which are more cosmopolitan. Kerr implied that the shared perspective of *Gemeinschaft* was largely absent in today's university, that universities were becoming more fragmented. Another way to explain this is that universities today are less integrated than they used to be in terms of what the French sociologist Emile Durkheim called "collective conscience"—that is, a sense of common identity is lacking among the faculties of the various schools.

But today the growth of knowledge itself is increasing pressure within universities to alter their structure to meet the needs of a multidisciplinary and more integrative approach to solving complex problems. The relative isolation of units, or schools, within the university is placing fetters on the growth of knowledge within them. The movement toward what the great Harvard biologist E. O. Wilson called "consilience," or reintegration of knowledge—or at least the realization that problem solving requires expertise drawn from all sectors of the university—may reduce the isolation of the various parts of the university that Kerr observed.

Kerr was right in suggesting that the multiversity was deeply integrated into the larger society in ways that were less apparent in the early twentieth century. But he underestimated the number of shared values of the university. I believe widespread consensus does exist across schools and faculties about some things. These core values are critical points of commonality and common identity within the university—and this agreement exists between faculties of arts and sciences and among business and law schools. The belief in the purposes of the university and the basic core values form the glue that holds the disparate parts of the university together in a fragile equilibrium.

Kerr's description also ascribes too much power to university administrators. Today, if a president or provost tries to close a school, department, or research institute, all hell is apt to break loose—not only among alumni and faculty members of the soon-to-be extinguished unit, but among concerned faculty and students in many quarters of the university. They agree about more than the parking.

Nonetheless, Kerr understood that the organism that has adapted to the new environmental conditions is very different from what existed at the time when Johns Hopkins University began its experiment as a center for research a hundred years earlier. And he understood that the idea of the university would continue to evolve as the needs of the larger society changed, and as the research university became increasingly central to the welfare of that society.

That has proved to be the case, as can been seen in a few ambitious efforts by leaders of American institutions of higher learning to extend Kerr's idea of maximizing both access and excellence while taking into account the new research environment of the early twenty-first century. For example, Michael Crow, president of Arizona State University since 2002, who worked with me at Columbia for a decade, is well aware of the California model. He is trying to craft a world-class research university that attracts the best scholars and scientists to a vibrantly new research environment that provides them with government resources and world-class facilities, but at the same time, he is making sure that Arizona State can provide a college education for a large population of Native Americans and other minorities, and that it can accommodate others who would be first-generation college graduates.

In creating what he calls "the new American university," Crow has consciously avoided imitating the Ivy League and the other older major private and public research universities. In particular, he wants to avoid the heavy emphasis they have placed, until recently, on a disciplinary structure. Without abandoning core disciplines, he has created a research environment that emphasizes multidisciplinary research in areas of national importance. A great deal of Arizona State's research is taking place in Pasteur's quadrant, in that it emphasizes the compatibility between curiosity-driven and utility-based research aimed at solving specific and important scientific and societal problems. Crow has a very precise idea of the thirteen criteria required for greatness, and, like both Terman and Kerr, he is systematically putting into place the elements needed to move Arizona State from a rather sleepy university into one that will be an active player on the world stage.[32]

Truly distinguished American universities are not built overnight or over a decade. In the past it was not uncommon for a great university president to stay around for several decades, putting ideas and strategies into place; collaborating with his provost, deans, and faculty; and working steadily to achieve long-term goals. But more recently, with the size and complexity of these institutions growing so rapidly, it is rare that even an exceptional leader stays in place for more than a dozen years. This creates the problem of succession for universities that have been fortunate enough to have extraordinary leadership.

Good leadership needs to be sustained if it is to be effective. Unfortunately, most universities—even those with large endowments and loyal patrons—can only run on autopilot for a short period of time. After a decade, the declines tend to be noticeable, and unless resources are available to plug the holes in the ship, the declines will continue. Places like Stanford and Chicago have been fortunate in selecting successors to their great leaders who have generally kept them on course—and in some cases strengthened them still further. But most universities have great difficulty with the problem of succession. Universities simply are not natural breeding grounds for leaders of large organizations.

Their trustees or regents tend to have only a modest understanding of what the institutions they guide need by way of leadership. If an organization is not breeding its own leaders, as most large corporations do, and is not particularly skilled at searching for the appropriate leaders when they are needed, dramatic gains in quality can remain tenuous. Exceptional gains that may have been made under a Kerr, a Terman, or a Crow must be consolidated and improved upon with sustained leadership of the first rank.

Over the next half-century, from the mid-1950s until today, the American research university would be characterized periodically, often from within the academy, as being in a state of crisis. And it seemed that way at times. At varying interludes, political leaders in Washington would criticize the universities for a variety of supposed failures, including, among others, their failure to be cost conscious, their avoidance of accountability for their research expenditures, the lack of fairness in the peer review system, the support of unimportant and trivial research with taxpayer dollars, and their failure to use their endowments properly. These attacks on the universities have led to periods of tension, requiring university leaders to spend enormous amounts of effort explaining the mission and functioning of their institutions. Federal support for research universities went through many cycles, and support by the states for their universities also oscillated over time.

Yet the research universities continued to expand and get stronger. The "founding fathers" of the American research university—people like Gilman, Harper, Eliot, Hutchins, Conant, Terman, and Kerr—created a system that worked. They laid a foundation on which great structures could and would be built. The core elements fit well with the conviction that the system should be detached from government bureaucratic control, and with the sense that competition among the universities to be considered the very best was healthy for the system. In short, the founders put into place the conditions necessary for true distinction.

CHAPTER 5

In Search of a Golden Age

The mission of the university is the discovery, improvement, and dissemination of knowledge. Its domain of inquiry and scrutiny includes all aspects and all values of society. A university faithful to its mission will provide enduring challenges to social values, policies, practices, and institutions. By design and by effect, it is the institution which creates discontent with the existing social arrangements and proposes new ones. In brief, a good university, like Socrates, will be unsettling.

—Kalven Committee Report,
University of Chicago, November 1967

The decade following *Sputnik*, and particularly the years between 1963 and 1968, has been called a Golden Age for research universities. The federal government increased its support for basic research at an unprecedented pace. Access to higher education grew so dramatically that a rapid expansion in educational services was required; the burgeoning rolls of students created opportunities for young scholars and scientists from almost all backgrounds to find remarkable jobs inside the academy. Some universities knew how to use the new resources to boost their comparative advantage, and the quality of these institutions went up accordingly. The United States assumed a leading international position in the sciences, including medical research, and a new synergy between the American research university and high-technology industries came into being.[1]

It seems paradoxical, in retrospect, that this Golden Age occurred at a time of such extraordinary turmoil in the university and in American society, a time when the very idea of the university was being challenged by both students and faculty. While Sterling and Terman were building their "steeples of excellence" in California, while basic science budgets were rising and fundamental discoveries were being announced as never before, while the industrial park at Stanford was in the process of becoming Silicon Valley, the social and political tensions on campus were approaching a breaking point. Many students and faculty members were up in arms about the university's links to the defense establishment. Yet the greatest universities continued spiraling upward toward an apex of prestige and scholarly and scientific achievement.

The decade opened with an ascendancy of youth, hope, a sense of style, and a renewed appreciation of intellect and culture. In his January 1961 Inaugural Address, President John F. Kennedy, the youngest president in our history, stood in front of the Capitol with his family, enjoining Americans to "ask not what your country can do for you—ask what you can do for your country." By March 1, he had signed an executive order establishing the Peace Corps, and three days later Sargent Shriver became its director. Earl Warren's Supreme Court was in place, and, much to the chagrin of President Eisenhower, who had appointed Warren, it had taken a sharp turn to the left in its interpretation of the Constitution. Our leaders were viewed as the best and the brightest, a new, younger generation of Americans to whom the torch of liberty was being passed.

This mythical Camelot was not to be sustained for long. The real world intruded on April 17, when Kennedy authorized (but ultimately did not support with American air power) the ill-conceived, ill-fated, and ultimately disastrous Bay of Pigs invasion by some 1,300 Cuban exiles. Conservatives felt that Kennedy had pulled the rug out from underneath the Cuban exiles, who were either killed or captured when the anticipated support from within Cuba failed to materialize. Even Kennedy's more liberal supporters criticized the invasion, questioning the intrinsic value of overthrowing Castro.

But the effects of that episode paled in comparison with the imprint of the twelve-day Cuban Missile Crisis of October 1962. This almost surreal event, perhaps marking the moment in the Cold War when we came closest to a nuclear exchange with the Soviet Union, changed perceptions around the world: A nuclear exchange was no longer beyond the imagination. And simmering beneath the surface, far removed from Cuba, was the conflict in Southeast Asia—the conflict that would trigger much of the activism on American college campuses later in the decade.

The civil rights movement had become a truly national phenomenon by the mid-1950s. Although a price had been paid in human lives, the movement had already chalked up many hard-fought legal, social, and cultural victories by August 28, 1963, when Martin Luther King, Jr., stood on the steps of the Lincoln Memorial and delivered his "I Have a Dream" speech before a throng of more than 250,000 people. Meanwhile, the great universities were making only slow progress in opening their doors to African Americans.

In the new social tapestry woven during these years, two strands stood out: They consisted of hope and despair. There still existed a hope that social institutions could be perfected and that we could be the agents of that change. Yet the contradictions were everywhere: The Civil Rights Act and the Voting Rights Act were passed, and blacks and whites were marching together in voter registration drives in the South, and yet the South remained in the grips of broad institutional racism. In the North and in the West, there was "white flight" to the suburbs as parents attempted to avoid sending their children to integrated public schools.

Another piece of the tapestry—one that disproportionately affected university life—was the choice by some to become part of a drug subculture. By the second half of the decade, a significant share of undergraduates at universities and colleges had experimented with drugs, mostly marijuana, and to a lesser degree "speed," "downers," and psychedelic drugs such as LSD. Some students found their guru in Timothy Leary, the Harvard lecturer in psychology who encouraged them to "Turn on, tune in, drop out."

Finally, during this era the divide between the sciences and the humanities that had begun to appear in the 1800s suddenly grew wider, causing, in C. P. Snow's words, "two cultures" to emerge. The sciences were rapidly advancing, yet, because of their complexity, they were less readily understood among those in the humanities. In its more sophisticated forms, the anti-science movement rejected the core Enlightenment ideals of rationality and reason in favor of more aesthetic and spiritual ideals. Meanwhile, the measure of greatness at universities was increasingly becoming their contribution to scientific and technical knowledge, with the contributions of the humanities, unfortunately, being devalued.

These elements of cultural change provided the backdrop for the student movement that would begin in earnest in 1964 in the form of protests against the enforcement of campus restrictions on free speech. These protests shifted into high gear as the war in Vietnam escalated and as students reacted against the very real possibility of being drafted into military service in a venture that they violently opposed.

CULTURE WARS ON CAMPUS

While the free speech movement was growing and the New Left was gaining new focus, military research and ROTC drills continued on the campuses across the country. Through the Congress for Cultural Freedom, which had offices in thirty-five countries, the CIA co-opted faculty members, writers, artists, musicians, and other intellectuals to wage a "cultural cold war" in an effort to move European intellectuals away from a commitment to communism.[2] It was the antiwar protests, however, that received the most attention, with Americans watching the chaos taking place on campus via nightly news recaps broadcast to their living rooms.[3] The students found welcome partners among many of the faculty at these universities who abhorred the war and questioned the growing hegemonic tendencies in U.S. foreign policy, to say nothing of their dismay at the slow pace of social change within the nation. Until they created a huge schism among the faculty over the use of tactics, students had ready allies among the predominantly liberal faculty. These forces clashed with university administrators who viewed the student attacks as efforts to undermine the core values of the university—and with a much less vocal cadre of conservative students, those who were more willing to be drafted or to voluntarily enlist. In short, the Cold War was as much a part of university life as it was a part of life on the national and international stages.

Although students began by mounting ideological protests against the war, they later turned their protests against the universities themselves, in part because the universities were perceived as a weak link in the chain of institutions responsible for the war and a plethora of social injustices. If student activists couldn't bring the Pentagon down, they could force the universities to their knees. Some thought at the time that the student re-bellions were harbingers of a long-term national movement for social change in the United States. But this was wishful thinking: Student protest movements are inherently unstable in organizational terms because the population of students turns over every four or five years. This makes sus-taining such a movement—and building upon prior episodes—virtually impossible. Social unrest tends to produce student unrest. And to a sig-nificant degree, that is what happened during the period of social upheaval in the sixties.

But the student antiwar protests reflected more than just general social unrest. Because of the Selective Service Draft, students had a very real in-terest in what was happening overseas, and they wanted to avoid being called for service in Vietnam. It is true that there was moral outrage on campus about the American intrusion into Southeast Asia, but it was the draft that caused student opposition to the war to build to such a high pitch. The number of American troops in Vietnam jumped from around 15,000 in 1963, at the time of the Kennedy assassination, to about 23,000 in 1964, 486,000 in 1967, and 536,000 in 1968. The antiwar consciousness grew apace.

The draft was grossly unfair, as it often has been historically, with the middle and upper classes the beneficiaries. In the early phases of the war, a male college student who could show he was making "satisfactory progress" toward his degree could qualify for a deferment. But the rules favored students whose grades were in the upper range. Colleges and uni-versities routinely gave class rank information to the draft boards—those lower in the class were more vulnerable to being drafted than those with higher grades. Graduate students could also obtain deferments. After the lottery system was introduced on December 1, 1969—for the first time since 1942—one's lottery number determined the order of call. The new procedure reduced the number of possible loopholes, but it hardly elimi-nated the anxiety of students and their families. Indeed, opposition to the war only intensified.

I am convinced that these rules had a significant impact on the educa-tional attainments of the children of the sixties. The high quality of an en-tire generation of young people choosing academic life in the 1960s and early 1970s was in part a consequence of draft deferment rules, with young people using advanced education as a means of avoiding the draft. As

Daniel Yankelovich, who examined a great deal of survey information about student radicals and their followers during the sixties, put it:

> The war and the draft forged an intensely personal link between the students and a far-off war which inspired loathing, fear, and revulsion on campus. The small core of political radicals, though never more than 10–15 percent of the college population, took the lead in interpreting the war in terms that were harshly critical of the United States, its motives, its institutions, and its moral impulses. Because they were so disturbed by the war, the great mass of college students accepted the radical critique and, especially in the Ivy League colleges, joined with the New Left in its attack on the universities and other institutions that were interpreted as being part of the web of immorality and misuse of power that students associated with the war.[4]

When this distrust coincided with what the literary critic Lionel Trilling called the "adversary culture" of university intellectuals—who tend to embrace antinomian attitudes and to oppose, if not scorn, aspects of the corporate world's ethic of functional rationality and bureaucratic efficiency, as opposed to creativity and originality—the ingredients for a strong social protest movement were brought together.[5]

At the universities, the confrontations centered on ROTC, black studies, military research on campus, student power and representation in the governance of the university, grievance policies, and admissions policies. As student militancy increased, political action against the New Left also increased—both in terms of the public characterization of the students and government political action to repress the student movement.

At the end of March 1968, with Vietnam troop levels at more than half a million, President Lyndon B. Johnson, facing a revolt in his own political party, announced that he would not seek reelection. Within a week of the announcement, Martin Luther King was assassinated at a motel in Memphis, Tennessee. Racial riots broke out across the country. When arsonists began setting fires on the West Side of Chicago, Mayor Richard Daley ordered police to "shoot to kill." Only three weeks later, all hell broke loose at Columbia University when students occupied a series of campus buildings and refused to leave until their demands were met. Before these protests had abated, Senator Robert F. Kennedy was assassinated in Los Angeles after making his victory speech following the California primary. These events set the stage for demonstrations that turned into riots at Chicago's Democratic National Convention in August.

The Columbia student demonstrations rocked the campus and eventually led to police action. Other universities would learn from Columbia's mistakes, but the former home of Alexander Hamilton and John Jay was entering uncharted waters—and the president and provost were poorly prepared to handle the unique set of unfolding events. An ideologically committed faction of radical students had little idea of where the strike was headed once it began. Flawed strategies on both sides produced a campus disaster. Before dawn on April 30, 1968, following the police bust, a Students for a Democratic Society (SDS) flyer read: "At 2:30 this morning, Columbia University died."

There was an element of truth to that statement. Some brilliant faculty members subsequently left the university. Columbia lost its sense of purpose, and its financial health declined. All told, it took Columbia more than two decades to recover from the casualties of the conflicts among faculty and students tied to those events. There followed, of course, many other campus protests against the war, not only at Columbia, but also at Harvard, the University of Chicago, and hundreds of other university campuses, before the Vietnam War ended. This series of events reached its tragic culmination at Kent State in 1970, when four student protesters died when they were shot by the Ohio National Guard.

THE AFTERMATH OF THE 1960S

Despite all these problems, during the years following the Vietnam War almost all disciplines in the American research university gained in relative standing against the world's best seats of higher learning. In the 1970s and 1980s, American universities gained preeminence in the sciences and were increasingly acknowledged as the leading places for humanities and social science scholarship. They were doing well in every area—but if certain disciplines suffered more than others, damaged disproportionately by the larger societal events of the 1960s, it was surely the social sciences and humanities. Skepticism off campus about the radical impulses of many social scientists, and the continual questioning within the humanities of the rational models of thought handed down from the Enlightenment, began to take a toll on these disciplines.

Funding was part of the problem. While humanists never received much external government funding, despite the creation of the National Endowment for the Humanities (NEH) in 1965, and therefore any loss of those resources had minimal effect on their research habits, the social sciences had become more dependent on funds to support increasingly empirical disciplines. When the flow of those funds turned into a trickle during the Reagan presidency, the effects reverberated throughout the academy.

But there were also tensions and internal schisms within both the humanities and the social sciences, and these had a bigger impact than any funding problem. Scholars began to question the values and norms that had guided the university's evolution. As the humanities became more open to points of view beyond the traditional Western one, admitting scholars into the club who had formerly been defined as outsiders, the leaders of the humanities had to confront challenges to their literary and social perspectives. This led to sharp intellectual conflict.

In 1997, Princeton humanities professor Alvin Kernan enumerated some of the internal struggles that had beset his discipline since the 1960s, writing that the humanities and social sciences had become "the battlefields of an extended *Kulturkampf* ": "These subjects have proven extremely sensitive to pressures for social change in the society at large, to the wave of populist democracy, to technological changes in communications, to relativistic epistemologies, to demands for increased tolerance, and to various social causes, such as black studies, feminism, and gay rights. Every liberal cause—from freedom of speech and the Vietnam War to anticolonialism and the nonreferentiality of language—has fought bitter and clamorous battles in these subjects."

"Deconstructive philosophies," Kernan wrote, "replaced knowledge with interpretation and dethroned objectivity in the name of subjectivity. Where the old humanities were once ethnocentric in their concentration on western Europe, they have become increasingly multicultural, pluralistic, and politicized."[6] In short, the humanities and social sciences after the 1960s were bogged down with internal debates, controversies, and theoretical schisms. Meanwhile, the sciences forged ahead, making discovery after discovery with relatively unimpeded progress.

The difficulties faced by the humanities were compounded by the increasingly self-referential quality of those disciplines. They seemed more and more to be talking only to themselves. The problem was not that they didn't have anything to offer the attentive, educated public; it was that what they did have to offer was rarely getting through to that audience. There were important new literatures opening up through translation, and valuable new perspectives and commentaries being produced, but no matter—the people across campus in the other buildings, let alone the average American, rarely heard about them. Scholars of the first rank were far more often writing books and articles for tenure and for professional audiences than for the educated public.

In addition, the subdisciplines within the humanities, particularly literary studies, seemed to embrace a form of scientism—creating a technical language not immediately accessible to the public—while simultaneously rejecting the Enlightenment idea of objectivity. This movement looked to works outside of literary studies, such as those by Thomas Kuhn, who seemed to imply, particularly in his highly influential book *The Structure of Scientific Revolutions,* that the dominant paradigm in a scientific field at any given time depended substantially on social forces, particularly power. Leading humanists emphasized and rewarded "theory," and insisted on "rigorous" theory, yet many seemed to be rejecting belief in objective knowledge—that "there is a there out there."

The skeptics within the humanities and social sciences questioned the foundations upon which these disciplines had been built. They also challenged the criteria for what constituted quality work, and such challenges struck at the heart of the peer review system and academic freedom. The scholars critiqued the norms of authority and power—asking who had the right to judge quality and control access to the profession and its lofty positions. And yet, for all the characterizations of the humanities in the United States as being in a chaotic free-for-all, what they were actually producing, in comparison with their counterparts in other countries, was still perceived as distinguished.

It's not that these internal debates were without redeeming value. On the contrary, those engaged in the debates of this era made contributions that focused on America's ethnocentricism and its exclusion of minorities, women, and other national class perspectives from the analysis of texts, politics, and social history. While the scientists attended to their business of making discoveries, the scholars in these other fields attended to theirs, turning to their historical role as critics of social values and of societal practices and policies. This continues to be an important function of the university—particularly for the humanities and social sciences—but it rarely makes those who criticize, or the institutions and disciplines that house them, popular with those in power. The last decades of the twentieth century were no different in that regard: Those in power did not take kindly to the skepticism and the critiques coming from those quarters of the universities.

The point of humanistic disciplines, according to many who practiced them during this period, was to move against the grain. It was not to affirm or consolidate what was known or felt by the majority, and surely not to validate anything done by those in positions of political power. Rather, it was their job to be questioning and upsetting—to challenge the commodified, uncontroversial, and codified certainties thrown at the public by the prevailing political powers and the unguided and unthinking media.

Much of this was captured by the great sociologist Max Weber decades earlier, in the 1920s, when he wrote, in "Science as a Vocation," that "the primary task of a useful teacher is to teach his students to recognize 'inconvenient' facts—I mean facts that are inconvenient for their party opinions."[7] The essence of humanistic studies, from Lionel Trilling to Edward Said, has been to be oppositional. Humanists and social scientists are *supposed* to discuss and question traditional values—not necessarily to overthrow them, but to elevate the basis on which they are embraced or altered. This is a point that many critics of these disciplines miss. Reactionary forces, witnessing the oppositional character of scholars, respond by vilifying individuals, trying to debunk the entire enterprise of teaching at the major universities as guided only by radical thought.

Not all humanists took up this critical stance. The majority, in fact, like most other intellectuals, demonstrated, in the words of University of Chicago professor Hans Morgenthau, "our conformist subservience to those in power." However, a sufficient number of prominent humanists and social scientists refused to yield to the pressure applied by advocacy groups and the government. Despite efforts to vilify them, the literary critics continued to criticize the way those in power—and conventional authors, both living and dead—represented "the other" in non-Western cultures. The literary canon came under fire, and new norms about scholarly research and criticism were forged. Every aspect of Western culture and its history became subject to reinterpretation and "deconstruction." The effort was sharply resisted by prominent scholars within the academy, which created an even greater sense outside of the academy that the humanities were in disarray. The problem was not the existence of highly contentious and competing points of view. It was that all too often the intellectual debates and differences in the social sciences and humanities became personal and political.

Humanities scholars and their leaders at our major universities also failed to argue effectively to their elected representatives and the broader public that the nation needed what they taught and wrote about. Humanities scholars tend to be even more leery than scientists and social scientists about government intrusion into the life of the academy and violations of free inquiry. Perhaps for that reason, they never successfully made the case that wrestling with questions of competing values, morality, and ethics, and thinking critically about these subjects, were essential for citizens, or that knowledge and understanding of other cultures, languages, and literatures were essential for the nation's welfare and security.

Whether the sources of their troubles originated from inside or outside the academy, the devaluation of the humanities was an extremely unfortunate result of the conflicts. Increasingly, universities were being judged by their utilitarian value—their contributions to the education of professionals and to useful knowledge. There is nothing wrong with training professionals and discovering useful knowledge—both should be supported and celebrated—but at the same time, it would be a mistake not to acknowledge the critical role that the humanities and the social sciences play at the universities and in the larger society.

Harder to quantify, but no less essential, the humanities are inextricably linked to the web of knowledge of a university. That is why any attempt by an emerging powerful nation, such as China, to build great universities without paying attention to the humanities is likely to fall short. Don Randel, the former president of the University of Chicago, now president of the Andrew Mellon Foundation, pointed out the inherent value of these disciplines: "The instrumental view of knowledge is surely not sufficient . . . and we ought to want to make that clear . . . [and] would be insufficient as the foundation of a democratic society. . . . The narrow, instrumental view of *knowledge* that often dominates our thinking needs at a minimum to be expanded or supported by *ideas* and *values* about which we may also reason. . . . The ultimate foundation of any society ought to be the human imagination, honed to the greatest degree and in the company of its faithful companion, curiosity."[8]

The persistent undervaluation of the humanities has been reflected since the inception of the NEH in the absence of adequate funding. In summarizing the state of affairs as of 2009, sociologist Harriet Zuckerman, senior vice president of the Mellon Foundation, and Ronald G. Ehrenberg, a professor of industrial and labor relations at Cornell who has written widely on higher education, concluded that "financial support for the 'academic humanities,'" while "never abundant, . . . is now scarce." NEH funding for the "academic humanities" in fact declined between the mid-1990s and 2008, and the humanities "did little better in securing support from private foundations," Zuckerman and Ehrenberg wrote.[9]

Perhaps the government's responses to the internal disarray of the humanities was to be expected, but the decline in interest by students in the humanities was equally unfortunate, given what these fields had to offer. A few simple statistics drawn from the 2008 Humanities Indicators project of the American Academy of Arts and Sciences convey a sense of the "roller-coaster" ride of undergraduate interest in the humanities between the 1960s and today. Undergraduate degrees in the humanities reached a peak in the late 1960s and early 1970s only to go into a steep decline over the next three decades. While humanities degrees represented about 18 percent of the total bachelor's degrees recorded in the late 1960s, by 2004 they represented only about 8 percent of the total. The picture is much the same for advanced degrees. As the Humanities Indicators report found, "By 2004 the humanities had lost over 75% of the share of master's degrees they were awarding in the late 1960s, while the share of doctoral degrees had decreased more than 45% from the peak levels of the mid-1970s."[10] Perhaps this decline reflects the impulse among so many recent students to take subjects that they believe will "pay off" after graduation. But one consequence is that the graduates of our great universities have weaker language and writing skills than earlier generations of graduates and limited experiences with literatures and cultures other than our own. Even worse, they have not confronted the kinds of moral and ethical questions critical for citizenship that are often debated in humanities courses.

The arts and sciences have always been at the core of the university mission. In any era, the balance can tip toward one or the other—and the late twentieth century exemplifies this principle. As the social sciences and the humanities were experiencing difficulties, the sciences, particularly the health sciences, were taking off—shifting the center of gravity at the university toward the medical schools and medical research centers.

THE EXPLOSIVE GROWTH OF THE HEALTH SCIENCES

The great American medical schools began to undergo an exponential expansion in the 1960s, and by the 1980s they were flourishing as never before. During the second half of the twentieth century, they were reshaped by the shift toward huge, research-oriented projects and enterprises within the postwar research university. Many became health science centers, incorporating new schools of public health, nursing, and dentistry into their traditional programs in medicine and the biological sciences. Departments were being recast to include specialties such as genetics, biochemistry, neuroscience, psychiatry, biostatistics, epidemiology, and other new fields. The older disciplines, such as medicine, anatomy, dermatology, and neurology, were still there as well; in fact, they grew, with department sizes expanding to accommodate both research and clinical practice. Teaching and training medical students became only one part of the larger mission of these medical schools and centers.

The rapid advances in scientific knowledge, new technologies, and health-related research produced extraordinary changes in the economy of universities in the postwar period. The quality of the work produced at the medical centers contributed significantly to the level of distinction that universities were able to achieve—and to their funding levels. As the medical schools grew in size and influence, the relative power and autonomy of their leaders became a matter to be reckoned with. Some have questioned whether such a dramatic shift in the relative size and power of a discipline within the university can become so fundamental that it represents a change in the "idea" of the institution itself. Christopher Ricks once said, "A substantial change in scale is a change in enterprise." This judgment may well hold for America's great universities after the expansion of their medical schools. Although I do not believe that this growth altered the fundamental values or ideas of the university, it is clear that the changes in scale had dramatic effects on the economics of universities and how they were run.

The size of the health sciences relative to other disciplines has changed so much since the 1950s that many leaders of universities today wonder whether the tails (the medical centers) are now wagging the dogs (the universities themselves). Two features of medical schools in particular altered the landscape: the growth in the number of doctors affiliated with the medical schools who operated their research and clinical practices through the schools, and the close corporate or quasi-independent relationships between the medical schools, the larger universities, and affiliated hospitals.[11]

The timing of the rise of the medical centers might be seen as paradoxical. It occurred in the midst of an increasing skepticism in America about the Enlightenment idea that science was invariably linked to progress. The anti-science movement in the United States focused more sharply on the physicists and engineers, however—those seen as being responsible for the atomic bomb and the nuclear weapons stockpiles, nuclear power and its attendant risks, pesticides, and other problematic enterprises—than on those working to cure or treat disease. The health-care industry, the medical schools, and the physicians and medical students were not perceived as being part of the "military-industrial complex," and thus never became the target of protests. So, while the public and members of Congress began by 1970 to draw back from the large-scale funding of science, ending what many considered to be the Golden Age of federal research support, the biomedical research community remained relatively immune from attack and in fact increasingly became the beneficiaries of government largess. From 1971 to 1981, the National Institutes of Health (NIH) budget for academic research increased by more than 300 percent in total and roughly 50 percent adjusting for inflation, going from just over $600 million to $2 billion annually. Support for medical research funding was bipartisan, as it was politically safe.

Moreover, members of Congress and the general public increasingly identified personally with the goal of finding cures for killers such as heart disease and cancer. In the midst of the disaster in Vietnam, President Richard Nixon proposed that the United States engage in a second war—the "war on cancer." On December 23, 1971, he signed the National Cancer Act into law. This new law brought an additional flow of money to

America's research universities—both for basic biological research and for clinical work. On all sides of the political spectrum, it was agreed that it was important to gain a better understanding of what caused the disease and to learn how to improve the quality of treatment for cancer patients. Nixon was articulating one of Vannevar Bush's basic goals of postwar science policy—to use national resources to conquer disease.

Lyndon Johnson's Great Society program had also promoted the exponential growth of the nation's medical schools.[12] In an effort to expand health care coverage for Americans, Johnson had been the driving force behind the Social Security Act, which became law in 1965. Medicare and Medicaid were featured in the bill, and as part of the legislation (and as a way to gain support for it), the government agreed to reimburse hospitals and physicians for the full cost of services provided. This gave physicians and hospitals a huge incentive to increase the services they could provide, and gave university medical schools a new source of revenue.[13]

New medical technologies, now being paid for by the federal government, began to abound. A number of truly important technological innovations and devices were introduced in the 1970s and 1980s, and hospitals and medical centers made enormous investments in new, state-of-the-art equipment. Along with this machinery came the economic imperative to make heavy use of the costly technologies in order to justify their purchase, sometimes before the real medical value of the technologies was proven.

The revenues of medical schools and hospitals rose steeply, as did the incomes of doctors and medical researchers. At Johns Hopkins, for example, income from sponsored research reached a high of over 75 percent of the university's total expenditures in 1970—most of it from federal sources, with physician practice plan income representing only 3 percent of the medical school revenues. By 1990, practice plan revenues represented a third of the medical school's budget. In dollar terms, revenues rose from about $1 million in 1970 to $140 million in 1990.[14]

During roughly the same period, 1968 to 1988, the faculty at twelve of the nation's leading medical schools grew by 39 percent in the basic biological sciences and by a whopping 160 percent in the clinical departments. The research budgets of the clinical departments grew so fast that by 1990 they were generating more sponsored research than basic science departments. Faculty members who were capable of bringing in NIH and private research funds became valuable commodities. Dangling large recruitment packages worth millions of dollars, medical schools and universities began to compete for talented clinical researchers who were capable of winning large federal research grants and contracts, and a researcher's funding history began to carry significant weight in the rationale for granting tenure—regardless of how important a given candidate's research outcomes were. NIH support for average scientists at top-rated medical schools skyrocketed—by 1990, the average annual NIH grant at Stanford had reached over $230,000 per scientist.[15]

Throughout the first half of the twentieth century, physicians had been the ones at the top of the totem pole at the medical schools. By the beginning of the 1960s, it was the basic biomedical scientists—particularly those with Nobel Prizes—who were the most highly esteemed. The basic scientists continued to garner the bulk of the Nobels and other honors, but Congress was just as interested in supporting the continued development of life-saving clinical applications and clinical trials of new drugs that could improve public health. With the growth in funding came a sharp rise in the published research and clinical literature in the health sciences. By 1990, clinical medicine and biomedical research accounted for almost half of the published scientific papers in the world, and because of the growth in American medical research, the United States' share of the literature in these fields increased proportionately.

The structural balance of research universities became heavily weighted toward the medical centers and other health-related departments and programs. These programs accounted for an increasingly large proportion of the revenues and expenditures of the universities between 1960 and the turn of the twenty-first century. The Columbia University Medical Center, for example, which consists of the schools of medicine, public health, nursing, and dentistry, accounted for 13 percent of Columbia's total expenditures of $19 million in 1949–1950 and only 11 percent of $67 million by 1960–1961. By 1972–1973, the medical center accounted for over 37 percent of the total budget. Its share of the budget leveled off at around 40 percent until 1989–1990 and then took off again. By 1995–1996, the Columbia University Medical Center expenditures represented almost half of the $1.2 billion budget, and it would grow still further after that, so that in 2005–2006 it accounted for 54 percent of Columbia's $2.4 billion annual budget.[16] Meanwhile, there was almost no external federal funding for the humanities, and little for the social sciences. That kind of quantitative difference translates into a major qualitative shift in the character of the university.

There can be no doubt that the discoveries made at medical centers have improved the quality of life of Americans in many ways. At their best, the great teaching hospitals and medical centers contribute increasingly to progress in health care and to the creation of the most fundamental new knowledge in the biological and biomedical sciences. But has the idea of the university been compromised by the changing relative size of these medical schools and departments? Aside from the revenues they generate, do clinical research activities and practice plans benefit the university or help them carry out their primary missions? Are the arts and humanities, and even the other sciences, suffering today because of the wealth of resources now available to health science centers? The medical faculty trains a relatively small cadre of students; the size of the teaching portfolio is very small compared with the size of the research enterprise. And because many of the researchers do not teach undergraduate students, some of the best minds at the university are not involved in teaching undergraduates at all.

These are very complicated questions, and those in charge of university budgets and policies are still in the process of working out the answers to them.[17] One thing is for certain: The medical departments and research activities are here to stay for the foreseeable future. And as the researchers continue to make discoveries, they will continue to develop closer linkages with the business world in their efforts to move knowledge more rapidly from the laboratory to the marketplace.

A NEW DEAL BETWEEN AMERICAN UNIVERSITIES AND AMERICAN INDUSTRY

The idea that universities should own and sell their discoveries was not part of academic culture until very recently. Industry held on to proprietary knowledge; universities were poorly organized for moving their discoveries quickly into the public domain where they could be freely used. The reason for eschewing ownership of intellectual property was simple: There was a fear that if research was motivated by profit, professors might forgo working on more important problems that had no potential for commercialization, influencing their students to do the same. As universities

increasingly occupied center stage in the creation of new knowledge with
the potential for practical use, however, the attitude toward intellectual
property began to change. University administrators reasoned that they
could maintain institutional integrity and avoid the corruption of its
work while creating important new revenue streams that could be reinvested to advance the central teaching and research missions of the universities. A corollary was that if universities could form a new
relationship with industry, they could move ideas with practical value
more rapidly to the market.

In fact, in *Science—The Endless Frontier*, Vannevar Bush had suggested
that changes in the patent system could help facilitate this transfer of discoveries to the marketplace. He proposed that formal ties between universities and industry could promote innovation by providing incentives. By
the 1950s, economists had demonstrated that technological investments
paid off in terms of economic growth. Robert M. Solow, who received the
1987 Nobel Prize in Economics for his work on this relationship, concluded that for the U.S. economy between 1909 and 1949, "technology remain[ed] the dominant engine of growth, with human capital investment
in second place." He credited "'the growth of knowledge' or technological
progress in the narrow sense" with being responsible for "34% of recorded
growth."[18] Bush's proposal to promote innovation through greater formal ties between universities and industry had a long gestation period in
academia—it was some thirty-five years before the universities acted upon
it in a significant way, although some universities, such as Stanford, did
take earlier steps in that direction.

In the 1970s, when American industry began to feel competitive pressures from Japan and other Asian nations, as well as from Europe, much
more thought was given to this issue. Pressure began to mount in Congress for a review of patent law as a means to greater American competitiveness. Still, not much happened at the federal level in terms of the
kind of patent reform that would create incentives for increased interaction between universities and industry until 1978, when, under the leadership of former Stanford psychologist Richard C. Atkinson, the
National Science Foundation tried to stimulate such connections through
a pilot program offering support for research at universities that demonstrated strong collaborative ties with industry. The program proved
highly successful, showing that it might be possible for universities and

businesses to work together more closely for the public good, despite the fact that the two communities had fundamentally different goals and value systems.

A much bigger step toward collaboration between business and academia was taken with passage of the Bayh-Dole Act of 1980.[19] The change in the law that this act engendered was simple but of profound significance: In the past, intellectual property rights resulting from federally sponsored research at universities had been assigned to the federal government; they would now be assigned to the universities themselves. The universities would be able to patent discoveries and license the patented material to businesses interested in developing marketable products. Universities could even sponsor start-up companies based on the intellectual property that they owned and hold an equity stake in them.

This was a critically important change and a remarkably important piece of science policy legislation. Almost immediately, research universities began to set up technology transfer offices designed to identify research that could be patented, to facilitate the patenting of discoveries, and to oversee the licensing of those patents to companies interested in them. A new arm of the research university was born—one that was often run more like a business enterprise than a school or department. It had the dual purpose of rapidly bringing the fruits of new discoveries to the public and generating new income streams for the university.

The Bayh-Dole Act made it clear that the intellectual property rights were not vested in the individuals who made the discoveries, but in the universities that employed them. Revenues from the intellectual property were to be reinvested in the educational mission of the university, and each university could establish its own internal revenue distribution policy. As it turned out, many different models of distribution were created. Columbia, for example, allowed the faculty member who made the discovery to retain almost all of the revenue below a rather low threshold. If the patent turned out to be lucrative, the revenues were divided among the discoverers, the research laboratory, the school at the university where the discovery was made, and the central university. As the returns grew, a higher proportion of the total revenues were returned to "the common" for redistribution and investment in new educational initiatives, including those proposed by departments that were unlikely to have faculty members who made patentable discoveries, such as the humanities and social sciences.

Some universities allowed the revenues from licenses to flow entirely back to the school housing the original scientist or engineer who had made the patented discovery. Getting these policies into place has often involved duels between academic administrators and members of the faculty. While the administration of most universities wanted a policy that provided flexibility in distributing the returns from royalties and the sale of equity stakes in incubator companies, some faculty wanted the economic benefits to be returned entirely to the individuals and teams who made the discoveries. Some faculty members opposed the idea of ownership altogether.

Interest in the potential commercialization of ideas discovered at research universities is not a recent development. There were efforts to commercialize ideas produced at the great universities throughout the twentieth century. However, the notion that scientists and engineers should be able to sell their ideas for profit flew in the face of traditional scientific norms. In the past, scholarly and scientific activity had been rewarded only by peer recognition, greater prestige, or possibly promotion; the idea that individual researchers and faculty members should profit directly from their discoveries was new to the academy.[20]

Perhaps the best-known early effort at commercialization of patents came from the University of Wisconsin, where Harry Steenbock, a biochemistry professor at Madison, set up the Wisconsin Alumni Research Foundation (WARF) in 1925. WARF, a nonprofit organization, was affiliated with but corporately independent of the University of Wisconsin. It was designed to work "with business and industry to transform university research into real products benefiting society at large."[21] Steenbock was moved to establish WARF because he had made an important discovery of his own—that by irradiating milk with ultraviolet light he could increase its vitamin D content. This finding was eventually responsible for eliminating the childhood disease rickets. Steenbock knew that his discovery could be valuable if it was managed properly. He also knew that discoveries placed in the public domain had often been poorly managed, thus depriving the public of the social benefits that might have come from the new knowledge. He thus set up WARF with the intention of making sure that all the proceeds flowing from the licensing of his discovery would be earmarked for reinvestment in the University of Wisconsin. WARF still exists today as the organization that licenses patents held by Wisconsin professors. It has been highly successful at fulfilling this purpose, making it possible for many profound discoveries to be used in marketable products. One example is Karl Paul Link's discovery of warfarin, the active ingredient in what is now the most widely prescribed anticoagulant medication in the world (Coumadin).[22]

In fact, the Bayh-Dole Act was modeled on the system that had been tested by WARF. The leaders of WARF had convinced the administrators of the Department of Health, Education and Welfare (DHEW) that the federal government was not using its intellectual property rights in a productive way. In the 1960s, federal agencies held about 30,000 patents that had resulted from scientific research conducted at universities with government funding, yet only a very small percentage of these inventions (5 percent) had been licensed to companies or developed into commercial products.[23] By 1968, WARF and the University of Wisconsin–Madison had produced a new kind of contract with DHEW, known as the Institutional Patent Agreement (IPA), that granted patent rights to the University of Wisconsin for discoveries made with federal funding. It also permitted the university to license new technologies to companies. By 1973, the University of Wisconsin and WARF had negotiated a similar agreement with the NSF.

The objective of WARF, and later of the Bayh-Dole Act, was to decrease the amount of time it took to transfer the fruits of university research to businesses that were interested in developing the ideas into products. Part of the motive was to benefit society: Many of the new discoveries, like Steenbock's discovery with milk or Link's discovery with warfarin, could benefit society. But altruism was hardly the only motive behind Bayh-Dole. The law opened up potentially lucrative new revenue streams for the universities. It also put them squarely in the business of commercializing ideas.

Scientists did share their ideas with industry prior to Bayh-Dole. Indeed, intellectual property created at the universities was being transferred to industry all the time. But the transfer came in the form of bilateral consulting arrangements, which were sometimes also quite lucrative, between individual professors and industrial business clients, rather than in the form of licensing agreements. The companies held proprietary rights over the ideas produced by their consultants, and the consultants earned fees.[24] Rules were put into place that governed the amount of time that professors could spend consulting outside the university; conflict-of-interest policies had to be developed to make sure faculty members were not improperly using university facilities, researchers, and students to pursue their outside work. The rules helped to prevent abuse of the system, but it was not a good arrangement for the universities. Faculty members were still essentially giving away intellectual property that had been developed, at least in part, using the resources and facilities of their university. With the passage of Bayh-Dole, universities became interested parties capitalizing on their greatest asset: the discoveries of their faculty.

Although the precise consequences of the Bayh-Dole Act are difficult to measure, there are some indications that the act has provided a valuable incentive to universities to forge agreements with industry. Universities have acquired more patents than in the past and have made more licensing agreements with firms wishing to exploit the ideas and discoveries originating on campus.[25] Universities acquired roughly 250 to 350 patents annually in the 1970s, before Bayh-Dole, but they acquire more than ten times that number today. About 5 percent of the patents granted to the U.S. private and nonprofit sectors today go to universities, up from 1.5 percent in 1981.[26] In 2006, almost 700 of the new products introduced into the market were based at least in part on something covered by a patent that a university had obtained. Universities have managed about 13,000 licenses, and a total of about 5,700 new spinoff companies have been launched since the passage of Bayh-Dole.[27] Thousands of professors have had their work patented or have begun their own start-up companies in order to see the practical fruits of their discoveries and to profit from them. Businesses, which have been pressured by their shareholders to show increasingly large quarterly results, have cut back on their long-term research investments (consider only the evisceration of the formerly great Bell Labs)—instead relying more heavily on university research to provide ideas for new products or improvements to existing ones.

Richard Nelson, an economist at Columbia who has studied the relationship between technology, universities, and innovation, commenting on the "division of labor" in university-industry relations, observed that in the postwar era, before passage of Bayh-Dole, "R&D to improve existing products and processes became almost exclusively the province of industry, in fields where firms had strong R&D capabilities." Work to bring the next generation of products and practices into commercial use was also the province of industry: "Industrial R&D is almost totally concentrated on this kind of work," Nelson wrote. "Basic research," however, "became increasingly viewed as the task of universities." In this division of labor, the universities also assumed the critical role of training the advanced students, who would enter industrial laboratories and work on both research and development in those locations after earning their Ph.D.s.[28]

Most of the returns from these new arrangements initially came from discoveries linked to the biological sciences; today, an increasing share of patents are being acquired by engineering and physical science programs. As the rate of discovery in genetics, biotechnology, electronics, computer science, nanoscience, and material science picks up speed, the potential for substantial economic returns from the intellectual property rights produced in these fields grows. And, although universities have already earned far more than $1 billion in royalties from their intellectual property, I am convinced that this represents just the tip of the iceberg. Research universities that take advantage of the new rules should be able to look forward to much greater returns in the future. And royalties on licenses is only one of the effects of the processes set in motion by Bayh-Dole. Another is the economic impact that the start-up companies have had on local and state economies and on the creation of knowledge-based, skilled jobs. Perhaps most important is the impact that Bayh-Dole has had on the world outside of academia and industry: The products developed under the act's new rules are helping to transform our lives. And yet, we are just scratching the surface of what is possible from the collaboration between research universities and industrial partners.

Not all universities have benefited from the new rules. Indeed, most universities have earned little from this new source of revenue. A few, however, have earned a lot and have positioned themselves to earn even more. It is a game of almost all strike-outs and singles, but with a few home runs. Relatively few patents earn a great deal of money. A few discoveries and inventions can earn hundreds of millions of dollars over the life of a patent. But to hit these home runs, you've got to go to bat quite a number of times. While you may have some idea of who the great hitters are, no one knows for sure when the next ball will go out of the park or who will be the one to hit it: It's just not that predictable. Usually, it will be someone on the team that already has the most money: The universities with the best funding have the best faculty and researchers; it stands to reason that these are the places where the batters will hit the most home runs.

So far, the most research-intensive universities, with depth of talent in the biomedical sciences, the physical sciences, computing, and engineering, have outperformed the universities with less talent and resources, both in the production of patentable discoveries and on the home run scoreboard. At Columbia, we pursued technology transfer aggressively, in part because we believed that the ideas of our scientists and engineers could improve the welfare of the nation—indeed, of the world. We also knew that if we succeeded, we could use the resources generated to compete effectively with wealthier universities. At the end of the day, we were very successful. In the late 1990s and early 2000s, we generated more than $150 million per year, principally from the revenues of a few important patents, such as the Axel "cotransformation" patents.

These generic patents, based on research by Nobel Prize winner Richard Axel and several of his colleagues, involved the discovery that foreign DNA could be inserted into a host cell to produce proteins of great value in pharmaceutical applications that were useful in treatments for anemia, heart attacks and strokes, multiple sclerosis, and hemophilia. Although not all of this revenue went to my office for redistribution during my time as provost, enough did to allow for considerable reinvestment in important new academic initiatives, such as the Columbia Earth Institute. The revenues also boosted our efforts to recruit great scientists and scholars working in many different fields, including physics, chemistry, biomedical engineering, health sciences, the social sciences, and the humanities. The funds also went toward research projects and programs sponsored by the Classics Department and the schools of architecture and journalism. In short, the return on these patents fueled much of the new multidisciplinary work and a number of new research initiatives at Columbia.

Stanford University led the way in technology transfer in the 1990s, earning more than $100 million a year on a number of its "home-run" patents. Fundamental research by Stanley Cohen of Stanford and Herbert Boyer of the University of California at San Francisco in 1973 had led to critically important discoveries about recombinant DNA and how to genetically engineer cells to produce human substances. Using a gene-splicing technique, they had found a quick and easy way to produce chemicals such as HGH (human growth hormone), synthetic insulin, factor VIII for hemophilia, and other chemicals that could be used by the new biotechnology industry. When Cohen and Boyer, who are both winners of the National Medal of Science and members of the National Academy of Sciences, decided to apply for a patent to protect some aspects of their discovery, it was a deeply controversial matter. Stanford received three patents for their work in 1980, and the revenues generated over the seventeen-year life of the patent totaled more than $250 million, based on over $35 billion in worldwide product sales that used the patent.

Looking back on the discovery, Cohen said, "Boyer and I didn't set out to invent genetic engineering. Our invention came from efforts to understand basic biological phenomena and the realization that our findings had important practical applications."[29] Cohen's point is an important one: Many of the most valuable discoveries that have been translated into successful commercial products emerged from an interest in basic scientific problems that were linked to the solution of practical problems—thus fitting squarely into Pasteur's quadrant.

If the commercialization of these discoveries represents only the tip of the iceberg, we are beginning to realize what lies below the surface. The returns on intellectual property will come not only from the patenting and licensing of discoveries, but also from fostering and developing new companies. Some of this is happening by design. MIT has focused a good deal of energy on entrepreneurial efforts by its faculty and students, as has Stanford and other universities with very strong biological science and computer science programs. And the returns from patents on computer algorithms and computer software, and from equity stakes in companies that are derived from those types of innovations, can be very large indeed. MIT made a small fortune by backing Akamai Technologies, a distributor of online content, and Stanford hit a spectacular home run when Sergey Brin and Larry Page developed the search engine Google as a research project while they were Ph.D. students at Stanford. Stanford received 1.8 million shares of Google in exchange for letting the company use the patented search technology that the university owned. When the shares were sold, Stanford received $336 million. That's equivalent to a lot of endowment; and it can be reinvested in educational activities that are apt to be less restricted than most university endowment gifts.

Given these kinds of returns, it should come as no surprise that over the past decade interest in technology transfer and entrepreneurship has grown at many of the great research universities. The entrepreneurial impulse is very much a part of American history, and faculty members, despite professorial stereotypes to the contrary, have responded to the incentives contained in the Bayh-Dole Act. In fact, many professors— and not only scientists and engineers—have demonstrated enormous interest in creating ideas that have commercial value, both because of the implications for business and for their educational value. It is also fair to say that the norm of disinterestedness—of not gaining personally from your own discoveries—has eroded in university culture over the past few decades.

By 2006, around thirty research universities were reporting revenues from patents and licenses exceeding $10 million a year, and an additional forty-two reported more than $5 million. The University of California system had licensing income of more than $193 million; New York University generated almost $157 million; and Stanford, which had lost the income from the Cohen-Boyer "home run" because the patent had expired, was still generating close to $61 million a year.[30] Columbia received almost $180 million in 2003, the last year that I was provost, and prior to that it had actually topped $200 million for several years. Universities would be unwise to count on these revenues for ongoing core support, such as financial aid, because patents do run their course. But to understand the magnitude of what the funds add to a university, one can calculate the size of the endowment that would be needed to generate similar revenues. The annual yield from a $1 billion endowment, for example, would be about $50 million, assuming a normal spending rule of 5 percent. (Taking the procedure the other way, you could multiply $50 million by 20, which is equal to $1 billion, to see what the size of the endowment would have to be to produce a given amount of funding.)

Based on these calculations, it's easy to see why the great research universities have gotten into the business of technology transfer. But the high returns are not the only factor motivating the universities to pursue patents, licensing agreements, and entrepreneurial activity. The original intent of the legislation was to speed up the transfer of knowledge, and this remains one of the chief reasons why universities care about intellectual property. Cynics say that it is about the money, and that is partly true. But American research universities have a long history of service to the nation. Educating citizens, building the knowledge base for new jobs, enhancing social welfare, reducing social injustices, and improving economic development and well-being throughout the world are also important parts of the mission of great universities.

Today, the mission of public service is taken very seriously by most of the leaders of higher education. And the ability to produce useful knowledge from research discoveries, a small fraction of which are patentable, has become more relevant to that part of the university mission in the twenty-first century. Some patents have been used in thousands of surgeries to relieve pain suffered by patients—for example, patents for artificial shoulders or knees. Indeed, scores of health-care-related discoveries have enhanced people's lives. Discoveries in engineering and computer science have spawned novel industries to produce electronic products and computer software programs that presumably have made positive changes in the ways we live and work.

The revenue has also become part of the culture of competition among the universities. Every administrator of a top research university wants his or her institution to become the best, and then to compete with the best to become still better. Bayh-Dole has not exactly set off another California gold rush, but it has stimulated interest in technology transfer, providing the incentive that it was intended to provide to ensure that useful ideas will be applied in ways that benefit all of us.

Many commercial firms would rather be able to obtain the information they need from universities without having to pay for it—becoming willing free riders on the backs of university research efforts. For most of the twentieth century that was in fact the situation. Since Bayh-Dole, many of the great research universities have guarded their intellectual property more vigorously than before, and some have sued companies for infringing on their patents. Are universities becoming greedy institutions, commercializing their valuable intellectual property instead of sharing it freely? Are they violating their compact with society and their nonprofit status? Sometimes business and industry leaders accuse the universities of such things—but when the attacks come from industry it sounds a bit like the pot calling the kettle black. Other times, it is federal government leaders who voice concerns about the effects of commercialization on the advance of knowledge. And sometimes the critics come from within the academy itself, with people from within academia posing fundamental ethical questions about whether the commercialization of intellectual property will undermine core values at the universities.

When the critiques come from government and from within the academy, they must be taken very seriously. Derek Bok, the former president of Harvard, has been perhaps the most insightful and articulate commentator on the potential darker side of commercialization.[31] In his book *Universities in the Marketplace*, Bok attends not only to technological transfer, but also to collegiate athletics and the recent infatuation at research universities with new digital media technologies that have potential commercial value. He does see the bright side—the benefits that American society receives from the extraordinary research discoveries made at our universities. And Bok recognizes the reasons for increased commercialization, such as the increasing competition between universities and the quest for new revenue streams. But he judiciously focuses on an array of potential harmful consequences of commercialization on the idea of the university. And when Derek Bok speaks, it is wise to at least listen.

Bok fears that research universities are entering a Faustian bargain. His main worry is that the incentives of commercialization will cause universities to focus their efforts on secondary rather than primary functions, and that the redirection of energy could subvert the essential idea of the university. He is rightly concerned that commercialization could have corrupting effects on both the individuals who work at universities and the institutions that house them, with each yielding to temptations of substantial monetary returns.

Bok asks whether proprietary interests in withholding important scientific discoveries from the public domain, in order to obtain patents for those ideas, could lead to delays in moving important discoveries into the public arena and consequently slow down the rate of scientific and technological progress. Progress in science is based on the norm of open communication, with scientists around the world sharing knowledge and building on each other's work to produce more knowledge. How will this system change if it becomes more likely for knowledge to be withheld until the patent is obtained? When real or potential conflicts-of-interest arise for faculty members who have financial stakes in start-up companies, will they be recognized for what they are by university administrators who are eager for the cash that might flow from the ideas?

If doctors at university medical schools and hospitals are receiving substantial monetary benefits from their links with pharmaceutical firms, will they cut corners in the way they report scientific results, or make biased choices about what drugs or medical devices to use? If they have a personal stake in the welfare of a company because they hold an equity share in the company, can their judgments remain objective? Will scholars and scientists misuse their influence with graduate students as they help them decide what problems to study and research? Will they shape students' interest around those problems that have potential commercial payoff, rather than focusing their attention on the scientifically most important set of problems, regardless of commercial possibilities?

Bok's concerns also ought to be ours. If individuals within institutions have a set of goals that are very important to them, it is possible that they will attempt to achieve them through illegitimate means, particularly if the pressure to reach them is extreme and socially appropriate means are unavailable. In short, as competition rises and it becomes more important to reach a goal, the pressure builds to commit deviant behavior. Pressure from academic administrators to bring income into institutions that are struggling can become very strong. Institutional pressure exists to keep the level of income rising—and this pressure can be felt by people at all levels of the university system. If individuals and their institutions yield to these pressures, and begin to redefine what is acceptable behavior, then the core values of a university are threatened.

Conflicts of interest pose a very real problem for universities today. The commercialization of the discoveries made by universities will undermine their culture if curiosity-driven research is driven out solely on the basis of its lower potential for utility and marketability. And there is enough evidence to suggest that big business and industry have successfully bought and paid for influence within the academy. Medical device manufacturers, for example, have paid surgeons to use their hip-replacement joints, without public disclosure, and there are scores of examples of pharmaceutical firms paying physicians with the expectation that they will prescribe their products.

Corruption of core values is more apt to occur if university leaders fail to introduce mechanisms to make potential conflicts transparent and to sanction members of the community who violate ethical standards of conduct. It's one thing for university leaders to encourage entrepreneurial behavior; it's another to encourage it at the expense of quality research or the erosion of core values. Extraordinary abuse of core values and cases of outright fraud continue to be quite rare—in part because in most fields such things are eventually exposed. When this happens, the violator is essentially excommunicated. As a general rule, faculty, administrators, researchers, and grad students uphold the university's core values, maintaining high standards of ethical conduct. Nevertheless, it only takes a few exceptions to the general rule to warrant vigilance in making sure that all members of the university community adhere to the commitment to these behavioral ideals.

What is more common is the tendency to finagle the results of research, unconsciously looking for confirmation of one's presuppositions and biases while neglecting disconfirming evidence. Out of a commitment to the "righteousness" of one's larger goals, one might attempt to justify cutting procedural or methodological corners, or even permit borderline violations of the conflict-of-interest rules. These insidious activities threaten the production of good science. If selling one's soul to the pharmaceutical firms is justified as part of a "larger good" purpose, we are in trouble.

In our culture, there are strong tendencies to commodify everything, to turn everything into dollars and cents—a cost-benefit analysis. That is not the basis on which great universities have been built. And yet, in a culture in which such tendencies are rife, it may be difficult for some individuals or institutions to avoid taking that path. We must build structural mechanisms to ensure that the values remain intact.[32] The great universities will not thrive without an agreement among those who lead them, work in them, and teach in them that the growth of fundamental knowledge cannot be sacrificed for expedient goals.

CHAPTER 6

Growing Pains

Using any reasonable definition of a scientist, we can say that 80 to 90 percent of all the scientists that have ever lived are alive now.

—Derek J. de Solla Price

S cience, engineering, and the full range of other academic activities at American universities have grown far beyond anything Vannevar Bush could have imagined possible when he crafted *Science—The Endless Frontier* in 1944 and 1945. We have entered an age of Big Science, with funding in amounts previously unheard of, teams of collaborators frequently numbering more than a dozen and sometimes reaching into the hundreds for a single published paper, and partnerships between universities and industry that are bringing scientific discoveries into our lives at an unprecedented rate. The tremendous growth of the university in such a short time period has caused some fundamental changes to take place in the way the university is run and in the tone of university life.

In some important respects, large universities are much the same now as they were in Bush's time. Their basic commitment to teaching and research, to excellence, and to core institutional values goes back to their origins as research institutions. There has been relatively little change over the past half-century in the number of schools within the large universities or in their basic internal organizational structure. But in many ways that are often not entirely appreciated, the Berkeley and Harvard of today are very different organisms from what they were in 1945. The fundamental difference is in their size and complexity and in their responses to the exponential rate of growth in the acquisition of new knowledge.

Research universities are now complex formal organizations. They depend less on patterns of stability, loyalty, and friendship—the hallmarks of the ecclesiastical model of academia—than on formal rules designed to reinforce core values associated with excellence. In concrete terms, for example, the better the university, the less likely it is that scholars will be granted tenure because they happen to be wonderful colleagues, deeply loyal "citizens" of the place—members of the family—and the more likely it is that they will be judged on more impersonal criteria, such as how academically productive they have been. Every other activity, program, and school or department will be judged on these same objective terms. Something may be lost in the adherence to such impersonal standards, but the overall quality of the universities is apt to be enhanced through their use.[1]

THE EMERGENCE OF BIG SCIENCE

Knowledge in the postwar years has undergone exponential growth of the type normally reserved for describing the law of compound interest. This knowledge explosion was first noted in 1963 by Yale historian of science Derek J. de Solla Price,[2] who spent a good deal of effort measuring the functional form of that growth and the time constant that produced it. His analysis resulted in the following conclusion: Eighty to 90 percent of all scientists who had ever lived on Planet Earth were alive at the time he was writing. The number of scientists around the world, if anything, has increased even more since Price made that observation.

Price also calculated the exponential growth that was then taking place in a number of other ways in science, and some of the patterns he noticed have continued into the twenty-first century. For example, the number of published scientific and scholarly papers in many fields doubles every five or ten years. Think about how difficult it must be to keep up with a literature that is growing that fast. Price applied his theory to a wide range of examples— the rate of important discoveries had doubled in twenty years, the number of B.A. degrees awarded had doubled in fifteen, the number of physicists had doubled in twenty, the number of known asteroids had doubled in ten, and so on. What Price noticed in the growth of new knowledge was also true for the growth in computing power. Gordon Moore, cofounder of Intel Corporation, received recognition in 1965 for "Moore's Law," his claim that the capacity, or data density, of computer chips was doubling roughly every two years. Moore's Law turned out to be an accurate predictor of the exponential growth of several aspects of computer technology for more than forty years and is projected to remain valid for at least another decade.

Obviously, Price and Moore recognized that there were limits to growth. If the number of scientists on earth continued doubling at an exponential rate, in short order there would be more scientists on earth than people. Similarly, experts in the field of computer technology keep trying to guess when Moore's law will no longer hold, since there must be an upper limit on the capacity of a silicon chip to hold circuits. As Price himself noted, at a certain point the rate of growth will have to slow down, because exponential growth cannot continue forever.

Despite the exponential growth in all of these areas, a disproportionately small number of scientists and scholars are producing most of the work. Exceptional scholarly and scientific talent is very rare. Roughly 10 to 15 percent of the people in any academic field account for more than 50 percent of all the scholarly literature in that field. As it turns out, there is an inverse law of scholarly productivity: The fraction of scholars or scientists publishing in a given field who will produce at least n papers in their lifetime is roughly equivalent to $1/n^2$. At the simplest level, the fraction of scholars or scientists publishing in a field who will produce at least 1 paper is $1/1^2$, or $1/1$, which means that 100 percent of the scholars or scientists who are publishing in the field produce at least 1 paper. But the fraction of scholars or scientists who will produce 10 papers is $1/10^2$, or $1/100$. That is, only 1 percent of the scholars or scientists who are publishing in a field will produce 10 papers. For every 100 authors in a field, there are roughly 25 who produce 2 papers, 11 who produce 3 papers, and so on. This seems to be true in almost any walk of life: Ten to 15 percent of the people engaged in almost any activity account for more than half of all the output.

This inverse law applies not only to scientific and scholarly productivity but also to the impact and quality of scientific work as measured by citations (references to a person's work in scholarly journals or books) and other indicators of quality. That distribution is highly skewed as well. Most scholars and scientists receive almost no citations to their work; a few garner vast numbers. Julius Axelrod, who won the Nobel Prize in Physiology and Medicine for his path-breaking discoveries on the activity of neurotransmitters, which eventually led to the production of antidepressants such as Prozac, claimed that "ninety-nine percent of the discoveries are made by one percent of the scientists."[3]

When we compare scientists and scholars whom the community has recognized as making significant contributions to their fields—those, for example, who have been elected to the National Academy of Sciences, the American Academy of Arts and Sciences, or the American Philosophical Society—with a random sampling of scientists and scholars at colleges and universities across the United States, we discover that those who have received substantial honorific recognition have, on average, far higher rates of scientific or scholarly productivity and citations to their work before they received recognition than the rank-and-file members do. There is also a strong correlation between the rate of production and citations suggesting that scientists who simply churn out papers are actually less likely to be highly recognized by their peers than those who publish fewer papers of higher quality.

The widespread aphorism that academics must publish or perish, which is often translated for the public as scholars caring only about their sheer output regardless of its content, is only trivially correct. Obviously, you can't produce great scholarship if you don't produce any. So there is apt to be a significant positive relationship between the sheer number of publications and their assessed quality. But, as I noted, it turns out that scientists and scholars with the highest percentage of quality publications tend to be those who are most highly honored—not those who churn out a mass of papers, few of which are of any importance. These highly productive scholars are disproportionately located at America's greatest universities, and, as you can imagine, they are the focus of a great deal of competitive zeal on the part of universities.

There has been a popular idea in academia that all academics contribute in one way or another, like bees in a hive, to the overall results of the system of scholarship. As Stephen Cole and I have demonstrated, this metaphor is far from correct. The vast majority of faculty members in the United States and elsewhere simply do not contribute much to the growth of knowledge. Relatively few scientists and scholars in fact influence their peers and the growth of knowledge.[4] Does this mean we could cut the number of scientists in half in America, cut the cost of training Ph.D.s, and still maintain our superior output? Not at all. Why? The most obvious reason is that in many fields it is often difficult to predict early on which scientists or scholars are going to turn out to be the most creative.

If it was easy to predict which young men and women, at age twenty or twenty-two, would turn out to make the most notable contributions during a lifetime of working in their chosen field, then we might well be able to reduce the numbers of those accepted to graduate schools for training. But a social system needs some slack, or redundancy. In addition, if young people who were thinking about careers believed it would be too hard to succeed in a field, many of the most gifted among them would self-select themselves out of that career path, and the system would not be apt to recruit many of the potentially most gifted scientists or scholars.

Academic departments fulfill many functions, and research excellence is only one of them—albeit an extremely important one. There is a great need for devoted teachers who spend relatively more time on undergraduate and graduate education, or who do administrative tasks that allow a department to run smoothly for its students and faculty members. Given the time commitments related to these roles, these scholars may publish less than some of their colleagues. Not all scholars and scientists can be star researchers.

American scholars and scientists have been very well represented in the exponential growth of knowledge internationally. As American universities ascended in quality and prestige, their production of knowledge began to increase dramatically, just as I. I. Rabi and Robert A. Millikan had predicted years earlier. The share of the world's academic literature flowing from American universities rose from World War II until the mid-1990s, leveling off thereafter. And the greatest universities have tended to produce the lion's share of the truly outstanding new work.

The United States still dominates the world in the production of literature in the sciences and engineering, where most major discoveries are reported. The relative decline in the production of research articles from the United States in general over the past decade can be attributed to two main factors: (1) Europe has recovered more fully from the long-term impact of World War II, and (2) rapidly growing nations have begun to recognize the value of science and scholarship to their larger economic aspirations and are starting to increase their participation in the international academic community.

In 2001, the United States produced roughly one-third of the world's science and engineering articles appearing in refereed journals included in the *Science Citation Index*. However, our share of the world's output actually declined for fifteen years before that, going from 39 percent of the total to 31 percent between 1986 and 2001. In fact, as of 2001, Western European nations, taken together, were producing a higher proportion of the world's literature than the United States. Highly industrialized societies are competing for excellence and true distinction internationally.

The share of work coming from the United States—or any other nation—is becoming difficult to measure, however. It is getting more and more difficult to say what nation has produced a given article or book, as research is increasingly collaborative over time and across nations. And even where the American share of the total literature has declined, the knowledge produced by U.S. scientists and engineers continues to have the greatest impact, at least as measured by citations by scientists and scholars to the work of others.[5] The value of research produced at our great universities continues to be recognized abundantly with the most prestigious prizes: In 2006, 2007, and 2008, American scientists continued to dominate in the receipt of Nobel Prizes, receiving 64 percent of all the science and economics awards.

The story of exponential growth can be seen within individual institutions as well as in the international arena. Part of the story plays out in the rising budgets of the research universities. Columbia University, for example, in Nicholas Murray Butler's final year as president, 1944–1945, faced a $1.6 million deficit, which Butler adroitly turned into a $65,000 surplus by the end of that academic year. This was on a total operating budget of about $11 million. Still struggling to balance its books, Columbia had an operating budget in fiscal year 2007–2008 of roughly $2.8 billion—more than 255 times greater than Butler's final budget. Even a cursory glance at the intervening decades reveals how quickly this growth—which corresponded to an equivalent growth in the number and size of academic programs—occurred: The operating expenses went from $11 million in 1944–1945 to about $57 million in 1959–1960, $170 million in 1969–1970, $317 million in 1979–1980, $800 million in 1989–1990, $1.1 billion in 1993–1994, and then $2.8 billion in 2007. Columbia's budget has more than doubled in some ten-year periods, and its annual expenses have increased at a compound rate of close to 10 percent for the past sixty years. Even allowing for the substantial inflation in some time periods, this is an enormous rate of real growth. The same pattern has been sustained by most of the other major research universities. Harvard's operating revenues totaled roughly $3.5 billion in its

2007–2008 fiscal year, with sponsored research making up about $670 million, or almost 20 percent of the total budget. Harvard's budget was only a small fraction of this at the end of World War II. Capital budgets for building and renovation projects on campus have grown at much the same pace. This rate of budgetary growth reflects the patterns of expanding research and teaching opportunities at America's top universities.

With increases in size have come increases in complexity. Universities have become large organizations with a substantial division of labor and responsibilities. The sheer number of people who work at them has increased at such a high rate that organizing the efforts of all of these groups to fulfill the missions of the university has become an enormous enterprise. Many of the large research universities are among the top employers in their communities, and their "business" has a profound economic impact on these communities. This is true even in cities like New York, Boston, and Los Angeles, where the universities are only one component of a larger economy, but still a major component. Along with the growth in complexity has come a growth in the types of revenues universities receive from various sources, a rising endowment, and increased fundraising activities (including courting alumni). University investment portfolios have become more diverse, and managing these portfolios has become more complex. Campuses have grown in size and in the number of buildings and other facilities, including classrooms, labs, athletic centers and fields, dorms, student services offices, health centers, parking facilities, and so on, all of which are essential to maintaining quality.

There are more lawyers because there are more legal disputes, more government regulations to follow, and more federal, state, and local relationships to be maintained. The number of patents for the intellectual property that the university owns has gone up, and patent applications, as well as the licensing agreements with industry for the use of intellectual property, must be handled correctly. There are more academic offerings, more faculty members, and more research staff than in the past, and the number of reviews needed to evaluate people for promotion and tenure has increased accordingly. An expanding number of institutional affiliations must be maintained, including joint academic programs with other universities within the United States and abroad. More contract and grant applications must be processed and submitted, and once these grants and contracts are awarded, they must be individually accounted for and monitored. Athletic teams have become more complicated to manage. The number of people involved in community relations has increased, and the number of staff employed to maintain the university's facilities has risen. Library collections have expanded, and various forms of information technology and new media have become important. The cost of attracting academic stars has also increased, brought about by competition among peer universities that are all interested in capturing the best scholars and scientists.

All of these aspects of university management have become matters requiring exceptional skill and expertise as well as a sharp division of labor—even between the president and provost of the university. They are no longer issues that can be handled in town meetings. Many have become too technical, or too far removed from the main interests of the typical faculty member, for the scholars, scientists, and students to pay them much mind. Few people inside universities today have a comprehensive idea of how they are actually run. They want things to run smoothly, and they don't hesitate to let leaders of the institution know when they are not, but they have only a limited idea about how "the business" operates. In fact, research universities have become big and highly complex organizations, even though they are still based on the set of values enumerated earlier that separate them from profit-making corporations.

Along with this rapid growth has come a steep rise in the number of Americans who have earned higher degrees over the decades since World War II. This growth parallels, of course, the general population growth in the United States. It also reflects the increasing number of high school graduates who could take advantage of improved opportunities for financial aid that made a college education affordable. Today, about two-thirds of high school graduates go on to some form of higher education. The United States continues to be among the international leaders in the proportion of its population entering advanced degree programs, but it is by no means alone at the top of that ladder. Opportunities in higher education have expanded in many other industrial nations as well.

In the 2004–2005 academic year, American colleges and universities conferred more than 1.4 million bachelor's degrees; roughly 87,000 professional degrees; and almost 53,000 doctoral degrees. Just after World War II, before the full impact of the GI Bill was felt, the numbers were dramatically lower. The growth in doctoral degrees did not, however, follow a clear exponential form. There was very rapid growth in the number of doctoral degrees conferred in the 1960s and mid-1970s, when it reached about 33,000. Then we saw a leveling off in this growth for about a decade.

The concentration of Ph.D.s has also shifted over time. Until the 1970s, it was the older public and private institutions that awarded the majority of these degrees, but between 1950 and 1970 the number of universities offering doctoral degrees grew from about 100 to about 600.[6] Since the 1970s we have seen a general expansion of doctoral programs, although the elite public and private universities still tend to award a high proportion of the degrees conferred. In 2004–2005, public institutions awarded about 60 percent of the doctorates.

The demographic composition of doctoral degree recipients has also changed remarkably over time. Today, fully 49 percent of the doctorates go to women. More than half of the doctorates received in the humanities are earned by women; almost half of those conferred in the life sciences go to women; and about a quarter of the doctorates in the physical sciences go to women—far more than in the decades immediately following World War II.

At America's great universities today, you will see a montage of student and faculty faces representing almost every nation in the world. A remarkably large number of our doctorates in the physical sciences—40 percent in 2005–2006—go to foreign-born students who study here on temporary visas. About 57 percent of the Ph.D.s in engineering go to foreign students, and between a fifth and a quarter of the Ph.D. recipients in the social and life sciences are earned by foreign students.[7] If we look at the number of foreign students enrolled at specific American universities, at the top of the list is the University of Southern California, with more than 7,000 foreign students in 2006–2007, which represented about 23 percent of its entire student enrollment; Columbia had almost 6,000, representing 22 percent of its enrollment, closely followed by New York University with 5,800, or almost 15 percent of its total. International students represent somewhere between 16 and 26 percent of enrollment at Harvard, Stanford, Cornell, and MIT. Somewhat below those numbers, there is the University of Texas at Austin at 11 percent, and Johns Hopkins at 12 percent. These schools are highly selective in their admissions to Ph.D. programs. In short, globalization has come to higher education, and the flow is to the United States. We are importing more advanced students than we are exporting, and the leading sources of talent for our universities have been Asian and Southeast Asian nations.[8]

The infusion of public dollars for university-based research since World War II has come principally from the National Science Foundation, the National Institutes of Health, and the Defense Department, although a healthy share of the financing has come from private industry and foundations as well. The growth in the NSF research budget is another indicator of the resources that have become available to fuel innovation and discovery. The first full-scale National Science Foundation budget request of $14 million turned into a $4.75 million appropriation in 1953. Just four years later, in 1957, the total NSF budget was $40 million, and more than fifty years later, in 2009, the total NSF budget was about $6.9 billion, roughly $5.7 billion of which was allocated to research and development funding.

The growth of the National Institutes of Health budget has been even more impressive over the decades. From 1947, the NIH's first year in operation, to 1954, its budget rose from $8 million to $71 million. The budget continued to grow rapidly between 1955 and 1968 under the leadership of Dr. James A Shannon, and by 1960 the NIH surpassed the Department of Defense as the largest supporter of university-based research.[9] By the 2009 fiscal year, the NIH budget had grown to more than $29.5 billion, with more than half allocated to support almost 40,000 competitively funded research grants conducted outside of the NIH—principally at research universities. Between 1997 and 2004, the NIH budget doubled. Since then, funding levels at the NIH have increased only marginally, and in fact between 2007 and 2009 funding was down in terms of real growth by 8 percent, reflecting the views of the Bush administration toward scientific and health-related research. Nonetheless, despite these lean years, funding over the long term at the NIH has approximated an exponential function since the integration of the institutes in the late 1940s.[10]

Some of the increases in funding, admittedly, are due to inflation. Using the Consumer Price Index (CPI), a less than perfect research expense deflator, we find that the inflation conversion of $1,000 in 2005 was equal to $135 in 1947, about the time of the reorganization of the NIH. The initial budget of the NIH has grown well over 3,000 percent since 1947; the NSF's budget more than 1,000 percent since 1953—each far surpassing the rate of inflation and indicating enormous real growth.

Federal support for academic research, which grew from roughly 25 percent to 60 percent of university research funding between 1935 and

1960, took off in the 1960s. Total academic research and development funds grew from $646 million in 1960, of which $405 million was federally sponsored, to about $16 billion in 1990, of which over $9 billion, or about 58 percent, was federally supported. Measured against the CPI, real resources grew about 12 times from 1935 to 1965, and rapid growth continued until around 1980. This huge expansion of resources undoubtedly changed the fundamental character of the American research university.[11]

Of equal importance are the investment choices by the federal research agencies supporting research and congressional support for the agencies' decisions. The research agencies and Congress tended to support the life sciences and the physical sciences, including the earth sciences, and engineering fields, including computer science and electrical engineering. For much of the past half-century, in part because of this national investment, these were the fields where a great deal of the action was taking place. Indeed, because of the scientific and technological revolutions in these fields, industry increasingly ceded its role as the incubator of new ideas—the leading force in directing the research component of research and development—to the research universities. This is important because it is these very areas of growth—the fields most highly favored by the people making decisions about federal research investments—that have had the most profound impacts on industry and business. And it is one of the reasons why the universities play a far more critical role today than in the past in the developing economy of the nation.

A detailed look at other federal agencies would tell much the same story: The American research universities have become highly dependent on the federal government for the resources needed for scientific discovery. This extraordinary support from the federal government has required Herculean efforts by academic leaders, who now spend countless hours in Washington explaining the value of investments in university research to members of Congress. And it is not just the public universities that have taken this route; private universities, too, have become dependent on public funding. The old distinction between public and private universities is withering away, even if parts of their mission, such as the commitment of the public university to meeting the needs of its state's student population and its local economic interests, remain very different.[12] With increased resources comes increased competition for them. And that competition has grown fierce, as a number of cases will illustrate.

THE COMPETITIVE SPIRIT

While I was provost at Columbia I spent a great deal of time recruiting academic stars; I spent an equal amount of time fending off efforts by others to raid some of our best scholars and scientists. Some of the deals might be illuminating. As early as 1990, three of Columbia's best young neuroscientists were approached by a first-rate university whose leaders wanted to build a world-class enterprise in neuroscience at their institution. The package that this institution was offering these young scientists, between new laboratory space, equipment, and resources to hire other extraordinary young scientists, came to somewhere between $30 million and $40 million.

We did our homework. How good were the people we might lose? What could we "buy" for that kind of money in talent outside of Columbia? How would losing these three young stars affect our ability to recruit other outstanding talent? How would it affect morale? How would it affect our ability to generate external research funds? A host of these questions were posed and answered through a good deal of consultation with leaders in the neurosciences. At the end of the day, we felt we had to meet this offer. These people were too talented to lose. Based on their work to that point, it was possible that any one of the three might win a Nobel Prize in the future. And we had to make a statement that Columbia would not be beaten in its pursuit of quality as a result of this kind of offer. We might not be able to control other factors, such as a scholar's interest in staying in New York versus moving to the West Coast, or getting away from a messy divorce situation, but we did not have to lose because of financial resources.

When the dean of the School of Medicine, Herbert Pardes, and I approached the president of Columbia with our recommendation, we were emphatic that we should keep these three faculty members. What we were not sure about was where we would come up with the money to counter the external offer. To his credit, the president, Michael Sovern, said that if I could assure him that these scientists were as good as I had said they were, he would find the money. I did, and he did—and so we parried one more effort to recruit some of our best. Ten years later, one of those scientists had won a Nobel Prize and the other two had been elected to the National Academy of Sciences. They all have had richly productive careers and are true leaders of neuroscience—a field in which Columbia continues to rank among the best in the world. But at the time, the price was steep, and it seemed that we were making a leap of faith, though it was an edu-cated leap.

Then there was our effort to recruit one of the country's outstanding humanists from Harvard. We got lucky here. He was perfectly happy at Harvard, but his spouse, an exceptionally talented young biologist, was not ready to be considered for tenure at Harvard. Our biologists saw great promise in this young woman and wanted to offer her a tenured position, but they were not familiar with the renown of her husband. When I was ap-proached about whether we would consider hiring both scholars, I became enthusiastic. But that's only the beginning of the story. Both of these schol-ars explored the quality of Columbia's facilities relative to Harvard's in great detail—for example, the quality of the art history and history collections in New York City and Columbia compared with those of Cambridge, Massa-chusetts. After negotiating salaries, space and set-up requirements, and other perquisites, we were able to attract these two brilliant scholars, who have both been extremely productive since coming to Columbia.

Recruitment of star faculty is an expensive proposition. Within the sci-ences that require labs and equipment, it can cost $1 million to recruit a junior scientist and many millions to recruit a well-known senior scientist. It may not have been as expensive in the past, but competition to acquire the best professors and students was a constant and important feature of the American system of higher learning throughout the twentieth century. Over the past several decades, the United States has found itself in an era of "academic free agency" that parallels the kind of competition we see in contemporary professional sports. The flow of "labor" in the system is con-strained by a system of academic tenure that provides security for those who earn it, but limits the movement of people more than in other indus-tries, because even unproductive tenured faculty members cannot easily be removed from their positions. The competition has driven up the cost of running great universities. It has also improved their quality and relative standing in the world of higher learning. Without the most talented fac-ulty members, it is difficult for universities to legitimately claim that they are among the best in the world.

Competition has driven the system—and the rate of discovery—on both the individual and institutional level. Individuals compete for prior-ity in discovery as well as for funds, which are, in many instances, essential for the pursuit of particular lines of inquiry. In the era of "little science," competition for ideas was more important than competition for resources. Today, universities are forced to invest resources in the most advanced and important areas of inquiry at the frontiers of knowledge. It has led to technological innovations, but it has also required universities to build modern laboratory facilities and stock them with the best equipment, to invest in libraries and research materials, and to stay on the cutting edge of information technologies. All of this is done principally to lure individual scholars and scientists of the first rank—or teams of them—from one university to another in an effort to enhance excellence.

Competition operates at the larger institutional level to open up new fields of scholarship and scientific inquiry. Pushing at the frontiers of knowledge, talented faculty members bargain with universities to place resources in new and potentially important areas of research. Academic competition puts pressure on the boundaries of knowledge and often leads to creation of new jobs and fields of inquiry within the larger system. What was once the field of biology is now a plethora of important subfields created by the interaction between competition and the development of disciplinary knowledge.

Competition forces universities to be innovative. For example, if some universities make it virtually impossible to do multidisciplinary research, aspiring universities can offer easier opportunities for faculty to engage in that type of research and teaching. Competition forces universities to experiment with new teaching and research technologies and to collaborate with other institutions, if that will make their programs better. It forces them to expand their search for talent, making their scope cosmopolitan rather than local, international rather than national or regional. Competition forces universities to think strategically about how to spend their resources—for example, whether to concentrate on new areas of research that will enable them to attract scientists and scholars whom they might not otherwise have been able to woo. Competition for students can produce better financial-aid and fellowship packages that will make graduate Ph.D. programs more attractive for the most able students. Finally, competition causes universities to explore nontraditional sources of funding that can be reinvested in the educational missions, research and teaching.

Indeed, competition has raised the overall level of excellence at our universities and has helped to produce the growing quality we have seen in them over the past fifty years. For a variety of reasons, European systems of higher learning have not fostered competition to the same degree. In fact, some nations, to the overall detriment of their universities, have actively discouraged competition in academia—a subject to which I shall return in the last part of this book.

The competitive spirit does have some negative consequences. There is far more horizontal mobility today among academics than in the past. Loyalty to a university is often subordinated to personal self-interest. Identification with one's discipline often replaces identification with one's university—and personal identity often trumps both. Faculty members have become world travelers, attending conferences and visiting other universities while on leave from their home institution. Some enjoy their winters in California and their falls in New York; others prefer Paris to either. These cosmopolitan professors are on the move between research facilities—high-energy particle accelerators or large-scale telescopes, one center for advanced study or another, one major museum or another—and their home universities either adjust to these schedules or find themselves in peril of losing some of their leading lights.

The competition behind the "star" system is intense and double edged. Great scientists and scholars attract resources, students, recognition, visibility, and prestige for the university. But at even the best universities, the star system also exacerbates inequalities—in salaries, compensation, and other resources. Stars are a necessary, if not sufficient, condition for great quality. The stars usually remain at the forefront of their fields, producing discoveries that generate pride in the university among faculty members, students, and alumni, heightening the morale of all who are part of the community. Problems do arise. Some fields really do not have great original thinkers at some points in their development, for example, and the field creates "stars" when there are none. Fields do need stars, for reasons that I need not pursue here. Suffice it to say that when universities spend large amounts of money to attract these "created" stars, they are often using resources that could be better spent on other activities. There is then ambivalence toward these stars—sometimes including resentment, particularly when they appear to be prima donnas.

The American university system essentially operates in an entrepreneurial way, driven by competition and innovation. One reason is that the great private universities have never been controlled by the state. And because of the tradition of academic freedom, professors at the state universities are not treated as "state employees"; nor do they have a "state employee" kind of mentality. The independence of the great universities from official state control has fostered excellence and independence, autonomy and innovation.

When the state "owns" the universities and controls the salaries and resources invested in them, the potential for competition is attenuated or nonexistent, unless there is an official state policy to encourage such competitiveness. Although there are many federal and state controls on what universities can do in America, our research universities have operated in a relatively free market as well as in a free marketplace of ideas. This has allowed them to pursue their own plans and to invest in areas of research and teaching that their leaders deem best in their quest to fulfill the mission of the university and to further the pursuit of excellence. The competitive spirit also produces incentives for universities to take risks in pursuing critically important research.

Of course, individual states have not always tolerated this independence, especially in difficult political times. In some periods, legislators or regents have constrained the universities by imposing such things as loyalty oaths, or regulations limiting the universities' latitude in shaping students. However, few national systems of higher learning have had the degree of freedom and autonomy enjoyed by universities in the United States. In fact, in Europe and Asia, most universities operate within a national system of higher education that is controlled by a national ministry of education. Richard C. Atkinson, a former director of the National Science Foundation and former president of the University of California system, once remarked that in countries where the universities are regulated by the government, "it is more difficult for individual universities . . . to distinguish themselves from one another and thus to compete effectively."[13]

What is the evidence that this type of competition has led to excellence in scholarship and boosted the rate of discovery? The growth of the university described at the beginning of this chapter is one kind of evidence. In the next chapter, I will try to present another kind of evidence by describing the breadth and depth of knowledge that our preeminent universities produce.

PART II

DISCOVERIES THAT ALTER OUR LIVES

CHAPTER 7

Finding a Smoother Pebble: A National System of Innovation

I do not know what I may appear to the world; but to myself I seem to have been only like a boy playing on the seashore, and diverting myself in now and then finding a smoother pebble or a prettier shell than ordinary, whilst the great ocean of truth lay all undiscovered before me.

—Isaac Newton

Americans have always been fascinated with inventions and scientific discovery, and we pride ourselves on our ability to find solutions to formidable problems. Yet most people do not know the origin of the most important discoveries of our time. Is it any wonder, given that the best-selling twentieth-century American history high-school textbooks devote more space to Madonna than to Watson and Crick, that our top university professors and researchers typically miss out on even their fifteen minutes of fame?[1] Nevertheless, we use products derived from ideas generated at our great research universities countless times a day—whether we realize it or not.

For example, in the morning you may brush your teeth with an electric toothbrush, then stagger into the kitchen, open the refrigerator, and take out some orange juice. The toothbrush can vibrate thousands of times a minute, creating fluid dynamics that can dislodge bacteria and plaque much more efficiently than an old-fashioned toothbrush; the refrigerator has a compressed gas circulating through its coils; and the orange juice has been preserved while being shipped from a distant location. All three are based on discoveries made in university research departments. Contemplating that night's dinner, you take some steaks out of the freezer and make sure you have the ingredients for a salad. Most likely, you are not thinking about the fact that the meat's fine quality is a result of artificial insemination and scientific breeding techniques, both the result of university work, or that the special tomatoes on your counter have been genetically modified. You put a nice bottle of California wine into the fridge to chill, with nary a thought of the heartier vines made possible by research conducted by university enologists, then turn on your favorite FM radio station, made possible through university inventions over in engineering, for a little background news.

The station gives you a weather update, based on knowledge originating in the meteorological wings of universities. Then there are news stories about an earthquake that measured 7.5 on the Richter scale, the number of hurricanes predicted for this year, and the latest public opinion poll on the upcoming election, all of which are based on information learned through university research. You swallow the antibiotic your doctor prescribed for you, and then, as your conscience gets the better of you, decide to go out jogging. You bring along some Gatorade (another university invention) so you won't get dehydrated. As you begin, you notice that your muscles are sore from your last run, and that reminds you to order some flowers for your elderly mother—her hip replacement surgery is tomorrow. On your way home you stop at the closest ATM machine for some cash, which, of course, uses another university discovery, and later, when you're driving to work, you flip on the GPS to navigate a construction detour. A few minutes later, back on route, you use your E-ZPass to glide through the bridge toll booth—which uses laser technology, not to mention computers—paying a premium for driving into the city during peak hours (congestion pricing is also a university invention).

Whatever your job, you are very likely to continue using methods and devices that are the fruits of university research once you reach the office. As the manager of a hedge fund, for example, you would be using sophisticated mathematical programs to help make investment decisions, and the mathematics and investment algorithms, of course, would be based on advances made in universities. When you entered the office, you would turn on the computer to find out how the foreign markets were doing. In fact, all day long you would be using the computer and the Internet, which also began with university discoveries. If your advertising agency was using focus groups, it would be basing its work on university research, and when you took your lunch break, and the clerk at the local deli swiped your sandwich and soda over the bar-code scanner, you would again be encountering a university discovery. Enough. The list could go on and on, but the point is clear. As we march through our daily lives, all of us are continually enjoying the benefits of discoveries made at our great universities.

The universities play a huge role in bringing all of these inventions and discoveries into our daily lives, but they do not do it alone. The research conducted at our great universities is part of a larger national system of innovation. That system is essentially a social system for producing and applying new knowledge. It is a complex network of affiliations, collaborations, associations, and formal relationships that includes our universities, government agencies and laboratories, and the private sector, including the nonprofit research sector. Each plays a critical role in enhancing the overall stockpile of knowledge that we possess and in bringing it piece by piece into our lives through the practical applications that make up our world.[2]

A PRODUCTIVE PARTNERSHIP: THE IMPACT OF UNIVERSITIES ON INDUSTRIES AND LOCAL ECONOMIES

Industry and research universities are interrelated in many ways—not only through licensing agreements (explored in Chapter 5), but also through production of the highly trained, talented individuals who work in industrial laboratories and through the founding of companies by university faculty or former students. As of 2003, over 70 percent of all science and engineering graduates were working in private industry. Forty-four percent of all the science and engineering students who had earned Ph.D.s were working in industry; 43 percent were working at institutions of higher learning; and 13 percent were doing other things. It is clear that research universities represent the main pipeline to our nation's industrial research laboratories.[3] And the 100 or so greatest research universities produce the majority of Ph.D.s in science and engineering. The great industrial laboratories could not function without these universities feeding them new, talented individuals on a consistent basis.

Although the universities supply the talent—people with the aptitude, the skills, and the training to contribute to industry—as well as many of the ideas that industry uses, however, the credit for creating and developing products and services based on discoveries in science and engineering cannot go solely to the universities. Industry picks up where the universities leave off, playing an equal role in the innovation process. In that sense, there is a very productive partnership between the universities and industry. And the knowledge produced at universities and then developed by industry has huge societal payoffs with an enormous impact on local, national, and international communities. The national system of innovation in America has many components, as mentioned above. Here we will take a closer look at the relationship between two of those components—the universities and industry—with an emphasis on how the universities have an impact on the economies of their local communities.

Stanford and Boston area universities, particularly MIT, have attempted to measure the economic and social impacts they have had on their local communities, and the data they have generated can help us estimate the impact of universities on local communities in general. Stanford University reported, for example, that since the funding of Hewlett-Packard in 1939, 2,325 members of the Stanford University community founded more than 2,454 companies. These companies included such giants as Cisco Systems, Google, Hewlett-Packard, Sun Microsystems, and Yahoo!, and their commercial prosperity led to the phenomenal success of nearby Silicon Valley.[4] These companies have consistently made it into the "Silicon Valley 150"—the list of the largest Silicon Valley firms, published annually in the *San Jose Mercury-News*. In fact, they have not only made the list, they have consistently been in the top ten or fifteen in terms of rank by sales. In 2008, Hewlett-Packard topped the list, Cysco was number two, Google and Sun were numbers six and seven, respectively, and eBay was number nine, with Yahoo! twelfth. These companies generated $261.2 billion, or 55 percent of the total revenues of the 150 companies, in 2008. The total market capitalization of the Stanford-founded companies on this select list totaled $415 billion, or about 50 percent of the total market capitalization of the 150 companies.[5] Silicon Valley is in a class of its own, but other cities have also benefited from their proximity to major research universities. A 1997 study by BankBoston concluded that the local economic impact of eight Boston-area universities was "more significant than at any other time in modern economic history." The study concluded: "As jobs become more knowledge-driven, the universities produce not only the research that can lead to the creation of new companies and industries in the Greater Boston area, but the ability to deliver a workforce educated in emerging technologies." It further noted that the universities had "served as a magnet to a number of national and international companies that have located or are developing major research operations in the Boston area," listing Amgen, Cisco, Merck, Novartis, Pfizer, and Sun Microsystems as examples.[6]

A 2003 study of the economic effects of Boston's eight research universities showed that in the year 2000, these universities provided a $7.4 billion boost to the regional economy. The universities employed almost 51,000 people directly in 2002 and provided employment indirectly for about 37,000 other workers in the region. (This does not include people employed by university-affiliated hospitals or research institutes.) A talent pool of roughly 32,000 graduates, many of whom remained in Boston, came out of the universities every year. Innovative research at these universities had led to 264 patents, 280 commercial licenses for technology, and 41 start-up companies as well as opportunities for more than 25,000 continuing education students, many cultural and community events, and general improvements in the housing, streets, and environment of Boston. The universities received about $1.5 billion a year in research contracts and grants, mostly from the federal government. The report noted that faculty members had founded major local companies such as Akamai Technologies, Biogen, Delphi Communications Systems, and Genome Therapeutics. They had also spawned hundreds of new start-up companies. In fact, 25 out of the 50 Boston-area start-ups that had attracted the most financing had been companies associated with these universities.[7]

MIT alone has a huge impact on the local economy. The BankBoston report found that "if the companies founded by MIT graduates and faculty formed an independent nation, the revenues produced by the companies would make that nation the 24th largest economy in the world. The 4,000 MIT-related companies employ 1.1 million people and have annual world sales of $232 billion. . . . That is roughly equal to a gross domestic product of $116 billion, which is a little less than the GDP of South Africa and more than the GDP of Thailand." Perhaps as important as the overall effects of MIT research and training is the type of companies that are being formed on the basis of discoveries and training at the university. Noting that the MIT companies tended to be "knowledge-based companies in software, manufacturing (electronics, biotech, instruments, machinery) or consulting (architects, business consultants, engineers)," the report said: "As you would expect from the most distinguished engineering school in the nation, about 50% of the firms had founders who majored in engineering and another 24% in physical science. But fully 25% of the founders of MIT-related firms majored in 'social studies,' and a significant number of firms generated by them were related to ideas produced in the social and behavioral sciences. The knowledge based companies have a disproportionate importance for their local economies because they usually sell to out-of-state and world markets and because they so often represent advanced technologies."[8]

The universities and the firms based on their research also were found to have a "multiplier effect" on the total number of jobs created in the local area because, for example, for every local job created by a pharmaceutical firm working on university-based discoveries, there tended to be three to five additional jobs created by the needs of that firm for suppliers of equipment and services. These data are now a decade old, but since 1997 MIT's research and development activity and its role in the establishment of new start-up companies has expanded dramatically. The 1997 data vastly underestimate the impact of MIT's faculty and students today on the formation of national and international companies and the value of their discoveries and innovations to our economic well-being.[9]

The fact that the universities have so strongly boosted the growth of technologically oriented firms is significant. The independent Milliken Institute in Santa Monica, California, found that it was the high-technology sectors of the economy that determined the success or failure of a metropolitan area. High-technology activity explained 65 percent of the difference in economic growth among metropolitan regions in the United States in the 1990s, and research centers and institutions were undisputedly the most important factor in incubating high-tech industries. Proximity to a research university has been a critical factor in determining where high-

technology industries locate their offices and laboratories, both because
the brains located at the university represent a greater asset than ever before, and because of the increased interest among universities to be involved in the early stages of company formation and the licensing of their
ideas to established businesses.[10]

SOCIAL, CULTURAL, AND ETHICAL IMPACTS OF UNIVERSITIES

For many generations, we Americans have thought of education as a
public as well as a private good. An investment in the education of our
young people was an investment in the nation. We created land-grant
colleges after the 1862 Morrill Act in an effort to train young people for
more skilled jobs and to improve the quality of our agriculture and related
industries through organized research. We knew that a better-educated
citizen had greater life chances and could potentially contribute more to
the general social welfare. In recent decades, we have moved away from
this rationale for higher education toward one that focuses on individual
payoffs rather than on larger societal returns. That is a mistake. Our personal and taxpayer investments in the American research university
should be seen by each of us as an investment in the public good—in the
larger welfare of the nation that will improve the lives of all citizens. That
commitment to the general good is a fundamental part of the mission
of great universities.

I don't want to dismiss the other side of the story. The great transformation that university research has created in our lives and society, sometimes beyond what we could have imagined even a decade or two ago, also
has produced a host of complex new scientific, moral, and ethical problems for us to address and solve. Our successes have spawned new dilemmas of choice. When modern biological science allows us to create new
and potentially lethal viruses; when nanoscientists, piecing together individual atoms, can create biological structures that can learn from their own
actions; when nuclear physics produces the possibility of Armageddon,
and creates problems of nuclear waste disposal even when its discoveries
are used peacefully to generate power; when computer-science technology
allows us to spy on our own citizens and abridge their privacy; when automobiles and other manufactured goods contribute to global warming; and

when we have the capacity to clone animals and potentially human beings, we are faced with a set of vexing and challenging problems of our
own making that are sometimes urgent and often controversial.

New social and economic costs are thus sometimes associated with discovery. A number of questions arise that we all must consider as the social
and ethical impacts of university-related research affect our world in ever
more surprising ways. When science and technology have the potential to
be misused and can potentially fall into the wrong hands, what should our
attitude toward the advance of knowledge be? When we can use our
knowledge for the welfare of others, what choices are we faced with? How
and whether we decide to use our knowledge depends on our values, and
sometimes it involves making complicated choices where both options
have advantages and disadvantages. These are issues that are usually the
province of the humanities, not the sciences, and yet they are questions
that scientists are now facing every day. This is why I insist that the great
centers of higher learning must include an emphasis on the humanities
and social sciences. Great universities cannot ignore the contributions of
any of these sources of ideas.

When we think about the contributions of the universities to industry
we naturally focus on the influence they have had on the growth of industrial innovation and the scientific and engineering feats involved in taking
ideas and translating them into useful products. But another kind of contribution to the social and cultural life of the nation is derived from the
ideas, inventions, and discoveries made by scholars working in the social
and behavioral sciences and the humanities. As with the contributions of
science and technology to industry, the contributions in the social and behavioral sciences and the humanities are made through the influence of
ideas, concepts, and methods as well as through the people who establish
and staff organizations and businesses that depend on the training that is
provided in these fields by our best universities.

Consider in blueprint form five domains where our universities have
had an enormous impact on the direction the society has taken over the
past fifty years: (1) independent "think tanks" that translate empirical
knowledge into policy advice; (2) consulting firms that are used by businesses and government to solve organizational problems; (3) nongovernment organizations around the world and other private nonprofit
foundations; (4) cultural institutions; and (5) individual social and politi-

cal advisers who work for the government.[11] There are hundreds of thousands, if not millions, of jobs created as well as thousands of businesses spawned as a result of the training and expertise gained at our universities in these fields.

There are hundreds of private think tanks, and they work on every imaginable subject, from military preparedness to health-care reform. Some are liberal (the Brookings Institution), and some are highly conservative (the Heritage Foundation), but the entire spectrum of political perspectives is represented in the range of think tanks that exist. Though most are independent, some are associated with universities (such as Stanford's Hoover Institution, the University of Chicago's National Opinion Research Center [NORC], and the University of Michigan's Institute for Social Research [ISR]). Some are extremely large, such as the Rand Corporation, while others are boutique-sized, specializing in just a few areas of knowledge. What almost all have in common is that they recruit highly knowledgeable and well-trained graduates of our major research universities, most of them with advanced degrees from Ph.D. programs or law schools. Many of the larger think tanks have endowments, but their revenues come principally from work on government contracts that require specific answers to questions posed by the funding agency or from private businesses. They exert increasing amounts of influence in the policymaking world, independent of universities. The quality of their work is often mixed, but they depend largely on our great universities for their talent.

The number of consulting firms that depend on advanced university training, either in the form of Ph.D. or advanced professional degrees, and that work for industry to solve market-research problems, is staggering. The very idea of systematic marketing research comes, as we shall see, from our universities. Polling and public-opinion firms alone hire thousands of people to staff their efforts to put their finger on the pulse of the nation. Hundreds of thousands of jobs have been created from the ideas and methodologies developed at research universities that have created advanced techniques to explore questions about peoples' preferences and purchasing behavior, and about their attitudes and opinions, and to place these views in some form of theoretical context.

Nonprofit organizations are largely staffed by those with advanced training at our great institutions of higher learning. Nongovernment organizations (NGOs), which now number in the thousands around the world, and which set out to achieve a host of objectives, ranging from empowering women in less developed countries to preventing disease, find their talent most often at the distinguished research universities. These graduates of our universities are contributing on the homefront as well as epidemiologists working for the Centers for Disease Control; they might become medical sleuths trying to uncover the genetic makeup of a bacteria or to piece together the history of a flu that is developing into a pandemic. As social workers with Ph.D.s or lawyers who work for organizations such as the Urban Justice Center, they may advocate for the poor. Brilliantly trained lawyers and Ph.D.s are working for organizations that are trying to limit the number of wrongful convictions in felony cases through the use and analysis of DNA evidence. In today's world, NGOs are having as much impact in many domains as governments are. And large, private foundations that support the arts, sciences, and humanities, as well as ongoing projects on themes designed to address major social, political, and economic problems, also depend increasingly on the skills and knowledge of Ph.D. and professional school graduates from our finest universities. Foundation leaders and program officers, who choose how and where to invest scarce resources, have been trained and often had teaching or research experience at these universities.

Finally, we should not omit the contributions of these universities to the cultural institutions of our cities and nation. Universities produce more doctorates than are needed on university faculties. Increasingly, these highly trained professionals, particularly in the humanities, are working at museums, libraries, media companies, and arts and cultural centers. The quality of curatorial work at museums, and the art and science of the restoration and preservation of valuable artifacts, depends on highly technical knowledge that can only be gained with advanced education. Work at museums on virtual learning centers and on documentary films exploring historical and cultural subjects depends on the talents emerging from the advanced university programs.

In some measure I'm simply extending the conclusion of Claudia Goldin and Lawrence Katz, which I mentioned at the beginning of the book, that the American century and the human capital century are closely linked. As we depend increasingly on knowledge as the source of social and economic advance, we require an increasing proportion of our young people to be trained, even beyond their undergraduate education. The universities are not only critically important to our economic and technical welfare; they are also, both directly and indirectly, essential in creating the richness of the social fabric of the nation.

In the next section of the book I will introduce you to some of the fruits of the process of discovery and training at these great research universities. Before moving on, however, a few words are needed about how I gathered the information about these discoveries, about who makes them, and about how I decided which ones to include as illustrations.

A NOTE ON THE SELECTION OF EXAMPLES

Arthur Schopenhauer, the nineteenth-century German philosopher, is reputed to have said, "Talent hits a target that no one else can hit; Genius hits a target no one else can see." Schopenhauer was perhaps half right. Geniuses are rare. Many of the people we will encounter hit the target and made truly interesting and important discoveries, but they were not the only ones with the ability to hit targets. They competed with others to be the first to hit the target, to formulate a new idea or achieve a breakthrough, and to gain recognition and reap the other rewards of their success. Many Nobel Prize winners have made marvelous and even breathtaking discoveries, but few are geniuses. Newton and Einstein, and a few others in the history of science and scholarship, were geniuses, but even they did not entirely see what no one else could see. Leibnitz, after all, developed calculus at about the same time that Newton did, and they had a priority fight over who actually was first.

Nobel Prize winners and others who make brilliant discoveries possess enormous talent and can hit a target. They have produced profound ideas and made significant discoveries because they can use their substantial imaginations and intelligence within a social system of science, engineering, and scholarship. Without that system, few discoveries would be made. And the system that most of these people have been embedded in, at least over the past half-century, is the great American research university. If that system deteriorates or loses its way, if it comes under siege in a way that deflects it from its central purposes, or if it is starved for resources, it will not function well or at all. And there are many mechanisms by which the system can be impaired, endangered, or destroyed. In some sense, threats to its welfare are always present in one form or another, but on some occasions those threats reach a level where the system of knowledge production can be particularly vulnerable. It is often an open question whether the system can adapt to these external and internal threats and disarm or neutralize its predators.

My argument throughout these chapters is based upon my many years of working to create an academic field that focuses on the social and structural conditions under which scientific and technological knowledge grows and thrives in university settings.[12] It is also based upon my years as provost and dean of faculties at Columbia University, where I was responsible for the academic life of one of our great research universities. For this book, I collected a great deal of data and information about discoveries made at these institutions.[13] In addition, I contacted the presidents or provosts of the leading fifty research universities in the United States. Many of these people are friends or acquaintances of mine. I asked them to provide me with a list of discoveries—perhaps ten or more over the past thirty or forty years—that had been made at their university and that have had an impact on our society. I did not limit them in any particular way. Forty-five of the fifty leaders responded to my request, providing many different types of lists, including discoveries made not only in science, medicine, and engineering—undoubtedly the easiest fields from which they could construct such a list—but also from the social sciences and humanities.[14]

There are scores of other sources where one can find lists and descriptions of important discoveries, and I have consulted quite a few of these as well. Many honorific societies produce materials on those who win their awards, such as the Nobel Prize, the Lasker Awards, and the National Medal of Science. The National Academy of Sciences and the National Science Foundation, the National Institutes of Health, and the Association of American Universities have published descriptions of important discoveries that have been supported by funds from government agencies or that have been produced by leading universities. For example, the National Science Foundation published "The Nifty Fifty"—a website established in 2000 to mark the fiftieth anniversary of the NSF that tells the story behind fifty major discoveries sponsored by the foundation since its inception in 1950.[15] A complete list of discoveries that have changed our lives would be impossible to fit into a single book. Therefore, this book contains brief descriptions of a small, highly selective number of discoveries that will be illustrative of the depth and breadth of what universities are producing. The stories told here identify what these discoveries have been, some of the people responsible for them, and the universities that have provided the research home for the scientists and scholars involved. They are organized largely by discipline categories. My initial focus is on biological and biomedical discoveries that affect our bodies, our health, our food, and our genes. I then turn to the physical sciences and engineering to describe another set of discoveries. Finally, I describe some of the notable ideas from the social and behavioral sciences and the humanities.

In addition, I have emphasized discoveries made since World War II. At the turn of the twentieth century, manufacturers of machine tools, firearms, clocks, sewing machines, agricultural implements, bicycles, steel, telegraphy and telephony, and electrification—none of which were highly dependent on research discoveries at universities—were among the leading industries of the day. Now our economy is knowledge driven and the leading industries are microelectronics, biotechnology, new materials science industries, telecommunications, computer technology (hardware and software), civilian aircraft, and robotics. The rapid, revolutionary changes that we are witnessing in modern biology and medicine, along with the revolutions in the physical sciences, have substantially increased the rate at which basic research knowledge created at universities gets translated into practical applications through linkages with industry in the national system of innovation. As a result of this exponential growth of knowledge, we would expect to find many more discoveries at universities produced during the second half of the twentieth century than during the first fifty years. And, as I've argued, the true take-off stage for our great universities was after the war.

I want to also provide you with an opportunity to grasp the full range of discoveries and the enormity of the production of knowledge and ideas. To that end, I have created an important appendage to this book—an interactive website (http://university-discoveries.com) containing descriptions of hundreds, and potentially thousands, of discoveries that can be sorted in various ways: by the name of the discovery, the scientists or scholars responsible for them, the universities that provided the intellectual environment for these discoveries, and the date and type of discovery. See Appendix B for more information.

Let us now turn to some of the research discoveries.

CHAPTER 8

It Began with a Fly: Genetics, Genomics, and Medical Research

There is no logical way to the discovery of these elemental laws. There is only the way of intuition, which is helped by a feeling for the order lying behind the appearance.

—Albert Einstein

Discovery consists of seeing what everybody has seen, and thinking what nobody has thought.

—Albert Szent-Györgyi

Though the discoveries of university scientists and engineers have often been born of war, they have ultimately made an extraordinary difference in our welfare in times of peace. Many Americans view the U.S. physicists of World War II as heroes. Working on the front lines of discovery, they made the triumph of the Allies possible. The invention of the atomic bomb and the development of radar played crucial roles in winning the war, and the basic science associated with these feats would later be used for peacetime purposes. Equally important in the war effort was the use of quinine and the spectacular advances in health care that came from the use of penicillin and other antibiotics, all of which had lasting effects on the public's health. A great many of our everyday medicines, medical treatments, tools, and instruments are products of discoveries made at our leading universities, not only during the war but since then, with the rate of discovery revving up throughout the remainder of the twentieth century and into the twenty-first.

Some of the most significant advances in recent years have been in genetics. The ongoing research at our universities has put us on the threshold of being able to map our own DNA relatively inexpensively, and we may soon be able to interpret this information in ways that will give us greater insight into our own health than ever before. From a few drops of blood and the analysis of thousands of proteins, scientists will be able to determine an individual's susceptibility and resistance to specific diseases. The age of truly preventive medicine will soon be upon us. We will be able to customize medical treatment based on a deep understanding of biochemistry. The current developments are the result of advances in the most basic scientific knowledge of atoms and biochemistry generated at our universities.

In some ways, the advances of science and meaningful transformative applications of knowledge always live off of the future. The search for antibiotics, or the search for ways to prevent our bodies from rejecting transplanted organs, took decades, along with a healthy suspension of disbelief, frequent assessment of the record of successes and failures, and the passing of the torch to multiple generations of scientists through university teaching and mentoring. Today, we can look forward to the possibility, indeed the likelihood, of even greater advances: the development of designer drugs and genetic therapies, vaccines for AIDS and cancer, and epidemiological understanding of the interaction between our genes and our environment. Every generation must embrace the possibilities for future progress.

Over the past century we have been stockpiling fundamental knowledge with an eye toward its eventual application, and this stockpile of fundamental knowledge coincided with the growing distinction of our universities. In this chapter I will look at some of the major discoveries found through research conducted at universities during that time, with a focus on the biological sciences. I begin by describing a few extraordinary advances in genetics and molecular biology that continue to affect our lives. I then turn to an overview of some of the most inspired innovations in cancer research, medical instrumentation and equipment, and treatments for children, quickly look at a potpourri of other university-research successes, and finish by noting some new methods in food production and the birth of sociobiology. Each of these subjects could be the subject of a much longer essay—or, indeed, of many books—but here, my objective is to provide a brief overview of a broad spectrum of discoveries in order to convey the scope of biological and medical research at universities.

OUR GENES

Very fundamental science often paves the way for medical miracles. In the United States this was the case in genetics, starting with Thomas Hunt Morgan and others in the "fly lab" at Columbia, and similar teams at other American universities, in the first two decades of the twentieth century. The fruit flies that Morgan and others chose to experiment with, from the genus *Drosophila*—to be exact, the species *D. melanogaster*—turned out to be perfect for studies in genetics and heredity. The small size of the flies meant that many of them could be studied at once in the laboratory, and the short (twelve-day) reproductive cycle meant that researchers could study many generations in a short period of time.

But genetics has also benefited from its share of breakthroughs—discoveries that allowed the field to make sudden leaps. When Oswald Avery, Colin MacLeod, and Maclyn McCarty at the Rockefeller University discovered in 1944 that genes are made of DNA (a famous example of a truly fundamental scientific breakthrough that did not win the Nobel Prize), the revolution in understanding basic biology began to take off. Avery's work opened up the entire field of molecular genetics. In the same year, Barbara McClintock, working initially at Cornell and then at Cold Spring Harbor, was elected to the National Academy of Sciences for her discovery of transposition and "jumping genes," part of her revolutionary research with maize plants. Before her work, according to one geneticist looking back several years later on advances in the field, most biologists believed that genes "were fixed units with precise boundaries, strung along chromosomes like beads on a thread, very stable, and almost immune to external influences."[1]

McClintock had discovered two elements that were part of the system by which genes are controlled: the regulating element that switches genes on or off to produce specific genetic traits, such as color (in this case, of the maize), and an activator element that can make the on/off switch jump around to different positions on the chromosome. McClintock's discoveries were important because the *transposons* (jumping genes) can cause mutations and affect the amount of DNA in the genome. McClintock was eventually awarded the Nobel Prize for this work in 1983, so unlike Avery, she did receive the recognition she deserved, though it was belated.

There was a reason that the full import of McClintock's maize research was not immediately apparent, however: It had to await further developments by Avery and then the discovery in 1953 of the double-helix model of the molecular structure of DNA made at Cambridge University by twenty-five-year-old American biologist James D. Watson and British physicist-turned-biologist Francis Crick, who was all of thirty-seven at the time. The work of intellectual émigrés such as Max Delbrück and Salvador Luria, in turn, was critical to the discoveries of Watson and Crick. But once Watson and Crick beat the most formidable chemist in the world, Caltech's Linus Pauling, to publishing the correct model of the DNA molecule, the implications for biology and for medicine became increasingly clear.[2] Early work by Edward L. Tatum at Stanford and George Beadle— who moved from Cornell to Caltech and then to Chicago—showing that genes act by regulating specific chemical processes, and Joshua Lederberg's work at Yale, the University of Wisconsin, and Stanford on the organization of genetic material in bacteria, set the stage for advances over the next twenty years that would begin to have very practical uses.

Following Watson and Crick, Arthur Kornberg was the first person to synthesize DNA-like material in a test tube. This was an essential step in understanding the relationship between DNA and disease. Kornberg, who was at Stanford, received the Nobel for this work in 1959. To identify the genetic basis of a disease, one must show how the DNA of affected people differs from the DNA of those who do not have the disease. Stanley Cohen of Stanford and Herbert Boyer of the University of California at San Francisco showed that segments of DNA from two species could be joined and put into a living cell, and that the cell would still replicate. This process, called gene-splicing, became the practical method for transplanting genes from one species to another and lies at the foundation of the biotechnology industry.[3] The discoveries of Cohen and Boyer not only made hundreds of millions of dollars for their respective universities but also benefited the public in myriad ways, leading to the creation of various medical products.

One of the scientific challenges of the post-Watson-Crick age was to figure out how to create "designer genes," genes with desired characteristics created in the lab through artificial manipulation. Early gene-splicing techniques were a step in this direction, but more precise techniques were needed before true genetic engineering could take place. A similar goal was to learn how we might repair damaged genes and DNA strands that produced a high probability of disease. Paul Berg of Stanford, Walter Gilbert of Harvard, and Frederick Sanger of Cambridge University shared a Nobel Prize in Chemistry in 1980 for their discovery of recombinant DNA technology, a new method of inserting genetic material from one organism into the genome of another. The Nobel Foundation noted their "fundamental studies of the biochemistry of nucleic acids" and "their contributions concerning the determination of base sequences in nucleic acids." The transformed organisms that resulted from the process of genetic manipulation were called "transgenic." The work of Gilbert and Sanger on rapidly decoding base sequences in DNA was applied to induce bacteria to produce medically useful substances, including interferon and insulin. Yale University's Frank Ruddle constructed the first transgenic mammal—a mouse—and transgenic mice are now widely used in research in the diagnosis and treatment of disease.[4]

Recombinant DNA technology has already had enormous practical implications. In the 1970s, three Columbia University scientists, Richard Axel (who later won a Nobel Prize with his former student Linda Buck for his discovery of the gene for the sense of smell—the largest gene in the human genome), Saul Silverstein, and Michael Wigler, invented the cotransformation process—one of the most important pharmaceutical success stories of the past forty years—a more advanced version of recombinant DNA technology. Their method allows almost any gene to be introduced into cultured animal cells, a discovery that has made it possible for drug companies to use cells as "factories" to generate specific proteins. Scientists insert foreign DNA into a host cell to produce proteins that can target specific disease-causing molecules. Human proteins rather than chemicals can now be used as the basis for creating new drugs. Their work also contributed to our understanding of gene function and regulation and advanced the research on the replacement of defective genes.

Their technique, which was patented in 1983,[5] has led to the creation of a host of drugs, including medications used to treat heart disease and strokes, hemophilia, rheumatoid arthritis, thyroid cancer, asthma, and non-Hodgkins lymphoma.[6] In addition, it was used in the development of a medication that helps to prevent kidney transplant rejection. These products have been developed by more than thirty companies and have improved the lives of hundreds of thousands of people suffering from these health problems while creating jobs and generating billions of dollars in sales.

Research is being done to explore the use of gene therapy to treat conditions that have a genetic cause. Theoretically, for example, it may be possible to remove the bone marrow cells of a child with attention deficit disorder (ADD), "repair" them via supplementation with a copy of normal DNA, and then return them to the child's body. Although gene therapy research is still in the very early stages, most distinguished biologists and medical researchers have little doubt about its future importance in medical treatment.

Recombinant DNA technology is used today in the production of transgenic plants that are far more tolerant of herbicides and more resistant to insects and viral pests than their natural counterparts. Although there continues to be resistance to genetically altered plants among consumers, particularly in parts of Europe, agricultural production throughout the world has been vastly improved using such techniques. Plants can be altered to grow under extreme conditions, for example, which expands the agricultural production of regions that previously had limited options. Berkeley scientists were the first to field-test a genetically engineered organism, paving the way for genetically altered plants and animals. In 1975, Steve Ludlow, for example, used recombinant DNA technology to alter a single gene of a widespread bacterium on certain crops in order to inhibit frost damage. His 1987 test demonstrated that companies could use variants of this bacterium to substantially reduce crop damage due to unexpected freezes.

Research in biotechnology has led to a variety of other innovations as well. DNA fingerprinting and polymerase chain reactions (PCR) are allowing scientists to uniquely identify individuals by DNA fingerprints.[7] We can now use these technologies to diagnose bacterial and fungal infections, to determine familial relations in paternity litigation, and to explore the family histories of people who are interested in their genetic roots (Oprah Winfrey and Henry Louis Gates are among those who have pursued this route). In addition, with a technique called "restriction fragment length polymorphism" (RFLP), scientists can use DNA fingerprinting to solve crimes and provide evidence in criminal proceedings, to uncover wrongful convictions, to match organ donors with recipients in transplant programs, and even to produce pedigrees for seeds or livestock breeds.

In short, a whole set of new industries was born as a result of fundamental research on DNA, and the technologies that have come out of that research have made possible a new generation of health-care-related products. Promising therapies for the future include those arising from current research into messenger RNA and its role in protein formation and gene expression. Within the past decade, scientists have learned more about how RNA works. RNA, like DNA, is a nucleic acid, but it is generally a single strand rather than double-stranded like DNA. It fulfills several different functions when it acts as a "messenger": It can carry information about a protein sequence from the DNA to the ribosomes; it can act as a transfer mechanism; and it can be a regulator of gene expression. In fact, it plays a more fundamental role than previously believed in gene expression and in the relationship between normal and abnormal genes.

RNA interference, which occurs in humans as well as in plants and in other animals, is critical to gene expression and participates in our defense against viral infections. It also keeps transposons under control to keep them from causing all kinds of damage. Today, RNA interference is used in basic research to study the function of genes, but in the future our knowledge of RNA interference may influence the development of new therapies. The boundaries of scientific knowledge continue to expand, and each new major breakthrough in our knowledge leads to multiple potential applications. New biological revolutions are either in their early stages of formation or in critical stages of elaboration. Some biologists believe that in the twenty-first century, advances in biology will center on the study of the brain—and the number of practical applications that may flow from discoveries about brain functioning seems practically limitless.

Below I describe the state of current genetics research for two diseases, diabetes and Huntington's disease, before turning to research dealing with cancer.

The Insulin Gene. I've heard some very capable scientists question whether in a practical sense we have really gained much from the biochemical revolution that started with the discovery of DNA. To answer this question, we need look no further than the treatment of diabetes. This disease affects millions of people around the world and places them at increased risk of heart attack, stroke, hearing loss, colon cancer, and a host of autoimmune diseases, including thyroid problems, celiac disease, and Addison's disease.

As is well known, insulin helps to control the amount of sugar in our bloodstreams. Millions of diabetics must take insulin every day to keep their blood sugar at normal levels. For many years, the insulin from cows and pigs was used to treat diabetics. But now, as a direct result of the basic discoveries in genetics described above, we can mass-produce insulin through genetic engineering processes.

William Rutter and others in the biochemistry department at the University of California at San Francisco isolated the gene for insulin in 1977, finding that it was located on chromosome 11. Building on Cohen and Boyer's earlier discoveries, scientists were able to use recombinant DNA technology to produce insulin using bacteria and yeast, and millions of diabetes victims now take human insulin that is compatible with their body chemistry.[8] Professor Rutter, along with others, founded Chiron, one of the world's first biotechnology firms, to mass-produce genetically engineered insulin in the quantities needed to treat diabetes patients.

The Gene for Huntington's Disease. In 1993, scientists at Harvard and Columbia located the gene for this relatively rare inherited neurological disorder that is untreatable and invariably leads to physical disabilities and painful death. The result of a ten-year search, the finding has led to promising new lines of research that may lead to treatments that can slow or prevent brain cell loss. Although the research on treatment is still in experimental stages, scientists have learned much through the use of animal models, and clinical trials with humans to test new drugs have begun.

Trained as a psychologist, but also an expert in areas of neuropsychology, Columbia professor Nancy Wexler, whose mother died of Huntington's, knew she had a 50 percent chance of contracting the disease. More than twenty-five years ago, as part of her quest to track down the genetic cause of Huntington's, she wound up in Lake Maracaibo, Venezuela, a small fishing village with a very high incidence of this disease—all traceable to a single woman. Wexler collected highly detailed anthropological family histories from people living in this inbred community, developing a pedigree of 18,000 individuals and taking 4,000 blood samples, and charted those with and without the disease. She befriended the families, gained their trust, and, with their consent, obtained blood and skin samples to share with her collaborators at various universities who were also pursuing a cure for Huntington's.

These collaborators included James Gusella, a geneticist at Harvard, and David E. Housman of MIT. Wexler's research enabled Gusella to identify the location of the gene and to create the first genetic mapping of a disease. The work proceeded far more rapidly than expected. Gusella discovered a complete chromosomal test that could be used to tell people if they would develop Huntington's. The DNA marker he found was 96 percent accurate in identifying the Huntington gene in individuals. Housman has been working on "modifier genes" that determine the age of onset of Huntington's. His group at MIT is trying to identify small molecules that show promise for effective intervention and treatment of Huntington's.

This deeply collaborative work, which continues to involve scientists at many leading research universities, has led scientists and ethicists to address important questions about patients' rights and issues of choice about testing for the genetic marker when no treatment is yet available.[9] Wexler's pursuit alerts us to the complexity of science and the never-ending search for answers. The cure for Huntington's was more elusive than was at first anticipated. Researchers had hoped that the cure would be found shortly after the discovery of the gene. Instead, the discovery only led to a series of new, vexing problems dealing with the mechanisms of expression of the gene, what produces the onset of symptoms—and, indeed, how the disease can be prevented and treated.

FIGHTING CANCER

In 1971, President Richard Nixon declared war on cancer with the enactment of the National Cancer Act. The increased attention to cancer, which continues to be the second leading cause of death in the United States—and the first cause of death among women between ages thirty-five and seventy-four—led to rapid growth in cancer research.[10] Many important university-based discoveries related to the basic biological causes of cancer followed, preparing the way for improved methods of treatment. Although great strides have been made in our understanding of causes of cancer, and we have vastly improved treatments for some forms of cancer, progress has been slower and more painstaking than many would have predicted at the time when the National Cancer Act was signed into law.

There have been few defining victories. Although molecular biologists, geneticists, biochemists, and medical research doctors have proposed many new ideas and conducted a great deal of clinical research with an eye toward developing new drugs and treatments for cancer patients, there have been many false starts and false hopes, a long series of treatments that have been tried and have not worked, and sustained efforts to develop vaccines that have not panned out. Nevertheless, progress has been made in our understanding of the basic biochemistry of cancer. In fifty years, what we do today in terms of radiation treatments and chemotherapy will seem utterly primitive—we are using blunt instruments to deal with the fine-grained properties of cells. Advances in knowledge have obtained, and certain cancers today are both treatable and curable, no longer representing death notices. Though these gains often seem too limited, they are gains nonetheless, and we can look forward to more in the years to come. The advances that have been made have come out of our great biological science departments and university-affiliated teaching hospitals. Some highlights in the story of our ongoing battle with cancer follow.

THE DISCOVERY OF THE ONCOGENE

Much cancer research has been devoted to investigation of "oncogenes," genes that contribute to the development of cancer. "Oncogenesis" refers to the process of malignant tumor formation, and an "oncogenic virus," or "oncovirus," is a virus that is cancer-causing. Oncogenic viruses come in several forms. One type is the retrovirus, an RNA virus that uses a process called "reverse transcriptase" to insert a copy of its genome into a normal cell and is then reproduced by that cell.

Although the first discovery of an oncogenic virus can be traced back to the work of Peyton Rous at the Rockefeller Institute in 1916, it took more than thirty years for university researchers to begin to recognize the importance of the "Rous virus" and other viruses that were part of the larger group called retroviruses. Rous, born in 1879, had attended Johns Hopkins Medical School. By 1909, he was working on a "beginners" fellowship at the Rockefeller Institute when Simon Flexner asked him to run the laboratory for cancer research. Rous was able to prove that viruses caused some "spontaneous" tumors in chickens. Other scientists, however, simply could not conceive that a relationship existed between invisible viruses and the growth of cancer cells. It was not until the 1950s that a new generation of scientists demonstrated that, under certain conditions, viruses could cause leukemia and other types of cancer. In 1966 Rous was finally awarded a Nobel Prize for his early work.[11]

In 1970, Peter Duesberg and Peter Vogt at Berkeley identified and mapped an oncovirus in birds. They showed that the birds with cancer had extra genetic material compared to the birds without cancer. At roughly the same time, Howard Temin at the University of Wisconsin and David Baltimore at MIT independently discovered the reverse transcriptase process used by the retrovirus—for which they and Ranato Dulbecco (their former professor and mentor at Caltech) shared the 1975 Nobel Prize. The normal process of transcription involves the synthesis of RNA from DNA. Reverse transcriptase takes place when the opposite occurs, that is, when the RNA enters into DNA and is reproduced. Temin, working on tumor viruses since the 1950s, had accumulated a tremendous amount of indirect evidence that the flow of genetic material could go in this reverse direction, even though it violated an element of the central dogma of the field during those years. The crucial breakthrough occurred with Baltimore's discovery of "a specific enzyme in RNA tumor virus particles that could make a DNA copy from RNA."[12]

Reverse transcriptase allows RNA to act as a template in assembling and producing DNA strands. When the encoded single-stranded RNA moves to the double-stranded DNA molecule and enters into the process of DNA replication, it sets in motion the dynamics for the spread of disease within the body. Oncoviruses are not the only viruses that can be retroviruses. HIV, for example, also uses reverse transcriptase to transfer itself into a person's DNA and reproduce. In fact, since these discoveries there has been a dramatic increase in our knowledge about the genetic materials found in RNA tumor viruses. Much of the recent work in the development of HIV "cocktails" consists of attempts to design specific drugs that inhibit the reverse transcriptase process, and this is why those drugs are called "reverse transcriptase inhibitors."

In the mid-1970s, Harold Varmus and J. Michael Bishop, collaborating on oncogenes at the medical school of the University of California at San Francisco, were able to explain the cellular origins of retrovirus oncogenes. We all know that every person carries genes that will determine their eye and hair color, height, and a host of other characteristics that we inherit from our parents. What was not known before 1976 when Varmus and Bishop published their dramatic discovery was that each of us also carries genes that can turn against us and cause cancer. Varmus and Bishop showed that cancer is a genetic disease in which some genes get damaged and cause the cells to run amok. We now know that chemicals, food, radiation, and environmental agents can cause this cellular damage; however, the genetic component makes some people more likely than others to develop cancer when this damage occurs. These two scientists produced the tantalizing possibility that we may be able to prevent cancer by influencing the way oncogenes behave. The oncogene has now been implicated in many human cancers, and although there is no unified theory of the causes of cancer, the role of oncogenes remains one of the most popular theories of the origin of cancer today. Meanwhile, university scientists were also hard at work trying to find ways to suppress the growth of tumors. In 1979, Princeton biologist Arnold Levine, who later became president of Rockefeller University and then returned to scientific work at Princeton's Institute for Advanced Study, codiscovered a molecule that inhibits tumor development, the p53 tumor suppressor protein ("p" refers to protein; 53 refers to its molecular mass). The cancer-fighting p53 molecule coordinates the behavior of more than sixty genes that prevent damaged cells from becoming cancerous tumors. Levine found that about 11 percent of the population has lower than normal levels of p53, that these individuals had a higher risk of developing cancer than those with normal p53 levels, and that they were at risk of developing it at an earlier age. His discovery was valuable because it identified a subset of the population that should be screened for cancer earlier than other members of the population. People with low levels of p53 are now advised to pursue cancer screenings on an earlier schedule. This is the beginning of personalized medicine.[13] Similarly, the well-publicized discovery of BRCA1 and BRCA2 (breast cancer 1 and breast cancer 2) genes by Berkeley's Mary-Claire King in 1991 made it possible to screen women who are at significantly higher risk of developing breast cancer.

Below we will look at four other areas of cancer research before moving on to inventions that revolutionized medical care in a completely different way.

Invention of Gleevac. As university researchers developed a better understanding of the biochemical basis for cancer and its relationship to both genetic and environmental factors, the pharmaceutical industry was trying to develop drugs for the treatment of cancer patients. In one of the more successful collaborations between universities and industry, a powerful and effective new anticancer drug, Gleevac, was produced and marketed by Novartis.

Basic research conducted by David Baltimore and Naomi Rosenberg in the 1970s at MIT played an instrumental role in the discovery of this drug, which has been effective in treating chronic myelogenous leukemia (CML)—a form of cancer characterized by an overabundance of white blood cells. The extraordinary feature of the drug is that it targets cancerous cells while leaving healthy cells alone. CML affects about 5,000 American annually. Gleevac has also shown promising results in treating other forms of cancer, including gastrointestinal stromal tumors (GISTs), which usually kill patients within a year of diagnosis.

David Baltimore and Owen Witte, professor of microbiology and molecular genetics at UCLA, experimenting with mice, discovered the basic mechanism by which CML occurs. A genetic anomaly is triggered by the rearrangement of chromosomes 9 and 22, forming what is called the "Philadelphia chromosome" or the "Philadelphia translocation." Further research conducted by Alex Matter of Novartis, Nicholas Lydon of Amgen, and Brian Druker of the Oregon Health Sciences University resulted in the development of Gleevac.

Invention of Alimta. Edward Taylor, a Princeton chemistry professor, invented a path-breaking chemotherapy drug named Alimta that has been highly successful in stopping the growth of solid tumors, easing suffering, and extending life. Alimta is manufactured and sold by Eli Lilly, and it is usually used to fight pleural mesothelioma and other forms of lung cancer. The Food and Drug Administration approved Alimta in 2004, and it is currently being tested for use against other forms of cancer, such as esophageal cancer.

Early on at Cornell, where he worked on his Ph.D. in the 1940s, Taylor became fascinated with a compound that had been isolated from the human liver and that also formed the recurring pigmented ring structure in the wings of butterflies. It had been shown to be an antibacterial agent and to be helpful in the treatment of childhood leukemia. It could be toxic to healthy cells, but it could also help in the fight against cancer. How could this contradiction be reconciled? It was a problem that had frustrated several Nobel Prize winners. After years of research, Taylor solved the mystery: The ring compound (later named folic acid) played a role in every form of life, including microorganisms, birds, trees, and mammals. Precisely what that role was became clear over the next thirty years. Scientists at other universities doing similar research found in 1948 that if they altered the structure of the compound slightly they could change it from being necessary for microorganism growth to being an inhibitor of growth. By pure serendipity, scientists found that this antibacterial agent also brought about remissions of acute lymphoblastic leukemia, a lethal form of cancer in children. Taylor was now on to solving a truly important puzzle. He said, "I just wanted to know what caused this cancer remission in the chemical derived from folic acid."[14]

Taylor found that the antibacterial agent caused the cancer to go into remission, but it was so lethal that it destroyed healthy as well as cancerous cells. As a synthetic organic chemist, he needed help in analyzing the compound from biochemists, and he wound up collaborating with scientists at Eli Lilly. The compound they developed was complex and difficult to work with, but they came up with an ingenious method of eliminating part of the molecule without destroying the essential features needed to stop tumor growth. Alimta was the result. Princeton patented the discovery, and Lilly developed it after a decade of clinical trials.[15]

Curing Childhood Leukemia. Childhood leukemia is now often curable as a result of the extraordinary imagination and dedication of medical researchers who built on decades of basic scientific work to develop new treatments.

We take up the story well after its beginning in the nineteenth and early twentieth centuries with the identification of the importance of enzymes in chemical reactions and the 1908 discovery by Paul Ehrlich that one could use chemicals to interfere with the growth of infectious agents. Much of this early work on chemotherapy was carried out in Europe and England. The work of George H. Hitchings and Gertrude B. Elion at the Wellcome Research Laboratories in New York, however, led to a major discovery that pointed the way to the cure. Hitchings, who had spent ten years at Harvard and Western Reserve University (now Case Western Reserve),[16] moved to Wellcome in 1942 and launched a research program to design and synthesize a drug that could interfere with the reproduction of pathogens without harming the host cells. This work focused on DNA bases, but it was begun well before Watson and Crick published the findings of their fundamental work on base pairs and the double helix structure of DNA. In 1944, Gertrude Elion joined Hitchings's group. She was remarkably talented and suffered from the widespread exclusion of women from equal opportunities in graduate Ph.D. programs. The efforts of Hitchings, Elion, and others over the next two decades revolutionized the methods used by researchers to search for chemicals that can be used to treat disorders. Their model has been instrumental not only in finding a cure for childhood leukemia but also for finding effective drugs for treating high blood pressure, heart disease, and infectious diseases.

Previously, drug development was based principally on the alteration of natural products. Hitchings and Elion introduced a more rational approach to drug screening and identification through an understanding of basic biochemical and physiological processes. They looked for differences in the nucleic acid and metabolism of normal human cells, cancer cells, bacteria, and viruses and then tried to identify drugs that would block the growth of cancer cells. They used one of these drugs, 6-mercaptopurine (6-MP), to produce two remissions in adults with leukemia, and by 1953 the FDA had approved it. After this, drug treatments were developed that dramatically increased the five-year survival rates for children with leukemia. Soon, 50 percent of the children diagnosed with leukemia could be expected to survive for at least five years. Using as many as a dozen drugs in complex combinations, Hitchings and Elion subsequently developed drug cocktails that produced a 95 percent four-year survival rate for children with the disease. The improvements continued, and today, the disease has become not only treatable, but virtually curable. In 1988, Hitchings and Elion received a Nobel Prize for their work developing principles of drug treatment.

Pap Smear. Early twentieth-century research by professors of anatomy and cell biologists led to methods of cancer prevention that have saved hundreds of thousands of lives and that are still in use. One prominent example is found in the work of an assistant professor of anatomy at Cornell University and New York Hospital in the 1920s, George Papanicolaou, who developed the well-known "Pap smear" as a method of detecting cervical cancer.

Papanicolaou began his research on vaginal cytology and focused on changes in the cells that led to cancer. In 1928 he published the research results in a paper entitled "New Cancer Diagnosis." The *New York World* reported on his contribution: "Although Dr. Papanicoloau [*sic*] is not willing to predict how useful the new diagnostic method will be in the actual treatment of malignancy itself, it seems probably that it will prove valuable in determining cancer in the early stages of its growth when it can be most easily fought and treated. There is even hope that pre-cancerous conditions may be detected and checked."[17] This hope was more than realized. Papanicolaou and his colleagues worked on improving the diagnostic capabilities of the Pap smear over the next fifteen years, and it rapidly became a worldwide diagnostic tool for cancers of the cervix. Millions of women have received the Pap smear, many of them annually, as recommended by the American Cancer Society, and thousands of lives have been saved because of its use.

BUILDING BETTER MOUSETRAPS: MEDICAL DEVICES AND INSTRUMENTS

Medical instruments, devices, and equipment can affect people's lives just as surely as new drugs and therapies can. This category of medical inventions is very broad. It includes everything from simple items that can be used in medical treatments—such as the nicotine patch—to highly complex machinery or devices—such as X-ray machines, magnetic resonance imaging (MRI) equipment (covered in Chapter 9, along with several other types of medical equipment), implants, artificial joints, and the like. Often, it involves objects that make new lines of research possible. Whatever their size and level of complexity, these tools are often underappreciated, but they are frequently among the most highly referenced works in the research literature.[18] Many university discoveries of this kind fall into what Donald Stokes refers to as "Edison's quadrant," where the principal interest is solving important practical problems. Below I examine just a few of the many contributions that university researchers have made in this area.

Sequencers and Synthesizers. Lee Hood, initially at Caltech and then at the University of Washington, changed the way biologists work on problems of genetics and human health. He invented four powerful devices for studying genomics and molecular biology: the DNA sequencer and synthesizer and the protein sequencer and synthesizer. Hood believed that if "one wants to invent a new area [of research], one must invent new instruments." Commenting on the new equipment that he devised, he said: "I realized that sequences [of DNA] would be generating lots of data, and so I pushed the instrumentation that generated that data. I worked under the premise that if one could put all of the genes of an organism on a chip, then we would be able to observe in a single inspection the changes as an organism or disease progresses."[19]

His work made the success of the human genome project possible. Yet when he was at Caltech, Hood said, the university president found it embarrassing to have so much instrumentation in a biology department. So Hood moved it to an independent company. Eventually, he was instrumental in founding biotechnology firms such as Amgen, Applied Biosystems, and Rosetta.

Nicotine Skin Patch. University of California researcher Jed Rose; his brother Daniel Rose, a physician; and psychologist Murray Jarvik of UCLA developed the nicotine skin patch in 1991. This simple device was to be worn on the upper arm to wean smokers from cigarettes. The team was interested in separating nicotine from sensory factors, such as taste, in the hope that this would help reduce the craving for cigarettes in people who were addicted to them. Jarvik had demonstrated through experiments with monkeys that smoking was an addiction and that nicotine was the primary contributor to that addiction. The skin patch would transmit low dosages of nicotine into the bloodstream through a person's skin at about the same rate that a smoker would absorb nicotine from smoking.

Jed Rose actually experimented on himself, rubbing his skin with tobacco leaves and measuring his own physiological responses. These studies led to the conclusion that nicotine could be absorbed through the skin and that nicotine administered in this way could reduce a person's cravings. They obtained three patents for the technology in 1990. Numerous studies suggest that nicotine patches roughly double the rate of successful attempts to quit smoking. This discovery has helped thousands of people to stop smoking every year and has reduced the medical costs associated with cigarette smoking.

Artificial Joints. There are innumerable ways that our joints can become damaged. It could be a sports injury, a car accident, falling off of a ladder— or having a ladder fall on you. Often, it is simply part of the aging process, sometimes from arthritis, but sometimes just from so many years of use. The wear and tear can add up. In the past, there was little physicians could do, other than hope an injured joint would heal on its own with time, or refer the patient to physical therapy. Now, however, with the invention of new artificial joints, surgeons can perform such feats as shoulder, hip, and knee replacements. These surgeries have become very common and are highly successful. University researchers have played a major role in perfecting these surgeries and making them more widely available.[20]

UCLA has been a leader in joint-replacement innovations. A durable artificial hip was developed at UCLA in 1975, and the first total shoulder replacement was performed there in 1976. In 1993, Dr. Louis Bigliani, a Columbia University orthopedic surgeon, and Dr. E. L. Flatow, a former Columbia professor, began developing a shoulder prosthesis that allows for the restoration of shoulder joint function for people who suffer from pain or disability from arthritis or from certain types of breaks in the shoulder bones. A patent for the device was granted in 1998 and the first prosthesis was used in 1999. Dr. Thomas P. Sculco, professor at Weill/Cornell Medical College and surgeon-in-chief at the Hospital for Special Surgery, has collaborated with biomechanical engineers to develop new prosthetic implants (artificial hips and knees) that are widely used to relieve patients of extreme pain and to enable them to again function normally.

Cochlear Implants. Hearing loss affects millions of people around the world. As a result of research conducted at Harvard, Princeton, Rutgers, the University of California, the University of Utah, Johns Hopkins University, Rockefeller University, and Baylor College of Medicine, among others, there is hope for those who suffer from this problem. Surgeons can now implant a transmitter in the temporal bone behind the ear and thread an array of six electrodes through the spirals of a person's cochlea. The typical hearing aid simply amplifies sound; the cochlear implant is far more sophisticated, effectively acting as an artificial inner ear.

The external part of the device includes a microphone to receive sounds, a speech processor to convert signals to a form that is recognizable to a person's auditory nerve, and a transmitter that sends the signals to the implant. Cases are reported of people who went from largely unsuccessful attempts at lip-reading to hearing 94 percent of what the people around them were saying. While these devices are not appropriate for all forms of hearing loss, thousands of people for whom the device can be helpful are beginning to hear normally again.

In the category of instruments that have saved lives we must also include the heart pacemaker, which was developed initially by Harvard scientists in 1952. Duke University scientists invented the childproof safety cap for pharmaceutical products in the 1950s, and a Hopkins research team led the way to produce child restraints in automobiles in 1979. Not to be out-done, in 1987 University of Washington researchers David Engel, Joseph Miller, and Roy Martin helped entrepreneur David Giuliani make the first Sonicare toothbrush, whose bristle tips could move at such a high frequency that they directed fluids deep between the teeth and below the gum line to remove plaque and prevent gum disease. Newer versions of the toothbrush have an even higher rate of vibration.

And although it is not technically a device, an instrument, or a piece of medical equipment, one other innovation that resulted from university research must not go unrecognized. It is the Heimlich maneuver, first described by Henry Heimlich of Cornell University in 1974. This procedure, first described in an article called "Pop Goes the Café Coronary," has saved thousands of people around the world from choking to death and is routinely taught in first aid courses.

Speaking of medical procedures, we shall now turn to procedures that were specifically designed for situations involving children.

PROTECTING THE HEALTH OF CHILDREN

Today countless medical procedures, including surgeries, are performed safely on babies right at birth or even before they are born. It was not too long ago that surgical procedures for the fetus and neonate would have been unthinkable. One of the first breakthroughs came when university-based researchers figured out how to help babies born with a condition known as cyanosis, a heart malformation that prevents their blood from being fully oxygenated.

In cyanosis, the lack of oxygen moving from the heart to the lungs causes the baby to turn a bluish color. In fact, the condition is sometimes called "blue baby syndrome." Dr. Helen Taussig of Johns Hopkins Hospital, one of the nation's leading pediatric heart specialists, believed that surgeons could reduce the constriction of the pulmonary artery by bypassing that portion of the artery that was overly constricted. In 1943, Taussig convinced Dr. Alfred Blalock, a superb vascular surgeon, to undertake a research project to treat cyanosis. After many experiments with animals, the two developed a successful bypass surgery, which became known as the "Blalock-Taussig Shunt." The operation, which was designed by Taussig and first performed by Blalock in 1944 at Hopkins, is also known at the "blue baby operation."[21]

Hundreds of physicians from around the world came to Hopkins to learn how to perform the operation. Today, it is used principally as a holding action until the baby is old enough for open-heart surgery. Taussig and Blalock paved the way for the modern era, when surgical treatment of congenital heart defects has become relatively safe.[22]

Below we will look at some other areas of pediatric care that have seen advances through the contributions of university research.

Prenatal Care. The pace of innovation in prenatal care increased rapidly in the second half of the twentieth century. Ultrasound technology and a variety of other safe and effective diagnostic tools were developed during this period. As a result of these advances, better nutrition among pregnant women, and better prenatal care in general, the U.S. infant mortality declined by 76 percent during that period. Literally scores of university scientists and engineers worked on various aspects of ultrasound technology to monitor the health and development of babies in utero. It is now used as a diagnostic tool in prenatal care around the world.

Early uses of ultrasound were not for prenatal care, however. Instead, similar technology was used for a variety of military purposes and for other diagnostic purposes in treating adults. A great deal of the early work was carried out at MIT. Between 1947 and 1949, Dr. George D. Ludwig, who was at the Naval Medical Research Institute before going to MIT, demonstrated that gallstones could be detected by an ultrasound pulse-echo method. The technique he used was similar to the underwater sonar and radar methods that the military used to detect foreign boats and airplanes. Physicists at the Naval Research Laboratory had also used ultrasound technology to detect flaws in metal. These military devices were all scientific precursors to medical ultrasonic equipment—basic scientific findings used for military purposes in fact often have important practical implications for medicine later on. Donald Baker, an electrical engineer at the University of Washington in Seattle, developed the idea of using pulsed ultrasound in the early days of cardiovascular research in the late 1950s. His creation turned ultrasound into one of the most vital, cost-effective diagnostic tools in the world today. Douglas Howry began pioneering work on the use of ultrasound techniques to monitor the development of fetuses in 1948 at the University of Colorado. Three researchers at Colorado began to develop these techniques in 1962. They left the university and formed Physionic Engineering, Inc., which produced the first hand-held ultrasonic fetal scanner in 1963.

In the 1970s, because of work being done at California universities, prenatal tests for diseases like sickle-cell anemia and thalassemia were developed. Many of the extraordinary accomplishments in the care of fetuses and neonates were initially conceived by female physicians. While on a research fellowship at Harvard in 1951, for example, Mary Ellen Avery, an international expert in neonatology, developed a treatment for acute respiratory distress in premature babies.[23] She identified the cause of the condition as a deficiency in "surfactant," the soapy coating in the lungs that allows the alveoli to inflate easily during inhalation. This was an important discovery because the respiratory system is one of the last to develop in babies; the lack of these agents was a significant cause of death among premature babies and neonates.

Building on Avery's success, scientists at the University of California at San Francisco, led by Dr. John Clements, produced an artificial surfactant—Exosurf, patented in 1981—to compensate for the absence of the lung coating in infants born with immature lungs. The drug, which received FDA approval in 1990, produced a 50 percent reduction in the number of neonatal deaths from respiratory distress syndrome (RDS), revolutionizing the treatment of premature infants. A year later, scientists at UCSF conducted the first successful corrective procedure on a baby still in the mother's womb, pioneering the clinical specialty of fetal diagnosis and surgery.

Hepatitis B Vaccine. The first recorded references to hepatitis epidemics date from 2000 B.C. In our time, viral hepatitis causes about 1.5 million deaths worldwide each year. Symptoms of this infectious disease include yellowish skin, fever, fatigue, nausea, loss of appetite, chills, and abdominal pain.

Ultimately, the virus eats away at the liver and the victim dies of liver failure or cancer. Although some people with hepatitis B never experience
acute symptoms, they may be chronically ill. In addition, they can pass the
virus on to their children and other people with whom they have contact.

This deadly disease is now treatable and even preventable because of
the insight of medical researchers who were curious about why some people were particularly prone to various ailments or became sick following
blood transfusions. Scientists did not know that a virus caused the disease
until after World War II. In the 1960s, discoveries by Baruch Blumberg,
who worked at the National Institutes of Health (where he collaborated
with Harvey Alter at the NIH blood bank) and later at the University of
Pennsylvania, and by other scientists following different leads, changed
the fate of hepatitis B sufferers. The incidence of the disease has been reduced dramatically because of a public health blood-screening initiative
and because of the production of a highly effective hepatitis vaccine. The
vaccine not only protects people from this disease but also turns out to
protect against liver cancer.[24]

In 1969, Blumberg and Irving Millman patented their idea for the use
of *Australian antigen* to prepare a hepatitis B vaccine. The antigen produced an antibody response, but it was not yet ready for general use. In the
1970s, there continued to be some resistance to their discovery among
scientists, and it took some time for the scientists to interest pharmaceutical firms in developing and producing the vaccine. Merck finally developed the vaccine and shared the foreign patent rights to the vaccine with
Blumberg and Millman. Other researchers refined the vaccine in ways
that made it safer and more effective. Scientists at the University of California developed a hepatitis B vaccine using recombinant DNA technology in the late 1970s. In the early 1980s, scientists at the University of
Washington used advanced recombinant DNA techniques to develop a
hepatitis B vaccine from altered yeast cells, which after years of study and
testing was approved for use in humans in 1986. By 2000, more than a
billion doses of the vaccine had been administered, and by 2003, according to Blumberg, "151 (79%) of the 192 members of WHO had national
vaccination programs. It is now one of the most widely used vaccines in
the world."[25]

The blood-screening initiative came about through federal legislation
passed in 1972 requiring that blood donors be tested for the hepatitis anti-

gen. The most accurate blood tests involved radioimmunoassay techniques developed by Rosalind Yalow, who received a Nobel Prize in 1977 for her research on insulin using radioactive tracers, and Solomon Berson at the Bronx Veterans Administration Medical Center in the 1950s. Yalow and Berson's technique was effective for identifying minute quantities of a substance as it binds to an antibody or other protein.[26]

Vitamin A Supplements. Advances in public health during the twentieth century may have been as responsible as advances in medicine for lowering mortality rates. Whether we consider how clean water reduces the probability of typhus fever, mosquito netting reduces the incidence of malaria, or the use of vitamins improves health, we cannot overlook the important ways that university epidemiologists and public health researchers have contributed to improving the lives of millions around the world.

Not every advance in medicine involves expensive treatments. A case in point is the result of a line of research that scientists at Johns Hopkins were pursuing between 1982 and 1986 in Indonesia. Professor of ophthalmology Alfred Sommer, researching childhood blindness, discovered that pennies' worth of vitamin A supplements could bring about a dramatic drop in infant death rates. The incidence of vitamin A deficiency was far more extensive in Indonesia than had previously been estimated, and this caused decreased resistance to infectious diseases such as measles as well as an increase in diarrhea, which can cause dehydration and even death. Other studies, being conducted in Africa, demonstrated that measles-associated blindness was also related to vitamin A deficiencies.

Sommer proved the causal relationship by running very large-scale randomized trials in several Indonesian communities between 1983 and 1992. These trials included some 20,000 children. The data surprised even Sommer. He found that children with eye problems such as night blindness and dry eye (evidence of vitamin A deficiency) were dying at a rate four to eight times that of children without eye problems. When the vitamin A–deficient children were treated with a small capsule of the vitamin, mortality dropped by 30 percent. Other scientists initially resisted Sommer's findings, but follow-up studies at Hopkins confirmed his results, finding, in fact, that an even higher percentage of mortalities—one-half instead of one-third—could be prevented by the treatment. The causal relationship was clear; even small increased dosages of vitamin A led to lowered child mortality rates. This was a classic case of a dose-response relationship. Sommer's studies led to similar vitamin treatments for children in other developing countries—ultimately saving millions of lives. Today, more than seventy countries have vitamin A control programs that cost only 2 or 3 cents per dose.

In 1999, Hopkins scientists showed that vitamin A supplements could reduce malaria and maternal death in developing nations, and that zinc supplements reduced infant mortality, pneumonia, and diarrhea. This work is testimony to the enormous positive effects that simple public health innovations and relatively low-cost applications can have on morbidity and mortality rates in developing nations.

Treatment for Head Lice. Purdue University scientists set out to find a better method of treating head lice (*Pediculus humanus capitis*), which annually infest, by various estimates, between 15 million and 25 million people in the United States, including about 10 million children. Symptoms included itching on the scalp and around the ears and neck, and secondary infections could also occur. Lice were very difficult to eradicate once they appeared, and many families used special shampoos that we now know are toxic. Shampoos containing the toxic substance lindane, a pesticide, are still sold in the United States (except in California, where it is banned). Available under several brand names, both by prescription and over the counter, they are recommended for use only when other, milder shampoos have been tried and have not been effective, as lindane can cause seizures and even death.

After more than twenty-five years of research at Purdue University, Dr. Jerry McLaughlin identified compounds in the bark of the pawpaw tree, called *Annonaceous acetogenins*, that are particularly effective in treating pesticide-resistant pests. McLaughlin devised a way to extract and concentrate the compound and then figured out how to ensure a consistent concentration in his end product. Purdue licensed the technology to Nature's Sunshine, a Utah company that specializes in herbal products and nutritional supplements. The product, PawPaw Lice Remover Shampoo, which became available in 2001, has worked well against the three phases of the head lice infestations. In follow-up clinical studies, the product has been almost 100 percent effective in removing head lice and their nits when used according to instructions.[27]

A POTPOURRI OF OTHER DISCOVERIES

There have been many health-care-related inventions and discoveries at universities that simply cannot easily be categorized. Here I describe a variety of these to give just a sampling of the many ways that university research in America has added to the health and well-being of our nation and the world.

Organ Transplantation and Tissue Typing. Some 28,000 Americans received organ transplants in 2007, and there were more than 100,000 people on organ-transplant waiting lists. Worldwide, more than 50,000 people receive organ transplants annually. Although there is an elaborate system in place in the United States to determine priorities for transplants, many people die while waiting for an organ match. A great deal of research is being conducted at our major universities in attempts to rectify this situation. Some of this research is not without controversy, however, as it involves tissue engineering and cloning.

Organ transplantation is a relatively recent phenomenon. We have come as far as we have with organ transplants because of international scientific cooperation and effective collaboration between research universities, hospitals, and private industry. Some of the basic techniques of transplantation have been known for more than a century. In the early 1900s, a Viennese surgeon attempted the first organ removal and reinsertion using an autologous animal kidney graft. His success led him to try to cross the species line, but that proved disastrous when an immediate and fatal tissue rejection ensued. In the 1940s and 1950s, Peter Medawar, who pursued his research at Oxford, Birmingham, and University College, London, recognized the cause of tissue rejection as the natural response of the human immune system. Medawar's research on skin grafts allowed him to establish theorems of transplantation immunity, and his research, for which he received a Nobel Prize in 1960, stimulated renewed interest in the subject. The goal of research was to overcome the immune system's efforts to reject foreign and invasive bodies.

In 1954, Dr. Joseph E. Murray, who had been trained at Harvard, took up the problem at Peter Bent Brigham Hospital (later Brigham and Women's Hospital) in Boston, which was affiliated with the Harvard Medical School. He performed the first human kidney transplant between living identical twins, launching the era of organ transplantation. By using identical twins, Murray had attempted to minimize the possibility of organ rejection. The patient lived for several years, but the problem of organ rejection persisted.

The success that surgeons have today in transplanting organs would not have been possible without the work of Dr. Paul Terasaki, professor of surgery at UCLA's School of Medicine. In 1964 Terasaki developed the *microcytotoxicity test*, which has become the international standard for tissue typing. This simple test has been critical in reducing the incidence of organ rejection. More than 1 million donors and recipients worldwide have been typed using this method over the past twenty years. No patient can receive an organ transplant without it. Terasaki also organized the world's largest Kidney Transplant Registry, which is sponsored by UCLA.

In 1968, Dr. Norman Shumway performed the first human heart transplant in the United States at Stanford University. In 1972, scientists at Sandoz (now Novartis) in Basel, Switzerland, developed the immunosuppressive drug Cyclosporine. In 1980, Dr. Thomas Starzl, who worked at the University of Colorado before moving to the University of Pittsburgh, performed the first successful liver transplant in the world using Cyclosporine, and the era of organ transplantation truly began.[28]

Tissue rejection was not the only problem that had to be overcome. In order to complete transplants successfully, doctors also needed to be able to preserve the organ between the time it was harvested and the time it was placed in the recipient. Wisconsin researchers Folkert Belzer and James Southard developed a synthetic solution in 1986, Viaspan, also dubbed the UW Solution, for cold storage of organs during this crucial time. This method of preservation was far superior to prior methods and remains in wide use.

Today, doctors are able to transplant kidneys, lungs, corneas, livers, pancreases, hearts, heart valves, intestines, bones, tendons, skin, and bone marrow because of what has been achieved in the science labs and operating rooms at university teaching and research hospitals. As researchers continue to work on organ transplantation, they hope to reduce waiting times and make the procedure more widely available.

Kidney Dialysis. Of course, before we think about the transplantation of organs, we try to treat the disease. Before resorting to a kidney transplant, for example, many patients undergo dialysis. There are several types of kidney dialysis. It often takes several hours a week to undergo the treatment on an ongoing basis.

Healthy kidneys filter the blood, removing waste products. When the kidneys are not functioning properly, dialysis can replace some of the lost kidney function, though it cannot do all the jobs that normal kidneys perform. It is thanks to a number of university discoveries that patients can live with kidney failure for an extended period of time without resorting to transplantation.

In 1951, a University of Pennsylvania medical student, William Inouye, devised a dialysis machine literally using a kitchen pressure cooker to hold the filtration system. Other dialysis machines had been precursors; his device, which used a coil system, was an improvement on the earlier models. A variation of this "pressure cooker" design was later adopted for worldwide use.

Researchers at the University of Washington pioneered long-term dialysis for kidney failure in 1960, and in the 1970s researchers at the University of Missouri in Columbia developed Continuous Ambulatory Peritoneal Dialysis, which allowed patients to receive dialysis treatments at home.

Development of Antibiotics. The story of antibiotics can be traced back thousands of years to the chance discovery that certain kinds of naturally occurring molds had curative powers. Two landmarks in that history closer to our time were Louis Pasteur's discovery in the 1860s that bacteria caused disease and British scientist Alexander Fleming's discovery of penicillin in the late 1920s. The invention and use of sulfa drugs came next, but their side effects led to a continued search for new classes of antibiotics that could fight bacterial infections without harming patients. This is where American research universities entered the picture.

Selman Waksman at Rutgers University, a microbiologist, isolated eighteen antibiotics throughout his career in the 1940s and 1950s by looking for antibacterial substances in soil. Neomycin was one of these; streptomycin—the first antibiotic helpful in treating tuberculosis, was another. Both had a wide variety of uses in health care. Waksman received the Nobel Prize in 1952 for the discovery of streptomycin and for the methods he had used to discover it and the other antibiotics. He worked closely with Merck to develop the antibiotics as drugs.

Rather than profiting personally from the lucrative sales of the antibiotics, Waksman helped to establish the Waksman Institute of Microbiology

at Rutgers, plowing the profits into the institute to support further research. Scientists at many of America's research universities have built on
his work to produce additional methods of treating infectious diseases.

The Discovery of Prions. The prevailing dogma in science until the early
1980s was that all diseases were caused by either bacteria or viruses. So
when Stanley Prusiner, professor of neurology at the University of California at San Francisco, along with his team of scientists, hypothesized
that "the infectious agent of scrapie (a fatal neurodegenerative disease
found in sheep and goats) was either a protein or a small nucleic acid sur-
rounded by a tightly packed protein," the idea was resisted. It challenged
received wisdom about what causes disease, and therefore, it was looked on
with a great deal of skepticism.

But Prusiner and his colleagues were right, and their hypothesis quickly
moved from the contentious frontier of knowledge to its core. The particle they had found was dubbed the "prion," a combination of letters deriv-
ing from the words "proteinaceous" ("pr") and "infectious" ("i"), with "on"
added on for good measure (as a parallel to "virion"). The discovery of prions has forced scientists to rethink prior assumptions about the causes of
disease. Prions cause bovine spongiform encephalopathy (BSE, or "mad
cow disease") as well as other neurodegenerative diseases, such as Parkinson's. In 1997, having persuaded almost everyone in the scientific community that prions were an infectious pathogen causing a group of fatal
diseases, Stanley Prusiner received the Nobel Prize.

The finding led scientists and public health officials to organize methods for dealing with diseases about which we still know very little. Public
health officials have the difficult challenge of preventing exposure to infectious agents within a population. In the United States, for example, actions have been taken to prevent the importation of BSE via the
importation of infected cattle; to prevent the spread of the agent throughout the U.S. cattle herd; and to prevent public exposure to the agent
through food and other products that are derived from cattle. A three-year
risk assessment study carried out at Harvard and Tuskegee universities suggested that if farmers and manufacturers complied with the measures already put into place, we could secure the food chain in the United States.
When BSE agents infected cattle herds in England in 1996, mass slaughter of the herds was required to prevent further infestation, costing an es-

timated $700 million in lost revenue for British farmers. Identifying the prions was a step in the right direction; preventing them from spreading was another. Next on the agenda will be discovering how to fight prions directly so that BSE and similar diseases will no longer be such a threat.

Stem Cells. Embryonic stem cells are cells that are not yet programmed for a particular bodily function. They are formed during the blastocyst stage of embryonic development—within the first four or five days after fertilization—when they exist in a cluster of somewhere between 50 and 150 cells. These cells are "pluripotent," which means that they can be turned into any of the 220 cell types found in the adult human body. When they can be harvested at this very early stage of development, they have the capacity for self-renewal. Since they could, in principle, be used to replace damaged or diseased cells, they offer the potential for regenerative medicine. This potential has captured the imagination of some of the world's great biologists while presenting a dilemma for politicians, ethicists, and informed members of the general public. Indeed, the discovery has ignited a controversy, with one side expressing concern about the ethics of harvesting embryonic cells and the other claiming that the potential for relieving human suffering outweighs the ethical problems. The weight of scientific and public opinion is to proceed with stem cell research.

A turning point in stem cell research occurred in 1981, when Martin Evans at Cambridge University in England and Gail Martin, professor of anatomy at the University of California at San Francisco, independently isolated precursor cells from mouse embryos. Gail Martin is credited with coining the term "embryonic stem cells." The discovery laid the groundwork for current worldwide research on the use of human embryonic stem cells to treat disease. UCSF has continued to be a leader in the field of embryonic stem cell research and was one of two academic institutions in the nation that derived embryonic stem cell lines that qualified for inclusion in the National Institutes of Health Stem Cell Registry in 2001. This was during the administration of President George W. Bush, who, because of political and ethical considerations, limited the number of stem cell lines that could be used in research funded by the National Institutes of Health to the few that had already been produced. Human embryonic stem cells were first isolated and cultured in 1998 by a group of University of Wisconsin scientists led by James Thompson. Scientists pursuing this line of research argued against the limitations placed on their field by the president, pointing out that access to human embryonic stem cell lines promised significant opportunities to study early development and could one day provide a near limitless supply of cells for transplant therapy.[29]

Despite the limited access, research proceeded, and some advances were made. In 2000, Hopkins scientists had successfully restored movement to recently paralyzed rodents by injecting stem cells into their spinal fluid. This experiment raised hopes for improved treatment of paralyzing motor neuron diseases such as amyotrophic lateral sclerosis (ALS). The laboratory of Professor Roger Pedersen at the University of Cambridge began distributing one of these cell lines to scientists around the world in 2002. His group identified key differences between human and mouse embryonic stem cells and found that the human cells were relatively stable during their derivation and extended growth. In 2003, scientists at the independent Whitehead Institute, who also hold faculty positions in the biology department at MIT, used embryonic stem cells to produce the total number of 23 chromosomes in human male gametes.

Even more recently, researchers have found ways to extract embryonic stem cells without destroying the embryo, a practice which could virtually eliminate the reasons for the ethical and religious concerns about stem cell research. As recently as November 2007, research groups in Japan and Wisconsin announced that they had succeeded in transforming ordinary human skin cells into cells that looked and acted like embryonic stem cells. This discovery meant that scientists may be able to generate patient-specific stem cells for use in cell-replacement therapies.[30]

The long-term goal of this research is to learn how stem cells might be used to treat heart disease, diabetes, Parkinson's disease, and Alzheimer's as well as spinal cord injuries. A great deal of recent stem cell research has come from nations other than the United States. Whether or not this would have happened under a different federal policy remains an open question, but many scientists and observers believe that the federal policies under President Bush caused American scientists in this area to lose ground. President Barack Obama repealed Bush's policy by issuing a new executive order in March 2009. The National Institutes of Health was instructed to propose revised guidelines for federal funding of stem cell research, which were produced in July 2009.

Cardiopulmonary Resuscitation (CPR). The search for ways of resuscitating people who had suffered heart attacks or drownings goes back to ancient times, and the first formal attempts to codify such procedures appeared in the middle of the eighteenth century, in Amsterdam. But it was not until the 1950s and 1960s that physicians at major hospitals and medical schools began to hone in on truly effective techniques.

About 300,000 Americans die from cardiac arrest every year. When blood does not circulate to the organs, particularly the brain, the possibility of resuscitation only exists for a few minutes. CPR is designed to delay the immediate effects of cardiac arrest and, when combined with quick defibrillation, to prevent death. New medications and surgical techniques have played a big role in saving the lives of the victims of cardiac arrest, but usually the victim is not near anyone who can provide medical assistance when the cardiac arrest occurs. If people who are nearby can assist for a few minutes, by providing CPR until medical help arrives, they can make a crucial difference. Therefore, educating the public about how to respond quickly is an important feature of these efforts.

The modern effort to develop mouth-to-mouth resuscitation and CPR can be dated to the work of James Elam, who received his medical training at Johns Hopkins, and Peter Safar at the University of Pittsburgh, both anesthesiologists, and to work on chest compression defibrillation at Johns Hopkins University. Rescue breathing had been described before, but Elam "rediscovered" the technique in 1946 when he applied the principle to a child in an emergency situation at a Baltimore hospital. Elam described the moment: "I was browsing around to get acquainted with the ward when along the corridor came a gurney racing—a nurse pulling it and two orderlies pushing it, and the kid on it was blue. I went into total reflex behaviour. I stepped out in the middle of the corridor, stopped the gurney, grabbed the sheet, wiped the copious mucous off his mouth and face, . . . sealed my lips around his nose and inflated his lungs. In four breaths he was pink."[31] This serendipitous moment inspired him to do further work in rescue techniques, and he ended up making a series of contributions while renewing interest in the field. Through their experiments, Elam and Safar convinced the world that rescue breathing was an effective method of oxygenation and could prevent organ damage and death. The U.S. military adopted their techniques and efforts to educate the general public got underway.

The element of chest compression in CPR was an accidental discovery by Hopkins scientists William Bennett Kouwenhoven, Guy Knickerbocker, and James Jude in 1962, who found that they could restore a pulse to dogs by applying electric shock paddles. Careful experimentation led to improved understanding of the best location for the paddles, the speed of application, and the intensity of the shock that would most likely restore a regular heartbeat in humans. Hopkins research doctors also found that placing weight on the chest of heart attack victims increased blood pressure.

HIV/AIDS. Many researchers at American universities have contributed to our understanding of HIV/AIDS. They have made fundamental discoveries pertaining to the biology of HIV and AIDS and have searched for methods of prevention through vaccines. Indeed, it would require a lengthy article to provide the highlights of their contributions. Here, we will look just briefly at some of the highlights of HIV/AIDS research, with a focus on the scientist David Ho, who was born in Taiwan in 1952 and educated at MIT and Caltech. Ho did not discover the fact that HIV caused AIDS; nor did he make the most fundamental discoveries associated with our efforts to understand HIV or to develop a vaccine. Yet he represents a quintessential case of "a man on a mission." Along with scores of others, he has helped to turn HIV from a death sentence into a controllable disease.

Ho's willingness to challenge received wisdom is part of what has made him famous. Before he began to prove otherwise, starting in around 1994, most scientists believed that there could be a fairly long latency period between a person being infected with HIV and the time that he or she experienced symptoms. Ho, who saw some of the first cases of HIV while working as a resident at Cedars-Sinai Medical Center and UCLA Medical Center, thought that in fact there was a continuous onslaught by the virus and that the virus and a person's immune system were in a death struggle. Once he was able to measure the amount of virus in the blood, he was able to confirm that billions of HIV particles were being produced every day.

Ho was treating AIDS patients before we even had a name for it— when the cause of the syndrome, HIV, was still a mystery. As a physician in the early 1980s, he was seeing patients—young gay men—who were being admitted to the hospital with a plethora of medical problems. Most of them had been healthy all of their lives until suddenly coming down with some sort of rare infection.[32] The common denominator in all of the patients was that their levels of CD4 T-cells was low. These cells were a subgroup of the lymphocytes that influence the effectiveness of the immune system.

In 1983, Luc Montagnier's lab at the Pasteur Institute in France found that when a portion of a French patient's lymph node was put into a culture, the culture propagated reverse transcriptase activity. This was the first major clue that retroviruses might be involved in causing AIDS. Robert Gallo, working at the National Institutes of Health at about the same time, demonstrated that the retrovirus was highly transmissible, convincing much of the scientific community that this new virus, which later was called HIV, was the cause of AIDS. Within the scientific community there followed a combative priority dispute between the labs of Montagnier and Gallo over which one was first to discover the AIDS virus (Montagnier and his colleague Francoise Barre Sinoussi, not Gallo, were awarded the Nobel Prize for this work in 2008). For those beyond the combat zone over priority, however, there was great enthusiasm. Many researchers assumed that with the cause of the disease now known, the discovery of a cure or vaccine would soon follow. Of course, the scientific problems involved in finding a cure proved to be far more complex and unyielding than originally anticipated.

A concerted effort to identify drugs that could combat the replication of the HIV virus began. By 1985, clinical trials were underway for AZT, and within two years it became the first drug to be used to treat the disease. In 1995, Ho developed a combination therapy, treating the patient early on with several antiviral drugs and protease inhibitors at once in an effort to suppress the virus to undetectable levels. These cocktails had dramatic effects, and his approach was considered a breakthrough. Patients on the verge of death rebounded after taking Ho's "triple cocktail" therapy. The combination therapy developed into what is now called "highly active antiretroviral therapy," or HAART, and it is still the treatment of choice for HIV/AIDS patients, though the specific combinations of drugs have changed.

David Ho is now the head of the Aaron Diamond Research Center in New York and professor at Rockefeller University. He is only one of the thousands of university-based researchers who are working to gain a greater understanding of the basic biology of HIV, its transmission, and its mechanisms of expression in an effort to find better treatments and ultimately a vaccine to prevent it. Wayne Hendrickson, a biophysicist at Columbia, is another. He has used X-ray crystallography to understand how HIV, like the flu virus, evades the immune system by "constantly mutating its protein coat and hiding under layers of sugar."[33] With all of the discoveries of university research, using billions of dollars of U.S. funding ($2.9 billion in 2008 out of a total of $23.3 billion for domestic and global HIV/AIDS activities),[34] some progress has been made. Using HAART regimens, survival rates can be increased by perhaps four to twelve years, and the quality of life of HIV/AIDS patients has been improved. Until the discovery of a vaccine, however, it is not likely that science will be able to eradicate the disease.

THE REVOLUTION IN FOOD PRODUCTION

For centuries, farmers around the world have been plagued by the devastation of crops by insects, microorganisms, and weeds. When President Lincoln signed the Morrill Act to support the creation of land-grant colleges and agricultural stations across the United States, the idea was that research done at these universities would lead to revolutionary advances in agriculture. Over many decades, the American research university has played a critical role in revolutionizing agricultural methods, production, storage, and transport. Many of the advances in cattle breeding and disease prevention in livestock can also be attributed to our research universities. But the research universities that have led the way in this revolution were not the Ivy League colleges or even the most prestigious state universities—with the exception of perhaps Cornell, where extraordinary work on cattle breeding has been done. Instead, it is the great Midwestern universities that have tended to produce the landmark discoveries, innovations, and techniques in agriculture.

Purdue University, among many others, has helped to shape this revolution. For example, Purdue's Philip F. Nelson, a professor of food science, invented "bulk aseptic," or sterile processing of food, which allowed orange juice producers to ship large quantities of not-from-concentrate orange juice. The process was patented by Purdue in 1972. Aseptic processing has benefited other food-processing industries as well. Combined with a type of packaging invented by William Scholle, a Purdue graduate, for example, it has made possible the long-term storage and transport of fresh fruits and vegetables. Advances in food preservation began to be made not long after the Morrill Act was passed. As early as 1919, researchers at the University of Illinois at Urbana-Champaign created the first antitoxin for botulism poisoning, and scientists at the University of California at San Francisco conducted research in the 1920s that led to the adoption of safety standards for the modern canning industry, another advance in fighting botulism.

Much of the university research in agriculture conducted over the past fifty years has involved attempts to make crops more resistant to pests or to invent novel ways of eradicating the pests themselves. Purdue scientists collaborated with an industrial partner to tackle the costly problem of the soybean cyst nematode, a pest that significantly reduced soybean yields. After many years of genetic analysis and selective breeding, they developed soybeans that were resistant to the cyst nematode in 2000.

In another area of food science, in 1965 in an effort to aid football players during hot summer practices, University of Florida scientists Robert Cade, Dick Malonis, Harry Free, and Dana Shires invented the world's most popular sports drink. This combination of water, sodium, sugar, potassium, phosphate, and lemon juice came to be known as Gatorade to honor the Florida team, the Gators. These scientists also developed the process for making frozen concentrated orange juice in collaboration with the Florida Department of Citrus.

Because California is one of the great agricultural centers of the world, the various campuses of the University of California have focused a good deal of attention on improving the quantity and quality of the food produced in California and protecting people from illness related to contaminated food. California's strawberry industry, for example, was saved in the 1940s when university scientists developed a hybrid plant resistant to a devastating virus. Since then, university scientists have developed about forty different strawberry varieties grown worldwide. In the 1960s and 1970s, they modernized farming with new machinery such as tree-shaking devices for harvesting fruits and nuts. Work to fine-tune farming equipment and develop new machines continues today. Researchers at the University of California at Davis developed farming technologies that improved the wine industry and the tomato industry. They invented a tomato harvester that is credited with saving the California tomato industry, and they have produced genetically altered tomatoes that turn ripe on cue and remain that way for as long as three months without spoiling. This discovery may help consumers, especially those in Third World countries, store fruit longer without refrigeration.

Artificial insemination (AI) techniques for dairy cattle were developed at several places, including Cornell, after World War II. The success of this line of work led to significant increases in milk production. In 1936, Cornell professor S. J. Brownell began inseminating cows in the Cornell herd, and similar efforts took place at the University of Minnesota and the University of Wisconsin.[35] An AI cooperative modeled after one in Denmark was established in 1938 in Ithaca, New York. This cooperative maintained ties with the researchers at Cornell. According to R. H. Foote, a professor of animal science at Cornell, the result was "the experimental insemination of hundreds of thousands of cows and publication of more than 100 research papers . . . on sire selection, testicular evaluation, semen collection, evaluation and processing, and fertility testing."[36]

The AI movement had to overcome obstacles, including the reluctance in the general public to any research involving sex. There were some who feared that AI would lead to genetic abnormalities, and there were cattle breeders who believed that AI would ravage their bull market. Nonetheless, the research led to significantly improved artificial insemination techniques, improving our understanding of frozen semen, superovulation, and embryo transfer. Eventually researchers began to experiment with cloning, chalking up some well-publicized successes and raising new ethical questions.

Genetic engineering of crops is another sometimes controversial subject. From 1993 to 2002, Allison Snow from Ohio State led a multiuniversity team in researching artificial genes (called "transgenes"). Transgenes have been inserted into the genomes of crop plants, but Snow's research team found that they are able to spread to wild plants much more easily than was previously believed. As a result, advice from ecologists is now being sought to help with the design and evaluation of genetically engineered plants.[37] The work has important implications for modern agriculture, food security in developing countries, and international regulations pertaining to safe uses of genetic engineering in agriculture.

Snow showed that crop genes are able to persist in wild and weedy plant populations for many years and that the presence of dispersed transgenic genes does not inhibit the growth or reproduction of other species. Specific transgenic traits, such as resistance to insect damage, can allow weedy plants to become much more widespread than before the dispersal of the artificial genes. In other words, a transgene that is beneficial for a crop could have the unintended effect of creating "superweeds." Snow's work, which was recognized as one of the top science stories of 2002 by *Discover* magazine, is shaping interdisciplinary efforts to assess the environmental risks and benefits of using biotechnology in agriculture.

Independent researchers like Snow who are unfettered by the kinds of restrictions placed upon researchers in the corporate world are in a critically important position because they can assess the pros and cons of agricultural bioengineering without feeling pressured to simply promote it. Bioengineering processes have faced widespread resistance from the general public despite the extraordinary effects that they have had on agricultural production. Snow's work has already had important positive effects on national and international biosafety policies.

THE BIRTH OF SOCIOBIOLOGY

The forces of academic specialization have caused the virtual extinction of the "polymath"—the scholar with broad knowledge who can synthesize the discoveries and theories of many different fields to produce something new. However, there continue to be a few members of that species, and these few thrive and make huge contributions to the growth of knowledge. One such person is the Harvard scientist E. O. Wilson, who has changed the way many academics think about evolution and human life.[38]

At an early age, Wilson attempted to synthesize Darwinian evolutionary theory and the great advances in Mendelian genetics, particularly in the work from Thomas Hunt Morgan to Theodosius Dobzhansky, a Ukrainian geneticist who wrote *Genetics and the Origin of Species*.[39] But despite his love for theory and synthesis, Wilson began with the data and ideas that emerged from his trips to study ants in New Guinea, other Pacific Islands, and the American tropics.[40] This detailed work with ants led him to a theory (with Princeton scientist Robert H. MacArthur) of island biogeography.

Essentially, Wilson uses biological factors and evolutionary principles as a lens for examining social behavior, both in insects and in other species, including humans. Wilson's ants and other insects had "evolved to perform tasks in just the right numbers and with just the right adaptations," and Wilson was able "to formulate mathematical equations to predict a wide range of behavior, right down to . . . altering birth rates to suit the prevailing conditions."[41] The theory has had great influence on the discipline of ecology, and it became the intellectual framework for the field of conservation biology. The work has also helped conservationists to plan parks and reserves around the world.[42]

In the 1950s and 1960s, Wilson's work influenced the emergence of the new field of chemical ecology. In a collaborative effort, Wilson "created the first general theory of properties of chemical communication." His idea was that societies were integrated by an elaborate system of chemical signals, and he proved the existence of "pheromones," chemical substances emitted by animals that influence the responses of other members of the species, through an experiment: "Pied Piperlike, he lured a stream of worker ants along a chemical trail laid down with pheromones extracted from a gland in the abdomen of a fire ant."[43] He then dipped "bits of paper in the juice of dead ants and found that live ants would carry the paper to their nests" just as they would carry "the corpses of their sisters."

Wilson extended his work to the analysis of vertebrates and related his ideas to evolutionary biology in his 1975 book *Sociobiology,* which the officers and fellows of the International Animal Behavior Society called the most important book on animal behavior ever written. Wilson had started a new field, sociobiology, sometimes called evolutionary psychology.

The discoveries I have chosen to describe in this chapter represent just a few of the highlights; there are many more examples of the ways that biologists, geneticists, and medical doctors have transferred public and private research support into new discoveries and practical applications that have changed our lives. They have taken on difficult problems and found solutions that are breathtaking in their scope and impact. In the next chapter, we will look at similarly breathtaking discoveries in the physical sciences and in engineering.

CHAPTER 9

Buckyballs, Bar Codes, and the GPS: Our Origins, Our Planet, Our Security and Safety

There is no excellent beauty that hath not some strangeness in the proportion.

—Sir Francis Bacon

The twentieth century was a time of monumental revolutionary change in our understanding of the basic laws of physics and chemistry. The physical sciences did advance in the eighteenth and nineteenth centuries,[1] but not until the twentieth were the basic laws of Newtonian physics revised and superseded by a different way of thinking about time, space, and matter. The revolution in basic theory was accompanied by leaps in our understanding and use of nuclear and particle physics, discoveries in solid-state and condensed-matter physics, and, still later, advances in nanoscience. Astrophysics and chemistry also underwent revolutionary changes. And at increasing speed, scientific discoveries were informing new technological and engineering advances that led to the creation of thousands of products that have altered the way we think and live.[2]

The United States has not led in the physical sciences and in engineering in the same way that it has in the biological and biomedical fields. The universities and industrial research labs of Germany, England, and France were the dominant sites for work in the physical sciences until the early 1930s, and the total number of scientific papers in these fields coming out of the nations of Europe and Asia surpasses the number coming from America. Europe has built some of the most modern facilities for conducting basic research in physics, and it has maintained its leadership in some areas of the physical sciences. The French have probably produced as many great mathematicians, per capita, as the United States.

To be sure, there is extraordinary international cooperation in these fields, particularly among the scientists of America, Europe, and Asia, which makes it difficult, if not impossible, in many cases, to assign "discovery" to any single nation or university. Many of the great scientists working at American research universities today were born and educated in other nations; indeed, many of those working in Europe or Asia were educated in America. The scientific community involves international collaboration and communication today as never before. That said, it is also the case that American society over the past sixty years has continued to create academic centers of excellence that consistently produce the most significant contributions to these fields.

Universities are singular places where knowledge and discovery have intrinsic value, where they are often pursued without "products" in mind. A friend of mine at Princeton, a theoretical astrophysicist, once described the joy that he experienced in trying to understand aspects of spinning stars within the larger universe. Each time a new discovery was made, he would become excited, as if another dot had been filled in on the vast canvas of some pointillist artist. Because we are curious about our origins, we are willing to make large and long-term investments in trying to understand the universe. University researchers spend billions of government dollars and decades of their lives pursuing the kind of research that promises to illuminate the workings of everything from the tiniest particles to the largest things we know of—stars, galaxies, and more. They build enormous cyclotrons to test abstract ideas and theories. They plan events—such as a NASA space mission—years in advance, bringing together the talents of hundreds of people for a single purpose. They look deeper and deeper into space, through ever bigger and better telescopes—including the ultimate to date, the Hubble—to explore the mysteries that still puzzle and intrigue us. All of this is testimony to our human commitment to knowledge of fundamentals and of our origins.

The search for knowledge causes us to look to the stars, but it also causes us to look into the depths of our own seas—which seem, at times, to be equally mysterious places. To have a greater understanding of our own planet, we must also understand the atmosphere that envelops it, and research concerning our ozone layer and other aspects of this delicately balanced protective layer has become important in the past century. And it has been the computer, with its unbelievable advances over the past half-century—including the Internet—that has enabled us to gather and analyze all of the data that have made many of the scientific gains possible. In this chapter, we shall look at some of the main contributions that researchers at American universities have made to our knowledge of the universe and our planet and then at the rise of the computer age and issues surrounding national security.

FUNDAMENTAL DISCOVERIES ABOUT OUR WORLD

Quantum mechanics—the study of the laws of physics operating at the atomic level—began with Max Planck, a German physicist who was born in 1858 and died in 1947, and took another great leap forward when Albert Einstein, one of the few physicists fully aware of Plank's theory in 1905, calculated his "independent energy quanta," challenged the wave theory of light, and demonstrated that quantum theory could explain the photoelectric effect in a way that the prior wave theory failed to predict. In that same year Einstein produced his special theory of relativity while questioning the concept of a stationary ether. This new physics was not taken up immediately. But when it began to take off as a result of profound work being done in Europe and by a new generation of American physicists, the world of science would rapidly change.[3] This new kind of physics shaped the thinking of American scientists of Einstein's time, and when Einstein and so many of his colleagues were displaced from Europe by World War II and came to America, they brought the quantum revolution with them. The Manhattan project applied some of their theoretical findings, contributing to the Allies' victory in the war.

When historians of science and technology reflect on the twentieth century, they tend to describe it as "the age of physics." The physicists who participated in the Manhattan Project and produced the atom bomb and radar, as well as other pathbreaking discoveries, became cultural icons.

The discoveries after the war went far beyond the technical feats that produced the bomb. American physicists, mathematicians, chemists, astronomers, and geologists were widely recognized for their creativity and discoveries, many of which would lead to practical applications. Their universities became known as the best producers of talent in the world.

The discoveries that I will describe in this chapter, each coming from one or more universities, sometimes in collaboration with major scientific laboratories, were built on a fundamentally new framework for understanding the laws of nature. To be sure, there were extraordinary accomplishments in the physical sciences in the eighteenth and nineteenth centuries. Benjamin Franklin's discoveries and technological inventions—from his experiments with electricity to his inventions of the lightning rod, the Franklin stove, the flexible urinary catheter, and bifocals—are a case in point, as are Joseph Priestley's and Antoine Lavoisier's simultaneous discovery of oxygen gas; the Scottish mathematician and theoretical physicist James Clerk Maxwell's equations in electricity, inductance, and magnetism, as well as his kinetic theory of gases; the discoveries of the French naturalist Georges Cuvier, which laid the groundwork for Charles Darwin's evolutionary theory in 1859; and the work of Yale's preeminent theoretical physicist and chemist, Josiah Willard Gibbs, who created the foundations for chemical thermodynamics and physical chemistry.

But in the course of the twentieth century, principally in the United States and Europe, physicists transformed the way we think about the world and set the stage for thousands of practical technological advances, inventions, discoveries, and devices that influence our daily lives.

Albert Einstein, whose theory of relativity had huge theoretical and epistemological implications, became, and remains, the most famous symbol of scientific genius. His theoretical discoveries were perhaps the most meaningful and dramatic since Newtonian physics in the seventeenth century. As towering a figure and presence as Einstein was, there were many other revolutionaries who altered the face of physics.[4] Ernest Rutherford, working in both England and Canada over the course of his life, discovered the atomic nucleus, and Max Planck, in Germany, introduced quantum theory. Niels Bohr was Danish but spent time in Sweden and the United States during World War II to escape Nazi occupation and became closely associated with the Manhattan Project.

His investigations into the structure of atoms and the radiation emanating from them made the idea of nuclear fission and an atomic bomb seem possible. Werner Heisenberg, in Germany, published his theory of quantum mechanics in 1925 when he was only twenty-three years old. The theory was to usher in the new physics of the atomic world.[5] And it was Heisenberg's famous "uncertainty principle" ("The more precisely the position is determined, the less precisely the momentum [mass times velocity] is known in this instant, and vice versa.") that altered philosophical as well as scientific views about the nature of the objective world.

The Niels Bohr–Werner Heisenberg theories, often called the "Copenhagen interpretation of quantum mechanics," had many initial detractors and elicited great scientific skepticism from many scientists, including Einstein. Reacting to the Copenhagen interpretation and its implications that probabilistic statements would replace the idea of objective certainty about the physical universe, Einstein critically observed: "I cannot believe that God would choose to play dice with the universe," to which Niels Bohr replied: "Einstein, don't tell God what to do." Bohr acknowledged, however, that: "Anyone who is not shocked by quantum theory has not understood a single word."

When Enrico Fermi, as the Nobel Prize Committee put it, "demonstrated the existence of new radioactive elements produced by neutron irradiation" and "nuclear reactions brought about by slow neutrons," he created the basis for discovering new elements that went beyond what could then be found in the periodic table.[6] Fermi, an Italian, arrived in the United States in 1938 and was appointed professor of physics at Columbia University. One of the putative fathers of atomic physics, Fermi ushered in the atomic age. When Otto Hahn and Fritz Strassmann, who were both German but opposed the Nazi government, discovered nuclear fission in 1939, Fermi recognized the possibility of creating a nuclear chain reaction from the emission of secondary neutrons. Their colleague Lisa Meitner, who left Berlin in 1938 as the Germans were closing in on anyone with Jewish ancestry, contributed enormously to this discovery, conducting her work in basement laboratories. Fermi's work led to the first controlled nuclear chain reaction, which took place on a squash court beneath the University of Chicago's athletic stadium on December 2, 1942.

He was one of the leaders of the Manhattan Project that developed the atom bomb.[7]

Nobel Prizes, which have been awarded since 1901, are a convenient indicator of the scientific standing of nations. In the years prior to 1940, the Germans won more than a quarter of all the prizes. Great Britain was in second place for having the highest number of recipients, and the United States captured only 11 percent of the prizes. Americans played a part in the revolution of the physical sciences before World War II, but most of their seminal contributions come after 1940. Fully 35 of the 125 émigrés from Europe who received Nobel Prizes in all categories up until 1976 did their prize-winning work in the United States. But only 11 of these were refugees from Hitler's Europe between 1930 and 1941. As much as the refugee physicists from Nazi Germany helped catapult American physical science toward preeminence—and they had a far greater impact than one would predict from their sheer number—they composed only a small fraction of the growing number of physicists in the United States at that time. They were important leaders, something that I. I. Rabi had said the United States needed, but the basic foundation for American preeminence in the physical sciences was being built from within the system of universities as better laboratories were built and smart young people were recruited into these fields. At the universities, these young people were provided with opportunities to identify and solve fundamental problems. By the late 1930s, American physics could hold its own against any other nation in the world.

The United States proved superb at producing scientists who had both scientific talent and organizational genius. Rabi, who taught at Columbia for many years, was one who fit this description. Focusing predominantly on the nature of the force that bound protons to atomic nuclei, his research with many others eventually led to the creation of the molecular-beam magnetic-resonance detection method. A Nobel Prize winner for his own work, Rabi helped to found the Brookhaven National Laboratories. He was devoted to the peaceful use of atomic energy and was instrumental in establishing Europe's CERN, the world's most powerful accelerator and particle collider as of 2009. Many of his intellectual progeny went on to win Nobel Prizes themselves or to achieve substantial recognition for their contributions to American physics. During World

War II, he was granted a leave from Columbia to become the associate director of one branch of MIT's Radiation Laboratory, where he was instrumental in the development of radar. The discovery of radar had extraordinary consequences for the war effort and innumerable valuable applications. Rabi's postwar work led eventually to the invention of the laser and the atomic clock.

Ernest O. Lawrence, a 1939 Nobel winner and a professor at the University of California at Berkeley, was cited by the Nobel Committee for "the invention and development of the cyclotron and for results obtained with it, especially with regard to artificial radioactive elements."[8] Lawrence proved as great an organizer and administrator of science as he was a bench scientist. He organized a massive effort to build accelerators that brought great scientists to the Lawrence Berkeley Radiation Laboratory.

The atmosphere at many of the rising physics department from the 1930s onward was vibrant and full of a sense of infinite possibilities. Students felt that they were participating in a great revolution. While working to develop laser spectroscopy as part of his research on superconductivity at Bell Labs, Arthur Schawlow (later at Stanford University) described the intellectual energy and excitement that permeated the physics community during his postdoctoral studies at Columbia and his subsequent collaboration with Charles Townes: "What a marvelous place Columbia was then, under I. I. Rabi's leadership! There were no less than eight future Nobel laureates in the physics department during my two years there. Working with Charles Townes was particularly stimulating." Townes, he said, "was extraordinarily effective in getting the best from his students and colleagues. He would listen carefully to the confused beginnings of an idea, and join in developing whatever was worthwhile in it, without ever dominating the discussions."[9]

Efforts by American physicists to identify elementary particles and to integrate their discoveries into a larger unified theory continued in the 1950s and 1960s and found expression in work by Murray Gell-Mann. The son of Jewish immigrants and a child who early on displayed a prodigious intellect, Gell-Mann attended Yale and MIT and spent most of his subsequent career at Caltech. His enormous contributions to physics came from his attempt to bring order to the rapid discovery of roughly 100 particles that were found in collisions involving atomic nuclei.

The major challenge to physicists at the time was to create a unified theory that made sense of the scores of new particles that physicists were discovering through their experiments. Toward that end, Gell-Mann proposed the theory of the "Eightfold Way" (a reference to Buddhism) and the idea of quarks as the fundamental building blocks of nuclear particles and their strong interactions.[10] His general theory, now called "the standard model," has been supported over the years by experiments, yet the search continues for the last elusive particle, the Higgs boson. This is currently the focus of research at CERN, the largest accelerator in the world today.[11]

Along with many other physicists, Gell-Mann went on to construct the quantum field theory of quarks and gluons (quantum chromodynamics), which attempted to account for all the nuclear particles and their strong interactions.[12] Collaborating with the brilliant physicist Richard Feynman (Caltech), he and a rival group were the first to identify the structure of weak interactions in physics—a result that followed on the early experimental work of Chien-Shiung Wu (Columbia University) and C. N. Yang (State University of New York, Stony Brook) and T. D. Lee's (Columbia) discovery of parity violation in weak interactions.[13] In comparing his Nobel Prize–winning work with his collaborative work with Gell-Mann on weak interactions, Feynman, one of the great science teachers of his time, said, "I won the prize for shoving a great problem under the carpet, but in this case there was a moment when I knew how nature worked. It had elegance and beauty. The goddamn thing was gleaming." The theory was so shiny, in fact, that when several eminent physicists produced experiments that seemed to falsify it, Feynman, a great believer in experimentation (remember his on-the-spot experiment on the "o rings" during the Challenger space shuttle disaster inquiry), insisted that they were wrong. And indeed they proved to be.

What is both wonderful and at times frustrating about trying to understand these fundamentals is that the answers always yield new, unanswered questions and problems. There is always room for new theory and experimentation. Think of the state of modern particle physics. With a cyclotron at CERN that is capable of setting protons in motion that virtually achieve the speed of light, scientists will be searching for the missing Higgs particles, for particles that have never been observed but in theory should exist as symmetrical partners for those that are known, such as a partner for the "quark," dubbed by physicists a "squark." They will be searching for evidence that might or might not support string theory. None of this has any practical application except to tease our imaginations and fulfill our desire to know more about the origins of the stuff that makes up our universe and what happened at the very beginning of its existence.

A remarkable number of scientists believe, I think incorrectly, in a hierarchy of sciences. This idea holds that the best minds in the academic community migrate to fields at the top of the hierarchy, such as mathematics and theoretical physics, where they attack the most difficult problems, while those with lesser talent search for fields lower in the hierarchy where they can excel. For most of the postwar period, the most brilliant theoretical particle physicists were the elite figures in the discipline and in science more generally. They were often treated like academic demigods. Their work was considered the deepest and most fundamental, and, along with the smartest mathematicians, they were deferred to throughout the field. Despite the elegance associated with the theory of particle physics, the work in other fields of physics, perhaps more low flying, began to have profound effects on the overall discipline and ultimately on the practical uses of physics. The emergence of solid-state and condensed-matter physics, and their growth into far larger specialty areas than particle physics, launched a new relationship between basic knowledge and utility.

If revolutionary changes were taking place at the top of the hierarchy in physics, led by physicists with extraordinary intellects, American scientists with equally extraordinary intellects were creating revolutions during most of the twentieth century in the fields of chemistry and the geosciences, and American universities, along with their remarkable partners in industrial and national laboratories, were supporting a substantial amount of the most consequential work. Our ideas about the nature of our planet, its evolution, and its geochemistry, and our knowledge of its oceans, atmosphere, and land masses, underwent a powerful transformation during this time that has not only altered the way we think about the earth as a living system but also led to amazing practical advances.

Caltech's Linus Pauling is perhaps the quintessential example of a university scientist who profoundly altered his field, paving the way for many practical applications. Many knowledgeable chemists would say that Pauling was the most accomplished chemist of the twentieth century. His long-standing interest in the then uncharted territory of molecular structures and the nature of the chemical bond, and his innumerable discoveries, influenced generations of chemists. His textbook *The Nature of the Chemical Bond* remains a classic in the field sixty years after it was first published. Pauling, a man with unbounded curiosity and intellect, was at once a quantum chemist and biochemist and contributed profound ideas to our understanding of crystal and protein structures. His work on the chemical bond was a central feature in the development of organic chemistry, and he could be considered one of the founding fathers of molecular biology. It was Pauling who was the rival of Watson and Crick as they competed to unravel the mystery of the structure of the DNA molecule. Pauling also proposed theories about the relationship between vitamin C and disease. He led the effort to halt aboveground nuclear testing—for which he was awarded a Nobel Peace Prize to place alongside the Nobel he had won in 1954 for his work on the chemical bond.

Theories in physics, chemistry, and the other sciences may not often be developed with practical applications in mind, but they nevertheless often generate a set of research problems that lead to technological innovation. If the basic science departments were producing monumental new discoveries, so were the best American schools of engineering and applied sciences. Technology, which is the focus of these schools, is the process by which humans modify nature in ways that meet their needs and desires. Often the stepchildren to the basic sciences in terms of prestige at American research universities, engineering programs deal with the built world, and with increasing frequency they are the sources both for novel ideas and innovations and for the advanced technical manpower working in American industry.[14] The boundaries between these disciplines and the physical sciences are increasingly blurred, with more interdisciplinary research being conducted that involves both. Engineering schools are also far more likely than science departments to create direct linkages with industrial labs, and they have become a major source of new intellectual property at the universities.

After World War II, as the Cold War escalated, the United States came to believe that the struggle would be shaped as much by scientific and technological competence and achievements as by economic theory. A new emphasis was placed on developing the scientific capacities of students, from high school to the top levels of university study. Young, bright high-school students in the 1950s were directed toward science and math at the expense of language training and the arts. American scientists were challenged to reach the goals that the nation's leaders had set, and they came through with stunning discoveries and inventions. Stiff competition developed between the Soviet Union and the United States in the sciences, and the area of scientific and technological advance that perhaps received the most attention was space exploration. The moon landing in the summer of 1969 and the numerous steps leading up to it were the most obvious symbols of this rivalry. Indeed, the technological innovations that emerged from NASA's space program, and the involvement of university-trained engineers and scientists in those endeavors, could easily be the subject of another book. Here, we shall focus on one small but essential part of space exploration: the telescope.

Although the optical telescope dates to the early seventeenth century, large optical and radio telescopes and X-ray, ultraviolet, and gamma telescopes are twentieth-century inventions. The Mount Wilson 60-inch reflection telescope was completed in 1908, and the Hasker telescope, with a 100-inch reflector, in 1917. In 1932, John Donovan Strong, a Caltech physicist, improved the technology of the reflecting mirrors to give added life to these telescopes. The Mount Palomar was the largest telescope in the world (200 inches) when it was completed in 1948 (eventually it was surpassed by the 238-inch Altazimuth telescope in Russia, completed in 1965). But the 1990s saw a revolution in telescopes, with the completion of the Keck I in Mauna Kea, Hawaii, in 1992, the Keck II in 1996, the Very Large Telescope (VLT) at four locations around the world in 1996, and others, all of which depend on new "adaptive optics."

In conjunction with the European Space Agency, NASA scientists helped to design and build the Hubble telescope, launched in 1990. The telescope is named after Edwin Hubble, an American astronomer, and astrophysicists are continuing to do path-breaking work based on the data that it has generated. The beautiful pictures taken by the Hubble camera have inspired people around the world. The idea for the Hubble can be traced to a 1946 article written by Lyman Spitzer, a Princeton professor, who became one of its leading advocates over the next several decades. Jim Gunn, another Princeton astrophysicist, was one of the designers of the telescope. The Hubble supports work by scientists such as National Academy of Sciences member Sandra Faber, who has made important discoveries on the formation, structure, and evolution of galaxies and clusters of galaxies at the University of California's Lick and Keck observatories.

Indeed, the study of the structure and evolution of stars has gained a great deal from the Hubble program. The study of black holes, quasars, and the like are part of this subfield of physics. In 1930, Subrahmanyan Chadrasekhar at the University of Chicago presented mathematical calculations supporting the existence of black holes, regions of space where the gravitational force would be so powerful that nothing, not even visible light, could escape its pull. In 1997, an international team of astronomers, including Doug Richstone of the University of Michigan, discovered a supermassive black hole in a galaxy 30 million light-years from Earth that seems to contain the mass of a billion suns. The researchers found that massive dark objects, most likely black holes, also lie at the center of Andromeda and M32, the two galaxies closest to Earth. These discoveries have led to speculation that black holes are the energy source of quasars. Other astronomers, such as Princeton's Joseph H. Taylor, Jr., and Russell A. Hulse, discovered gravitational radiation and found that neutron stars were losing energy at exactly the rate that Einstein predicted.

In the quest to understand the composition of the universe, astrophysicists have hypothesized the existence of "dark energy" and "dark matter" that in theory permeates space. A large international group of astronomers, many from English and American universities, and including Berkeley astronomers Alex Filippenko and a young post-doc, Adam Reiss (now at Johns Hopkins), developed the current theory that the universe is expanding at an accelerating rate. As of 2001, estimates obtained from NASA satellites suggest that dark energy accounts for 74 percent of the total mass-energy of the universe, while dark matter accounts for another 22 percent. The parts of the universe that make up stars and planets that can be "seen" make up only about 4 percent of the universe's total mass-energy.

It would be a mistake to think that basic physics and chemistry have not been translated into uses that affect our everyday experiences. In truth, some of the inventions flowing from these fields have been remarkable. Here I shall describe just a few that have had important implications.

The Laser. Originally dubbed "a technology in search of an application" when it was invented, the laser has played an essential role in every branch of science, from physics to geology to microbiology.[15] American research universities and the Bell Laboratories were instrumental in the discovery and development of lasers and laser technologies. In 1958, Charles Townes and his brother-in-law, Arthur Schawlow, showed that, theoretically, masers (an acronym for "microwave amplification by stimulated emission of radiation") could be made to operate in the optical and infrared region. He then proposed that this could be accomplished with "lasers" (an acronym for "light amplification by stimulated emission of radiation").

We hear about lasers all the time, but what are they? It is light, of course. Light is an electromagnetic wave with brightness and color that vibrates at a particular angle. In a laser, every part of the beam of light moves in virtually the same direction, so that the light waves are running parallel to each other. You can concentrate the light energy in a laser so precisely that it is possible to cut and drill with it. Schawlow, who later moved from the Bell Labs to Stanford and would share the Nobel Prize for the discovery of the laser, liked "to entertain students and other audiences by shooting a laser beam through a transparent balloon to pop the dark Mickey Mouse balloon inside. The demonstration showed that the laser could be tuned to pass through the transparent outer balloon without burning it."[16] Lasers are powerful instruments. University of Michigan scientists collaborated with scientists at the French National Atomic Energy Commission to create the most powerful pulse of laser light up to that time, a 55-terawatt pulse that was the equivalent of a hundred times the total electrical power generated in the United States.

If scientists were searching for applications for the laser, they have surely found them, as they are now ubiquitous. Consider just a few examples from a variety of industries. Lasers are widely used in medicine. They are used in various eye surgeries, including repair of retinal detachment, glaucoma surgery (the laser creates a small opening in the iris in order to allow fluid to circulate and reduce pressure), and surgery for vision correction of nearsightedness. They are also used in cosmetic surgery to treat birthmarks, to perform skin resurfacing, and to remove tattoos, and they are used to treat problems related to snoring (by reshaping the uvula without making an impact on the airway). Dentists are beginning to use lasers to drill teeth with less pain and to remove excess gum tissue, and in general surgery, lasers are being used to shatter kidney stones and to assist in angioplasty to reopen blocked or narrowed arteries.

Lasers have revolutionized the electronics and communications industries. Without lasers, we would not have CDs and CD players or related technologies such as CD-ROMs. Audio CDs are made by converting music to digital code, which the laser writes as tiny holes on a master disk, and the disk is played by focusing a laser beam on the aluminum and plastic layer that coats these holes. The holes in the disks reflect light differently, and sensors measure the difference; electronics decode the signal and reveal what is on the disk. Lasers are now widely used in "laser jet" printers as well.

Professor Joe C. Campbell, professor of electrical engineering at the University of Texas at Austin, is widely credited for having developed the modern-day detectors of laser light used in telephone technology and other telecommunications systems to receive voice and data over fiberoptics. As he has explained, "Anytime you make a long distance phone call, you use a laser and our patented detector." The Internet takes advantage of laser fiberoptic bundles to transfer vast amounts of data instantaneously. These same fiberoptic bundles can be used to transmit voice and television signals. They are more efficient than radio waves, and because they operate at a higher frequency, they can carry more information.[17]

Lasers are also being widely used by the military and in police work. What was very recently only possible in our imaginations—military combat involving light beams, as in *Star Wars*—is quickly on the way to becoming reality. Lasers are now used extensively to hone in on targets and to direct weapons to those targets. Today, lasers are used as "designators": A sensor in a "smart bomb" finds the target after a laser has marked it with invisible infrared light.

Closer to home, as many of us have found out, police are often using lasers, which are more accurate and less prone to user error, instead of radar technology to monitor the speed of automobiles. Other uses for medical, military, and industrial purposes will almost certainly be developed in the coming years.

LEDs (Light Emitting Diodes). Today, we all benefit from the use of LEDs: They are in our cars, our computers, and many other everyday items. Few people realize, however, that it was a professor of electrical engineering at the University of Illinois at Urbana-Champaign, Nick Holonyak, Jr., who invented these tiny semiconductor-based lights that are at the heart of CD players and computer optical drives. Some believe that LEDs will eventually replace incandescent and fluorescent lights in most lighting applications. And in the process, they will help cut energy consumption worldwide, since LEDs are more efficient and last up to a hundred times longer than incandescent lightbulbs.[18]

Bar Codes. The bar code, a combination of 30 lines and 29 spaces, is attached to almost everything we buy, from books to bubble gum, from airline tickets purchased online to iPods purchased at the Apple Store. Bar codes are used to inventory purchases and to glean information about who makes the purchases. A substantial amount of research was done at universities and in private industry to develop and introduce bar codes and scanners in the 1970s.

The first bar codes were developed at Drexel University in 1948, but they were not put to practical use until a bar-code system was installed in an Ohio supermarket in 1974. Initially, bar-code scanners involved the use of lasers—so utilizing them depended on the application of laser technology to this purpose. Scientists at the State University of New York at Stony Brook produced major advances in the algorithms for bar-code readers.[19] In the 1990s, other scanner technologies began to replace lasers as the preferred method for reading bar codes.

Radar. Work conducted at MIT's "Rad Lab" and other radiation labs during World War II led to the development of radar systems. Although this work was based on pure scientific research, it was undertaken with very immediate military needs in mind.[20] Radar systems have been used in automobiles to help prevent collisions. They can track weather formations and aircraft; detect speeding cars and wind speed; and are used in missile guidance systems and in air traffic control. They can be used to track migration patterns of animals, and have even been used to help us pin-point sites for archaeological excavations. Radar has been such an effective military tool that a great deal of scientific work has gone into identifying materials that might be used in military aircraft to avoid radar detection. Stealth technology, which can limit but not entirely avoid radar detection, is an example of such an effort.

Transistors. The transistor, the result of fruitful collaboration between physicists at university labs and physicists at industrial labs, transformed the world of electronics and modern communications. Much of the early work was done at the Bell Labs, where John Bardeen and Walter Brattain, along with William Shockley, built the first practical point-contact transistor in 1947.[21] A series of improvements followed, and the transistor turned out to be the fundamental building block of the circuitry that is used in computers, cell phones, and virtually all other modern electronics. Although Shockley was reluctant to share credit for the invention, the three men received the 1956 Nobel Prize for its creation, and its importance for modern technology cannot be overestimated.

Transistors are used in both digital and analog functions. They can be used individually, but they are almost always part of an integrated circuit. Today more than 1.5 billion transistors may be on a very small computer microchip. The low cost and reliability of transistors have made their use in digital computing and in electromechanical devices for machinery and household appliances almost ubiquitous. Transistors have many advantages over the older vacuum tubes that they replaced, although the old tubes continue to have advantages in some electronic devices, such as the high-end amplifiers used by audiophiles.

Superconductivity. Equally consequential discoveries were being made in the emerging field of condensed matter physics, which grew out of the field of solid-state physics. Now the largest field in American physics, it focuses on the macroscopic properties of matter. One of its concerns is superconductivity, the lack of electrical resistance in some materials at very low temperatures.

John Bardeen, who moved from Bell Labs to the University of Illinois following his participation in the development of the transistor, along with Leon Cooper of Brown University and John Robert Schrieffer, then a graduate student and Bardeen's research assistant, using the initial letters of their last names, proposed the fundamental "BCS theory" of superconductivity in 1957—although the phenomenon of superconductivity itself was first discovered in 1911. (Schrieffer's work on the BCS theory constituted his doctoral dissertation. He has since held numerous university positions.) The BCS theory solved a host of theoretical problems that had stymied some of the great minds in physics for almost thirty years.[22]

The more recent discovery of high temperature superconductors is being applied in a variety of ways in, for example, magnetic shielding devices, magnetic resonance imaging (MRI) systems, analog signal processing devices, infrared sensors, maglev trains, and microwave devices. Since superconductors allow us to conduct electricity with almost zero resistance, the applications for electrical transmission lines hold great promise. Because the size and speed of computer chips are constrained by the amount of heat that is generated, superconducting electronics are being widely used in digital technologies. In short, the basic ideas that emerged from this field of physics have proved their value, creating large new industries and their associated products.

Medical Diagnostics. In 1952, Stanford radiologist Henry Kaplan collaborated with Edward Ginzton at Stanford's Microwave Laboratory to build the first linear medical accelerator in the Western Hemisphere, a 6-million-volt, 6-foot-long machine to be used in radiation therapy for cancer patients. The first patient to be treated was a two-year-old boy who had lost one eye to retinoblastoma; his second eye was saved as a result of the X-ray treatment.[23]

When Kaplan came to Stanford he had one goal: to turn the ideas of physicists about linear accelerators into a medical device that could save the lives of people with cancer. According to Stanford University's description of the invention, "Fifty years and 40 million patients later, medical linear accelerators have become the backbone of radiation therapy for cancer worldwide. Roughly half of all cancer patients receive radiation therapy, primarily from the rays generated by a linear accelerator."[24]

MRI Technology. Many physicians believe that magnetic resonance imaging (MRI), which became viable in 1973, was the most important advance in diagnostic medical techniques in over a century. This tool allows physicians to quickly understand what is causing patients' symptoms so that they can receive proper treatment without delay.

Diagnosing medical problems is not always a straightforward process with clear-cut answers. A patient who is having severe headaches, for example, could be simply suffering from migraines, but it is also possible that he or she is in the first phase of a stroke. Physicians often have to decide what is going on in such situations very quickly. In the past, it sometimes involved a bit of guesswork. Today, however, physicians can use MRI equipment to help them make diagnostic judgments. Within a few minutes, in this example, a physician could determine whether there had been a stroke, and if so, whether brain damage had occurred, and pinpoint the part of the brain that might be at risk. MRI provides physicians with a window into all parts of the body without using invasive techniques, helping them to detect arterial sclerosis, ruptured disks, torn cartilage, and tumors, among a host of other physical abnormalities.

The origins of MRI can be traced to 1938 and the work of the physicist I. I. Rabi, who first described nuclear magnetic resonance and measured it in molecular beams. That work was interrupted by the war. But after World War II ended, Edward Purcell of Harvard rediscovered nuclear magnetic resonance in 1946. At Stanford, Felix Bloch (a Jewish émigré scientist who had left Germany in 1933) independently arrived at the same basic idea almost simultaneously. Purcell and Bloch received a Nobel Prize for this research. Herbert S. Gutowsky of the University of Illinois at Urbana-Campaign showed that nuclear magnetic resonance could be used to establish molecular structure and to measure rates of chemical and biological reactions and motion in solids. As a result of his work, nuclear magnetic resonance became a standard tool in chemistry, molecular biology, and medical imaging, foreshadowing the development of the MRI for medical diagnostics.

MRI technology shows once again how scientists can succeed through collaboration, building upon each other's work. Scores of scientists and engineers in the United States and Britain contributed to the instrument that hospitals and clinics use today. These include people in universities from the University of California and Washington University in St. Louis to the State University of New York at Stony Brook and to the work of Russell Varian, Richard Ernst, and Weston Anderson working at Varian Associates in Silicon Valley. MRI systems use a powerful magnet and radio waves to produce detailed images of organs and structures of the body. It is safe and painless, exceeding the quality of X-rays without the use of radiation. With MRI, a computer pieces together a three-dimensional image of the body part being scanned that is much clearer than any image that could be obtained through other methods. But MRI technology would not have become a reality without the development of high-speed computers that could handle enormous amounts of complex data. Nor could we have created the machinery without some British engineering feats that combined an X-ray machine and a computer that could scan the body from many directions. The computed tomography (CT) scan is another extremely useful diagnostic tool, but unlike MRI, it uses radiation to generate the images. MRI technology is especially valuable because, unlike X-rays, it can "see" through bone and define fluid-filled soft tissue. Some patients have found that the MRI apparatus induces claustrophobia; however, new machines have now been designed that should help to solve this problem.

A late twentieth-century extension of the MRI, known as functional magnetic resonance imaging (fMRI), can be used to map and explore human brain function. The fMRI allows researchers and clinicians to obtain high-resolution images of neural activity as detected by a signal that is dependent upon blood oxygen levels.[25] Seiji Ogawa of Bell Labs and Kenneth Kwong of Massachusetts General Hospital (affiliated with Harvard) have been among the pioneers in developing fMRI techniques, but the scientific and practical value of fMRI is being explored and extended at many of our great universities today. Researchers at Columbia University, for example, foresee the ability to directly observe brain function and believe that fMRI technology will allow us to advance our understanding of brain organization. It will also, they hope, help neuroscientists to create new standards for assessing neurological status and neurosurgical risk.[26]

At Columbia and other universities, scientists are applying fMRI methods to "identify brain structures uniquely involved with visual perceptions, language generation, comprehension of sequential information as in a movie, the execution of visually guided responses, and complex problem solving."[27] Although scientists know the general location of these brain functions, individual differences exist. The fMRI technology enables doctors to obtain the exact locations of these functions in individual patients who have suffered injuries and disease, which can cause shifts in the location of functions in the brain. Doctors can use fMRI technology to plan surgeries, to hone in on the areas to be included in radiation therapy, in stroke treatments, and in treating other types of brain disorders and injuries. Medical researchers are also using fMRI techniques to explore how to better manage pain in patients who are experiencing it.[28]

There are a few diagnostic alternatives to the MRI: CT scans, mentioned earlier; computerized axial tomography (CAT) scans; and positron emission tomography (PET) scans. All of these are derived from university-based research in the physical sciences. Like MRI, tomography allows the clinician to obtain three-dimensional images, enabling technicians to take pictures of body layers of any size and variable thickness. It has been used to monitor brain activity and in cancer detection, and it has revolutionized many areas of care and research.

The research that led to the PET scan was done at Massachusetts General Hospital, Ohio State University, the University of Pennsylvania, the University of California at Berkeley, and Sloan Kettering Institute in New York between the mid-1950s and the early 1990s. UCLA scientists Michael Phelps and Edward Hoffman developed the first functional PET system, and the UCLA Medical Center was the first to provide clinical PET services in the 1980s. The scanner developed at the University of Pennsylvania, called HEAD PENN-PET, incorporates the latest advances in the technology, with improvements in the sensitivity of the equipment and in the quality of the image resolution. Over the past decade, an increasing number of physicians have been using PET scans for brain imaging and other medical diagnostics—for example, for detecting malignant melanomas or diagnosing renal disease.[29]

Finally, diagnostic sonography, which uses safe ultrasound technology (involving frequencies above human hearing), images soft tissue, muscles, and bone surfaces. We can trace the origins of this technology back to the nineteenth century and the work of Pierre Curie in France and then to the work on radar and ultrasonic antisubmarine technology by physicists at MIT and elsewhere in the early 1940s. It is now widely used in prenatal care, allowing obstetricians to visualize the embryo and fetus and take measurements that can show whether there are abnormalities in the pregnancy. Besides enabling physicians to identify the sex of the fetus, ultrasound helps physicians to date pregnancies and allows them to monitor the growth and position of the fetus. In 1962, Joseph Holmes, William Wright, and Ralph Meyerdirk, working at the University of Colorado, produced the first compound-contact B-mode ultrasound scanner. Wright and Meyerdirk left the university to form a company, Physionic Engineering, to produce these scanners. They were the most popular devices at the time but have now been replaced by scanners using more advanced technology.

Biomedical Engineering. Biomedical engineering is a relatively new and multidisciplinary field that has gained substantial prominence at our major universities. Biomedical engineers most often work collaboratively with physicians and other health professionals designing new instruments, medical devices, and tools that promise to solve medical problems.

Among the more important areas of specialization are bioinstrumentation, which applies basic ideas drawn from electronics to diagnose and treat diseases. Biomaterials is another fascinating specialty in which scientists and engineers work to use live tissue and artificial materials for implantation.[30] Bioengineers work to develop metal alloys, ceramics, and composites that are nontoxic, noncarcinogenic, chemically inert and stable, and mechanically strong so that they can be implanted into the human body and withstand the rigors of everyday life. One other important focus of attention is in biomechanics, which applies the classical mechanics of fluids, solids, and thermodynamics to biological or medical problems. This research has led to the development of artificial hearts and heart valves, cardiac pacemakers, artificial kidneys, synthetic blood vessels, and artificial joint replacements. It may not be long before we will be able to grow cartilage and use the body's own materials rather than mechanical devices as substitutes for arthritic knees and worn-out shoulders. Almost all of this research is being carried out at top American universities. It is a very practically oriented field that has helped thousands of people already and holds even greater promise for therapeutic use in the future.

Although biomedical engineering is still in its neonatal stage of development, it has been growing rapidly, largely owing to the efforts of pioneers in the field at great universities. One of those is Chinese-born Professor Y. C. Fung, who was a faculty member at Caltech before moving to the University of California at San Diego. Considered the father of biomechanics, Fung focused on the interface between body movement and medicine[31] and coined the term "tissue engineering." His research has transformed the field of automotive safety design, since crash studies depend on studies of tissue response. The more than 36,000 sports medicine and body movement specialists who work in orthopedic surgery, occupational and physical therapy, and clinical athletic training follow the breakthroughs in biomechanics closely.

Another internationally renowned pioneer in bioengineering is Van C. Mow, who received degrees in applied mechanics and applied mathematics from Rensselaer Polytechnic Institute (RPI) in 1966. After working on mathematical models of ocean waves and acoustics for the development of sonar used to detect submarines, Mow turned his attention to the biomechanics of soft tissues.[32] At Columbia University, he has been particularly interested in articular cartilage in joints and worked to understand how these biological materials functioned in the body under unusual stress. Mow has worked with scores of students to develop both theories and experiments to study biological tissues.

EARTH SCIENCES: UNDERSTANDING OUR PLANET

The earth sciences have always attracted the attention of top scientists around the world. However, over the decades, Woods Hole Oceanographic Institution (affiliated with MIT), Scripps Institution of Oceanography (affiliated with the University of California at San Diego), and Lamont-Doherty Earth Observatory (affiliated with Columbia) have consistently made important contributions to these disciplines. My primary focus will be on the scientific contributions of these three institutions and the many practical results of their work.

Although Europeans did extraordinarily innovative work in the earth sciences preceding World War II, many of the most important discoveries in this field came after the war. Until then, we knew little about weather patterns or climate change. We did not know what produced the oceans, continents, mountains, and islands. Scientists assumed that the Earth's surface was essentially permanent and rigid, which could not have been further from the truth. In 1915, German scientist Alfred Wegener had proposed the idea of continental drift—that the continents were once a single mass that had drifted apart over time. Wegener's theory was resisted, and for good reason. He had little evidence to support his idea and he failed to provide a mechanism for continental drift.

Vilhelm Bjerknes, a Norwegian physicist and meteorologist, was a pioneer in applying mathematical techniques to weather forecasting. By 1917, he had formed the "Bergen School of Meteorology," and many of his students helped to develop the theory of the polar front. His rather primitive climate models laid a scientific foundation for later, more sophisticated attempts at modeling the motion of the oceans and the atmosphere. His son, Jacob Bjerknes, formulated some of the early theories about El Niño and the Southern Oscillation (ENSO)—the climate patterns of the tropical Pacific Ocean that have consequences for local weather patterns from droughts to hurricanes. One of Vilhelm's Swedish-born students, Carl-Gustav Rossby, carried on the intellectual tradition of the Bergen School at Woods Hole and later at the University of Chicago, where he made pioneering discoveries on the relationship between oceans and atmosphere and on problems of turbulence. At Chicago, he identified both the jet stream and "Rossby waves" in the atmosphere. After World War II he became interested in mathematically describing atmospheric dynamics in weather forecasting and in how this could be done with the use of electronic computers.[33] Rossby essentially founded the meteorology departments at MIT and Chicago. These were important early efforts that made modern weather forecasting feasible.

In the 1930s, Maurice "Doc" Ewing came along, a geophysicist who wanted to construct a larger theory of what created the oceans, continents, mountains, and volcanoes. Ewing believed it was necessary to accumulate vast amounts of data—drawn not only from the limited surface of the Earth, but also from the floors of the world's oceans—to devise truly scientific theories of the planet. He and his colleagues—and many of their students—became virtually obsessed with the collection and proper storage of core samples, which came to be called "Ewings." These efforts began in the 1930s while Ewing was at Lehigh University and continued after he moved to Columbia in 1947. When not taking cores, Ewing and his colleagues would work on developing new scientific instruments that would improve the data gathering. One of these was the first deep sea camera, which was "housed in a glass test tube about eight inches in diameter and four feet long, affectionately called the 'Pyrex Penis.' Its watertight seal was made from inner tubes, its reflectors out of coffee cans."[34]

Ewing and his team collected thousands of sediment cores that have been used for years in analyzing the ocean floors. Their work became the basis for the plate tectonics revolution and a theory of the movement of these plates over time that essentially demonstrated the drift of continents, the mechanisms behind the drift, the basis for large and small earthquakes, and a way of monitoring tension in the plates as they collided with each other. The techniques they developed for measuring how sound traveled through the oceans was used by the U.S. military in antisubmarine and mining operations during World War II.

At this time, Woods Hole scientists also took on military-related research and produced the bathythermograph, an instrument that was used to measure and record subsurface water temperature at various depths. The Navy used some aspects of Woods Hole discoveries to devise ways to search for enemy submarines and to prevent detection of U.S. submarines. Scientists at Woods Hole also worked on underwater explosives research and on improving underwater photography. With their knowledge of water currents that was based on precise measurements, they helped to predict the drift of aviators in life rafts and made wave and swell predictions for amphibious landings.[35]

Discoveries in the geosciences were based on the ability to amass huge amounts of data; scientists worked inductively from those data to test theoretical ideas. Ewing and his colleagues charted a series of mountainous ridges—some rising miles high—running north and south down the middle of the Atlantic. The ridges had a continuous V-shaped rift at their crests. Using these maps, Bruce Heezen and Marie Tharp, two of Ewing's collaborators, found that the earthquake epicenters tended to line up within the rift valley. The task was arduous and often tedious, but Ewing continued to map the oceans and take his samples and readings in all kinds of weather. The ships in the academic fleet were small at this time; like the early whaling vessels, they sometimes ran into real trouble. In the geosciences, gathering data could be hazardous, and it was not without drama, on some occasions.

Although the big breakthroughs in plate tectonics did not take place until the 1960s, the data were being put into place that would allow the ideas to come together.[36] When Bruce Heezen presented data on mid-ocean ridges in 1957, the Princeton geologist Harry Hess said, "Young man, you have shaken the foundations of geology!"[37] The ridges that

Ewing, Heezen, and Tharp had discovered "served as a border separating the face of the earth into sections, or plates," wrote Walter Sullivan, an exceptionally able science writer, in 1974. "At the edges of some oceans, however, particularly in the Pacific Ocean, Hess and others discovered trenches plunging miles below the seafloor," Sullivan explained. "Hess assembled the emerging assortment of geological clues to fashion a comprehensive theory, coined 'seafloor spreading' by . . . Robert Dietz [an Arizona State University geophysicist and oceanographer who collaborated with Hess]."[38] Unlike Wegener, Hess attempted to answer the question, How do the continents move? The theory of seafloor spreading held that continents were carried along as the ocean floor spread from the ridges. The scientific community remained skeptical until Fred J. Vine and Drummand Matthews of Cambridge University discovered "magnetic stripes" that formed at spreading centers of the mid-ocean ridges, which led to the Vine-Matthews hypothesis in 1963.[39]

Scientists working at several great research institutions, including Columbia, Princeton, MIT, Caltech, and Scripps, among others, now had sufficient empirical evidence to formulate the theory of plate tectonics. (Since that time substantially more evidence has been found.) The theory, according to the U.S. Geological Survey, holds that the Earth's surface is

> broken into a number of shifting slabs or plates, which average about 50 miles in thickness. These plates [roughly a dozen] move relative to one another above a hotter, deeper, more mobile zone at average rates as great as a few inches per year [about at the rate that a fingernail grows]. Most of the world's active volcanoes are located along or near the boundaries between shifting plates and are called "plate-boundary" volcanoes. . . . The peripheral areas of the Pacific Ocean Basin, containing the boundaries of several plates, are dotted by many active volcanoes that form the so-called "Ring of Fire."[40]

Scientists attempted to use the concepts of seafloor spreading and "plate tectonics" to explain volcanic eruptions and earthquakes. They also related them to other large-scale geologic features. Following the Vine-Matthews discoveries, Canadian geophysicist J. Tuzo Wilson of the University of Toronto, who had studied at Princeton in the late 1930s when Hess was a young lecturer, and American geophysicist Jason Morgan of Princeton

University, among many others, began to outline the theory of plate tectonics. Wilson's paper on "hot spots" was published in 1963 in a relatively obscure Canadian journal after having been rejected by the major scientific journals. It became a classic paper. He suggested that the Hawaiian and other volcanic island chains may have resulted from plates moving over stationary "hot spots" in the Earth's mantle. Morgan's paper establishing the kinematic framework for plate tectonics, published in 1968, is considered by many to be one of the most important milestones in twentieth-century American science.

Public interest in plate tectonics led extremely talented younger scientists into the fields of oceanography, geochemistry, atmospheric sciences, and seismology. The result has been a much better understanding of the dynamics of our planet and a host of practical returns. Today, for example, we typically receive four-day weather forecasts on our local television news programs that have a reasonably high level of accuracy. This was not possible twenty-five or thirty years ago. Scientists can predict and trace the path of tropical storms and hurricanes over vast parts of our oceans until they hit landmasses, and they can warn people well in advance about the intensity and likely effects of these storms. We can also predict extreme weather conditions in various parts of the world with increasing accuracy.

The quality of forecasting today can be illustrated by the 2008 monitoring of Hurricane Ike, which covered most of the Gulf of Mexico and hit Galveston and Houston, Texas, with winds exceeding 100 miles an hour. Although the hurricane caused great physical damage, given the intensity of the storm, public officials were able to save many lives by forewarning the local population and evacuating affected areas. As a result, the death toll was minimal compared to what it could have been without accurate forecasting. In fact, on the same day as the storm, more deaths occurred in Los Angeles as a result of a train collision. Much of the increased understanding of weather patterns is the result of research carried out by university professors at the leading earth observatories, places where modern oceanography was defined.

Using an early computer system, ENIAC, Jule Charney, R. Fjortoft, and John von Neumann produced the first successful numerical weather forecast in 1950 as part of a group at the Institute for Advanced Study at Princeton. Charney, one of the dominant figures in atmospheric science for three decades after World War II, moved to MIT and continued to produce important theory about the nature of atmospheric motions. Then, in the 1950s, Victor Starr and his collaborators at MIT created a description of the transformation of energy in the atmosphere. In the 1960s, Edward Loreng of MIT showed that there are systems so "sensitive to initial conditions" that small differences, within weeks, can lead to very large differences in the state of the atmosphere. In other words, weather is not entirely predictable. This proved to be a transforming revelation. At the same time, Richard Lindzen at Harvard solved a problem of atmospheric tides that had been formulated by Pierre-Simon Laplace in a set of linear partial differential equations 150 years earlier.[41] This effort to make meteorology into a science was a truly international effort, involving leading university scientists from England, Sweden, and Norway as well as the United States.

Columbia University professor of oceanography and climate change Mark Cane, and his former student Steve Zebiak, worked on tropical oceans in the mid-1980s, devising the first numerical model to simulate El Niño and the Southern Oscillation. In 1985, they "used this model to make the first physically based forecasts of El Niño."[42] The Zebiak-Cane model is one of the most important tools scientists have for work on ENSO. There are now a fair number of similar models for El Niño, and they help meteorologists predict weather patterns and hurricanes around the world. Although Cane and Zebiak's contribution to our knowledge has been significant, many other scientists and researchers at other American universities have been working on the same set of problems and contributing to our understanding and prediction of weather patterns.[43] The ability to forecast long-term weather patterns and extreme changes in weather on the basis of the El Niño models is a benefit to both rich and poor nations.

Although the ability to predict earthquakes with precision has lagged behind weather forecasting, seismologists and geoscientists have learned much about fault lines and tectonic plates. Local governments can use this information to craft building codes that take the likelihood of earthquake activity into account, and architectural engineers have devised building methods that can reduce the likelihood of earthquake damage. The Richter scale, widely known as the standard for measuring the severity of earthquakes, was the result of work at Caltech by Charles F. Richter and his collaborator Beno Gutenberg in 1935.[44]

Years later, in the 1990s and 2000s, seismologists Paul G. Richards and Xiodong Song from Columbia University, aided by four of their students, discovered that the inner core of the Earth is rotating eastward with respect to the mantle and crust. In Richards's words, the "seismic waves through the inner core on path from the South Sandwich Islands to Alaska have a travel time that gets smaller by about a tenth of a second per decade." This means that the inner core of the Earth will rotate through one revolution inside the mantle every 1,000 years.[45] In addition, Richards and his colleagues, along with colleagues in Russia and Kazakhstan, have become the world's experts in differentiating underground nuclear tests from other seismic phenomena, such as earthquakes.[46] Richards's research on explosions has become the basis for the detection, identification, and location of underground tests of varying sizes. As he says, "these issues are critical in evaluating present and prospective arms-control treaties."

Many scientists are collecting data and presenting evidence on the causes of global climate change and suggesting possible methods for slowing down the rate of change. In 1958, years before people like James Hansen of NASA's Goddard Institute for Space Studies and Columbia University began documenting the trend toward global warming and the role that human-caused forces have played in the warming tendency,[47] Charles David Keeling at Scripps began to conduct continuous monitoring of atmospheric CO_2. Taking readings at the South Pole and the Mauna Loa Observatory in Hawaii, he worked on the impact of the carbon cycle on changes in climate. The patterns he documented produced the "Keeling curve," the cornerstone of climate change research. Keeling reported a rising level of CO_2 within a few years of beginning to record these measurements, and as a result, the National Oceanic and Atmospheric Administration (NOAA) began monitoring atmospheric CO_2 worldwide in the 1970s.

Working at Columbia's Lamont Geological Observatory, Wallace S. Broecker, then a graduate student, soon became fascinated by the Keeling Curve and began studying geochemistry and climate change. Broecker, who would become perhaps the world's most distinguished interpreter of the Earth's operation as an integrated biological, chemical, and physical system, advanced methods of "measuring the radiocarbon content of ocean water and the accumulation of deep sea and lake sediments, using this data to trace ocean circulation patterns over time."[48] His research led to a far greater appreciation of the ocean's influence on atmospheric carbon dioxide levels and on processes of global climate change. And, he coined the phrase "global warming," which first appeared in one of his scientific papers in the mid-1970s.

Although the study of global warming has been an international collaboration, few scientists have been equal to Wally Broecker and James Hansen in demonstrating the science behind the conclusions of global-warming theories and the effects of human behavior on climate change. American university science has produced a good deal of the work that has modeled the process and rate of increase of global warming.

The ozone layer of Earth's atmosphere, like global warming, is an issue that has garnered attention internationally among both political leaders and the general public. In the 1970s, scientists in England and the United States began demonstrating that an ozone hole existed in the atmosphere above Antarctica, that it was expanding, and that, if left unchecked, it would eventually pose great health hazards to humans, such as overexposure to harmful ultraviolet (UV) radiation that could cause skin cancer. They proved that this ozone depletion was being caused by manmade compounds called chlorofluorocarbons (CFCs), which had uses in a variety of modern conveniences, such as air conditioning and cooling systems, aerosol sprays, and even Styrofoam cups. These discoveries had huge policy implications. In 1987, the Montreal Protocol was opened for signatures. One hundred and fifty nations agreed to phase out CFC production in order to reduce the number of CFCs released into the environment. The protocol was amended seven times in the 1990s. Scientists predict that if signatories continue to follow the protocol, the ozone layer could recover by 2050.

CFCs had been invented in the 1920s in an effort to find nontoxic substances that could be used as refrigerants. Although the ban on CFCs instituted by the treaty is having an effect, it will take another forty or fifty years for the ozone layer in Antarctica to return to the levels of the 1970s.[49] In 1978, the United States banned the use of CFCs in aerosols. In 1995, F. Sherwood Rowland and Mario Molina from the University of California at Irvine and Paul J. Crutzen from Max-Planck-Institut für Chemi (Otto Han Institute) in Mainz, Germany, received the Nobel Prize for showing "how sensitive the ozone layer is to the influence of anthropogenic emissions of certain compounds." The scientists had also explained the mechanisms that influenced the thickness of the ozone layer, thereby, according to the Nobel committee, contributing to "our salvation from a global environment problem that could have catastrophic consequences."[50]

British scientists were actually the first to report a drop in the ozone layer. But among the important contributors to the discovery that human activity could harm the Earth's atmosphere was Harold Johnston, a professor of chemistry at Berkeley. Although Johnston's work was initially resisted and attacked, subsequent discoveries proved him to be correct. In 1973, University of Michigan scientists Richard Stolarski and Ralph Cicerone[51] discovered the stratospheric chlorine chain reaction that was responsible for depletion of ozone. In 1984, British scientists led by geophysicist Joseph Farman detected a 40 percent ozone loss over Antarctica during spring in the Southern Hemisphere, and in 1986–1987, leading climate scientist Susan Solomon from Berkeley and other scientists found that the ozone loss was associated with atomic chlorine and chlorine oxide radicals. Further confirmation of the ozone hole's existence came with NASA satellite data produced in 1985.

The CFCs in the atmosphere have been reduced, and the ozone layer is very gradually recovering. Many other environmental problems remain, however, particularly the threat of global warming. As we will see in Chapter 13, under the George W. Bush administration there were attempts to censor science when it offended those in political power. But issues such as these are examples of how science can play a crucial role in policymaking. There are many times when scientific research can help to solve mysteries that capture the public imagination—for example, scientists from Woods Hole in 1985 were able to use a small underwater research submersible to find the sunken RMS *Titanic* and reveal the interior of the ship. But it is through research on monumental problems such as earthquake detection, hurricane predictions, the ozone, and global warming that science—and university research—can have their greatest impact on the future.

THE BIRTH AND DEVELOPMENT OF COMPUTER TECHNOLOGY

Few people would dispute the claim that the modern computer and the ensuing information revolution have dramatically changed our lives. Only sixty years ago, few could have imagined this transformation; we barely knew what computers were capable of doing. The history of the computer, in which American science and technology have played the dominant roles for decades, is a complex one involving the interdependence of our research universities, our military, our major government funding agencies, and our most innovative industrial laboratories.

The division of labor throughout this period of revolutionary change involved all four of these segments of society. The federal government, initially through the Department of Defense, made substantial investments in computer science, targeting military uses. Later, the National Science Foundation and other federal agencies supported the discipline at American universities. This infusion of taxpayer dollars—which increased from roughly $65 million in 1976 to $265 million in 1995—went largely to research universities, fueling the rapid expansion of computer science at these institutions.[52] Federal dollars also created opportunities for faculty to launch "spin-off" companies such as Sun Microsystems. The increasing number of professionals in the field, in turn, helped in the quest to build faster and more reliable computers, leading eventually to the emergence of the Internet and the World Wide Web.

The strategic role of the federal government in this endeavor should not be underestimated. The effort was organized as an open, quasi-academic enterprise that did not give private firms or industries a competitive advantage in patenting innovations fundamental to the development of the field. This changed over time as the costs of innovation grew; the government by the 1970s was moving toward greater privatization of the effort to build faster and better computer chips, turning instead to support for new software applications and search engines. In all of this, the research universities played a critical role in several ways: They developed basic knowledge in areas of computer science and technology that could be used for creating the framework of a computer system and for building faster and smaller components of computers, ultimately in the private sector, and they trained highly skilled programmers and hardware and software experts who went to work for new, innovative start-up companies. Individual firms, often led by visionary and entrepreneurial leaders who held Ph.D.s in science or engineering, built enormously successful businesses that moved mainframe computers from large research or industrial settings to the home. Each of these elements was essential for the revolution in computers and later for the development of the Internet. Industry played an important role as well, taking young, highly talented and entrepreneurial science and engineering Ph.D. students and giving them intellectual freedom (similar to what they would have experienced at research universities) and support. It became, in fact, difficult for universities to compete with industry for some of the best minds in the emerging field of computer science.

Many of the most notable innovations in computer technology—such as microprocessors, chips with random access memory, Ethernet connectivity for local area networks, and the first personal computers—have been made by highly trained individuals working in industrial laboratories and offices. The universities have provided a steady flow of this talent, with many of the leaders of the technological revolution earning several degrees from top universities before working in the private sector. Robert Metcalfe, co-inventor of the Ethernet, is a good example of this. After receiving two degrees from MIT, one in electrical engineering and the other from the Sloan School of Management, he traveled across Cambridge for his graduate work, receiving master's and doctoral degrees in applied mathematics from Harvard by 1973. His doctoral dissertation was on packet switching (discussed below), and he wrote it while working at MIT's Project MAC (Project on Mathematics and Computation), a project established in 1963 with a $2 million grant from the federal Defense Advanced Research Projects Agency (DARPA) to focus on problems of artificial intelligence. By 1973 Metcalfe was working at Xerox PARC. It was at this time that he co-invented the Ethernet, which has become the international standard for connecting computers over short distances. The other inventor was David Boggs, a Ph.D. in electrical engineering from Stanford who was also working at Xerox PARC. By 1979, Metcalfe had left Xerox and founded 3Com, a company that manufactured computer networking equipment. Boggs later co-founded LAN Media Corporation.

It would be impossible in one chapter to describe every major breakthrough made by university-trained personnel working at America's technology firms. Here we will look just briefly at a few of the major milestones and discoveries of the computer revolution. Initially, most of the research and innovations were centered on the hardware that made up computers; later, the focus changed to innovative software and the remarkable applications that were developed for specific purposes. Computers have at once made the world smaller and the pace of our lives faster, while creating unprecedented opportunities for people around the globe to access knowledge. Because of these now-ubiquitous machines, certain jobs have been eliminated while others have been created, with a revolutionary impact on almost all sectors of our economy. The computer has become an indispensable tool for virtually all forms of academic research and training. It is equally indispensable for almost every kind of business, institution, and nonprofit group.

Although the idea of computers was first conceived centuries ago, most historians of technology begin the modern history of computers with the work of Konrad Zuse, a Berlin construction engineer who invented a series of automatic calculators around the beginning of World War II to help with engineering calculations. These were the first freely programmable computers.[53] Working at Iowa State University between 1939 and 1942, Professor John Atanasoff and his graduate student Clifford Berry built the first electronic digital computer—the Atanasoff-Berry Computer. Their major innovation was to include a binary system of arithmetic, parallel processing, regenerative memory, and a separation of memory and computing functions.[54] Atanasoff and Berry found themselves later in a priority fight with J. Presper Eckert and John Mauchly, who were the first to patent a digital computing device, the ENIAC computer.

ENIAC I (the name is an acronym for Electrical Numerical Integrator and Calculator) was born in 1946. The U.S. military sponsored Eckert and Mauchly's research with the goal of producing a new device for writing artillery-firing tables. Scientists at the Ballistics Research Laboratory (BRL) had heard of Mauchly's research on calculators at the University of Pennsylvania in the early 1940s. In 1943, the military commissioned the development of a new computer and named Mauchly as the chief consultant, and Eckert, who had met Mauchly as a graduate student in 1943 at the Moore School of Electrical Engineering, became the chief project engineer. After one year of design work and another eighteen months of construction, costing the government the not inconsiderable sum at the time of $500,000, the ENIAC was built. The military immediately put it to work making calculations that went into the design of the hydrogen bomb. It was also used to help make weather predictions, in cosmic-ray studies, and in random number studies and wind-tunnel design.[55]

The ENIAC contained about 17,500 vacuum tubes, 70,000 resistors, 10,000 capacitors, 1,500 relays, 6,000 manual switches, and 5 million soldered joints. It covered 1,800 square feet of floor space, weighed 30 tons, consumed 160 kilowatts of electrical power—and was far less powerful than one of today's MacBook Pro laptop computers. But the ENIAC, which was then 1,000 times faster than anything that had preceded it, could perform 5,000 additions, 357 multiplications, or 38 divisions in a second. Vacuum tubes were key—they increased the speed. In 1948, mathematician John Von Neumann modified the ENIAC so that it could do serial operations. In 1946, Eckert and Mauchly launched a computer company and built the BINAC, which used magnetic tape to store data. The company was purchased by the Univac Division of Remington Rand, which developed the UNIVAC (Universal Automatic Computer) in 1951.

A patent infringement case actually voided the ENIAC patent, with the court ruling that it was an infringement of Atanasoff's invention. In fact, Eckert and Mauchly received the lion's share of credit for the development of the electronic computer, although many historians now believe that the Atanasoff-Berry computer was actually the first.

By 1944, Howard Aiken and Admiral Grace Hopper designed the Mark I computer at Harvard University. It was 55 feet long and 8 feet high and weighed 5 tons; it contained about 760,000 separate pieces and was controlled by pre-punched paper tape. Used by the U.S. Navy for gunnery and ballistic calculations, it was in operation until 1959. Although it took this somewhat clunky machine three to five seconds to perform a single multiplication operation, it was capable of handling special logarithmic and trigonometric functions using numbers with up to 23 decimal places.

Aiken and Hopper were extraordinary innovators. An electrical engineer and physicist who received his Ph.D. from Harvard, Aiken had remained in Cambridge to work on the idea of the Mark I with three other engineers, including Grace Hopper.[56] Hopper was born in New York City in 1906 and educated at Vassar College and then Yale, where she earned a Ph.D. in mathematics in 1934. She resigned her academic appointment at Vassar to join the Navy in December 1943. Originally commissioned as a lieutenant, she was assigned to work on the Bureau of Ordnance Computation Project at Harvard under Aiken, who was a professor and naval research lieutenant.

Hopper's most significant contributions to computing were the invention of the computer language APT and verification of COBOL, the computer program that takes English language instructions and translates them into the computer language of the targeted computer. Her work foreshadowed a great deal of what would develop in more sophisticated form in digital computing, including subroutines, formula translation, relative addressing, the linking loader, and code optimization. Hopper coined the term "bug" for a computer flaw and was the first person to "debug" a computer, which turned out to be a moth that was causing hardware problems in the Mark I. She also designed the first English-language data-processing compiler, known as Flow-Matic. In a 1981 extended interview with Harriet Zuckerman and me, Hopper spoke of her vision for the future of computers and computer science: "At any given moment I think we underestimate where the computer is going. Just as the people who built the first prop airplanes couldn't have dreamed of jets. I have no idea what we'll see. But I know we're only at the beginning. . . . We're going to see a change in the computer industry as great as Model Ts made."[57]

In 1952, the Digital Computer Laboratory at the University of Illinois combined the administrative and technological talent of Louis N. Ridenour, the mathematical ability of Abraham H. Taub, and the electrical engineering background of Ralph E. Meagher to develop the first digital computer built and owned entirely by an educational institution. Called the ILLIAC I, it weighed 5 tons and contained 2,800 vacuum tubes. The ILLIAC series continued with ILLIAC II, a transistorized computer, and culminated in the mid-1960s with the ILLIAC IV supercomputer, the largest and the fastest in the world at the time.

It did not take long for smart businessmen to recognize the potential market for computers and to set up research and development operations to produce them. At this time, it was the large mainframe computers that were to be manufactured; the smaller personal computers did not appear for almost thirty years. International Business Machines (IBM) entered the picture in a big way in 1953 with the production of the IBM 701 EDPM, developed as part of the Korean War effort, which turned out to be the first commercially successful general-purpose computer. Apparently, Thomas Watson, Jr., had to convince his father, who was the CEO of IBM, that the production of these computers wouldn't undermine IBM's lucrative punch-card processing business.

IBM manufactured nineteen 701s and rented them out for a monthly fee of $15,000 apiece. The machine led to the development by John Barkus and IBM of the important high-level computer language FORTRAN in 1954. There followed a 700 series of IBM computers, each with significant upgrades in speed. The IBM 7090 computer was the fastest in the world in 1960, and for the next two decades IBM dominated the mainframe and minicomputer market. With great intelligence, IBM began to court the potential market for computing at universities, offering them 60 percent discounts on some of their equipment with an eye to establishing a close manufacturer-client relationship. Finally, in 1981, IBM manufactured its first personal computer, called the IBM PC.

In 1955, the Stanford Research Institute (SRI), Bank of America (BofA), and General Electric began working on the first bank industry computer and methods for reading checks using magnetic ink character recognition. Today, we take it for granted that banks must use computers to keep records of deposits and withdrawals and to keep their accounts up to date; to read optically scanned checks and signed overdrafts; and to perform a host of other functions. Sophisticated online banking capabilities and computers that handle most back-office work are standard. But computers did not exist to perform these functions back in the 1950s; it all began when the nation's largest bank at the time, BofA, asked SRI to create the capabilities. The first phase of the project was launched in 1955 when SRI rolled out ERMA (the Electronic Record Method of Accounting).[58]

Another major stage in the development of computers involved three visionaries, Gordon Moore and Robert Noyce, cofounders of Intel, and Andrew Grove, one of Intel's first employees, director of operations. Grove, an émigré from the Hungarian Revolution, had been a student at the City College of New York and the University of California at Berkeley, where he had earned a doctorate in chemical engineering in 1963. He'd had a brief stint at Fairchild Semiconductor. Moore, who had worked with William Shockley and had Ph.D.s in both chemistry and physics from Caltech, had not yet formulated the famous "law" bearing his name that stated that the capacity of computer chips would double every two years. Noyce had co-founded Fairchild Semiconductor, and that is where Grove and Moore had met him. When Intel manufactured the first dynamic random access memory (DRAM) chips in 1970 and the first commercial microprocessor chip in 1971, it started an electronics revolution.

Noyce and Grove had contrasting management styles, with Grove being far more competitive than Noyce. Grove is famous for his motto: "Only the paranoid survive," and Grove is credited with making Intel the world's largest producer of sophisticated microprocessors. As the speed and capacity of the chip increased, the price per unit of operation fell precipitously, enabling individuals and families to purchase affordable computers for home use.

The interaction between industry and research universities is illustrated again in the invention of the integrated circuit by Jack L. Kilby, who worked at Texas Instruments (TI) and at several universities, including Texas A&M, from 1958 through 1970. In fact, in 1958, Kilby and Noyce both discovered the integrated circuit, working independently of each other. Both were able to place what had previously been separated—transistors, resistors, capacitors, and all the connecting wiring—onto a single crystal, or "chip." Kilby used germanium as a semiconductor material, whereas Noyce used silicon. Both companies applied for and received patents on their discoveries in 1959.

The companies cross-licensed their patented materials and created a global business. A worldwide integrated circuit market, whose sales in 2006 totaled roughly $210 billion, grew from Kilby's simple circuit design.[59] Kilby also headed teams of researchers at TI that built the first computer incorporating integrated circuits, as well as the handheld calculator and the thermal printer. He received the 2000 Nobel Prize in Physics for his discovery of the integrated circuit. President Bill Clinton wrote of his achievement: "You can take pride in the knowledge that your work will help to improve lives for generations to come."[60]

Considerable interaction has taken place between industry and academia in the development of advanced microprocessors, semiconductors, software, and the like. Many people have worked to make computers user-friendly for those who are not familiar with programming, computer languages, and other highly technical subjects. Over the past few decades, university researchers have contributed greatly to the development of new uses for the computer, designing software applications, computer games, and other applications widely used by professionals, students, and the general public.

A number of America's great research universities have been particularly strong in computer science, contributing disproportionately to some of the innovations in the field. Few have been as active in this field as Carnegie Mellon University (CMU). Researchers at CMU were the first to create a distributed computing environment with what we now call "e-mail" (their "Andrew" system), including the concept of "attachments" to e-mail. CMU was also the first university to develop and implement the idea of the "search engine." Researchers there formed a spin-off company named Lycos that produced one of the first search engines available for wider use.

Scientists and engineers from many universities worked with National Science Foundation support to develop computer-aided design (CAD) and computer-aided manufacturing (CAM). Every major architectural school or significant architectural firm in the world relies heavily today on CAD, and CAM has revolutionized manufacturing processes in the United States as well as in many foreign nations. With these tools, architects, as well as designers in other fields—such as engineers designing aircraft and satellites, automobiles, manufacturing equipment, and a variety of products—can create three-dimensional images and detailed plans that can easily be modified as desired over time as the item undergoes further development. Another application of these technologies has been in creating "virtual" models of products and the assembly of those products.

The work on CAD and CAM began at Carnegie Mellon and elsewhere in the early 1970s. Faculty members at the University of Rochester produced the first practical software for three-dimensional designs. By 1982, computer software had advanced to the point that the Boeing 777 aircraft could be virtually modeled and assembled through the use of CAD and CAM. In the late 1980s and early 1990s, Professor Christos Yessios did the initial research for the development of Form-Z, a world-renowned 3-D modeling software (a type of CAD), while in the School of Architecture at Ohio State University. Yessios went on to develop one of the leading 3-D modeling software companies in the world. Form-Z was the most popular CAD software among architectural and design firms in the United States and the developed world as of 2003.

In 1980, a Ph.D. student at the University of Michigan, Thomas Knoll, wrote a program to produce grayscale images on a monochrome display. The program, called Display, intrigued his brother John, who encouraged

Thomas to turn it into a full-fledged image-editing program. Taking a half-year break from his graduate work, Thomas Knoll collaborated with his brother and created a program named ImagePro. In 1988, Thomas renamed the program Photoshop. John pitched the program to engineers at Apple Computer as well as to Russell Brown, the art director at Adobe Systems. The sales pitch worked. In September 1988, Adobe purchased the license to distribute the program. Thomas worked on program code in Ann Arbor while John was working on plug-ins in California. Photoshop 1.0 was released in 1990 for Macintosh exclusively. As of 2007, Photoshop has become the industry standard for image-editing programs.[61]

In 1985, the NSF began to support five national centers for supercomputing. These facilities were located at major universities but could be used by academic researchers from around the country. One of the major goals was to establish partnerships with business, and although the businesses would not set the agenda for research or exert any control over the results, they were well positioned to benefit from the research. The scale and scope of the research conducted at these national centers has grown dramatically since they were founded, and the number of national, international, and industrial collaborative projects has risen accordingly. In 2006, as part of its science education program, the San Diego supercomputer was used to produce animation showing the birth of our solar system for a show at Hayden Planetarium, for example.[62] And in 2009, biophysicists at the University of Pennsylvania used the facility at Illinois to "clarify a mysterious interaction between cholesterol and neurotransmitter receptors."[63]

Thousands of researchers and students used the computing and data systems at these supercomputing centers in support of hundreds of projects every year—there were 800 projects represented in 2006 alone. The five original sites were the University of California at San Diego, the University of Illinois at Urbana-Champaign, Cornell University, the University of Pittsburgh, and the John von Neumann Center at Princeton University.

The University of Illinois site played a role in the development of Mosaic, the first widely used web browser, as it was written by Marc Andreessen (who later cofounded Netscape) and Eric Bina while they were working at the university's supercomputing center. Mosaic allowed users to display and interact with text information, videos, music, and other images, and it was an important factor in the emergence of the World Wide Web and the Internet. Mosaic was eventually licensed to Spyglass and became the foundation for Internet Explorer. The Illinois center has been a pioneer in computer visualization as well. Donna Cox of the School of Art and Design, director of the advanced visualization laboratory at the university's supercomputing center, created the Oscar-nominated IMAX film *Cosmic Voyage* and many PBS *Nova* episodes that have captivated millions of viewers, such as "Hunt for the Supertwister" and "Runaway University."[64]

Computer visualization techniques are used in weather prediction, architecture, surgical and radiation therapy planning, medical diagnosis, mapping and cartography, industrial and interior design, urban planning and design, and mathematics. In the social sciences, it is used in modeling decision-making systems as well as in making graphic data displays. In education, there are uses in programs designed to improve visual thinking skills. Computer visualization has become an essential tool in scientific research and is now used in a wide range of science applications. The subfields of computer visualization, which include computer graphics, animation, and virtual reality, have been pioneered at many research universities with the support of NSF funding. In 1993, scientists at New York University created the first three-dimensional animated model of a beating heart. At about the same time, researchers at the University of Illinois "created a model that provides a closer look at updrafts, downdrafts and strong horizontal changes in wind speed—all of great use to air traffic controllers, airline pilots, flight trainers and meteorologists."[65]

Next we will look at four aspects of computer technology that demonstrate the important role that universities have played in its development in recent years. We begin with the Internet, then look at Google, the MIT Media Library, and MEMS technology (along with nanotechnology).

The Emergence of the Internet.[66] The Internet began as a focused, government-funded project with its origins in NSFnet, which linked a few universities together in a computer network that transferred 56,000 bits of information per second. It is now a massive international phenomenon with more than 625 million hosts, as of 2009. It is accommodating more voice and video than ever before, and its capacity has been projected to be exhausted by 2010 unless billions of dollars are spent to enlarge the infrastructure.[67] The Internet is part of almost every American's daily life.[68] (The Internet should be distinguished from its sister, the World Wide

Web, which is a software innovation that enabled many millions of people to access the Internet for easy personal use.[69])

Simple new ideas often turn out to have huge consequences. A change in the way computer scientists thought about networks, for example, made the Internet possible. Rather than trying to link all individual computers, researchers began to recast the idea of a network in terms of "a network of networks." As historians of technology David C. Mowery and Timothy Simcoe have said, "The distinction turns on the idea of open standards. By adopting a set of publicly available protocols and ensuring that any suitably constructed network can communicate with any other using these standards, the Internet allows network users to share information and applications despite idiosyncratic differences in local computing and communications technologies."[70]

By creating these standards, the government maximized the network's chances for rapid growth and paved the way for further innovations in the protocols while reducing the risk of any individual innovator or company gaining too much market power. Mowery and Simcoe characterized this structure for innovation as "quasi-academic" in its use of government, industrial, and academic expertise to grow the network's capabilities. A massive collaboration between these various sectors produced an environment with many of the core values found at universities, including a collaborative system of open communication.

Between 1960 and 1985, a set of major innovations in the structure of the Internet facilitated its growth. Leonard Kleinrock at MIT and Paul Baran of the RAND Corporation developed the theory of "packet switching." This was an architecture, still used today, that allowed information in a single communication, such as an e-mail message, to be broken up into a series of discrete packets by the sending computer. Unlike a single circuit in a telephone call in which each communication is allocated its own connection, packet switching allowed the packets from a single communication to take very different routes from the sender to the receiver. This architecture had both efficiency and performance advantages over the older Bell system and allowed others to create modifications and improvements on the original design.

The breakthrough led the Defense Advanced Research Projects Agency to fund the construction of a prototype network. In 1969, DARPA granted a contract to a Cambridge, Massachusetts, firm, BBN Technologies, which was in fact a spin-off company founded by two MIT professors, Leo Beranek and Richard Bolt, to do the development work. The company produced a switch called an Interface Message Processor (IMP) that linked computers in a wide-area network.[71] This was the beginning of ARPAnet, which led to the invention of e-mail.

Vint Cerf is perhaps the person most often referred to as "the father of the Internet." He was educated at Stanford and then took his Ph.D. at UCLA, where he participated in Leonard Kleinrock's data-packet networking group. At UCLA he met Robert Kahn, who was also working on the ARPAnet hardware architecture. Cerf became an assistant professor at Stanford. There, from 1973 to 1976, he focused on packet-networking protocols and, with Kahn, codesigned the Department of Defense TCP/IP protocol. TCP (Transmission Control Protocol) allowed "peer" networks (distinct and physically separated networks) to connect in order to exchange data. The idea of connectivity among networks, which were linked by "gateways," represented a major advance. The TCP protocol was eventually subdivided into two pieces, TCP and IP (Internet Protocol). The TCP/IP protocol was reliable and has several advantages over earlier network architecture. It is still used today and, perhaps most importantly, it was an open standard. That meant that others who were using it could make improvements in it, because anyone who belonged to the networking community had free access to a complete description of the protocol.

The "spin-off" companies and new start-ups proved instrumental in the commercialization of the Internet. Some companies, such as BBN, Novelle, and 3Com, had major roles to play in Internet infrastructure, and others, such as AOL, Prodigy, and Compuserve, became Internet Service Providers for the general public. Most companies like these had close ties to the research universities; many were conceived of by graduates and professors.

One can imagine the potential democratizing effect of the Internet in bringing knowledge to those who have access to high-speed computers and connectivity but who are physically remote from the seats of higher learning in the United States. I have no doubt that future generations of the Internet and the World Wide Web will be widely used by research universities for educational purposes, both for free and as commercial enterprises. The Internet business phenomenon will continue to expand throughout the world, and many new and complex public policy problems will arise, including issues related to intellectual property rights, issues related to tax policies for Internet businesses, and cross-national or global policy issues.

If Cerf is the putative father of the Internet, then Tim Berners-Lee holds the same title for the World Wide Web. When the Web was born, he was not at a research university but at the world's largest particle physics laboratory, CERN (originally the Conseil Européen pour la Recherche Nucléaire). CERN is akin to a multi–research university consortium. It houses hundreds of university scientists working on basic physics problems, many of whom hold faculty positions at leading universities around the world. Berners-Lee was attempting to solve a problem for the scientists working at CERN. Educated at Oxford's Queen's College, where he built his first computer and graduated in 1976, he wrote a program called "Enquire" in 1980 while consulting for CERN, and it formed the basis for the development of the World Wide Web.

In 1989, Berners-Lee proposed a hypertext project that would allow people to collaborate or work together by combining their knowledge in a web of hypertext documents. He called it the World Wide Web. The innovation was to link hypertext to the Internet. Berners-Lee wrote the first World Wide Web server, "httpd," and the first "WorldWideWeb" hypertext browser and editor. This program, "WorldWideWeb," was first made available on the Internet in the summer of 1991. Berners-Lee continued to improve it based upon user feedback across the Internet.[72] In 1994, he moved to MIT, where he founded the World Wide Web Consortium at the Laboratory for Computer Science. He continues to coordinate Web developments through the collaborative work of researchers from around the world.

Google. "To google" has become a part of our lexicon, achieving the status of a verb in the Oxford English Dictionary (OED). The development of ever more sophisticated search engines has been part of the history of computer science for years, and an increasing number of university researchers have taken an interest in how computer algorithms could make searching through vast amounts of information more practical and efficient. The results have been mind-boggling, but despite Google's current position, many university computer scientists see a future in which today's Google will seem primitive and inefficient compared to search engines using even more sophisticated methods.[73]

The "Google Boys," Larry Page and Sergey Brin, were graduate students at Stanford University working on their doctoral degrees when they developed the algorithm for their Internet search engine. Page invented PageRank, patented by the Trustees of Stanford University in 2001—a way of calculating the popularity and relevance of web pages based on the number of links to it from other web pages. Page and Brin had suspected that analyzing the relationships between websites would produce better ranking than previous techniques, which were based on the number of times a search term appeared on a given page. The two Ph.D. students found that pages that had the most links to other highly relevant web pages would also be the most relevant for the person who was searching for information. Originally dubbed "BackRub" because it checked backlinks, their search engine initially used the domain name google.stanford.edu. It operated on Stanford servers in 1996 and 1997. The company google.com came into being in September 1997 and was fully incorporated as Google, Inc., a year later in a friend's garage in Menlo Park, California.

Stanford held the intellectual property rights to the algorithm until the company paid the university handsomely in stock and cash, plus annual royalties for the exclusive licensing rights in 1998 (an agreement subsequently amended several times). This was like déjà vu, recalling the much earlier development of Hewlett-Packard in another garage on the Stanford University campus. In that same Stanford tradition, but now in a much more mature Silicon Valley, the "Google Boys" built one of the largest and most successful computer software companies in the world—and one that many of us depend upon on a daily basis. As of 2009, Google employed approximately 20,000 people in offices around the world, about 8,000 of whom work at the famous "Googleplex" campus in Mountain View, California. This is far fewer than other computer-industry companies, such as Hewlett-Packard, which employed more than 300,000 employees, or IBM, with almost 400,000 employees in 2009. Google is famous for the unusual set of fringe benefits it offers, including free meals, an on-site health-care center, and on-site gyms, massages, game rooms, dry-cleaning services, and even haircuts. Employees can spend up to 20 percent of their worktime each week pursuing a special project of their own choice—a rule that has led to several innovative advances.[74] The company's success is largely due to its online advertising. By 2008, the market capitalization of Google was estimated to be near $158 billion, roughly the same value as that of IBM and Apple Computer. Both Google and Apple have a way to go if they hope to catch Microsoft, which as of 2008 was valued at about $255 billion.[75]

Many young, extremely bright doctoral students, faculty members, and even undergraduates have used their knowledge, training, and entrepreneurial spirit to create innovative companies that have brought new "killer applications" to the marketplace—while making a lot of money. We may be approaching the limiting case in Mark Zuckerberg, who at the tender age of twenty founded the popular social networking site Facebook in 2004 while still an undergraduate at Harvard. Initially available only to Harvard students, Facebook expanded to include other Ivy League colleges and as of April 2009 had more than 200 million active users.

The MIT Media Laboratory. MIT established the Media Laboratory in 1984 in an attempt to "design technology for people to create a better future." The brainchild of MIT professor Nicholas Negroponte and former MIT president Jerome Wiesner (who was also science adviser to President Kennedy), the Lab is renowned for its innovative educational programs in music, film, graphics, holography, lasers, photography, television, and other media technologies.[76] The Lab combines rigorous research and graduate degree programs where traditional disciplines get checked at the door.

From its inception, the Lab has received a significant amount of support from industry, but the Lab faculty and students determine the research agenda. I've included the Media Lab here to emphasize the point that innovative research laboratories have an explicit teaching mission. In developing innovative technologies and important new scientific knowledge, universities have a key advantage: their ability to create truly multidisciplinary programs and projects. The Media Lab is within MIT's School of Architecture and Planning, but the students and faculty there research and develop a broad range of technology-related projects, taking knowledge and ideas from many different disciplines and combining them in new ways.

The Lab began to produce useful results within its first few years of operation. For example, in 1986, MIT professor Stephen Benton and his students invented the alcove hologram that projected a computer-generated 3-D image—an automobile "parked" in mid-air—into space.[77] The focus of the Media Lab is on projects, with each research group being led by a faculty member and a research scientist. Graduate students and sometimes undergraduate students, regardless of discipline, are on each research team. In 2008, Media Lab faculty and students focused on "machines with common sense, viral communications, 'smart' prostheses, advanced sensor networks, innovative interface design, and sociable robots."[78] Projects in 2009 included a prototype for a wearable device, such as a pendant, that "projects information onto the surfaces and physical objects around us, making any surface into a digital interface." Other researchers were attempting to use techniques from Disney-style animation to improve robotic social expressions, or developing "intelligent sticky notes." Clearly, the projects cover a very broad spectrum of interesting new ideas.[79]

At the January 2005 World Economic Forum in Davos, Switzerland, Negroponte unveiled the idea of bringing $100 laptop computers to 150 million of the world's poorest schoolchildren by the end of 2008. He started an educational nonprofit effort to that end, and although he did not meet his target goal, the One Laptop initiative—along with formidable competitive efforts by Microsoft, Intel, and others, which jumped on the bandwagon when they saw Negroponte's effort as a competitive threat—is likely to help millions of people around the world join the online community at low cost.

MEMS: A Still Smaller World. MEMS, or Micro-Electro-Mechanical Systems, are very tiny instruments that are capable of doing big jobs. Engineers at many universities have been at the cutting edge of their development. Berkeley researchers, for example, have developed tiny gears, motors, sensors, and other mechanical devices that could "fit into the period at the end of this sentence."

MEMS technology, which involves integrating various components on a silicon substrate via microfabrication, already has a host of applications, and engineers see even more in their future. They can be very cost effective. When used in accelerometers in automobile air bags, for example, they can reduce the cost of the accelerometer from $50 to $5 per automobile. Another popular application, developed at Berkeley, is in tiny sensors that can be scattered throughout a building to return data on temperature and light in order to help reduce energy use. MEMS can also be used to provide reconnaissance data over an entire battlefield.

MEMS and nanotechnology are not exactly the same thing, but they are related in that they both work on a very small scale. Nanoscience focuses on the control of matter the size of 1 micrometer, or between 1 and 100 nanometers. In what has been described as a "triumph for the new field of nanotechnology," Berkeley physicist Alex Zettl and his collaborators built the first nano-scale motor—"a gold rotor on a nanotube that could ride on the back of a virus." This proved that small, synthetic motors, nanotubes, and other nanostructures that are several hundred times smaller than a human hair can be assembled and used as actual devices.

Scientists and engineers working at the nano level can be found in their laboratories moving individual atoms around in the process of building new structures. They are now building both mechanical and biological devices with applications in everything from tissue engineering to wastewater treatment to air-purification devices. As a field nanotechnology has its origins in very fundamental nineteenth-century research by James Clerk Maxwell, who worked at Edinburgh and Cambridge universities, and, in the 1920s, in research by the physicists Irving Langmuir of Columbia and Katharine B. Blodgett of General Electric. Richard Feynman, in a 1959 talk at Caltech, described a process by which one could manipulate individual atoms and molecules using a set of very precise tools. Today, the growing interdisciplinary field of nanoscience involves work by physicists, chemists, biologists, and engineers.

Many members of the general public became aware of the idea of nanostructures when "buckyballs" bounced onto the scene in 1985. This occurred when British chemist Harry Kroto and Americans Richard Smalley and Robert Curl at Rice University discovered a previously unknown carbon molecule that typically contained sixty carbon atoms. The structure of this molecule turned out to be a series of interlocking hexagons and pentagons of the type that had also formed the basis of the geodesic dome designed by architect and engineer R. Buckminster Fuller for the Montreal World Exhibition in 1967. The Rice University researchers named the new molecule "buckminsterfullerene," which was quickly shortened to either "fullerenes" or "buckyballs."

The potential usefulness of buckyballs was immediately clear to many scientists as soon as the discovery was published in the prestigious journal

Nature. Curl, Kroto, and Smalley received Nobel Prizes for this work in 1996. We now know that there are hundreds of different combinations of interlocking pentagon/hexagon formations, but buckyballs remain the most famous of the fullerenes. Donald Hoffman at the University of Arizona discovered a method for bulk manufacturing of fullerenes, and scientists at Lucent Technologies' Bell Labs have shown that buckyballs can act as superconductors at relatively warm temperatures. This suggests that they may have great potential use in applications such as quantum computers and power loss–free organic electronics.

Using buckyballs, it may be possible to manufacture aerospace hardware a hundred times lighter than the hardware being manufactured with current materials, but just as strong. Buckyballs could be used in the construction of other products that need to be strong but light, too, such as yacht masts.[80] Other potential applications include the creation of nanoparticles that can deliver drugs to specific diseased cells in the body; waterproof, tear-resistant cloth fibers; combat jackets that are ultrastrong; sturdier concrete; more durable, lighter sports equipment; and stronger suspension bridges.

Artificial Intelligence. The impulse to create intelligent machines is hardly new. Philosophers and scientists have been interested in thinking machines for thousands of years. But AI was not considered a practical field of study until 1955, when Herbert Simon and Allen Newell at Carnegie Mellon University began to work in this area.

Simon is reputed to have told his class: "Over the Christmas holiday, Al Newell and I invented a thinking machine." In fact, even then, the formal birthing of "artificial intelligence" had to await a 1956 summer research project on artificial intelligence at Dartmouth College, where John McCarthy coined the term as part of a proposal for a study "on the basis of the conjecture that every aspect of learning or any other feature of intelligence can in principle be so precisely described that a machine can be made to simulate it." In that year, Simon, Newell, and J. C. Shaw demonstrated the first running AI program, the Logic Theorist (LT). Simon would eventually win a Nobel Prize in Economics for his theory of bounded rationality, one of the cornerstones of AI known as "satisficing."

From 1956 to the present, the field of artificial intelligence has made great strides, but in fits and starts. Its development has certainly been less dramatic than the overall growth and penetration of computer technology into everyday life. Research universities have played a central role in the growth of the field, which has actual and potential applications in such areas as linguistics, psychology, and mathematics, sometimes with worrisome implications.

John McCarthy of MIT invented the Lisp Processing Language in 1958. Only FORTRAN is older than Lisp, which is actually a family of programming languages. Lisp dominated AI applications for several decades and has been used in AI robots, in computer games, and in pattern recognition and air defense systems. In 1961, James Slagle, in his Ph.D. dissertation at MIT, produced the first symbolic integration program, SAINT, which solved calculus problems at the college freshman level. Not to be outdone, Thomas Evans developed the program ANALOGY as part of his dissertation work at MIT in 1963, showing that computers could solve the kind of analogy problems that appear on IQ tests. And to demonstrate still further that very smart graduate students often make more important discoveries than their professors, Ivan Sutherland of MIT introduced the idea of interactive graphics into computing. Danny Bobrow showed in his 1964 MIT doctoral dissertation that computers could use natural language sufficiently to solve algebra word problems correctly.

Richard Greenblatt, also a student at MIT, built MacHack in the 1960s and published it in 1969. Also known as the Greenblatt Chess Program, it was the first computer program to actually play in tournaments; the first knowledge-based chess program to be rated good enough to achieve a Class C tournament rating; and the first to actually win against a person under tournament conditions. Twenty years later, IBM would send its computer chess program, "Deep Blue," into an exhibition competition with the world champion of his time, Gary Kasparov. Deep Blue emerged victorious (2 games to 1, with 3 draws), and the world's human champion demanded a rematch. None was granted, and Deep Blue was retired. In fairness to Kasparov, he had defeated an earlier version of Deep Blue, so that over the two exhibitions, Kasparov led the computer by a score of 6.5 to 5.5.

Most knowledgeable academics would count Seymour Papert of MIT as among the most innovative scholars interested in how technology can help people learn. Papert was ridiculed in the 1960s when he suggested that computers would become fundamental tools for learning and enhancing young people's creativity. But time has proved him right. The research coming from Papert's laboratory has demonstrated what is now obvious—that children can creatively use computers to produce graphics and to write. The Logo programming language was created in Papert's laboratory. A mathematician by training, Papert, with Marvin Minsky, co-founded the Artificial Intelligence Laboratory at MIT. Papert was also one of the faculty founders of the Media Lab.

Finally, some of the basic tools and techniques developed in artificial intelligence have been applied to clinical medicine. Physicians are faced with making diagnostic decisions based on an exponentially increasing amount of medical data. Those data can only be helpful to the clinician if they can be sorted and if patterns can be discerned. This is especially important for physicians working in rural communities, who do not have access to the types of data found at teaching hospitals. The development of the field of medical informatics, which grew out of university research on artificial intelligence, is a response to this need. Dr. Edward Shortliffe, who was educated at Stanford, is one of the pioneers in this new area of study. He was the principal architect of the first clinical expert system, called MYCIN, which obtained clinical data from physician users and turned it into information that could be used to diagnose and treat severe infections. The development of MYCIN preceded the local area networking and therefore was never used in clinical practice, but Shortliffe and others were able to demonstrate that the quality of the diagnoses based on MYCIN were sometimes more accurate than that of Stanford's clinical specialists in infectious diseases. After moving to Columbia University, Shortliffe founded the first university department of medical informatics in the United States. The field is considered so important today that many universities have followed suit, creating their own medical informatics departments. Increasing the use of medical informatics lies at the center of President Obama's 2009 effort to produce a near-universal health-care system that is more cost effective and efficient.

Our Personal and Collective Security

From the Office of Naval Research after World War II to the Defense Department and Department of Energy, the federal government has played an active role in supporting research innovation at our universities.

At times this role has been hotly debated on campuses, but whatever one's beliefs on the subject, it is clear that university research made possible through military-related funding has had a host of applications, some with a profound reach beyond military uses. In recent years federally funded research often focuses on ways that the nation might protect itself from potential biological attacks by domestic or foreign terrorists.

Much of the university research devoted to military and national security needs is mission oriented in nature. For example, in 1949, Professor H. Schector and R. B. Kaplan at Ohio State University developed compounds that could be used in solid fuel rockets, and these compounds were indeed used in over 20 percent of the rocket propellants used in Polaris submarine missiles beginning in 1960. Similarly, chemists at the University of California at San Diego developed a silicon polymer "nanowire" (2,000 times smaller than a human hair) in 2001 that is capable of detecting trace amounts of the chemicals commonly used in terrorist bombs; they also developed an inexpensive, portable nerve gas detector as well as dust-sized chips of silicon capable of detecting a variety of chemical and biological agents.

Some military research turns out to be useful in law-enforcement applications. For example, a University of Southern California professor of computer science, Christoph von der Malsburg, has worked extensively on advanced face-recognition software that has many applications for commercial as well as military customers. At the University of Arizona, professor of management information systems H. Chen and his colleagues developed a data-mining computer technique that has been used nationwide to link law enforcement agency databases. The technique has been useful in solving high-profile crimes, such as the D.C. sniper case in 2002.

Since the late 1950s, the Defense Department has sponsored "blue sky" research—that is, theoretical research as opposed to practical, application-oriented research—in the hope of creating a strong foundation upon which significant innovation can be built. The Defense Advanced Research Projects Agency, one of the many responses by the federal government to the Soviet's launching of *Sputnik*, was established with this goal in mind. It is an agency within the military, but it is relatively independent of the services and reports directly to high command in the Department of Defense. Its own research focuses on the development of new technology for use by the military, and over the course of its history it has sponsored hundreds of university-based projects—some classified and others unclassified. Its annual budget is over $3 billion.

The development of ARPAnet, the precursor to the Internet, has been among the most notable achievements of DARPA. Charles M. Herzfeld, former director of ARPA (its name in 1958 when the agency was first established), claimed that the ARPAnet idea "came out of our frustration that there were only a limited number of large, powerful research computers in the country and that many research investigators who should have access were geographically separated from them."

The first exchange of data over the new ARPAnet, as noted above, occurred in 1969 between researchers at UCLA and the Stanford Research Institute. Nonmilitary uses of ARPAnet increased dramatically over the next seventeen years, and in 1986, a new competing network, called NSFnet (National Science Foundation Network), was formed by first linking the five national supercomputer centers, and then every major research university in the United States. NSFnet began to displace the slower ARPAnet, which was shut down in 1990 when its faster competitor became generally available.[81] The American public adopted the Internet far more rapidly than it had adopted most other innovative technologies: It took thirty-eight years before 50 million people tuned into the radio, and thirteen years for TV to reach that plateau, but only four years for 50 million people to go online. In 2008 the Census Bureau found that 62 percent of American households said they used the Internet and over 50 percent had broadband connections to it.[82] A PEW Research Center survey found that 63 percent of American adults had broadband connections at home in April 2009.

DARPA is supporting other projects, some of which may seem farfetched today but in time will be reality. In fact, the actual basis for some of these projects can be found in science-fiction writing. For example, DARPA is sponsoring a project to create what is called the DARPA Vulture, which is intended to fly unattended for up to five years at 65,000 feet to monitor terrain. It is also funding the development of a "trauma pod battlefield treatment system," which is intended to speed up the treatment of wounded soldiers on the battlefield with miniature, tele-operated instruments that will load wounded soldiers onto the trauma pod, give them oxygen if needed, fully scan their bodies for injury, and possibly even allow actual surgeons removed from the battlefield to perform surgery with remote-controlled surgical instruments. This is a collaborative project that brings together an independent research group, an industrial firm, and a university medical school.

Military research has already given us the Global Positioning System (GPS) device, now a standard piece of equipment in automobiles, iPhones, and Blackberries. Brad Parkinson, a professor of aeronautics and astronautics at Stanford, led the military team that developed the Global Positioning System, which used an integrated set of earth satellites to locate a user's position to within a few hundred feet.

A U.S. Air Force colonel, Parkinson was instrumental in beginning the revolution in navigation during the 1970s. In fact, the interest in such a system goes back to the late 1950s, when the United States wanted to be able to precisely track the location of satellites circling the Earth, beginning with *Sputnik*. William Guier and George Wiefenbach, two Johns Hopkins University researchers in its Applied Physics Laboratory (APL), were able to precisely determine *Sputnik*'s orbit by measuring the Doppler-induced changes in the frequencies of the very simple radio signal that it transmitted.[83] Some time later, the U.S. military also became interested in tracking the exact location of its Polaris nuclear submarines and finding a way for the submarines to locate themselves. Frank McClure, also at Hopkins' APL, had the insight that by "inverting" the approach of Guier and Wiefenbach—that is, by measuring a radio signal from a satellite whose position was known—a submarine would be capable of finding its own position precisely. In 1964, Richard Kerschner, a colleague of McClure's, designed a system of satellites that could provide the navigation information needed for positioning. The various military services, working on similar projects, favored different solutions, however, and conflict followed. Finally, Parkinson led a coordinated team representing the various service branches; the result was a superior system now known as the Global Positioning System, or NAVSTAR. The first satellite was put up in 1978; today there are at least twenty-five GPS satellites in orbit (there must be at least twenty-four operational at any given time for the system to work).

The commercial value of the GPS quickly became clear, and today there are millions of units being produced and sold to members of the general public. When Parkinson moved to Stanford, he and a team of collaborators developed the Stanford Differential GPS, which is used in, among other things, the automatic landing of aircraft, and it has rendered much of the original military system obsolete.

I have thus far focused exclusively on those biological, biomedical, and physical science and engineering discoveries that have changed the way we think about our planet and universe, as well as our bodies and our health. Many have altered our daily lives. But there is another domain of discovery that has affected the way we make sense of our world. This work, which has come from work carried out at our great research universities in the social and behavioral sciences, as well as in the humanities fields, also represents a form of discovery. It is an articulation of some of those ideas, concepts, and discoveries that forms the content of the next chapter.

CHAPTER 10

Nosce te Ipsum: Culture, Society, and Values

If men define situations as real they are real in their consequences.
—W. I. Thomas and Dorothy Thomas

W hen people think about the discoveries of our time, they usually think about the inventions of scientists and engineers—the scientists-turned-entrepreneurs who have started multibillion-dollar companies in their garages, or the star professors who have made breakthroughs in their labs. Few people would think about social and behavioral scientists, and even fewer would consider the scholars in the humanities. And yet, scholars in these fields make discoveries all the time. We tend not to classify the results of their work as particularly profound or consequential. This is a mistake.

Discoveries in the social sciences and the humanities, often taking the form of basic ideas, concepts, theories, and the results of empirical research, have turned out to be highly influential over the past few decades. The shape of these discoveries is different from those made in the physical sciences. But when scholars translate great authors whose works have been totally unfamiliar to us previously, these are discoveries. When linguists identify the fundamental structure of language and linguistic forms, or when philosophers propose philosophical ideas about causality, or falsifying theories, these, too, are discoveries. And these discoveries help to shape the way we think.

Yet there have been almost no systematic attempts to identify the most important social and behavioral science discoveries of the past fifty or sixty years or to catalog the greatest achievements in the humanities during that same period.[1] In 1971, Karl W. Deutsch, a Harvard professor of government, and two colleagues identified sixty-two important achievements in the social sciences that were made between 1900 and 1965.[2] Deutsch's list was highly subjective, based on his own judgment after consulting with various experts. He found that in the social sciences, Europe dominated the United States as the source for discoveries from 1900 to 1929, but that the reverse was true from 1930 to 1965, just as in the "hard" sciences: America caught up to and surpassed Europe, especially in the postwar years. If Deutsch were alive today, and decided to update his paper, he would find that the United States had played an even greater role in producing the advances of the social sciences in the final third of the twentieth century than it had in the period he examined.[3]

Deutsch estimated that in the social and behavioral sciences, the diffusion of the knowledge took time—ten to fifteen years, in fact, on average. That interval is shorter today. The diffusion of knowledge in these fields into cognate disciplines and then into the wider culture is now helped along by the many academic journals that exist and by the media. Major discoveries in one field quickly diffuse into another—say, from economics to sociology, or from psychology into economics. In short order, powerful concepts move from the initial field to cognate disciplines and from there into the language of everyday life. Thus we have all heard of "human capital," "the self-fulfilling prophecy," or "relative deprivation." The origins of the ideas themselves may then be largely forgotten, but not completely: It is simply left to the historians to identify them for posterity.

Each subdiscipline of the social and behavioral sciences has produced dominant schools of thought, some lasting far longer than others. Many schools eventually wither away; some undergo significant modifications as a new generation has its say. Entire areas of specialization, such as physiological psychology, have yielded to new fields—in this case, neuroscience. A particular theoretical framework, such as John Maynard Keynes's extraordinary take on economic theory, can be transformed when fundamental assumptions are influenced by ideas and concepts from other allied disciplines, such as cognitive psychology or game theory. Each discovery and new idea is thus integrated into a much larger intellectual context, helping to shape not only the future of the social science disciplines themselves, but also the way we think about ourselves, our choices, our relationships, and our society in our daily life.

In this chapter we will look briefly at many of these discoveries. I've organized them into five general categories: concepts related to our decisions and reasoning; values and opinions; culture, economy, and society; ourselves and our sensibilities; and our "thinking about thinking"—that is, the discoveries made in philosophy, literary theory, and the like. Although the methods I used initially to identify discoveries in these fields were the same as those I used for the biological and physical sciences and engineering, I found that the presidents and provosts of universities provided little guidance here, as their lists did not include many social and behavioral science advances or discoveries in the humanities. To enlarge the scope of discoveries, I spoke with a number of Nobel Prize–winning economists and other leading scholars in these fields to obtain their views about major discoveries. Being a social scientist myself, I had, of course, some of my own favorites. In short, this is a set of illustrations of the many ideas that have influenced our society and culture. This set of discoveries plainly is *not* intended as a comprehensive or systematic sampling of major discoveries in these fields. Many very important technical and methodological innovations are underrepresented here, and I have consciously omitted a number of significant social science advances.[4] Emphasis has been placed on more substantive concepts and ideas—some that may be quite familiar to you.

OUR DECISIONS AND REASONING

Psychologists Daniel Kahneman and Amos Tversky wrote: "The making of decisions is perhaps the most fundamental activity that characterizes living creatures. Consequently, the attempt to understand, explain, and predict individual choice behavior has been a major goal of the behavioral and social sciences."[5] Each of us makes hundreds of decisions every day. We have to make these decisions—some trivial, others important—when there is a good deal of uncertainty about whether the decision is right or wrong, or when the alternatives and their possible outcomes are distorted by the limited information available to us at the time. What affects our judgments and decision-making under these conditions? Do we act rationally in making these choices; do we act in self-interest? Are there patterns of behavior in the choices—and in the errors we make—that can be described and analytically understood, so that we have a better sense of how choices are made?

What follows is a set of very brief descriptions of some of the main theories in the social sciences focusing on how we make decisions—and some of the concepts and counterintuitive findings that psychologists, sociologists, and economists have proposed when considering decision-making under various conditions.

The Self-Fulfilling Prophecy. One of the leading American sociologists of the twentieth century, Robert K. Merton, a professor at Columbia, coined the phrase "self-fulfilling prophecy." As Merton put it in his original essay: "The self-fulfilling prophecy is, in the beginning, a *false* definition of the situation," but it ends up "evoking a new behavior which makes the original false conception come 'true.'" "The specious validity of the self-fulfilling prophecy," Merton wrote, "perpetuates a reign of error. For the prophet will cite the actual course of events as proof that he was right from the very beginning."[6] Examples of the self-fulfilling prophecy are easy to find, as this principle can work on both the level of the individual and the level of the group. For example, if I do not think a person is trustworthy, and I begin to treat him as if he is not, he can begin to act in ways that are in fact not trustworthy. Or, if people believe that a young person is apt to become a juvenile delinquent, they may set up conditions, such as an unwillingness to employ them or support them, that lead to his actual delinquency. Likewise, if people in positions of authority or power define the members of a minority group as less able scholastically than the members of other groups and therefore less likely to succeed in school, they may allocate fewer resources to educating the minority students. Allocated fewer resources on the basis of a false definition, the schools will have inferior teachers and school environments, and the students, on average, will do poorly in school compared to the students in the majority group. The original prophecy seems to be confirmed, even though the students might have done well if their schools had been given the same resources as the other schools. Merton also coined other terms that have gained widespread currency, such as "role model."

Election Polling. When political pundits discuss voting behavior on television, projecting winners and losers on the basis of "exit interviews," they are applying theories that resulted from a long history of empirical research in the social sciences. It began with Paul Lazarsfeld's research in the 1940 and 1948 presidential elections[7] and the contributions of Angus Campbell and Philip Converse from the University of Michigan at about the same time.

These social scientists produced predictive models that helped us understand voter preferences and the reasons for those choices. Lazarsfeld introduced the idea of panel analysis, where researchers systematically collect information from the same sample of voters at multiple points in time during the election. Unlike trend data, which are collected from different samples of people at multiple times, panel analysis allows social scientists to analyze "turnover"—changes in preferences over time—and the possible causes of those changes. Panel analysis has become a standard method of determining why changes in preferences, attitudes, and behaviors occur. When the entrepreneurial pollster George Gallop began to use these kinds of techniques and models to predict voting outcomes, a new industry was born.

Although political candidates continue to downplay the importance and accuracy of voting preference polls, polling has been quite accurate in predicting election outcomes. In the 2008 presidential contest between Barack Obama and John McCain, the predictions of the best of the pollsters were amazingly accurate—not only in terms of the popular vote but also in terms of the state-by-state Electoral College decision. Political polling has become more than an art; it is a science. Like any scientific work, however, it can be conducted well or poorly. A poll that does not take selection bias into account, for example, will end up with a skewed outcome.

Robert K. Merton also developed the idea of the focused interview, which was originally intended as a method of exploring a set of concepts in an informal way to add supplementary data to large empirical studies. After conducting focused interviews, where the interviewees were organized into "focus groups," sociologists would formulate questions that would appear in survey questionnaires for a broader sampling of respondents, using a variety of sampling techniques to ensure that the inferences drawn from the data were reasonably robust. Today, the focus group is used in political campaigns, in advertising and marketing studies, in scientific jury selection, and so on, but it has become an end in itself. Market researchers, for example, might use focus groups, but without following up with the survey questionnaires. This technique can lead to false inferences about relationships among variables, as the association among the variables themselves have not been further tested.

Problems with Eyewitness Testimony. One of the most powerful forms of evidence in jury trials is eyewitness testimony. As social psychologist Elizabeth Loftus, professor at the University of California at Irvine, observed, "When a victim gets on the stand and says, 'I was there, I saw it, that's the guy, I'll never forget that face, I'm absolutely positive,' it's extremely compelling testimony and it's very hard to shake that testimony." But how accurate and reliable is eyewitness testimony? What kinds of errors do people make and why? It was Loftus, in her book *Eyewitness Testimony,* who completely changed the way we think about eyewitness testimony in court cases, in line-ups, and as a general form of evidence.

Through a series of ingenious experiments, Loftus demonstrated that, in fact, eyewitness testimony can be highly unreliable and that witnesses often use poor cues to make false identifications. Her work has led to national changes in the way police line-ups are conducted and in the way this kind of evidence is used in court. Eyewitness testimony remains a major factor in criminal court cases. In recent years, however, the use of DNA evidence has supported Loftus's research, exonerating innocent people who were convicted principally on the basis of eyewitness testimony. In the late 1990s and in the 2000s, Loftus's work on "false memories" led her to examine problems with recovered memories about childhood experiences, especially in cases of alleged sexual abuse. She has testified at several high-visibility trials and has received much criticism from some segments of society; nevertheless, her research is highly regarded in the field and has been recognized by her election to the National Academy of Sciences in 2004 and to the Royal Society of Edinburgh in 2005. She has revolutionized her field and her work has had broad social applications.

The Theory of Cognitive Dissonance. Psychologist Leon Festinger, who worked at the University of Iowa, the University of Rochester, MIT, the

University of Minnesota, the University of Michigan, and finally, during the most influential segment of his career, at Stanford during the 1950s and 1960s, developed the theory of cognitive dissonance, another term that has now entered the vernacular. In simplified form, the theory holds that when there are inconsistencies between someone's beliefs and his or her behavior, this causes psychological tension, and the individual will change his or her beliefs to be consistent with the behavior rather than changing the behavior to fit the beliefs. The theory is explored in his book *When Prophecy Failed* (coauthored with Henry W. Rieken and Stanley Schachter), which focused on a UFO doomsday cult. The idea is linked in practical terms to the tendency of people to resist information that is apt to create cognitive dissonance. Festinger also made important contributions to social network theory in his famous study of how the architecture of a housing project could affect friendship patterns.

Impossibility Theorem. Economists have also thought about social choice and behavior. In many social situations it is necessary, or at least highly desirable, for example, to aggregate individual preferences. The "impossibility theorem," devised by Nobel Prize–winning economist Kenneth Arrow in 1951, states that no voting system can transform the ranked preferences of individuals into a community-wide ranking while also conforming to a set of reasonable voting-system criteria.

In other words, say we list the rules that we think should apply to the procedure for making a choice that will have consequences for a number of people. People are going to rank their individual preferences, and we want the result to be a ranked system of preferences for the group. Let's say that a group of several friends wants to decide which movie to see. There is a list of several movies, and the group members are going to rank their individual preferences to come up with their top choice as a group. Arrow in fact came up with a list of rules to apply in such cases in order for the procedure to seem "fair." For example, it would not be fair if one person alone could decide, as a dictator would; everyone must get an equal say. Also, social preferences should be "transitive," in the sense that if an individual prefers movie A over movie B, and prefers movie B over movie C, then it follows that movie A is preferred over movie C. But, having devised these rules, Arrow proved mathematically that there was no form of decision-making that could construct social preferences from arbitrary individual preferences. Arrow's proof for his impossibility theorem was quite complex, but even in its simplest form it has changed our thinking about how to aggregate individual preferences. Arrow taught at Stanford for many years; his theorem was first presented in his Ph.D. dissertation for Columbia.

Game Theory. The branch of economic and mathematical analysis called "game theory" has had a great deal of influence on the development of the behavioral sciences and has crept into the way we analyze the situations we face and the choices we make. Consider only two ideas drawn from game theory: the zero-sum game and the Prisoner's Dilemma.

The zero-sum game is a form of a constant-sum game in which all losses and gains must equal zero. It is impossible for two people to win. Chess is an example of a zero-sum game; so is checkers. But zero-sum games are not always "games" in the traditional sense; there are many social and political situations that operate by similar zero-sum logic. John von Neumann, a mathematician at the Institute for Advanced Study at Princeton, and Oskar Morgenstern, a Princeton economist, explored zero-sum-game logic in 1944. It has been debated by many others since then.

The Prisoner's Dilemma was first posed by RAND Corporation thinkers but was later named by Albert W. Tucker, who taught for many years at Princeton and contributed his ideas to the discussion. Basically, the dilemma explores the limits of rationality and self-interest by examining what would happen in a hypothetical situation involving two prisoners arrested for being accomplices in the same crime. They are held in isolation and cannot communicate with each other. Each prisoner is offered a deal by the police: If he testifies against the other prisoner, he can possibly go free (unless the other one also testifies against him). Correlatively, if he remains silent and his partner confesses, his accomplice goes free while he does serious time. Each prisoner is better off if he testifies than if he remains silent; but if both confess, both have a reduced sentence and are worse off than if they had both remained silent.

There are now many descriptions of this game with different variations—for example, when each of the prisoners has a different amount of information, or where there are multiple moves that each prisoner is allowed. It has been a source of rich scholarly debate but has also been used by policymakers. Game theorists began to create these kinds of puzzles during the Cold War and used them to think about, among other things, global nuclear strategy. There have been thousands of scholarly articles written about various forms of the Prisoner's Dilemma. In game theory more generally, many different types of games, in addition to the Prisoner's Dilemma, have been explored.

Thomas Schelling, a Harvard economist who contributed to game theory, revolutionized our thinking about both conflict and cooperation. In 1960, Schelling showed that a party can strengthen its position by overtly worsening its own options, that the capability to retaliate can be more useful than the ability to resist an attack, and that uncertain retaliation is more credible and more efficient than certain retaliation. These insights have proven to be of great relevance for conflict resolution and efforts to avoid war.[8]

Bounded Rationality. Herbert Simon, a Nobel Prize–winning scientist at Carnegie Mellon University, studied the basic assumption of rationality in standard "expected utility theory" in economics, which deals with decision-making in situations where various outcomes have different probabilities of occurring—such as in betting and lotteries. The standard theory says that in such situations, people will calculate the probabilities of various possible outcomes, weigh their likelihood, and construct some average of these weights, or "expected utility," before making a decision. In other words, they act rationally. But in his influential book *Models of Man,* Simon questioned this idea, implying that rational choice models of action have to take errors of cognition into account. He developed the idea of "bounded rationality," that is, that there are many situations in which people act only partially rationally; they also act partly out of emotions and in response to other constraining factors. His theory applied not just to betting and lotteries, but to many situations in which the outcome is uncertain. Simon enjoined social and behavioral scientists to pay close attention to how people make actual decisions, and his ideas have had a significant impact on the work of behavioral economists and political theorists.

Conditions of Uncertainty. Expected utility theory and game theory have been built on several very strong assumptions. One is that individuals will act rationally; another, that they will act to maximize their self-interest; and still another, that they make decisions with the benefit of full information.

Since their initial theoretical formulation, these assumptions have been questioned and contested. Analysis of uncertainty and asymmetric information challenges one of the abiding assumptions underpinning economic theory since Adam Smith: that markets operate efficiently. Joseph Stiglitz of Columbia, George A. Akerlof of the University of California at Berkeley, and Michael Spence of Stanford shared the Nobel Prize in Economics in 2001 for research focusing on an extremely important basis for market inefficiencies—imperfect information.

In his classic 1970 paper, "The Market for 'Lemons': Quality Uncertainty and the Market Mechanism," Akerlof tried to explain why used car dealers had difficulty developing a market for their cars: Since buyers were uncertain about the problems that resided under the hoods of the cars, they would reason that some of the cars could be "lemons." Not knowing which ones were the lemons, they would be reluctant to pay a good price for them. Stiglitz's research suggested that lack of information, access to poor information, and different levels of information could have a large number of economic consequences, from unemployment to lending shortages. Asymmetric information affects decisions in transactions where one person or company has more or better information than another, creating a potential imbalance in power. In effect, Stiglitz assumed that markets are efficient only under unusual circumstances. If asymmetric information exists, then there should always be potential government intervention in markets that would result in Pareto superior outcomes that would make everyone better off. Stigliz advocated a balance of markets and government action to produce more social justice and more efficient economic outcomes.

Columbia economist Edmund Phelps, who won the Nobel Prize in 2006, had made important contributions in this area in his 1960 study of the relationship between inflation and unemployment. Phelps challenged the prevailing view that the price for lower unemployment rates was a one-time rise in the inflation rate. His analysis showed that problems of information within the economy were not equally distributed and could affect decisions based on expectations.[9] Buyers and sellers often had access to different amounts of the information they needed to make optimal choices. This line of research has had widespread practical consequences and has led to further debate over when and how government should intervene in inefficient markets.

It was not until the late 1970s that some scholars, trained in psychology but highly conversant with economic theory, began to produce both a theory of decision-making and an experimental research program that fundamentally challenged a good deal of the received wisdom in neoclassical economics. These scholars demonstrated that the assumptions of rationality and self-interest were demonstrably violated in many situations, and perhaps more importantly, that these violations led to different behavioral results than would obtain had we assumed rational and individual maximizing behavior.[10] Daniel Kahneman and Amos Tversky, followed by many behavioral economists, have built an important and expanding scientific field that begins to answer these and related questions.

Both born in Israel, these two pioneers eventually moved to the United States and worked at several different American research universities. The remarkable Kahneman-Tversky collaboration began in the 1968–1969 academic year. Together they would father an alternative and revolutionary new theoretical perspective on how decisions are made. Drawing from the fields of psychology and economics, the students and colleagues of these two men expanded decision theory and essentially created the field of behavioral economics.[11] Distinguished economists who were drawn to this alternative point of view, such as Richard Thaler, who had been at Cornell and is now at the University of Chicago, have developed theoretical and empirical models distinguishing between normative theory—what people should do if they are acting rationally—and what they actually do in real life situations.

Although there are many features of this work, Kahneman and Tversky's work on "prospect theory" and "endowment effects" has been particularly influential. Their work takes on the game theorists' basic assumption of rationality. They demonstrate that people do not tend to look at the level of their final wealth when considering gambles. They look at potential gains and losses from some psychological reference point, which varies from one situation to another, and display "loss aversion." In other words, when people are making decisions that involve risks, out-of-pocket losses weigh more heavily than opportunity costs or foregone gains. The underweighting of opportunity costs is called the "endowment effect."[12] "Loss aversion" is a concept that helps to explain, for example, the strong reluctance of investors to sell stocks that have lost value. In short, prospect theory addresses how we frame our decisions and how those decisions are affected by our attitudes toward risk.

Kahneman and Tversky give us the following example of prospect theory:

> Suppose you are compelled to play Russian roulette, but are given the opportunity to purchase the removal of one bullet from the loaded gun. Would you pay as much to reduce the number of bullets from four to three as you would to reduce the number of bullets from one to zero? Most people feel they would be willing to pay much more for a reduction of death from 1/6 to zero than for a reduction from 4/6 to 3/6. Economic considerations [that is, expected utility theory] would lead one to pay more in the latter case, while the value of money is presumably reduced by the considerable probability that one will not live to enjoy it.[13]

The credit card business offers an example of endowment effects in prospect theory. Until the 1980s, credit card companies would not allow stores using their cards to charge higher prices to credit card users. Congress took up a bill that would ban such restrictions. The credit card companies cleverly then turned their attention to how to frame the price differential so that it would have the best outcome from their perspective. They decided it would be better for the price differential to take the form of a cash discount than for it to take the form of a credit card surcharge. As Richard Thaler, who was working at Cornell at the time, noted, "The preference makes sense if consumers would view the cash discount as an opportunity cost of using the credit card but the surcharge as an out-of-pocket expense."[14]

Thaler and his colleagues also examined the "status quo effect." He demonstrated that people facing decisions about altering the ratio of stocks to fixed-income bonds in their portfolios tended, despite aging, to stick with the same ratios that they'd had since they had first made a choice. In other experiments, Thaler found that people faced with choices about complex problems, such as selecting among health-insurance plans, tended to make their choices based on the order of the choices and whether one was the default option. People tended to pick the default option, when one was given. This research shows how paternalistic policymakers can influence choices by careful selection of a default option.

Kahneman and Tversky also studied how people, as they put it, rely on "a limited number of heuristic principles (rules of thumb)," which "can lead people faced with complex tasks or decisions to make errors."[15] This work is related to the problem of estimating the psychological value individuals place on "sunk costs," costs that cannot be recovered once they have been incurred. Standard economic theory suggests that decisions are affected by incremental costs and benefits, not historical or sunk costs. But do people in fact ignore sunk costs in making their decisions? A good deal of evidence suggests that they do not.

A simple example involves individuals in a hopeless conflict situation who want a rationale for continuing the conflict. You've heard the argument: We must stay the course so that those who have already died will not have died in vain. The death of those soldiers, however tragic, represents sunk costs, and while a rational decision-maker would not take those costs into account when deciding on future strategy or policy, we know that people often do take such things into account. Another example can be found in the behavior of an undisciplined gambler at the racetrack. Having lost his bets for most of the day (sunk costs), and wanting to recoup his losses, the individual makes increasingly long-shot bets and winds up losing even more. Psychologists and economists are building increasingly sophisticated models that allow us to understand how such decisions are made.

Congestion Pricing. Introduced by William Vickrey at Columbia in 1952 and elaborated upon by other economists, the idea of congestion pricing has been used around the world in efforts to control traffic. It is a market-based strategy that provides users of automobiles monetary incentives or disincentives to travel on certain roads or into specific highly congested locations at specific times of day. Also known as "value pricing," "variable pricing," and "peak-period pricing," it charges drivers different rates during rush hours and may allow automobiles with a certain number of passengers to drive in faster lanes than those with fewer passengers. Congestion pricing involves another form of choice theory, reasoning that, given a monetary disincentive to travel at peak times, people will be more likely to arrange their travel to avoid peak times, thus improving traffic flow for everyone.

Tragedy of the Commons. An ancient problem of how to treat public goods has received a great deal of attention by political scientists and economists over the past fifty years. Aristotle observed ironically that "that which is common to the greatest number has the least care bestowed upon it." In his 1833 book on population, William Foster Lloyd, a British economist, discussed the problem as well. More recent systematic research began with the ecologist Garrett Hardin, a professor at the University of California at Santa Barbara, who picked up this theme in his 1968 essay "The Tragedy of the Commons."

Hardin pointed out that when a resource is shared, people are often unwilling to help pay for the resource or to preserve it. In fact, they may attempt to make the most possible use of the resource while paying the least possible amount. In one example, he shows that owners of cattle sharing a pasture have incentives to use the pasture as much as possible but little incentive to help maintain it. He then extends the concept to natural resources such as our air and water. People do not generally want to pay for efforts to reduce air pollution, for example, even when they are significant contributors to the pollution. These people become "free riders," relying on others to pay the price that is required to have cleaner air. There is a problem with free riders, however, and it arises when individuals or groups use more than their share of a collective resource or pay less than their share of the cost of producing the resource. Ultimately, the tragedy of the commons is that the resource becomes degraded. Mancur Olson, working at Princeton and the University of Maryland, also made important contributions to our thinking about the tragedy of the commons.

Others have questioned the assumption of self-interest, or the lack of altruism, inherent his Hardin's theory by showing that individuals often act in a way that would not seem to maximize their economic self-interest. For example, there are many people who contribute to public television. Though public television depends on viewer contributions, people can still get the benefits of public television even if they do not contribute.

OUR VALUES AND OPINIONS

For centuries, philosophers have attempted to improve methods for determining causal relationships among variables. Social and behavioral scientists took on this same task from the earliest days of its development as a field. It is a task that involves complex analyses of logical relationships, and it has proved to be a daunting one.

To understand the problems involved in determining causal relationships, consider an argument that appeared in the popular book *Freakonomics* by University of Chicago economist Steven D. Levitt and journalist Stephen J. Dubner. Levitt addressed the complicated problem of what caused the rather dramatic drop in felony crimes in major American cities during the 1990s. Many explanations have been offered by criminologists, sociologists, and economists, including factors such as improved police techniques for dealing with neighborhoods with high crime rates, changing demographics of the American population, and the like. Levitt offered a clever and curious alternative hypothesis. He suggested that it was the U.S. Supreme Court decision in *Roe v. Wade* in 1973 that caused the decline in crime in the 1990s. Of course, the decision itself was only part of a causal chain, according to Levitt. It led to an increased number of abortions, particularly in the subgroups of the population that would have children who would grow up in poverty and consequently be more likely to commit felony crimes between the ages of eighteen and twenty-five. Levitt examined a great number of causal links. But was this a true cause, or did Levitt make an incorrect inference based on correlations? How might one demonstrate that Levitt's causal argument was wrong? How do we in fact establish causality? This is one of the central and most difficult questions facing social and behavioral scientists. The number of times we encounter assumptions about causal linkages (for example, in studies reporting that eating certain foods reduces one's chances of getting cancer or heart disease) is staggering—and most often, the causal relationship has not been established.

The field of econometrics is devoted to causal analysis, and the field draws heavily from mathematical statistics. Pioneers in the field include the Norwegian Trygve Haavelmo from the University of Oslo, who was the first to use mathematical statistics to estimate complex economic relations. More recently, James J. Heckman from the University of Chicago and Daniel L. McFadden from the University of California at Berkeley have developed methods for resolving some of the basic problems that arise in analyzing data about individuals, such as selection bias and endogeneity (where the independent variables in a regression model are correlated with the error term in the equation). The problem is especially difficult to solve when economists are examining longtime prices in causal analysis.

But efforts at American universities to establish causal explanations through social research go back more than a century—to the "Pittsburgh Surveys" of 1907–1908 and the Brandeis brief (discussed in Chapter 2). Monumental efforts at collecting systematic data, particularly economic data, were made during the 1930s by economists such as Simon Kuznets at the University of Pennsylvania, who produced and organized the "national income accounts" of the United States. These reports calculate the monetary value and sources of output that the nation produces as well as the distribution of income generated by this production and examines statistical correlates of economic trends, growth, seasonal fluctuations, and use. Kuznets also tried to explain different levels of income inequality and processes of growth in nations at varying stages of economic development.

But the systematic development of causal analysis in social research, at least in American sociology (Emile Durkheim worked on these problems in France in the late nineteenth century), would have to wait until the 1930s and 1940s and the work by Paul Lazarsfeld at Columbia and the Bureau of Applied Social Research. Most of his work searched for elusive causal explanations, particularly those that might be counterintuitive. He also brought this kind of thinking to the world of applied social research, also known as market research. Many of his former students have also made important contributions to this field.

OUR CULTURE, ECONOMY, AND SOCIETY

Social stratification and social mobility in the United States have been important themes in social science research. What determines differences in social status? What determines social mobility among different social classes? These have been two of the abiding social science questions throughout the history of the discipline. Large numbers of economists and sociologists have attempted to answer these questions. In this section we will examine a few of them.

Human Capital. The idea of "human capital" is not new—Adam Smith wrote about it in the eighteenth century, and Alfred Marshall wrote about it in the nineteenth and twentieth. But the concept was given new force by twentieth-century economists Milton Friedman and George Shultz, and most importantly, by Gary Becker at the University of Chicago and Jacob Mincer at Columbia.

The concept of human capital may not be intuitively obvious. Most people think of capital as an asset that yields income, such as a bank account, shares of stock, or a factory in China. What Becker and Mincer did in the 1950s and 1960s was to describe a different form of capital that society can invest in—"human capital." As Becker wrote, "economists regard expenditures on education, training, medical care, and so on as investments in human capital." He went on to explain that "people cannot be separated from their knowledge, skills, health, or values in the way they can be separated from their financial and physical assets. Education and training are the most important investments in human capital." But investments in human capital are no less important than investments in other things, because these investments also "raise earnings, improve health, or add to a person's good habits over much of his lifetime."[16]

Mincer and Becker expanded the concept of human capital during a now-famous labor workshop that met at Columbia in the 1960s. Human capital and labor supply, they said, were the causes of wage differentials between men and women. Although Mincer and his students acknowledged that some portion of the hourly differential in the earnings of men and women was the result of discrimination, it also was, they argued, a result of differences in investments in on-the-job training, in work histories, and in depreciation of skills—each an element in a person's human capital. Mincer's and Becker's empirical studies and ideas had enormous potential for elaboration, and some of his students and colleagues, such as Nobel laureate James Heckman, had a sense that they were creating a new field of labor economics. As Heckman said, their work "changed the way we think about skills and the role of education."[17]

The theory has had enormous effects on our understanding of the payoffs that accrue to those who develop skills and attain higher levels of education. Labor economists have analyzed data (often incomplete data requiring sophisticated methodological adjustments to account for potentially confounding selection and other biases) to obtain usable estimates of the effect of an additional year of education (at various levels) on earnings, apart from the effects of age, experience, and other variables. The work on human capital has influenced the study of gender and race differences in the marketplace, including the "taste," as Becker puts it, for discrimination.

The practical value of this work lies in the potential for a better allocation of public resources to education. Becker extended the framework of research on human capital to include a study of social behavior that had not yet been addressed to a significant degree by economists. The term "human capital" has become part of our everyday vocabulary. In 1992, Gary Becker received a Nobel Prize in Economics. Mincer probably deserved to share the prize with Becker, but he was overlooked despite his enormous contribution to the elaboration and empirical development of the idea.

Social Mobility. In 1967, Peter Blau from Columbia University and Otis Dudley Duncan from the University of Michigan published *The American Occupational Structure,* which launched an extensive effort at the universities of Michigan and Wisconsin and the University of Chicago to answer important questions about social mobility. Literally hundreds of young sociologists became interested in explaining social stratification by developing new quantitative models, models that borrowed, to some extent, from advances made in both econometrics and statistics. These scholars examined how family background, particularly a father's education and occupational status, influenced a child's educational, occupational, and income attainment.

The "Blau-Duncan" status attainment model attempted to measure both direct and indirect effects of background variables and early individual achievement. Using rather simple econometric techniques, sociologists created theoretical causal models called "path diagrams" to estimate the effects of these individual characteristics on social mobility and stratification. The potential for elaboration on the simple forms of the model led to a cottage industry of scholars producing work in this area. They examined differences in gender, race, individual aptitude, and nationality in the attempt to find answers, devising new theories of social mobility.

Trying to discover the reasons for the persistent disparity in the achievement of white and minority children was a major subject of social science interest during the years following *Brown v. Board of Education (1954).* The effort to understand the causes of these racial differences attracted some of the best minds in the social and behavioral sciences. In response to the Civil Rights Act of 1964, the U.S. Department of Health, Education, and Welfare commissioned James S. Coleman, a renowned sociologist at Johns Hopkins University (later at the University of Chicago), "to assess the availability of equal educational opportunities to children of different race, color, religion, and national origin." Published in 1966, the Coleman Study was the second-largest empirical research study in history, involving surveys of more than 500,000 students and 50,000 teachers and principals. It was one of the first major studies to be used to inform national policymaking.

Coleman tried to weigh various factors in determining educational outcomes. He expected to find that schools with a majority of black students would have poor resources compared with white-majority schools and that these differences in resources would explain the difference in outcomes for these children. Almost everyone, including Coleman and his colleagues, was surprised to find that measures of school quality, such as instructional facilities, curriculum materials, and even teacher salaries, were not as unequal across predominantly black or white schools as they would have expected. These factors simply did not explain the differences between the two racial groups. Coleman found that instead, it was the social background and socioeconomic status of the students that influenced outcomes.

While supporting much of what Coleman found, Christopher Jencks elaborated on Coleman's analysis, most notably in his 1972 book, *Inequality*. Jencks demonstrated that the composition of student bodies in terms of academic, economic, and social attributes affected the academic standing of schools. The social composition of secondary schools had a greater effect on students' cognitive achievement than the social composition of elementary schools. Still, family background was the best predictor of achievement at all levels. Since early academic performance is known to predict later occupational achievement and income, the results of these classic studies were important discoveries that informed both educators and public policymakers struggling to understand what would produce equality of opportunity for racial and ethnic minorities in the United States.

Wealth and Poverty. In his extraordinarily successful book *The Affluent Society* (1958), John Kenneth Galbraith documented the way postwar America was becoming affluent in the private sector while remaining poor in the public sector—leading to inequalities in wealth and underinvestment in public goods. Galbraith, Harvard's rebellious economist (who coined the phrase "conventional wisdom"), was one of the great skeptics and critics of American society, but he was addressing an issue that social scientists have been interested in for decades.

Other theorists have taken various approaches, from doing fieldwork in poor communities to undertaking large-scale economic and sociological quantitative studies of the correlates and determinants of poverty. Anthropologist Oscar Lewis of the University of Illinois first developed the idea of "the culture of poverty" in his 1959 book *Five Families: Mexican Case Studies in the Culture of Poverty*. The core idea was that those who lived in poverty were marginal and suffered from a sense of not belonging along with dependency and helplessness. They were, in effect, aliens in their own country, and the subcultural values they had developed prevented them from rising out of their poverty. Although Lewis was writing about Mexicans, his work had a strong impact on Daniel Patrick Moynihan, who adopted the orientation both in his policy work and in *The Moynihan Report* (1965). Over the past two decades, Lewis's and Moynihan's representation of the cycle of poverty and their descriptions of poverty have been widely criticized, although the ideas have a good deal of persistence within the thinking of the broader public.

University of Wisconsin and University of Michigan economists and sociologists have made landmark discoveries through their theoretical and empirical work related to poverty. Research conducted at Wisconsin in the 1930s led to the development of the federal Social Security program and to government employment programs. Wisconsin social scientists examined various alternatives to welfare policy in the 1970s and 1980s. Researchers at the University of Michigan created the "Panel Study of Income Dynamics," which since 1968 has followed the same individuals and families to gather information on their economic and social behavior and their health. These data have improved our understanding of the determinants of family income and its changes over time. Federal and state policy options about how to address problems faced by low-income families have been based, in part, on this research.

The Lonely Crowd. Middle-class and affluent America has been subjected to analytic inquiry since the inception of social science research at American universities. In the 1950s you did not have to be living in Levittown or attending cocktail parties in any other New York suburb to hear conversation about national character, conformity, and individuality. David Reisman, a Harvard University sociologist, generated a lot of that conversation with the 1950 publication of his book (with Nathan Glazer and Reuel Denny) *The Lonely Crowd: A Study of the Changing American Character.* After World War II, many educated people became interested in questions about conformity and whether you could generalize about a national character—whether, for example, the German people tended toward authoritarian personalities. David Reisman tried to describe changes in the American character that paralleled the larger changes in mass culture and an increasingly urban, industrial society.

Reisman identified three types of personalities: the tradition-directed, the inner-directed, and the other-directed. Tradition-directed people tended to obey ancient rules and seldom thrived in a modern, fast-changing society. Inner-directed people tended to be more rigid but also more confident; they embodied certain Protestant values and were motivated by individual aspirations and ambitions. The other-directed people aspired to be loved rather than esteemed. They wanted to feel in harmony with the people around them, and they were largely conditioned by what they thought other people would think of them. Reisman argued that Americans were shifting from a society where people were predominantly inner-directed to one where people were other-directed; the personality of the other-directed person fit more easily into a world increasingly influenced by large corporations and government bureaucracies. While Reisman was not nostalgic for the older inner-directed type, he was concerned, as he put it, that Americans would "lose their social freedom and their individual autonomy in seeking to become like each other." They were becoming "a lonely crowd."

Many sociologists at the time were skeptical about these generalizations because they believed that the variations in personality types within societies were greater than those between societies, making generalizations about national character misleading. The skepticism of his colleagues aside, Reisman had a huge following and many admirers. He appeared on the cover of *Time* magazine, becoming a household name, and the idea of the "lonely crowd" developed into a common point of reference. His book has sold more than a million copies—an unheard of number for a book by an academic social scientist.

Sociolinguistics. William Labov, considered the father of sociolinguistics, turned his attention while at Columbia and the University of Pennsylvania to understanding the linguistic patterns of people in different social classes, particularly within economically disadvantaged, black, urban communities. His book *The Social Stratification of English in New York City* (1966) found that African American vernacular English, or "Black English," was a variety of English with its own grammatical rules, and that it should not be stigmatized, as it was at the time.

Effective Scope. David Caplovitz's *The Poor Pay More* examined consumer practices in New York City. Caplovitz taught at Columbia and produced his research at Columbia's Bureau of Applied Research. His major finding was that low-income people tended to pay more than middle-class people did for the same products because they were less likely to shop around for better buys. In this discussion, he extended the concept of "effective scope," first introduced by Paul Lazarsfeld in his famous study of unemployment in the Austrian town of Marienthal in the 1930s and later in his study of academic freedom during the McCarthy period.

Lazarsfeld wrote: "External circumstances can restrict or widen an individual's effective scope. Studies carried out during the depression of the 1930's indicated that long-lasting unemployment made the effective scope of workers and their families even more limited than before. Paradoxically, the longer workers were unemployed, the less they kept track of employment opportunities outside of their communities; the unemployment of parents also led to an impoverishment of their children's fantasy world."[18] In his study of the purchasing habits of low-income people, Caplovitz found a significant correlation between a person's social class background and his or her awareness of alternative opportunities.

For example, he found that people's effective scopes were very different when they listened to the radio: Lower-class people tuned in to only a few stations, and these stations were generally close to each other on the radio dial, while middle-class people might scroll from one end of the band to the other. Their effective scopes, and thus their opportunities, were far broader.

Unintended Consequences. One of the core ideas in the social and behavior sciences is that purposive action directed toward a set of results may actually turn out to produce some different results. One thing we can almost count on is that there will be unintended consequences of some of our actions. Hints of this idea can be traced at least as far as the Scottish Enlightenment, and one can find anticipations of it as well in Joseph Schumpeter's work, for example. But it was Robert K. Merton in 1946 who began to systematically analyze and classify types and determinants of the unanticipated consequences of purposive action. Unintended consequences are so pervasive, in fact, that social and behavioral scientists now systematically anticipate these consequences and try to analyze when and why they occur. This topic is important to studies of culture and society because unintended consequences on a broad scale can, and often do, result from government policy decisions.

Deviant Behavior and the American Dream. The continuing widespread belief in the American Dream lies, in part, behind the scholarly interest in social mobility. Immigrants used to come to the United States believing the streets were paved with gold, and social scientists have attended to the reality of that dream and what has frustrated people in their attempts to realize it. Sociologists have analyzed the relationship between strongly internalized social values, such as becoming a success in America (measured by occupational, educational, or financial success), and the opportunities actually open to people who embrace those values.

Robert K. Merton and many other social scientists began to work on this problem as a way of understanding "deviant behavior" and to explain the causes of crime and juvenile delinquency. Drawing upon and refining Emile Durkheim's nineteenth-century work, Merton applied the idea of *anomie* to social situations. Anomie is caused by a sharp disjunction that exists in society. On one hand, there are almost universally shared values and aspirations; on the other, the individuals located in different social strata of society have very different opportunities. Some have a good chance of achieving these aspirations by legitimate means, while others have very little opportunity to do so. Merton focused, in fact, on the American Dream, examining the responses of individuals to frustrated opportunities, and concluded that structurally induced anomie could lead to deviant behavior. He hypothesized that when people's aspirations are thwarted when they use legitimate means to reach those highly valued goals, because of a lack of opportunities, they will under certain conditions turn to illegitimate means to achieve them.

Merton's social structural theory of deviant behavior led to efforts to empirically test it and use it to turn deviant behavior around, particularly in urban areas where youth gangs and juvenile delinquency were seemingly intractable problems. One of the most famous efforts to turn juvenile delinquent behavior into socially acceptable behavior was carried out in a multiyear project, called "Mobilization for Youth," in New York City during the 1960s. The social researchers and social workers tried to transform the values and aspirations of youngsters who were prone to delinquency by setting up things like local cafes where the teenagers could spend time, dance, listen to music, and get a better understanding of schooling as a means of social mobility.

Social Structures and Social Networks. Each of the social and behavioral sciences has its own unique angle of vision on behavioral patterns. Psychologists see psychological causes behind the same pattern of behavior that sociologists see as a result of social structural forces. In fact, for decades, sociologists and anthropologists searched for structural theories of behavior in an effort to differentiate their explanations from those that were fundamentally social psychological.

Structural analysis goes back a long way—it was adopted as a mode of explanation by the great anthropologists of the early twentieth century and revived by Harvard sociologist Talcott Parsons, who tried to construct a theoretical basis for the analysis of social structures in the 1950s. In more recent years, the discoveries of structuralism have been augmented and extended in a new line of theory and research called "network analysis." One of the leading figures in this area has been Harrison C. White, who taught at Carnegie Mellon University, the University of Chicago, and Harvard before moving to the University of Arizona and then Columbia University. White was trained as a physicist, and his mathematical models led the way in developing network theory and analysis. The signature ingredient of his work, and of the work by the extraordinary number of talented students whom he trained, has been his focus on social structures based on patterns of relationships rather than on attributes of individuals. In the first decade of the twenty-first century, social network analysis is perhaps the principal way of examining social structures and organizations in sociology.

If Harrison White is the putative father of "network analysis," his disciples have done him proud. Mark Granovetter, who received his Ph.D. at Harvard and studied with White, and has taught at the State University of New York at Stony Brook as well as at Stanford, used network analysis to demonstrate that people were more apt to find jobs through acquaintances than through close friends. His paper "The Strength of Weak Ties" (1973) was one of the most influential pieces of work in network theory. He demonstrated that in marketing and politics, the use of acquaintances ("weak ties") enables people to reach audiences that would not be accessible through the use of close friends ("strong ties"). He compares information flow where there is a low-density network (where many lines indicating direct relationships are absent) with information flow in a high-density network (where most of the possible lines among friends are present).

Granovetter wrote that "the weak ties between Ego and his acquaintance" were "a crucial bridge between the two densely knit clumps of close friends," pointing out that "these clumps would not, in fact, be connected to one another at all were it not for the existence of weak ties." People without weak ties, he concluded, "will be deprived of information from distant parts of the social system and will be confined to the provincial news and views of their close friends."[19] Weak ties lead to more rapid innovations, to an increased ability to coordinate efforts, and to greater access to resources—and in the case of the labor market, to greater job opportunities. Following the work of Thomas Schelling, Granovetter also developed a model of the formation of "fads," which found its popular expression in Malcolm Gladwell's book *The Tipping Point*. These ideas have had enormous potential for elaboration and are among the most influential and highly cited works in contemporary sociology. A second generation of sociologists working on network analysis, including Ronald Burt, Peter Bearman, and Duncan Watts—all former students or colleagues of Harrison White—has now applied it to the structure of business firms, to historical analysis, and to interpersonal relations.

War-Related Research. Some of the most influential and lasting social science "discoveries" have come from war-related research conducted by social scientists. Although the military funds far less social and behavioral science than "hard" science, it has supported work that has led to important discoveries. Perhaps the quintessential example of this is the research during World War II on the impact of the war on the attitudes, opinions, and psychological adjustment of soldiers.

The findings of this research were used to formulate social policy related to the war effort and the demobilization of the troops after the Allied victory. Much of this work involved a team of psychologists and sociologists, led by a Harvard sociologist, Samuel Stouffer, author of the two volume classic *The American Soldier* (1949). Among hundreds of findings, the team of social scientists discovered that soldiers fought not only to end the war and to be able to go home, but also because they did not want "to let their buddies down." The influence of comrades and social cohesion on willingness to do battle has become an axiom of our knowledge of behavior in battle situations. It was found to be true among German soldiers as well as Americans. In a 2003 study of American troops in Iraq, social scientists wanted to see if these older findings remained valid. In response to the question, "Generally, in your combat experience, what was most important to you in making you want to keep going and do as well as you did?" American troops responded as they had in the past.[20]

Stouffer's empirical research led to the elaboration of other important concepts that continue to influence our thinking as well—for example, the concept of "reference group behavior"[21] and the idea that "relative deprivation" may have a greater impact on individual behavior than "absolute deprivation." Soldiers, for example, tended to compare their situations relative to others, including their comrades and buddies, rather than looking to some absolute scale of deprivation.

Stouffer's research on the American soldier also played an important role in legitimating sociological survey research for the public. Many readers of sociological findings during the first half of the century found them to be entirely obvious and wondered whether in fact social science research could teach us anything. The findings from *The American Soldier* helped to reduce this skepticism. For example, people believed that "as long as the fighting continued, men were more eager to be returned to the States than they were after the German surrender." But it turned out that the exact opposite was true: Men were more eager to return to the States after the German surrender than while the fighting was still on. The "obvious" turned out not to be so obvious. In some cases, once the facts were known, people could construct narratives and explanations that made them seem obvious. But in this case, the contribution of the study to our understanding of a common behavior was clear.

Political Science. The contributions of our political scientists can be grouped into four fields: international relations, comparative politics, theory, and American politics. The boundaries between these four specialties have become increasingly blurred, but within each discipline, significant work has been produced to improve our understanding of the political processes and institutions of the United States and other societies.

As early as the 1940s, V. O. Key, who taught at UCLA, Johns Hopkins, Yale, and Harvard during his career, began to emphasize empirical studies of elections and voting behavior, a major part of political science both then and now. Based on analysis of empirical data on election returns, Key, in his textbook *Politics, Parties, and Pressure Groups,* began to emphasize the role of interest groups in understanding political contests. In later work he analyzed the influence of public opinion on government policies.

Robert A. Dahl, while at Yale, entered into extended debate with the sociologist C. Wright Mills over the nature of the American elite. Mills thought of them as more unified and homogeneous, and Dahl argued that there were elites in many groups and that they were hardly unified in their views or political positions. Perhaps his most influential work was *Who Governs?* This was a study of power structures and relations in the town of New Haven, Connecticut.

Richard Neustadt, a political scientist who taught at Cornell, Columbia, and Harvard over several decades, led a group of scholars who focused on the American presidency as an institution. His most influential book, *Presidential Power* (1960), examined the actual power of the president within the structure of American government. He argued that the president had to use personal persuasion, professional reputation within Washington, and public prestige to effect change within a system that had significant checks on the president's authority. Because of the power of his ideas, the newly elected president, John F. Kennedy, quickly recruited Neustadt as an adviser—a position that he continued to hold during the Johnson administration. He later returned to Harvard, where he founded the Kennedy School of Government.

The work on presidential power illustrates that discoveries in the social and behavioral sciences differ significantly from those made in the physical sciences, in part because the conditions of social and political life are constantly changing. Moreover, the discoveries and results of those discoveries can be forces themselves, changing the phenomenon under study. The social scientists are always chasing a moving target. It is not clear how Neustadt, for example, would analyze presidential power in light of the Bush administration's effort to extend the power of the presidency through a series of unilateral actions. It is no longer clear, for example, what checks Congress really has on the power of the president to wage war without actually declaring it.

Economics. As the saying goes, "It's the economy, stupid." And so it often is in determining people's actions, attitudes, and voting patterns. Sociologists, anthropologists, and political scientists surely have increased our knowledge and understanding of patterns of behavior and social life and have influenced social policies, but economists have had a far greater impact on our lives—either directly or indirectly—by making discoveries and devising theories that influence economic policy, business and investment decisions, and financial markets. In each case, scores of people have worked on the problems; I will only allude to a few of the major contributors.

At the turn of the twentieth century, the economist Thorstein Veblen, who studied at Johns Hopkins under Charles Peirce, one of the founding fathers of pragmatism, developed the concept of "conspicuous consumption," which he introduced in his widely influential book *The Theory of the Leisure Class* (1899). He was a professor of economics at the University of Chicago at the time. Conspicuous consumption refers to the tendency of people to spend money to enhance their status in the eyes of others— carrying with it the pejorative connotation that such spending is a waste of money and other resources.

The classic and hugely influential work of Cambridge University's John Maynard Keynes on macroeconomic theory during the 1930s shaped government policies on how fiscal and monetary policy could influence rates of economic growth that affect the occurrence of recessions, depressions, and inflation. Although he was not an American, he had a major influence on economic thought in America in the twentieth century. In America, Paul Samuelson at MIT transformed the study of economics through his research in three main areas: stock pricing, with a particular emphasis on the importance of information and expectations; welfare economics and public finance; and international economics and consumer theory. He emphasized mathematical precision, and he was the intellectual father of scores of economists who themselves made seminal contributions to our knowledge and to the growth of the field. He also fulfilled the role of éminence grise, as an adviser to political candidates and officeholders, and influenced the public's understanding of economics through his column in *Newsweek*, which ran from 1966 to 1981.

Many people know Samuelson as the person who codified core economic theory and research in his 1948 textbook, *Economics: An Introductory Analysis*, which has sold more than 4 million copies. For several generations, most undergraduate students of economics cut their teeth on this text. One must not underestimate the way a highly successful textbook can influence the thinking of practitioners and shape a discipline. Samuelson surely was aware of this when he once remarked, "Let those who will, write the nation's laws, if I can write its textbooks."[22] Samuelson's and Keynes's discoveries lie in the background of much of the research that emerged in economics for the rest of the twentieth century.

In another important development, economists subsequently produced an empirically valid and theoretically sound understanding of how monetary policy works in the short-term bond market, often now embodied in the "Taylor rule," developed by Stanford economist John Taylor, a former member of the Council of Economic Advisors. The rule holds that the "real" short-term interest rate (adjusted for inflation) should be determined by the Federal Reserve according to three factors: "(1) where actual inflation is relative to the targeted level that the Fed wishes to achieve, (2) how far economic activity is above or below its 'full employment' level, and (3) what the level of the short-term interest rate is that would be consistent with full employment." Furthermore, "The rule 'recommends' a relatively high interest rate (that is, a 'tight' monetary policy) when inflation is above its target or when the economy is above its full employment level, and a relatively low interest rate ('easy' monetary policy) in the opposite situations."[23] This is a precise statement of how central banks should act, under common conditions, in the interest of economic stability. It turns out to describe quite well how they do in fact act.[24]

Economists have also developed a precise model of the pricing of risky assets in a competitive securities market. This has led to standard measurements of relative risk, universally used by investment bankers and others, and has thus been the basis for the "financial engineering" that underlies the practice of diversification and the market of derivatives and that enables the packaging of risk to be sold to those who prefer to bear it. Some say that the most important insight in the evolution of these core investment ideas came in a paper published in 1952 by a twenty-five-year-old University of Chicago graduate student in economics, Harry Markowitz. His paper was called "Portfolio Selection" and appeared in *Journal of Finance*. The idea was premature, according to some; indeed, it was not widely used in economics for another ten years, when it was rediscovered after the specialty of finance economics had matured. He shared a Nobel Prize thirty-eight years later for his work on portfolio selection.

Markowitz was interested in how to minimize risk among those who were willing to invest their money with the knowledge that investing in a portfolio of stock inherently produces risk. The Markowitz Efficient Portfolio is one where an increased diversification will lower the portfolio's risk for any given expected rate of return, or, put differently, the most efficient portfolio is one that will yield the highest expected return given the level of risk assumed by the investor. Markowitz's idea was critical to the long-term development of the capital asset pricing model (CAPM), which describes the relationships between risks and expected returns in setting prices for risky securities. The CAPM was developed by William Sharpe at Stanford, John Lintner at Harvard, Jan Mossin at Carnegie Mellon, and Jack Treynor from the Arthur D. Little management consulting firm.

The sophistication of the financial models increased over time, and a major contributor to that progress was the Black-Scholes formula of pricing options, named after Fischer Black of the University of Chicago and Myron Scholes, who worked at both Chicago and MIT. Pricing options are contracts that give the buyer the right, but not the obligation, to buy a security or commodity at some later date for a specified price. The Black-Scholes model, which Robert C. Merton improved, became the basis for a great many hedge-fund investment strategies during the 1990s. Merton used "continuous time analysis" to take the capital asset pricing model and transform it, making it more dynamic by taking into account changing conditions over a series of time periods.

Various hedge funds used the model, including Long Term Capital Management, which was founded in 1994 by John Meriwether, former vice chairman and head of bond trading at Salomon Brothers. Scholes and Merton, both Nobel Prize winners, were on the board of directors of LTC. The fund initially had spectacular success, earning annual returns of up to 40 percent, and led all other hedge funds in performance for some time. Then it suddenly failed because a series of highly improbable events related to Russian currency occurred. The firm was very highly leveraged and could not raise sufficient capital to avoid its own destruction. The Federal Reserve and several investment banks stepped in to stop the bleeding because of the implications for financial markets beyond LTC. In short, economists may have developed models to manage and reduce risk, but no one can eliminate it entirely—especially if you are looking to outperform the market substantially. And if we combine extreme risk-taking with market imperfection of information; extremely high, unregulated leveraging of assets (used to multiply gains, and, of course, potentially resulting in losses as well) by financial institutions, including insurance companies, banks, and hedge funds; and very low interest rates, you have the ingredients for financial meltdown. The bitter truth of this became abundantly apparent in the financial crisis of 2008.

The research and discoveries of economists like Kenneth Arrow of Stanford and Robert Solow of MIT have produced a far greater general understanding of the process of long-term growth in advanced economies. Arrow produced a theory of growth that moved technical change from an assumption to something to be seriously studied within the framework of neoclassical economics. He argued that innovation and technical change are determined endogenously and can be measured, and therefore studied, as part of economic activity. Solow's research has led to a useful analysis of the extent to which governments are well advised to subsidize activities such as basic research, applied research and development, capital investment, and even vocational education.

OURSELVES AND OUR SENSIBILITIES

Studies in such fields as linguistics, social and cultural anthropology, social psychology, and human sexuality, and from professional schools such as law schools, have helped to shape our understanding of the human condition;

they have given us insight into many areas of human life, sometimes influencing policy debates and decisions. Here we shall look at some of the highlights in these areas that are related to university work.

Linguistics. Formerly an Institute Professor at MIT, Noam Chomsky, the son of a Hebrew scholar, was born in Pennsylvania and completed his undergraduate and doctoral work at the University of Pennsylvania. Part of his doctoral dissertation research was carried out over four years as a Junior Fellow at Harvard, one of the most coveted positions in American higher education. His best-known works are on aspects of syntax, or what came to be called "generative grammar," and on an innate body of linguistic knowledge that is referred to as "universal grammar."

According to his theory, knowledge of this universal grammar is innate in children, who can easily learn their native language by applying certain features of it. Chomsky used the speed with which children learn their native language as support for his theory. His work represented a challenge to behavioral psychologists, such as B. F. Skinner at Harvard, who thought of language acquisition as an example of operant conditioning. While always controversial, Chomsky's theories have been exceptionally influential in linguistics and in cognitive psychology and the impact of his work remains extraordinary.

Other influential discoveries related to language and perception have been carried out by linguistic anthropologists. Edward Sapir, one of the prize students of the founder of American anthropology, Franz Boas, and Benjamin Lee Whorf, a linguist, produced the "Sapir-Whorf Hypothesis." This work argued that there was a direct relationship between the grammatical categories of a person's language and the way in which that person understood the world and behaved in it. In short, different language patterns produced different ways of thinking. Sapir and Whorf identified some of the grammatical mechanisms that influenced thought.

An example of the idea of linguistic determinism can be found in George Orwell's novel *Nineteen Eighty-Four*, where he creates a fictional dystopia in which words and language are used to manipulate society. The words used to express ideas about revolution, rebellion, and freedom are removed from the language, for example, in Newspeak—the new language that replaces English—thus making the people incapable of revolting because they have no language with which to do it. Although there is no consensus about the Sapir-Whorf hypothesis, work by Peter Gordon in 2004 at Columbia University provided some support for its validity.

Social Anthropology. Social anthropologists have produced a cumulative body of work that has attempted to change the way we think about other cultures, and through that understanding, to learn how to better evaluate our own. English and French anthropologists of the late nineteenth and early twentieth centuries, such as Bronislaw Malinowski, Radcliffe Brown, and Marcel Mauss, used ethnographic fieldwork to develop theoretical ideas about other cultures, paving the way for the American social anthropologists of the later twentieth and early twenty-first centuries.

The subject of cultural variability began to draw great interest in American society with the widespread dissemination of works by Columbia's Ruth Benedict in *Patterns of Culture* and Margaret Mead in *Coming of Age in Samoa* (Mead worked as a curator at the Museum of Natural History in New York and was an adjunct professor from 1954 to 1978 at Columbia). Their anthropological travels and discoveries intrigued others in the academy, including literary critics, who began to incorporate their ideas in their literary criticism. These works crossed the divide between the academy and mass culture and opened up to the popular imagination the idea that particular aspects of the human experience (for example, the experience of adolescence or gender roles or the nature of political authority) were neither divinely given, nor biologically mandated, nor logically necessary.

Clifford Geertz from the University of Chicago, and later the Institute for Advanced Study at Princeton, extended this tradition through his work on "thick description," as expressed in his 1973 book, *The Interpretation of Cultures.* Geertz's point was that without understanding social context it is difficult to interpret most actions. He argues that the role of cultural anthropologists is to provide thick descriptions, which attempt to explain behavior within specific types of social contexts.

Obedience to Authority. In some of the most ingenious and disturbing social psychological experiments ever conducted, Stanley Milgram of Yale University examined the question of the banality of evil in the 1960s and early 1970s. Milgram's experiments began in 1961 following the capture of

Adolf Eichmann, the German officer who was tried in Israel for the murder of thousands of Jews in the concentration camps, and his subsequent trial and execution. Eichmann's defense was that he was merely following the orders of his superiors. Hannah Arendt, a prolific political philosopher, followed the trial for *The New Yorker* magazine and authored a controversial book for the general public, *Eichmann in Jerusalem: A Report on the Banality of Evil* (1963). In the book she argued that we are all capable of committing morally opprobrious and horrendous acts under certain conditions, particularly in an effort to conform to mass opinion.

Stanley Milgram wanted to test Arendt's hypothesis. In his experiment, conducted in a laboratory at Yale University, the stated purpose was to reward or punish a "student" for correct or incorrect answers to a series of questions in a simple learning experiment. If the "student" was unable to answer a question correctly, the subject of the experiment was asked to give the student an electric shock. The experimenter stood next to the subject and enjoined him to continue shocking the student for wrong answers, increasing the level of the shock for each incorrect answer. There was a meter in front of the subject that had labels indicating the intensity of the shock. The student, who was actually not being shocked at all, acted as if he were increasingly in pain, until he would scream out in agony for the subject to stop (when the meter read severe shock). The design of the experiment was to determine at what point the subject would refuse to shock the subject any longer. As it turned out, a very high percentage of subjects were willing to continue the experiment (under the urging of the experimenter) to a level that could have caused severe harm or even death to the student if the shocks had been real.

In *Obedience to Authority*, published in 1974, Milgram concluded that under certain conditions we are all capable of acting in ways that are morally repugnant, and that perhaps Arendt's notion of the banality of evil was not far-fetched. This experiment had a huge effect on the ways in which we think about morally opprobrious actions. It also caused a furor among researchers and observers who felt that Milgram had not adequately informed his subjects about the nature of the experiment and how it might affect them psychologically. In fact, the experiment, like thousands of other social psychological experiments at the time, depended on deception and today probably could not be conducted; the need for informed consent would have undermined the experimental situation.

Human Sexual Behavior. Before Alfred Kinsey's famous research into human sexual behavior, we had little knowledge of the patterns and practices of sexual activity in men and women in the United States. Kinsey's pioneering and controversial 1948 research at the University of Indiana raised our awareness of sexual practices, which only then began to be studied in a more systematic way. While research into sexual practices has remained controversial—to the point where Congress has tried to limit or undermine surveys of sexual behavior using government funding—other researchers have continued to make major advances in our understanding of patterns of sexual behavior.

In 1992, Edward Laumann, a sociologist at the University of Chicago, began a large-scale and highly collaborative project that became the most systematic study of sexual behavior ever done in the United States. The National Health and Social Life Survey was the first scientifically based examination of sexual behavior among Americans, and the results disputed a host of myths. Other surveys followed that also shattered prevailing myths. For example, based upon a representative survey of more than 3,000 Americans between the ages of fifty-seven and eighty-five in 2007, Laumann and his colleague Stacy Tessler Landau found that more than three-quarters of those questioned had remained sexually active well into their seventies and eighties, proving that there is hope for us all. They found that older people "value sexuality as an important part of life" and continue to be very much interested in sex.[25] Other sociologists, such as Columbia's Peter Bearman, have also helped to dispel myths about sexuality. In a large-scale empirical study, Bearman and his colleagues found that, by the time their teenage years were over, teenagers who had signed abstinence pledges had been just as sexually active as those who had not signed the pledges.

Law and the Other Professions. A good deal of the core knowledge used at law schools and other professional schools has been derived from the knowledge produced within the traditional arts and sciences disciplines. For example, much of the value added in business school education comes from social science disciplines, and it is being produced at business schools by the exceptionally brilliant economists, sociologists, and psychologists who happen to be located there. This is not entirely fair, of course, since many major innovations in fields like accounting have developed inside business school programs. To suggest several types of contributions that professional schools have made through their "discoveries," let me focus on just a few from the law schools.

Northwestern University's Center on Wrongful Convictions has been actively trying to identify—and rectify—serious miscarriages of justice. It has successfully applied scientific techniques developed in other fields, such as using DNA and other types of evidence, to overturn cases that were decided improperly. Similarly, the Innocence Project, founded in 1992 by Barry C. Scheck and Peter J. Neufeld at the Benjamin N. Cardozo School of Law at Yeshiva University in New York City, "works to exonerate the wrongfully convicted through post conviction DNA testing; and develop and implement reforms to prevent wrongful convictions."[26] Finally, James S. Liebman, Jeffrey Fagan, and Valerie West, at Columbia University's School of Law, have documented the extraordinarily high error rates associated with the judicial process leading to capital sentences. The work of these groups has led to a reconsideration of the use of the death penalty in the United States, and in a number of states the suspension of the death penalty.

One of the most influential ideas in economics, known at the Coase Theorem, came from the work of Ronald Coase at the University of Chicago Law School. The basic idea can be simply stated: "In a world where there are no transaction costs, an efficient outcome will occur regardless of the initial allocation of property rights." The theorem, which has been used in such varied fields as tort law, pollution regulation, farming policy, and voting rights, has been one of the most influential of all ideas in the growing field of law and economics.[27] In fact, following the work of Coase and others at the University of Chicago as well as at a number of other major American law schools, the field of law and economics occupies an important position in the interpretation of law. The many books by Judge Richard Posner, who teaches at Chicago, use basic economics concepts and ideas, such as utilitarian theory and cost-benefit analysis, to analyze a set of social and legal issues.

On a different front, Ruth Bader Ginsburg's scholarly work on gender equity and the law, done while she was on the faculty of Columbia University before she became a Supreme Court justice, profoundly changed the way courts considered gender discrimination cases under Title VII of the 1964 Civil Rights Act, under the Equal Pay Act, and under the Equal Protection and Due Process clauses of the Constitution. Gender cases still do not have the same formal standing in judicial review as race discrimination cases do, but Ginsburg made gender inequalities far more visible than before and fostered a legal movement dealing with gender issues. A generation later, University of Michigan law professor Catherine MacKinnon's innovative work led directly to the expansion of the definition of discrimination to include sexual harassment—and to its treatment as such in the law.

Finally, through their work on separation of ownership and control, Adolf Berle, professor of corporate law at Columbia, and Gardiner Means, a Harvard economist, have had an enormous effect on corporate law. Berle, who advised Roosevelt on aspects of business law as part of his brain trust, affected New Deal legislation, modern scholarship, and judicial decisions in business law. In the 1930s, Berle and Means held that corporations were economic organizations that had public responsibilities and accountability. They wrote that separation of ownership and control "destroys the very foundation on which the economic order of the past three centuries has rested." The increased interest in accountability led to the formation of the Securities and Exchange Commission.

America's professional schools also influence our lives indirectly through the students they produce who hold influential positions in government, business, law, architecture, social work, journalism, and other areas requiring specialized training. Even if specific law journal articles do not directly affect opinions of the courts (and there is an ongoing debate over how much influence law professors have on actual decision-making), their students, who clerk for judges and who work in litigation, carry with them ideas learned at law school that shaped their thinking.

THINKING ABOUT THINKING

With the ascendance of science and engineering, and the overemphasis on the pre-professional training of undergraduates, the humanities remain underappreciated for the important roles that they play at our great universities. The scientific, social science, and humanities disciplines at these institutions of higher learning are actually quite interdependent, and, as previously stated, I cannot imagine being able to create a top-tier university without a distinguished humanities program at the core of its activities. There is a web of influence that cuts across disciplines and schools.

Although they may be labeled somewhat differently from one university to another, included under the general rubric of the humanities are English and comparative literature, philosophy, the multiple languages and cultures departments, art and art history, music, religion, and, increasingly, history. Beyond these traditional subjects are new, interdisciplinary subjects such as African American studies, women's and gender studies, urban studies, film studies, and communications, among a host of other emerging fields of study. The so-called culture wars of the 1980s and 1990s, and the movement toward scientism in the humanities, surely hurt the image of these disciplines in public opinion (and this was not without some justification). Nevertheless, brilliant scholars in these fields continue to shape the values, the aesthetics, and the moral character of our culture in critically important ways. They also represent in good measure the critical voice of the universities as social and intellectual antagonists and as public intellectuals who write for wider audiences.

In the assessment of the rankings of the world's universities, the humanities are an undervalued component in part because it is harder to quantify measures of distinction here than in science. But there is not a single great multiversity—placing to one side now those boutique universities that specialize in one or two specific areas of knowledge acquisition—that does not have distinguished humanities departments. Better methods of assessing the overall quality of universities would include refinements in how to measure the impact of the humanities on research discoveries, on students, and on our everyday lives.[28]

Having made this claim, I will only suggest a few of the forms of discoveries that humanists have made—and continue to make—that have had a large impact on the way we think about our world, our culture, and ourselves.

John Dewey is familiar to many of us as one of the leaders, along with psychologist William James and the logician and philosopher Charles Peirce, of American pragmatism. The school of pragmatism included, during the years 1894 to 1904, George Herbert Mead, James H. Tufts, James R. Angell, and Edward Scribner Ames and had affiliates such as Jane Addams, founder of Hull House in Chicago. Dewey studied at Hopkins and taught at the University of Chicago just after its founding, from 1894 to 1904, but left for Columbia when the University of Chicago refused to hire his wife at the new Chicago Laboratory School. Dewey's work has had extraordinary influence, not least upon our thinking about early childhood progressive education.[29]

Many contemporary philosophers consider Harvard University's John Rawls's *A Theory of Justice* (1972) to be the most important contribution to social contract theory since the work of Thomas Hobbes, John Locke, and John-Jacques Rousseau in the late seventeenth and eighteenth centuries. Rawls's theory is complex, but his ideas about justice in a liberal democracy have had a substantial, if indirect, influence on the way we think about justice.[30]

If the world of philosophy is somewhat removed from the public arena, the world of the literary critic is not. Our research universities have had a tradition of literary critics who are also public intellectuals. Lionel Trilling, the widely read Columbia University literary critic, introduced several generations of academic readers as well as the general public to the modern novel—and particularly, but not exclusively, to the interpretation of literary works using Freudian concepts. Trilling and many of his colleagues who wrote for *The Partisan Review*, including, among others, Harold Rosenberg, Dwight MacDonald, Mary McCarthy, Irving Howe, Saul Bellow, Leslie Fielder, Daniel Bell, Hannah Arendt, and Susan Sontag, became public intellectuals who introduced works of literature and social science to a more general reading public.

The rise to preeminence of American art historians coincided with the growth of American research universities.[31] Until the turn of the twentieth century, art history followed German and Italian models. The art historian Aby Warburg traveled to the United States in the 1890s. The founder of the Warburg Institute associated with the University of London, he had been born in Hamburg, Germany, and had been the first heir to the Warburg Bank. But he gave up his position in order to pursue art history, with the understanding that his life of learning and scholarship would be supported by his brothers. Warburg introduced two new approaches around the turn of the twentieth century: the iconographic and the social historical methods. The iconographic line of inquiry was taken up by Erwin Panofsky, an intellectual émigré who began teaching at the Institute of Fine Arts at New York University and then moved to the newly formed Institute for Advanced Study at Princeton in 1935.

American art history was particularly blessed by the migration from Europe. Distinguished German art historians who took up residence at

American universities included William Heckscher, Richard Krautheimer, Adolf Katznellenbogen, and Julius Held. Rudolf Wittkower moved to London in 1934 and worked under the incomparable E. H. Gombrich at the Warburg Institute before emigrating to the U.S. and joining Columbia, where he remained from 1956 to 1969. The other line of inquiry, the social historical approach, was quintessentially and powerfully represented by Meyer Schapiro at Columbia. Influenced by Marxist social thought in the 1920s and 1930s, Schapiro produced the social historical paradigm that still dominates the discipline, particularly, but not exclusively, in the Anglo-Saxon world. Schapiro became an important public intellectual, and his graduate lectures at Columbia were widely attended by New York art lovers.

European academics tended to look down at American humanists, including art historians, because the Americans lacked, in the Europeans' view, both philological and archival skills—and were shamefully less adept at foreign languages. But from about 1980, much of the work in the field was being dominated by art historians at American universities. This was because of the influence of both the Panofsky and Schapiro lines of analysis—and the influence of their intellectual offspring. It is perhaps interesting that at the end of the nineteenth century, the American Bernard Berenson combined the aesthetics of British writers such as John Ruskin and Walter Pater with the connoisseurship skills of Italians such as G. B. Cavalcaselle and Giovanni Morelli, and dominated the world of art history outside of Germany.

Berenson essentially created the market for the "old Masters," and, as an intermediary between collectors and dealers, earned fees that made him a fortune. The art historical world had to await Panofsky and Schapiro to detach the academic discipline firmly from the world of art dealers. In more recent times, the movement to introduce various forms of theory into art history—especially in regard to contemporary art related to the abstract expressionist works of Jackson Pollock, William de Kooning, and Hans Hofmann—was led by the controversial art critic Clement Greenberg (1909–1994). Greenberg influenced a new generation of theoretically oriented modern art historians, including Rosalind Krauss at the City University of New York (CUNY) and Columbia, and Michael Fried at Johns Hopkins.

American thinkers in the humanities have done much to introduce major writers from other cultures to the American public. Edward Said tried for years to get American publishers to support translations of the novels and short stories of the Egyptian writer Naguib Mahfouz. He was told there was no audience for this writer until Mahfouz won the Nobel Prize for Literature in 1988. There are many examples of American scholars translating the works of others in order to have them reach a wider public, such as Gregory Rabassa, of Queens College and CUNY, and his translations of Julio Cortázar, Jorge Amado, and Gabriel Garcia Márquez.

If the focus of Said and others was on contemporary literatures, Theodore de Bary and Donald Keene, among others, created a window into the history of civilizations that had rarely been studied by American students. They created a core curriculum at Columbia that focused on China and Japan rather than on Western literatures, modeling it after the famous Columbia and Chicago undergraduate general education courses. In the 1960s, with support from the Carnegie Corporation and the U.S. Office of Education, de Bary, Keene, and Burton Watson started a series of translations that now has 150 titles. It is used as part of general education courses on Asia. Many other scholars also began translating essential literatures. For example, Barbara Stoler Miller, a Barnard College scholar, helped Americans discover Sanskrit literature with her marvelous translations, particularly of the *Bhagavad Gita.*

Over the past thirty or forty years, one of the most profound changes in historical study has been the emergence of subdisciplines that concentrate on specific forms of identity, such as gender and race. Gender studies can be traced back to Gerda Lerner's work at the University of Wisconsin. Called the "godmother of women's history," Lerner was a radical student in Nazi-occupied Austria. When she came to the United States and went back to school at age thirty-eight, she continued to think about the history of injustice. In the late 1950s, there were no women's studies departments, no women's history courses taught at colleges and universities, and indeed little mention of women's history in the standard history curriculum.

As Lerner has said, "People didn't think that women had a history or a history worth knowing." She focused her energy on finding a place for marginalized people at the center of historical discourse. While still an undergraduate, she created the first women's history course in the United States. She went on to develop and direct the first women's history doctoral program at the University of Wisconsin.[32] Today, women's history occupies a central place in history departments, and the angle of vision of historians who work in the field, such as Carolyn Walker Bynum, who taught at the University of Washington and at Columbia before moving to Princeton's Institute for Advanced Study, has changed the way historical analysis is done.

On a different front, a good deal of modern music has been produced or invented at our major research universities. Composers working at these institutions have created electronic music, new forms of opera, and the field of computer-based music. John Chowning, a Stanford professor for twenty-five years and director of the Center for Computer Research in Music and Acoustics (CCRMA, pronounced "karma"), which is also at Stanford, invented FM synthesis, the computational technique that ushered in the era of digital synthesizers, MIDI (musical instrument digital interface), and desktop music production. CCRMA has been called "one of the most successful think tanks for music technology in the world." According to Paul Lehrman in a 2005 article, "Some of the most important research in music synthesis and digital signal processing that we use today emerged from there, and among the many major figures who worked there were Andy Moorer, developer of the legendary SoundDroid for Lucasfilm and founder of Sonic Solutions; David Ziccarelli, writer of Opcode's original DX7 patch editor and now head of the wildly innovative software company Cycling '74; and Julius O. Smith, creator of what was to become known as physical modeling synthesis."[33]

Of course, computer music depended on the evolution of highly sophisticated computers. Prior to that development, professors who were also composers at Princeton University, the University of Illinois (particularly Lejaren Hiller), the University of Pennsylvania, and Columbia developed electronic music, particularly during the 1950s and 1960s. In fact, the Columbia-Princeton Electronic Music Center used the RCA Mark II Synthesizer in 1958, and some of the most innovative professors and composers included Milton Babbitt, Peter Mauzey, Vladimir Ussachevsky, Otto Luening, Alice Shields, and Mario Davidovsky.

Many people believe that the arts, whether it is creative writing, film, or visual arts, cannot be taught—and that university programs that aspire to do so are of little value. Nevertheless, there is a good deal of evidence that the graduates of these schools, after receiving master's degrees, often go on to stellar careers. Perhaps they would have done so anyway, but the scores of writers who have come from the University of Iowa writing workshop, and others who have earned degrees from top-ranked programs such as those at Hopkins, Columbia, New York University, the University of Houston, Cornell, and Boston University, as well as from public university programs such as the University of Virginia, the University of Michigan, and a number of the California universities, suggest that these programs leave some value added. Much the same can be said for young filmmakers and screenwriters. Beyond the value of training, the programs in the arts at these universities have brought the voices and words of people such as Saul Bellow and Maya Angelou to the students at our universities.

Above I touched on the notion of "public intellectuals," those scholars, from any field, who speak and write on a wide variety of subjects or attempt to communicate the ideas of their discipline to a broad audience. Today there is a sense that the number of public intellectuals who work at universities has dwindled, but I doubt that this notion could be confirmed if rigorously studied. Scores of public intellectuals continue to work from a university base and to contribute to broader public education and debate, although *The New York Review of Books* and *The New Yorker* may occupy the space previously filled by magazines like *The Partisan Review*. And far greater exposure for the thinking of university-based public intellectuals now comes from their appearances on television and in the new media; many have constructed their own blogs.

Simon Schama of Columbia, for example, an internationally renowned historian, wrote and directed a television series on the history of Britain that had an audience of roughly 3 million viewers in Britain and millions more in the United States. He has also written and directed a series on art history as well as several other shows for PBS and the BBC. Harvard's literary critic Henry Louis Gates reaches millions of viewers through his PBS programs *African American Lives*. William Julius Wilson also writes about race in America. Edward Said became one of the world's leading literary critics through the creation, with others, of a new subdiscipline, postcolonial studies.[34] He wrote about music for *The Nation* and about the Palestinian experience for the public interested in Middle East politics and literature. He collaborated with Daniel Barenboim to create a Palestinian-Israeli orchestra, the West-Eastern Divan Orchestra, that performed in many countries. Scientists and scholars in many other fields have become public intellectuals in this way as well. Working in such venues is a particularly attractive method of educating a wider audience about exciting discoveries in any field.

The American research university remains an amazingly fertile place for the creation of novel ideas, whether in the sciences, the social sciences, or the humanities. It has been remarkably successful in realizing its research goals, and its increasingly strong linkage to industry makes it all the more central to the economic and social dynamics of our society. But it is young and fragile. If we want to preserve its preeminence and its effectiveness, we must do more than recognize its value; we must also recognize how it can be threatened. Only then can we respond intelligently to those threats and ensure the ongoing health of our universities.

PART III

FACING CHALLENGES AND LOOKING FORWARD

CHAPTER 11

Academic Freedom and Free Inquiry

The essentiality of freedom in the community of American universities is almost self-evident. No one should underestimate the vital role in a democracy that is played by those who guide and train our youth. To impose any strait jacket upon the intellectual leaders in our colleges and universities would imperil the future of our Nation. . . . Scholarship cannot flourish in an atmosphere of suspicion and distrust.[1]

—Chief Justice Earl Warren

The United States has created a system of higher learning which at its best is the most distinguished in the world. Yet at some points in our history, its position of preeminence has been threatened. The latest threats to the fundamental values of free inquiry and academic freedom have been quite recent, under the George W. Bush administration in the post-9/11 years. Although there is good reason to hope that universities will recover during the administration of President Barack Obama, the problems of the early 2000s remind us that we must not take our universities for granted. In this chapter I shall put the threats to free inquiry during the Bush years into historical perspective.

From 2000 to 2008, roughly half a century after the 1954 House Un-American Activities Committee (HUAC) held congressional hearings on

Communists in American universities, faculty members experienced once again a rising tide of anti-intellectualism. They were increasingly apprehensive about the influence of external politics on university decision-making. Attacks on professors, coupled with other actions by the federal government in the name of national security, represented nothing less than another wave of intolerance and repression, forces that have always made it difficult for institutions of higher learning to thrive, whether during the McCarthy era in America or in other countries at difficult times in their own histories.

The United States paid a heavy price in the 1950s when the leaders of its research universities failed to defend some of their greatest scientists and scholars. If an assault on free inquiry and academic freedom similar to the one that marked the post-9/11 Bush years were to continue for an even longer period of time, or become even more repressive, the negative consequences for the quality of American universities could be dramatic. Universities today are more dependent on federal support than they were during the Cold War. During the McCarthy period they were relatively small institutions, and government contracts and grants made up a smaller portion of their overall revenues. Recall that, in the early 1950s, Columbia University's annual expense budget was substantially less than $50 million. In 2008 it was almost $3 billion, and more than a quarter of this comes from the federal government. Other large research universities are in the same situation, which means they are more vulnerable to political manipulation and control than ever before.

Universities are also more deeply embedded in the broader society than ever before. They are linked to industry, business, and government in multiple ways. These connections inevitably lead to public criticism when faculty members or students express ideas or behave in ways that some people find repugnant. But the kind of free inquiry that leads to discovery must include the freedom to pursue lines of research that may be offensive to some. When the government, or a university administration, cannot tolerate the research efforts of faculty members, and sanctions professors whose work fails to conform to the orthodoxy of the moment, violations of these critically important values also obtain.

There are two powerful defenses of academic freedom. The first is that there is an intrinsic value to free inquiry and to the creation of the conditions necessary for the expression of thoughts to take place in an unfettered way. How else would it be possible for faculty members and researchers to explore new ideas and concepts, attack received wisdom and entrenched ideological beliefs, correct wrongs, and search for truth? The free expression of ideas lies at the heart of what the United States stands for and represents the potential triumph of democracy, where the value of discordant ideas can be presented, defended, accepted, or rejected on the basis of rational argument and evidence. These ideas need not have any practical application that is immediately discernible for them to be valued. Great universities are special places that protect such activities, and those activities must occupy a free zone removed from the powers that be. Universities are places that help us realize the potential of our imaginations and our search for fundamental truths.

The second main defense of academic freedom and free inquiry is a pragmatic and "consequentialist" argument: If we threaten academic freedom and free inquiry, we threaten the ability of universities to make great discoveries, and we potentially sacrifice the fruits of both the transmission of knowledge and the creation of new knowledge—knowledge on which our society greatly depends. I could be proven wrong if someone could point to a system of higher learning that was under the thumb of external political forces that managed nonetheless to be as creative as the system that we have produced under the principles of academic freedom and autonomy from the state. There are some totalitarian societies, such as the Soviet Union, that have managed to produce some extraordinary science, but generally in these cases the creative work has taken place at academies, universities, or research institutes that have been granted a great deal of autonomy from strict government controls under special institutional arrangements.

Granted, it is difficult to establish a clear causal connection between the presence of academic freedom and university discovery. There have been no systematic empirical studies of this relationship, so we must depend on historical examples and anecdotal evidence. In our look at Nazi Germany, I have already described the most blatant example of warped ideology curtailing academic freedom, and in that case, the repressive regime systematically destroyed a university system that arguably had been the best in the world. But there are many other examples that are perhaps less egregious. One of the most notable is the destruction of Soviet biological sciences during the first third of the twentieth century by Trofim

Denisovich Lysenko. His story illustrates the point that when external political ideology trumps scientific method and findings, a body of knowledge can be damaged or destroyed and progress delayed.[2]

Born in the Ukraine in 1898,[3] Lysenko was an agronomist who published about 350 works between 1923 and 1951. He believed in the inheritance of acquired characteristics, an idea often associated with the eighteenth-century French biologist Jean-Baptiste Lamarck, who espoused the theory that characteristics acquired during one's lifetime could be passed on to the next generation genetically. Lysenko's theories had great appeal to Soviet leaders who saw a parallel between his work with plants and animals (to increase the productivity of farms) and the idea that the population itself could be "improved through central state planning." As Loren Graham, the foremost authority on Soviet science, has noted, Lysenko actually rejected the claim that his theories had applicability to human beings. Lysenko did believe in their applicability to other species, however. He was hailed within the Soviet Union as the discoverer of "vernalization," a process by which, he claimed, he could change a winter variety of wheat into a spring variety by subjecting the wheat to different temperatures. The process he was referring to had actually been discovered years earlier in the United States, but received its widest application under Lysenko. Where Lysenko was scientifically wrong was in his claim that the vernalized state could enter the genome of the plant itself and be inherited by the next generation of plants, which would not require vernalization.

Perhaps more important than Lysenko's theories, which after all could have been tested by skeptical colleagues, was his effort to gain control over his scientific field. He wanted to purge the best Soviet geneticists, such as N. I. Vavilov, who was committed to the theories and applications of modern genetics, and he wanted to control the scientific job market in the Soviet community of biologists. He succeeded in doing both. In 1935, Stalin praised him and his work. Lysenko argued that vernalization could vastly increase the production of wheat in the Soviet Union. By 1935 and 1936, Lysenko and I. I. Prezent—a lawyer, not a scientist, by training—were jointly publishing articles declaring that the discoveries of other scientists in the field of genetics were antithetical to the state's political ideology. Prezent constructed facile arguments on Lysenko's behalf showing the snug fit between his form of biology and the ideas of dialectical materialism. Together they attacked Vavilov's work and the evolving theories of modern genetics, which were accused of slowing down the development of agricultural production—a serious offense in Stalin's regime.[4]

Although some Soviet scientists—as well as Americans, such as the Nobel Prize–winning geneticist H. J. Muller—tried to resist the attacks on genetics, they failed to convince other Soviets. Sound science had been discarded in favor of an unsubstantiated belief because Lysenko's science was so consistent with Marxist-Leninist ideology. Then the purges began, and they not only affected geneticists but also anyone else who opposed Lysenko. Being an advocate of genetics was a dangerous matter in the mid-1930s' Soviet Union, as Vavilov discovered. As Theodosius Dobzhansky, an American geneticist and evolutionary biologist who had emigrated from the Ukraine in 1927, said: "In the last years he had to suffer the anguish of seeing the results of his efforts being pulled down by incompetents. He met death in a prison on the bleak and forbidding shores of Eastern Siberia."[5]

Today, Lysenko's theories have been totally discredited, of course, but he came to power because Stalin and his various advisers staunchly supported his efforts and his desire to purge alternative views from the Soviet scientific community. Lysenko's rise occurred at almost the same time that Hitler was purging scientists who were Jews or who opposed Nazi policies. Both became quintessential examples of gross violations of academic freedom and free inquiry; both are powerful illustrations of the consequences for science and the universities of using brute political force to shape or limit the growth of knowledge. The norms of science and the university were violated, and science in Germany and Russia has never recovered from the trauma of those violations.[6]

CAN WE LEARN FROM OUR PAST?

The actual consequences of the McCarthy period for faculty at American universities were far more profound than what we saw during the Bush administration's war on terrorism. During the McCarthy era, universities were represented by some in the FBI and in Congress as safe havens for Communists, former Communists, "fellow travelers," and radical students. A price was paid in ruined careers and lives for those at the great universities who refused to "name names" during the "witch hunts" of the 1950s.

We have not experienced this kind of repression of speech or group affiliation in the 2000s. Nor have the costs in morale, lost research opportunities, and fear reached the pitch found during the McCarthy period. We should take little comfort in these facts, however. For, as will be discussed, many of the actions taken after September 2001 to restrict civil liberties and rights had a substantial impact on the value system and operations of research universities. New forms of government interference with the research mission of our universities did take shape in the years of the Bush administration. We can all learn from the history lessons of the past, including the very recent past.

And there is much to learn. Periodically, in times of actual or perceived national crisis, Americans have been asked to consider the appropriate balance between the rights of individuals and the need for national security. The Alien and Sedition Acts of 1798, President Lincoln's suspension of *habeas corpus* during the Civil War, the Espionage Act of 1917, the internment of Japanese Americans after Pearl Harbor, and the Smith-McCarren Acts passed during the McCarthy period all stripped Americans (or some Americans) of basic civil liberties in the attempt to ensure national security. In each instance, the curtailment of freedoms, which may have seemed necessary at the time, became in short order almost universally judged to have been excessive and overreaching; unnecessary, if not futile; and a subject of national shame and regret. In a recent address to the U.S. Supreme Court, Geoffrey Stone, a constitutional law scholar and the former provost of the University of Chicago, concluded that: "In time of war, or more precisely, in time of national emergency, we respond too harshly in our restriction of civil liberties, and then, later, regret our behavior."[7]

The price paid in civil liberties during national emergencies has become a subject of considerable interest to legal scholars and historians.[8] As we shall see, as we consider several of these episodes, the patterned responses to national crises have often begun with the targeting of noncitizens or new citizens, then continued by extending the scope to all Americans. Although the precise form of intolerance has varied over time, it has typically involved race or nationality, the content of opprobrious ideas, and guilt by association. Whether the targets have been the French or Germans during the eighteenth century; the Germans, Austrians, or Jewish immigrants of the early twentieth; the Japanese and Japanese Americans during World War II; or Arabs and Muslims today, efforts to heighten national security have often involved racial and ethnic stereotyping, prejudice, and fear. The mechanisms used to express distrust and to produce repression have involved restrictive legislation, executive orders, and administrative authority to limit the right of personal privacy (while increasing the government's power to search, seize, incarcerate, or limit access to legal counsel), to deny due process, to criminalize expression of beliefs, and to violate the right of association. While many of these liberties are restored after the crisis has abated, the cost of the repression has already been felt by hundreds or hundreds of thousands of individuals as well as by institutions. In each of these episodes, a drama has unfolded with its heroes and villains.

Although the dilemma of how to balance individual rights and national security interests has been with us since the birth of the nation, it is the two "Red Scares" of the twentieth century that best illustrate the dangers of intolerance and repression for the spirit of academic freedom and free inquiry at our universities. As the research university in the United States was not truly born until after the Civil War, and did not evolve into a significant educational force until the early twentieth century, the national responses to these later crises bear more directly on higher education than earlier episodes. And, because education is viewed as an essential instrument in shaping American values, the academy in the twentieth century often became the target of organized groups intent on restricting liberty in times of national emergency.

WORLD WAR I AND THE RED SCARE

Eugene V. Debs once called Scott Nearing, a professor at the University of Pennsylvania, "the greatest teacher in the United States." This opinion echoed those of the chairman of the Economics Department at Wharton, who said that he considered Nearing "a man of extraordinary ability, of superlative popularity, and . . . the greatest moral force for good in the University."[9] Nearing was also a radical thinker who supported socialist ideas and socialist organizations. His timing was not as good as his teaching, apparently. The administration, alumni, and trustees of the university did not appreciate his outspoken views, which came at a time of gathering national hysteria about the conflict in Europe and our role in that war.

In July 1915, the board of trustees of the University of Pennsylvania notified Scott Nearing that despite the recommendations of the faculty, he would not be rehired for the following year. His firing, one of the more famous early academic-freedom cases, became a cause for the American Association of University Professors (AAUP), which had recently been formed expressly "for the purpose of maintaining academic freedom of speech."[10] Their protest had little practical effect, however.[11] Writing for the *New Republic*, Randolph Bourne, a progressive public intellectual, responded to Nearing's firing by posing the question: "Who owns the universities?" He insisted that "the issues of the modern university are not those of private property but of public welfare," and that "irresponsible control by a board of amateur notables is no longer adequate for the effective scientific and sociological laboratories for the community that the universities are becoming."[12]

As the United States moved closer to war, intolerance toward dissent grew more extreme. After the declaration of war and the passage of the Espionage Act and the Sedition Act, which made it a crime to utter "any disloyal, profane, scurrilous, or abusive language . . . as regards the form of government of the United States, or the Constitution, or the flag,"[13] more than 1,000 people were convicted of crimes under these laws. There was little tolerance for dissent on American university campuses. Efforts to defend "academic freedom" by the AAUP may have had some symbolic value, but they led to few victories.[14]

There may have been a handful of professors who were agents of the German government, but if so, no one could find them. There were, of course, a very limited number of outspoken professors who were opposed to American entry into the war, and there were individuals who were attracted to socialist ideas. Leaders of universities, often out of personal conviction, shut down visible dissent. And where intolerance was not based on conviction, leaders limited dissent because their trustees and alumni, and even other faculty members, pressured them to do so. The need to defend the institution's "reputation" and to mollify wealthy benefactors trumped individual rights.

The simple fact was that at the time of World War I, the faculties at universities were subjected to the same constraints on speech as everyone else in the United States, and there were few who had the power, the organization, or the will to defend dissent. The courts were populated predominantly with conservative judges; the attorney general would not support dissent; and public opinion reflected the fear that gripped the nation. As Geoffrey Stone noted, "After the excesses of World War I, a more expansive view of free expression began to emerge. . . . Nowhere was this shift more evident than in the Supreme Court."[15] It is a strange irony that the first steps toward a far more expansive definition of protected speech and protest emerged from this period of intolerance reinforced by the Supreme Court decisions (which upheld the convictions of the few dissenters who challenged the Espionage and Sedition Acts)—an evolution in thinking set in motion by Oliver Wendell Holmes, Jr.'s, opinions in *Schenck v. United States*[16] and *Abrams v. United States*,[17] and later in his dissent with Justice Louis Brandeis in *Gitlow v. New York*.[18]

If the repression of dissent during the war was excessive, given the actual threat within the United States, the aftermath of the war produced even more extraordinary limits on dissent. Fear of Marxist-Leninist ideology, of the spread of communism in Europe where revolutions were taking place, of anarchists, and of internal conspiracies to overthrow the government did not end with the war. Following 1919, the year of the *Schenck* and *Abrams* decisions, came "the Palmer raids," organized by Attorney General A. Mitchell Palmer and carried out by a freshly minted graduate of George Washington Law School, J. Edgar Hoover. Hoover would cut his teeth on Palmer's efforts to rid the nation of potential subversives, and for fifty years at the FBI would use a variety of techniques to ferret out those whom he perceived as subversive threats to the nation.[19]

The Palmer raids were responses, in part, to actual "terrorist" attacks—mail bombs during April 1919, and then bombings in eight American cities on June 2, 1919. The bomb targets were prominent Americans, including the attorney general himself; Senator Lee Overman, chair of the Bolshevik Investigation Committee; Justice Oliver Wendell Holmes, Jr.; Postmaster General Albert Burleson; John D. Rockefeller; and J. P. Morgan.[20] The bombers were never caught, but that November the first raids brought in about 650 people who were suspected of "radicalism." Many were innocent people simply caught up in the wide dragnet. Some 249 of these people were deported in December 1919. The following month, another 4,000 suspected radicals were rounded up in thirty-three cities, and "virtually every leader of every local communist organization was taken into custody."[21] Leading figures at American law schools and prominent judges such as Learned Hand and Charles Evans Hughes despaired at the extremism of the raids.

The Red Scare of 1917–1920 demonstrated to those within the teaching and research community that principled support for ideas that had been labeled as seditious was just as scarce in the halls of the university as it was in the larger society. If the university was to be a special place that would tolerate the free expression of ideas in difficult times—even ones that a majority of people feared—it was not yet ready to take that role.[22] In sum, little effort was made to "balance" the freedoms of speech and association against the needs of a nation at war. The general climate of opinion that prevailed effectively halted dissent in the universities and larger American society.[23]

THE COLD WAR

The "reign" of Joseph McCarthy lasted only four years, from 1950 to 1954, but many of the conditions necessary for the rise of McCarthyism were already in place well before he emerged as a powerful national figure (and they were alive and well after his death in 1957).[24] From the time of the initial Red Scare after World War I until the full-blown crusade against Communists in the academy that began in the late 1940s, the government, in fact, never ceased its investigations into potential subversive activities. Nor did the universities stop firing professors for "unacceptable" political beliefs and associations.[25] Congress had passed the Smith Act, which made it unlawful to advocate the overthrow of the government, in 1940.[26] J. Edgar Hoover had already built an elaborate administrative apparatus at the FBI that institutionalized surveillance and information-gathering activities to secure secret information on tens of thousands of U.S. citizens.

By the mid-1940s, HUAC had already existed for more than five years and was searching for new rationales for its continued existence. The nation, which had emerged from World War II as the sole nuclear and dominant world power, soon found that Eastern Europe had been lost to Russia and would become part of the Soviet bloc, and that communist parties were growing in influence in Italy and France, and it seemed quite possible that they might gain control of those governments through democratic elections. The rapid development of nuclear capabilities by Russia, the fall of China to Mao Zedong and communism in October 1949, and the threat of war in Korea followed by the June 1950 attacks by North Korea on the South, contributed to the growing fear in the United States that communism posed a real external threat to the United States.

The highly visible HUAC testimony of Alger Hiss in 1949, responding to espionage accusations made by Whittaker Chambers, an editor of *Time* magazine, and the follow-up indictment of Hiss for perjury, contributed further to the misperception that internal security was lax and that there were widespread conspiratorial efforts among Communist groups (the incident also propelled Richard Nixon, then a young Congressman, to national prominence for his role in the hearings). Added into the mix were the "atom spy" inquiries in 1950 and 1951, those questioning the loyalty of J. Robert Oppenheimer in 1953 and other atomic scientists who had worked on the Manhattan Project, and Klaus Fuchs's 1950 admission to British intelligence that he had passed secret scientific information about the atomic bomb to the Soviets. Fuchs's charge that David Greenglass, the brother of Ethel Rosenberg, had spied for Russia while working as a machinist on the Manhattan Project led to the investigation of Julius and Ethel Rosenberg, their arrest on espionage charges in July 1950, their conviction (after a deeply contested trial), and their execution (after a set of appeals) at Sing Sing prison in 1953 for conspiracy to commit espionage.

Congress passed the Internal Security Act ("McCarran Act"), which required registration of the American Communist Party and affiliated organizations with the attorney general, in 1950. The act also required that people seeking government employment or a U.S. passport reveal whether they were Communist Party members, and those who made such revelations could be denied passports and deported from the country. President Truman vetoed the act, saying that it "would make a mockery of our Bill of Rights [and] would actually weaken our internal security measures." Subsequently, Congress overturned the veto by an 89 percent majority vote. The Republicans had found a mechanism, the congressional investigation and hearing, by which it could portray the Truman and Roosevelt administrations as "soft on communism."

The courts took a sympathetic stance toward legislative and other restrictions on civil liberties that were linked to fighting subversive activities and possible internal Communist conspiracies.[27] Even where the judges and Justices of the Supreme Court found HUAC tactics abhorrent, they "respected" the "investigatory authority" of Congress and acquiesced to the limits placed on civil liberties. Perhaps it was out of respect, but it may also have been the result of practical political calculation as judges weighed the effects of opposing the furies of McCarthy and his supporters on the courts. Whatever their justification, they legitimated the "witch hunts" and "red baiting" by finding room in the Constitution for limits on core civil liberties.[28]

By 1953, the federal government was investigating roughly 10,000 citizens and 12,000 aliens for possible deportation. Senator Joseph McCarthy was at the apex of his powers. About one-fifth of the labor force in the United States was working under the penumbra of a loyalty program. Finally, President Dwight D. Eisenhower, pressing his anticommunism campaign, signed the Communist Control Act of 1954, which "outlawed" the Communist Party.

In order for repression to take place, those who were investigating potential subversive activities needed people whose personal histories could make them potential suspects. There were many who would qualify, principally because of the appeal that the ideas and works of Karl Marx, Friedrich Engels, V. I. Lenin, Leon Trotsky, and other democratic socialist thinkers, such as Rosa Luxembourg, had for a generation of young people who came of age during the Depression in the 1930s. Some were searching for a better world and a social theory that would offer them hope. Hardly revolutionaries, a number of students at places like the City College of New York, Columbia, Harvard, and the University of California at Berkeley had flirted with or joined either the Communist Party or communist-oriented organizations. This added ingredient, a group of available suspects, reinforced the fear of internal conspiracies. As we would expect, many younger scholars and scientists on college and university campuses were attracted to alternative ways of seeing the political and social world. It was fertile soil for a campaign against Communists.

Political leaders and men like J. Edgar Hoover used their knowledge of the past histories of prominent Americans, along with the knowledge they gained from "professional" red-baiters and former party members who were willing to "name names," to create an exaggerated narrative of a large number of subversive activities. The actual membership in the Communist Party declined precipitously during the years between World War I and the Cold War. At its peak membership in around 1940, the party had roughly 140,000 paying members. By 1950, this number had shrunk to about 50,000, half being located in New York; and by 1957, there were an estimated 10,000 members of the party. Many of these were members of minority groups, particularly first- or second-generation Jews living in the Northeast. So, by the time McCarthy came to prominence, only 1 in every 2,000 adult Americans were members of the Communist Party—hardly a political threat. Nonetheless, 44 of the 48 state governments passed laws between 1949 and 1955 that "were designed to root out subversives and suppress communist activities."[29]

The internal political atmosphere in the middle to late 1940s contributed to the fears that there were Communists within the United States who were conspiring to overthrow the government. The Republican Party, out of office during the Roosevelt years and faced with the real possibility of defeating Truman in 1948, used the fear of an internal threat to its advantage, suggesting that Truman was insufficiently tough on those who might pose a threat from within the belly of the nation. Responding to the increasing attack that he was "soft on communism," Truman, who was not sympathetic to the hysteria over communism that the Republicans were creating, launched a loyalty security program in 1947, which required federal government employees to gain security clearance to retain their jobs.[30]

Ironically, this changed everything. The Executive Order prohibited the federal government from hiring Communists, fascists, and the amorphous group of "other totalitarians" and excluded from employment those who were guilty of "sympathetic association" with the undesirables or their organizations. The FBI was assigned the responsibility to check out all who might fall under this umbrella before they could be hired.[31] In short, Communists or Communist sympathizers could now be fired from their jobs because of their political beliefs. Truman's order had a ripple effect, setting in motion the adoption of loyalty oaths by states and by organizations and institutions that could use them to fire people whose ideas or affiliations were portrayed as signaling disloyalty. All of this led up to the passage of the McCarran Act in 1950. The House Un-American Activities Committee, recently reinvigorated, began its investigations into Communists in the entertainment industry, but most visibly into the Hollywood film industry and into the "Hollywood Ten" in October 1947. The Hollywood Ten—ten Hollywood writers and directors who refused to testify, claiming that the hearings violated their First Amendment rights—were jailed and blacklisted from employment in the entertainment industry.[32]

When HUAC had finished with Hollywood, its members looked for other "high-profile" targets and found them in the scientists who had worked on the Manhattan Project and scholars at universities. HUAC was not, however, the first to tread this path. Some state governments had already set up their own committees to investigate security risks, targeting many of the nation's leading universities. Still more were passing legislation to bar Communists from the classroom. The actual victims of the purge of "subversives" from universities and colleges—those who lost their jobs— were more often former members of the party who had quit long before they were questioned by their university administrators or HUAC. Victims also included those who in fact were members of the Communist Party when they faced the inquisition; those who had rejected party membership, but who knew people who were members; former members who had joined for a brief period of time, but who left early on for any of multiple reasons, including their disgust with the Russo-German pact and their rejection of party discipline. Within these groups were people who were willing to talk to investigators about themselves, but refused to implicate others by "naming names." Finally, there were professors who never were members of the party who refused on principle to sign loyalty oaths required by their states and universities.

Ellen Schrecker, in her exceptionally well-documented histories of the witch hunts, concluded that:

> From Harvard to Hollywood, the process followed the same trajectory— from initial tolerance for dissent and hesitations about violating people's civil liberties to the conviction that Communists were so uniquely dangerous that their rights could be ignored. . . . In almost every instance, the process of eliminating communism from the nation's public and private institutions followed a two-stage procedure. In the first stage, the alleged subversives were identified, usually by an official body like HUAC or the FBI. In the second stage, they were punished, usually by the imposition of economic sanctions.[33]

The University of Washington's investigation of un-American activities was perhaps the most significant because it became a model of how universities would deal with charges of communism against faculty members made by external investigators, whether they were state committees or the FBI. It began the process of defining communism as inconsistent with academic values and, by extension, excluding Communists on the faculty from the protection of academic freedom and participation in university life. In fact, what emerged was a tautology in which the very definition of academic freedom excluded Communists, who were "subject to party discipline," and, by virtue of their membership in the party, according to University of Washington president Raymond B. Allen, "slave[s] to immutable dogma." The Communist faculty member, Allen said, had "abdicated control over his intellectual life."[34] The Washington case became an exemplar of how boards of regents and university administrations would work in tandem to purge the system of Communists.

The "Canwell Committee" (the Joint Legislative Fact-Finding Committee on Un-American Activities), chaired by the committed anticommunist Albert Canwell, a Republican from Washington, investigated the faculty of the University of Washington in 1948—a hotbed of Communist activity, in his view. He subpoenaed eleven faculty members and heard testimony from "a mélange of professional witnesses, local informers, and alleged Communists."[35] Following the hearings, the university set up its own special committee to investigate the six tenured faculty members who had either refused to testify before the Canwell Committee or refused to name names. The committee members did believe that membership in the Communist Party was sufficient grounds for dismissal, but the cases before it involved more than the simple issue of current party membership. Faculty members were often complicit in the effort to purge their colleagues from university positions. In 1949, President Allen, who realized that this investigation would make national headlines—and would be precedent setting—sent the report by the faculty committee, along with his own recommendation, to the board of regents. He suggested that three of those charged be fired, principally because they had lied about their past and current affiliations. Notably, President Allen did not rest the university's case on the substantive content of the faculty members' work or on the content of their teaching. Eager to dismiss all six who were charged, but ready to support President Allen, the regents fired the three tenured faculty members.

The national debate over exclusion of Communists and left-wing faculty members engaged the major figures in American higher education of the day. Most fully supported the exclusion of people from the ranks of the teaching faculty solely on the basis of party membership. Aside from President Allen, who became a national figure in higher education after the Washington case was concluded, major intellectuals, such as Sidney Hook and Arthur O. Lovejoy, supported the firing of Communist professors, claiming to be doing so in the name of preserving academic freedom. Hook, head of the philosophy department at New York University, whose earlier romance with the left had ended, and others argued that if the universities could not police themselves, their traditional independence in determining the criteria for hiring and promotion would be limited by outside authority. Lovejoy, who had taught philosophy at Hopkins and was one of the founders of the AAUP, argued that communism itself was a threat to academic freedom, and that fighting its spread on campus was therefore justified:

> A member of the Communist Party is . . . engaged in a movement which has already extinguished academic freedom in many countries and would—if it were successful here—result in the abolition of such freedom in American universities. . . . No one, therefore, who desires to maintain academic freedom in America can consistently favor that movement or give indirect assistance to it by accepting as fit members of the faculties of universities, persons who have voluntarily adhered to an organization one of whose aims is to abolish academic freedom.[36]

The most acrimonious and lengthy debate over loyalty oaths, which lasted three years, took place in California, which passed a loyalty-oath requirement for teachers in 1949. This was a largely symbolic act, since the state already had enacted a ban on Communist teachers in 1940 and two years later required teachers to take an oath to uphold the Constitution. When the Regents adopted an anticommunist disclaimer in 1949 that it required professors to sign, it was intended to show that the University of California could police itself and that it was "on top" of the issue.[37] Thirty-one faculty members who refused to sign the oath, but who were acknowledged not to be Communists, were fired.

Institutionally, almost all of the states fell into line after the Washington firings and the establishment of the pledge of loyalty in California. Barring alleged Communists, uncooperative past members, and "fellow-travelers" from teaching faculties was no longer potentially embarrassing—in fact, it had become dogma. The universities certainly went after the "small fish"—the untenured faculty members who were young and relatively unknown, but whose past affiliations had brought them to the attention of the FBI. But, following the lead of HUAC and the FBI, they also went after the "big fish in the big ponds."

Some university leaders underestimated the gravity of the situation and bowed to wealthy benefactors who threatened to withdraw their support. Others dismissed professors out of fear of bad publicity. Still others supported these purges because they believed in them. The Ivy League and other highly distinguished institutions that point with pride to their principled defense of faculty rights during the Cold War years were less tolerant of dissent than they would have us believe. Their rhetorical defense of faculty rights and civil rights was often contradicted by their actions. For example, Stanford's president, Wallace Sterling, who had, as we've seen, so much to do with the rise of that university to preeminence, took much the same position as other administrators: "I doubt very much that a member of the Communist Party is a free agent. If he is not a free agent, then it would seem to follow that he cannot be objective. If he cannot be objective, he is by definition precluded from being an educator."[38]

Yale also fell into line. "There will be no witch hunts at Yale because there will be no witches. We do not intend to hire Communists," said President Charles Seymour. A. Whitney Griswold, who followed Seymour to the presidency, actively resisted appointments of former Communists at Yale and in March 1953 became the principal author of the position paper unanimously adopted and signed by the thirty-seven presidents of the nation's leading research universities who were members of the Association of American Universities (AAU). It proclaimed "the main threat to academic freedom to be 'world Communism'; accordingly, teachers who were associated with that movement, dependent on thought control and deceit, disqualified themselves from the teaching profession. Universities and faculties owed cooperation to official inquiries; not defiance."[39]

HUAC hearings in February 1953 focused on university professors. At those hearings, Daniel Boorstin, a University of Chicago professor who later would become the Librarian of Congress, told the committee that he had been a member of the Communist Party, but had left, and that he thought "a member of the Communist Party should not be employed by a university." He added, "I would not hire such a person if I were a university president."[40]

James B. Conant illustrates the "tortured liberalism" and ambivalence of the period. Conant had done more than any prior Harvard president to open the university to talented young people on the basis of their ability rather than their pedigree. He once said: "There are no known adherents of the Communist Party on our [Harvard] staff, and I do not believe there are any disguised communists either. But even if there were, the damage that would be done to the spirit of the academic community by an investigation aimed at finding a crypto-communist would be far greater than any conceivable harm such a person might do."[41] Despite these visible public statements of concern with the McCarthy demagoguery, however, there is substantial evidence that there was at least one exception to Conant's liberal perspective—the hiring of Communists—for he also said this: "In this period of a cold war, I do not believe the usual rules as to political parties apply to the Communist Party. I am convinced that conspiracy and calculated deceit have been and are the characteristic pattern of behavior of regular Communists all over the world. For these reasons, as far as I am concerned, card-holding members of the Communist Party are out of bounds as members of the teaching profession."[42] And in congressional testimony in February 1953: "If the Government has evidence that there are such people there [Communists at Harvard], I say I hope they will ferret them out by FBI methods and prosecute them."[43]

In fact, using the Freedom of Information Act (FOIA), which had not been available to earlier scholars, Sigmund Diamond produced evidence that President Conant; Provost Paul Buck, who served as acting president when Conant left the presidency; and dean of arts and sciences McGeorge Bundy were in close touch with the FBI's Boston office and the CIA, exchanging information about faculty and staff at Harvard who were identified as sympathetic toward communism.[44]

Diamond's experience with intolerance at Harvard was personal. Upon receiving his Harvard doctorate in 1953 in American history, he accepted an offer of an administrative position from McGeorge Bundy. The following year, Bundy offered him another administrative position, but with some teaching duties. According to Diamond, "The offer was withdrawn when, after telling me that he had reason to believe that I had once had an association with the Communist Party, Bundy asked what my position would be if I should be asked about the matter by 'civic authority'—meaning the FBI or a congressional investigating committee—and I answered that I would speak about myself but not about others."[45] Diamond did not get his Harvard job and was fortunate to land one at Columbia.[46]

Others at Harvard were subjected to similar inquiries, including sociologists Robert Bellah and Talcott Parsons. There were scores of cases of scientists and scholars who either were fired from their positions or found it very difficult to move from one position to another. Almost all of the major universities have sad stories to tell of actions taken at the time to deny appointments to former party members or about firings that they regretted in retrospect.

The story of the inquiries and harassment of the leader of the Manhattan Project, the physicist J. Robert Oppenheimer, is relatively well known. Fewer are aware of the treatment of Linus Pauling, whom James D. Watson described in *The Double Helix* as "the greatest of all chemists." At the height of the competition to win the race to discover the structure of DNA, which was made of course by Watson and Crick in 1953, McCarthyism was in full flower and the political assault on professors in the United States was cresting. While Watson and Crick were in England, Linus Pauling, their chief competitor, was simultaneously contending with the inquisitors from the FBI and with those who wanted to purge him from Caltech.

Aside from his scientific work, for which he had been awarded a Nobel Prize, Pauling, like many other distinguished scientists, became involved after the war with an effort to develop international treaties banning the use and testing of nuclear weapons. He also believed that disputes between nations needed to be settled by international law rather than through "the barbaric method of war, made especially barbaric by the nuclear weapons," as he put it in an interview. Summing up his experiences at this time, Pauling said, also in an interview, that "the McCarthy period came along [and] many of the other people who had been scientists who had been working on these same lines, gave up." Pauling admitted that "it was a difficult period" for him. Support, in the form of grants from the National Science Foundation and the National Institutes of Health, was withdrawn. The State Department declined his requests for a passport for two years, thus preventing him from attending one conference, in particular, on his work that was held at the Royal Society of London. And it became clear that he'd have to move from Caltech.

The most famous scientist of our times, Albert Einstein, was deeply distressed by the fear generated by HUAC. In a letter published in the *New York Times* on June 12, 1953, he wrote:

> The problem with which the intellectuals of this country are confronted is very serious. Reactionary politicians have managed to instill suspicion of all intellectual efforts into the public by dangling before their eyes a danger from without. Having succeeded so far, they are now proceeding to suppress the freedom of teaching and to deprive of their positions all those who do not prove submissive. i.e., to starve them out.... Every intellectual who is called before one of the committees ought to refuse to testify, i.e., he must be prepared for jail and economic ruin, in short, for the sacrifice of his personal welfare in the interest of the cultural welfare of the country.[47]

Although the number was depressingly small, there were some extraordinary leaders who were passionate and articulate defenders of civil liberties on campus and beyond who openly resisted McCarthy and those in state governments who led the crusade against "subversives" on campus. For example, when Owen Lattimore, a China scholar at Johns Hopkins, was accused without foundation by Joe McCarthy in 1950 of being the Soviet Union's top espionage agent in the United States, and indicted by a federal grand jury on charges that he had lied to the McCarran Committee, Johns Hopkins president Detlev Bronk resisted the enormous public pressure from McCarthy to fire Lattimore. Among the most notable faculty members who fought against McCarthyism was civil libertarian Zechariah Chafee, Jr., at Harvard Law School.[48] And a group of very distinguished social scientists joined Columbia sociologist Robert MacIver's effort to define and defend basic principles of academic freedom while pointing to the costs of their abridgement.[49] The group reached eight conclusions, including the belief that although the Communist Party was bound by a discipline that was destructive of academic freedom, "no competent educator should be dismissed or disciplined [because] the majority disapproves of his opinions."[50]

If one person could be crowned as *the* champion of academic freedom before and during the Cold War, it would be Robert M. Hutchins, the president and later chancellor of the University of Chicago.[51] No other person had as sharp a defense of the university and no one placed it as well in the context of educating the public about the role of universities in modern America. Hutchins understood the tension between national security and civil liberties and how the fabric of a university could be cut and destroyed by a crusade to limit speech and association based on specific content.

During a good portion of Hutchins's stay in office, the University of Chicago faced attacks on its faculty and students for their political views and affiliations. From 1931 to 1949, anticommunist "red baiters" periodically viewed the University of Chicago as a "seat of subversion"; the National Association of Manufacturers referred to Hutchins as a "parlor red." Undaunted by powerful opposition from Illinois senators and groups such as the American Legion, to say nothing of vocal concerns from some members of his own board and alumni, Hutchins consistently defended the idea that the work of the university was to judge competing and often conflicting ideas. Such judgments could only take place in an open, free, and tolerant space unfettered by concern with political reprisals.

Consider only one of many possible examples of Hutchins's views—his testimony in 1949 against Illinois legislation, known as the "Broyles bills," which bestowed somewhat notorious eponymous recognition on the chairman of the commission investigating subversive activities in the state, Paul Broyles. The bills made any person in the state of Illinois who was a member of the Communist Party ineligible for "public office" or for any position "as a teacher, instructor or professor in any school, college or university." After students had marched on the state capital to protest against the passage of these bills, President Hutchins appeared as the first witness before the 1949 state commission and boldly argued for tolerance.[52] His remarks represent the courage that one looks for in great academic leaders:

> These students exercised their right as American citizens to protest against pending legislation of which they disapproved. They were entirely right to disapprove of this pending legislation. The Broyles Bills . . . are, in my opinion, as a former professor of law, unconstitutional. And worst of all,

they are un-American. . . . It is now fashionable to call anybody with whom we disagree a Communist or a fellow-traveler. . . . One who criticizes the foreign policy of the United States, or the draft, . . . or who believes that our military establishment is too expensive, can be called a fellow-traveler, for the Russians are of the same opinion. One who thinks that there are too many slums and too much lynching in America can be called a fellow-traveler, for the Russians say the same. One who opposes racial discrimination or the Ku Klux Klan can be called a fellow-traveler, for the Russians claim that they ought to be opposed. Anybody who wants any change of any kind in this country can be called a fellow-traveler, because the Russians want change in this country, too. . . .

The whole educational system . . . is a reflection of the American faith in thought and discussion as the path to peaceful change and improvement. The danger to our institutions is not from the tiny minority who do not believe in them. It is from those who would mistakenly repress the free spirit upon which those institutions are built. . . .

The policy of repression of ideas cannot work and has never worked. The alternative to it is the long, difficult road of education. To this the American people have been committed. It requires patience and tolerance even in the face of intensive provocation. It requires faith that when the citizen understands all forms of government, he will prefer democracy and that he will be a better citizen if he is convinced than he would be if he were coerced. The University . . . asserts that the policy of education is better than the policy of repression.[53]

After Hutchins and several other educators testified, the Broyles Commission hearings collapsed. The Broyles bills were defeated in the legislature, and the state and the university remained free of political tests for employment. Hutchins's courage was widely praised by defenders of academic freedom and civil liberties. Indeed, his forceful counterattack on the "red hunters" has led scholars of the Cold War period to speculate that some of the damage of McCarthyism might have been mitigated had more academic leaders had his courage to defend the idea of the university.[54]

The mass hysteria over communism, coupled with the insecurity produced by university policies, had its effects on the morale and actions of the faculties at these universities. At the time it was difficult to assess the impact of McCarthyism on the academic community because there were few empirical studies that attempted to measure it. One, *The Academic Mind,* by Lazarsfeld and his colleague Wagner Thielens, Jr., obtained responses from almost 2,500 interviews with social scientists at 165 American universities and colleges to questions related to McCarthyism and apprehension on campus.[55] Many in the academy, in fact, agreed with the efforts to exclude Communists, past and present, from the universities. Many, however, did not, and for them it was a time of apprehension. Fear was pervasive on most college and university campuses.

As might be expected, anxiety was linked to age, with younger faculty members, often unprotected by tenure, more apprehensive than their older colleagues. Lazarsfeld and Thielens found that over 25 percent of the social scientists had exercised some form of self-censorship in either their public or private lives. Faculty members became more cautious in what they said or did. For example, while 80 percent said they would support an invitation to Owen Lattimore to speak at their schools, only 40 percent said they would "protest vigorously" if "the president of the college were to ban the event." In general, the professoriate felt safer on their campuses than outside of them. The fear felt by faculty derived in part from their correct perception of the level of intolerance toward Communists in the general public.

Consider a comparison of teachers in the Lazarsfeld study with a national sample of almost 5,000 Americans who were asked the same questions by Harvard social scientist Samuel Stouffer.[56] Fully 89 percent of the general public, compared with only 45 percent of the social scientists, felt that "a college teacher who is an admitted Communist should be fired." Even 22 percent of the public, compared with 4 percent of the teachers, felt that "a college teacher whose loyalty has been questioned should be fired."[57] The fact that people had been fired was problem enough—the firings cut off voices of dissent, punished people for their political views, and often victimized people unfairly. But what these data suggest is that this was not the whole story. As Robert Hutchins said so perceptively, "The question is not how many professors have been fired for their beliefs, but how many think they *might* be. The entire teaching profession is intimidated."[58]

As we reflect on these episodes in our history where civil liberties have been curtailed in the name of national security, where universities were pressured to limit academic freedom and free inquiry, we can now see that the pattern of excesses threatened to erode the basic structures needed for great research universities. In the name of national security, the Bush administration also took actions that affected our institutions. Some were similar to the actions that were taken during the Red Scares, and some were different, and yet the results of the Red Scares can inform our analysis of the impact of the Bush era on universities.

One similarity between the 1950s and the 2000s can be found in the response of academics to the measures that were taken. During the Red Scares, few leaders in the academy distinguished themselves by speaking out, and the same thing occurred during the Bush era. During the war on terror, there were few clear and steady voices raising appropriate questions about both the measures taken by the government in the name of national security and their actual and potential impact on colleges and universities. The fear of governmental power, of being labeled "soft on terrorism," seems as potent today as the fear of being labeled "soft on communism" was in McCarthy's time. Where have you gone, Robert Hutchins?

THE SCOPE OF THE ASSAULT ON
ACADEMIC FREEDOM IN THE POST-9/11 ERA

To many university administrators, faculty members, and observers, the most recent attacks on academic freedom seemed both more subtle and more extensive than the attacks of the McCarthy era. This perception was due in part to the fact that so many aspects of the idea of the university and its core missions were under fire, and in part to the variety of antagonists, from private advocacy groups, professors, donors, and trustees and regents to congressional committees, all of whom were pressuring universities to abridge their norms and values. Indeed, these things did not all disappear with the end of the Bush administration. Conservatives on the far right are still writing about the evils of the university and speaking vociferously on the radio and in other venues. Those criticisms, as we shall see, were not limited to conservatives. Nor did criticism of universities begin in 2001. The attack on free inquiry has been a feature of the culture wars for decades. The advocacy groups surrounding these efforts have long had the resources to lobby government figures, and to organize alumni and students, with the goal of generating public outrage and eventual pressure on the university to abandon some of its basic commitments. But during the Bush era, they had a powerful voice in the White House and the ranks of their followers swelled, largely because of the 9/11 attacks and the fears of terrorism that came to the surface.

In an October 2007 statement published by the Ad Hoc Committee to Defend the University, which I helped to draft, the consequences of these efforts were spelled out:

> In recent years, universities across the country have been targeted by outside groups seeking to influence what is taught and who can teach. To achieve their political agendas, these groups have defamed scholars, pressured administrators, and tried to bypass or subvert established procedures of academic governance. As a consequence, faculty have been denied jobs or tenure, and scholars have been denied public platforms from which to share their viewpoints. This violates an important principle of scholarship, the free exchange of ideas, subjecting them to ideological or political tests. These attacks threaten academic freedom and the core mission of higher education in a democratic society.[59]

Looking back on the assaults on free inquiry and academic freedom since World War I, we see that these episodes almost invariably attacked dissenters at universities; the primary targets, however, were different each time. In some ways, attacks on academic freedom have evolved like lethal viruses, mutating over time and taking on new forms that, at least temporarily, are resistant to prior lines of defense. For example, between 2001 and 2008, the government left most of the attacks on free expression to private groups; it concentrated its own attacks on free inquiry to restricting the university research community, something we will look at in detail in Chapter 12.

Besides the research restrictions, the recent assault has involved attempts to infringe on the freedom of faculty and administrators to express their views, both inside and outside of the classroom; to develop the curriculum of courses without outside interference; to invite controversial speakers to campus; to offend or unsettle people in a diverse community; to criticize American policies and those of other countries; and to conduct research on topics that are of interest to faculty and to an academic discipline.

At Columbia we have had a series of incidents over the past several years that resulted in alumni, journalists, and our own faculty members attacking the university for standing behind its faculty and defending the value of free inquiry. One could be sure that any public statement in support of the Palestinian people by the preeminent literary critic Edward Said would elicit hundreds of e-mails, letters, and journalistic accounts calling on us to denounce Said and to either sanction or fire him. Until Said's death in 2003, however, the university stood fast in defending his right to voice his opinions in his books and speeches—works that were followed throughout the world but abhorred by those who objected to the content of his work. These critics often failed to understand that it was critically important for us as leaders of Columbia to defend his right to air his opinions about literature, politics, and their intersection.

The sources of protest have been varied—it is not just members of the general public who object to the political views of professors or to activities taking place on the Columbia campus. At a 2003 antiwar teach-in, a Columbia assistant professor of anthropology, Nicholas de Genova, speaking out against the U.S. war against Iraq, made a comment that was carried all over the country in the news media. He said that he wanted to see a million Mogadishus—a reference to the 1993 military incident in Somalia in which eighteen American soldiers were killed. De Genova's remarks were immediately—*immediately*—criticized as totally inappropriate by other distinguished faculty members who took part in the teach-in. Those refutations were largely ignored in the press. But this case is important because the type of protest took on a different character from the protests of previous years, which had been marked primarily by floods of irate e-mails from members of the public and alumni. In this case, Lee Bollinger, Columbia's president, received a letter from 104 Republican members of the House of Representatives asking that Professor de Genova be fired.

De Genova, the letter said, had "brought shame on the great institution that Columbia University is. As an assistant professor, de Genova has not yet earned the promise of lifetime academic employment. We hope that you will take steps immediately to ensure that he never gets it." It is deeply troubling that nearly a quarter of the members of the House of Representatives should have such a profound misunderstanding of the basic principles governing a university—in particular, the process of self-policing through application of organized skepticism, a process that actually worked at Columbia in this case through the criticism of this speech by colleagues.

Of course, those who protested these activities at Columbia and elsewhere had a right to do so, and in such cases they should be responded to in an appropriate way. But the letters, e-mails, and other communications were not simply from individuals who were spontaneously reacting to news of these events. They were coming from websites that were supplying the text to be used in the protest messages. They were the result of organized efforts by members of conservative groups to pressure universities to take action against professors whose ideas they find repugnant.

The commitment of American universities to academic freedom and free inquiry has been challenged by these attacks. A significant number of the protests have focused on the efforts of universities to expand their expertise into areas of the Middle East and to hire exceptionally able scholars of that region. In fact, the tensions in the Middle East have been mirrored in the university. Untenured scholars who have been openly critical of Israeli government policies toward the Palestinian people and its neighbors have been particularly vulnerable.[60] Some of these targets of criticism have been American citizens, and some have been from the Middle East.

The case for the tenure of Joseph Massad at Columbia took years to be decided. He was finally granted tenure in June 2009. Massad, a professor of modern Arab politics and intellectual history, has published three books with highly reputable publishers and more than a score of peer-reviewed articles. His scholarship received overwhelmingly favorable evaluations by some twenty scholars in his field or in related fields who were asked to evaluate his work, and he has a stellar teaching record, at least as judged by the course evaluations of his students. Even when nobody loses his or her job, these assaults take a toll. As Massad explained on his website in 2005: "With this campaign against me going into its fourth year, I chose under the duress of coercion and intimidation not to teach my course [Palestinian and Israeli Politics and Societies] this year."[61] Despite all of his accomplishments, Massad continues to be vilified and demonized in the press, where the quality of his work as judged by peers—and even an accurate account of its content—is never referenced. He and others in Columbia's Middle Eastern Languages and Cultures Department have been subjected to malicious attacks that are limited to their views on Middle

East politics. In November 2007, Joel Mowbray, a regular contributor to the *Washington Post,* baselessly attacked Massad in a story entitled, "No Tenure for Hatred."

Meanwhile, an untenured Barnard College archaeologist, Nadia Abu El-Haj, a Palestinian Arab, was unmercifully attacked in the press for defending Edward Said's work and for her own work on aspects of the archaeology of the ancient Middle East, which was taken as critical of the Israeli writing of that history. Paula R. Stern, a Barnard alumna, led the initial charge, producing totally unsubstantiated charges, which led a number of scholars—most of whom were far removed from Professor El-Haj's field—to join the bandwagon of those opposing her tenure. A petition of scholars supporting the archaeologist was formed and a public battle was joined. The Barnard president, Judith Shapiro, herself an anthropologist of note, wrote a courageous piece defending academic freedom and the fundamental necessity of allowing peers to be the final judge of El-Haj's work. Professor El-Haj received tenure, but the case raised the central issue of who the appropriate judges are for evaluating specialized scholarship.

Although junior faculty members bear the brunt of attacks in these cases, the efforts to vilify senior scholars for their published views has expanded as well. John J. Mearsheimer, the R. Wendell Harrison Distinguished Service Professor of Political Science at the University of Chicago, and Stephen M. Walt, the Robert and Renee Belfer Professor of International Affairs at the John F. Kennedy School of Government at Harvard, published an extended essay in the *London Review of Books,* which then appeared in revised form as a book, *The Israel Lobby and U.S. Foreign Policy.* Their argument was that there is a highly organized and well-heeled lobby in the United States that generates extraordinary pro-Israeli support within Congress for policies that might not be of strategic value to the United States, and a powerful set of advocacy groups that are organizing American campuses to discredit professors who oppose Israeli policies. The level of attack on Mearsheimer and Walt, not only on scholarly grounds, but also on political grounds, was unusually harsh and relentless. There are many substantive claims in this book worthy of debate. However, arguments about the scholarly merits of the book's thesis took a back seat to the personalized assaults on its authors. Similarly, the British-born Jewish intellectual and social historian Tony Judt's criticisms of Israeli policies and his advocacy for a single-state solution to the conflict between Israel and the Palestinians unleashed a torrent of vitriol against him and successful efforts by prominent Jewish organizations to have speaking invitations to Judt rescinded.

Of course, there are other advocacy groups that are party to attacks on academic freedom, but the role of Jewish groups in these recent episodes represents a tragic irony. In several cases Jewish advocates and intellectuals have used high-octane fuel in an effort to exclude a largely disenfranchised minority group from access to mainstream discourse in the great universities. Nothing can or should prevent these advocates from criticizing ideas that they believe have no merit, but the efforts go far beyond intellectual discourse. They include attempts to politically interfere with tenure appointments by using students, advocacy groups, legislators, and alumni to pressure the universities to deny tenure and to run the scholars out of town altogether. The irony of these cases is self-evident: This is precisely what happened to Jewish scholars when they began to be a force in graduate studies and began to seek positions at the best American universities. What would have happened had the universities and other advocacy groups resisted hiring the Jewish scientists and scholars from Nazi Germany who were able to find homes at many of our great universities in the 1930s, despite the high level of anti-Semitism that existed in the United States? Jewish academics had to overcome powerful political opposition and bias toward them.[62]

Parts of the limits on speech can be found in the increasing number of invited guest speakers or scholars who are finding it difficult to express their views at universities, even after faculty or student groups have followed all of the university's rules before issuing invitations. Former Harvard president Lawrence Summers was invited to speak by the University of California Board of Regents only to have the invitation rescinded after female faculty members petitioned the regents to cancel the event because of the content of some of his ideas. Jim Gilchrist, founder of the *Minutemen*, a conservative volunteer border-control group that favors a very strict immigration policy, was unable to speak at Columbia after hecklers and protesters took to the stage with a large banner and proceeded to get into a nasty scuffle with those who supported Gilchrist's right to speak.

Similar disruptions at Michigan State University prevented Congressman Tom Tancredo, another staunch opponent of liberalized immigration policies, from speaking. Phil Donahue's commencement address at North

Carolina State University was interrupted by a jeering group of students because of his liberal views on the Iraq War. And Stanford University's Israel Alliance "disinvited" Daniel Pipes citing the controversy over his website, Campus-Watch.org, which is a project of the Middle East Forum. The website says that it "reviews and critiques Middle East studies in North America, with an aim to improving them," but it in fact allocates almost all of its space to critiques of Palestinian and Arab scholars who criticize Israeli government policies.

There is, of course, nothing new about student protests against speakers whose ideas are distasteful or repugnant to the protesters. Such protests were a hallmark of the 1960s and 1970s. But the reemergence of the campaign to stifle open dialogue today is harmful because it restricts the access of students to ideas that they may find troubling, but which they should confront as part of their university experience.

We should remember that the proper goal of higher education is enlightenment—not some abstract ideal of "balance." Indeed, those who demand balance on some issues never demand it on others. The University of Chicago's school of economics is widely admired for its accomplishments. Must Chicago seek balance by forcing its economics department to hire scholars with contrasting points of view?

Occasionally, students have to do the hard work of seeking alternative points of view across institutional boundaries. They cannot expect "balance" to be delivered in neat packages. It is the professor's pedagogical role that grants him or her the authority and the right to judge which scientific theories or historical facts are presented in the classroom. We cannot deny the asymmetry in these roles. If we do, we fail to understand a legitimate goal of higher education: to impart knowledge to those who lack it. Of course, one can question the competence of a professor—that happens routinely at a good university. But the evaluation of that competence must be, and is, left to the professor's peers—not to students, and surely not to trustees, regents, congressmen, advocacy groups, or members of the press.

With the support of a faculty committee, a liberal professor of law and political science from Duke University, Erwin Chemerinsky, was offered the job as the first dean of the new University of California at Irvine Law School in 2007. Conservative groups found the appointment offensive and vehemently opposed it, and Irvine's chancellor, Michael V. Drake, withdrew the offer because the appointment was "too politically controversial." Beyond political controversy in this case was the fact that the university had agreed to "periodically and confidentially consult" an Orange County billionaire on the selection of the dean in exchange for his $20 million gift.[63] The university was hit with intense adverse publicity, and faculty and others expressed outrage at this infringement on academic freedom within two weeks. Later, the regents and Drake bent to the pressure and reversed the decision. Chemerinsky got his job after all.

In another incident, a twenty-four-year-old conservative alumnus of UCLA, Andrew Jones, started a Bruins alumni organization to combat UCLA's lurching to the left. He also offered to pay students at the university to tape-record the lectures of left-leaning professors. Convinced that UCLA was slipping into the hands of leftist political partisanship and indoctrination, Jones rescinded his pecuniary efforts after being counseled by university leaders, but not before he enumerated a "Dirty Thirty" list of UCLA professors whom he judged as too liberal.[64]

Boards of regents and university administrations sometimes justify their hiring, firing, and tenure decisions by citing reasons that sidestep the issue of a person's political views. This was the case when the regents of the University of Colorado pressured the university to fire Professor Ward Churchill, who once compared some victims of the September 11, 2001, attacks to Nazi bureaucrats. Whatever one thinks about the quality of Churchill's ideas, there can be little question that the ostensible reason for his dismissal, which was that he had made false claims on his curriculum vitae, was a proxy for discontent with the content of his ideas. In 2009 the University of Colorado lost a First Amendment lawsuit brought by Churchill over his firing. However, as of the summer of 2009, Churchill's victory was only symbolic: A state judge held that the university was not obligated to rehire him despite its losing the academic freedom case.[65]

In other cases, the restrictions on academic freedom can take unusual forms. From May 2006 until August 2008, Florida professors were not allowed to travel to Cuba to conduct research. Although the U.S. government, which hardly has benign policies toward Cuba, allows such research, the Florida legislature banned faculty members at public universities from having any contact with the island nation. "Florida's taxpayers don't want to see their resources being used to support or subsidize terrorist regimes at a time when Americans are fighting a war on terror," said David Rivera, a Republican Cuban-American state legislator who introduced the bill that banned the travel to Cuba.[66]

Consider Students for Academic Freedom (SAF),[67] an organization launched in 2004 by veteran conservative activists. The group's very name implies a commitment to a core liberal value, and the group promises to empower aggrieved students. Since its inception in 2003, the SAF has encouraged students nationwide to organize and lobby university leaders, alumni, and state legislators (as well as members of the U.S. Congress) to adopt a "student bill of rights."

But SAF's language and tactics are misleading. Under the banner of seeking balance and diversity in the classroom, these students are trying to limit discussion of ideas they disagree with. They want students to become judges, if not final arbiters, of faculty competence. They have supported the campaign against Massad at Columbia and have urged students to report "unfair grading, one-sided lectures, and stacked reading lists" as an abuse of student rights. The Duke University chapter of Students for Academic Freedom asked arts and sciences professors in 2005 to sign an "Academic Freedom Pledge" signaling their support of "intellectual tolerance and diversity." The names of faculty members who refused to sign this oath would be listed on a website for public viewing—a contemporary form of blacklisting.

People who would have us fire, censure, or withhold invitations to professors because of their political opinions and remarks often fail to comprehend that they are the current beneficiaries of a predominant point of view, and that if content and ideology became the basis for hiring and firing decisions at universities, the tables could turn quickly. The moment has rarely failed to arrive when the prosecutors become the prosecuted. People must be able to imagine that their thoughts, beliefs, and speech might make them the victims of the unbridled power of the government, of a university, or of a nation. And we, in defending the idea of the university, must educate the public about why we defend the faculty members whose ideas may offend people.

There is of course no place in the American research university classroom for physical intimidation, physical assault, or violations of the personal space of students. There is no place for faculty members to use their positions of authority to coerce and cow students into conforming to their own point of view. They must never discriminate against students based on their race, ethnicity, religion or gender. No university will protect a professor's use of a string of epithets directed toward a particular student in a gratuitous manner. There are workplace rules in place at universities that govern and control such forms of behavior. And there must be, by law, mechanisms for students or others at the university to lodge complaints against professors who violate these rules. This basic commitment to civility and professional responsibility is part of the code of conduct at Columbia and at every other major American research university.[68]

But the codes that place limits on conduct must never be directed at the content of ideas—however offensive they may be to students, faculty, alumni, benefactors, or politicians. Critics of the university—such as those who produced the highly controversial film *Columbia Unbecoming*, an attack on professors who taught Middle East studies, such as those affiliated with the David Project Center for Jewish Leadership in Boston—tend to blur the distinction between speech and action. They accuse professors of inappropriate action and intimidation when they are actually trying to attack the content of their ideas. They also tend to expropriate key terms in the liberal lexicon, as if they were the only true champions of freedom and diversity on college campuses.

Most of the recent attacks on university professors have been leveled against social scientists and humanists. Many critics of the university seem to believe that sanctioning one group of professors will have no effect on those in other disciplines. This is dangerously naive, both in principle and in practice. The stakes are high. The destruction of university systems has historically been caused by the imposition of external political ideology on the conduct of scholarly and scientific research. Defense of faculty members in the humanities and social sciences from external political pressure protects all members of the university community.

The goal of academic freedom is to establish an environment in which it is possible for the inquisitive mind to flourish. In contrast to private enterprise, the university places the welfare of the community above individual gain. The coin of the academic realm is the recognition that professors and students receive based on the quality of their contributions to the creation, transmission, and understanding of knowledge. The university strives to be a meritocracy. Ideally, quality, as expressed through teaching, research, and learning, is rewarded without regard to race, religion, nationality, gender, or sexual orientation.

Researchers at America's universities do not typically investigate questions for which there are "right" or ready answers—answers at the back of a book. The goal of academic discourse is not merely to convey information, but to provoke thought, to stimulate ideas, and to teach students and provide them with the intellectual and analytical tools that will enable them to think *well*. Great universities are designed to be unsettling. They challenge orthodoxies and dogmas as well as social values and public policies. They are the most effective instrument for creating skepticism and discontent with established institutions. Distinguished universities must entertain and not suppress the most radical thoughts—whether they are from scientists who challenge the longstanding belief that only bacteria and viruses cause disease, or social scientists and humanities scholars who attack the foreign policy of the United States.[69]

Great teachers challenge the biases and presuppositions of their students and colleagues. They present unsettling ideas and dare others to rebut them and to defend their own beliefs in a coherent and principled manner. The American research university pushes and pulls at the walls of orthodoxy and rejects politically correct thinking. In this process, students and professors may sometimes feel intimidated, overwhelmed, and confused. But it is by working through this process that they learn to think better and more clearly for *themselves*.

Unsettling by nature, university culture is also highly conservative. It demands evidence before accepting novel challenges to existing theories and methods. The university ought to be viewed in terms of a fundamental interdependence between the liberality of its intellectual life and the conservatism of its methodological demands. Because the university encourages discussion of even the most radical ideas, it must set its standards at a high level. We permit almost any idea to be put forward—but only because we demand arguments and evidence to back up the ideas we debate and because we set the bar of proof at such a high level. These two components—tolerance for unsettling ideas and insistence on rigorous skepticism about all ideas—create an essential tension at the heart of the American research university. It will not thrive without both components operating effectively and simultaneously.

Here we must acknowledge an area where the university today faces a real and difficult problem with the mechanisms it uses to evaluate the work of its scholars. For the threats to free inquiry do not come only from government policies, from local or national politicians, from external lobbying groups, or from lazy journalism. Some of the most subtle threats come from within the academy itself. An unspoken but widespread aversion to airing topics that are politically sensitive in various fields sometimes limits debates that ought to take place. The growth of knowledge is greatly inhibited when methodological thresholds for evidence are relaxed and when claims to truth are advanced on the basis of shoddy evidence, or on the basis of supposedly possessing privileged insight simply as a result of one's race, gender, religion, or ethnicity.

Most scholars and scientists at leading universities would more than likely exercise their right to remain silent before placing on the table for debate any number of controversial ideas: for example, the idea that differences in educational performance between different racial groups are not a result of discrimination; that occupational differentiation by gender may be a good thing; that dietary cholesterol above and beyond genetic predispositions has only a minimal effect on coronary heart deaths; that the children of crack cocaine mothers will nevertheless experience normal cognitive development; or, until recently, that prions, as well as bacteria or viruses, can cause disease.

Fear of sanctions is one basis for faculty not upholding their simple responsibility to engage in debate on potentially controversial subjects on which they have some knowledge and expertise. But the sanctions do not always come from outside the university or even from the university administration or from conservative student groups. As the Columbia philosopher Akeel Bilgrami has pointed out, academic dogmatism is also a threat to academic freedom. Dogmatism threatens academic freedom when powerful members of a discipline or an academic department "circle the wagons around our own frameworks for discussion such that alternative frameworks for pursuing the truth simply will not even become visible on the horizon of our research agenda."[70] In short, through the expression of internal academic power, it is possible for faculty members to systematically exclude from the conversation those whose views offend the central dogma of a field; in other words, alternate views are sometimes perceived as intellectual threats because, if given the chance, their proponents may produce counter-evidence and arguments refuting conventional claims.[71]

I have suggested that we entertain radical and even offensive ideas at universities because we simultaneously embrace rigorous standards in determining the adequacy of truth claims. But if scholarly skepticism is sometimes compromised by a lack of courage or an intolerance of competing points of view, then the primary mechanisms by which universities ensure the quality of research will not always reliably function. To complicate matters, different disciplines have evolved somewhat differently in institutionalizing mechanisms to ensure that rigorous standards exist to evaluate ideas and the results of research.

I have defended the right of academic freedom within the community of scholars. But what, if any, right to freedom of expression does a student have as against his or her professor? The rise of groups like Students for Academic Freedom raises this important question. Students clearly have the right—indeed, the obligation—to enter the general debate within the university community. They have the right to express their ideas forcefully in the classroom and to argue against their professors' views. At the same time, there is a clear differentiation of roles between professors and students. We expect professors, not students, to offer their own best judgment on competing truth claims. A student may argue for creationism or intelligent design, but that does not oblige a biology professor to take these views seriously as a rival to the evolutionary accounts favored by virtually all contemporary biologists. One student, following the political dogma and propaganda of one side in the Middle East conflict, may deny the Holocaust; another student, following propaganda from the other side, may make the claim that the Israeli government was not responsible for the 1982 Sabra and Shatila massacres in Lebanon. But professors are under no obligation to take such views seriously—they are views that are not based on evidence.

The university cannot and should not attempt to decide what ideas or perspectives are appropriate for the classroom. For one student, a professor's ideas may represent repugnant stereotypes or efforts at intimidation; for another, the same ideas may represent profound challenges to ostensibly settled issues. For example, a professor's discussion of our culture's bias against female circumcision may seem to one student an affront to what is self-evidently a basic human right; to another student, it may seem a provocative illustration of cultural imperialism, raising serious moral questions that ought to be put on the table for debate. Are we to take seriously those who would have us sanction the professor for raising this subject in a seminar? And if we did, who would be cast in the role of the "Grand Inquisitor"?

The broadest possible protection of freedom of expression is of a piece with another important aspect of the academy. We have understood for some time now that the university is not a place where we exclusively house or train the kind of scientist or scholar who advises the prince— those who currently control the government. There are members of the faculty who sometimes voluntarily give advice to the prince—and there may even be academic programs (such as Russian studies during the Cold War) that exist in part to inform government policy—but it is not the point or the rationale of universities to furnish such advice, nor to have the thematic pursuits of inquiry in the university shaped by the interests of the prince. That is why universities will often find in their midst those who air the most radical critiques of the prince and his interests. Were we to silence or even to inhibit such people, we would not only be undermining free inquiry, we would also gradually reinforce the countervailing power of conformism.

Despite the commitment of the American research university to freedom of thought, the natural tendency of professors and students, as we have seen, is to avoid expressing views that may offend others. But the responsibility of the university is to combat this tendency and to encourage, rather than squelch, freewheeling inquiry. The university must do everything it can to combat the coercive demand for political litmus tests from the right and the left, and the pressure to conform to established academic paradigms.

By affording virtually absolute protection to classroom debate, the university encourages the sort of open inquiry for which universities exist. Those members of the university community who are willing to take on prevailing beliefs and ideologies—be they the pieties of the academic left or the marching orders of the politicians currently in power—need to know that the university will defend them unconditionally if they are attacked for the content of their ideas.

The attacks on academic freedom have gone beyond issues of speech on and off campus. If we confine our thinking to defending individuals from attacks on their academic freedom, we will fail to see that the threats are as much to the institution as to the individuals. The obsession of the Bush administration with national security since 9/11 did not lead to the rebirth of rampant McCarthyism with its loyalty oaths, or to extensive academic firings of those who sought a public platform for dissent. Faculty members felt intimidated, they may have ducked for cover, and they may have feared inappropriate surveillance of their classroom teaching and public speeches, but fewer were purged from their jobs than during the Cold War. However, if we shift our angle of vision from the individual to the institutional level, and focus on more subtle attacks on the structure of the university itself—and the principles of academic freedom and free inquiry—we can find a host of examples of attacks during the Bush years that may have been more harmful to the structure of universities than we found even in the McCarthy period.[72]

Although we have seen that politicians have used the media to pressure universities to purge themselves of professors, relatively few ambitious politicians used demagogic methods in the media to get their fifteen minutes in the sun by offering up to the nation a set of dangerous subversives working at our universities. But the critics were attacking the normative foundation of universities and the derived social structures. One reason that some observers of the university are hopeful, based on their sense that the recent wave of repression was not as ominous as the repression that occurred during the dark days of McCarthyism, is that they are focusing on the effects of the repression on individuals rather than its effects on the institution. In this case, however, I believe it is the institution that is the appropriate unit of analysis. The victims often were the institutions and the consequences were not trivial—in fact, they are consequences that the new leadership in Washington, both in the executive and legislative branches, would be wise to address.

There is also mounting evidence that professors and researchers at the nation's universities and colleges are increasingly apprehensive about the erosion of academic freedom. A 2007 survey of 1,417 professors at 927 institutions, as reported by Neil Gross at Harvard and Solon Simmons at George Mason, suggests that there is widespread concern within the academic community about attacks on academic freedom. One question the researchers asked professors was the same as one that was asked by Lazarsfeld and Thielens in their study of the effects of McCarthyism among social scientists at American universities: "In the past few years, how much have you felt that your own academic freedom has been threatened in any way?"

In Gross and Simmons's survey, roughly 28 percent of the respondents said either "a lot" or "some." About one-third of the social scientists felt some kind of threat. In Lazarsfeld and Thielens's survey in 1955, only 21 percent of the respondents reported feeling this way. Gross and Simmons concluded: "Although the two samples are not strictly comparable—we include a broader spectrum of institutions, and define social scientists in a somewhat different way—we can still reasonably say that social scientists today perceive as much if not more of a threat to their academic freedom than during the McCarthy era."[73]

We often conflate the idea of freedom of speech at universities with academic freedom and free inquiry. As critically important as the dimension of freedom of expression in or outside the classroom is to academic freedom, the concept goes beyond issues of expression. As I suggested earlier, academic freedom goes beyond the defense of oppositional or even opprobrious views expressed by professors and students. It establishes a set of structural relationships and values that govern the university. Robert Post, a constitutional law professor at Yale, made this critical point clear when he said that "academic freedom sought to redefine the employment relationship between professors and universities."[74]

Properly understood, the obsession with free inquiry and academic freedom at universities is to defend governance rules that define the boundaries of faculty prerogatives over parts of the enterprise. It is therefore worth reemphasizing the point made by Louis Menand and referred to earlier that academic freedom "is the key legitimating concept of the entire [academic] enterprise." It is the mechanism that establishes control and authority over the critical decisions in the university. It places in the hands of highly trained, competent professors, who have met standards set by the disciplines, the power to create criteria for entrance into the profession, to set standards of admission, to establish what is and what is not valued or labeled as "high quality work," to determine standards for hiring and promotion to coveted positions, to construct the examinations, and to determine what will or will not be taught in classes run by those professors.

The alternative is, as Menand notes, a political free-for-all where external or internal political power makes up the rules of governance and the relationship between academic administration and the faculty. So a natural question is: What level of legitimacy should we offer to assessments of work that do not come from peers? If we abandon academic freedom, or we think of it as something that is simply a protective shield surrounding privileged professors who want no control over what they say or do, we will be misunderstanding the functions that these values fulfill in great universities. And without placing these forms of authority in the hands of a group of knowledgeable peers we run the risk of creating chaos and a void that could be filled by self-appointed government "experts" from outside the university.

Without these structural relationships and freedoms, a university cannot achieve greatness. It goes to the heart of the critical compact that universities have established over the past century with American society.[75] American society has given our universities a great gift of substantial autonomy and has been, by and large, willing to accept that the decisions that universities make will benefit both the universities and the society.

The compact relies fundamentally on trust—the initial axiomatic belief that these missions will be better fulfilled if the universities are granted this autonomy and are not interfered with by external political pressure groups. The assumption is that without academic freedom and free inquiry, without freedom from external political and economic influence, the universities cannot meet these national goals effectively. Academic freedom is a form, then, of what Sir Isaiah Berlin called "negative liberty"—freedom from interference in one's pursuits.[76] It is "negative liberty" with a purpose. One does not require a deep philosophical basis for defending academic freedom, although many would argue for its intrinsic value. We can defend academic freedom at the academy by demonstrating the good that these universities do for the society, which is precisely what I'm trying to do in this book. If our cumulative experience with universities tells us anything it is that the only thing far worse than letting universities order their own affairs—that is, letting faculty members battle out what constitutes quality and merit—is to leave the ordering of those affairs to others.[77]

Another essential feature of the American research university that is related to academic freedom is that no one speaks "for" the university—not even its official leaders. Although the president, the provost, and the board of trustees have the responsibility and the authority to formulate and carry out university policies, the essence of a university lies in its multiplicity of voices: those of its faculty, its students, its researchers, and its staff. Presidents and provosts are often asked questions of the following kind: "What is the university's position on the writings, or remarks, or actions of Professor X?"

In fact, there is no "university position" on such matters. The university does not decide which ideas are good and bad, which are right and wrong. That is up for constant debate, deliberation, and discourse among the faculty and students. For the university to take such positions would stifle academic freedom and alienate those whose views differ from those of the institution's leaders. The responsibility of these leaders is not to decide whose ideas are best, but to create an environment in which all ideas may be explored and tested.

Finally, academic freedom creates tension within the role of leaders of great research universities. On the one hand, many of their constituents, particularly alumni and trustees, would like to see presidents visibly use the bully-pulpit to articulate views on broad societal issues, to use the weight of the institution and its prestige to shape policy issues, and to bring visibility to the work of the university. They might not flinch at public positions taken by leaders, and in some measure, many presidents believe that the job should afford them the opportunity to have their voice heard in public discourse. This is potentially a part of a difficult job that brings personal and institutional rewards for university presidents. But, on the other hand, to the extent that university leaders who take positions are interpreted as "speaking for the university," their decision to articulate these views can have damaging effects on the kind of discourse that Hutchins and other proponents of academic freedom expect at the university.

The defense of academic freedom is never easy. It is understandable that university leaders will react to outside attacks with caution. There is always a risk that taking a public position on a controversial matter may alienate potential donors or offend one of the modern university's many and varied constituencies. In response to negative publicity, it is entirely natural for presidents and provosts—and for trustees and regents—to work feverishly "to get this incident behind us" and to reach for an accommodation that calms the critics and makes the problem go away.

However, to act on such understandable impulses would be a grievous mistake. There are few matters on which universities must stand on absolute principle. Academic freedom is one of them. If we fail to defend this core value, then we jeopardize the global preeminence of our universities in the production and transmission of new knowledge in the sciences, in the arts, indeed in every field of inquiry. Whenever academic freedom is under fire, we must rise to its defense with courage—and without compromise. For freedom of inquiry is our reason for being.

As the threat to academic freedom and free inquiry increased over the past decade, few lined up to defend the university against those who were seeking to undermine its core values. Failure to defend these values from further attack will threaten the preeminence of universities. It is far more difficult to rebuild greatness once it has been lost than to preserve it while it exists. The broader attack on the ethos of the university includes but also goes beyond the value of academic freedom. The federal government played a central role in threatening the university during the two Red Scares as well as following the fateful 9/11 attack. I turn now to an examination of the policies and legislation that posed these threats during the Bush era.

CHAPTER 12

The Enemy Is Us

They that can give up essential liberty to obtain a little temporary safety deserve neither liberty nor safety.

—Benjamin Franklin

It has often been said that the first casualty of war is the truth. In the American experience, the second and third casualties of a perceived national crisis may be civil liberties and the role of an independent judiciary. In times of war, or its recent, modern equivalents, national security tends to trump all else. The mass psychology of the moment is dominated by fear. After the tragic events of September 11, 2001, many Americans were so uncertain about what would follow, about the size, location, and shape of the "enemy," which they could not identify clearly or locate in any traditional sense, that they dramatically changed their daily behavior as they waited for "the other shoe to drop." The economic impact of this modified behavior was immense. Then, within weeks of 9/11, the other shoe did seem to drop. The nation faced an "anthrax" scare that initially was thought to be the work of terrorists unleashing another part of their arsenal—biological weapons to kill innocent people. This fear proved misguided.

At these moments, political leaders can attempt to reduce public fear, anxiety, and uncertainty by sharing information about the nature of the enemy and its size and location, and they can begin to educate the public about the likelihood of events occurring that can so easily be imagined.

Political leaders can use fear to rally a nation to respond to the emergency—to foster patriotism and the will to sacrifice to heighten national security. In an effort to deal with fear and the desire for "revenge," they also can manipulate and use public fear and uncertainty about risks to gain support for dramatic legislative and administrative action—for a larger agenda—that might have deeply offended many Americans under normal conditions. President George W. Bush, like so many presidents before him who faced national emergencies, used public fear to extend his power and to push through "preemptive" law-enforcement methods that have had a substantial adverse impact on civil liberties. As the political scientist Stanley Hoffman wrote:

> A technique that the administration has used brilliantly is the manipulation of fear. Americans have been "shocked and awed" by September 11, and the President has found in this criminal act not just a rationale, hitherto missing for his administration, but a lever he could use to increase his, and his country's power. All that was needed was, first, to proclaim that we were at war (something other societies attacked by terrorists have not done), second, to extend that war to states sheltering or aiding terrorist groups, and third, to allege connections between Islamist terrorists and "rogue states," such as Iraq and Iran, engaged in efforts to obtain or build weapons of mass terror.[1]

The tools, techniques, and rhetoric used by President Bush and his colleagues in the government to fight terrorism had important consequences. If the balance between national security and civil liberties is upset to the point that there are significant abridgements of the freedoms and rights that have been in place, individuals at universities will be affected as much by them as others in the society. The legislation passed in the post-9/11 era and the administrative procedures adopted by the Bush administration have, in fact, had both a direct and indirect affect on the research university. The direct effects were embodied in the provisions of the legislation designed to influence behavior at universities. The indirect effects were felt when the implementation of laws and processes created a "chilling climate" within the society, and, specifically, on the campuses of research universities, in ways that began to change the value systems of these intellectual communities, alter their research agendas or missions, and influence the types of people who chose to work there. The larger societal context in any era helps to shape, constrain, embolden, or dampen efforts to create and disseminate knowledge. Just as the larger social context had such effects on campuses, for different reasons, during the McCarthy period and the Vietnam War years, the social context of the Bush years adversely affected the great universities. Now that we have a change in government, perhaps the damage will be undone and our universities can return to their proper path of heightened creativity.

The response of the Bush administration to the September 11 attack was swift and bold. The administration used legislative authority and executive orders, as well as some actions unknown to the public at the time, to deal with terrorists, terrorist organizations, and their supporters. Two pieces of legislation, the USA Patriot Act, passed by Congress with overwhelming support and signed into law by the president on October 26, 2001, and the Public Health Security and Bioterrorism Preparedness and Response Act, passed on June 12, 2002, are central to our concerns here.[2] Both laws attempted to control the use and movement of dangerous biological agents, pathogens, and toxins and to extend the government's access to private records and surveillance of personal actions. Despite five years of sustained criticism of major provisions of the Patriot Act, Congress approved reauthorization of the act's most controversial powers in March 2006 with little or no change under a Congress where the Democratic Party held the majority. (As of August 2009, nothing has been done by Congress under the Obama administration—with a strong Democratic majority in both houses—to repeal the most onerous parts of these pieces of legislation.)[3] Other important pieces of legislation[4] and executive orders that were being used by the government to wage war against terrorism, such as the National Security Administration's ability to spy on Americans without court warrants, have been highly criticized, and their constitutionality has been challenged in the courts and in the theater of public opinion. In fact, the full impact of the so-called "war on terrorism" on our research universities is only now being revealed.

Since its reauthorization in 2006, there has been a great deal written about the Patriot Act. There is no need for me to rehearse the act's provisions in detail, other than to focus on those relevant parts that bear directly on the value system of the scholarly communities at our universities. The Patriot Act broadened the powers of the government to obtain information about potential terrorist activities. In broadening the investigatory capacity of law enforcement agencies, provisions of the act bear directly on issues of personal privacy; the rights of immigrants, refugees, and minorities; the rights of people who have been detained by the government; the right of the government to withhold information from the public; and issues of international law and basic human rights.[5]

In fact, many features of the act lead to the question: How far can the government go in investigating the personal lives and property of individuals without violating their Fourth Amendment rights? Many of the most consequential and controversial provisions of the Patriot Act built on prior legislation. Features of Title II of the act (Sections 205, 213, 215, and 218) authorized the executive branch, when it deemed it appropriate, to bypass, if not eliminate, the probable cause requirement of the Fourth Amendment.[6] These sections of the act expanded the ability of law enforcement agencies to combat terrorism through the surveillance power and information-gathering techniques of the FBI, such as the use of wiretaps, so-called "sneak and peek" searches of offices and homes, and e-mail and Internet communications tracking methods.

Section 215 amended the Foreign Intelligence Surveillance Act (FISA), enacted by Congress in 1978 to curtail widespread abuses of intelligence information-gathering operations in the name of national security. FISA was enacted to limit the authority of law enforcement agencies, including the FBI (those related to J. Edgar Hoover's counterintelligence activities), which in the 1970s had carried out illegal surveillance investigations into the personal lives of antiwar protesters and civil rights activists (including Martin Luther King, Jr.).[7] The FISA law required that the FBI obtain a special court order on the basis of probable cause before gathering information about people for *foreign* intelligence purposes. Under the 1978 act, there was court oversight of FBI requests for foreign surveillance.[8] Frankly, obtaining such orders from the FISA Court (FISC), which met secretly to hear the government's request, was easy. The success rate of the FBI and the Justice Department would fill any prosecutor with envy—only five of the roughly 15,000 requests were even modified before the surveillance request was granted. Nonetheless, a court did stand between the FBI and the people, presumably possible foreign spies, who were being investigated.

FISA surveillance, like wiretaps, could be used "for *the* purpose of" gathering foreign intelligence.[9] The Patriot Act weakens that constraint.

Now, the collection of foreign intelligence can be only a "significant purpose" of the surveillance, but is not limited to foreign intelligence.[10] Section 215 "repealed a restriction that had required the government to specify in its applications for court orders . . . 'specific and articulable facts giving reason to believe that the person to whom the records pertain is a foreign power or an agent of a foreign power.'"[11] It also repealed a provision that limited the reach of inquiries to "records" and extended it to the universe of all "tangible things." These tangible things might be found anywhere—in public or university libraries or bookstores, for example.[12]

In fact, in 2007 the government was given expanded authority by Congress to essentially bypass this limited form of judicial review. The director of the FBI or a designee of the rank of special agent or higher can use "National Security Letters" (NSLs) that are served to people who are required to provide information related to personal records of U.S. residents or visitors. The use of NSLs goes back many years, but following 9/11 their use was expanded significantly. For example, in 2000, about 8,500 NSLs were issued to investigators. That number jumped to some 49,000 in 2006. An FBI field office can now compel an organization—such as a university—to release private information—in this case, about faculty, students, and staff—without prior authorization by a grand jury or a judge. Moreover, a "gag order" exists that prevents those served with the letter from informing the person of interest that he or she is under investigation. And in 2007, a Justice Department investigation found "pervasive errors in the FBI use of its power to secretly demand telephone, email, and financial records in national security cases."[13] The Justice Department's inspector general issued a report in 2007 that detailed widespread abuse of the FBI's authority in the use of NSLs. Since the Obama administration took office we have learned of other widespread abuses of executive power in surveillance of U.S. citizens—including some programs that existed without the knowledge of congressional leaders.

The Patriot Act also amended the Family Educational Rights and Privacy Act (FERPA) to require educational institutions to disclose educational records to federal law-enforcement agents without the consent of the student. Until the act was passed, only "directory" information about students could be revealed to outside authorities without specific court orders. Otherwise, students had to give permission for their records to be shared with others. The act gives the president and the Justice Department the

power to search the private records of American citizens, including educational records, book purchases, financial records, and medical records,
without having to show that the targeted individual has any involvement
whatsoever with terrorism or international espionage. There has been essentially no judicial oversight of these FBI activities.

Perhaps the most extraordinary expansion of executive authority after
9/11 was linked to the treatment of individuals whom the attorney general or the president felt were security risks who should be detained. It is
not hard to imagine why governments would want to detain people during wars or national emergencies. Clearly, there may be good reasons and
a basis in evidence to detain people who are suspected of being terrorists
or who have been linked to terrorist organizations. But we now know
that the Bush administration operated secret prisons in Europe and the
Middle East and used "extraordinary renditions" by seizing suspects on
foreign soil and interrogating them at secret locations in foreign countries. The Justice Department condoned forms of extreme interrogation,
such as water boarding, that clearly violated the Geneva conventions and
that most people would consider torture. In addition, it conducted covert,
massive data-collection enterprises on U.S. citizens to create profiles
(with high levels of inaccuracies) of potential terrorists and to monitor
various forms of communication between the United States and abroad.
In 2009 it has become very apparent that even Congress was not given
full information about these methods of law enforcement and the surveillance programs.

As Diego Gambetta, a sociologist at Oxford University, has observed,
social trust became another casualty of the war on terrorism: "Trust in the
truthfulness of information . . . has been seriously dented on both sides of
the Atlantic. . . . Much of the breakdown of trust is due to what appear to
be deliberate misrepresentations and exaggerations by both the U.S. and
U.K. governments, especially in connection with the war in Iraq."[14] The
erosion of trust is like a cancer in the academic community, which relies a
great deal on trust in carrying out its work. If scholars and scientists believe
that the government is eavesdropping on their e-mail conversations; or is
investigating their library-book selections; or is preventing able students
and scholars from entering the country to lecture, conduct research, or
study; or is biased against certain types of research; or is investigating researchers for the purpose of determining whether to indict them for vio-

lation of national security laws; or is influencing hiring and promotion decisions on the basis of politics rather than on the basis of quality, then the university itself will be perceived as under threat and trust will erode. It is difficult to believe in such circumstances that the government will not abuse its policies affecting the institution.[15] The repeated revelations of the abuse of the government's new extended powers produced apprehension among already skeptical minds in the academic community and concern that the government could be using its new powers to gather information on scholars and scientists.

The antiterrorism legislation was intended, in part, to help law enforcement agencies increase biological safety in the United States. But the efforts to monitor and control the activities of scientific researchers seemed to have a perverse, unintended consequence that may well be increasing the risk of bioterrorism. As I have tried to suggest, there is an almost unimaginable amount of impressive biological and biomedical research going on today at American research universities, with researchers attempting to understand the nature of infectious diseases, the means of their transmission, the way the immune system works, and how we can develop vaccines against various viruses as well as defenses against bacterially caused diseases. Bonnie Bassler's work at Princeton is only one example of such extraordinary work. And an increasing number of American researchers are interested in developing knowledge that could be used by public health officials and doctors to prepare the nation adequately for attacks of bioterrorism. Microbiology and immunology have become "hot" fields. Of course, most of the research conducted with these agents has nothing whatsoever to do with bioterrorism itself, but the results of that work could, nonetheless, eventually help us to fight bioterrorism and develop methods of prevention and treatment of diseases.

When the SARS virus was identified in China in 2003, an international community of scientists and public health leaders mounted a targeted effort to understand the origins and genetic organization of the virus so they could develop an effective vaccine and contain its spread. These medical sleuths are like warriors entering a highly dangerous battlefield, sometimes placing themselves at great personal risk in an effort to forestall the spread of diseases that could cause thousands of deaths. The simple fact is that the government and research scientists have a great deal of common interest in learning more about anthrax, botulism, smallpox and other pox viruses, plague, and other causes of infectious diseases that could cause harm to the public, whether or not they are used by terrorist organizations. Inability to understand and treat new viruses and bacteria that can spread rapidly from one continent to another could cause many more deaths to innocent civilians than is apt to result from terrorist attacks.

For some time after 9/11, the Bush administration and Congress increased government funding for this kind of work. This funding, which is administered through the National Institute of Allergy and Infectious Diseases (NIAID), the Department of Defense, and other government agencies, included about $1 billion for basic research for therapeutics, drugs, and vaccines. Normally, when funding is available, scientists flock to these research areas, especially if the work is potentially of great scientific value. Instead, scientists abandoned work in these areas during the Bush years. Why? What we have here is an example of "too much of a good thing." With its focus only on national security issues, the government had created a chilling climate for research in an area where there was a great need for breakthrough discoveries. The irony was that, in an effort to improve national security against bioterrorism, the policies adopted could actually have led to increased risk for the nation. How is this possible?

To work with any of the eighty-odd viruses, bacteria, or toxins that could be used as weapons, scientists have to register with the federal government and fill out FBI forms for security clearance that essentially allow the FBI to look into any aspect of their background; they have to put their fingerprints on record, have their labs inspected, and catalog and report on any changes in the amounts of select agents in their laboratories—accounting for all samples of these agents and for their destruction. Only certain students may work with these agents. In addition, researchers must follow multiple regulations promulgated by different government agencies, and these regulations often conflict with one another.

The heightened controls on the transportation, storage, and disposal of these select agents is a good thing. This stuff should not just be hanging around, and it could be dangerous if not monitored very closely. One cannot argue with the need for tighter controls on the agents themselves. But in their zealousness to heighten national security, the government created such fear of noncompliance and its consequences that scientists were getting out of the business of doing research with these agents. In addition, the government's inability to create simple but effective processes for guaranteeing greater controls caused bureaucratic nightmares for scientists still willing to work with the pathogens.[16]

Much of the fear among scientists that would cause them to abandon their work with select agents was reinforced by the highly visible case of Dr. Thomas C. Butler. After 9/11 and the anthrax incidents, Butler's career seemed to be peaking. Head of the division of infectious diseases at Texas Tech University, he was working in Dar es Salam, Tanzania, with sixty Tanzanian bubonic plague victims, charting how they responded to a new antibiotic. His clinical trials in Tanzania seemed to hold promise for biodefense. The new interest in pathogens such as anthrax and plague bacteria increased Butler's visibility. In fact, according to *Science* magazine, "Butler was on the verge of becoming perhaps the United States' hottest plague scientist."[17] The university was familiar with Butler's plague research, the board of regents had approved his sabbatical to work in Tanzania, and the university had approved his laboratory for plague research.

In April 2002, on a return trip from Tanzania, Butler packed the plague samples in dry ice and transported them to London and then back to Texas. Carrying infectious disease samples for research on commercial airlines had been common practice for years. Butler did not ask either U.S. or U.K. officials for transport permits before boarding his plane to London, although he did have a letter from Tanzania authorities indicating that he was carrying these fluid materials. Butler was apparently following practices that he had used before 9/11, and before the new antiterrorism laws were passed. When Butler arrived at the Dallas airport, he failed to declare the plague bacteria samples as "commercial merchandise" for U.S. Customs. The government charged Butler with violation of the Patriot Act for improperly transporting, labeling, and reporting biohazards. He was also charged with smuggling and accused of other violations, including failing to obtain the appropriate permits before driving approximately 700 miles from Lubbock to the Fort Collins labs of the Centers for Disease Control, where he was having his samples tested.

But more critically, on January 13, 2003, Butler told Texas Tech safety officials that 30 of 150 vials of plague bacteria in his laboratory had been stolen. Upon Butler's revelation to the university officials, "sixty F.B.I. agents swept through the campus and surrounding Lubbock to look for the missing vials. They found no signs of forced entry into the laboratory, and after two days of intense grilling Butler reversed himself."[18] It was then that the FBI arrested Butler and charged him with multiple counts of lying to its agents, all on top of the Patriot Act violations he had already been charged with committing. While the FBI was investigating possible violations of antiterrorism legislation, they were also investigating other aspects of Butler's scientific life at Texas Tech.

Some agents combed over materials related to Butler's grants and his other activities at the university, while others reviewed his tax returns. Ultimately, the indictment was expanded to include fifty-four unrelated charges of embezzlement, tax evasion, and mail fraud. Later, in an interview on CBS's *60 Minutes*, Butler said that the FBI had tricked him into a confession. At the end of the day, at age sixty-two and at the peak of his career after thirty years of research, Thomas Butler was placed on trial facing a sixty-nine-count indictment "that carried a maximum of 469 years in jail and $17 million in fines."[19] To add to his reversal of fortune, Texas Tech placed Butler on a paid leave, denied him access to his laboratory, and began proceedings to fire him.[20]

The Butler case became a cause célèbre for the science community, which feared that the prosecution of Butler was being used "to scare scientists into obeying strict new bioterror-prevention laws" and that the result would have the unintended consequence of driving able scientists away from biodefense research, which would undermine national security.[21] Peter Agre, winner of the 2003 Nobel Prize in Chemistry, who is an acquaintance of Butler's, said, "As far as I can tell, it is based on some kind of misunderstanding or maybe some absent-minded bumbling. . . . I can't imagine he would do anything intentionally malicious. . . . It looks like there was no bioterror. There was a false alarm. It seemed that might have been the end of it. In Butler's case, that was just the beginning of it."[22] Agre donated part of his Nobel Prize money to Butler's legal defense fund.

Stanley Falkow, winner of the 2008 Lasker Award, professor of microbiology and immunology at Stanford, and the putative father of molecular microbial pathogenesis, told reporters that he had destroyed his plague cultures and therefore the new laws were "not going to have that big of an effect on me, because I'm not going to deal with it."[23] In a letter to Attorney General John Ashcroft, Falkow made it quite clear what he thought would be the consequences of the new regulations:

Trying to meet the unwarranted burden of what the government considers 'biosafety' is simply not coincident with the practice of sound, creative scientific research. . . . How could I possibly permit my students and myself to be subject to the same nightmare [as Butler] if we also made an inadvertent mistake? . . . I know this fearful feeling is true not only of American scientists but also of colleagues from abroad. . . . You have your regulations but I believe you will have fewer knowledgeable scientific practitioners of infectious diseases research.[24]

Another prominent research scientist, who declined to be identified, said that the regulations are full of catch-22s. For example, the regulations require "that clinical labs that grow new cultures of select agents must destroy them within seven days. . . . But another part requires labs to get permission before destroying any cultures—and this takes more than seven days." The problems of compliance are so acute that one other scientist opined, "Every single lab involved in select agents has violated the regulations somehow. . . . The FBI can come in and find you out of compliance whenever it chooses."[25]

Of course, no one should be above the law. On December 1, 2003, the jury convicted Butler of forty-seven of the sixty-nine counts against him. He faced up to 240 years in jail and millions of dollars in fines. However, a close look at the verdict is highly instructive. It shows that Butler was found not guilty on almost all of the charges related to illegally transporting, smuggling, and importing plague bacteria—the most significant original charges against him related to bioterrorist activities. None of the forty-seven convictions were directly related to the original incident; forty-four involved contract disputes with Texas Tech. These convictions, with the notable exception of his failure to obtain transport permits, had nothing to do with his plague research in Tanzania. He was "acquitted of charges of lying to the FBI and university officials about the missing vials, smuggling plague samples into the United States from Tanzania and illegally taking them to government laboratories in Colorado and Maryland."[26]

After the verdict, facing dismissal from Texas Tech, Butler resigned from his position, repaid the university more than $250,000, and lost his medical license. On March 10, 2004, he was sentenced to two years in prison followed by a three-year term of supervised release; fined $15,000;

and ordered to pay \$38,675 in restitution to Texas Tech University. Federal District Court Judge Sam R. Cummings (nicknamed "Maximum Sam" by local lawyers) surprised some when he imposed a sentence that was lower than the standard set by federal guidelines, citing testimony that the bacteria shipment was done for humanitarian reasons and that the Department of Commerce would have approved a permit had Butler applied. The U.S. Court of Appeals for the Fifth Circuit denied Butler's appeal in October 2005. In May 2006, his petition for certiorari to the U.S. Supreme Court was denied. The perceived and potentially actual costs to scientists of conducting research with "select agents" are apt to trigger reactions similar to Peter Agre's, who found the message of Butler's convictions "chilling. . . . It still strikes me as an episode from the McCarthy era."[27]

Thomas Butler's case is not unique. Other faculty members and researchers have been subjected to various forms of investigation without any result except for the consequences for people's careers. One worthy of note is the saga of Dr. Steven J. Hatfill, who was labeled by Attorney General Ashcroft as a "person of interest" in the FBI investigation of the anthrax mail attacks in the fall of 2001. Several letters containing anthrax had been sent to members of the media as well as to senators Thomas A. Daschle and Patrick J. Leahy. The anthrax caused the death of five people, and seventeen others became ill. The FBI interviewed hundreds of scientists and others who worked in fields related to biological weapons. Hatfill, an army biodefense researcher at Fort Detrick in Maryland, had never worked with anthrax and willingly cooperated with the FBI. He volunteered to take a lie detector test—which he passed, according to the examiner, suggesting that he had nothing to do with the anthrax attacks. Nonetheless, in the months that followed, the attorney general focused the public's attention on Hatfill as if he were a suspect.[28]

The defense contractor that employed Hatfill fired him, and soon thereafter he got a new job as associate director of the National Center for Biomedical Research and Training at Louisiana State University. On September 3, 2002, the chancellor of Louisiana State University, Mark A. Emmert, who has gone on to become president of the University of Washington, issued a press release announcing his decision to "terminate the employment of Steven J. Hatfill." Chancellor Emmert said, "In taking this action, the university is making no judgment as to Dr. Hatfill's guilt or innocence regarding the FBI investigation. Our ultimate concerns are the ability of the university to fulfill its role and mission as a land-grant university, to fulfill its contractual obligations to funding agencies and to maintain academic integrity. In considering all of these objectives, I have concluded that it is clearly in the best interest of LSU to terminate this relationship."[29]

Upon an inquiry from U.S. Senator Charles Grassley, Department of Justice officials did not deny that they had requested that the university not employ Hatfill on any DOJ funded projects—one of the sources of support for Hatfill at LSU—even though "at that time, Dr. Hatfill had not been arrested, he had not been charged and, according to official statements made by law enforcement officials, he was not even a suspect in the anthrax investigation."[30] The chancellor's statement makes one wonder what the role and mission of LSU actually is, if it is not to defend principles of freedom of inquiry and attacks on a member of its faculty against whom no charges have been made. Although Hatfill's reputation was shattered and it became impossible for him to find a job, the outcome for him was somewhat better than for Butler. Hatfill sued the Department of Justice in 2003, and in June 2008 the suit was settled for $5.82 million.

Scientists looked at this case and wondered whether being involved with select-agent research was worth the trouble. Their actions tell it all. In 2004, Nobel Prize winner Robert C. Richardson gave an example from Cornell:

> The Patriot Act, which was passed after 9/11, has a section in it to control who can work on "select agents," pathogens that might be developed as bioweapons. At Cornell, we had something like 76 faculty members who had projects on lethal pathogens and something like 38 working specifically on select agents. There were stringent regulations for control of the pathogens—certain categories of foreign nationals who were not allowed to handle them, be in a room with them or even be aware of research results. So what is the situation now? We went from 38 people who could work on select agents to 2. We've got a lot less people working on interventions to vaccinate against smallpox, West Nile virus, anthrax and any of 30 other scourges.[31]

These scientists were not prevented from working on these problems by law or regulation. They chose to get out. And many scientists since the

Butler case are opting out of work with select agents. In late 2007 the National Research Council and the American Association for the Advancement of Science conducted a survey of 2,000 scientists about their behavior in light of security concerns. Fifteen percent said they had changed their behavior in one or more of the following ways: avoiding "dual-use" research projects with the potential for harm; "shying away from international collaborations"; or "excluding foreign graduate students and postdocs from certain lines of work and censoring themselves while talking about their research." Ron Atlas said, "It is a surprisingly high number."[32]

Clearly, the debate over the new emphasis on national security is not only a matter of whether or not the government should be investing in efforts to improve defenses against bioterrorism or the misuse of discoveries, or investing to develop new vaccines and treatments that would mitigate the impact of bioterrorist acts. Of course it should. The debate is also about whether the means actually adopted to improve security really achieve that outcome, and of equally great importance, whether the cost to the growth of the scientific knowledge needed to combat these toxins and agents is too great, given the nature of the threat that we face. This is a calculus that we must do.[33]

RESTRICTIVE VISA POLICIES

The American research university remains far and away the place that the most talented young people who are willing and able to venture abroad want to come to. At this time, we have better and more prestigious programs than most other nations. The incentives for coming here are obvious: better economic opportunities and returns for graduates than alternatives. And the American system of higher education is huge. As a 2007 National Research Council Report has noted, with fewer American students choosing careers in science and engineering, the American preeminence in research and development cannot be sustained without the influx of the most talented foreign students. Jacques Gansler, a former Pentagon official who cochaired the National Research Council committee, noted that despite continued security concerns about foreign students, "both the security and scientific communities agree that losing our leading edge in science and technology is one of the greatest threats to national security. . . . Unnecessary or ill-conceived restrictions could jeopardize the scientific and technological progress that our nation depends on."[34]

In fact, we train more advanced graduate students in a few of our leading universities than most entire nations have the capacity to train—even if they wanted to increase the numbers of foreign students in their advanced degree programs. And a remarkably high proportion of these highly trained students stay in the United States after receiving degrees, finding jobs in all walks of life, but particularly in our universities and industries. A significant percentage of those who do return home assume leadership positions at their nations' leading institutions—thus solidifying bonds between the United States and these other nations. Having internalized the values associated with the universities and collaboration, these American-trained scientists and engineers continue to be engaged in the international community of scientists and scholars. More often than not, they become our unofficial ambassadors in their own country. However, storm clouds began gathering as a result of the Bush administration's obsession with national security and its visa policies after 9/11.

Foreign students from a host of nations that send a great many exceptional students to the United States were being treated as if they were enemy aliens. Men over sixteen who were last admitted to the United States on or before September 30, 2002, were required to register within a designated period of time with the Immigration and Naturalization Service (INS), which in 2003 would have its functions placed under three agencies (U.S. Citizen and Immigration Services [USCIS], Immigration and Customs Enforcement [ICE], and Customs and Border Patrols [CBP], all within the Department of Homeland Security). Those who came from Middle East nations were often subjected to interrogations and threatened with deportation. Over a million foreign students studying in the United States in 2008 were tracked using the government's Student and Exchange Visitor Information System (SEVIS), which requires schools to provide information to the government about the enrollment status of each foreign student.

The government's Visa Mantis program tries to identify those visa applicants who pose a threat to national security and may transfer sensitive technologies to terrorist organizations and their supporters. The review system, at least between 2001 and 2005, caused long delays in processing visas for students and scholars who were already studying or working at

American universities, as it required each of them to go through a lengthy security-clearance procedure every time the visa was renewed, even if it was just following a short visit home. Until 2005, the FBI clearance procedure in Mantis cases, which had been put into effect in 1998, took about twenty-nine days to complete, and sometimes much longer, with seventy days being the average in 2003. Under a February 2005 change in the rules, the repeated security clearances were no longer necessary, and the visas became valid for up to four years for students and two years for researchers. Much of the visa authority was handed over to the State Department as part of this change in the procedures, and the change was widely hailed as an improvement because of the shorter waiting times and reduction in red tape. But there was a tradeoff: The FBI was given access to the information in the SEVIS system.

The improvements in the efficiency of the Visa Mantis system since 2005 have not cured the problems that are involved in recruiting the most talented foreign students—particularly in science and engineering. Delays in obtaining visas of two or three months were not uncommon as of 2008. As Amy Scott, assistant vice president for federal relations at the Association of American Universities (AAU), said in March 2009: "We are very concerned that we are losing ground here, that people are missing opportunities to come to the U.S. to teach, conduct research or just participate in a conference."[35] In a January 2009 National Academy report, "Beyond 'Fortress America,'" the academy makes it clear that the barriers we create for the most talented students translate into opportunities for foreign universities that now have the research equipment and infrastructure to compete with us. As Danielle Guichard-Ashbrook of MIT said: "There are other countries that want these folks. They are the best of the best. They have other options."[36] Guichard-Ashbrook told one of her Middle East students, whose father was dying, that if he went home to see his father, he was apt not to be let back into the United States to complete his courses. He went home and his return was, in fact, delayed.

It is difficult to know the total number of students and researchers affected by these policies, but there are scores of similar recorded cases, especially for students from India, Russia, the Middle East, and China.[37] Some have been denied visas; others have been arrested and either held for deportation or actually deported by federal authorities. In the aftermath of September 11, 2001, the tightening of policies for foreign students and researchers led to the collapse of the collaboration between chemists Arthur D. Broom and Tarek Aboul-Fadl, who had been working to create new HIV drugs. Aboul-Fadl had been working with Broom at the University of Utah, but after 9/11 he could not get a visa to come back to the United States after returning to Egypt for a family visit.[38] In another case, Narendra Banad, who had graduated from the University of Wisconsin Business School, tried to return to the United States from India via Los Angeles in 2008, but immigration officials detained him at the airport, revoked his visa, and deported him back to his native India. Another University of Wisconsin student, Tope Awe, was held in federal custody by immigration and customs enforcement authorities in 2008. Awe, who had been born in Nigeria but had lived in the United States since she was three years old, was slated for deportation despite the fact that 1,000 students and many of her professors were trying to prevent this from happening.[39] Many others around the country continue to be told that they are "in deportation status."[40]

Two other visa problems persist as of 2009. It remains difficult for foreign scholars who hold controversial views to obtain visas to speak, attend conferences, or become temporary professors at some American universities. On March 18, 2009, a group of academic free-speech and civil-rights organizations sent a letter to Secretary of State Hillary Clinton asking that the Obama administration revise the practice of the George W. Bush White House of denying visas to foreign scholars, as well as artists and writers, based on ideology—or viewpoint-based exclusions. The letter said: "While the government plainly has an interest in excluding foreign nationals who present a threat to national security, no legitimate interest is served by the exclusion of foreign nationals on ideological grounds. To the contrary, ideological exclusion impoverishes academic and political debate inside the United States. It sends the message to the world that our country is more interested in silencing than engaging its critics. It undermines our ability to support political dissidents in other countries."[41]

Perhaps equally problematic for talented graduates of our major universities is the difficulty they have obtaining visas to work in the United States or obtaining visas for their young wives and children. Many foreign students wish to remain in the United States after earning their degrees so that they can use their skills in existing industrial labs or begin new start-up companies. These young scholars, scientists, and engineers are often

forced to leave the United States against their wishes. The net result for the
nation is the loss of a huge investment in human capital. Given the current
quality of our universities and their prestige, young people around the
world are still willing to tolerate indignities and delays in order to have
the opportunity to study in the United States. But such tolerance won't
last forever.

The real effects of the unwise immigration policies will not cause an
immediate erosion in our relative or comparative position in the world of
higher education, but it could be felt significantly in the rate of our own
growth in fields of science and technology. We are currently making very
rapid progress in these fields and clearly lead the world, but to maintain
this superiority we must have access to the best students and researchers
from around the world. Unwise policies that restrict foreign talent from
studying here and becoming faculty members may slow down the rate of
discovery and innovation coming from U.S. universities and from the industries that depend on its graduates. We must not be too complacent.

Beyond these immediate problems for the university and industry, closing down the borders of the United States to foreign students and scholars from some nations nurtures American isolationism. It not only fosters
xenophobia in the United States, but also leads to false characterizations of
the United States and the growth of fundamentalism abroad. It reverses
America's history of receptivity to people of talent from anywhere in the
world, reduces the opportunities for our understanding and appreciation of
different cultures, and denies these same opportunities to foreign students
and scholars who wish to come here. In short, these policies are counterproductive in the "war on terrorism."

Scholarly Publication and Open Communications

Because of its importance to the growth of knowledge, I have repeatedly
emphasized the value of the open communication of ideas. Scientists typically publish the results of their work in scientific journals that are easily
accessible to the world's scientific community—a world without national
borders. Scientific publication not only allows science to grow, but also allows it to be critiqued. Only through publication, with the accompanying
detailed description of techniques and methods, can work be replicated
and confirmed or falsified. Indeed, limitations on such communications

would limit scientists' understanding of the basis of claims of novel discoveries and impede the process by which scientists build on each other's work. At a minimum, discoveries should not be withheld from the scholarly and scientific community for proprietary reasons; only those experiments that must be deemed classified research should be withheld from public scrutiny. Moreover, the government and other sponsors of research should not be permitted prior review or prior restraint on the will of scientists and scholars to publish their work.

However, in today's world, given the potential misuse of science and technology, serious and important questions are being raised about whether the right to publication of unclassified research should be viewed as an "absolute." Are there conditions under which unclassified research should be withheld from the larger scientific community because it could be misused by terrorist groups and individuals or others who present a threat to security? If so, what are those conditions, and who should decide what discoveries to withhold from the public domain? Furthermore, would prior restraint really prevent those who would do evil things with the discoveries from obtaining the information that would be contained in these scientific and technical papers? This problem has become known as the "dual use" problem.

Some scientific and technological discoveries, when published, may move a field forward in important ways, leading to the development of new treatments, vaccines, and the like, while simultaneously providing information to those who would misuse the knowledge for undesirable purposes. The Bush administration's public position, which was to search for a proper balance between prior restraint and open communication, betrayed its private efforts to limit scientific communications to serve its political ends. Using various forms of political pressure, the administration's views created tension and conflict with most leaders of universities and the scientific community.

John H. Marburger III, President Bush's science adviser and director of the Office of Science and Technology Policy, said that open communication should be abridged "when there is a risk to the public, when there is a possibility of hurting people or infringing on widely-acknowledged human rights." When asked if he could give an example of such a situation where withholding information actually proved useful, he could not think of one, "although," he added, "the terrorists are becoming more sophisticated at accessing knowledge."[42] Of course, because science grows in a worldwide community with a great deal of advanced work going on in many nations, the policy of a single nation, albeit one as important as the United States is in the international community, will not prevent the misuse of scientific results. Unless there was some international agreement about criteria and standards for publication, U.S. policy on the matter makes little difference. Censorship of publications by the United States alone will not have much of a deterrent effect on terrorists' efforts.

Few would deny that the government has a right and a duty to take an interest in the misuse of science. It has a legitimate interest, for example, in knowing where certain bacterial agents and toxins are stored and who is working with them. The fundamental problem facing research universities is how much they should be willing to compromise their long-standing principles about open, free communication for unclassified research to meet the government's idea of what is needed to heighten national security in an age of terrorism. For biologists, more specifically, the problem is how they should handle "sensitive research" results that are not classified.

Many universities, including the most distinguished research universities, do not accept classified projects from the government, and those that do conduct the research in facilities that are separate from the main campus. Since the National Security Decision Directive of 1985 was issued, the research universities have worked with a clear understanding of the distinction between unclassified and classified research.[43] After the 9/11 attacks, the Bush administration tried to introduce a new classification: research that involved "sensitive but unclassified information."[44] The administration tried to have this intermediary classification accepted by universities despite the ambiguity over what might fall into this new category.[45] Some universities accepted contracts with these new restrictions on publication, whereas others, such as MIT, refused to accept government contracts that contained "sensitive but unclassified" provisions.

Research universities report having continuing problems with unclassified public domain contracts, mostly with the Department of Defense and the Army Research Laboratory, in which there are restrictions on publication without prior review and on the employment of foreign nationals without prior review and approval by the government contracting officer. For many universities these provisions are "deal breakers" in that they compromise the essential openness of the scientific research system and the ability of scientists to freely communicate new knowledge. Unless the funding agency is willing to remove these clauses, the universities will not take on the research project. Moreover, these kinds of unclassified but restrictive contracts conflict with the antidiscrimination policies of most universities, which state explicitly that participation in research cannot be based upon the ethnic or national background of a student or faculty member.

When these conflicts over security issues fail to be resolved, both the government and the universities lose. But university-based science and engineering would suffer a greater loss if the universities compromised their basic values in order to receive these kinds of government research contracts. As Bruce Alberts, the former president of the National Academy of Sciences, said at the time of the original proposal for the new classification, "We were furiously trying to defend our right to publish things and not cave into this sensitive but unclassified category which you could put everything into. It has been, and often was, used as an excuse by people in government to try to restrict what people know."[46] Harvard science policy expert Lewis Branscomb went even further. It was not the controlling of the dissemination of information by a single government agency that he feared, but that the web of controls from multiple agencies "looks, smells, and tastes like 'classification.'" He went on to say that prohibiting some foreigners, marijuana smokers, or people with clinical depression from seeing research "reminds me of McCarthyism."[47] Ambiguous classification affects individual scientists' decisions about research projects. "Scientists are afraid of something so nebulous," said Stephen Morse, director of the Center for Public Health Preparedness at the Mailman School of Public Health at Columbia University. "The bottom line is they want to know what they can publish before they are up to their necks in research."[48]

The dual-use publication dilemma facing the biological sciences community is real and must be taken seriously by both the scientific community and the government. The stakes are high. Not since the Cold War had the tension between national security and the rights of scientists to publish freely been so dramatic as during the Bush years following 9/11. During the early phases of developing nuclear fission and the atomic bomb, American physicists faced the dilemma of whether they should publish results of experiments that were important and would be of use to

German scientists. The government clearly wanted to restrict the release of this information. At the end of the day, the small band of extraordinary physicists decided to restrict access to some of the knowledge that they had developed. Today, the dual-use dilemma is somewhat different. In seeking to develop vaccines or defenses against old or new forms of lethal viruses or bacteria, biologists employ materials that could be used as biological weapons and that are far easier to obtain than the materials that nuclear scientists worked with in developing the atomic bomb.[49]

Some believe that concern for national security defeats the need for open scientific communication. Others, including most members of the scientific community, remain extremely skeptical of the government's efforts to control the content of science prior to its publication. Craig Venter, the former president of Celera Genomics—a company that contributed mightily to the mapping of the human genome—told one reporter, "Some people argue that publishing each genome is like publishing the blueprint to the atomic bomb. But it's also the blueprint for a deterrent and the blueprint for a cure."[50]

Clearly, it would be foolish to deny the potential for the misuse of biotechnology. It would also be foolish to place the growth of science at risk by imposing impossible restrictions on the ability to carry out and publish scientific work on important biological problems. One of the continuing challenges that we have in making judgments about policy is the absence of hard evidence about the nature and scale of the potential problem. As it is virtually impossible to obtain a good reading of the "enemy," it becomes very difficult to make policy judgments that could have substantial consequences.

So, what is to be done to deal with the potential threat of misuse of biological research? A 2003 report from the "Fink Committee" of the National Academy of Sciences proposed that a new system of review be set up to ensure "that advances in biotechnology with potential applications for bioterrorism or biological weapons development receive responsible oversight."[51] The system recommended by the committee relies heavily on a mix of "voluntary self-governance by the scientific community and expansion of an existing regulatory process" and would require periodic review of research and research results at specific stages of development.[52]

As Gerald R. Fink put it: "The issue of whether these results should be published needs to be resolved within the scientific community, not within the federal government."[53] Concurring with this view, Ronald M. Atlas, past president of the American Society of Microbiology (with 42,000 members), noted, "We must not adversely impact science. . . . It is the advance of science that provides the real future protection [from diseases]. . . . We have provided an architecture that helps prevent the subversion of science."[54] "We could shut down the life sciences," Atlas also said recently, "but the problem is we'd never have a cure for cancer and a lot of the diseases people are dying from every day."[55] Through mechanisms of voluntary self-governance, the scientific community is trying to keep the government away from overregulating science to the point where both science and national security suffer.

As Robert Gates, the former director of the CIA—and president of Texas A&M University before being named secretary of defense—concluded in 2003, "The beauty of trying self-policing is that it still leaves other options open if it fails. If you immediately move to government control, the situation becomes quickly irreversible and the consequences to the scientific process are catastrophic."[56] Stephen Morse summarized the sentiments of most members of the academic and scientific community when he said, "The antidote to this kind of dangerous knowledge is more knowledge."[57]

The rules for biosecurity did not end with the end of President Bush's term. If the regulations hindered international cooperation in dealing with SARS, they also slowed down our response in 2009 to the H1N1 influenza virus. In 2009, Mexican officials shipped "200 samples of the new H1N1 virus to Canada for identification rather than to the U.S. Centers for Disease Control and Prevention, because of the U.S. rules on importing biological materials."[58] As *Science* magazine pointed out, the rules governing the handling of biological agents, which were under review in 2009 by the National Academy of Sciences as well as several federal agencies, "may also affect both the climate for U.S. science and how inviting America will be to international scientific guests."[59]

INCREASED SURVEILLANCE

Perhaps the feature of the Patriot Act that has produced more national skepticism and hostility than any other is its "relaxation" of the Fourth

Amendment's protections of personal privacy. The heightened surveillance and erosion of the need to demonstrate probable cause has been felt by university librarians, by students in terms of FBI access to their records, and by faculty in terms of surveillance of their research and communications. This potential intrusion on individual freedoms and rights is perhaps the most difficult to measure. Under the law, those librarians or university officials who are asked for information by the FBI are not allowed, under threat of criminal penalties, to inform a faculty member or student that he or she is under surveillance and investigation. Consequently, it becomes nearly impossible to obtain accurate data on the use by the FBI of its new powers. Nonetheless, other types of information do speak to the "chilling effect" that this legislation is having on the gatekeepers of information at the universities. If students, faculty, and librarians believe surveillance of their personal records, computer traffic, and reading choices is real and is taking place on the campus, then it is real in its consequences for them. The situation is akin to the one that Robert Hutchins reacted to in the 1940s when the faculty at colleges and universities felt great fear during the McCarthy period: "The question is not how many professors have been fired for their beliefs, but how many think they *might* be. The entire teaching profession is intimidated."

When we think about libraries in the United States we rightly think of the extraordinary evolution of our public library system. Few factors have been as important in the social mobility of talented but economically deprived youngsters as the presence of books in the local library. It is probably less widely known, however, that the majority of the large and unique library collections in the United States belong to research universities.[60] These university library systems are rapidly expanding their use of digital materials and fostering the online use of their resources, which can be accessed from anywhere in the world by using Google or other online search engines. But where collections remain private and have not yet been digitized, scholars need to visit the great libraries for their research.[61] Access to books, manuscripts, government documents, scientific and scholarly journals, ancient prints, and the like is central to scholarly work. If the privacy of library records is compromised and those records are open to surveillance with minimal cause, then the basic functions of the research universities and their gatekeeper librarians are threatened.

A 2003 interpretation of the American Library Association's Bill of Rights concluded:

> In a library (physical or virtual), the right to privacy is the right to open inquiry without having the subject of one's interest examined or scrutinized by others. . . . Protecting user privacy and confidentiality has long been an integral part of the mission of libraries. . . . The *Library Bill of Rights* affirms the ethical imperative to provide unrestricted access to information and to guard against impediments to open inquiry. . . . The library profession has a long-standing commitment to an ethic of facilitating, not monitoring, access to information.[62]

The librarians and academic information staff members of universities are critically important to the quality of these institutions. They are, in many ways, custodians of culture. Extraordinarily talented librarians and new digital-media information scientists and staff members are as scarce as exceptional faculty members, and the great research universities compete to attract the best talent from around the world to fill key positions. So, the effects of the privacy policies can have a chilling effect on those who staff the libraries as well as on those who use them.

The librarians at research universities have reacted vocally with skepticism and anger and have vehemently opposed the potential intrusion of the FBI into the personal reading habits of those using their libraries.[63] Indeed, public librarians have taken unusual action to warn the public about the provisions of the Patriot Act. One librarian in Monterey Park, California, posted a sign on each of its publicly accessible computers: "Beware," the message says, "anything you read is now subject to secret scrutiny by federal agents."[64]

We actually know very little about how this aspect of the Patriot Act is being used by the government, in part because of the difficulty of gathering the information. We in fact do not have reliable data on efforts by the FBI and the police to obtain information from the research university libraries. On an anecdotal level, we understand that the fear of inquiries into the computer use of patrons worries many directors of libraries more than inquiries about reading habits. Whatever the actual level of surveillance that has gone on thus far, the nation's librarians have vigorously supported new federal legislation. The Freedom to Read Protection Act, introduced in 2004 by Congressman Bernie Sanders of Vermont, would exempt libraries and bookstores from the provisions of the Foreign Intelligence Surveillance Act, which requires "the production of tangible things for certain foreign intelligence investigations, and for other purposes."[65]

The Freedom to Read bill, which had 145 cosponsors, lost in the House after Bush threatened to veto it. Under the 2006 reauthorization of the Patriot Act, this provision of FISA was extended until December 2009, but as the ALA states: "In spite of years of work done by ALA members, our allies in the civil liberties arena, and dedicated Members of Congress, the [reauthorization] legislation does not include most of the meaningful reforms we hoped would restore the privacy rights of America's library users."[66] The reauthorization was passed (with some slight relaxation of disclosure requirements and slightly more control of federal investigators) under a Congress controlled by Democrats, leading one to wonder if changes will occur in these provisions even with the even larger Democratic majority in Congress in 2009.

We also do not have good information about how often the federal government has made requests for student records that were previously protected under FERPA. University officers, such as the registrars who keep these records, are bound to confidentiality under the law. We do know that a tremendous amount of information is being organized to identify and follow the paths of foreign students who are studying in the United States. As of 2009, the fundamental obligations of colleges and universities to the Justice Department have not changed. There is an expectation at our universities that under the Obama administration these surveillance provisions of the Patriot Act will not be used without substantial evidence of probable cause. This provision (Section 215) of the Patriot Act will sunset on December 31, 2009, if it is not reauthorized—and there is pending legislation in both the House and Senate to curtail abuses of the use of NSLs in gathering information from libraries.

EFFORTS TO IMPOSE IDEOLOGICAL POSITIONS

In some cases the attack on universities has had bipartisan support. For example, in 2003, extreme political pressure was placed on a number of the nation's largest private foundations to withdraw grant support made to organizations that had been labeled by critics as directly or indirectly supporting activities that are anti-Israel. This political pressure led to changes in foundation policies that go far beyond current law and that placed unconscionable pressure on research universities to monitor the speech and actions of their students, faculty, and the people most affected by the grants if they wished to continue receiving support from the foundations.

Perhaps the most troubling case involved the Ford Foundation, one of the largest philanthropic foundations in America, with assets that reached $13.5 billion in 2007 and roughly $11 billion as of September 2008. Only five universities have endowments larger than Ford's, which under law must spend about 5 percent, or $600 million, annually in grants and operations. These roughly 2,500 awards go to organizations in the arts, education, development, and social justice. For more than forty years, Ford has supported almost all of the major American research universities in one form or another. Among the many recipients of its grants have been groups supporting social justice in Israel and groups associated with the Palestinians.

In October 2003, Edwin Black, reporting for the Jewish Telegraphic Agency (JTA), "an international news service that provides up-to-the-minute reports, analysis pieces and features on events and issues of concern to the Jewish people," published "Investigating Hate," a "four-part investigative series" accusing the Ford Foundation of providing extensive financial support to Palestinian nongovernmental organizations (NGOs) that were intent on subverting the state of Israel, on fostering the distribution of anti-Zionist and anti-Semitic materials, and on supporting Palestinians whose activities encouraged terrorism against the state of Israel.[67] It focused initially on the Ford Foundation's support for groups that Black claimed had hijacked the 2001 Durban, South Africa, conference on human rights for the purposes of gaining support against Israel. The series of articles suggested that, in effect, knowingly or not, the Ford Foundation was supporting organizations favoring anti-Israel terrorist activities.[68]

Following the publication of the series, leaders of the American Jewish community, including Yehudit Barsky of the American Jewish Committee; Abraham Foxman, national director of the Anti-Defamation League; and Malcolm Hoenlein, executive vice chairman of the Conference of Presidents of Major American Jewish Organizations, denounced the Ford

Foundation for its support of organizations such as LAW (which today is the Palestinian Committee for the Protection of Human Rights and the Environment based in Jerusalem) and the Palestinian NGO Network, an umbrella organization of about ninety nongovernmental organizations representing different Palestinian causes.

Calling for a congressional investigation of Ford Foundation grants to these groups, Hoenlein said, "At a time when government and society are demanding transparencies on the part of corporations and charities, it is hard to justify the apparent exemption of the Ford Foundation, which uses tax-free dollars to fund what is at best questionable organizations and causes—and at worst organizations undermining the interest of the United States and its allies. It is now incumbent on Congress and federal agencies to conduct their own examination." Yehudit Barsky added, "We need two kinds of accountability from Ford—not just where did the money go, but how was it spent. Ford owes the public not only a financial accounting, but also a moral accounting."[69] How Ford would provide a "moral accounting" remains totally unclear.

The "Funding Hate" series and the responses to it by influential Jewish organizations in the United States triggered a series of threats and placed extraordinary pressure on the Ford Foundation to alter its grants policies and to publicly issue a "mea culpa." Where did the pressure come from? The leader was Jerrold Nadler (D-N.Y.), a member of Congress with a liberal voting record who represents one of the largest and most influential Jewish populations in the United States. Congressman Nadler circulated "a petition signed by 20 members of Congress demanding that Ford halt its funding of anti-Israel hate groups." Nadler and conservative senators Rick Santorum (R-Pa.) and Charles Grassley (R-Iowa), the chairman of the Senate Finance Committee, called for congressional investigations of Ford and other foundations to review their funding practices. The intense pressure and not very subtle innuendo sent Ford a clear message: Get your grant policies in line or face congressional inquiries into your tax-exempt status and financial operations.

The Ford Foundation has been one of the few foundations willing to endure criticism and still fund Palestinian groups interested in advocacy and social justice. The foundation has also supported many efforts by Israeli organizations working for social justice. Under extreme pressure from Nadler and others in New York and Washington, the leadership of Ford capitulated and announced a change in its oversight policies. I don't know the details of what transpired between Ford and Nadler and others who pressured Ford to change its policies, but I do know that Ford suddenly not only reversed its position by 180 degrees but also publicly admitted that its prior policies were in error. It embraced "advisors" from the Jewish organizations to help assess Ford's grant activity in this program area. Of course, the Ford Foundation and other philanthropic foundations can create their own rules for distributing their funds as long as they do not violate laws governing foundations, but in redefining their rules Ford and others may undermine their mission to support organizations that actually do work to promote social justice. For our purposes, suffice it to say that the changes that Ford made had a direct impact on research universities that were receiving grants from the Ford Foundation, and from other foundations that fell into line behind Ford's capitulation to political pressure.

But what in fact did Ford do to call forth the wrath of the politicians? In his articles, Edwin Black did not present any evidence that the Ford Foundation had violated American laws or that its funds for Palestinian groups were being misused for support of "terrorist" activities. There is not one piece of direct evidence that suggests that the flow of Ford dollars went to support "terrorists," unless one applies the broadest possible definition of both "terrorism" and "support." In short, unless the reporter omitted damaging information on Ford's inadvertent links to terrorist groups, or unless he considers all Palestinian groups "terrorist" supporters, there is nothing in the articles that demonstrates the misuse of Ford funds for this implied purpose. The Black series does make a number of specific accusations of inappropriate use of Ford funds that were not properly accounted for by the grantee organizations,[70] but nothing whatsoever to suggest that these funds were being used to support terrorist activities.

A sad aspect to this entire episode is that by capitulating rather than fighting the claims made in the articles, and by issuing a formal apology, the foundation has ensured that the assertions of fact that remain unsubstantiated in the Black articles will become socially constructed "historical facts." At the end of the day, one may approve or disapprove of the decision by the Ford Foundation to make these grants in the first place, you may criticize their "peer review" system, one may argue that the accounting standards for the grants were lax and that Ford was unable to identify funds misappropriated for personal use, and one may disagree with the ideas and ideology of the organizations receiving the grants, but there is absolutely nothing in the content of Edwin Black's exposé that would indicate that the Ford Foundation had violated U.S. law, even after the passage of the 9/11 antiterrorism legislation. Nor had the foundation supported any type of activity that would not be protected by the First Amendment had the organizations been active in the United States.

It is remarkable that Ford's grants to groups that opposed the Sharon government's policies toward the Palestinians and that produced advocacy materials and pamphlets were apparently sufficient to trigger such extreme political pressure, to the point where Ford essentially required all grantees to sign a loyalty oath for their institutions and all others who were associated in any way with their institutions. One can imagine Representative Nadler finding the content of these Ford programs objectionable, but one can hardly imagine him waging a campaign against the rights of these groups to produce these materials, however opprobrious to him, had these forms of speech been produced in the United States. But he and others in Congress, in a heavy-handed way, forced Ford's leadership to "reassess" its values and to alter its policies, and Ford appears to have been too weak to resist the political pressure.

What the Ford Foundation does internally to change and improve its grants management procedures and accountability practices and, to some extent, its peer review system are of limited concern to us. But the requirements that it places on grant recipients, particularly research universities, are of great concern. Ford now requires any university that accepts its financial support through grants or contracts to sign a statement with the following terms: "By countersigning this grant letter, you agree that your organization will not promote or engage in violence, terrorism, bigotry, or the destruction of any State, nor will it make subgrants to any entity that engages in these activities." The Rockefeller Foundation also required similar affirmations for its awards: "In accepting these funds . . . certify that your organization does not directly or indirectly engage in, promote, or support other organizations or individuals who engage in or promote terrorist or other violent activity."

The nation's leading private research universities found these clauses to be fundamentally objectionable to the very idea of the university. Nine chief academic officers of large universities, including the University of

Chicago, Columbia, Cornell, Harvard, MIT, the University of Pennsylvania, Princeton, Stanford, and Yale, wrote to Ford's president, Susan Berresford, and Gordon Conway, then president of the Rockefeller Foundation, expressing their objections to the new funding requirements.[71]

Berresford responded, "In our view, our grant letter is a statement of our institutional values. We think that's a very important aspect of the relationship with Ford."[72] For his part, Congressman Nadler said of the letter from the nine universities, "There is no constitutional mandate for the Ford Foundation to give you or me money. The foundation can set conditions that reflect its values."[73] Of course, this is technically true, but essentially disingenuous. It is also true that as a private institution Ford is governed by different rules than public and government agencies. But all of this misses the fundamental point. Putting aside the vagueness of the conditions being set, Ford is pressuring universities to compromise some of their most fundamental values of free inquiry and discourse, their belief that there is no single way to view the world or to discuss it, that there is no single definition of what constitutes bigotry or prohibited speech, and that no single voice speaks for the "university." And if Ford and other foundations had held to its extreme position of requiring this pledge of allegiance to "Ford's values," and the universities had refused to sign, would these foundations, or the world, have been better off? Ford can see that proposals for grants conform to "their values" through its peer review process, but it would be a sad day if that process included a political litmus test for grant recipients. For Ford to knuckle under to crude political pressure and then to insist that universities accept its vaguely articulated conditions in order to be funded undermines the integrity of the foundation and the quality of its work.

Given the conflict between the foundations and the universities on the one hand, and the foundations and politicians who are catering to their constituents on the other, how was the matter resolved? In fact, the resolution by the Ford Foundation will not go down as an example of institutional courage. The nine universities that wrote as one to Ford negotiated a sidebar agreement that diluted the language that Ford was insisting on, but they did not succeed in having the policy retracted. It would be a blunder of significant magnitude for these foundations to cut off funding to the research universities. And although many members of the faculty who receive support from foundations do not want their personal ox gored, the research universities would be unwise to accept funds that must comply with the original language that Ford offered.

In times of war or national fear, civil liberties have often come under attack. This was true in the post-9/11 period. The effects of attacks on these values are not only felt by individuals but also by institutions, and when the weight of these assaults become heavy enough, the ability of institutions to fulfill their mission is disrupted and sometimes seriously undermined. Efforts to politicize "truth" and "discovery" also affect the ability to pursue that mission.

CHAPTER 13

"Political" Science

I believe it is true that there is such a thing as objective scientific reality, and if you ignore that or try to misrepresent it in formulating policy, you do so at peril to the country.

—Wolfgang H. K. Panofsky

The United States has never come even close to disrupting university life with ideological demands the way Germany did under the Nazis or the way the Soviet Union did during the "Lysenko" years under Stalin. I certainly do not want to suggest that I believe we have reached that level of government intrusion into the work of our great universities. Nevertheless, the eight years of the Bush administration offer us a frightening example of how the distrust of scholarly and scientific work—because it challenges the ideological views of the prince—can begin to seriously erode the structure of knowledge production that has made our universities the finest in the world. If the policies of the past eight years are not reversed under the new administration, the future of our most distinguished institutions of higher learning is in jeopardy. The evidence to support this view seems reasonably clear.

In February 2004, the Union of Concerned Scientists (UCS), which includes many of America's most distinguished scientists as members, including twenty Nobel Prize winners, published a report that accused the Bush administration of misusing science for political purposes.[1] The report argued that the integrity of American science was at stake and that the Bush administration, in an unprecedented way, had been undermining the basic values of science and science-based policymaking. Others were highly critical of the administration's willingness to ignore scientific "facts" because they might undermine the political agenda of the administration. For example, reports from the office of Congressman Henry A. Waxman (D-CA) noted many of the same examples of abuse that the UCS identified,[2] and numerous distinguished scientists who were unconnected to the UCS became harsh critics of the administration's attitude toward "uncooperative" scientific findings and facts and its willingness to tailor science to fit politics. The criticism focused on discrete policies and actions taken by the administration rather than on a comprehensive policy. In fact, a clearly articulated science and technology policy was not a high priority for the Bush administration. This was in contrast to the Clinton administration, and even the administration of President George H. W. Bush, both of which supported rather clear statements and policies advocating the growth of science and technology in a knowledge-based society.[3] During the first eight months of his administration, President Barack Obama gives every indication that he understands the need for defending the integrity of scientific facts and the role that our universities play in developing innovations that drive our economic system—matters to which I will return in the final chapter.

The way the integrity of science and university research has been undermined can be demonstrated through a few examples. And although the White House and the president's science adviser, Dr. John H. Marburger III, denied the UCS accusations, there is little question among scientists and science policy experts that the weight of the evidence is against what the Bush administration actually did.[4] It systematically tried to "rewrite" scientific results, censor scientific reports, muzzle some of the world's leading scientists, and exclude the best scientific evidence when the results didn't fit its political ideology or agenda.

EMBRYONIC STEM CELL RESEARCH

Over the past decade, the scientific community has come to believe that the use of embryonic stem cells holds great promise in the fight against diseases, from Alzheimer's to juvenile diabetes and from spinal cord injuries to Parkinson's disease. The claim within the scientific community is that federal funding for new stem cell research, including the creation of new stem cell lines, could save lives, produce remarkably important new knowledge, and help ensure continued American superiority in this area of biomedical research. Although stem cell research is viewed as a highly promising line of inquiry, it is, like most important areas of research, "living off its future." Great rewards could come from this research, but only if the research necessary to substantiate the claims and expectations is pursued. In fact, this is true for all promising lines of research.

The opposition to the use of embryonic stem cells in scientific research comes from those who believe that it poses an ethical problem about the termination of life that could otherwise have developed into human beings, and for believers, this is a grave dilemma. Others believe that using embryonic stem cells for research will lead us further down a slippery slope toward cloning human beings and to producing "designer parts" for individuals who are not suffering from specific diseases. The debate thus pits the politics of antiabortion groups and religious fundamentalists against the views of most scientists and, as we shall see, most Americans.

In an effort to sidestep this moral or ethical dilemma, scientists since 2006 have been experimenting with adult cells in an effort to get them to regress to a stage that is equivalent to embryonic stem cells. These cells are called "induced pluripotent stem cells" (iPS). Questions remain about whether these cells are really equivalent, despite promising work done in 2009 by a number of Chinese scientists of the Chinese Academy of Sciences.[5]

Unfortunately, adult stem cells, despite their value in scientific research and medicine, probably cannot totally solve the ethical dilemmas involved in this debate. Embryonic stem cell research may offer a unique path to finding a cure for a wide variety of health problems.[6] Princeton philosopher Peter Singer has summarized succinctly why embryonic stem cell research is important for biomedical research:

> Only stem cells derived from human embryos have been shown to possess the ability to develop into virtually all the tissues of the human body. These are therefore the ones that scientists believe hold the most promise of cures of major diseases. Once a cell has been taken from a human embryo, it can be maintained in the laboratory, and will produce more

cells, which will in turn produce further cells, and so on, until there are millions of cells available for research. This creates a line of cells that are all descended from the original cell taken from an embryo. Scientists speak of "cell lines" to refer to the entire group of cells, past and present, that have this kind of relationship to a particular original cell, much as we might speak of the "line of descent" from an ancestor. Cell lines can grow indefinitely, but they all start with an original cell taken from an embryo. The embryo does not survive the removal of the stem cells. That is why the use of stem cells is ethically dubious for those who think that a human being has right to life from the moment of conception.[7]

But the problem of whether or not to use embryonic stem cells for re-search is more nuanced than it might at first appear—even for "right to life" advocates. The embryonic stem cells that are used to create cell lines are almost invariably taken from cell banks where people who are at-tempting in vitro fertilization (IVF) have stored multiple embryos for pos-sible future use. When a pregnancy occurs—or a pregnancy does not occur after multiple efforts and the "parents" give up—the remaining embryonic stem cells are destroyed. By 2004, an estimated 400,000 IVF embryos had been frozen and were "likely to be destroyed if not donated, with the in-formal consent of the couple, for research."[8] These are the cells that would be used for research purposes and the creation of cell lines. So the choice is not really between using these cells for research or impregnating a woman through in vitro fertilization; it is about whether these "surplus" stem cells will be used for potentially life-saving research or will be de-stroyed because they will not be used.

Facing increased pressure from the scientific community and concerned members of the public to embrace research using these stem cells, Presi-dent Bush presented his views to the American public in a televised ad-dress in August 2001. The question before the president was whether or not federal taxpayer dollars, through the National Institutes of Health (NIH) and other federal agencies, should be used to support embryonic stem cell research. Acknowledging that scientists believe that further re-search using stem cells held great promise for improving the lives of peo-ple who suffer from terrible diseases, the president suggested that using embryonic stem cells "raises profound ethical questions, because extracting the stem cell destroys the embryo, and thus destroys its potential for life."[9]

The president's position was shaped, he said, by "deeply held" but conflicting beliefs.

On the one hand, he said, "I'm a strong supporter of science and technology and believe that they have the potential for incredible good—to improve lives, to save life, to conquer disease." On the other hand, the president believed that "human life is a sacred gift from our Creator. I worry about a culture that devalues life." In the end, the president, in an effort to be Solomonic (or at least to satisfy as many political constituencies at once as possible), decided to permit continued research on the existing lines of stem cells, which he estimated as greater than seventy-five, while banning federal funding for the development of additional stem cell lines to be used for research and therapeutic purposes. He also set up a council on ethics, chaired by Dr. Leon Kass, a highly regarded, conservative bioethicist from the University of Chicago, "to monitor stem cell research, to recommend appropriate guidelines and regulations, and to consider all of the medical and ethical ramifications of biomedical innovation."

After the president made that speech, it turned out that there were far fewer existing cell lines that could be used, in fact, for biomedical research—a total of nineteen rather than seventy-eight. The value of these lines for therapeutic use for humans was quite uncertain because all of them had been contaminated with mouse feeder cells. The issue of federal funding gained renewed attention during the 2004 presidential election year after Nancy Reagan, who is viewed as royalty in some quarters of the Republican Party, openly supported federal support for stem cell research in a speech she delivered to the Juvenile Diabetes Research Foundation in May. The scientific community continued to push for a review of the Bush policy.

In June, the Coalition for the Advancement of Medical Research, representing 140 different organizations, wrote the president, stating: "Mr. President, now is the time to update the current policy. For those of us with a personal stake in the possibilities of embryonic stem cell research, this really is a race against time. In the past three years, more than 4 million Americans have died from diseases that embryonic stem cells have the potential to treat."[10] Letters from 58 members of the U.S. Senate and from 206 members of the House of Representatives were sent to the president also calling for an immediate reevaluation of the policy and noting that the current restrictions on funding stem cell research were making it increasingly difficult to recruit new scientists into this area of research. "Despite the fact that U.S. scientists were the first to derive human embryonic stem cells," the coalition's letter said, "leadership in this area of research is shifting to other countries such as the United Kingdom, Singapore, South Korea, and Australia," where more liberal policies toward embryonic stem cell research had been adopted.[11]

In response to a poll conducted in 2004 by Research!America, a significant majority of Americans (62 percent) said "they believe that research into therapeutic cloning (to produce stem cells) should be allowed." And in another poll, conducted by the Juvenile Diabetes Research Foundation, among "conservative voters," 44 percent favored expansion of the 2001 policy "to include federal funding for research on stem cells developed from excess embryos in fertility clinics."[12] A majority, 56 percent, of those conservative voters said they either strongly supported (34 percent) or somewhat supported (22 percent) "using embryonic stem cells from embryos frozen in fertility clinics."[13] By 2007 and 2008, a strong majority of Americans favored stem cell research (73 percent) when the question included a mention of how it could find treatments for a variety of diseases, such as Alzheimer's, and more than half (53 percent) favored the research even if it involved destroying human embryos (35 percent opposed).[14] Despite the growing bipartisan support for a review and change in policy, President Bush never altered his position on banning federal financing of embryonic stem cell research. In the meantime, a number of states independently began to fund local stem cell research at their universities, but the efforts were hardly a substitute for federal funding, and keeping the federal funds and the local ones separated involved substantial logistical problems.

Meanwhile, other nations, not without their own local ideological resistance from religious and antiabortion groups, were moving forward with stem cell research programs. The British are about to begin to clone embryonic stem cells for research purposes using eggs that are left over from IVF treatments, and they are hopeful that they can lure top American scientists to places like Cambridge University, King's College London, and the Center for Life in Newcastle, where they can work in a more permissive environment than currently exists in the United States.[15] The rush to establish national leadership in stem cell research has placed so much pressure on scientists to come up with path-breaking results that it has led to deviant behavior, including the falsification of data by scientists at Korea's Seoul National University.

In reflecting on the consequences of delaying stem cell research, Dr. Gerald D. Fischbach, Columbia University' former executive vice president for health sciences and a member of the National Academy of Sciences, wrote:

> The cost in dollars of delaying new stem-cell research is difficult to estimate. It might measure in the hundreds of billions of dollars. . . . A less obvious, but real, cost is the damage to the fabric of America's extraordinary culture of inquiry and technological development in biomedical sciences. . . . A crippled research enterprise might add an unbearable stress with long-lasting effects on the entire system. If revolutionary new therapies are delayed or outlawed, we could be set back for years, if not decades. To steer clear of controversy, some investigators will redirect their research. Others will emigrate to countries where such research is allowed and encouraged. Some will drop out entirely.

Fischbach warned of the consequences of mixing fundamentalist political ideology with science: "When you begin arguments based on convictions and not open to scientific discourse, the whole process starts to crumble, and that worries me, not only with stem cells but in the whole sphere of scientific inquiry. . . . I think it is very threatening . . . as threatening as any time in my lifetime, including the McCarthy era."[16]

Embryonic stem cell research remains a contentious issue, but not among scientists. President Bush cast the dilemma as one that pitted the potentials of science against ethical considerations, although it remained unclear whether his real intent was political—to secure the support of the religious right. One of the problems with the former president's staunch opposition is that the biological material used in stem cell research is the surplus of embryos that would otherwise be killed—they are not needed for the fertilization of women who are trying to become pregnant. Moreover, the president assumed that the embryos used in the research represented "human life." As many scientists have noted, every year millions of embryos die. Even apart from those that may die in laboratories or fertility clinics, or as a result of abortions, millions die as a part of the natural process of fertilization—those that fail to implant in the woman's uterus. "The truth is," said Peter Singer, "politics aside, virtually no one except couples who want to have a child really cares about the loss of embryos. And even couples seeking to conceive only care about whether they will be able to have a child. They don't really care for the particular embryo that is lost. More often than not, they aren't even aware it ever happened."[17]

The president's conduct in relation to the Council on Bioethics, which he established, was also a source of controversy. The council was chaired by Kass and made up of leading scientists, doctors, ethicists, lawyers, theologians, and others. After its inception in 2001, the committee members held sharply different views about the issues before them—a healthy state of affairs, indicating that open debate and expression were encouraged in the council. However, in February 2004, President Bush dismissed two members of the council—both outspoken advocates for human embryonic stem cell research. One, Professor Elizabeth Blackburn, was a biologist at the University of California at San Francisco, a member of the National Academy of Sciences and the Institute of Medicine, and winner of the 2009 Nobel Prize in medicine. She received a call from the White House indicating that some changes were going to be made in the composition of the council and that she was herewith dismissed from its membership. The other dismissed member, professor emeritus of moral philosophy at Southern Methodist University William May, also had taken positions opposed to those of conservative members of the council. Kass said that these changes were "in no way political," that there were still strong differences among council members, and that seven remaining members in fact opposed the president's position on stem cell research.

In their letter to the president protesting the two dismissals, Representatives Henry Waxman (D-CA) and Louise Slaughter (D-NY) concluded: "We understand that many social conservatives who represent part of your 'political base' are opposed to stem cell research. But their opposition should not obscure the fact that your policy is inhibiting research. Nor does political ideology justify turning an independent advisory committee into an echo chamber."[18]

Urging the president to reconsider his dismissal of the two council members, Bettie Sue Masters, president of the 12,000-member American Society for Biochemistry and Molecular Biology, argued that the dismissals were contrary to the processes of discovery in science:

Dr. Elizabeth Blackburn is a world-renowned scientist with expertise in the very subject the Council on Bioethics has been dealing with in recent months. . . . This action confirms the accusations of a "litmus test" being applied by the Administration to every appointment to scientific panels. . . . Science is not political; rather, it seeks to uncover truth about the origins and mechanisms of life and the world and universe in which we live. Scientific truths are sometimes uncomfortable and do not always conform to ideological convenience. This is precisely why scientists are valuable members of any policy-making body that considers scientific and biomedical issues—political positions ought to be based on science, rather than the other way around.[19]

The two departing scientists were replaced by three new members, whose views, based upon their prior stated beliefs, seemed more in tune with Bush's.[20] The president's rhetoric on stem cell research reawakened a streak of anti-intellectualism that is older than our national identity. This attitude is one that periodically resurfaces, as it did during the McCarthy period and the Eisenhower administration when the "egghead" became the brunt of ridicule, or later on during the Nixon administration when Vice President Spiro T. Agnew attacked the "effete intellectual snobs" of the Northeast.

Bush's tone and rhetoric in the stem cell research debate, and his attitudes toward scientific evidence in general, suggested a resurfacing of the ambivalence toward scholars and scientists among some segments of society. His religious sensibilities, and his religious beliefs about the "beginnings of life," about "life as a sacred gift from our Creator," about a "culture that devalues life," and finally, about how he hoped America would "always be guided by both intellect and heart, by both our capabilities and our conscience," were closely related to his political religious base of support. They also attested to a person who was a tad bit suspicious of the values and motives of the scientists who supported embryonic stem cell research—the intellectuals and experts at the universities—who failed to address the moral questions that Bush identified as crucial in such decisions. The scientists and others who favored embryonic stem cell research were portrayed as people devoted to the creation of new ideas rather than to the words of their Creator.

There was, of course, no evidence that scientists were any less concerned than the president with the ethical problems that cloning presents. On the contrary, there was some evidence that the scientists, after taking into account the source and nature of the embryos that would be used for research purposes, and the good and harm that could obtain from the research, simply reached a conclusion that was quite different from the president's. In short, it is precisely because of the extraordinary value that physicians and biomedical researchers place on human life and the number of lives that might be saved as a result of stem cell research that scientists were urging the president to revise a policy that seemed based on religious and political rather than scientific criteria.

Whether President Bush's opposition to stem cell research—or the right of women to have abortions—or, for that matter, his ambivalence toward science and technology more generally, was a matter of conviction, or politics, or both is beyond my powers of inference. There was, however, a very strong correlation between Bush's sources of political support and opposition to fundamental scientific ideas. And in fact, this same kind of opposition has historically been linked to fundamentalist religious beliefs and to anti-intellectualism in America.

In the history of science, there have been many periods when the forces of objectivity and subjectivity have clashed.[21] Although we might think that in modern America we are beyond such juxtapositions, I believe that the arguments against stem cell research and the skepticism about science and its methods that Bush embraced can be linked to an anti-intellectual posture. A problem arises when the president of the United States allows his personal feelings and beliefs to influence his views on scientific questions to the extent that he attempts to silence alternate views and restricts scientists from exploring promising and ethically justifiable lines of research. President Barack Obama has already taken action of two kinds to reverse the position of the Bush administration. First, almost immediately upon taking office, he sent a memorandum to the heads of executive departments and agencies making clear his commitment to the integrity of scientific results. The March 2009 memo said: "The public must be able to trust the science and scientific process informing public policy decisions. Political officials should not suppress or alter scientific or technological findings and conclusions. . . . The selection of scientists and technology professionals for positions in the executive branch should be based on their scientific and technological knowledge, credentials, experience, and integrity."[22] Second, he changed (through an Executive Order dated March

9, 2009) the federal government's position on funding of embryonic stem cell research. Instead of only nineteen stem cell lines, an unlimited number of embryonic stem cell lines may be used in federally funded research. This order was in accord with his presidential campaign rhetoric. On the campaign trail, he had said, "I strongly support expanding research on stem cells. I believe that the restrictions that President Bush has placed on funding of human embryonic stem cell research have handcuffed our scientists and hindered our ability to compete with other nations."[23] While reversing the Bush policy, Obama acknowledged that embryonic stem cell research continues to be a difficult ethical issue for some people. Both positions were greeted warmly in the academic and scientific communities.

GLOBAL CLIMATE CHANGE

Over the past several decades a wealth of scientific data has accumulated to suggest that humans are causing disruptions in the Earth's climate. Fossil-fuel emissions and various greenhouse gases are producing changes in the climate that could have long-term, catastrophic effects on the environment. In fact, recent evidence suggests that the time frame for these changes is much shorter than we previously believed. Climate scientists and former vice president Al Gore received the 2007 Nobel Peace Prize for their work in bringing this critical issue to the attention of the world's population.

Efforts have been made to deal with the increased levels of carbon dioxide in the atmosphere with limited success. International agreements, such as the Kyoto Protocol, hardly represent a panacea, but such agreements among nations represent steps toward gaining control over the complex causes of global warming and climate change. The United States is a signatory to the Kyoto Protocol, which was initially adopted at a conference in Kyoto, Japan, in 1997, but Congress has not ratified the treaty and thus the United States is not bound by its terms. The United States is one of the few advanced industrial nations unwilling to commit to the Kyoto accord. The scientific community has urged the government to take a leading position in international efforts to slow down the rate of climate change. The policy position advocated by earth scientists is based on research conducted throughout the world. The policy implications for certain sectors of the U.S. economy are not trivial—especially for the industries that profit from the sale of fossil fuels; nevertheless, scientists believe the situation is urgent enough to take serious steps to slow or reverse global warming.

When George W. Bush came to office, he asked the National Academy of Sciences to review the findings of the Intergovernmental Panel on Climate Change (IPCC) and provide the administration with an impartial assessment of the state of knowledge in climate change science. The academy produced a strong endorsement of the IPCC that was consistent with the report produced by the American Geophysical Union, the world's largest organization of earth scientists. Yet, according to the Union of Concerned Scientists, "Bush administration spokespersons continue to contend that the uncertainties in climate projects and fossil fuel emissions are too great to warrant mandatory action to slow emissions."[24] The UCS noted that "in May 2002, President Bush expressed disdain for a State Department report ... to the United Nations that pointed to a clear human role in the accumulation of heat-trapping gases and detailed the likely negative consequences of climate change; the president called it a 'report put out by the bureaucracy.' In September 2002, the administration removed a section on climate change from the Environmental Protection Agency's (EPA) annual air pollution report ... even though the climate change issue had been discussed in the report the proceeding five years."[25]

The concerned scientists also noted that White House officials tried to introduce so many qualifiers into the text as to produce a report that would convey a sense of uncertainty where, in fact, there was a high level of scientific agreement. In commenting on the Bush administration's efforts to intrude on the formulations of the scientists at EPA, Russell Train, the EPA administrator under both presidents Nixon and Ford, said the "interests of the American people lies in having full disclosure of the facts. In all my time at the EPA, I don't recall any regulatory decision that was driven by political considerations. More to the present point, never once, to my best recollection, did either the Nixon or Ford White House ever try to tell me how to make a decision."[26] Dr. Rosina Bierbaum, appointed by President Clinton to the Office of Science and Technology Policy (OSTP), who also served for one year under President Bush, said: "The scientists [who] knew the most about climate change at OSTP were [from the start] not allowed to participate in deliberations on the issue within the White House inner circle."[27] The exclusion of some of the most knowledgeable scientists from a conversation about climate change is problematic in itself, but the active effort to censor the opinions of government and university scientists by the government is even more disconcerting.

There may be a few better climate scientists in the world than James E. Hansen, but they would be hard to find. Hansen has been the director of the Goddard Institute for Space Studies and works for the National Aeronautics and Space Administration (NASA) as one of its leading scientists. He also holds professorial appointments in Columbia University's Department of Earth and Environmental Sciences and in its Earth Institute. Hansen joined the space agency in 1967 and has been one of the world's leading scientists in trying to produce computer simulation models that predict the effects of a variety of factors, such as greenhouse gases, on global climate change. He had opportunities to brief Vice President Gore during his years in office as well as Vice President Dick Cheney in 2001. Hansen's scientific interventions have not always been welcome. As early as 1988, he was issuing public warnings about the damaging effects on the climate of heat-trapping emissions, dominated by carbon dioxide, that are unavoidable by-products of burning fossil fuels such as oil and coal.

But never before had Hansen run into efforts to control what he said publicly about his scientific results as he did during the years of the Bush administration. Hansen has asserted that various officials in the hierarchy at NASA headquarters ordered the public affairs staff to review his scientific papers, his upcoming lectures, his Goddard website postings, and requests for interviews with him. "They feel their job is to be this censor of information going to the public," Hansen said in a 2006 interview with the *New York Times*.[28] According to the *Times* story and a book by Mark Bowen that focuses on the Hansen case, *Censoring Science,* there was nothing in Hansen's thirty-year career that equaled "the push made since early December [2006] to keep him from publicly discussing what he says are clear-cut dangers from further delay in curbing carbon dioxide."

The drama started after Hansen delivered a lecture at the meetings of the American Geophysical Union on December 6, 2006, in which he said that the United States could achieve significant reductions in emissions with existing technologies, particularly through control of emissions by motor vehicles. He added that without leadership from the United States, we would experience climate change that would leave Earth "a different planet." In effect, Hansen was echoing an observation made by E. O. Wilson: "Do we want to destroy the creation? That's the question. That's what we're doing at an accelerating rate."[29]

After releasing the data on which his lecture had been based that showed that 2005 was probably the warmest year in over a century, officials at NASA had the public affairs officers relay a warning to Hansen saying there would be "dire consequences" if such statements continued. In fact, Hansen was concerned that he could lose his job, although that was not going to stop him from speaking out. The public affairs people at NASA tried to restrict his access to the media, including controlling whether they would have someone else stand in for him in any news media interviews.[30] According to Leslie McCarthy, a public affairs officer responsible for the Goddard Institute, George Deutsch, a political appointee and public affairs officer at NASA headquarters, would not permit Hansen to talk to National Public Radio about his findings, calling NPR "the most liberal" media outlet in the country. According to McCarthy, Deutsch said it was his job "to make the president look good." McCarthy went on, "I'm a career civil servant and Jim Hansen is a scientist. That's not our job. That's not our mission. The inference was that Hansen was disloyal."[31]

Hansen's understanding of NASA's mission was quite different from Deutsch's. He felt that his science needed to be communicated to the public, that it was part of NASA's mission to communicate important scientific findings, and that it was entirely inappropriate to censor or alter the science produced by government scientists. Once the Hansen muzzling efforts broke in the *New York Times,* other government scientists began to chime in on their experiences with censorship. Many scientists at the National Oceanic and Atmospheric Administration (NOAA) who worked at climate laboratories said that what would have been routine conversations with reporters five years ago could no longer occur without the prior approval of administration officials in Washington, and "then only if a public affairs officer is present or on the phone."[32] Some were hesitant to go public. "One later admitted [to Hansen] that he kept his silence out of fear that he might lose funding for a project he had been working on for a few decades—most of his career."[33]

NASA was not, of course, the only federal agency where government-employed scientists complained about political interference with their work. In fact, complaints of ideological interference with the scientific process by the Bush administration emanated from virtually every federal agency involved with science: NOAA, the NSF, the NIH, the Food and Drug Administration, the U.S. Department of Agriculture, the U.S. Geological Survey, the National Forest Service, the Environmental Protection Agency, and the Centers for Disease Control. David Baltimore, the Nobel Prize–winning biologist whose discoveries I've described, spoke out at the annual meeting of the American Association for the Advancement of Science (AAAS) in 2006, saying that the suppression of science by the Bush administration was "no accident." After learning of each new incident of interference, Baltimore said, he would "shrug and say, 'What do you expect?' . . . It is part of a theory of government, and I believe it is a theory that we must vociferously oppose."[34]

All of this did not escape members of Congress. Representative Sherwood Boehlert (R-NY), chairman of the House Science Committee at the time and one of the strongest advocates for science within the Republican Party, said to NASA Director Michael Griffin that "good science cannot long persist in an atmosphere of intimidation." Boehlert went on to say: "NASA is clearly doing something wrong, given the sense of intimidation felt by Dr. Hansen and others who work with him. Even if this sense is a result of a misinterpretation of NASA policies—and more seems to be at play here—the problem still must be corrected. . . . Political figures ought to be reviewing their public statements to make sure they are consistent with the best available science." He concluded that "scientists should not be reviewing their statements to make sure they are consistent with the current political orthodoxy."[35]

Whether the policies at NASA have changed is difficult to say, but the case of James Hansen has not been an isolated one, and it further suggests why the American research university is so important to scientific discovery: It presents opportunities that often do not exist in science enterprises that are subject to direct government control, which may be run by political appointees. Hansen managed to weather the storm related to his whistle blowing, but we don't know whether scientists of lesser distinction have fared as well. When scientists are essentially civil servants and state employees and have to submit their scientific papers and discoveries, as well as their public statements, for review by bureaucratic offices influenced by political partisanship, there is a greater probability of censorship and control of science than in the university environment, where research is at least at arm's length from political control. The

Hansen case offers us still further evidence of the key role that academic freedom and free inquiry play at our universities.

REPRODUCTIVE HEALTH AND OTHER HEALTH ISSUES

The general consensus in the scientific community and among top public health officials is that the use of condoms helps prevent unwanted pregnancies and the spread of sexually transmitted diseases such as HIV/AIDS. George W. Bush and many of his "pro-life" followers consistently opposed public education that emphasized the use of condoms. While governor of Texas, Bush was a passionate proponent of "abstinence-only" educational programs and a staunch opponent of educating young people about other scientifically proven methods of preventing sexually transmitted diseases. When he became president, Bush and his appointees not only ignored the evidence about the efficacy of abstinence-only programs—that they don't work very well—but sought to have data on the effectiveness of such programs, such as charts documenting birthrates among female program participants, removed from the website of the Centers for Disease Control and Prevention (CDC). According to the Union of Concerned Scientists, "In place of such established measures, the Bush administration has required the CDC to track only participants' program attendance and attitudes, measures designed to obscure the lack of efficacy of abstinence-only programs."[36]

The CDC is one of the world's premier public health organizations. It has a proven track record of responding quickly and effectively to reported outbreaks of new forms of deadly diseases that could spread around the world. It has also played a leading role in efforts to increase public awareness and understanding of the causes of AIDS, the ways it is transmitted, and how individuals can help prevent or reduce the probability of infection. In short, it has earned its reputation as an authoritative and trusted scientific organization. So, it was no trivial matter for President Bush and others in his administration to be pressuring the CDC to distort science by altering the information that it distributed through its website on public health issues. Yet, in addition to distorting information about abstinence-only programs, the Bush administration "suppressed other information at the CDC at odds with preferred policies," according to scientists with the UCS. "At the behest of higher-ups in the Bush Administration . . . the agency was forced to discontinue a project called 'Programs that Work,' which identified sex education programs found to be effective in scientific studies. All five of the programs identified in 2002 involved comprehensive sex education for teenagers and none were abstinence-only programs. In ending the project, the CDC removed all information about these programs from its website."[37]

The CDC had placed information on its website showing that the use of condoms helped to prevent the spread of HIV/AIDS. The Bush administration pressured the CDC to alter the wording in such a way as to raise doubts in a reader's mind about the scientific value of condom use as a method of prevention. Furthermore, a "fact sheet on the CDC website that included information on proper condom use, the effectiveness of different types of condoms, and studies showing that condom education does not promote sexual activity was replaced in October 2002 with a document that emphasizes condom failure rates and the effectiveness of abstinence."[38]

Trampling on medical facts did not stop there. There is overwhelming medical evidence that the quality of health care for racial and ethnic minority groups is far poorer than the quality available to the more affluent members of society who are disproportionately not minority group members. The incidence of many diseases, especially those that are dependent on controllable environmental factors, is unquestionably higher among these racial and ethnic minority group members. Addressing this problem, a 2002 report from the Institute of Medicine (one of the National Academies) concluded that "the real challenge lies not in debating whether disparities exist . . . but in developing and implementing strategies to reduce and eliminate them."[39] One year later, the Department of Health and Human Services released *National Healthcare Disparities Report*, in which health-care disparities were not described as a national problem. However, that conclusion was not present in the draft report that HHS sent up for review by political appointees (not by knowledgeable scientific peers).

After review, the final version of the report emphasized "that in some ways racial and ethnic minorities are in better health than the general population." Accordingly, it "delete[d] most uses of the word 'disparity'"; "eliminate[d] the conclusion that health care disparities are 'national problems'"; "drop[ped] findings on the social costs of disparities and replace[d] them with a discussion of 'successes'"; and "omit[ted] key examples of health care disparities," such as the higher incidence among racial and ethnic minorities of deaths from HIV and suboptimal cardiac care. When criticism of the HHS changes and alterations in the conclusions came from members of Congress and was covered in the press, HHS Secretary Tommy Thompson admitted that "there was a mistake made" in revising the scientific conclusions of the report and pledged that it would "be rectified."[40]

There is no need to produce a litany of examples of altered reports from federal agencies, particularly the Environmental Protection Agency, or of distorted scientific facts that have been the product of the administration's policies. The critical question is whether this disdain for scientific facts and for those who work to produce useful knowledge will be reversed by the Obama administration.

THE PEER REVIEW SYSTEM

The Bush administration and Republicans in control of Congress intensified their scrutiny of research projects that focused on sensitive subjects. They were intruding into the peer review process, the critical mechanism that universities and the scientific community use to ensure that quality work is supported. For example, a funded NIH project on sex trafficking and the transmission of HIV (with an interest in intervention and prevention) produced an inquiry from a Republican staff member of the House Subcommittee on Criminal Justice, Drug Policy, and Human Resources. Here is an excerpt from the inquiry to the NIH:

> The Subcommittee strongly supports President Bush's efforts and is gravely concerned about the efforts at the National Institutes of Health that contradict the President's mission and instead seek to legitimize the commercial sexual exploitation of women. One particular program the NIH is funding . . . in San Francisco seeks to "promote protective work environments" and "protective behaviors" for "commercial sex workers" from Asia. By doing so, the NIH is, in effect, advancing the sex trade as a legitimate form of commerce that simply needs to be made "safer." . . . The behaviors being examined by the NIH are immoral and illegal, as they should be, in the United States. Knowledge of such illegal exploitation should be reported to the appropriate legal authorities for investigation and prosecution. The NIH and its collaborator on this project, are instead, providing legitimacy and financial support to the continuation of the sex trade. . . . Please provide the Subcommittee with the following in-

formation: (1) Ethical reviews, if any, that the NIH conducted for the San Francisco and Miami studies. (2) The name(s) of the NIH employee(s) who approved funding for the San Francisco and Miami studies, including the names of the individuals on the panels that reviewed the studies' applications. (3) A list of all efforts, if any, by the NIH and collaborators on these studies to notify law enforcement of illegal activities being conducted that were observed or witnessed. . . . (6) A full listing (including funding amounts) of all NIH funded studies over the past decade involving commercially sexually exploited women, including prostitutes or "commercial sex workers."[41]

This was nothing more than crass political interference with the way NIH proposals are evaluated for scientific merit, which includes, among other criteria, assessments by qualified scientists of the quality of the proposed work, the scientific track record of those who are conducting the study, and the potential usefulness of the project.

Many of the projects that came under attack when Republicans controlled Congress were social science projects that dealt with sensitive social issues on which the Bush administration had taken a "moral" position, such as studies of gay men and prostitutes who may have transmitted the HIV virus. There is evidence that staff members at the NIH and the CDC suggested to social scientists submitting applications for research grants on sensitive subjects that they "cleanse" their language, eliminating, if possible, words such as "transgressors," "prostitutes," "men who sleep with men," "anal sex," and "needle exchange." Medical researcher Dr. Alfred Sommer, dean of the Johns Hopkins Bloomberg School of Public Health, said that "what is frightening" was that NIH staff felt grantees needed to disguise their work. He told the *New York Times* in April 2003 that a researcher at Hopkins had been advised to change the term "sex worker" to something more euphemistic in a grant proposal. Dean Sommer made the critical point that "if people feel intimidated and start to cloud the language they use, then your mind starts to get cloudy and the science gets cloudy," adding that although from a management perspective HHS technically has the right to oversee NIH affairs, the federal support of medical research has in fact traditionally been free from political interference.[42]

The effort to intimidate scientists went even further. Apparently, the NIH was asked to "justify" about 200 approved or funded projects to the

House Committee on Energy and Commerce on topics such as "sexual behavior." The list, which Representative Waxman called "the hit list," was compiled by a highly conservative advocacy group, the Traditional Values Coalition, and forwarded to the Commerce Committee, which in turn sent the list to the NIH for explanation. Andrea Lafferty, the coalition director, called the research on projects such as AIDS risk among drug users and on teenage pregnancy "smarmy," and a waste of taxpayers' money.[43] In an October 27, 2003, letter to Secretary Tommy Thompson, Waxman, from California, who has become a major "watchdog" against the intrusion of politics into science, wrote:

> I urge you in the strongest possible terms to denounce this scientific McCarthyism. . . . One researcher wrote: "We are seriously concerned that extra-scientific criteria are being introduced into the NIH grant making process that until now has been based solely on the scientific merit and public health importance of proposed research." This atmosphere of intimidation is unacceptable. These researchers, who are tackling serious and intractable health problems, have done nothing wrong. . . . It would be appalling for the Department to be directly involved in the creation of a "hit list" of scientists and peer-reviewed research. Such involvement would send a clear message to scientists around the country that the Bush Administration is prepared to attack leading researchers and sacrifice scientific integrity at the NIH to further a narrow right-wing ideological agenda.[44]

Thirty-six scientific organizations wrote letters to Congress defending the peer review system at the NIH, and specifically, its support for research on HIV/AIDS, human sexuality, and risk-taking behavior. Although a spokesman for HHS, Bill Pierce, denied the existence of any "hit list" and said that the list prepared by the Traditional Values Coalition should not have been passed on to Congress, NIH Director Elias Zerhouni was called before Congress, where he defended both the peer review process of selection and the importance of these particular grants.

The attacks on the peer review system do not stop with concern about individual grants. It extends to the integrity of the system itself and how members of special advisory committees, speakers at government conferences, and members of study review panels are chosen, and to efforts by the Bush administration to control the peer review of information in federal agencies. Many scientists and scientific organizations claimed that the administration was using litmus tests to veto membership on national advisory committees. Some scientists who were interviewed about possible service were asked who they voted for in the 2000 election, a fact totally unrelated to their expertise or to the tasks of the advisory panel. (This procedure was apparently not unlike the one used to select U.S. Attorneys by the Justice Department.) Others claimed that people were being appointed to national advisory committees who had clear conflicts-of-interest—often people from industry who had a stake in the outcome of particular scientific inquiries.

Dr. Gerald T. Keusch, assistant provost for global health at Boston University Medical Center, resigned from the directorship of the Fogarty International Center at the National Institutes of Health over disputed "procedures" for appointing members of advisory boards. Keusch said that prior to the Bush administration the process was simple. He would propose members to the NIH director, and if those names were approved, officials at the Department of Health and Human Services and in the Clinton administration signed off on them. The officials invariably agreed with his choices. But HHS Secretary Tommy Thompson's office had rejected nineteen of twenty-six candidates, including Torstein Wiesel, a Nobel Prize winner and former president of Rockefeller University.[45] "There is increasing bits of evidence at attempts at control over the business of science," Keusch said. His opinion was not an isolated one.

The report in which his experience was detailed was issued by the Union of Concerned Scientists and signed by more then 4,000 scientists, including 48 Nobel Prize winners and 127 members of the National Academy of Sciences.[46] The list of signers was nothing short of an all-star cast of prominent American scientists. Finding the Bush administration "unresponsive" and "dismissive" of the concerns raised in the first report, the UCS offered more evidence that the administration was "distorting and suppressing science to suit political goals." For example, Richard Myers, director of the Stanford Human Genome Center, had been rejected for a seat on the National Advisory Council for Human Genome Research after he resisted telling an administration official his opinion of President Bush, until an NIH director interceded on his behalf.[47] Jane Menken, one of the nation's most respected population experts, was turned down when nominated to serve on an advisory board after having served on such boards under both presidents Reagan and George H. W. Bush. "I was nominated and I was turned down," she said. "No official reason was ever given," but "it is very hard not to reach a conclusion that it was based on something different from scientific qualifications."[48] It did not go unnoticed that Professor Menken had openly supported the availability of legal abortions.

Ironically, the Bush administration tried to use the peer review system to slow down regulatory decision-making within federal agencies and to alter the composition of peer-review advisory panels more generally. In 2003, the Office of Management and Budget (OMB) created a row by proposing sweeping changes in the peer review process for information to be published by federal agencies. The proposal, which was put out for public comment, received scathing reviews from the scientific community. The scientists were not opposing peer review itself, but the lengthy and unmanageable process of peer review that would apply to almost all information having to do with regulating industrial behavior affecting public health. In short, behind the technical aspects of the process, the scientists saw a political motivation—a way for the Bush administration to impede the introduction of new health and safety regulations.[49]

After reviewing the large volume of criticism, the administration modified the proposal, allowing individual agencies to propose their own form of review, exempting time-sensitive data, modifying the conflict-of-interest clauses (which would have excluded many scientists from serving on peer review panels because they were receiving grant funds from other federal agencies), altering the threshold for review, and limiting the requirements to those regulations that would involve at least $500 million in regulatory costs. Bruce Alberts, president of the National Academy of Sciences, was pleased with the changes the administration had made. In fact, there was "a collective sigh of relief," according to David Michaels, an epidemiologist at George Washington University, who had been among twenty federal officials asking for changes in the initial bulletin. "This is a much better-thought-out proposal."[50]

The OMB claimed it was trying to improve the quality of the information produced for regulatory purposes. In responding to the claims of the UCS and others about misuses of science, Scott McClellan, the president's spokesman, defended the administration: "I can assure you that this is an administration that makes decisions based on the best available science."[51] The president's chief science adviser, Dr. John H. Marburger

III, the director of the Office of Science and Technology Policy, added, "From all the evidence I can find, it's certainly not true that science is being manipulated by this administration to suit its policy. It's simply not the case."[52] Most of the scientific community, including three former presidential science advisers, disagreed with Marburger, pointing out that he was not to blame for these transgressions. They viewed these policies as attacks on meritocracy and further evidence of anti-intellectualism in the Bush administration.

Dr. Lewis M. Branscomb, a former IBM vice president and chief scientist, past president of the American Physical Society, and recently retired professor from Harvard's John F. Kennedy School of Government, as well as one of the nation's most respected science policy observers for forty years, director of the National Bureau of Standards during the Nixon administration, and chairman of the National Science Board during the Carter years, told the *Christian Science Monitor* in 2004: "I don't believe there's any precedent for it, I really don't, at least since World War II. . . . I'm not aware that [Nixon] ever hand-picked ideologues to serve on advisory committees, or dismissed from advisory committees very well-qualified people if he didn't like their views. . . . What is going on now is in many ways more insidious. It happens behind a curtain. I don't think we've had this kind of cynicism with respect to objective scientific advice since I've been watching government, which is quite a long time."[53]

There was a pattern to the assaults by the Bush administration on science and to its efforts to selectively use scientific evidence only when it supported Bush's prior policy position. Initially, when challenged about their disregard for scientific evidence, administration officials denied the claim and suggested that the motives behind the claim itself were political. Then, if there was sufficient criticism of the politicized position, if it became a minor cause célèbre within the scientific and health communities, and especially if the mass media began to cover the story, the administration backed away from its initial position. It then tried alternative channels to create the policy position it desired. And this pattern occurred repeatedly, not only with policies that had detrimental effects on science and the research universities, but also with policies regarding the Patriot Act. President Obama's memo of March 2009, which I mentioned earlier, was an initial effort to reassure the scientific community that assaults on the peer review system would stop.

THE CONTENT OF THE UNIVERSITY'S CURRICULUM

The Bush administration and its supporters in Congress did not spare the humanities and social sciences from assault. Indeed, they treaded on sacred ground within the university: its prerogative to shape and articulate the content of it curriculum and the freedom of professors to teach their subjects without external interference. External political monitoring of the content of courses strikes at the very heart of free inquiry and the most basic values of the university. The case in point is the assault on the National Resource Centers, Title VI programs under the Higher Education Act that can be found at many research universities and that are typically associated with schools of social policy and international relations.

There are about 120 international study centers that divide up almost $100 million of annual support from Title VI dollars to support graduate fellowships, language instruction, lectures, and public programs. Very few, if any, of the centers hire faculty members or have their own curriculum, relying instead on faculty in related academic disciplines and on the courses already offered throughout the university. These centers tend to be multidisciplinary, drawing on the interests of faculty members across the university, but most draw heavily from social science and humanities disciplines.

On September 11, 2001, the national security of the United States was compromised in part because of the virtual absence of people in the intelligence community with sufficient knowledge and understanding of Middle Eastern languages and cultures to be of value in gathering and analyzing intelligence information. At the time of the assaults, there were apparently no more than a handful of individuals in the CIA who were fluent in Arabic and who could act as "native speakers" in those countries. Recent histories of the CIA suggest that the intelligence agency placed far greater emphasis on clandestine operations than on information gathering and analysis, an orientation that marked a significant difference between the CIA and its European and Soviet (and then Russian) counterparts.[54] The lingering bitterness between U.S. intelligence agencies and the universities that goes back at least to the Vietnam War has cut off the pipeline for talent that existed in previous decades between the university programs that produce people with skills and the intelligence community that so desperately needs their expertise.

Federal Title VI programs, through the support of the National Resource Centers, are designed to create expertise in foreign languages and increased understanding of the economic, social, and cultural dynamics that play out through politics in foreign countries. The effort to develop expertise about different regions of the world—expertise that could help in formulating policy alternatives for the government—began after World War II and gained substantial recognition in the 1960s. In fact, our national investment in knowledge of just the languages of these societies has declined markedly since the 1960s. The centers are part of what has come to be known at universities as "area studies," and they have drawn on historians, social scientists, and humanists to flesh out their programs. So, there is support in Title VI programs for work on Russia (and the former Soviet Union), Africa, South Asia, East Asia, and most notably in recent years, the Middle East. Many of the best research universities hold multiple grants for support in a number of these different areas. The one that has attracted the greatest attention recently, as might be expected, is the Middle East.

An important feature of these programs is to lead students to question whether there are universal moral absolutes and ethical principles that govern all people or legitimate cultural differences that we must understand in order to truly appreciate what is going on in these societies. Many skeptics of this kind of cultural psychology and anthropology believe that the field is dominated by cultural relativism. In fact, many faculty members who teach in the programs are acutely aware of patterns of behavior that are highly valued in these other societies but that differ significantly from what many Americans value, and they teach their students about these differences. They often encourage students to question forms of moral and ethical absolutism that are part of our usual way of thinking.

Problems arise when we insist that we have a moral imperative to promulgate and impose our values on other cultures that have different ideas about, for example, appropriate patterns of behavior for women and men, or appropriate attitudes toward technology and science. The "missionary moral progressivism" that the anthropologist Richard Shweder associates with President Bush's approach to these questions is typically laid out by the president in black and white, as may be seen in his April 2004 description of Iraqi insurgents:[55] "We love freedom and they hate freedom—that's where the clash occurs. Freedom is not America's gift to the world; it is God's gift to the world." For people with these views, Title

VI programs, which hardly take this point of view, are considered "biased" and lacking "balance."

The attack on the content of these programs began with criticism from leaders of conservative policy "think tanks"—some of whom were associated with major universities—who thought in this way. In particular, there have been three hawkish prime movers in the almost messianic movement to reshape Middle East studies programs at our research universities. Martin Kramer, who published an attack on the failure of Middle East studies in his book *Ivory Towers on Sand*, is affiliated with the conservative Middle East Forum and served as an adviser to Israeli intelligence for a number of years. Stanley Kurtz is a research fellow at Stanford University's Hoover Institution and a contributing editor to *National Review Online*. Daniel Pipes is a conservative polemicist appointed by President Bush to the board of the government-funded United States Institute of Peace, a colleague of Kramer's at the Middle East Forum, and the creator of *Campus Watch*. In 2002, this organization, a project of the Middle East Forum, produced scathing personal attacks on eight Middle East or Islamic scholars in American universities. Pipes asserted that these professors, as well as fourteen American universities, had unacceptable views about Palestinian rights, U.S. foreign policy in the Middle East, Islam and Islamic fundamentalism, and terrorism. When asked by the *Chronicle of Higher Education* about this list, he said that it was "actually too short."[56]

The eight professors were accused of using biased and fundamentally anti-American materials to create hostile attitudes and beliefs toward the United States among their students. *Campus Watch* created a "blacklist" of professors who were purportedly supporters of Palestinian rights, were anti-Israel, and against U.S. foreign policy in the Middle East. Pipes encouraged students to act as "informants" on their professors—reporting to *Campus Watch* those professors who were highly critical of U.S. policies toward Israel or the Middle East in the classroom, who could then be put on display as perpetrators of anti-American views on campus. Many did, writing to *Campus Watch* about professors who were in their opinion espousing anti-American views. When a hundred other professors defended the "blacklisted" eight and accused *Campus Watch* of stifling free inquiry and open dialogue on campuses while insinuating that the scholars were unpatriotic or even apologists for terrorism, *Campus Watch* simply added the protesting 100 to the blacklist—names later withdrawn from the website.

The subtext of a great deal of this discontent and criticism of American area studies scholars is the perceived attitudes toward the Israeli-Arab conflict. For Kramer, Kurtz, and Pipes, those openly critical of the Israeli government's policies toward the Palestinians, and favoring a more balanced approach to the Middle East conflict, are suspect if not subversive. This is not about anti-Semitism or Israel's right to exist. It's about a zero-tolerance policy toward anyone who criticizes the Israeli government's policies—and this intolerance of criticism seems greater in the United States than it is in Israel. Professor Zachary Lockman, director of the Hagop Kevorkian Center for Near Eastern Studies at New York University, characterizing the attack on the area studies programs, said, "The priority of those behind this is defending Israel from any criticism. They understand that the universities are one of the few places where debate and argument take place that cannot be heard in the media or anywhere else."[57]

Nonetheless, these conservative critics created quite a stir, and they persuaded members of Congress to hold congressional hearings in June 2003 on the content of Title VI centers. Their objective was to persuade Congress that these programs were "biased" and "one-sided" and that they did not support U.S. foreign policy objectives. Kramer, Kurtz, and Pipes wanted Congress to pass legislation, which they would help to craft, that would impose external authority on internal educational curricular matters. If they had had their way, all programs funded through Title VI would have had to agree to oversight by a new International Higher Education Advisory Board with the power to "monitor, appraise and evaluate a sample of activities supported under [Title VI] in order to provide recommendations to the Secretary [of Education] and the Congress for the improvement of programs under the title and to ensure programs meet the purposes of the title." If the universities didn't like this form of oversight, Kramer suggested, they could stop taking taxpayers' money. "Get off the public dole and find other subsidies," he said, " . . . perhaps from one of those rich Saudi princes on an academic shopping spree. . . . You won't be missed."[58]

They found some sympathetic ears in Congress, and not only among Republicans, but also among Democrats who were attuned to anything that could be construed as anti-Israeli policy. According to the original legislative proposal, the advisory board would have seven members, four of whom would be appointed by Congress; at least two of the remaining three would represent government agencies concerned with national security.

Following the set of hastily put together hearings, legislation was introduced in the House of Representatives. Linked to the Higher Education Act (H.R. 3077), the proposal was designed (and initially written) to have political appointees of the government act as external reviewers of area studies programs. Again, Zachary Lockman, among others, responded harshly to this proposed legislation, saying it "raises the specter of an unprecedented partisan political intrusion into university-based area studies."[59]

Of course, these critics on the right did not really understand the idea of the university—or chose to ignore it for political purposes. It's hardly news that university professors are, on average, more politically liberal than the general population. As sociologists Paul F. Lazarsfeld and Seymour Martin Lipset have shown, this has been true for decades. And in 2007, Neil Gross and Solon Simmons provided evidence that although liberally oriented faculty members represent a clear majority on campus, many of these liberals have centrist leanings, and their views on a wide variety of subjects can hardly be characterized as radical.[60] There are also many extraordinarily influential conservative voices within the academy. Indeed, one might consider Kramer and Kurtz as examples of such conservative voices.

The demand for "balance" from the critics of areas studies sought to force professors to abandon their own points of view. The central goal of a university's curriculum should be to pursue the difficult task of getting at the truth and examining the evidence for various truth claims; it is not mandating balance. One assumes that the norms of tolerance and skepticism permit the criticism of almost any position, including received wisdoms, although unfortunately that is not always the case at our universities today. To reiterate a central point, one of the goals of universities is, in fact, to be upsetting to students. And there is little evidence that indoctrination of ideological positions is going on, or has been successful, or, for that matter, that professors with liberal views teach in a biased manner.

In some quarters on American college campuses, the critics of Title VI did strike a real chord. Among some Jewish students and Jewish organizations, as well as among some university trustees, the critics opened up the question of "balance" in the curriculum, especially as professors portrayed the Israeli-Palestinian conflict. None of the critics ever really collected evidence beyond the anecdotal to demonstrate overall imbalance in the curricula of these universities; nor did Congress. But assertions of "bias" from external sources and from some internal student groups and faculty members suggested that the content of some programs had led to subversive attitudes and beliefs among students. When one examines the full array of the offerings on the Middle East at the great universities, one sees that this is simply not the case. Nevertheless, criticism of Israel's policy toward the Palestinians became the wedge to open up a frontal attack against campus programs with the suggestion that oversight might actually become reality.

At the June 2003 congressional hearings, Kurtz became inflammatory, reiterating his claims that the Title VI programs were anti-American. The criticism triggered a vocal response from some individual professors and professional organizations representing American colleges and universities. The American Council on Education sent Terry W. Hartle, its senior vice president on government and public affairs, to testify before the House committee. Hartle noted that college and university leaders were concerned that the proposed legislation would allow the government "to get into the business of reviewing syllabi and approving reading lists." However, he missed a golden opportunity to educate members of Congress on the broader point that government interference with free inquiry among university scholars would be counterproductive even in terms of the government's own interest in national security. Nor did he explain why it was so critical to universities that the norm of open debate and free inquiry be supported by Congress.

Lisa Anderson, professor of political science and former dean of Columbia's School of International and Public Affairs, did not miss the opportunity. In a remarkable presidential address to the Middle East Studies Association in 2003, she defended the idea of the university that was being attacked in the proposed Title VI legislation:

Self-appointed guardians of the academy now use websites like Campus Watch to invite student complaints of abuse, investigate their claims, and (when warranted) make these known, presumably to university presidents. . . . The assault on the region [the Middle East academic programs] . . . was accompanied by an offensive against the associated US area studies community. . . . This plan to monitor and evaluate the universities and their area studies programs is not about diversity [of perspectives], or even about truth, but about the conviction of conservative political activists that the American university community is insufficiently patriotic, or perhaps simply insufficiently conservative.[61]

Anderson suggested that these attacks, along with the highly restrictive and burdensome post-9/11 visa policies, were damaging scholarship about the Middle East. And yet she insisted that despite the attacks, the scholars who truly understood the mission of the research university must continue to persevere, adhering to rigorous rules of collecting and assessing evidence while formulating policy choices.

> We, as the community of scientists and scholars devoted to the production and deployment of evidence, a project we sometimes call the search for truth, must remain faithful to that purpose, even, perhaps especially, when policymakers seem distracted or uninterested. We must also make evidence accessible. This neither requires nor excludes scholars, or their students, serving on the government payroll or endorsing a particular policy position. . . . We must be constantly, restlessly open to new ideas, searching for new evidence, critical of received wisdom, old orthodoxies, and ancient bigotries, always creating and criticizing ourselves, each other and our world. This is the life of scholarship and we must embrace it for what it is and do it well.[62]

Kurtz, Pipes, and Kramer did influence congressional reauthorization of the Higher Education Act. Although the Title VI features of the bill did not include an oversight board, they did include a provision stating that international studies programs applying for federal grants must "explain how they 'will reflect diverse perspectives and a wide range of views' and how they will deal with disputes regarding whether they are meeting that goal."[63]

It would surely be in the best interests of the nation if members of Congress turned their attention away from whether or not the Title VI National Resource Centers were producing advocates for American democracy, and instead focus on how investments in these area studies programs could improve our understanding of other cultures, improve mechanisms by which we could build alliances with these other cultures through economic and social aid that was not tied to "nation-building," and increase our ability to gather needed information about these societies. We would accomplish far more by increasing the number of exchange grants for students and scholars working in these nations than by attempting to monitor the content of the programs for some form of conservative and ideological "political correctness."

There is, after all, nothing in the history of these universities to suggest that they would truly work to undermine the core values of the United States. Where they have been critical of American policies, their skepticism has helped rather than hindered American interests, causing students and others to undertake sober reflections on what the nation has been trying to do abroad. Even the 9/11 Commission embraced the need for better understanding of other cultures and a willingness to tolerate criticism of our own foreign policies. As most people would realize—unless they are committed to the kind of "war for the minds" that the CIA pursued during the Cold War in Europe—a highly restrictive policy toward the growth of knowledge about other societies would not further the national security interests of the United States.[64]

The policies developed and implemented by the Bush administration and Congress after 9/11 represent a case study in ways to damage a great university system. If the assault on the values and structures of the universities had continued, it would have threatened the preeminence of these institutions of higher learning, even if that was not what was intended. Unfortunately, the change in the political control of Congress that began with the national elections of 2006 did not produce significant changes in these policies. The Democratic Congress did not improve the research resources flowing to the universities. In fact, the budgets of the NIH remained essentially flat for two years after the Democrats assumed leadership in Congress.

If the Congress elected in November 2008 refuses to act to modify the laws and regulations produced by the prior administration, and if those laws stand up to judicial review in a conservative judicial environment; if the Justice Department continues to prosecute faculty members, such as Thomas Butler, and foreign students who covet the opportunity to study in the United States; if the personal privacy of our students and faculty continues to be invaded without probable cause; and if scientific and scholarly research continues to be constrained by political and ideological litmus tests, then our universities will begin to wither. If we continue to accept the effects of the policies I've been describing because we believe that the risks of changing them outweigh the benefits, or that we will be labeled as "soft on terrorism," then we at least should be fully aware of the consequences: further growth of anti-intellectualism and further restrictions on the academic freedom of those responsible for innovation and discovery at the world's greatest universities. If we embrace Bush-era policies rather than actively opposing them, then economic, social, and cultural consequences for the nation will follow.

These matters should not only be the concerns of members of the academic community. Policies affecting our universities affect all of us, either directly or indirectly. The centrality of the modern research university to the welfare of our society is too important for us to be complaisant. The situation calls for public debate and displays of discontent—and for a robust defense of the scientists and intellectuals at our great universities. The attentive public should not remain silent about these measures; nor should it be silent in the future whenever new policies threaten to undermine our nation's greatest comparative advantage—our ability to develop and exploit new knowledge for the public good. We must not allow ideology to trump science and scholarship.

With the enlarged majority of Democrats in Congress in 2009 and with the election of Barak Obama as president, there is room for hope that science and scholarship at our great universities will once again be esteemed and supported. In his inaugural address, President Obama said: "We will restore science to its rightful place, and wield technology's wonders to raise health care's quality and lower its costs. . . . And we will transform our schools and colleges and universities to meet the demands of the new age. All this we can do. All this we will do." If Obama's vision is realized, our great universities have the potential to make still more dramatic contributions to our society. However, if the Congress and the president fail to revisit and change the Bush administration policies and enforcement strategies, then the nation will continue to risk the slow decline of its great universities, which could lose their preeminent standing in the world of higher learning if we are not careful.

CHAPTER 14

Trouble in Paradise?

Of all the threats to the institution, the most dangerous come from within. Not the least among them is the smugness that believes the institution's value is so self-evident that it no longer needs explication, its mission is so manifest that it no longer requires definition and articulation.

—A. Bartlett Giamatti

There is reason to believe that unless the United States "blows it," its institutions of higher learning will remain among the best in the world—even if they lose their overwhelmingly dominant position among the most elite universities. But how secure is that dominant position? Does foreign competition present a threat to our preeminence, or should we applaud the growth of distinguished university systems in other nations? What are the dominant threats to the continued excellence of our universities? Do they come from rivals abroad, or do they come from within our own country and the great universities themselves? Perhaps the source of our greatest apprehension should be our own failure to promote higher education and free inquiry here in the United States, rather than the potential for the competition abroad to eclipse our institutions. In this chapter I will try to unravel these complex and interrelated questions.

GLOBAL COMPETITION

For the better part of the past half-century, the United States enjoyed an open playing field in shaping its comparative distinction. The efforts to recover economically from the devastations of World War II dominated Europe's priorities. And after Europe's recovery, its leaders had to rethink the role of the region in a new world order. Europe has always had some of the world's finest universities, and this is still the case, but since the war most of these institutions have faced structural problems placing them at a comparative disadvantage against American universities. Asian nations, particularly Japan, Korea, and China, have come to realize the enormous social and economic returns that come from a highly trained workforce and from a set of universities that produce world-class research. Recent literature on globalization often suggests that the United States may soon lose its comparative advantage in higher education and its lead in the production of new knowledge. This literature cites some good evidence.

The European nations would seem to be in an extremely strong position and could present a formidable challenge to American excellence. In recent decades each of these nations has attempted to increase the human capital needed for both technological innovation and the development of a highly paid, skilled workforce. Historically, Europe's elementary and secondary school preparation for advanced work has been superior to ours, and recently the proportion of Europe's population attending institutions of higher learning has risen to levels previously achieved only in the United States. Europe has an enormous reservoir of human capital to use, if it is properly organized.

A 2006 international assessment of math and science ability found that fifteen-year-olds in the United States were "near the bottom worldwide in their ability to solve practical problems that require mathematical understanding." The scores of U.S. students from ages nine through thirteen had "improved" over the past thirty years, but scores "remained stagnant" for seventeen-year-olds.[1] And the United States ranks near the bottom of nations in the proportion of twenty-four-year-olds who have earned degrees in the natural sciences or engineering compared with other majors. European and Asian nations have the highest proportions. Perhaps more ominous is the fact that in America only 33 percent of the teachers of high school physics and only 40 percent of the high school chemistry teachers have a degree in the subject, compared with 70 percent of those who teach high school English. There is in fact an alarming paucity of qualified teachers in science and mathematics, and that, among other factors, negatively affects the numbers of able students entering these critically important fields. We have created for ourselves, compared with other nations, a training gap. The lack of trained teachers disproportionately affects minority groups, who represent an increasing share of our total population. In addition, Europeans can now hold their own against the United States in manufacturing exceptionally fine advanced technology products—from automobiles to electronic devices.

Of course, the United States is a large nation, and given the wide variations in the quality of its pre-college education, it produces a significant number of extremely talented young people who are prepared to do high levels of science and math by the time they graduate from high school. But are we producing enough to support our current and future needs? The absence of adequate K-12 education in many areas, but particularly in science and mathematics, is widely acknowledged by now, but little has been done to address the problem or to recognize its potential harm for American society. A 2007 National Academy of Sciences report, *Rising Above the Gathering Storm*, acknowledged these national needs and sounded an alarm, pointing out that our economic future may well depend on our ability to solve these problems. Just as the United States has had a growing dependency on foreign oil, over the past several decades we have become increasingly dependent on the flow of foreign talent. The flow of human capital is as important as the flow of raw materials and goods and services, and the United States is backing itself into an extremely vulnerable corner by refusing to come to grips with its dependency on foreign talent. There would be nothing wrong with this dependency if we could be assured of its continued flow. But as the economies and social organization of European and Asian nations become comparatively stronger, and their investments in the quality of their universities and research enterprises grow more robust, we are at risk of seeing the best foreign talent deciding to stay home.

American society today is not preparing enough of its talented students for work in fields that will be critical for the growth of knowledge in science and engineering; nor is it adequately preparing those who will become lawyers, businessmen, members of Congress, or members of the judiciary by giving them the tools they will need to deal intelligently with decisions related to the science and technology policies that will be critical for the nation's future. As our dependency on science and technology grows, our literacy diminishes. Perhaps as alarming as our lack of scientific knowledge and literacy is our growing unwillingness to take seriously the study of foreign languages, which in an age of a global economy has become more rather than less important. Perhaps we are waiting for the rest of the world to learn English. But our lack of language training is not acceptable because it damages our ability to understand different cultures as well as our ability to gather the information that is needed for national security purposes. If this state of affairs persists, we are apt to find it difficult to compete effectively with societies that do a better job of training their young people in these areas of knowledge.

Some European nations, such as Germany, have begun to view superior production of university-based knowledge as worth substantial public investment. Asian societies, including Japan, Korea, China, and Indonesia, are already pouring billions of dollars into scientific and engineering research designed to benefit their economies and garner international prestige. The academic potential of European and Asian nations became clear when the latest data on the production of the world's scientific literature was released. The United States still far outstrips all other nations in the proportion of literature produced. In 2005, it had a 29 percent share of the total, and no single European nation came close to that: The United Kingdom and Germany produced slightly more than 6 percent each. The United States ranked first in every area of science and engineering.

However, the European Union, taken as a whole, is similar in size to the United States, and it now produces more of the world's scientific literature than the United States does—33 percent.[2] Russia, which for decades had exceptional human capital to work with, has experienced a brain drain in recent times and occupies a relatively low position in the hierarchy, contributing only about 2 percent of the total literature, a decline of 50 percent over the past decade. The most rapid growth over the past decade came from China, which is now producing roughly 6 percent of the world's scientific literature, just a few percentage points less than Japan. In fact, Asian nations now contribute one-fifth of the literature compared with about 13 percent a decade ago. The rates of change in growth are by far the highest in China and Korea. In short, strong competition is emerging in these two regions of the world, and to the extent that Europe can get its act together, it is likely to be our most formidable competitor for the next few decades, with the large Asian nations rapidly moving into the next tier.

If European and Asian societies are leaping ahead of us in the training of their youth, catching up with us in the production of scientific knowledge, and beginning to invest significantly in their systems of higher education, does this mean our universities are facing a bleak future, where they will be displaced as the most distinguished in the world? I do not think so. Competition from abroad may create incentives for us to allocate appropriate resources to our universities. The increase in international collaboration could cause a corresponding increase in the number of truly important discoveries taking place in areas of mutual interest. If our universities experience a relative decline, the most probable cause of this decline will be our own actions— and our inaction in areas where action is required. If we fail to act wisely toward these engines of discovery and innovation, and if the universities prove poor guardians of their core values, managing to corrupt them, we could indeed face a relative decline in quality and in the number of talented faculty members and students who choose to teach and study here.

So, I do not believe that European and Asian nations pose an imminent threat to our position in higher education. Here I will elaborate on that point and provide additional evidence to support this view, particularly as regards the French, German, British, and Chinese systems of higher education today. Each of these systems must overcome some significant obstacles if they are to achieve great distinction as research universities. At the end of the day, the relatively poor conditions of these systems of higher education reflect larger social and political problems in the societies in which they are embedded.

When we compare the great universities in the United States with those in France, Germany, or Britain, we tend to think of these as equal competitors or potential competitors—as if we were on a level playing field. We tend to think of these systems of higher learning as bigger and stronger than they really are because they are located in countries that have "big" histories, which included, at one time, producing the best universities, scholarship, science, and literature in the world. But in fact these countries are only a fraction of the size of the United States and cannot in any real sense be expected to compete on an equal footing with our system of higher learning. China and India are large countries with huge populations and great potential in terms of human capital. But they also have great hills to climb before their universities will be fully competitive with the most distinguished American research universities.[3]

Limits on French Excellence

During the fall of 2008, I gave some public lectures on the subject of this book at the Collège de France and had an opportunity to meet leading French scholars. During this time I learned more about the French university system and about what its leaders can hope to achieve over the next several decades. Few of their universities today are considered serious rivals to ours. As part of my conversations with my French colleagues, I posed several intentionally provocative questions. First, does France want a truly great, preeminent university system—one that is well represented among the top one hundred in the world? Second, do the French need a great university system, or should they become "free riders" on the backs of the United States and other great, emerging systems of discovery and innovation?

There are many features of French society that might lead one to expect that its universities would be able to compete with ours.[4] France has a population that admires intellectual achievement and discovery, for example, and it trains its young people in the pre-university years certainly as well as, if not better than, most other nations. It has a history of excellence in scholarship and learning and prides itself on that history. It has a tradition of respect for public intellectuals, who often influence national opinion. Its core values support the idea of free inquiry; academic freedom is taken for granted in French society. It supports the free and open communication of ideas. It has a long history of an ideal of universalism, and in fact its system of examinations is based on principles of merit, although it perhaps classifies children too early on. In short, many of the necessary conditions for greatness in a university system exist in France. And France continues to provide us with examples of its ability to match the best in the world in terms of scientific and scholarly excellence. For example, France produces as many great mathematicians as any other nation, and its work in certain fields of biology and engineering are absolutely world class. But fundamental systemic problems seem to forestall greater progress toward renewed preeminence.

I do not wish to distort the situation. Of course, the French do have some distinguished seats of higher learning and discovery. The Collège de France is a unique place of the highest possible quality. But it is a boutique institution with fewer than fifty faculty members and no students—hardly appropriate for comparison with America's best private and public universities. The grandes écoles are extremely competitive, high-quality seats of learning, although they are not the principal sites for research activity in France and educate less than 5 percent of France's university students. Then there are the eight universities that constitute the University of Paris, each specializing in a specific area of knowledge. These universities are physically removed from each other and operate essentially as separate institutions. The Sorbonne, for example, specializes in the humanities, and Paris VI is a distinguished science and engineering center in Paris—ranking forty-second in the Shanghai Jiao Tong rankings of world universities. There are pockets of international excellence in provincial universities as well, such as the exceptional work produced in economics at the University of Toulouse. And we cannot forget that the French have some truly world-class research institutes, such as the Pasteur Institute, where the quality of many discoveries is equal to what is produced at the best centers of learning in the world. But overall, the French system has not been able to compete with the best universities in our system, despite the abundance of human capital in France. Why are the French failing to compete?

The flow of talent into and out of a higher education system is one indicator of its health and standing. Although the French pride themselves on the absence of a brain drain to other nations, they have overlooked the distinction between absolute and relative numbers. Since only 5 to 10 percent of all scientists produce well over 50 percent of all scientific work—and an even higher proportion of significant, high-impact work—what really matters is how many of that top 1 to 5 percent a nation gains or loses to its competitors. If the losses contain a disproportionate number of the true scientific and scholarly elite, then the loss can be highly problematic for a small system of higher learning like the one that exists in France. The French are losing too many of their most brilliant scholars, even if that may not be so in a few fields, such as mathematics.[5]

Another problem is that France seems to operate two parallel systems of higher education—one of which occupies a position of far greater prestige in the public mind than the other. The French, it turns out, are competing against themselves—and unfortunately, not in a way that improves quality. The competition is between the French university system and the famous grandes écoles. I was told, perhaps with some hyperbole, that almost all leaders in France aspire to have their children enter the grandes écoles rather than the university system, and that many top government leaders and business leaders simply don't know what the French university system looks like. And despite the meritocratic façade of the admissions process for the grandes écoles, the children of current elites are far more likely to gain admission to these prestigious schools than those with lower social class origins. A system of higher learning cannot afford to siphon off the top talent in the nation.[6] And although there is this unfortunate form of competition between the universities and the grandes écoles, there is little competition among the universities themselves. That may be by design, but it does not push individual universities in the system to improve their quality, as I've suggested is the case in the United States.

The French system of higher learning is a far more structurally rigid system than its counterpart in the United States. There is little flexibility in the system to allow young people to move from one interest to another; the classification of individuals tends to take place early on, and it becomes cumbersome, if not virtually impossible, for young people to alter their career choices after a certain age. That lack of flexibility can have unfortunate consequences for students. Young women who specialize in science and mathematics, for example, are more likely than men to discover their interest and talent in these areas only after they have entered college. In France that student probably has already been tracked for a different career path and would find it to be almost impossible to change her occupational choice.

Moreover, the organization that supports most of the research in the nation, the Centre National de la Recherche Scientifique (CNRS), operates with a tenure system that really does not require researchers to prove their ability. CNRS researchers receive lifetime tenure at the time that they are hired, with only perfunctory or pro forma subsequent reviews. This would be unheard of in the United States, where very elaborate systems of evaluation for tenure take place after professors spend seven to ten years as untenured faculty members. Having no formal teaching obligations, CNRS researchers operate in a system lacking incentives and disincentives for performance. France, like most other European nations, also lacks a significant tradition of private philanthropy to support research. To improve their university system, the French need to increase their national investments in critical areas of knowledge growth and create a system of peer review and accountability, which could be modeled after America's National Science Foundation and National Institutes of Health. Changes are needed that reflect their commitment to both the quality of the individuals within the system and to the components of the system that make it possible for brilliant and highly motivated scholars to compete favorably at the international level.[7]

Certain structural changes would need to be made in the French system of higher learning in order for it to compete at that level. The system is very closely linked to state control, for example, with national policies controlling the operations of individual units in the system to an excessive degree. No individual state-supported university in France can announce that it will forthwith establish its own admissions standards, for example, or decide to charge higher tuition or fees than the ones established by the state. The faculty and student unions would not tolerate it, and the state would not sanction it. Changes in admissions criteria or tuition rates would probably send students into the streets and could easily topple a government. Unionization of faculty members in the United States, at least at the level of universities, has not, unfortunately, stimulated excellence. Too often these unions adopt a trade-union mentality in collective bargaining and the result is a "regression toward the mean," an outcome focusing more on the average performer and on seniority than on the individuals who perform brilliantly and expect to be rewarded accordingly for that performance. Reform efforts in France tend to be weak because of popular reaction against change.

Efforts from 2007 to 2009 to reform the university system by French president Sarkozy have met with angry faculty and student protests and claims that "universities are not an enterprise" and "knowledge is not merchandise." What, in fact, are the faculty protesting against? The Sarkozy reforms would give state-run universities greater control over their finances, their hiring and evaluation system, and their infrastructure. In short, French universities would have greater self-governance and greater ability to compete for top-quality faculty. Leaders of American state universities and most of their faculty members would welcome such increased autonomy.[8] But French professors and students have taken to the streets to oppose these reforms.[9]

Since reform is almost impossible to obtain politically, the French universities are shackled with a system where, with the exception of students in a few fields, such as medicine, any French student who passes the *baccalauréat* (known colloquially as *le bac*—the national high school diploma achieved through examination, a procedure begun under Napoleon) is entitled to enroll in any French university. In 2007–2008, the success rate on the examination was over 80 percent in mainland France. Consequently, at the "undergraduate" level, the students studying at places like the University of Paris number in the tens of thousands, far more than the system can truly accommodate. Most of these students are enrolled for one or two years before being turned out or leaving. Many never see the inside of a classroom for lack of space. There are not enough professors to staff a university system of this size, and the facilities for teaching are rarely adequate. Things are quite different in the competing system, the grandes écoles. In short, the problems facing the French undergraduate system of higher education run deeper in many ways than those we face in the United States.

The selection of university presidents presents yet another structural problem. In France they tend to be elected by the faculty rather than appointed by some external board that can search throughout the country to find appropriate leaders. In the United States they are elected by university boards of trustees or regents—and there are serious problems with this system of leadership selection as well, principally because the members of these boards are not academics and often know almost nothing about universities despite having ultimate governing authority over them. But the matter of faculty members electing leaders is fraught with obvious dangers, not least of which is that faculty members are not much better than trustees at knowing the qualities required for great leadership.

France could decide to be a free rider, sending many of its students abroad to benefit from other university systems, but this option would limit its freedom to choose for itself the directions of growth that it would like to promote for the well-being of French society. Knowledge free-riders may benefit in some ways, but they are at the mercy of other decision-makers, and that is a poor place to be when you are looking forward to a world where knowledge increasingly implies power. Free-rider nations will be constrained in the choices they can make about investments that are consistent with their national values and priorities.

Can Germany Regain Its Past Preeminence?

Surprisingly, the German university system—the greatest in the world a century ago, and the model on which our research universities were built—faces many of the same problems faced by the French system. The German university system seems to have lost its intense aspiration to be the best—something one certainly could not say about the university systems of the

United States or China, for example. German universities have never reestablished their ability to play a formative role in the future of a dynamic world. This may or may not be a good thing, but it surely differentiates German universities today—and indeed European universities in general—from the universities of the United States.

To understand some of the German problems one needs to know a bit about how the system is organized. There are relatively few private universities in Germany, and those that exist are small and not at this time particularly consequential. There are sixteen states in Germany, and each state controls its own universities. There are thus more than 115 universities throughout the nation.[10] There is a high level of bureaucratic state control of the system as well as fairly strict laws specifying what university professors may be paid. University professors, including those several ranks lower than the top full professors, are civil servants, and their compensation is determined by the civil service laws. It is very difficult to have a highly competitive system when university leaders have such little flexibility in determining salaries and other aspects of competitive packages for scholars and scientists. Recall the intense competition among universities for star professors that is so commonplace in the United States. So, although German universities need not worry about competitive offers coming from other universities within Germany, they do face competition with American universities that try to recruit the best German professors. Keeping good professors can thus be a real struggle for German institutions. Moreover, the absence of competition within Germany itself creates stagnation in the system and hurts the quality of higher education within the country.

Over the past several years, Germany has promoted a program of competitive excellence that its leaders hope will improve the quality of some universities and lead to internal structural reform. The German government has initiated a plan to pour $2.8 billion into an "Excellence Initiative" that is designed to focus resources on a small number of institutions that will in theory be capable of world-class research in specific areas of knowledge. Ultimately, they want to create incentives for structural reforms at these universities, both to make them more competitive and to create differential quality among the German universities. To this end, the federal government set up a competitive process to support new research initiatives, often involving efforts to create an interdisciplinary culture. It began with five years of support that at the end of that term could be renewed for another five-year period.

This program has produced disproportionate funding for the winners of the competition in specific areas. These are really like large five-year NSF or NIH grants, but whether the grants will lead to real structural reform is very difficult to predict. These universities would have to be able to support these research efforts on their own after the grant period has ceased, which might require them to eliminate or downsize other programs on their campuses—something that universities tend to find virtually impossible to do. In sum, real structural reform, which is needed in Germany, has been difficult to come by, and it remains unclear whether Germany will be able to make the changes that would be necessary for German universities to regain their past distinction.

In America, as I've noted, the linkage created between the advanced teaching mission and research that was so wisely established after World War II has paid hefty dividends. The divide between the teaching and research missions has not been bridged successfully in Germany. The research at eighty research institutes funded by the Max Planck Society ($2.1 billion annually), with each institute focusing on a different area of the natural and social sciences, is often of world-class quality. But many of these institutes remain small and autonomous. In 2008, an international advisory group, including Nobelist Günter Blobel of Rockefeller University, questioned the wisdom of having the two-tiered research institutes siphon off Germany's leading researchers away from its universities. The report suggested that "the society's institutes should be merged into nearby universities, and its researchers should become professors with all the attendant privileges and responsibilities."[11] The report affirmed Max Delbrück's earlier observations about the Kaiser Wilhelm Society, the precursor of the Max Planck Society, that "it takes the best people out of teaching and impoverishes contact with students."

There is, however, strong resistance toward moving the institutes into the penumbra of the universities. Consequently, like the French, the Germans have also set up a structural nightmare in which their universities compete for talent with highly prestigious research institutes that carry out a good deal of the truly distinguished research in the nation. But appointments to a Planck Institute, which carries with it greater compensation and prestige than is found in the universities, results in much of the best talent moving away from the better universities to research institutes that have almost no teaching requirements. Some educational reformers in Germany want to force the Planck research activities into the university structure; others have suggested that the institutes be permitted to offer doctoral degrees, an idea that sends shivers down the spines of current university leaders who believe that this would transform the universities into nothing more than glorified high schools. These proposals are apt to go nowhere. What seems clear is that German society currently does not know how to effectively link advanced educational training directly with the research community.

The Germans, like the French, have also created an unwieldy and almost nonfunctional system of admissions to their universities. Essentially, any German student who graduates from secondary school and passes the required examinations can apply and expect to be admitted into any German university. There is limited federal support for higher education—indeed, there is far more funding, proportionately, for the Planck Institutes than for the universities. Since the state is expected to pay for higher education, it is virtually impossible to increase tuition or fees to increase the number or quality of professors.

China Aims to Be a Contender

A look at the Chinese university system reveals some problems that are similar to those in Europe as well as some that are different.[12] The Chinese have made it their goal to create one of the world's top twenty-five research universities within twenty-five years, but it is debatable whether this is a realizable dream. Today, by their own reckoning, there is not one Chinese university among the top two hundred in the world. Even if that estimation of China's position is slightly exaggerated, it is not far off. Nonetheless, in the West it is commonplace to hear these days that within a quarter of a century China will lead the world in almost everything, and that the Chinese universities are becoming major competitors to U.S. universities. Similar prognostications were widespread in the late 1980s and early 1990s about almost everything made or built in Japan, until the bottom fell out of Japan's financial system and the Japanese economy went into a decade-long dive. We should not be too quick to assume that China can reach its goal, despite the fact that, like Europe, China has so many conditions in place that could promote greatness in higher learning and discovery. And China, unlike Europe, does have a sense of destiny.

The Chinese do have a wealth of raw talent. A significant number of the most brilliant Chinese students study for higher degrees in the United States and eventually hold jobs at our leading universities and industrial research laboratories. Chinese society values education as much as any other that I'm familiar with. China's size also makes a big difference. The number of students becoming scientists and engineers is staggering, even if the current quality of their education is not. The absolute number of brilliant students is mind-boggling.[13] In 2009, 10 million Chinese high school students took the "gao kao"—the test that determines whether they will be admitted to a university, and, if so, the level of quality of the university. This nine-hour test is the sole determinant for admission to virtually all Chinese colleges and universities.[14]

The political leaders of China want to be contenders in everything—from Olympic gold medals to advances in science and engineering. They are convinced that advances in science and technology represent tickets to economic growth and prosperity. They covet Nobel Prizes and the attendant esteem that could be achieved by abundant numbers of Chinese winning them. They increasingly have the resources, at least in some of the wealthier provinces and in the national treasury, to invest heavily in building world-class facilities. They are capable of mobilizing large labor forces to rapidly build world-class university facilities, especially since they do not have to work within the types of constraints that democratic nations must deal with—in terms of labor and environmental laws, for example. They are very hard working and have global aspirations to the point where every grade-school child in China today learns English as one of his or her three compulsory subjects.

But the Chinese also face real challenges in becoming an educational and innovative superpower. Perhaps most important, it is not clear that they truly recognize the degree of autonomy and freedom that they must give brilliant scholars and scientists if they want them to be creative. There is tremendous pressure from the state to succeed—to the point where it too often leads to acts of scientific fraud and deviance. The state tends to be reluctant to admit Chinese errors in educational and research policy, and it resists exposure of poor decisions and management—as was, for example, the case in their very tardy scientific responses to the SARS scare of a couple of years ago.[15] The system is not flexible and tends toward very hierarchical learning arrangements—with students sitting at the feet of masters rather than questioning and challenging them. Indeed, Chinese educational institutions do not foster the kind of creative problem-solving skills that are nurtured in the educational system of United States.

The Chinese have also institutionalized a highly prestigious research structure that runs in parallel to their universities and competes for talent with them. The Chinese Academy of Sciences is an institution of the State Council of China. With headquarters in Beijing, it has created research institutes throughout China as well as hundreds of commercial enterprises. So, like the French and the Germans, the Chinese have created a structure that is state controlled and highly prestigious, and that siphons off much of the top scientific talent that remains in China today.

If the most brilliant of the Chinese advanced students can pursue highly successful careers in American and British universities, where they are relatively free to conduct their research without any external interference, why would they tolerate the uncertainty that the state might introduce curbs on the way they work, the problems they choose to investigate, or the research results that can be published? The Cultural Revolution and the treatment of dissidents linger in the minds of Chinese scholars and scientists, even those who might prefer to go home. And China's treatment of dissenters would give pause to any outspoken academic who expects academic freedom and the right to question official policies.[16] Although educational leaders claim they understand the concept of academic freedom and free inquiry, it remains an open question as to whether the larger political order has really internalized this core value. Without that, preeminence is apt to be elusive.

The pressure to address other societal needs in China and to grow the general standard of living also interferes with achieving research and educational goals. The understandable interest of the Chinese in rapid industrialization has created an environmental nightmare in most large Chinese cities, where their best universities are located. It is hard to believe that many of even the most loyal Chinese scholars who would like to return to China, given the health hazards associated with living in an environment similar to England's during the high point of the Industrial Revolution or Pittsburgh's in the first decade of the twentieth century.

Finally, the Chinese are so intent on trying to be international leaders in science and engineering, and on the ability to transfer the resulting intellectual property rapidly to the marketplace, that it remains unclear whether they fully understand that totally neglecting the social sciences and the humanities will make it harder to achieve their goal. The best science and engineering universities in the United States, places like MIT, Illinois, Stanford, and Caltech, all have very strong faculties, even if small ones, in most of the disciplines of the social and behavioral sciences and humanities.

British Achievements and Their Limits

Perhaps the British already represent the most formidable competition for the United States. A far smaller nation, it nonetheless has some of the world's finest universities with a great scholarly tradition dating back many centuries. The British honor curiosity and work of imagination regardless of its practical or commercial value, and they understand the link between national needs and the production of knowledge. This has been true at least as far back as the time of Isaac Newton and other scientists who made profound basic discoveries as well as working on practical military and navigational problems. The British hold all of the same fundamental values for their universities as we do, they recognize the value of investments in research in new areas of advanced science and technology, and they have taken some steps to increase funding in these areas. On several occasions, some British universities have entered into collaborative agreements with some of our best research universities.

These agreements have not gone altogether smoothly, however, and it remains unclear whether the British government is truly willing to pay the price for expanding its competitive position in the future. Britain maintains a bizarre, overly formulaic mode of evaluating university productivity, which is linked to resource allocations, and its policies toward tenure have not been enlightened. The salaries of its faculty members and the quality of its facilities are not competitive with those of American universities, except at very few places, and as a consequence, the flow of talent over the past several decades has been in the direction of the United States. But as Britain recognizes that its future welfare depends more on its human capital and on the production of knowledge through its universities, its universities may well become even more competitive with U.S. institutions of higher learning. Recently, it has made a strong push to recruit very able foreign students in an effort to compete directly with America in this area.

Whether the American model for institutions of higher learning can be imitated by these other nations with equal success remains, of course, unclear. There are several initiatives underway that attempt to link the systems of higher education of the nations of the European Union. The goal is to increase their international competitiveness and to create degrees at the undergraduate and graduate levels that are of comparable quality and that permit students to maximize their training opportunities by transferring from one institution to another. In light of sectarian national beliefs about differences in the quality of universities and other local interests, it remains to be seen if these initiatives will succeed.

There is yet another important reason why it will be difficult in the shorter run for these systems of learning to compete with the United States' best universities. My concentration on the role of our great universities in the innovation process simplifies the other elements that are also crucial for that process—namely, the role of industrial and other technologies in the development of actual products. The role of universities in the innovation process is critically important, but it is not sufficient to producing a plethora of actual products. As Amar Bhidé, a professor at Columbia's School of Business, observed, successful innovation involves both *products* and *know-how*.[17] To understand successful innovation, Bhidé argued, we must take three levels of know-how and three levels of products into account.

Know-how, he said, ranges from "high-level general principles, to mid-level technologies, to ground-level context-specific heuristics or rules of thumb." For example, the development of microprocessors required know-how associated with the laws of solid-state physics (high-level general principles), circuit design work by engineers (mid-level technologies), and the "tweaking of conditions in a specific semiconductor fabrication plant to maximize the quality and yield from the microprocessors produced" (ground level heuristics).[18] In short, the discoveries in solid-state physics that are apt to happen at universities or industrial labs will not lead to innovative products without the other elements falling into place.

New products also can be ordered hierarchically, from high level products such as microprocessors (or the silicon used to develop them); to products in the mid-range, such as basic products used in computers; to lower-level products, such as the laptop computer. So, in the national system of innovation, by focusing on the role of universities I have been focusing on know-how at various levels and omitting almost entirely the discussion of the various product levels that are part of the innovation process. "Innovation that sustains modern prosperity," says Bhidé, has "a variety of forms" and is "developed and used through a massively multi-player, multilevel, and multiperiod game."[19] The discovery and development of the transistor, which revolutionized the electronics industry, is a good illustration of an innovation that required multiple actors in many locations and in many layers of the system of innovation.

If we keep in mind that the university is part of this larger system of innovation, some of the alarmist voices and paranoia about the imminent threat of competition from places like China and India as a product of rapid globalization can be muted. It takes decades or more to build a system that can successfully produce innovation. The Japanese and Korean experiences are good examples. They have produced discoveries and products that have benefited us, but their systems of innovation in terms of the production of know-how and products at the three levels has lagged well behind ours. The same is true, I believe, in the case of China and India. It will take those nations much longer to reach a point where they are full competitors with the United States because it takes time to build the necessary structures and to culturally assimilate values necessary for greatness. In fact it helps us to help them—we can benefit by producing more minds in the international community that are competing to solve significant scientific and technological problems, because the solutions that are found will help to increase our "know-how" at many levels. In short, it may be a bit premature to assume that we will be relinquishing our preeminent standing anytime soon. The rationale behind large increases in the resources needed to move forward with scientific and technological discoveries should not be that there will be dire consequences for our competitive position if we fail to do so, but rather, that by allocating resources to solve very fundamental problems, we will support the development of technologies that will lead to products that can be used anywhere.

In fact, advances abroad in the production of "know-how" at great universities will actually improve living standards in the United States. The obsession with "national competitiveness" is ultimately wrong-headed. Once again, Bhidé said that "the erosion of the U.S. lead in cutting-edge research isn't just harmless: an increase in the world's supply of high-level know-how provides more raw material for mid- and ground-level innovations that increase living standards in the United States."[20] I believe this is true, and it is why the development over time of great universities in Europe, China, Japan, Korea, and India should not be viewed as a principal threat to the truly distinguished institutions of higher learning in the United States. Since knowledge is not a depleting resource like oil—that is, we don't have less of it if others acquire more of it—we collectively gain by allowing new knowledge and discoveries to flow freely among countries. Of course, this includes our ability to obtain fundamental knowledge or know-how to use in our own system of innovation.[21]

If the threats to preeminence are not from other nations, then perhaps the potential enemy is in fact us. We must fortify and protect our great universities, or, to paraphrase Winston Churchill in another context, we are apt to crumble from within before we crumble from without.

I want to be very clear about the way I view competition with other countries. I am not interested in an international Olympic games of academic winners and losers. Nor am I interested in counting gold medals or Nobel Prizes held by Americans with the objective of feeding ethnocentric pride. Quite the contrary is true. I believe the evidence shows that competition is beneficial for the growth of knowledge, and that the growth of knowledge is good for the larger society. Of course, as many have pointed out, there can be unfortunate consequences of knowledge growth. Nevertheless, by and large, the growth of fundamental knowledge (as well as goal-oriented knowledge) has led to innovations that have improved the health, the social well-being, and the economic welfare of the citizens of the world. Since the academic world is already highly interconnected at the level of substantive interests, there is no real need to fear growing excellence and competition from other nations.

In fact, the better the universities of other nations become, the more likely it is that their scholars, scientists, and engineers will become collaborators with Americans. International collaboration and cooperation among equal partners would be good for scholarly and scientific growth and good for the depth of commitment each society has for the others. It would benefit the growth of knowledge and thus the outcomes if European nations, China, Japan, India, and other nations competed effectively with the powerhouses that the universities of the United States have become. It would intensify the competition to reach solutions to vexing and important health problems and to solving other problems that affect everyone, not just Americans.

If these other systems of higher learning became truly distinguished, perhaps equal to or better than our own universities in some areas of science and scholarship, our country might lose the dominance it currently has in translating these ideas and discoveries into new, practical applications, and in building the new industries and jobs that accompany those innovations. But that would increase the chances for economic development and social progress throughout the world. Although American universities might not be able to claim that they had 80 percent of the top twenty universities in the world, or 70 percent of the top fifty, the total number of great universities around the world would increase, with the result that the entire group would contribute to still more rapid scholarly and scientific progress. So, in arguing that France, Germany, or China cannot compete for preeminence for a host of reasons, or even come close to the level that American universities have reached today, I am arguing for what is to me a discouraging conclusion, one that I do not find to be either pleasing or good for the international system of higher education.

THE PARTNERSHIP BETWEEN UNIVERSITIES, GOVERNMENT, AND INDUSTRY

When Vannevar Bush and others created an enlightened federal science policy more than sixty years ago, they put in place some of the essential conditions for the flowering of American science and the academy. However, changes in the organization and structure of the academy have created a new landscape that requires us to revisit the expanded relationship between our universities, the federal government, and the increasingly important partner, entrepreneurial businesses. Can the partnerships be strengthened to enable even more rapid growth of university discoveries and rapid applications without the universities entering into a Faustian bargain? Much of Vannevar Bush's postwar document *Science—The Endless Frontier* remains relevant today, but there are features of our great universities, and needs of the nation, that Bush and his partners could not have anticipated. Whatever changes may be required in the earlier Bush model, the federal government must continue to be the principal supporter of basic research through the nation's universities on matters of military security. But will it invest heavily in more difficult economic times with an eye to maintaining the dominant role of our universities as incubators of innovation?

The simple fact is that in 2009 there is a crisis developing at our great state universities. Over the past decade, many of these states, which have refused to increase taxes because of the political fallout—or have been unable to increase taxes because of measures constraining them—have been expecting their universities to do more with a lot less. Unable to make any significant increases in tuition pricing, again because of the politics involved, faced with significant cuts in their operating and capital budgets (where the states actually support educational capital projects), and with a mandate to educate an increasing number of students, the state universities, which represent true jewels in the nation's crown, are being starved to death.

The proportion of the total budgets of public universities that comes from state sources is rapidly moving toward single digits. Faculty salaries and financial aid for students are limited, and increasingly these universities are finding it difficult to compete against private universities with large endowments for the best students and faculty—and even to provide quality education for the mass of undergraduate students who are admitted to their schools. The actions by many of the states suggest that they simply undervalue what their universities are doing and do not realize how important it is to adequately invest in these institutions. Unless legislators begin to realize that the infusion of significantly greater resources into their academic institutions leads to a better trained local labor force, local economic development, and the creation of desirable communities, many of our best research universities in these states are going to erode in quality. That would have a devastating effect on the larger system of higher learning in the United States.

The federal government also seems to lack 20/20 vision when it comes to the various payoffs that the nation receives for its support of higher learning and research. Nothing less than the economic and social health of the nation is at stake. The availability of adequate resources surely does not guarantee scientific breakthroughs or success in solving some of our most troubling health and welfare problems, but without a growing investment in the research and discovery process, the quality of our universities will deteriorate. Investments in the growth of knowledge pay off, and the tradition of funneling resources for that growth through our universities has been enormously successful, as we have seen. Recent cuts in the rate of funding of the NIH, to the point where we witnessed a decline in real growth in 2008 and 2009, have created troubling conditions for young scholars and scientists at universities.

It has become more difficult for extremely talented young scientists to start their own laboratories, for example. On average, they don't receive such funding until they are well into their forties; and the rejection rates for grant applications at the NIH have skyrocketed. For some study sections at the NIH today, only around 10 percent of proposals are being funded. When college and graduate students become aware of the difficulties involved in getting one's academic career started, they tend to back away from such careers. Moreover, when the government prohibits funding for specific research areas on ideological grounds, such as stem cell research, interest in careers in science and engineering wanes. A revised national science policy should search for ways to promote fundamental research, create incentives for the production of work in "Pasteur's quadrant," institute mechanisms for developing the human capital needed for continued preeminence, and articulate national needs that can be met through research and discovery. As it turns out, all of President Obama's major national objectives—everything from improving our environment to making America less dependent on foreign oil or creating jobs that require high levels of educational training—will require significant investment in university-based research.

Although the federal government has oscillated in the rate at which it has increased the federal budget for research, it has failed consistently to appreciate the importance of investing resources in national science and engineering infrastructure at research universities. The government emphasizes support for individuals and groups, which is essential, of course, but it has largely ignored support for new laboratories. Until very recently, the NIH and NSF allocated minuscule proportions of their budgets to infrastructure projects, leaving to universities the job of speculatively investing in new buildings. For the universities, the decision to self-finance these types of facilities typically involves a wager that the faculty for which they are designed will be able to produce scientific work that will help to pay for them, but even then the science produced usually pays for only part of the costs of maintaining and running the facilities.

This needs to change. Private universities must find the resources to build modern laboratories, and those dollars are extremely hard to generate. Budgets for infrastructure need to be increased dramatically, and awards of those resources should be based on an open competition using peer-review mechanisms for making choices among competing proposals. Until the past decade, many state legislatures have been more enlightened than the federal government about the use of their capital budgets for investments in research facilities. This has given state universities some comparative advantage in rapidly building great science programs. The absence of federal resources for laboratory buildings has had the unintended consequence of universities using Washington lobbyists to try to obtain special earmarked legislation for scientific facilities at private research universities. These policies stand in sharp contrast to the kinds of investments in laboratories and equipment being made by many Asian nations, particularly China, Korea, and Japan.

Finally, the federal government needs to dramatically increase its support for the humanities. The funding for the National Endowment for the Humanities (NEH) continues to be pathetically low and demonstrates a lack of awareness of the importance of these disciplines for studying questions that are not apt to be addressed by the science and engineering disciplines. The humanities, as well as the sciences, contribute to improved critical thinking and analytic ability and a better understanding of culture, literature, and alternative ways of thinking. Confronting philosophical and practical dilemmas are more often than not found in humanities courses. The federal government's compact with the universities now needs to be extended to the humanities.

INTERNAL TROUBLES: THE RICH GETTING MUCH RICHER

One pattern of university growth stands out in bold relief: Over time there has been a substantial degree of accumulation of advantage that has gone to some universities and not to others. As mentioned earlier, the accumulation of advantage arises when there is an unequal amassing of resources necessary for greatness among the various universities. This is a simple concept. If one university has greater resources at some point in time, it increases its chances of getting still more resources in the future—and all the things that those resources can bring to the university. With greater endowments, it can offer more competitive salaries to the faculty members it is recruiting (freeing less restricted money, such as tuition, for other uses); with better laboratory facilities, it can attract the most talented young students; if it already has more creative faculty members than other institutions, its chances of hiring the best of the younger potential faculty members is greater, because they will want to join great departments that are already distinguished, desiring the prestige and other forms of recognition that go along with being among the best. The result of this process is that some institutions have a much better chance of getting still better than others over time. Inequality begins to grow. Up to some point, which is not always clear, levels of inequality and the concentration of resources can transform very good institutions into great ones. Beyond a certain point, however, there can be too much of a good thing—a level of inequality that becomes unhealthy for the larger system of higher learning.

In the process of moving from very good to the world's best, the American research universities felt the consequences of cumulative advantage. In competing for talent, and in an effort to become still greater, the participants in the competition do not compete on a level playing field—as if individuals and institutions ever do. However, the irony is that since World War II, we have actually seen growth in the absolute number of great American research universities while simultaneously seeing a widening gap between the greatest universities, which tend to have long histories of excellence, and the universities that have only recently entered these ranks.

There are multiple factors responsible for both the growth in absolute numbers and for this widening gap between the "haves" and "have nots." And there are some exceptions. The growth over time in the state financing of large-scale capital programs to build great university laboratory facilities and hospitals has transformed the quality of some institutions. One of the best postwar examples of this can be found in California's investments in its UCLA and San Diego campuses, where the state has built laboratory facilities for the biological and biomedical sciences that rival any produced by the older private universities. Within two generations, the University of California at San Diego has become one of the greatest biological sciences universities in the nation, largely because of state investments, outstanding leadership, and the university's ability to successfully recruit scientists of the first rank. And yet, efforts by federal agencies to allocate resources to specific universities in order to create new centers of excellence have largely failed. Inequalities, resulting, for example, from variations in the distribution of resources based on the peer review of research grants and contracts, as well as from differences in the size of university endowments, have widened the gap between the very best and the rest.

The alarming growth of inequality among university endowments over the past two decades has produced an unnerving potential for a few institutions to be able to dominate the competition for talent.[22] Think of what

Harvard has at its disposal today compared with the University of Chicago—and these are two institutions that were arguably roughly equal in quality during the first half of the twentieth century. Harvard's endowment in June 2007 was over $34 billion, compared with $6 billion at the University of Chicago. Harvard's endowment reached a peak of $36.9 billion in June 2008 (Yale's was $22.9 billion, or 40 percent lower, and Stanford's was less than half of Harvard's, at $17.2 billion). The financial crisis of late 2008 and 2009 hit Harvard's endowment hard. Estimates vary about its loss in value, but it was over 30 percent, and some say closer to 50 percent. The other great private universities, which were also heavily invested in private university and hedge funds, did not fare much better. Yale, Columbia, and others lost 20 to 30 percent of their endowments. The point is that a few universities maintained, even after the losses, large comparative advantages over almost all other universities.[23]

Given the inequality in resources, it is actually quite remarkable that no single American research university yet dominates the market for talent, although the prospect looms on the horizon. If we examine the relationship between the assessed quality of research universities and the size of their endowments (or the size of the endowment per student or faculty member), we find a remarkably high correlation. The private American universities with the top six endowments were all ranked as being within the top ten universities in the world in the recent Chinese study.[24] Although we should not make too much of small differences in ranks, Columbia, which was ranked seventh in the world in quality, had a total endowment of over $7 billion, which is not much larger than the roughly $6 billion that Harvard added to its endowment in one year, 2006–2007. If the process of doubling continues as it has, we will see the day—not very far off—when the resources available to three or four American universities will be so much greater than those available to all of the rest that competition with them will become almost impossible. How long can Chicago and distinguished state universities with smaller endowments compete against a university whose endowment is growing at such a pace that in short order its annual growth will be larger than the total endowment of its competition? Another way of describing the current situation is that Harvard's annual endowment *growth* in 2006 was greater than the *total* endowment of all but the top dozen or so universities in the nation. If universities believe that they can't play in the same game, that it is impossible to ever win, they will have little incentive to play or to try to become great. At some point, they cannot, in fact, play in the big leagues.[25]

I've argued that competition to be the "best" not only has been good for the quality of American universities, but also has been one of the fundamental drivers of change and innovation in the system. But what would happen to our system if we fell into a situation where a very small set of universities had such disproportionately large resources that they could outbid all others for the best scientists and scholars in the world? Is the United States headed for the situation that exists in Britain, where two universities, Oxford and Cambridge, and in selected fields a few others, such as Imperial College, London, or the London School of Economics, dominate the landscape of higher learning?[26] We're a large nation, so that number might grow to six or seven universities, but the end result could be devastating for some of our greatest seats of learning.

Let's take as examples the University of Chicago and the University of California at Berkeley. These institutions have been rivals of Harvard and Yale in almost every scientific and scholarly discipline for generations, and they still rank among the very best institutions in the world. But they are becoming relatively "impoverished" compared with Harvard, Yale, Princeton, and Stanford. The public won't cry for universities with endowments of $6 billion or $7 billion, but it also may not realize that these institutions are competing against others with $30 billion or $23 billion endowments. The public is also largely unaware of the cost of doing top scientific work today. It is not unusual for recruitment packages for several world-class scientists to run to $40 million or $50 million price tags, not including the investments of hundreds of millions of dollars in new laboratory buildings, scientific equipment, and highly trained personnel. Today, relatively few universities can afford to support such recruitment efforts. As great as this current inequality is, the prospects for the future look bleaker. If the rich schools' endowments appreciate at roughly the same rate as the "poorer" ones, which is surely likely to happen, the inequality will grow even greater: In seven or eight years, Harvard's endowment may be well over $60 billion, while Chicago's will perhaps be $16 billion; then $120 billion compared with $32 billion, and so on.

Can Chicago and Berkeley stay in the game? Presently, they continue to hold onto top professors and attract great new talent. This is due to a variety of factors, such as the prized culture of Chicago, or the desirable living conditions in the Bay Area. But over the past decade or two, these institutions have found it more difficult to keep their best talent and have had to compete with the most highly endowed universities. And there are many less wealthy institutions than these that have had even more trouble recruiting and keeping top faculty members.

There are limits to how much of the total talent a few universities can succeed in capturing. After all, the very rich universities have a finite size, and their departments and schools, even if populated with extraordinary people, will not totally deplete the pool of exceptional scholars, scientists, and engineers. And there are many important but idiosyncratic reasons why some professors choose to make their homes at less wealthy and less prestigious institutions: for example, dual career issues, geographic preferences, and attraction to extremely strong but small groups of world-class scholars and scientists embedded in what are very good, but not truly distinguished, universities, among other factors. But the distribution of talent in its most extreme form is nevertheless sharply skewed. Even at the great American universities, there are significant inequalities of talent. The greatest discoveries are made by a very small proportion of the population of professors at even the best schools. If the wealthiest dominate the "acquisition" of this group, they will in fact reduce the competitors to a farm system of universities, whose function will increasingly be to prepare those who demonstrate the greatest talent to move up to the "final eight" or the "final four."

Berkeley's situation is no better in comparative terms than Chicago's. Ever affected by the vicissitudes of California's budget situation, the university faces slow growth or cuts in its operating budget. During much of the 1970s and 1980s, Berkeley's faculty could hold its own against any of the other best universities in the United States. It still is among America's greatest universities. But it is being bled by the state as it tries to remain fully competitive with the wealthiest academic institutions, including its neighbor to the south, Stanford. The funding problems betray a lack of understanding on the part of California legislators of the incredible role that Berkeley (and the other great institutions in the university system) plays in the economy of California, in providing opportunities for the state's residents, and in attracting talent to the state from all over the world, to say nothing of the value of having one of the world's most prestigious universities in the state.

Berkeley is not alone, of course. Over the past decade, all the great public institutions have had to struggle to remain competitive with their peers in the private sector. The great state universities in this country provide the bulk of access to higher education for those without substantial means. Their quality will diminish unless the states begin to invest much more heavily in these universities. In short, the growing inequalities of wealth are surely not dependent only on the appreciation of endowments, but also on the investments of state government in higher education and in the research enterprises at these institutions.

What, if any, effects will the financial crisis of 2008 and 2009 have on the quality of our great universities and on this pattern of growing inequality?

Overall, America's leading universities have sustained remarkable growth over the past half-century. The financial resources available to them have swelled as a result of the increased federal and private research investments in them, and the growth in tuition revenues has outpaced inflation. In some cases, enlightened state stewardship has made a great difference to universities as well. On the false assumption that the future would be much like the past, many of these universities expanded their faculties, their staff support, and their student financial aid packages and built new research facilities or expanded existing ones. The financial tsunami of 2008 and the new economic reality mean that universities are now hard pressed to meet these commitments.[27] A period of sharply slowed growth or retrenchment will require universities to make adjustments that could affect the rate of knowledge production.

In 2008 and 2009, Ivy League and other private university endowments saw losses in the 20 to 40 percent range with accompanying illiquidity problems (since many of these endowments enjoyed years of 20 percent per year returns from private-equity and hedge funds that required placement of funds for up to five years before those funds could be withdrawn). A university that loses roughly a third of its endowment in a single year, if it happens to be fortunate enough to have a large endowment, will obviously have to limit faculty salary increases, eliminate or reduce searches for new faculty members, and slow down or shelve ambitious capital projects for improved research and teaching space. As a consequence, growth in crucial areas of the economy that desperately need innovations from our universities, such as the production of green technologies or discoveries aimed at customizing treatment for specific diseases, is apt to slow down significantly. As of the summer of 2009, few of us can predict how the financial crisis will play out. Will the economy and universities rebound from this deep recession, as they have in the past, or will the 2008–2009 financial collapse have more lasting effects? Either way, analysis of the current conditions gives us an opportunity to assess the immediate and possible longer-term consequences of the hits that have already been taken by some of our best universities.

Although the immediate effects of the 2008 and 2009 financial crisis may be most visible in the erosion of the endowments of Ivy League schools and other private universities, our best public universities are at greater risk. Faced with budget crises, states have cut deeply into their funding for universities. The great flagship universities in California, such as Berkeley, UCLA, and San Diego, are being hammered in their 2009 and 2010 budgets, with cuts by the state of up to 20 percent. This will translate into eleven- to twenty-six-day furloughs for faculty members and staff. Simultaneously, bright students in California will be less likely to be admitted to one of the state's universities, since the universities project enrollment reductions totaling about 300,000 as a result of the cuts.[28] The stress on these institutions is not only affecting their ability to conduct world-class research and teaching; it is preventing them from competing for the highest-quality talent. The average salary for full professors at Harvard in 2008–2009 was almost $193,000. At Stanford, Princeton, Columbia, and the University of Chicago, it was above $175,000. At the great California schools, the average full professor salary was around $144,000; it was around $142,000 at the University of Michigan and the University of North Carolina.[29] In short, professors at these world-class public institutions make only about 75 percent of what their peers make at the great private universities. This disparity, if continued or exacerbated, does not represent a good formula for continuing competitiveness and preeminence.[30]

State universities are facing even more ominous economic restrictions as state legislators tackle 2009 budget deficits. Many legislatures have slashed their already dwindling support of higher education as a means of closing budget gaps. Arizona State University, an excellent state university that has been on a fast track to true international distinction, faced a $120 million cut from the Arizona legislature in 2009. This puts enormous strain on the university to meet its dual mission of producing original knowledge with potential for widespread practical use and offering college opportunities for those who have academic potential but lack the financial means to attend college. The dream of creating research universities that provide both access to economically disadvantaged students and world-class research may be fading with the choices taken by shortsighted state legislators.

In the long run, the depletion of endowments and the declining support for our best state institutions will do little to curb the increasing inequality of wealth among these institutions. The less well-heeled institutions have lost 25 to 35 percent of their endowments. When the markets readjust, the same doubling process will begin again, leading to enormous relative inequalities.

For all of its vast challenges, the financial crisis also affords the nation an opportunity to rethink how federal and state governments can best invest in our research universities. Stimulating the research enterprise is important, but it must be done with the longer-term effects on universities in mind. I think the evidence I've presented testifies to the tremendous societal yield that is brought about by increasing long-term investments in university-based fundamental and applied research. But throwing large amounts of short-term money at research agencies is not the key to our nation's longer-term research strength and ability to produce technological innovation. Although President Obama's economic stimulus package, which will pour an unprecedented $21 billion into research efforts, is surely needed to jump-start our economy, its goal is to create jobs more than to create a stockpile of knowledge that will have longer-term payoffs. Undoubtedly, the stimulus package for research shows President Obama's commitment to innovation through research, and it will undoubtedly fund a great many worthwhile and potentially important research projects. But its limited expected duration makes it somewhat problematic for research universities that work for the long term.

The prospects for annual budget growth for the key funding agencies for research are, in fact, not bright; they will barely rise above inflation in the 2010 fiscal year. The NIH received $10.4 billion as part of the economic stimulus program, which must be committed by September 2010. With this pot of gold on the table, it received 21,000 applications for grants. Ninety-nine percent of them will be denied—an unhealthy situation for the growth of knowledge. Simultaneously, the NIH is to receive a 1.5 percent budget increase for 2010. The NSF gets $3 billion of the stimulus pie, but the NSF is to receive a healthy funding increase of 8.5 percent in 2010, bringing its total to $7.04 billion, of which $5.73 billion would support research.[31] Brief infusions of research capital into the universities fails to account for the fact that optimal growth at these institutions requires steady, long-term investments. What the United States needs is breakthrough knowledge in basic areas of science and technology. We need to know far more about the basic biology of diseases such as Huntington's and various forms of cancer before we will have cures or vaccines. Short bursts of expenditures can produce great technological feats, such as the building of the atomic bomb or the ability to send a man to the moon (each of which rested on basic knowledge but depended more on technology than science), but for cures of diseases such as HIV/AIDS and cancer, long-term investments at the highest levels of fundamental research are needed. President Obama, in speaking to the National Academy of Sciences in the spring of 2009, promised to increase the steady flow of increased funding to the key agencies that support university-based science. It remains an open question whether Congress will approve such long-term measures in light of a growing national deficit.

The doubling of the NIH budget that took place in the late 1990s and into the twenty-first century had many positive effects, but it also had unanticipated consequences that exacerbated some of the nation's most vexing research funding problems. Rather than directing resources toward setting up the nation's most able young scientists and engineers in their own laboratories and helping them launch their careers as independent investigators, universities expanded the amount of space dedicated to these fields and hired additional faculty. On its face, this was not a bad idea, but it dispersed funds over a larger number of scientists rather than targeting those brilliant scientists who had had to wait until reaching their early forties before beginning the independent research programs they should have been commencing in their early thirties.

Increased research funding should bring improved returns to society, and the particulars of how to make such investments have become critical. It is important for our universities to conduct research into alternative energy sources, environmental pollutants, poverty eradication, and some of the world's most devastating diseases, but not at the expense of increasing the general stockpile of knowledge associated with basic science. We must increase the base budgets of the federal agencies that sustain the university research mission. It would also be wise for the federal government to begin to seriously address the infrastructure problems at American universities by establishing a well-funded, competitive, peer-reviewed system to support the maintenance and expansion of laboratory space—so long as it is not at the expense of the welfare of brilliant young academics. If the nation cannot support the growth of its laboratory facilities by making use of peer review, then universities will continue to work through the legislators to introduce special "pork-barrel" projects that have not been peer reviewed.

The 2008 and 2009 financial crisis could have some unanticipated positive consequences for our great universities. Over the past twenty years, increasing numbers of our brightest undergraduate students have majored in fields designed for business careers, with high income potential as an obvious incentive. The gold rush was on, and many undergraduate science, social science, and humanities students were attracted by the prospect of working in lucrative jobs after receiving MBAs or law degrees. In the 1960s, a generation of students who opposed the Vietnam War and feared being drafted sought protection in graduate Ph.D. programs that offered them a temporary safe haven. I've always believed that an extraordinary generation of academics came from this set of students. They were pursuing academic careers not only because of their appeal at a time when the academic marketplace was expanding and the prospects for excellent jobs existed, but also in order to avoid the draft. The current financial crisis may well lead many of our brightest young students to reassess their priorities and look to careers in public service, teaching, research, and other less lucrative, but perhaps at least as rewarding, fields.

The catch-22 is that there may not be many academic jobs available unless the financial crisis ends and substantial economic growth returns. We need to create greater liquidity in the academic marketplace, where the decimation of retirement plans for current tenured faculty members will cause many of them to put off retirement over the next decade. At our private universities that rely on tax-deferred contributions into retirement plans, this problem could prove especially intractable. Since currently there is no mandatory retirement age for tenured faculty, faculty members can defer retirement until they can better afford it. Even if we "grandfather" current faculty members, it may be time for the federal government to revisit age-discrimination statutes to enable universities to reestablish mandatory retirement policies. This change would open opportunities for younger faculty members, so that many of the brilliant scholars with new ideas would be able to take their place as leaders of our major universities.[32]

Finally, the financial crisis provides academic leaders with the opportunity to assess the true value and payoff of many Ph.D. programs in the United States that are of inferior quality. There has been an enormous growth in the number of Ph.D. programs in this country over the past forty years—more than we can support at a very high level of excellence. Ph.D. programs should not be designed simply to meet teaching needs of large state universities—or private universities, for that matter. If the sustained quality of these programs is not high and is not improving significantly over time, then they ought to be shut down. This is a very difficult thing to do in the academic community, but it nevertheless needs to be done, and real leadership is needed in this area.

What, if anything, can be done to slow this growing rate of inequality? In the larger society, the inequalities can be reduced through a variety of mechanisms, including tax policies. But within the system of higher education itself there are no clear mechanisms for attenuating them. We cannot tax Harvard's endowment, nor should we be interested in doing so. For one thing, even Harvard's endowment does not invariably increase, as we saw in 2008. We have no "league," like major league baseball does, that can supply a mechanism for putting salary caps into place, or luxury taxes to keep the leagues competitive through cross-subsidization from one team to another. Believe me, the Ivy League is not likely to agree to any system whereby Harvard, Princeton, and Yale would donate funds to strengthen the economic and competitive position of the University of Pennsylvania, Columbia, or Cornell. Most Harvard alumni are unlikely to be persuaded that they should donate to Berkeley, and the private foundations that support higher education, such as Mellon, Rockefeller, and Hewlett, cannot be expected to eliminate their support for the wealthiest institutions. Nor can we expect the peer review system to take into account the wealth of the institutions whose scholars and scientists are producing the best work and the best research proposals. There are in fact few degrees of freedom available to reverse the trend of growing inequality, despite the threat that it poses for the system of American higher learning.

Several responses to these conditions, however, are possible if the larger society realizes the value of their great universities. A major effort needs to be undertaken to educate those who have accumulated great private wealth

over the past twenty-five or thirty years about the value of academic competition for the good of our society and for the world beyond our borders,
and the way their wealth could be used not only to benefit individual institutions but the system of education itself. There were roughly 71,000 grant-
making foundations that distributed about $40 billion in 2006. American
foundations had assets valued at about $550 billion in 2005. There are only
a few private foundations that over the course of many generations have
had anything like the impact on society that our greatest universities have
had. Of course, there have been some great private foundations, and today
there are some that have supported extremely important causes—from
health-related issues to the arts and sciences. Many of them sustain cultural institutions that have few sources of government revenue in the United
States. But would it make a bigger difference to the world's population for
someone like Warren Buffet to add his personal wealth of, say, $30 billion
to the Gates Foundation, or for him to place those resources in the form of
an endowment at one of our great research universities?

If someone like Buffet were to give three great universities $10 billion
each to increase their ability to remain among the truly greatest institutions of knowledge production in the world, I would think that, in the long
run, a greater good would be achieved than would result from contributing
to the philanthropy of a private foundation. In fact, that is exactly what
John D. Rockefeller did when he started the University of Chicago, and
what Leland Stanford did for the Palo Alto institution. One way, then, to
attenuate the inequalities is for our wealthiest citizens to see clearly how
investments in the form of endowments at our great universities (that are
not already among the top five or so) would not only further their personal interests but also help to ensure continued competition among our
great universities. In a less dramatic way, state universities have seriously
entered the fund-raising game that has long existed at the private universities. With very large alumni bases, the potential for giving is high, but
these efforts are very late in flowering and thus may not help enough to
maintain true competition.

In fact, if states were far more enlightened than they seem to be in 2010,
they could make heavy investments in their universities that might well
allow them to compete directly with the wealthier private institutions.
After all, they can use tax dollars to create their own long-range stimulus
packages for higher education that could recreate the situation in the 1970s

and 1980s, when Berkeley was in many ways the equal of Harvard, Yale, Columbia, Chicago, and its rival on the peninsula. That could be done in California, Florida, North Carolina, Michigan, Wisconsin, Illinois, and Minnesota as well as New York, creating stiff competition for the rich private universities.

Some universities may be able to stay competitive through income from patents and licenses of intellectual property. It is likely, however, that the wealthiest institutions will also be leaders in generating this form of income. Universities could also deemphasize endowment growth and work to enhance their quality by spending gift money and other forms of income in order to compete with those who depend more on their endowment incomes. This, however, is a risky strategy.

If individual states realize the economic value of having one or more of the top twenty or fifty universities in the world, they might think more seriously of using special assessments, taxes, or other mechanisms to create the equivalent of endowments for their flagship universities. The international prestige of having such universities is the least of the positive outcomes for the states. New jobs would be created around these universities; highly skilled people would be attracted to the state; and the universities would make profound contributions to the social welfare of the nation. The value of Silicon Valley to Stanford, to the state of California, and to the nation is obvious. As we've seen, the conditions that made for the success of Silicon Valley are not easily reproduced, but there are other examples of successes like it, both in California and in other states.

Ensuring the future of our universities will also require closer bonds between the universities and industrial partners, and national and state legislation can create incentives for the development of such collaborative bonds. Legislation in this area might well allow for a more effective and efficient collaboration between those who generate new discoveries and those with the ability to exploit these discoveries as creative new business enterprises. The resulting new revenue streams would not eliminate the inequalities, but they may allow particularly entrepreneurial universities to continue to compete with their richer peers. The tension that exists between the missions and values of universities and industrial companies will, however, require our universities to remain vigilant, so that the potential for financial gain does not influence the selection of problems for inquiry, allowing financial interests to trump intellectual curiosity.

One danger is that if science and engineering departments become unaffordable, great universities with distinguished records in these areas could simply decide to get out of the business of trying to reach the top tier in those fields. They could pursue "selective excellence" and concentrate on the less costly fields in the humanities and social sciences. This is not likely to happen. Although universities, even the great ones, should consider backing off from being "full-service" enterprises, an institution cannot really give up on competing in the sciences, in engineering, or in biomedicine without abandoning its position among our greatest academic institutions. That decision would have very damaging consequences for a university's reputation, betraying a gross misunderstanding of the extent to which these high-priced fields influence the entire intellectual map of the modern research university. The cascading effects would be enormous, affecting almost all of the other branches of the university. One can be selective, but one cannot build or maintain a great modern university without being among the best in these costly disciplines.

Finally, although we live in a world full of mergers and acquisitions and partnerships, at least in the corporate world, great research universities have yet to fully explore or exploit these types of arrangements. They remain extremely conservative institutions when it comes to forging innovative collaborative enterprises. University culture tends to reinforce isolated, autonomous, individual efforts, which rarely look for cost-saving, quality-enhancing ways to collaborate. And unfortunately, some of the most highly publicized efforts at academic mergers between prized medical schools and hospitals in the 1990s turned sour.

If academic competition has been so valuable for the American system of higher learning, why would we want to think about more collaborative efforts? The answer is simple. In such a costly world, there can be too much of a good thing, even too much intellectual redundancy. A rebalancing of competition versus collaboration would pose a major challenge for our great universities, but it also holds the potential for great good, as it could help them to achieve efficiencies and improvements in quality. There have been some successful collaborative efforts, such as in building and maintaining joint remote storage library facilities. I initiated such a plan for Columbia, Princeton, and the New York Public Library. The facility, a state-of-the-art site for storage of old, rarely used books and valuable documents, proved of great value to faculty and students of all three institutions. It was located at Princeton, which had land to use for this purpose, and the three institutions shared the costs of construction, maintenance, and storage based on a simple model of proportional sharing—those who used the facility the most, paid the most. Library sharing is a good example of collaboration at its best in the academic world.

There have been some joint degree and joint curricular programs among universities that are physically close to one another. New York University and Columbia collaborate in the teaching of certain foreign languages, for example. During the 1990s, I started a program at Columbia known as the "Passport to New York" program. It allowed Columbia students and faculty members to gain free admission into many of New York's greatest museums; in exchange, museum staff members were allowed to take a number of courses at Columbia for free. There were formal agreements signed, but there never were any formal transactions—it was based on a principal of simple exchange. We had joint programs with the Juilliard School of Music in which a limited number of Juilliard students who were interested in the broad offerings of liberal arts courses at Columbia could enroll in our programs in exchange for a limited number of our students studying at Juilliard with some of their music faculty. These were all modest programs of limited size, but they became part of what I called Columbia's "virtual endowment," assets that could be used by its students and faculty because of our collaborative agreements.

There have been larger collaborative efforts, such as the one that is now in place between Arizona State University and a branch of the Mayo Clinic to work on clinical and medical research innovations, but these are few and far between. Arizona State and the University of Pennsylvania cooperate in the transfer of intellectual property from their universities to the market, sharing expertise and offering packages of inventions that complement each other. There have also been a number of linkages formed between American research universities and foreign universities—either for joint programs or for the exchange of faculty and students. For years, Columbia and a few other institutions have had exchange programs in place with Oxford and Cambridge for a small number of highly talented undergraduate students. The executive education joint-degree program between the Columbia Business School and the Haas School of Business at Berkeley, which takes advantage of access to both Wall Street and Silicon Valley, is another example of a collaborative arrangement designed to be a win-win effort.

To my knowledge, remarkably few universities have attempted to develop joint ventures with other universities in the arts and sciences. Faculty members are often skeptical about these matters, fearing the loss of their autonomy and an increased administrative workload. Yet the potential payoffs for well-crafted collaborations seem high. I once broached the idea to the Princeton provost of joining our two history departments, which I thought in combination would be far and away the best and most attractive in the country to potential students and faculty members. I thought it would be easier to produce a joint venture between two powerful universities and elite departments than to forge agreements where there was a strong partner and a weak one. In this case, we would keep separate admissions standards, which were very high already at both institutions, merge the course offerings, and allow students to take courses and fulfill degree requirements at either of the two universities. We would allow faculty members at either institution to sponsor doctoral dissertations of students admitted to either institution; we would even allow faculty members at Columbia to spend some time at Princeton, and Princeton faculty to spend time in residence at Columbia.

Although my Princeton counterpart had real interest in exploring the possibility, the idea gained no traction because there was not enough enthusiasm for this "merger" within the faculties of the two departments. Of course, Princeton had far more resources than Columbia to expand its faculty and student population as it saw fit, but the general idea of informally merging academic programs to the benefit of both places was met with chilling resistance. Nonetheless, in the future it may well be possible and necessary for research universities, even superb ones, to seriously consider various new combinations and alliances in academic programs to enhance their quality and to remain competitive with wealthier institutions.

BIG PROBLEMS REQUIRE BIG SOLUTIONS: NEEDED STRUCTURAL CHANGES

For most of the twentieth century, universities organized the transmission and production of new knowledge around schools and disciplines. This allowed faculty members to dig deeply into scientific and scholarly problems. They became experts in subfields within their disciplines, developed fundamental knowledge, and made path-breaking discoveries, some of which I've described. Because of this tradition, over time we developed extraordinary specialists with a great deal of knowledge, but they thought little about integrating their knowledge with what was known or being discovered in related fields. The membranes separating departments and schools were hardly penetrable. Faculty members in one department rarely collaborated with those in other departments and schools. They often did not even know the professors in those disciplines. The work of universities went on in departments of English, chemistry, physics, and anthropology, and in schools of law, business, medicine, journalism, architecture, and the arts and sciences. This is what Clark Kerr meant by referring to the modern university as the "multiversity."

The university also began to structure its internal economy in terms of these basic units of schools and departments. Within the past several decades, many of our great universities have moved to budget systems that are highly decentralized, which give a great deal of authority to "local" leaders—deans and chairs of departments—to make academic choices and to develop incentives for their local units to be fiscally responsible. Sound business principles were at work: Give authority to faculty and administrative leaders to construct strategic plans for their own areas of expertise, create incentives for their growth (allowing them to keep the differences between their revenues and expenses, subject only to a central tax for university common costs), and through this local empowerment, make gains in attracting better leaders of the schools and departments. There are still many variations of this general budget model. At one extreme is Harvard, where for decades each academic unit has operated more or less independently, which is in contrast, for example, to Stanford, where far more budgetary control and authority lies in the hands of the university provost.

The irony of this pattern of decentralization was that the quality of local leadership was improved, but the level of local isolation was increased. It became difficult for knowledge to move across the internal borders of the university's schools and departments. The budget systems at many universities put fetters on the growth of knowledge, and the free trade of ideas across disciplines became incompatible with the best way to manage financial affairs. Nevertheless, it became increasingly obvious that to solve truly monumental intellectual problems, more rather than less collaboration among departments and schools was required. For important discoveries to take place—and for big problems to be solved—it turns out that we need both the depth of knowledge produced by disciplinary work and the breadth of knowledge produced by interdisciplinary sharing of ideas and expertise. This is especially true when it comes to tackling problems such as global climate change, economic development, and finding the causes of disease or poverty and eradicating them.

Indeed, there are few profound, large-scale biological problems today that do not require the expertise of people trained in specialized fields of biology as well as people trained in chemistry, physics, mathematics, and computer science, to name only a few. Yet it still causes friction within universities to graft major new multidisciplinary institutes onto existing structures, because they invariably compete for resources with the traditional units. They fight for the right to hire and promote their own faculty independently of the individual departments, want to play a role in shaping curricula, and the like. Great universities will have to actively support the movement toward interdisciplinary teaching and research, which should begin at the undergraduate level.

The process of building these multidisciplinary units will need to be well thought out. For example, both faculty and students will need to learn "new foreign languages"—that is, the languages of the other disciplines that are involved—for without the knowledge of the "language" of your collaborators, the collaboration cannot be effective. Pursuing this path will also require us to rethink features of the reward systems at our great seats of learning. Today, scholars and scientists are rewarded for mastery within their own discipline; there must be greater opportunities for recognition, including promotion to tenure, for young scholars who take up difficult interdisciplinary problems early in their careers.

Foreign nations that are developing world-class universities may well be able to avoid these conflicts by creating new structures that focus on the "laboratory" or the "institute" as the primary unit instead of the "department" or the "school." Alternately, they could create multidisciplinary units to focus on a set of complex problems. Our great universities will have the challenge of adapting to these new imperatives.

The research university will also have to come to grips with other structural challenges, including the evolving meaning of "disinterestedness." Intellectual property will become a more salient issue in the years ahead. The size of the university-industrial complex is very likely to grow over the next several decades, especially in fields like neuroscience, biomedicine, nanotechnology, biomimicry, bioengineering, and information technology and computer science. These complex social networks will provide universities with many opportunities, but they will also create risks related to their autonomy. If universities and individual scientists are going to profit from ideas, they will have to rethink the arrangements that have traditionally prohibited academics from personally profiting from their discoveries. Institutionalizing appropriate behavior and controls over valuable faculty members who see dollar signs in front of them—and who may feel they have leverage to negotiate special deals—will require sound policies and enlightened leadership. If there are multiple threats to the core values of the university, none is clearer than the corruption that could result from the commercialization of intellectual property unless universities successfully control and regulate potential abuses.

I've suggested that research universities are highly accountable for many of their actions, and they are obsessed with measuring how well they are doing—particularly in terms of their research mission. But these great institutions must improve their financial accountability to the public if they are to generate the essential public trust that they need. They must provide a clear idea of how they are trying to moderate the costs of higher education. They must demonstrate that they are not only masters of creating innovative programs, but actually capable of terminating some—which is, truth be told, something they have not proven to be particularly skilled at doing. They must provide the public with a better understanding of how, say, one dollar of tuition is used in the university—a more complex assignment than it might seem. They have to persuade the public that their budget process does not simply involve adding up all of their expenses and revenues and filling in the gap through increases in tuition rates—or "solving for tuition."

Universities must also convince the public that they are doing everything possible to deter their faculty members from having potential conflicts of interest. This is a particularly acute problem in medical schools, where many clinical faculty members have very close relationships with pharmaceutical companies and are often on the payrolls of these companies as consultants. Virtually every day we read about payments to physicians—direct or in-kind—for prescribing one pharmaceutical drug over another when there may be no difference, or when the risks of alternative treatments are not discussed with patients.

In 2009, the American press reported large numbers of obvious conflicts of interest by faculty members at some of our greatest universities. The majority of these involved physician researchers who received large sums of money from pharmaceutical companies and medical-device manufacturers to use or publicize their products over those of competitors. Consider just two examples. One case involved Harvard professor of psychiatry Dr. Joseph L. Biederman, who is internationally recognized for developing diagnostic techniques for bipolar disorder in children. When Senator Charles Grassley, a member of the Senate Finance Committee, began investigating ties between physicians and pharmaceutical companies, he found that in 2000–2007 Biederman had been paid $1.6 million by the drug companies "in consulting and speaking fees."[33] The fees drew criticism largely because the companies included "those that make drugs [that Biederman] advocate[d] for childhood bipolar disorder." Dr. Alan F. Schatzberg of Stanford, head of the psychiatry department, held a large amount of stock in Concept Therapeutics, a company he cofounded. The company was investigating the abortion drug known as RU-486 as a treatment for psychotic depression. But Schatzberg was also the principal investigator in a National Institute of Mental Health study to research the same thing, and he had coauthored papers on the subject as well. Scores of additional examples of conflicts of interest involving physicians could be cited.

The problem lies, in part, in the fact that many top research physicians do not realize that such activities are conflicts of interest. Even if they receive large payments for touting a particular pharmaceutical company's product, or hold significant equity stakes in companies linked to their supposedly independent and disinterested research, they don't think there is anything wrong with what they are doing. But the fact remains that these exceptionally able research physicians have become guns for hire. When the values of academic research are so compromised that such things are common, and when there are insufficient safeguards against such conflicts of interest, the university's core values are under attack. The penetration of corporate America into the professoriate through income incentives places the university in precisely the position that Derek Bok feared.[34]

Universities must assiduously avoid even the appearance of conflicts of interest in conducting medical and other forms of research—particularly clinical trials that may involve the research of one of their faculty members who stands to gain financially if a new drug proves efficacious in clinical trials. Policies that prevent conflicts and emphasize the value of independent inquiry must be well articulated and enforced. This means that universities must reinforce the structural mechanisms that create firewalls to avoid conflicting business arrangements that pose dangers to the integrity of the research and clinical enterprises. The public's trust in the larger research enterprise will be eroded if people suspect that universities are cutting corners in their industrial relationships. As the boundaries between universities and business enterprises become blurred, it becomes even more important for universities to demonstrate that they are upholding their basic values.

In addition, the trustees and regents of our great universities must become more accountable in their role as "governors" of these academies. Although I have known deeply committed and knowledgeable trustees who have given generously of their time, energy, and means to support the growth and improvement of the universities they served, they have tended to be in a distinct minority. Most trustees of private universities see their selection as largely honorific, viewing themselves as potential benefactors. Good, decent, well-meaning people, who are interested in their alma mater or the institution that has chosen them to serve, they nonetheless know almost nothing about them. The leadership of universities rarely attempts to educate their trustees about the institution, and more often than not they fear trustees as potential micromanagers rather than as knowledgeable partners. Trustees are more concerned with their fiduciary responsibilities than anything else, which, given their legal liabilities, is understandable. But they rarely try to increase their knowledge of the educational and research programs. Thus, they remain blissfully or unhappily ignorant of what the university is actually trying to do.[35]

This lack of awareness tends to show up in the selection of new leaders. Ignorance of the "business" of the university often results in searches without real knowledge of the skill set and talents that are needed for leadership. It is not unusual, for example, to find presidents and provosts of multibillion dollar universities, as well as deans of schools, who simply cannot read a spreadsheet or a budget. There is, in short, no career path to becoming a leader of a university. These people are selected from the ranks of the faculty or after serving in some administrative post at another institution. The selection is often made without serious vetting to discover how competent they really are as administrators. Almost all of the presidents and provosts of the great universities whom I have known are in fact highly talented, hardworking people. But they vary enormously in their ideas about the role that a university president, provost, or academic vice president or dean should play, and they have highly variable capabilities as leaders and administrators. This variability exists, of course, in all businesses. But among the great universities there are many examples of untested and ill-suited academics moving into major leadership positions after having had essentially no experience to prepare them for their highly responsible administrative roles.

THE HERD OF INDEPENDENT MINDS: THE TENDENCY TOWARD INTELLECTUAL ORTHODOXY

Academic freedom and tenure combat the tendency of professors and students to sit on their hands and remain mum when they believe that their ideas and research may offend those who adhere to an ideologically "correct" way of thinking. But there is huge pressure toward ideological conformity within universities, as elsewhere, and universities, like other institutions, tend not to be tolerant of those in their midst who are courageous enough to challenge prevailing systems of thought. If the essence of a university is to be open and tolerant of all points of view that can be supported by evidence, then the most basic beliefs must be open to questioning within the academy. Yet they often are not. The limits placed on free inquiry within the academy threaten the realization of that ideal as much as threats from beyond the university campus.

In truth, there is both intellectual and personal risk involved in challenging the presumptions of the group. The weight of the community on the individual scholar is found in the way those who challenge "group think" are treated. More often than not, it's the faculty, not administrators, who define and enforce dominant orthodoxies. I doubt that any young social scientist who challenged the idea that the paucity of women in science and engineering was a consequence of a series of complex social and cultural processes that led women to select themselves out of these occupations, rather than adopting the belief—deeply held in academia—that the cause of the limited number of women was gender discrimination, would have as great a chance of obtaining a position at a major research university in the United States today as a scholar holding the orthodox view, regardless of the quality of the evidence. The same might be said of faculty members who offer tentatively genetic explanations for social or psychological behavior; those who challenge the efficacy of many medical practices taken as received wisdom; those who argue against postmodernist views in fields where this approach dominates faculty opinion; and those who propose radically different scientific ideas that run against the grain of prevailing scientific consensus. The tendency toward orthodoxy is also felt in campus life and in the treatment of students. At universities it has become difficult even to discuss certain topics or to suggest ideas that offend some significant part of the academic community.

What academic leader not looking for a good fight would tell "Take Back the Night" students, who were marching to protest the administration's failure to show greater concern about sexual assaults on campus, or to toughen up the university's sexual harassment policies, that they questioned the validity of the group's data on the percentage of young women who were victims of date rape? When any group of students asserts that the university is not sufficiently protective of its rights, to say nothing of its feelings, most administrators think first about how to redress the grievance rather than about how they might investigate whether there is a basis for grievance to begin with. Bad things do happen at universities, which are no more immune than the larger society to the malicious and unsavory behavior of some of its community members. But rather than viewing unconventional thinking as an appropriate challenge to received wisdom and ideology, those being challenged often become defensive, and these questions, even if posed in the most neutral of forms, get people into trouble.

The remarkable thing about these retreats from the ideal of freedom of expression and inquiry is that liberals have been as responsible for them as conservatives. In the 1990s, there were cases involving opprobrious speech by students on campus that led to the adoption of speech codes, sensitivity training, and *pro forma* statements of moral outrage from deans, university presidents, and provosts, to say nothing of faculty members. They all tended to lose sight of the principles of academic freedom and protected speech. One case at Yale Law School followed the rape of a white female law student by two black men in New Haven. Following the incident, according to one account, "ten black law students found in their mailboxes a note about the incident which ended with the sentence: 'Now do you know why we call you *NIGGERS?*'"[36] The author of this letter was not identified. The law school faculty surely did the right thing by expressing its sympathy for the affected students and condemning the content of the letter. But the dean of the law school went further, linking the incident to the racism of the institutions in which we live and therefore suggesting that all of the Yale Law School community was implicated in this despicable act—transforming the situation of an unknown individual letter writer to collective guilt.

When asked what ought to be done to the letter writer, the dean replied, "For myself, I am convinced that there is no place in this school for such vicious cowards." Some three hundred students subsequently signed a petition to the same effect. At the time, the question of sanctions was put to Yale's president, Benno Schmidt, himself a former dean of the Columbia School of Law, who aptly responded: "Freedom of speech protects cowards, too." I use this illustration not only to convey the power of collective thinking in subverting the principles of free speech, but also to point out its coercive effects on dissenting views. Schmidt may have been right, but I'm sure he was not a popular man at Yale for his comment. And what about the rush to judge and expel three lacrosse students at Duke University in 2006 who attended a stripper party and were accused by one of the strippers of rape? The North Carolina attorney general later dropped the charges against them, finding that the allegations were false, and the media exposed a series of missteps by law enforcement authorities in the case.

The academy's success at opening doors to students and faculty with different identities is to be praised. But in its fear of offending any of these groups, and in its resolution to reinforce distinct identities rather than to make a common effort to pursue truth that incorporates varying perspectives without privileging any identity, the university has often hindered open debate. The consequences of privileging groups on campus, according to David Bromwich, is to restrict freedom of inquiry and thought:

If academic life in America becomes less free in the near future, one way it may happen is by a series of concessions to the sensitivities of the advocacy groups. Divided by sex, race, class, or geography, these groups have little to say to each other: an educational address by Louis Farrakhan, solicited and admired by one group, will prove to be not what the others had in mind at all. But communication is not what they seek in any case. Beneficiaries of institutional compassion, they want to control the scene of education to assure that nothing wrong, or strange, or possibly injurious to the group-esteem of their members, gets said in the public forum of the classroom or the quad. Success on their terms means that the liberal ideal of tolerance, which drew no comparable limits around permissible speech, will have been exposed as part of the imperial ethic of the West. The defeat of the latter entity will have been worth the sacrifice. But that is to look far ahead. In the meantime, sects like these in their present state can weaken the resources that make for uncoerced discussion at a university. For they naturally defend against one kind of knowledge—the kind that challenges the protective instinct of group identity.[37]

Bromwich was criticized for these comments by the powerful majority in the academy, despite the fact that he was simply enjoining us to risk giving up our primary identities and privileges for the possibility of gaining through knowledge generated by truly free discussion.

Tenure does provide limited protection from formal sanctions for scholars taking on generally ideologically prohibited subjects. But it does not secure those same scholars from contempt from their colleagues. Take the example of the topic of female circumcision, or female genital cutting. There are very strong ideological forces both inside and outside of the academy that conclude, without much evidence, that this widespread practice among African cultural groups is repugnant, morally despicable, and clearly an example of the oppression and coercion of women in those cultures. Nonetheless, Professor Richard Shweder, a University of Chicago anthropologist, and others have had the intellectual courage to confront the prevailing ideology that attacks this custom without much evidence about local culture.

Shweder has raised serious questions about this cultural practice, speculating about why millions of African women not only accept but embrace it. Why have we passed laws against the female-circumcision practices engaged in by some subcultural groups, such as Somali immigrants, in America, despite the fact that we fully accept male circumcision? Regardless of whether Shweder and his colleagues are right, or whether you accept or reject his evidence, he is right to raise the questions and to expect that we will consider examining the evidence, trying to overcome whatever biases and presuppositions we brought with us to the discussion in order to understand his viewpoint and that of the

African cultures engaging in the practice. The fact that Shweder is at the University of Chicago may have something to do with his willingness to talk about the subject in the first place—given its traditions and cultural demands for discourse with evidence. But without tenure, I'm not sure that even a person with his intellectual courage would have made this project his first as a junior faculty member.

In fact, though, academic rank may have less to do with the willingness to take personal as well as intellectual risks than with sheer intellectual courage. And intellectual courage, which is needed in abundance within the academy, is unfortunately in short supply these days. It takes a great deal of intellectual courage for individuals within the academy to stand their ground and make their arguments, no matter how brilliant these arguments may be, in the face of overwhelming group pressure. And it takes intellectual courage as well to come to the defense of those who raise such questions, especially among academic leaders who may be able to use the opportunity presented by the situation to reinforce the value of free inquiry.

All of this suggests that despite the ideal of free inquiry at universities, there are numerous social pressures acting to limit or subvert it. In fact, over the past decades we have witnessed a growing intolerance of tolerance itself. Part of this seems to be an impulse to construct a protective shield around our undergraduate students—*in loco parentis* carried to the extreme. God forbid that teenagers of nineteen or twenty should hear something said that they feel is offensive—as if that has not already happened to them in their young lives. I'm afraid that one of the fallouts of the intense competition among universities to collar the very best students has been to treat students and their parents as "customers" who require luxurious student centers, athletic facilities, and extracurricular club spaces. Having residence halls that seem more like hotels has become more important in many cases than having modern classroom and laboratory spaces or environments conducive to learning.

The task of a committed and useful teacher is to force his or her students to recognize "inconvenient facts," as the great sociologist Max Weber put it. The aim is not to offer a "balanced" view, or to present materials in such a way that no one is offended by the content, but to speak truth as the professor, as an expert in the field, knows it. It in fact would be paternalistic, patronizing, and even insulting to treat very bright students to a benign presentation of difficult subjects—an insult to their ability to distinguish arguments that are nothing more than assertions of fact, poorly formulated hypotheses, or theories without evidence from ones that are grounded in logic and supported by evidence. Education is a hard thing to obtain; so is an independent point of view that relies on higher levels of critical reasoning and analytic skills. But it does not come more easily in an atmosphere that refuses to challenge students and their prior beliefs about what must be true or factual. As a former president of the University of California once said, "The University is not engaged in making ideas safe for students. It is engaged in making students safe for ideas." Derek Bok asked the rhetorical question, "Whom will we trust to censor communications and decide which ones are 'too offensive' or 'too inflammatory' or too devoid of intellectual content?"[38] The answer, of course, is that no one can be trusted to do this. Instead, there must be an open dialogue, with each person weighing the arguments against the evidence for himself or herself.

If universities coddled their students and other community members and prohibited expressions or displays that could be taken as offenses, or as affronts to someone's self-esteem, much would be lost in the academy. Limits on expression have found their way into a host of codes designed to prohibit offensive speech on campus. None of these codes at public universities have stood up to judicial scrutiny, and for good reason: They prohibit speech that would be protected for any citizen of the country.[39] Moreover, the idea that people have a right to self-respect and self-esteem, as Ronald Dworkin has pointed out, is absurd.[40]

The value of speech codes has been questioned by the Harvard literary scholar and public intellectual Henry Louis Gates, Jr., who is African American. Gates offered an example to demonstrate that prescribed limits on "hate speech" fail to address the real problems of stigmatization. He asked readers to contrast the following two statements addressed to a black freshman at Stanford (which, like the University of Michigan, had a speech code):

[A] LeVon, if you find yourself struggling in your classes here, you should realize it isn't your fault. It's simply that you're the beneficiary of a disruptive policy of affirmative action that places underqualified, underprepared, and often undertalented black students in demanding educational environments like this one. The policy's egalitarian aims may be well-intentioned, but given the fact that aptitude tests place African-Americans almost a full standard deviation below the mean, even controlling for socioeconomic disparities, they are also profoundly misguided. The truth is, you probably don't belong here, and your college experience will be a long downhill slide.

[B] Out of my face, jungle bunny.

As Gates said, "Surely there is no doubt which is likely to be more 'wounding' and alienating to its intended audience. Under the Stanford speech regulations, however, the first is protected speech; the second may well not be, a result that makes a mockery of the words-that-wound rationale."[41]

All of this is to say that there is today at our great universities an insidious tone to a significant amount of discourse that avoids taking on orthodoxies and prevailing wisdom. In fact, there is false satisfaction in intellectual consensus and conformity that has not been earned. Conformity may sometimes occur because people are afraid to confront politically correct thinking; other times, it may be a calculated form of careerism, a way of pulling one's intellectual punches when one holds evidence to question beliefs that most in the academy take for granted. But either way, the result is a perversion of the ideal of a great university.

The growth of knowledge, insight, and understanding is better served through the contest between ideas than through the blind acceptance of dominant ideologies and the silencing of criticism. In fact, without those contests we cannot easily distinguish between truth and falsity. Truth rests less in product than in process. Great universities need to create a culture in which the brilliant intellectual maverick or iconoclast, who supports ideas with evidence, is not apt to be a social isolate, if not vilified for questioning those "facts" and "truths" that are believed to be beyond doubt.

SUPPORTING INNOVATION AND EXCELLENCE

The faculty and students of great universities typically know very little about their histories, about their structures, or more broadly, about the values that form the foundation of these institutions. They are *at* the institution, but not *of* the institution. The students are merely passing through.

They take courses, they form friendships with other students, and they prepare themselves for the next phase of their lives, but they do not plan to stay beyond a few years and know very little about their temporary home. Much the same can be said for contemporary faculty members. When faculty members move into administrative positions, I often hear them say, "I had no idea what the university was about—how it was organized, how it was run—until I held this position."

In one sense, there is nothing lost by this. Students and faculty concentrate on their immediate goals—completing their assignments and projects, pursuing their work as teachers and researchers, and the like. They can leave the running of the university to others—more than they might admit to. But in another sense, the lack of deeper knowledge about the university and its core values limits their understanding, their range of responses to crises, and even their decisions about the choices they face. Some universities do a better job than others of socializing their faculty into the culture of the larger institution; some faculty members choose to teach at a particular university because they are familiar with its history and culture and wish to be part of it.

The quintessential example of this is the University of Chicago. There is an ethos at the university, fostered by its presidents from Hutchins to Levi to Hannah Gray to its current president, Robert Zimmer, that professors and students are truly proud of. It incorporates all of the values that I've described as being a part of great universities. One idea that is central to that ethos is the notion that each individual, regardless of his or her ideological position, and regardless of any personal attribute, is measured and valued by the quality of his or her ideas and ability to defend those ideas with evidence. There is also the belief that narrow disciplinary sectarianism should be avoided if possible, giving way to conversations across disciplinary boundaries.

When Robert Hutchins, along with the historian John U. Nef, the economist Frank Knight, and the anthropologist Robert Redfield, set up the Committee on Social Thought in 1941, with the aim of attending to substantive problems by including many angles of vision, they were expressing a value about the way the acquisition of knowledge ought to be organized.[42] Many other such committees and famous multidisciplinary workshops exist at Chicago with some of the same objectives. In each of these settings, great value is placed on encouraging different, counterintuitive, extraordinary, and even radical ideas; of harboring extreme skepticism about the assertion of facts without data; of testing theoretical ideas with data and other forms of evidence. These elements of the culture made the university an exemplar of successfully translating the ideal type of a university into a reality.

I hold the University of Chicago, with which I've never been formally affiliated, in such high regard because it offers us a reference point for how a value system associated with greatness (but not necessarily with the greatest wealth) can pervade an institution in ways that advance free inquiry and open discourse. Of course, like virtually any other university today, there are no doubt subjects that Chicago faculty members shrink from uttering, controversial and challenging ideas that may not be expressed because they run against the grain of orthodoxy, but this kind of self-censorship seems less prevalent there than at most other places, and therefore the University of Chicago offers us an example of what is possible. What we need is not just a culture of tolerance, but a culture that encourages difference and intellectual risk-taking, wants to hear conflicting arguments and ideas that may offend our own presuppositions and biases, challenging our commitments to theories and facts as well as our understanding of the world.

If an ideal type exists for the great American university, most universities do not, in fact, usually attempt to orient and educate new faculty members, students, and academic leaders about what it is, or to inform them about the history of the particular institution that they have chosen to make part of their lives. Universities do not often talk about the core values of the university—the values at the heart of university culture, which they are nevertheless expected to understand. There are no discussions with newcomers about what is meant by free inquiry and academic freedom; about the acceptance and encouragement of debate, dissent, and controversial opinions; about tolerance of ideas that may seem hurtful or repugnant; or about how and why great universities are organized as vehicles for discovery and criticism. Somehow, we assume that people have considered these issues, have come to understand them, and don't need to discuss the idea of a university or how to reinforce or challenge appropriately its core norms and values. Universities need to make a better effort at developing a culture that recognizes and rewards the contests that take place in the marketplace of ideas.

FIRST IMPRESSIONS:
BARACK OBAMA AND OUR RESEARCH UNIVERSITIES

The election of Barack Obama in 2008 and the monumental international financial crisis of 2008 and 2009 are two developments that bear directly on the quality of our best universities. Although the financial crisis has depleted university resources and endowments, there is hope on university campuses that the damage done over the past eight years by the Bush administration will be quickly reversed by President Obama. There surely is a sense that a new political enlightenment about universities and investments in innovation is at hand. Obama showed early on that he understood the role of university discoveries in the innovation process and the importance of the universities to the economic future of the nation. In an April 2009 speech at Georgetown University, he sketched his larger vision for the nation's future as "a future where sustained economic growth creates good jobs and rising incomes; a future where prosperity is fueled not by excessive debt, reckless speculation, and fleeting profit, but is instead built on skilled, productive workers; by sound investments that will spread opportunity at home and allow this nation to lead the world in the technologies, innovations, and discoveries that will shape the 21st century."

Obama recognizes the close linkage between the development of human capital through education and the welfare of the nation. He acted quickly to reverse the Bush administration's restrictions on embryonic stem cell research. He sent a clear message to federal agency leaders asking them to expunge the use of political criteria in evaluating scientific evidence within government agencies. He has brought in an exceptionally able group of science advisers. In a speech at the National Academy of Sciences, he pledged to commit federal resources to scientific research and innovation, promising to "devote more than three percent of our GDP to research and development." He went on: "We will not just meet, but we will exceed the level achieved at the height of the Space race, through policies that invest in basic and applied research, create new incentives for private innovation, promote breakthroughs in energy and medicine, and improve education in math and science." "This work begins," he said, "with an historic commitment to basic science and applied research, from the labs of renowned universities to the proving grounds of innovative companies."[43] Obama has echoed this theme repeatedly, as he did in his August 1, 2009, radio address to the nation: "Innovation has been essential to our prosperity in the past, and it will be essential to our prosperity in the future."[44]

I have little doubt that President Obama appreciates the creative role that our universities play on the national and international stages more fully than his predecessor did; however, these values must be translated into enlightened policies if they are to make a real difference.[45] His focus on the role of science and technology in transforming the U.S. economy into one that can compete more successfully in the twenty-first century should be the basis for discussion of a revised social compact that builds on Vannevar Bush's *Science—The Endless Frontier*. This compact must take into account the changed national needs and the transformation in the organization of our universities and industries. A longer-term strategy for investments in the production of knowledge to meet new needs, with dual emphasis on curiosity-driven basic knowledge and useful knowledge, needs to be developed now if President Obama's vision for a continued American leadership is to be realized. Beyond a commitment to noble ends, we need well-defined and structured mechanisms for achieving those ends.

If our universities are to retain their distinction, the commitment to them must extend far beyond the White House. Legislative bodies at both the national and state levels will have to understand the indispensable role that our universities play. Congress must craft policies embedded in legislation and appropriations. We cannot, for example, destroy our great university-affiliated teaching hospitals as a by-product of making much-needed health-care reforms. Nor can we expect that pouring money into research will contribute to advances in medicine and other crucial areas if the funds are not wisely spent.

The work carried out by state legislatures far removed from Washington may well prove more critical than what takes place in Washington. It is possible that these legislatures are doing more damage to research universities today than Congress. That damage will have to be repaired if our great public universities are to retain their world renown. With their myopic view about the value of their universities, state legislatures throughout much of the United States are disinvesting in higher education. This trend must be reversed or the result will be catastrophic for many of our nation's greatest universities. The federal government must create incentives for states to take actions to support the transmission and creation of knowl-

edge in a national system in which the core funding of higher learning remains remarkably uneven and decentralized. Correlatively, states that dis-
invest in their systems of higher education should be at risk of losing some
of their federal student and research support. In fact, if the quality of these
institutions declines, their competitiveness for federal peer-reviewed grants
will also fall, leading to fewer federal grants and contracts for research
going to these universities. This result could cause local economies to suffer in an increasingly severe downward spiral.

As the Obama administration looks toward enhancing the quality of
the nation's great universities, it may find that translating values and ideals
into action is not always easy. Some policies related to higher education
need immediate attention; changes in these areas would strengthen our
universities for the better almost immediately while further solidifying
their international reputations. It's imperative that President Obama and
Congress rethink our immigration policies as they relate to students and
scholars. Visa problems continue to drive many talented foreign students
and researchers away from American universities and industry. There are
other nations that would happily become the place of choice for this talent.
The United States was once viewed as the most hospitable of nations, but
it is losing that reputation. Historically, a substantial majority of foreign
Ph.D.s have remained in the United States and worked at our universities, at industrial laboratories, or at new start-up companies. However, a
March 2009 survey of 1,957 foreign students by researchers at Duke,
Berkeley, and Harvard found that only 6 percent of the students from
India, 10 percent of those from China, and 15 percent of the European
students wanted to stay in the United States, although a majority of the
Asian students and about 40 percent of Europeans expressed a desire to re-
main for a few years after graduation if they had the choice.[46]

Some of this represents a natural urge to return to be with family and
friends, but that impulse is not new. Students surveyed in 2009, for the
most part, developed more positive views of Americans while studying in
the United States than they had anticipated.[47] They also gave very high
grades to the quality of American education compared with higher education in their home country. But more than 70 percent of these foreign
students—from every part of the world—were worried about whether they
would be able to obtain work visas and jobs in their fields. More than half
of the Chinese students in the United States now feel that their best job

opportunities will be in China rather than in the United States. This is true for those who are entrepreneurial and hope to start their own businesses. The Obama administration can and should reverse this pattern. Moreover, it can alter immigration policy to make it easier for very talented foreign students, scholars, and their families to enter the United States to study and work here.

Perverse disincentives built into national security legislation since 9/11 have not only harmed our universities but also hindered the national effort to reduce the very real threat of terrorism. There is no reason for the FBI to have such close oversight of the use of select agents—even if universities need to increase their own internal controls over the use and abuse of lethal toxins and bacteria used in research. There is no reason for qualified students from Iran or Cuba who have never been linked to any subversive activity to be denied access to research laboratories using select agents. The government ought to be facilitating rather than impeding immunological research that promises great returns in the form of vaccines and other methods of dealing with potentially lethal and pandemic-causing agents. The federal government needs to work with the National Academies to develop policies that do not undermine the essential value of open communication. Self-policing among scholars and scientists should be explored.

Beyond reasserting the integrity of scientific research and its results, the Obama administration can influence the way the White House, Congress, the courts, and the American people understand the contributions of scientific research. Obama could give his science adviser a role similar to that of his key economic advisers. The administration could help the public differentiate between research results about which there is virtual consensus—such as the scientific agreement about the role that we play in increasing global warming—and the much larger body of published research that represents initial findings or results at the frontiers of science that are still deeply contested in the scientific community—such as the role of specific kinds of foods in *causing* cancer.

President Obama needs to ask Congress to reverse the perverse effects of the antiterrorism legislation of the Bush years, and he should use his executive powers to reverse other prior actions that have had detrimental effects on our universities with little apparent gain for national security. Congress should free our nation's libraries from surveillance and our universities from the disincentives for creative science that were built into the USA Patriot Act and other legislation passed after the 9/11 terrorist attacks. It must carry through on its pledge to take politics out of science. The national science advisers and the various bodies that are in place to advise the federal government, such as the National Academy of Sciences and the National Research Council, must occupy a place of prominence at the table equivalent to that held by the national economic policy adviser. By aggressively promoting the significance of science and technology to our welfare, President Obama can combat the dangerous anti-intellectualism and the anti-science movement in the nation.

Our universities cannot flourish without an effort to expand the opportunities for K–12 students from every social and economic background to participate in the creation of new knowledge. This will require a major initiative to improve the quality of the teachers who are entering the teaching profession. Educational policy cannot only be about "no child left behind." It also must create opportunities for brilliant children to forge ahead. Leaders of the Democratic Party in Congress need to generate incentives for states to provide increased funding for student financial aid and for research by creating matching programs as part of federal support for higher education and research.

Finally, Obama's science policy leaders will need to develop federal policies that reduce the opportunities for conflicts of interest to arise at our universities. Such policies already exist, but they must be sharpened to prevent inappropriate relationships from forming between the sponsors of research and entrepreneurs at our universities. The potential for the commercialization of ideas has reached a point where we can no longer assume that the power of norms will constrain bad behavior within the faculty and administration of our universities. And with the potential for patenting so much basic knowledge that will be developed in the future, the president and others need to lead a national debate within the scientific and academic communities about what ideas and discoveries should and should not be patentable.

The Obama administration would do well to take a close look at the remarkable underfunding of the humanities and the arts that has taken place historically. The discrepancy between the growth of federal investments in the sciences and the humanities is appalling. The humanities are essential to our understanding of other languages and cultures, of the values we hold, and of the moral arguments we make. In a world that increasingly depends on such knowledge for both our economic welfare in a globalized world and our national security, the absence of significant programs to improve our grasp of it represents nothing short of a national disaster. The Obama administration should consider an effort to double or triple the budget of the National Endowment for the Humanities every five to seven years until the total is respectable. It should set national priorities for the acquisition of language skills and should support research projects linked to understanding the cultures (and subcultures) and literatures of less-developed and emerging nations. We cannot assume that because the *lingua franca* is increasingly English we do not need to understand foreign languages or different cultural perspectives. The world turns out not to be so flat and uniform as some would like us to think.

In short, if we are to escape the tangle of policymaking that has distracted us from the central purposes of our universities for much of the past decade, President Obama will need to act forcefully and purposefully to articulate an agenda to sustain and improve our great seats of learning and discovery. Acting in concert with both the Congress and state legislatures, he can enact new legislation that unleashes the existing reserve potential at our great universities and help them to create social structures and mechanisms that assure their superior performance into the distant future. Although it is too early in Barack Obama's administration to know if he will be able to accomplish these goals, it is certainly not too early for him to get started.

The moment has come to take stock of what this nation has achieved in its greatest institutions of higher learning and what is required to further enhance them and protect them from attack and decline. I have focused attention on the historical roots of our preeminence in higher education and the elements that are required for discovery and innovation in any university system. Our universities have risen to the top in a remarkably short period of time. The achievements of our greatest universities have been honored throughout the world, and the best possible measure of our distinction lies in the numbers of extremely talented people, both students and faculty members, who covet positions at these institutions and wish to stay at them when offered the opportunity. There remain many opportunities for building on our current position, particularly in those public and private institutions that have the potential for combining great research with exceptional teaching for students of every social group in the nation and the world, regardless of background or personal attributes. The goal of meritocracy is within reach.

The potential for research discoveries in our universities seems limitless. We have before us the opportunity to change the world through the development of new knowledge. There is a national need to retain our preeminent position in the world of learning, discovery, and application, but we do not have to be the sole occupants at the top of the food chain of knowledge. We can share excellence and collaborate with those who will partner with us in expanding our knowledge in basic and useful ways. We can find grounds of common interest in the production of useful knowledge as well. But if we lose our position among the greatest educational institutions in the world, and allow ourselves to be replaced by others, the consequences, known and as yet unknown, are apt to be substantial for our national welfare.

For there can be little doubt that the United States has experienced unparalleled prosperity and improved public health, and that it has helped to serve the needs of other nations, largely because of the growth of all types of knowledge that has come from America's great universities. We should not fear the rise of great universities in other nations, or that they will replace ours as the source of extraordinary discoveries—at least not for the foreseeable future. Rather, we should fear that, as a society, we might allow anti-intellectual forces, which seem always to loom in the background of American society, to come forward and successfully attack the structure and values of our institutions of higher learning. We have survived several such attacks in the past, but if this should happen again, and the public should fail to recognize what is at stake and to repel these attacks, then the tapestry of knowledge woven so carefully over the past century could easily unravel. Beyond preventive medicine, we need positive policies regarding our universities, strong investments in the production of new knowledge and the training of young people, if we are to sustain and increase the rate of knowledge growth. Surely we are capable of this, and capable of making many new discoveries that will add to our knowledge, to our understanding of the world, and to our health and well-being in the years ahead.

But it is our choice—the choice of all Americans. Will the people of the United States choose to have great engines of innovation and discovery?

Will they appreciate that great scholarship in the arts, in the humanities, and in the social sciences contributes to our national welfare? And will they be willing to allocate the resources necessary for maintaining and expanding the number of the nation's great universities? The cost of one *Nimitz*-type aircraft carrier with a fifty-year life expectancy is roughly $4.5 billion; the annual operating expenses for one carrier amount to approximately $160 million. In 2008, the Pentagon budget was about $625 billion; roughly $150 billion was spent on the wars in Iraq and Afghanistan. The total National Institutes of Health budget for 2008 was about $29.5 billion, with no proposed increase for 2009; the budget of the National Science Foundation was about $6 billion, with about $5 billion of that amount allocated for research.

Are we willing to trade some of the resources that go into defense and other types of spending to train teachers who will teach physics or chemistry to our young people? Do we think it is important to improve our scientific infrastructure? To fund laboratories for some of the most able scientists, engineers, and scholars in the world? Are we willing to make the choices that are necessary to keep our great American universities the best in the world? These are the choices—and perhaps it is the test—that we face.

Acknowledgments

My understanding of the great American research university is a result of personal experience, my own scholarly background prior to becoming Columbia University's chief academic officer, and the many exchanges I've had with leaders of American universities, faculty members, students, and friends. It would be impossible to express my appreciation to all of these people, some of whom I consider close friends and others whom I know only as acquaintances but who nonetheless have influenced my thinking. I would, however, like to acknowledge many individuals and groups of people who have not only influenced my views about universities but who have also been generous enough to comment on, criticize, and raise questions about various features of this book during its gestation period.

Some of my ideas about universities come from decades of studying and writing about the sociology of science—particularly science at major universities—and from my training in empirical social research. So I begin with my gifted teachers and subsequent colleagues at Columbia, Robert K. Merton and Paul F. Lazarsfeld, whose work and encouragement set me on a path that led in a circuitous way to this book. The father of the sociology of science, Merton profoundly influenced my views about social systems, science, and universities, as will be apparent to those familiar with his extraordinarily original work. Lazarsfeld taught me more about causal thinking and empirical research than anyone else, and he engendered in me a deep sense of skepticism about claims to fact and truth. My colleague and friend Harriet Zuckerman, now at the Andrew W. Mellon Foundation, has been an intellectual partner in developing the sociology of science. Together we spent hundreds, if not thousands, of hours studying the place of women in the academic science community. The fruits of that collaboration are embedded in this book. Other exceptional historians of science, including Gerald Holton and Daniel Kevles, have taught me much about the way knowledge grows and about the compatibility of science and the humanities in a university. They have influenced my sense of the university as a web of interconnected conversations and relationships.

My closest collaborator over the years has been my brother, Stephen Cole, a distinguished professor of sociology at the State University of New York at Stony

Brook. Unwaveringly committed to discovering facts and truth no matter where they might lead him, he has had the courage to stand up against received wisdom, to challenge it, and, if necessary, to suffer the consequences of expressing unpopular views. Steve is also a demanding critic who influenced this book indirectly through many years of scholarly collaboration and directly through pithy analysis of an early draft and invaluable comments on how the book's arguments might be strengthened.

I am indebted to other academics as well, including my close friends Jon Elster, Richard Shweder, and the late Edward Said, who, along with many others, have been willing to take on intellectual orthodoxies. Their intellectual courage has helped me better understand the core value of academic freedom and free inquiry at our most distinguished universities.

Scores of faculty members, students, and academic administrators at Columbia and elsewhere have listened to the arguments in this book and provided me with useful comments and criticism as I worked on the manuscript. Some have been unusually generous with their time, reading and commenting on portions or the entire book or offering feedback on lectures and essays that have been the basis for parts of the book. In particular I would like to thank Geoffrey Stone, Jon Elster, Akeel Bilgrami, Thomas Goldstein, David Cohen, and Peter Bearman. I have learned a great deal about foreign universities from conversations with Antoine Compagnon, David Freedberg, Jean Tirol, and Diego Gambetta, as well as from conversations with leaders of many of the great universities around the world.

Over the years I have been interested in the qualities of mind and temperament that are associated with successful academic leadership. I have worked at Columbia with three extremely talented presidents, and they all possessed very different styles of leadership: Michael Sovern, George Rupp, and Lee Bollinger. I want to thank each of them for their support and their confidence in my ability to steer the academic ship for so many years. The leaders of the Columbia University Board of Trustees while I was provost deserve my thanks for their willingness to learn about all aspects of university life without trying to micromanage it. These leaders include the chairs of the board while I was provost: G. G. Michelson, Lionel Pincus, Jerry Speyer, Stephen Friedman, and David Stern.

Many of my academic administrative colleagues while I was provost helped to shape my thinking about innovation and discovery, including Michael Crow and David Cohen, with whom I worked very closely. Although not a Columbian, the chancellor of the City University of New York, Matthew Goldstein, helped to shape my ideas about the ideal of a university that provides both access and excellence. No one more fully embodies the qualities of leadership I most admire than my colleague and friend Herbert Pardes, the head of the health sciences at Columbia when I was provost, and more recently, the president and CEO of New York Presbyterian Hospital. Herb's ability to solve thorny and complex problems, in combination with his deep humanity, intelligence, range of interests, and willingness to take prudent risks—to say nothing of his indefatigable energy, good humor, and ability to get to the theater just on time—have taught me more than he can imagine about what it takes to be a visionary and successful academic leader.

I also want to thank the scores of other university presidents and provosts whom I have gotten to know and who have influenced my thinking about research universities. I particularly appreciate the responses of forty-four of the fifty leaders of world-class universities to my request for their Top Ten list of influential discoveries made at their universities. From 1989 to 2003 a group of provosts from nine private universities met twice a year, without an agenda, to discuss common problems. Those informal conversations proved invaluable in helping me to understand and tackle large university problems. Some of them subsequently became presidents of great universities themselves. Their leadership and ideas have influenced this book. I would like to thank Geoffrey Stone (University of Chicago), Gerhard Casper (University of Chicago and Stanford University), Robert A. Brown (MIT and Boston University), Jerry Ostriker (Princeton University), Amy Gutmann (Princeton University and the University of Pennsylvania), Alison Richard (Yale University and Cambridge University), John Etchemendy (Stanford University), Don Randel (Cornell University and University of Chicago), Biddy Martin (Cornell University and University of Wisconsin at Madison), and Mark Wrighton (MIT and University of Washington, St. Louis).

In addition to the many books written by university presidents and provosts in the first half of the twentieth century, whose work I have cited, a subset of more recent books about universities by friends and acquaintances holding high academic positions has influenced my understanding of institutions of higher learning and the challenges they face. Among the most influential of these scholars are: Richard C. Atkinson (University of California), William G. Bowen (Princeton University and the Andrew J. Mellon Foundation), Henry Rosovsky (Harvard University), Neil L. Rudenstine (Harvard University), Harold T. Shapiro (Princeton University), Charles M. Vest (MIT), Derek Bok (Harvard University), Frank T. Rhodes (Cornell University), the late Martin Meyerson (University of Pennsylvania), Vartan Gregorian, and A. Bartlett Giamatti (Yale University).

I want to thank my literary agent, Kathy Robbins, for her belief in the importance of this project as well as for her ideas about how to focus the subject for my intended audience. Peter Osnos, the founder and editor-at-large of PublicAffairs, has understood with exceptional clarity the message that I wanted to send to people around the world who harbor an interest in the essential features of truly distinguished universities. He has applied his brilliant analytic and editorial skills throughout the publishing process to sharpen the focus of the manuscript. Susan Weinberg, publisher of PublicAffairs, has given me continuing encouragement and patient support, for which I am grateful. I have benefited enormously as well from the keen analytic editorial advice that I've received through PublicAffairs and want to thank Mindy Werner and Kathy Streckfus for their exceptional work. Their intelligent queries and suggestions helped to shape the structure of the manuscript and helped me cut a very long initial draft. For her intelligence and youthful wisdom, I thank Lindsay Jones, who has kept a keen eye on the manuscript and helped to steer it through the editorial process, as has Meredith Smith during its final stages.

I have been fortunate to have had two extraordinarily talented young assistants, Esther Shin and Sarah Hospelhorn, who have helped me to collect data and materials for the book, and who have been of immeasurable assistance in using new media technology to locate information about discoveries from sources on the web. Sarah designed the website about university discoveries that supplements this book. I surely could not have created the site without her. Thanks are in order to Gabriel Bach for his astute suggestions about the organization and appearance of the site.

Over the past four decades, I have received generous support for much of my research from foundations and federal funding agencies, but none has been as important as the funding I received from the National Science Foundation. The NSF is a national treasure that has been instrumental in supporting university research. As anyone who has read this book will realize, it is one of the most important instruments of discovery and innovation in the United States. I owe much to the leaders of the NSF over the years and to the many program directors who ran the peer review process for NSF grant support.

I am also deeply grateful to my close nonacademic friends who have listened to my stories and have heard ad nauseam about this or that university discovery. There are too many to mention individually, but I so appreciate the way these friends have tolerated me over the years and have helped me—through discussions both serious and playful—to retain some semblance of sanity during the book's creation. I want to thank Joan Lewis, who has always been there when I've needed her. It saddens me that Sylvia Cole did not live to see the fruits of our many conversations. My deepest thanks and love go to Daniel, Nick, Susanna "Nonnie," Gabe, and Lydia, who lived the experience of this book over and over again during the innumerable dinner conversations at our apartment on Manhattan's Upper West Side, on Martha's Vineyard, and elsewhere. Finally, there is no one more important than my wife, Joanna. She has been responsible for much of what is most wonderful in my life—and she lets me know when I have the right to remain silent or when I am well enough to sit up and take criticism.

Appendix A:
Top-Ranked American Research Universities
(according to 2008 study by Shanghai Jiao Tong University Institute for Higher Education)

Institution[a]	World Rank	National Rank	Member of the Association of American Universities[b]?
Harvard Univ.	1	1	yes
Stanford Univ.	2	2	yes
Univ. California–Berkeley	3	3	yes
Massachusetts Inst. Tech. (MIT)	5	4	yes
California Inst. Tech.	6	5	yes
Columbia Univ.	7	6	yes
Princeton Univ.	8	7	yes
Univ. Chicago	9	8	yes
Yale Univ.	11	9	yes
Cornell Univ.	12	10	yes
Univ. California–Los Angeles	13	11	yes
Univ. California–San Diego	14	12	yes
Univ. Pennsylvania	15	13	yes
Univ. Washington–Seattle	16	14	yes
Univ. Wisconsin–Madison	17	15	yes
Univ. California - San Francisco	18	16	no
Johns Hopkins Univ.	20	17	yes
Univ. Michigan–Ann Arbor	21	18	yes
Univ. Illinois–Urbana Champaign	26	19	yes
Univ. Minnesota–Twin Cities	28	20	yes
Washington Univ.–St. Louis	29	21	yes
Northwestern Univ.	30	22	yes
New York Univ.	31	23	yes
Duke Univ.	32	24–25	yes
Rockefeller Univ.	32	24–25	no
Univ. Colorado–Boulder	34	26	yes
Univ. California–Santa Barbara	36	27	yes
Univ. Maryland–College Park	37	28	yes

Institution[a]	World Rank	National Rank	Member of the Association of American Universities[b]?
Univ. North Carolina–Chapel Hill	38	29	yes
Univ. Texas–Austin	39	30	yes
Univ. Texas Southwestern Medical Center	41	31	no
Pennsylvania State Univ.–Univ. Park	42	32–33	yes
Vanderbilt Univ.	42	32–33	yes
Univ. California–Irvine	46	34	yes
Univ. California–Davis	48	35	yes
Univ. Southern California	50	36	yes
Univ. Pittsburgh–Pittsburgh	52	37	yes
Rutgers State Univ.–New Brunswick	54	38	yes
Univ. Florida	58	39	yes
Carnegie Mellon Univ.	62	40–41	yes
Ohio State Univ.–Columbus	62	40–41	yes
Purdue Univ.–West Lafayette	65	42	yes
Brown Univ.	71	43	yes
Univ. Rochester	73	44	yes
Univ. Arizona	77	45	yes
Univ. Utah	79	46	no
Boston Univ.	83	47–49	no
Case Western Reserve Univ.	83	47–49	yes
Michigan State Univ.	83	47–49	yes
Texas A&M Univ.–College Station	88	50	yes
Indiana Univ.–Bloomington	92	51	yes
Arizona State Univ.–Tempe	93	52	no
Univ. Virginia	95	53	yes
Rice Univ.	97	54	yes
Baylor College of Medicine	101–151	55–70	no
Dartmouth College	101–151	55–70	no
Emory Univ.	101–151	55–70	yes
Georgia Inst. Tech.	101–151	55–70	no
Mayo Clinic College of Medicine	101–151	55–70	no
North Carolina State Univ.–Raleigh	101–151	55–70	no
Oregon State Univ.	101–151	55–70	no
Tufts Univ.	101–151	55–70	no
Univ. California–Riverside	101–151	55–70	no
Univ. California–Santa Cruz	101–151	55–70	no
Univ. Georgia	101–151	55–70	no
Univ. Hawaii–Manoa	101–151	55–70	no
Univ. Illinois–Chicago	101–151	55–70	no
Univ. Iowa	101–151	55–70	yes
Univ. Massachusetts–Amherst	101–151	55–70	no
Univ. Massachusetts Medical School	101–151	55–70	no
Colorado State Univ.	152–200	71–90	no
Florida State Univ.	152–200	71–90	no
George Mason Univ.	152–200	71–90	no
Iowa State Univ.	152–200	71–90	yes

Institution[a]	World Rank	National Rank	Member of the Association of American Universities[b]?
Oregon Health & Sciences Univ.	152–200	71–90	no
State Univ. New York–Stony Brook	152–200	71–90	yes
Univ. Alabama–Birmingham	152–200	71–90	no
Univ. Cincinnati–Cincinnati	152–200	71–90	no
Univ. Colorado–Denver	152–200	71–90	no
Univ. Connecticut–Storrs	152–200	71–90	no
Univ. Delaware	152–200	71–90	no
Univ. Maryland–Baltimore	152–200	71–90	no
Univ. Medicine & Dentistry, New Jersey	152–200	71–90	no
Univ. Miami	152–200	71–90	no
Univ. Nebraska–Lincoln	152–200	71–90	yes
Univ. Tennessee–Knoxville	152–200	71–90	no
Univ. Texas Health Science Center–Houston	152–200	71–90	no
Univ. Texas M.D. Anderson Cancer Center	152–200	71–90	no
Virginia Commonwealth Univ.	152–200	71–90	no
Virginia Tech.	152–200	71–90	no
Brandeis Univ.	201–302	91–114	yes
George Washington Univ.	201–302	91–114	no
Georgetown Univ.	201–302	91–114	no
Louisiana State Univ.–Baton Rouge	201–302	91–114	no
Mt. Sinai School of Medicine	201–302	91–114	no
Rensselaer Polytechnic Inst.	201–302	91–114	no
State Univ. New York–Albany	201–302	91–114	no
State Univ. New York–Buffalo	201–302	91–114	yes
Univ. Houston	201–302	91–114	no
Univ. Kansas–Lawrence	201–302	91–114	yes
Univ. Kentucky	201–302	91–114	no
Univ. Missouri–Columbia	201–302	91–114	yes
Univ. New Mexico–Albuquerque	201–302	91–114	no
Univ. Notre Dame	201–302	91–114	no
Univ. Oregon	201–302	91–114	yes
Univ. South Carolina–Columbia	201–302	91–114	no
Univ. South Florida	201–302	91–114	no
Univ. Texas Health Sci. Center–San Antonio	201–302	91–114	no
Univ. Texas Med Branch–Galveston	201–302	91–114	no
Univ. Vermont	201–302	91–114	no
Wake Forest Univ.	201–302	91–114	no
Washington State Univ.–Pullman	201–302	91–114	no
Wayne State Univ.	201–302	91–114	no
Yeshiva Univ.	201–302	91–114	no
Syracuse Univ.[c]	303–401	115–139	yes
Tulane Univ.	303–401	115–139	yes

Source: Data from 2008 study conducted by Shanghai Jiao Tong University, Institute for Higher Education study. The institute has been updating these rankings on an annual basis. See Shanghai Jiao Tong University, "2008 Academic Ranking of World Universities," http://www.arwu.org/ARWU2008.jsp. For a description of the methodology used, see Shanghai Jiao Tong University, "2008 Academic Rankings of World Universities: Ranking Methodology," http://www.arwu.org/Methodology2008.jsp.

Notes: Four Canadian Universities—University of Toronto, University of British Columbia, McGill University, and McMaster University—are represented in the top 100 world rankings, and two others are in the group 101–151. Two of these Canadian universities (University of Toronto and McGill University) are also members of the Association of American Universities.

The Shanghai Jiao Tong study tends to weigh research performance and honorific recognition of faculty members more heavily than other factors. The quality of teaching tends to be downplayed in rankings of this sort because it is difficult to measure. Since it is also easier to measure performance in the sciences and engineering than in the humanities, rankings tend to give greater weight to scientific and engineering research performance than to performance in the humanities. There have been other efforts to rank universities worldwide and in each of these cases there are slightly different criteria for judging quality. It is important not to think of the rankings in terms of fine distinctions. The differences between two universities that are ranked seventh and ninth, for example, may be inconsequential. In addition, within each of these universities there may be significant disparities in the quality of individual departments and schools.

[a]Institutions within the same rank range are listed alphabetically.

[b]The Association of American Universities, established in 1900, is a membership organization that includes 62 of North America's leading research universities, 60 of which are American and 2 of which are Canadian. Of the American universities that are members, 34 are public and 26 are private. There are other distinguished American universities that are not members of the AAU but contribute significantly to the growth of knowledge. This table shows the overlap between AAU membership and the Chinese rankings.

[c]Syracuse University and Tulane University are ranked lower in the world rankings, but are members of the AAU.

Appendix B:
An Online Source of Information About University Discoveries

In researching this book, I collected information about thousands of discoveries, inventions, innovations, devices, concepts, techniques, and tools that were born at great American universities and that have changed our lives and the world in which we live. I considered how to present both the breadth and depth of the fruits of research at these institutions. It was clear that listing hundreds of discoveries would be tedious and that concentrating on only a few would deny readers a sense of the wide range of discoveries that have been made over the past seventy-five years or so. In the end, I decided to create a website that would serve as a point of collection, or a clearinghouse, for university discoveries. The website, http://university-discoveries.com, is intended as a supplement for the material found in this book.

This site culls information about discoveries from a host of different sources, some of which I've mentioned in the body of this book. Many of them come from the universities themselves, which describe on their own websites some of the major products of their research enterprise. Some universities, such as Stanford and MIT, do a terrific job of presenting a sampling of the discoveries that their professors and students have created over time; other distinguished universities do not do justice to the products of their research. Some discoveries found on the website come from sources such as the National Institutes of Health, the National Science Foundation, and the National Academy of Sciences. I've gathered information about innovations and discoveries collected by professional organizations such as the Association of American Universities as well as from organizations that have honored some of the major breakthroughs in science and engineering, including sites such as the Nobel Foundation and the Lasker Foundation.

This is not a systematic catalog of, for example, the most highly cited papers written by university scientists or the best-selling books by humanists. You can find that elsewhere. Nor does the website include the discoveries and innovations that have come from industrial or national laboratories (although there is some overlap, since many of the great scientific industrial labs have made significant contributions to the evolution and development of discoveries at our universities). The sharp focus is on our most distinguished institutions of higher learning.

The information on the site is divided into two basic categories and three subcategories. The major groups are "Discoveries" and "Resources." Within the "Discoveries" section, there are three subcategories: Biological and Biomedical Sciences; Physical Sciences and Engineering; and Social and Behavioral Sciences and Humanities. In each category discoveries can be identified and sorted by the years in which they were made and the institutions where they took place. Very brief descriptions are provided, and, when available, the scientist(s) or scholar(s) who made the discoveries.

The "Resources" section offers additional sources for learning about university discoveries, ranging from the National Science Foundation's Nifty 50 (fifty top NSF-funded inventions, innovations, and discoveries highlighted to celebrate the NSF's fiftieth anniversary in 2000) to university websites that you can link to from the site. I have also provided visitors with "Notable University Links," where you can find out more about the research achievements and ongoing research projects of specific universities. Finally, you will find the top ten picks of the presidents and provosts (and a few deans) of forty-four of the top fifty research universities in the United States as of 2010.

My hope is that this will become an interactive, dynamic website with content that evolves over time. The site will be periodically updated, and viewers will have the opportunity to make comments on the content of the site as well as to suggest additional discoveries that they believe ought to be included.

Notes

Introduction

1. Http://www.hhmi.org/research/investigators/bassler_bio.html. See also Bassler's Princeton University website, http://www.molbio.princeton.edu/index.php?option=content&task=view&id=2, for a description of her laboratory's activities.

2. Http://www.hhmi.org/research/investigators/.

3. The top-ranked American universities in the 2008 Shanghai Jiao Tong University Institute for Higher Education study (Shanghai Jiao Tong University, "2008 Academic Ranking of World Universities," http://www.arwu.org/ARWU2008.jsp) are listed in Appendix A. It makes little difference whether a university is ranked number two or number five. The important point is that among the set of the best, American universities occupy most of the very top positions. This is not to say that there are not some universities in other parts of the world that are equal to the best in the United States. Oxford and Cambridge universities are such examples. And there may be true excellence in some areas of study in universities that are less than exceptional overall.

An increasing number of organizations have gone into the business of ranking universities. Each uses slightly different criteria. The London Times Higher Education rankings, which in 2007 placed less emphasis on research discoveries and more on whether employers said they would want to hire students from these universities, and the extent to which they had an international staff and student body, also put the American universities in a dominant position. Where research discoveries have been the principal focus of the ratings, the American research universities have tended to dominate the top tier. These rankings can be misleading and should not be reified, however. They tend to emphasize scientific achievement and "undervalue" work in the humanities, primarily because it is easier to obtain quantitative measures of excellence in the sciences and engineering.

One must also look at these rankings in terms of the overall picture they present—the predominant presence of American universities in the top 20 or 50—rather than as precise evaluations of standing. There is a tendency to reify small differences in ranks when in fact the difference between a school with a ranking of 6 or 8 may be purely a function of the variables used that are subject to measurement error.

Finally, rankings of the kind I'm referring to often miss nuances, such as the structure of a system of research and teaching in France, where a great number of scientists hold appointments with the Centre National de la Recherche Scientifique (CNRS), the agency in France that supports research. Although these scientists may also hold appointments at French universities, the statistical "value" of their work may be given only a fraction of its total value because of the dual affiliations. In short, I use these rankings because I think they provide a very good picture of the overall landscape of higher learning in the world, but do so with the understanding that there are limits to what such rankings can convey.

4. It remains unclear whether our Chinese hosts fully understood that each of these elements, including academic freedom and free inquiry removed from state control, are necessary conditions for true distinction. I will return to this topic in the final chapter of the book.

5. Besides the United States, England has come closest to creating a model with these elements in place, and it has a significant number of world-class universities because of this. It has a great tradition of undergraduate education that became the basis for part of the American model. But its efforts to expand the number of great research universities within Britain has not been highly successful over the past twenty-five years, and the intrusion of government involvement during that period has not been conducive to excellence. The very well-endowed colleges in Oxford and Cambridge have done well, as have a few of the colleges associated with the University of London. But even the London School of Economics has struggled in the past decade over appropriate financing for its activities, as the government has attempted to base funding on questionable measures of excellence.

6. Yale awarded the first American doctorate in philosophy in 1861. By 1890, only 164 degrees had been conferred. Richard Hofstadter and Walter P. Metzger, *The Development of Academic Freedom in the United States* (New York: Columbia University Press, 1955), 378.

7. "The Carnegie Classification of Institutions of Higher Learning," 2005. See http://www.carnegiefoundation.org/classifications/.

8. In 2005, the Carnegie Foundation for the Advancement of Teaching published a revised list of the most research-intensive American universities. They divided universities into three groups: those with very high research activity, those with high research activity, and others. Ninety-five research universities were classified in the first group. The distribution of research activity is highly skewed even within the most intensive group. The most active members of this group account for a far higher percentage of the total research expenditures and the discoveries that flow from them than the majority in this group. ("Institutions in Research Categories, New and Old," *Chronicle of Higher Education,* March 3, 2006.)

Chapter 1: The Idea of a University

1. Lawrence A. Cremin, *American Education: The Colonial Experience, 1607–1783* (New York: Harper Torchbooks, 1970), 210. See also Harvard University website, http//www.hno.harvard.edu/guide/intro.

2. Yale University website, http:www.yale.edu.

3. Frederick Rudolph, *The American College and University: A History* (New York: Vintage Books, 1962), 32.

4. Richard Hofstadter and Walter P. Metzger, *The Development of Academic Freedom in the United States* (New York: Columbia University Press, 1955), 221. Hofstadter breaks down the denominational affiliations of the colonial colleges as follows: 49 Presbyterian; 34 Methodist; 25 Baptist; 21 Congregationalist; 14 Roman Catholic; 11 Episcopalian; 6 Lutheran; 20 of miscellaneous sects; 21 state institutions; 3 semi-state; and 3 municipal ones (p. 214).

5. Hofstadter and Metzger, *The Development of Academic Freedom,* 214.

6. Clark Kerr, introduction to Abraham Flexner, *Universities: American, English, German* (New Brunswick, N.J.: Transaction, 1994 [1930]).

7. John Henry Newman, *The Idea of a University,* ed. Frank M. Turner (New Haven, Conn.: Yale University Press, 1996), 3. Newman delivered the first five lectures in Dublin in 1852. He worked on these sermons for some time after 1852, however, before they appeared as a collection of essays. Newman founded the Catholic University of Ireland, which evolved into University College, Dublin, Ireland's largest university in 2009 with more than 17,000 students and 1,300 faculty members.

8. Hofstadter and Metzger, *The Development of Academic Freedom,* 374.

9. In contrasting American higher learning with the German universities, the young Henry Wadsworth Longfellow, who studied at Göttingen in 1829, said, "What has heretofore been the idea of the University with us? The answer is a simple one: Two or three large brick buildings, with a chapel, and a President to pray in it." In contrast, Longfellow found in Göttingen the idea "of collecting together professors in whom the spirit is moved—who were well enough known to attract students to themselves, and . . . capable of teaching them something they did not know before." In speaking of the University of Berlin after his travels there in 1884, Nicholas Murray Butler, president of Columbia University, said that it "left an ineffaceable impression of what scholarship meant, of what a university was and what a long road higher education in America had to travel before it could hope to reach a place of equal elevation." A generation earlier, Columbia's distinguished political scientist John W. Burgess "argued that the college was an educational anomaly, unable to become a university and unwilling to become a *Gymnasium;* and that therefore it should cease to exist."

10. Andrew Dickson White, *Autobiography of Andrew Dickson White*, 2d ed. (New York: The Century, 1922 [1904]), 1:291, cited in Hofstadter and Metzger, *The Development of Academic Freedom*, 375.

11. Quoted in Hofstadter and Metzger, *The Development of Academic Freedom*, 376.

12. Quoted in Abraham Flexner, *Daniel Coit Gilman* (New York: Harcourt, Brace, 1946), 54–55.

13. Flexner, *Gilman*, pp. 5–12.

14. Roger L. Geiger, *To Advance Knowledge: The Growth of American Research Universities, 1900–1940* (Oxford: Oxford University Press, 1986), 8–13.

15. Edward Shils, "The Order of Learning in the United States: The Ascendancy of the University," in Alexandra Oleson and John Voss, eds., *The Organization of Knowledge in Modern America, 1860–1920* (Baltimore: Johns Hopkins University Press, 1980), 28.

16. Ibid., 14.

17. Hofstadter and Metzger, *The Development of Academic Freedom*, 377.

18. John C. French, *A History of the University Founded by Johns Hopkins* (Baltimore: Johns Hopkins Press, 1946), 41ff.

19. Flexner, *Gilman*, 105–106.

20. Quoted in Geiger, *To Advance Knowledge*, 8.

21. Quoted in Richard Hofstadter, *Social Darwinism in American Thought* (New York: Beacon, 1955), 45. Stephen Jay Gould brilliantly discusses social Darwinism and the vogue of scientism in nineteenth-century America in his *The Mismeasure of Man*, rev. and exp. ed. (New York: W. W. Norton, 1996).

22. Ibid.

23. Daniel J. Kevles, *The Physicists: The History of a Scientific Community in Modern America* (New York: Vintage Books, 1979), 68.

24. Ibid., 69.

25. Rudolph, *The American College and University*, 251–252.

26. Eliot pioneered many innovative changes at Harvard, introducing a novel elective system that allowed undergraduates to choose among a variety of courses of study. In the 1870s he revolutionized the curriculum of its law school by bringing in as dean Christopher Columbus Langdell, a scholarly New York lawyer, in the hope that he would shake up the faculty and develop a new method for studying law—the case method, which is still in use today. A chemist by training, Eliot also had traveled extensively in Europe with an eye toward reviewing its educational systems. He was responsible for the expansion of Harvard's graduate schools, for the growth in its facilities for research, and for restructuring Harvard around schools, including professional schools and academic departments. His efforts led to major improvements in the quality of higher learning. He expanded Harvard's reach beyond New England and became a

major public figure in the Progressive movement in the early twentieth century. When Eliot handed over the presidential reins to Lawrence Lowell in 1909, Harvard actually returned, at least in part, to its roots. Lowell built undergraduate houses, emphasized changes in curricular content, and focused on the quality of student life. But the work of Eliot was not to be undone. There are many useful sources for the history of Harvard University during this time. One of Eliot's friends and admirers was Henry James. His biography *Charles W. Eliot, President of Harvard University*, 2 vols. (Cambridge, Mass.: AMS Press, 1930), is useful and very Jamesian. See also Samuel Eliot Morrison's *Three Centuries of Harvard: 1636–1936* (Cambridge: Harvard University Press, 1936).

27. Rudolph, *The American College and University*, 245.

28. Ibid.

29. Gould, *The Mismeasure of Man*, 82–83.

30. As quoted in Nicolas Lemann, *The Big Test: The Secret History of American Meritocracy* (New York: Farrar, Strauss and Giroux, 1999), 69.

31. Daniel J. Kevles, "Testing the Army's Intelligence: Psychologists and the Military in World War I," *Journal of American History* 55 (1968): 561–581. Two other sources discuss the testing movement in instructive ways: Gould, *The Mismeasure of Man*, and Lemann, *The Big Test*.

32. For example, when elite private universities, such as Harvard and Columbia, saw the proportion of Jews swell to about 20 percent of the college's student body in the second decade of the twentieth century, President Butler at Columbia brought in Edward Thorndike and his "test for mental alertness" in an effort to solve "the Jewish problem." The content of Thorndike's test, hardly measuring some innate trait, was clearly culturally dependent. In fact, the early versions of the test were biased toward those who came from the Midwest, such as Thorndike himself, rather than toward those who were raised on the Lower East Side of Manhattan. One section of the test asked, "What joint is situated between the transmission and the differentials of an auto?" and "What is the name for the pointed end of an anvil?"—hardly the stuff that immigrant kids were absorbing in their childhoods. When the use of these tests failed to hold down the number of Jewish students to the level desired by university leaders, formal admissions applications were introduced that required applicants to give information about their family background and religious affiliation. And if this failed to do the trick, school principals were asked to assess their applicants' "leadership qualities and social skills." Eventually, the colleges shaved the number of Jewish students down to levels they could live with—hardly the finest moment in the history of the admissions processes of these great institutions. As quoted in Rosalind Rosenberg, *Changing the Subject: How the Women of Columbia Shaped the Way We Think About Sex and Politics* (New York: Columbia University Press, 2004.) Also see Michael Rosenthal, *Nicholas Miraculous: The Amazing Career of the Redoubtable Dr. Nicholas Murray Butler* (New York: Farrar, Straus and Giroux, 2006), 332–343.

33. Eric Kandel, "Thomas Hunt Morgan at Columbia University: Genes, Chromosomes, and the Origins of Modern Biology," http://www.columbia.edu/cu/alumni/Magazine/Legacies/Morgan/index.html.

34. Ibid.

35. Ibid.

36. A. H. Sturtevant, "Thomas Hunt Morgan: Biographical Memoir," *National Academy of Sciences* 33 (1959): 295, quoted in Kandel, "Morgan."

37. From an interview conducted by Harriet A. Zuckerman and reported in her book *Scientific Elite: Nobel Laureates in the United States* (New York: Free Press, 1977), 141–143.

38. Rudolph, *The American College and University*, 249, as quoted in Frank H. T. Rhodes, *The Creation of the Future: The Role of the American University* (Ithaca, N.Y.: Cornell University Press, 2002), 5.

39. The charters for the Agricultural College of the State of Michigan (later Michigan State University) and Pennsylvania State University became the models for the Morrill Act of 1862.

40. Rudolph, *The American College and University*, 249.

41. Rhodes, *The Creation of the Future*, 5.

42. Ibid., 6.

43. Ibid. Geiger's two volumes on research universities are an excellent source for detailed information about their growth.

44. Ron Chernow, *The Titan: The Life of John D. Rockefeller, Sr.* (New York: Random House, 1998), 308.

45. Geiger, *To Advance Knowledge*, 10–11.

46. Chernow, *The Titan*, 318.

47. Joseph Ben-David, *The Scientist's Role in Society: A Comparative Study* (Chicago: University of Chicago Press, 1971).

48. The next five included Wisconsin, Pennsylvania, Stanford, Princeton, and New York University. The fractions represent professors who are retired or give only part of their time to the university. See J. McKeen Cattell, ed., *American Men of Science: A Biographical Dictionary*, 2d ed. (New York: Science Press, 1910), 560.

49. Edwin E. Slosson, *Great American Universities* (New York: Macmillan, 1910), ix, x.

50. Clark University, established in 1887, was the first all-graduate university in the United States. Even Hopkins had undergraduates. Clark had an illustrious early history. Its first president, G. Stanley Hall, was the first psychology Ph.D. in the nation (studying under William James at Harvard) and founded the American Psychological Association. Clark became quite well known as the host for Sigmund Freud and Carl Jung's first major lectures in the United States in 1909. And in 1907, the physicist A. A. Michelson, a Clark professor, became the first American to win a Nobel Prize in the sciences. Yet Michelson was no longer at Clark by 1907: In 1892 he had become the first chairman of the physics department at the newly created University of Chicago, recruited away by Harper in his raid on Clark.

51. Geiger, *To Advance Knowledge*, Appendix D, 276–277.

52. The size of these endowments fluctuates over time, and there have been some sharp declines in these numbers since the financial fallout of 2008, but the overall growth has taken an exponential form. Despite the 2008–2009 declines in these endowments, the *relative* differences remain much the same.

53. Quoted by Kerr, introduction to Flexner, *Universities*, xix.

54. Clark Kerr, *The Uses of the University*, 5th ed. (Cambridge: Harvard University Press, 2001), 4.

55. Ibid.

56. Andrew H. Beck, "The Flexner Report and the Standardization of American Medical Education," *Student JAMA*, http://jama.ama-assnorg/cgi/content/full/291/17/2139.

57. Ibid.

58. Ibid., 5.

59. Kerr, *The Uses of the University*, 14, 15.

60. Thorstein Veblen, *The Higher Learning in America: A Memorandum on the Conduct of Universities by Business Men* (New Brunswick, N.J.: Transaction, 1993 [1918]), 12–14.

61. Ibid., 177.

62. Flexner, *Universities*, 178–179.

63. Ibid., 177.

64. Ibid., 23–24.

65. Ibid., 30.

66. William Howard Taft and Theodore Roosevelt (who broke with the Republicans, formed the Bull Moose Party, and ran for president as a Progressive Party candidate) divided the Republican vote.

67. Michael Rosenthal, *Nicholas Miraculous: The Amazing Career of the Redoubtable Dr. Nicholas Murray Butler* (New York: Farrar, Straus, and Giroux, 2006), 156–159.

68. Voluntary academic societies have ancient origins. In Europe they began to take on their modern form with the establishment by Cardinal Richelieu of the French Academy in 1635 and in the creation of the Royal Society in England in 1660. In the United States, Benjamin Franklin founded the American Philosophical Society in 1743 in Philadelphia for the advancement of practical knowledge. John Adams, concerned that Boston might lose prestige to Philadelphia, convinced the Massachusetts General Court to charter the American Academy of Arts and Sciences in 1780. These societies covered many areas of knowledge and scholarship. They were not yet linked to the highly specialized knowledge that would begin to emerge in the later part of the nineteenth century with the creation of numerous separate disciplines in the sciences and humanities. Nonetheless, it was Henry Oldenberg, one of the two secretaries of the Royal Society in 1664, who set in motion the creation of a system of experts judging the quality and publishability of submitted scientific articles, created the role of the peer reviewer, and began the formal process of institutionalizing a reward system based on establishing intellectual priority for publication in scientific journals.

69. Nicholas Murray Butler, *The Rise of a University*, vol. 2, *The University in Action* (New York: Columbia University Press, 1937), 44–45.

70. Henry James, *Charles W. Eliot* (New York: Houghton Mifflin, 1930), 2:12, quoted in Geiger, *To Advance Knowledge*, 35.

71. A. Bartlett Giamatti, *A Free and Ordered Space: The Real World of the University* (New York: W. W. Norton, 1988), 17.

Chapter 2: Coming of Age in Tumultuous Times

1. Louis Menand, *The Metaphysical Club: A Story of Ideas in America* (New York: Farrar, Straus and Giroux, 2001), x.

2. Walter P. Metzger, "Origins of the Association: An Anniversary Address," *AAUP Bulletin*, Summer 1965, 229.

3. Geoffrey Stone, *Perilous Times: Free Speech in Wartime from the Sedition Act of 1798 to the War on Terrorism* (New York: W. W. Norton, 2004), 151–152.

4. George Creel, "Public Opinion in War Time," *Annals of the American Academy of Political and Social Science* 78 (1918): 185–186, quoted in Stone, *Perilous Times*, 589, n27.

5. Harry N. Scheiber, *The Wilson Administration and Civil Liberties: 1917–1921* (Ithaca, N.Y.: Cornell University Press, 1960), 16.

6. Alan Brinkley, "Civil Liberties in Times of Crisis," *Bulletin of the American Academy of Arts and Sciences*, Winter 2006, 26–29.

7. *Schenck v. United States*, 249 U.S. 47 (1919); *Frohwerk v. United States*, 249 U.S. 204 (1919); *Debs v. United States*, 249 U.S. 211 (1919). The "bad tendency" doctrine diverged from Judge Learned Hand's more prescient theory in *Masses Publishing Co. v. Patten*, 244 F. 535 (S.D.N.Y., 1917), in which Hand tied the constitutionality of the speech to the specific content of speech rather than to the intent of the speaker or the consequences of the speech. The *Schenck* case, in which the defendants had been charged with trying to obstruct the draft through the circulation of pamphlets to men who had been recruited and called up for military service, was the first major Supreme Court free-speech decision. In *Schenck*, decided after the 1919 armistice had been signed, the Court supported the government's position toward dissent. Justice Holmes, as a member of a conservative Court, wrote the majority opinion.

8. See Thomas L. Haskell, "Justifying the Rights of Academic Freedom," in Louis Menand, ed., *The Future of Academic Freedom* (Chicago: University of Chicago Press, 1996), 43–90, esp. 48–53 on the Ross case.

9. In *Lochner v. New York*, 198 U.S. 45 (1905), the Supreme Court found unconstitutional a New York state law that said that no employee shall "work in a biscuit, bread or cake bakery or confectionary establishment more than sixty hours in any one week, or more than ten hours in any one day." *Lochner* is one of the most controversial decisions in the history of the Court. Four justices, including Justice Holmes, dissented, finding that the Court's majority upheld a laissez-faire economic theory that a large majority of the nation's citizens rejected. Legal scholars have argued that the "liberty of contract" that the majority defended in *Lochner* is not in the "liberty" protected in the due process clause of the Constitution. And it would certainly be the case that legislation that reinforces market forces without constraints is itself a product of social choices.

10. Nicholas Murray Butler, *Columbia Alumni News* 7 (July 1917): 883.

11. There are many sources of this well-known incident. For one, see Michael Rosenthal, *Nicholas Miraculous: The Amazing Career of the Redoubtable Dr. Nicholas Murray Butler* (New York: Farrar, Straus and Giroux, 2006), 225–239. The firings and resignations at Columbia led directly to Beard, Dewey, and others founding the New School for Social Research.

12. Although Dewey and Lovejoy tried to redefine the rules of engagement between the faculty and the university administrative authorities, as crafters of principles of academic freedom and free inquiry neither supported the hiring of Communist Party members. They believed that the allegiance of Communist Party members to the dogma and discipline of the party and its goals would lead them to undermine free inquiry.

13. Richard Hofstadter and Walter P. Metzger, *The Development of Academic Freedom in the United States* (New York: Columbia University Press, 1955), 468.

14. Brinkley, "Civil Liberties," pp. xi, xii

15. Richard Hofstadter, *The Age of Reform: From Bryan to F.D.R.* (New York: Vintage Books, 1955), 153–154.

16. Bernard Barber, "Some Problems in the Sociology of Professions," *Daedalus* 92 (Fall 1963): 669–688.

17. Daniel T. Rodgers, "In Search of Progressivism," *Reviews in American History* 10 (December 1982): 123. Rodgers focused on three clusters of ideas upon which Progressives drew. He noted, "Of the languages, antimonopolism was the oldest, the most peculiarly American, and, through the first decade of the century, the strongest of the three" (p. 123). "The second cluster of ideas from which the progressives drew—the language of social bonds—was more specific to the Progressive years, and at the same time much less peculiarly American. . . . The most common explanations most Americans gave to political, economic, and social questions at the end of the century were couched in terms of largely autonomous individuals: poverty and success were said to hinge on character; governance was a matter of good men and official honesty. Part of what occurred in the Progressive era was a concerted assault on all of these assumptions, and, in some measure, an assault on the idea of individualism itself." It had social and political dimensions "in economic terms," Rodgers said. "It took the form of a newly intense sympathy with what now seemed the innocent casualties of industrialism (women and child workers, the victims of industrial accidents, the involuntarily unemployed), and a keen desire for industrial peace and cooperation" (pp. 124–125). Furthermore, he said, "The last of the three clusters of ideas to arrive . . . was the one we associate with efficiency, rationalization, and social engineering. . . . Like the rhetoric of social bonds, the rhetoric of social efficiency was a transatlantic language. Large pieces of it could be picked up in the scientific laboratories through which a good number of the progressives moved. . . . But clearly it was the merger of the prestige of science and the prestige of the

well-organized business firm and faculty that gave the metaphor of system its tremendous twentieth-century potency—and it was presumably for this reason that the metaphor flourished more exuberantly in the United States, along with industrial capitalism itself, than anywhere else" (p. 126).

18. Daniel T. Rodgers, *Atlantic Crossing: Social Politics in a Progressive Age* (Cambridge: Belknap Press of Harvard University Press, 1998), 5.

19. Olivier Zunz, *Why the American Century?* (Chicago: University of Chicago Press, 1998).

20. Ibid., xi

21. Ibid., xi–xii.

22. Claudia Goldin and Lawrence F. Katz, *The Race Between Education and Technology* (Cambridge: Harvard University Press, 2008), 1–8.

23. Booth was an industrialist, not a social scientist. He had inherited a shipping business from his father and added to that a highly successful glove-manufacturing company. Because of his disbelief in the current estimates of the London poor, he organized a team of investigators who canvassed the streets of London, producing maps and surveys in an effort to estimate correctly the proportion of the London population that lived in abject poverty. The product of his labor left us seventeen remarkable and still valuable volumes, *Life and Labour of the People of London*. The third edition of Booth's studies appeared in 1902–1903.

24. Jack Barbash, "John R. Commons: Pioneer of Labor Economics," *Monthly Labor Review*, May 1989.

25. *Muller v. Oregon*, 208 U.S. 412 (1908). The Brandeis brief was presented to the Court in October 1907.

26. It is perhaps ironic that during this time, which coincided with the women's movement to gain the vote and improve the standing of women in society, the winning argument in *Muller* was based on a highly paternalistic image of women as frail and weaker than men and therefore in need of "protective legislation." At one point in the opinion, the Court, in what many took at the time to be a truism, concluded: "It is still true that in the struggle for subsistence she is not an equal competitor with her brother." The larger agenda for the reformers was, of course, to create a limit on working hours more generally, but they were willing to attack the current defense of the right to contract one step at a time.

27. Of the dozen values that are described here, the first, third, fourth, and fifth were initially discussed in an essay on the ethos of science by the sociologist Robert K. Merton. Robert K. Merton, "The Normative Structure of Science," in his volume of essays, *The Sociology of Science: Theoretical and Empirical Investigations* (Chicago: University of Chicago Press, 1973 [1942]), Chap. 13, 267–278.

28. Nicolas Wade and Chloe Snag-Hun, "Researches Faked Evidence of Human Cloning, Koreans Report," *New York Times*, January 10, 2006. Dr. Hwang Woo Suk, a South Korean researcher at Seoul National University, claimed to have cloned human cells, when in fact the data were fabricated. In disgrace, he became a symbol of scientific fraud and lost his job.

29. Louis Menand, "The Limits of Academic Freedom," in Louis Menand, ed., *The Future of Academic Freedom* (Chicago: University of Chicago Press, 1996), 4.

30. Robert Maynard Hutchins, "The Freedom of the University," *Ethics* 61, no. 2 (1951): 95, 104.

31. Ibid., 104.

32. Testimony of Robert M. Hutchins, Associate Director of the Ford Foundation, November 25, 1952, in Hearings Before the House Select Committee to Investigate Tax-Exempt Foundations and Comparable Organizations, pursuant to H. Res. 561, 82nd Cong. 2d Sess, quoted in *Wieman et al. v. Updegraff et al.*, 344 U.S. 183, 199.

Chapter 3: The Path to Greatness

1. The intellectual migration actually began earlier than 1933. The threat of the Nazis was apparent in the gains that they made in the parliamentary elections of 1930. They moved from 12 to 107 seats, increasing their percentage of the electoral votes by 800 percent. Some of the most prominent refugees began to migrate before 1933, especially among atomic scientists and psychoanalysts. But the purges did not begin until 1933, and the scope of the migration widened dramatically after Hitler actually came to power. A few scholars who have written about the intellectual migration have chosen to start their stories in 1930 because the National Origin provisions of the 1924 Immigration Act, which went into effect on July 1, 1929, effectively slammed the door to mass migration to the United States. See Laura Fermi, *Illustrious Immigrants: The Intellectual Migration from Europe, 1930–41* (Chicago: University of Chicago Press, 1968). From 1926 to 1930, almost 1.5 million people immigrated to the United States; over the next five years the total was roughly 220,000. Despite this closing of the gates, there was a provision of the immigration laws that left a crack in the door open to intellectuals. Clause 4d allowed nonquota immigration for ministers, bona fide teachers of higher education who would be teaching in the United States, and their families. This provision proved extremely valuable to intellectuals because these visas were more easily obtained than ordinary visas, even for countries that had not fulfilled their quota (Fermi, *Illustrious Immigrants*, 25–26).

2. For example, during the first twenty years that Nobel Prizes were awarded, German scientists had won about half of all the prizes in the natural sciences and medicine. Wilhelm Konrad Röntgen received his for the discovery of X-rays; Max Planck for discovery of energy quanta; Fritz Haber for the synthesis of ammonia from its elements; and of course Einstein for his revolutionary discoveries in basic physics. Even as late as 1950, Europeans, most working at universities, had captured 79 percent of all Nobel Prizes in the sciences, compared with 18 percent by Americans. From 1951 to 2003, Americans won 56 percent of all Nobels compared with 37 percent by scientists from all European nations.

3. Fritz Stern, *Einstein's German World* (Princeton, N.J.: Princeton University Press, 1999), 155.

4. The group included, among others, the great physicists Eugene Wigner and Edward Teller and the mathematician John von Neumann.

5. Leo Szilard, "Reminiscences," in Donald Fleming and Bernard Bailyn, eds., *The Intellectual Migration* (Cambridge: Belknap Press of Harvard University Press, 1969), 95.

6. This fact, that no one was spared, was perhaps best illustrated in the case of Fritz Haber, who was born into a prosperous Jewish family, and who converted at age twenty-four to Christianity with some sense that this would help him fulfill his ambitions for a significant academic career. He was a brilliant, inventive scientist who considered himself thoroughly German. His work on ammonia (the Haber-Bosh process, which is still used today and is considered one of the great discoveries of the twentieth century) won a Nobel Prize, and his work became critically important for the German war industry during World War I. His institute developed Zyklon B—the poison gas that would end up being used to annihilate millions during the war. When "Jewish science" was purged, Haber was, much to his amazement and chagrin, purged with the other Jewish physicists and chemists. There was almost no protest. Haber remained loyal to Germany, but ultimately had his spirit broken. He concluded: "My fate and that of my Institute will not constitute a unique situation. To continue to pursue great developments in Germany with the help of people selected principally for their political conviction seems to me to be hopeless."

7. Charles Weiner, "A New Site for the Seminar: The Refugees and American Physics in the Thirties," in Donald Fleming and Bernard Bailyn, *The Intellectual Migration* (Cambridge: Belknap Press of Harvard University Press, 1969). Weiner's important contribution defines "refugee scholars" as "those who were either dismissed or resigned from their positions as a result of the

Fascist policies, rather than those physicists who came as émigrés prior to 1933." Although Peter Debye, Albert Einstein, Enrico Fermi, James Franck, and Victor F. Hess were awarded their Nobel Prizes before coming to the United States, Hans A. Bethe, Felix Bloch, Emilio G. Segrè, Eugene Wigner, Maria Goppert Mayer, and Otto Stern earned Nobel recognition after they emigrated.

8. John Cornwell, *Hitler's Scientists: Science, War, and the Devil's Pact* (New York: Viking, 2003), 139–140.

9. Fritz Stern, "Einstein's Germany," in Gerald Holton and Yehuda Elkana, eds., *Albert Einstein: Historical and Cultural Perspectives* (Princeton, N.J.: Princeton University Press, 1982). See also Gerald Holton, *Victory and Vexation in Science: Einstein, Bohr, Heisenberg and Others* (Cambridge: Harvard University Press, 2005), 87. John S. Rigden wrote an excellent biography of Rabi. See his *Rabi: Scientist and Citizen* (New York: Basic Books, 1987).

10. Quoted in Gerald Holton, "The Migration of Physicists to the United States," in Jarrell C. Jackman and Carla M. Borden, eds., *The Muses Flee Hitler: Cultural Transfer and Adaptation, 1930–1945* (Washington, D.C.: Smithsonian Institution Press, 1983), 184–185.

11. Ibid., 222. Wigner's students went on to distinguished careers in physics. Perhaps the most notable one was John Bardeen, who, along with two colleagues, discovered the semiconductor and the transistor, which opened up the field of solid-state physics and in turn led to discoveries fundamental for generating high-speed computers.

12. Ibid., 223.

13. It is reasonable to ask why these scholars and scientists did not choose nations other than Britain and the United States. In fact, there were few other options that combined some reasonable level of safety along with a growing and dynamic university system. If they wanted to continue working as academics, the options were limited. Even England was less attractive to many of these émigrés, but some used England as a way station in their ultimate movement to the United States.

14. Born in 1906 in Berlin, Germany, Delbrück grew up in a fairly affluent suburb of Berlin that was populated by academics, professionals, and merchants. After 1914, these conditions changed into ones of economic hardship. Delbrück seems to have always been interested in science—initially in astronomy and then in theoretical physics, which he studied as a grad student at Göttingen. His acquaintance with Wolfgang Pauli and Niels Bohr in Switzerland and Denmark shaped his attitudes toward science. In fact, it was Bohr who stimulated Delbrück's interest in biology. After returning to Berlin in 1932, Delbrück joined an informal seminar among physicists and biologists that was examining the potential intersection between the two fields of study.

15. Http://nobelprize.org/nobel_prizes/medicine/laureates/1969/delbruck-b.

16. Donald Fleming, "Émigré Physicists and the Biological revolution," in Donald Fleming and Bernard Bailyn, *Intellectual Migration* (Cambridge: Belknap Press of Harvard University Press, 1969), 152–189. Quotation from p. 152.

17. The lure of Weimar culture was hardly confined to the sciences. Nor was the cultural energy limited to Germany. Europe between the wars, despite all of the social and economic turmoil that grew out of Versailles, continued to be a Mecca for those interested in advanced study and modern culture. It would prove to be a short flowering period between the establishment of the Republic after the war and the rise in fascism around 1930. Among the extraordinarily creative people who would be forced to migrate from Germany, Austria, Poland, Hungary, Russia, Italy, and France were writers and playwrights Thomas Mann and Bertold Brecht; artists Wassily Kandinsky and Max Ernst; architects Ludwig Mies van der Rohe and Walter Gropius; art historians Erwin Panofsky and Walter Friedlaender; philologist Erich Auerbach; composers Paul Hindermith, Bela Bartók, Arnold Schoenberg, and Igor Stravinsky; conductors Bruno Walter, Otto Klemperer, Erich Leinsdorf, and George Szell; theologian

Paul Tillich; psychoanalysts Sigmund and Anna Freud; psychologists Eric Fromm, Freida Fromm-Reichmann, Karen Horney, and Herta Herzog; social scientists Wassily Leontief, Paul Lazarsfeld, Kurt Lewin, Herbert Marcuse, Max Horkheimer, Theodor Adorno, Hannah Arendt, Leo Strauss, Franco Modigliani, Oskar Morgenstern, and Albert Hirschman; historians Paul Oskar Kristeller and Alexandre Koyré; philosophers Rudolf Carnap, Carl Hempel, and Philipp Frank; and mathematicians John Von Neumann and Paul Courant. An inclusive list of the hundreds who fled from their countries in the wake of fascism would read like a Hall of Fame list of artists, writers, and intellectuals. Until the end of the 1920s, many Americans were attracted to Europe for their advanced studies. The acceptance of the German intellectuals must be viewed against the backdrop of great resistance in the United States toward accepting Jews who were trying to escape Germany and other Nazi-occupied countries. The United States had a sorry history of closing its borders to most Jews who sought a safe haven in America.

18. Paul Lazarsfeld and Robert K. Merton were my two principal teachers during my doctoral studies at Columbia in the mid-1960s.

19. This follows closely the discussion in David L. Sills, "Paul F. Lazarsfeld, 1901–1976," *Biographical Memoirs*, vol. 56 (Washington, D.C.: National Academy Press, 1987), 254.

20. Seymour Martin Lipset, who was in fact a self-exemplifying case, has written extensively of the overrepresentation of Jews among the faculties of the great American universities in comparison with their numbers in the general population.

21. See, among other works, Jonathan R. Cole, *Fair Science: Women in the Scientific Community* (New York: Free Press, 1979); Harriet Zuckerman, Jonathan Cole, and John T. Bruer, eds., *The Outer Circle: Women in the Scientific Community* (New York: W. W. Norton, 1991).

22. Gerhard Sonnert and Gerald Holton, *What Happened to the Children Who Fled Nazi Persecution* (New York: Palgrave McMillan, 2006).

23. Eric R. Kandel, *In Search of Memory: The Emergence of a New Science of Mind* (New York: W. W. Norton, 2006), 12. See also Kandel's "The Molecular Biology of Memory Storage: A Dialog Between Genes and Synapses," reprint from Les Prix Nobel, 2000, 283–373 (quotation from p. 287); http://nobelprize.org/nobel_prizes/medicine/laureates/2000/kandel-lecture.html.

Another compelling story of a youngster being stranded without family while trying to avoid the Nazi police and finally making it to the United States is presented by Jacob Mincer, the renowned economist who worked on developing the idea of "human capital" while at Columbia with Nobel Prize winner Gary Becker.

24. Sonnert and Holton, *What Happened to the Children*, 7–8.

25. We know very little about what causes differential rates of decay of fame. Few people today could identify Vannevar Bush; more could locate James B. Conant; and probably more still J. Robert Oppenheimer. But why has Vannevar Bush's fame decayed faster than that of the other two? Perhaps it relates to anchors: For some, Oppenheimer is linked to the Manhattan Project and the creation of the atomic bomb; Conant is retrievable as the former president of Harvard University. Absent these types of anchors, individual fame, like that of Vannevar Bush, may decay more rapidly.

26. G. Pascal Zachary, *Endless Frontier: Vannevar Bush, Engineer of the American Century* (New York: Free Press, 1997), 218.

27. Members of the committee included Karl T. Compton, president of MIT; Richard C. Tolman, dean at Caltech; Frank B. Jewett, director of the Bell Telephone Laboratories and president of the National Academy of Sciences; James B. Conant; Conway P. Cole, commissioner of patents; and Brigadier General George V. Strong and Rear Admiral Harold G. Bowen, representatives of the army and the navy, respectively.

28. James B. Conant, *My Several Lives: Memoirs of a Social Inventor* (New York: Harper and Row, 1970), 235–237.

29. Roger L. Geiger, *Research and Relevant Knowledge: American Research Universities Since World War II* (New York: Oxford University Press, 1993), 5–6.

30. Ibid. Geiger also usefully pointed out that during World War I there were efforts to organize science and scientists. However, by the time the United States got into the war, most of the scientific applications for military technology had been produced—many of the "innovations" being established by German scientists. Perhaps more important by way of anticipating Bush's later ideas was the position of George Ellery Hale, who helped create the National Research Council in 1916 to coordinate scientific efforts among the academy, industry, and the government. Hale insisted that the organization of the scientific research effort must be granted a high level of autonomy if it was to be effective.

31. Don K. Price, *The Scientific Estate* (Cambridge: Harvard University Press, 1965), 65.

32. Conant, *My Several Lives*, 247.

33. For a rich description of Bush's early years and his impulse to invent, see Zachary, *Endless Frontier*.

34. Ibid., 5.

35. Ibid., 4–5.

36. In fact, he had always been interested in inventing things. He created, constructed, and patented machines like a surveying device, the "profile tracer," which was actually a rather primitive calculator. As early as the 1920s and 1930s he conceptualized what an advanced computational system would look like and how it could change our world. After tinkering with the idea for fifteen years, he would publish "As We May Think" in *Atlantic Monthly* (July 1945), which anticipated with uncanny brilliance the idea of the Internet and of digital libraries. He worked on calculators that were intended to be "thinking machines"; and he tried to invent methods that would rapidly match large numbers of fingerprints, which he called the "rapid selector." Many of his ideas went nowhere; others proved their value or were precursors of what would be discovered years later.

37. Zachary, *Endless Frontier*, 34–35.

38. Bush was a man of considerable courage. After World War II, the nation turned its back on one of its war heroes, J. Robert Oppenheimer, who was later accused of disloyalty by those in government who were part of the Cold War national paranoia about communism. At one point, Oppenheimer's security clearance for his role on the Atomic Energy Commission (AEC) was not renewed. AEC chairman Lewis Strauss and others were out to use Oppenheimer as a symbol of scientists with questionable loyalty. At an extended hearing of the AEC to review Oppenheimer's security clearance (Oppenheimer had vigorously opposed the crash development of the hydrogen bomb), Van Bush was one of the few witnesses to defend Oppenheimer and others like him. He came right to the point, saying that most scientists believed that Oppenheimer was "now being pilloried and put through an ordeal because he had the temerity to express his honest opinions" (Kai Bird and Martin J. Sherwin, *American Prometheus* [New York: Knopf, 2005], 529). In response to questions about Oppenheimer, Bush said, at the hearing, "I think this board or no board should ever sit on a question in this country of whether a man should serve his country or not because he expressed strong opinions. If you want to try this case, you can try me. I have expressed strong opinions many times, and I intend to do so. They have been unpopular opinions at times. When a man is pilloried for doing that, this country is in a severe state" (ibid.).

39. Letter from President Franklin D. Roosevelt to Dr. Vannevar Bush, November 17, 1944. Reproduced in Vannevar Bush, *Science—The Endless Frontier*, 40th anniversary ed. (Washington, D.C.: National Science Foundation, 1990), 3–4.

40. Among the members of the committees were Isaiah Bowman, president of Johns Hopkins University and chair of a key committee; Oliver E. Buckley, president of Bell Labs; I. I. Rabi, physicist at Columbia University; Linus Pauling, chemist at Caltech; Edwin Land, pres-

ident and director of research at the Polaroid Corporation; Rev. J. Hugh O'Donnell, president of Notre Dame; James B. Conant; Karl T. Compton, president of MIT; Warren Weaver, director of natural sciences, Rockefeller University; W. W. Palmer, Bard Professor of Medicine, Columbia University, and director of medical services at Presbyterian Hospital.

41. Daniel J. Kevles, one of the premier historians of science in the United States, has written with great insight about *Science–The Endless Frontier* in two works that I have found particularly useful here. See Kevles, *The Physicists: The History of a Scientific Community in Modern America* (Cambridge: Harvard University Press, 1971), and his preface to the fortieth anniversary edition of the report, "Principles and Politics in Federal R&D Policy, 1945–1990: An Appreciation of the Bush Report," in Bush, *Science—The Endless Frontier*, 40th anniversary ed.

42. Bush, *Science—The Endless Frontier*, 40th anniversary ed., 6.

43. Ibid., 7–8.

44. Ibid., 9.

45. Ibid.

46. Ibid.

47. Quoted by Gerald Holton in his unpublished paper presented on December 9, 1994, at a symposium at Columbia University, *Science: The Endless Frontier, 1945–1995: A Policy Evaluation and Formulation.*

48. After the war, virtually every major research university in the nation created policies that excluded contracts or grants on campus for classified research. This policy was reinforced during the Korean and Vietnam wars (when student protests were focused on the links of universities to secret research efforts) and still is in force at almost all universities. Research universities continue to do classified research and are often affiliated with laboratories that do, but those facilities are almost always physically separated from the universities even if they are affiliated with them.

49. Bush, *Science—The Endless Frontier*, 40th anniversary ed., 5–6.

50. Although much has been written about the conflict between the Bush and Kilgore models for science and technology policy, two particularly good sources can be found in the work of Daniel Kevles and Roger Geiger, all cited above.

51. Donald Stokes, "Science the Endless Frontier as a Treatise," paper delivered at the symposium *Science: The Endless Frontier, 1945–1995: A Policy Evaluation and Formulation*, Columbia University, December 9, 1994.

52. Ibid.

53. Kevles, "Principles and Politics in Federal R&D Policy," xiv–xv.

54. The NIH took off and was consistently funded at higher levels than the NSF because of the intuitive appeal to Congressmen of focusing on improving health and preventing or treating disease. They were not all as impressed with arguments for the fruits of fundamental research in the physical sciences.

55. One way members of Congress have been made to feel better about the overall distribution of NSF funding has been through the allocation of the science education program funds that are not based solely on peer review.

56. Donald E. Stokes outlined his criticism of the Bush linear model at the Columbia University symposium *Science: The Endless Frontier, 1945–1995: A Policy Evaluation and Formulation, December 9, 1994*, and later published the important book *Pasteur's Quadrant: Basic Science and Technological Innovation* (Washington, D.C.: Brookings Institution Press, 1997), in which he pays great homage to Bush's achievements but also demonstrates how the model was insufficient conceptually to recognize the far more complex relationships between mission- or use-driven research and curiosity-driven research.

57. James S. Coleman, "Science Advice and Social Science Advice to Government," in William T. Golden, ed., *Science and Technology Advice to the President, Congress, and Judiciary* (Washington, D.C.: AAAS Press, 1993), 90–94.

58. That position has had its own curious history. It was used effectively early on by presidents Eisenhower and Kennedy only to be emasculated by President Nixon, then brought back to life under President Clinton (who had a very strong science and technology agenda and who also created a cabinet level group called the National Science and Technology Council) only to be diminished in importance again during the administration of George W. Bush. Other organizational structures, such as the President's Science Advisory Committee (PSAC) and the Office of Technology Assessment (OTA), were created in efforts to improve scientific understanding among our legislators and policymakers. Suffice it to say that the challenge of creating quasi-independent organizations that would evaluate scientific and technological innovations and information in terms of their policy implications, create arguments for various policy options, and produce results in language understandable to members of the three branches of government who are often unfamiliar with science and technology remains a major unresolved problem—and one that was not part of the Bush treatise.

59. Quoted in Gerald Holton, "From Endless Frontier to Ideology of Limits," in *The Advancement of Science, and Its Burdens* (Cambridge: Cambridge University Press, 1986), 217.

60. If we return to one of the great scientific moments in history, seventeenth-century England—a century where war and revolution were rife—we find a deep interconnection between basic research and practical use. The focus of scientific attention was often determined by the need to solve practical problems. In his classic book *Science, Technology, and Society in Seventeenth Century England* (New York: Howard Fertig, 1970), Robert K. Merton made a strong case for the point that great advances in physics and other sciences were linked by intent to military and industrial needs in England at the time. Although Merton tells the story of seventeenth-century England, he emphasizes that we can go back as far as Leonardo da Vinci or Galileo to find critical linkages between scientific prowess and military engineering. One of the great military problems of the seventeenth century was ballistics. Robert Hooke studied the fall of "steel" bullets, for example, and the resistance produced by air to projectiles. Christopher Wren, the architect of London's St. Paul's Cathedral, collaborated with John Wallis and Christiaan Huyghens on inventing "offensive and defensive engines." The great astronomer Edmund Halley demonstrated the value of Newton's work in *Principia* for the problem of figuring out the trajectory for projectiles. As Merton asserted: "Halley may be considered as perhaps the clearest example of a seventeenth century scientist who found justification for his scientific labors in the immediate fruits which they afforded. . . . Halley was truly a child of the utilitarian age in which he lived: he constantly reiterates the economic advantages which obtain from the proper utilization of scientific knowledge" (p. 193).

Work on finding longitude is one more example of how practical considerations determined the focus of interest of many of the great scientists of the day, including Hooke, Huyghens, Halley, Leibniz, and Newton. The problem of finding longitude at sea continued to vex scientists for decades, including the unrivaled Newton, whose lunar theory not only advanced astronomy but also promised to be of some value to navigators and geographers. This pattern hardly ended in the seventeenth and eighteenth centuries. For example, in the nineteenth century, the work of the great Scottish mathematician and physicist William Thomson, Lord Kelvin, was inspired by his view of the needs of an expanding English empire. In short, many of the greatest scientists down through the ages have pursued problems that were driven by their interest in gaining a deep, fundamental understanding of nature as well as in helping to solve very practical problems that served the interests of their nation or that had economic and technological implications.

61. Donald Stokes, *Pasteur's Quadrant* (Washington, D.C.: Brookings Institution Press, 1997), 12–13.

62. Quoted in ibid., 61.

63. Quoted in ibid., 63.

64. Take one recent example: When American law schools denied military recruiters full access to their schools because the military's "don't ask, don't tell" policy toward homosexuality conflicted with the university's explicit antidiscrimination code, the federal government forced the universities to comply by threatening to withhold all federal funds, contracts, and grants if recruiters were denied full and equal access to law school students. While nominally the universities could choose to give up their federal research projects, this was a practical impossibility. The universities capitulated.

65. President William J. Clinton and Vice President Albert Gore, Jr., *Science in the National Interest*, Executive Office of the President, Office of Science and Technology Policy, August 1994.

66. Ibid.

Chapter 4: Building Steeples of Excellence

1. There is, of course, a critically important distinction between prediction and causation. Here I am referring to a set of elements that are associated with or correlated with great universities. Whether they "cause" greatness is a more complex matter related to how one defines greatness—and greatness toward what end—as well as how the various elements are related to each other and how they have to be organized over time to produce outcomes that we would say resulted in a great research university. If, however, we are trying to understand, for example, the basis for the way the world's greatest universities have been ranked in published lists in recent years, it is a different story. Many of the elements that I'm describing here have been used in those studies because they are widely taken to be indicators of quality.

2. To some extent, this indication of quality can be distorted when a university has a high volume of research activity but is also the home of a large national facility, as in the case of Johns Hopkins, which houses the Applied Physics Laboratory, a technology resource for the Department of Defense and other government agencies that receives $680 million of support each year from the federal government.

3. Jonathan R. Cole and James A. Lipton, "The Reputations of American Medical Schools," *Social Forces* 55, no. 3 (1977): 662–684.

4. Wallace Sterling, a historian, was selected as Stanford's fifth president in the fall of 1948 following his rapid rise as a researcher and teacher at Caltech. He did not take up the position until March 1949.

5. In academic circles, the career of Frederick Terman, as an engineer, as a leader of the engineering school at Stanford, as the great university provost, and as the putative father of Silicon Valley, is reasonably well known. But his work at developing Stanford is not widely appreciated in many quarters in the academy today and even less so among most educated Americans. Here I rely on recent outstanding work that has been done to chart the rise of Stanford and Terman's role in that ascendance. Particularly helpful is the full-length biography of Terman by C. Stewart Gillmor, *Fred Terman at Stanford: Building a Discipline, a University, and Silicon Valley* (Palo Alto, Calif.: Stanford University Press, 2004). For anyone interested in the life of Terman and his role in Stanford's ascendance, this is a critical source. There is also an excellent discussion of Terman's role in Stanford's history, and of some of his critics, in Roger L. Geiger, *Research and Relevant Knowledge: American Research Universities Since World War II* (New York: Oxford University Press, 1993), 118–135 (Geiger also discusses the factors that led to the rise of a number of public research universities after the war, notably UCLA); David A. Hollinger, *Science, Jews, and Secular Culture: Studies in Mid-Twentieth-Century American Intellectual History* (Princeton, N.J.: Princeton University Press, 1996), 136–137; Stuart W. Leslie and Robert H. Kargon, "Selling Silicon Valley: Frederick Terman's Model for Regional Advantage," *Business History Review* 70 (Winter 1996): 435–472. There are also a number of very valuable oral histories that Frederick Terman produced that are in the Hoover

Library at Stanford and part of the oral history collection located at the Bancroft Library, University of California, Berkeley. See also Hollinger, *Science, Jews, and Secular Culture*, pp. 121–154, for a comparison of Michigan, Stanford, and Columbia during this period. For a more critical view of Stanford's growth and Terman's role, see Rebecca Lowen, *Creating the Cold War University: The Transformation of Stanford* (Berkeley: University of California Press, 1997).

6. Gillmor, *Fred Terman at Stanford,* 189. Gillmor noted some uncanny parallels in the lives of Terman and Bush: Both had boyhood interests in radio, electronics, and communications; both became engineers, but both were also very knowledgeable in chemistry, mathematics, and physics; both had suffered from early illness, Bush from appendicitis at age twenty-one, Terman from tuberculosis, which nearly killed him, and appendicitis by age twenty-four; both were members of engineering fraternities; both already had taught while still in college; both held U.S. patents while still in their twenties; both were influenced by the potential relationship between the university and its industrial partners; both became distinguished young leaders of their academic departments who would go on to become formidable deans of their respective engineering schools; and both would play important roles working for the national defense during World War II. Gillmor also noted real differences between the men. For example, Bush was a particularly public man, whereas Terman was a rather private person; Bush liked the national stage, but Terman liked to stay closer to home.

7. This may seem like a small detail, but control over budgets, which are, after all, the main policy instrument at a university, is critical for placing academic priorities ahead of other administrative needs. In many research universities today the provost does not control basic budget decisions or formulate budget priorities. This often leads to tension between the academic and the administrative arms of the university. At Stanford, Terman gained basic control over budget priorities and that made a great difference.

8. By the end of the 1950s, Stanford's endowment was not equal, on a per student basis, to that of any of the Ivy League schools, with the possible exception of Cornell; it was only about a quarter of the size of the endowments of Harvard, Yale, and Princeton. Gillmor, *Fred Terman at Stanford,* 358.

9. By the time the complex opened—comprising three hospital and four medical school buildings and designed by Edward Durell Stone—the price tag had surpassed $21 million. Gillmor's book provides a more detailed description of Terman's effort at building steeples and is certainly worth reading to gain information about the processes used by the Stanford leadership. See Chap. 7, "Raising Steeples at Stanford: 1958–1965," in Gillmor, *Fred Terman at Stanford.*

10. Gillmor, *Fred Terman at Stanford,* 350.

11. George Beadle had been at Stanford for more than a decade before leaving for Caltech in 1947, and Ed Tatum was there for most of twenty years (with a short stint at Yale) before 1957. So Kornberg and Lederberg did not have to build great science out of whole cloth. In fact, the successful recruitment of Kornberg made Lederberg take a closer look at Stanford, which had been trying to lure him to Palo Alto for some time.

12. Gillmor, *Fred Terman at Stanford,* 354.

13. Ibid., 359.

14. For a summary of Stanford's improving rankings, see ibid., Appendix D. For a more fine-grained report on the results of each of the ranking studies, see, among others, Allan M. Cartter, *An Assessment of Quality in Graduate Education: A Comparative Study of Graduate Departments in 29 Academic Disciplines* (Washington, D.C.: American Council on Education, 1966); Kenneth D. Roose and Charles J. Andersen, *Rating of Graduate Programs* (Washington, D.C.: American Council on Education, 1970); Lyle V. Jones, Gardner Lindzey, and Porter E. Coggeshall, eds., *An Assessment of Research-Doctorate Programs in the United States,* 4 vols. (Washington, D.C.: National Academy Press, 1982); Marvin L. Goldberger and Brendan Maher, *Research Doctorate Programs in the United States: Continuity and Change* (Washington,

D.C.: National Research Council, National Academy Press, 1995). The next wave of evaluations is currently being carried out and should be available by 2010. Of course, a small cottage industry has grown up around "the ratings game." Individual universities are producing rankings of universities, as are an increasing number of major newspapers and magazines in the United States and abroad. See, for example, the annual reports from the Lombardi Program on Measuring University Performance at the University of Florida, http://thecenter.ufl.edu.

15. For a very valuable assessment of the rise of state universities over the past half-century along with some of the privates, see Hugh David Graham and Nancy Diamond, *The Rise of American Research Universities: Elites and Challengers in the Postwar Era* (Baltimore: Johns Hopkins University Press, 1997).

16. Stuart W. Leslie and Robert H. Kargon, "Selling Silicon Valley: Frederick Terman's Model for Regional Advantage," *Business History Review* 70 (Winter 1996): 435–472. Quotation on p. 437.

17. Geiger, *Research and Relevant Knowledge,* 120.

18. Ibid., 441–442.

19. Ibid., 436.

20. John M. Findlay, *Magic Lands: Western Cityscapes and American Culture After 1940* (Berkeley: University of California Press, 1992), 117–159.

21. Over the past century, the American research university has produced the scientific and technological talent on which future innovation would depend. Only some of these talented individuals worked at the universities; far more of them worked in industrial laboratories after receiving their Ph.D.s. Terman believed that a close connection between those working inside and outside the walls of the university produced the best conditions for innovation. Great laboratory leaders, such as William Baker of the Bell Labs in New Jersey, took note in the early 1960s of the impending shortage of talent for Bell and also recognized the importance of these links. He noted that Boston, San Francisco, and parts of North Carolina all had an advantage in this regard. Northern New Jersey, however, with its a high concentration of industrial laboratories, suffered from a relative dearth of these connections. RCA and Bell Labs tried to affiliate with several universities. These efforts were not successful and they developed their own training programs, which closely resembled the structure and values of the university research environment.

22. Fritz Stern, "Grayson Kirk, Biographical Memoirs," in *Proceedings of the American Philosophical Society* 143, no. 4 (1999): 675–678.

23. Geiger, *Research and Relevant Knowledge.* Geiger usefully discusses the resistance of some to the new multiversity, enumerating some of the problems associated with the rapidly expanding research university of the 1960s.

24. As quoted in Gillmor, *Fred Terman at Stanford,* 361.

25. Barzun saw his task as dean of faculties and provost in the following terms: "It was clear that in the previous dozen years, certain deans and heads of departments had become quasi-independent powers.... [His job was] to recapture the university from past neglect and the several 'warlords.'" See Thomas Vinciguerra, "Jacques Barzun: Cultural Historian, Cheerful Pessimist, Columbia Avatar," in Wm. Theodore de Bary, with Jerry Kisslinger and Tom Mathewson, eds., *Living Legacies at Columbia* (New York: Columbia University, 2006), 383–395. Barzun became concerned with such things as centralizing the budget process, formulating uniform rules for sabbaticals and promotions, and establishing the Office of Art Properties and a journal, *The Columbia Forum.* He was a tireless supporter of the liberal arts and was highly critical of the recent trend toward professionalism in the undergraduate curriculum. He wrote and published books and articles on these important subjects, but was better at expressing his concerns in written form than at creating a larger strategy for Columbia and implementing it in the context of the evolving American research university.

26. Clark Kerr, *The Uses of the University*, 5th ed. (Cambridge: Harvard University Press, 2001), 28.

27. In fact, Kerr would use the California model as the basis for proposing federal financial-aid legislation, which later took the form of Pell Grants for students whose families fell below a relatively low income level.

28. Quoted in an obituary by Emma Schwarz and Kim-Mai Cutler, "Clark Kerr, 1911–2003: Revered, Embattled UC President Dies at 92," *The Daily Californian*, December 2, 2003.

29. For an excellent and comprehensive discussion of the effects of the GI Bill on higher education, see, Geiger, Research and Relevant Knowledge. Geiger offered one of the best discussions and analyses of research universities more generally and his book contains a wealth of useful information about them during the postwar period.

30. Ibid., 41.

31. Kerr, *The Uses of the University*, 15.

32. Matthew Goldstein, chancellor of the City University of New York, is experimenting with another variation on Kerr's California model. With the advantage that all schools in the City University system report to the chancellor, which Clark Kerr did not have, Goldstein is implementing a tiered system that is aimed at providing access at different levels to students with varying levels of academic achievement. He is also taking major steps to enhance the research potential of the university, including pursuing the development of focused programs of scientific research in areas with high potential for important discoveries.

Chapter 5: In Search of a Golden Age

1. Roger L. Geiger, *Research and Relevant Knowledge: American Research Universities Since World War II* (New York: Oxford University Press, 1993), 195–197.

2. Frances Stonor Saunders, *Who Paid the Piper? The CIA and the Cultural Cold War* (London: Granta Books, 1999).

3. There is a long history of student activism for political and social causes that dates far back into the twentieth century and before. In fact, according to Seymour Martin Lipset and David Riesman, *Education and Politics at Harvard* (New York: McGraw-Hill, 1975), and Everett C. Ladd, Jr., and Seymour Martin Lipset, *The Divided Academy: Professors and Politics* (New York: W. W. Norton, 1975), the student movement of the 1960s probably did not include a higher proportion of the total student body than the protests prior to World War I and during the Great Depression. Low levels of student activism punctuated the century as well, with fairly quiescent student bodies during the 1920s, 1950s, and following the Vietnam War. Unlike earlier eras, in the 1960s there was no single radical group or coalition around which the activity coalesced—yet perhaps a million or more people identified with the militant protests.

4. Quoted in Ladd and Lipset, *The Divided Academy*.

5. For a discussion of this adversary culture, see Daniel Bell, *The Coming of Post-Industrial Society* (New York: Basic Books, 1973), 477–478; Seymour Martin Lipset, *Rebellion in the University* (Chicago: University of Chicago Press, 1976), xlii–xliii. Trilling's formulation and discussion of adversary culture can be found in his *Beyond Culture: Essays on Literature and Learning* (New York: Viking Press, 1965), xii–xiii.

6. Alvin Kernan, "Change in the Humanities and Higher Education," in Alvin Kernan, ed., *What's Happened to the Humanities?* (Princeton, N.J.: Princeton University Press, 1997), 3–4.

7. Max Weber, "Science as a Vocation," in *From Max Weber: Essays in Sociology*, translated and edited by H. H. Gerth and C. Wright Mills (New York: Oxford University Press, 1946), 129–156.

8. Don Michael Randel, "The Public Good: Knowledge as the Foundation for a Democratic Society," *Daedalus* (Winter 2009): 9–10. This is one essay in an issue of *Daedalus* that is devoted

to the humanities and linked to the almost simultaneous publication of the Humanities Indicators of the American Academy of Arts and Sciences, which publishes *Daedalus*. See http://www.humanitiesindicators.org/humanitiesData.aspx.

9. Harriet Zuckerman and Ronald G. Ehrenberg, "Recent Trends in Funding for the Academic Humanities and Their Implications," *Daedalus* (Winter 2009): 124–146. Quotations from pp. 124, 129.

10. The American Academy began publishing these statistics in 2008 as part of its larger effort to have the public and opinion leaders better informed about the humanities disciplines. The academy is not only publishing useful statistical indicators of the health of the humanities, however, but also simultaneously publishing a series of scholarly, yet highly readable articles on the health of the humanities. The model for this type of analysis has been the semi-annual publication by the National Science Board of Science and Technology Indicators over the past several decades. I was a member of the committee of the academy that conceptualized this humanities indicators project. The source for the data used here is http://www.humanitiesindicators.org/content/hrcoImageFrame.aspx?i=II-1a.jpg&o=hrcoIIA.aspx__topII1. For the general website, see http://www.humanitiesindicators.org.

11. Some universities own their own hospitals, which may be lucrative at times, contributing to their general funds, or sources of substantial losses, on occasion threatening the existing endowments of these universities. The University of Pennsylvania is a good example of a university that has at times benefited from the profits of its hospital, while at other times having its financial stability threatened by the hospital's deficits. Many universities have had long-standing formal affiliations with hospitals but do not own them and are corporately independent of them. Columbia, for example, has historically been closely affiliated with Presbyterian Hospital, which in 1999 merged with New York Hospital to become New York Presbyterian Hospital. But the doctors who practice at the hospital have their formal appointments at Columbia University and are part of Columbia's practice plans. Some doctors affiliated with teaching hospitals have appointments with the hospital rather than with the university. Many different configurations have developed over the past half-century.

Health science centers also differ in their organization. Some schools of public health are free-standing, independent schools that report directly to the president or provost, while others are integrated more directly into the medical school complex. Harvard University has affiliations with multiple hospitals in Boston, and its School of Public Health is an independent entity in its larger structure of governance. Different universities handle physician practice plans in very different ways: Some have one integrated plan, while others have multiple plans. Schools of medicine tax revenues from practice plans at varying rates, generating different levels of income from the doctors. The doctors use the facilities for seeing patients but also contribute much of their teaching time to medical students for free. Indirect costs from government and nongovernment grants and contracts pay a great number of bills related to research at medical schools, although not the full cost of that research.

There exists great pressure at medical schools to generate revenues through indirect costs linked to successful grant and contract applications. Space is costly, and without grant support it is almost impossible for medical schools to support adequate facilities. All of these elements in the organization of the health sciences keep deans of medical schools and presidents of universities awake at night in efforts to make ends meet while still expanding the research enterprise. It takes the extraordinary leadership qualities possessed by people such as Dr. Herbert Pardes of New York Presbyterian Hospital to orchestrate financial stability and exceptional patient care while maintaining a commitment to innovative research.

12. Hugh Davis Graham and Nancy Diamond, *The Rise of American Research Universities: Elites and Challengers in the Postwar Era* (Baltimore: Johns Hopkins University Press, 1997), 122–133.

13. Ibid., 122–123.

14. Ibid., 125–126. Many physicians who are affiliated with universities run their clinical practices in the medical school or hospital buildings and see their patients at their offices in these medical centers. They charge fees for the clinical visits through a "practice plan" that is administered by a department, such as medicine or dermatology, and their income depends on the volume of their practice and the amounts charged. They use medical school and hospital facilities and are charged for space and other services provided by the school. These same physicians do the lion's share of teaching of medical students, for which they are paid little or nothing by the medical school.

15. By 2008 the average dollar amount of each grant to the Stanford School of Medicine was more than $400,000.

16. Scott Norum, formerly Columbia vice president for university budgeting, provided me with these data.

17. The fundamental idea of the university would perhaps be less distorted if it emphasized basic biological and biomedical research (along with public health) while supporting a much smaller but still elite clinical enterprise to create new clinical knowledge and work to perfect new methods of treatment and cures for disease. This would reduce the role of clinical practice at medical centers and transfer that enterprise to the great affiliated teaching hospitals. We would be recreating a structure that was more like those of earlier days, when, for example, basic research at the Rockefeller Institute for Medical Research was complemented by smaller scale clinical research exploring the efficacy of new therapies and treatments of disease.

18. Http://nobelprize.org/nobel_prizes/economics/laureates/1987/solow-lecture.html. Solow's discovery was consistent with Vannevar Bush's beliefs that investments in human capital and in knowledge production would eventually be translated into new technologies and industrial products that would become the major drivers of innovation and economic well-being in the postwar era. Somewhat later, University of Pennsylvania economist Edwin Mansfield, a lonely pioneer in studying technological change, began to measure the effects of academic research on industrial innovation. He estimated that there was at least a 28 percent return to society from funds invested in academic research. In some later and admittedly limited studies, his estimates of the social rate of return on seventeen innovations was about 50 percent. The returns varied, as one would expect, according to the type of discovery and its impact on different industrial sectors. Despite his own acknowledgment of the limits to his models, his general conclusion, that academic discoveries either directly or indirectly had a significant positive effect on innovation and economic growth, was fairly well established by economists between World War II and 1980.

19. The Bayh-Dole University and Small Business Patent Act of 1980 (Public Law 96-517).

20. In the early part of the twentieth century, scientists who tried to profit from their discoveries were frowned upon and denied positions if they tried to patent their ideas. When T. Bailsford Robertson, for example, tried to patent his discovery of tethalin, Johns Hopkins rejected his candidacy for chair of its physiology department. The Rockefeller Foundation threatened to withdraw its funding of Herbert Evans at Berkeley when he indicated that he intended to patent ideas that were based upon work funded by the foundation.

21. Http://www.warf.org/about/index.jsp?cid=26.

22. Http://www.warf.org/about/index.jsp?cid=26&scid=34.

23. Http://www.warf.org/about/index.jsp?cid=26&scid=35.

24. The changing meaning of the norm of disinterestedness is illustrated here. These core values are ideals and have never been fully realized in the academy. They are in fact constantly under some form of pressure for change, if not assault.

25. One reason it is difficult to measure the effects of a policy change such as that represented by the Bayh-Dole Act is that we have no way of knowing what might have happened without

it. There is, in short, no control group situation by which we can measure the independent effects from other possible sources of change in the relationship between research universities and industry.

26. *Science and Technology Indicators 2004*, vol. 1, pp. 5:53–5:54. The number of patents belonging to universities pales in comparison with the annual patenting of ideas by leading industrial firms. For example, in 2004, IBM was awarded 3,248 patents.

27. Http://www.autm.net/AM/Template.cfm?Section=FY_2006_Licensing_Activity_Survey.

28. Richard R. Nelson, *The Sources of Economic Growth* (Cambridge: Harvard University Press, 1996), 212–215.

29. Http://web.mit.edu/invent/a-winners/a-boyercohen.html.

30. Http://chronicle.com/weekly/v54/i16/16a02202.htm.

31. Derek Bok, *Universities in the Marketplace: The Commercialization of Higher Education* (Princeton, N.J.: Princeton University Press, 2003).

32. An extraordinary case of conflict of interest is the disaster that befell Dr. Nancy Olivieri, a professor of medicine at the University of Toronto, who worked at the Hospital for Sick Children in Toronto, when she was involved in a clinical trial experiment abroad. After about a year, she found the experimental drug was having very harmful effects on the subjects in the trial. When she tried to "go public" with the results, violating the agreement between the pharmaceutical firm that was paying for the trial and the University of Toronto, and Dr. Olivieri was fired. It took her years to regain her position, and she succeeded only after the case was highly publicized and became a cause célèbre in the academy. The case was the basis for the movie *The Constant Gardener*. For an in-depth analysis of the case, see *The Olivieri Report* (Toronto: James Lorimer and Company, 2001).

Chapter 6: Growing Pains

1. Make no mistake: Even great universities make errors in appointments to tenured positions because of efforts by faculty members to promote friends or individuals who are loyal to a particular ideological point of view. Sometimes this is a result of conscious deception in the presentation of the candidate's credentials in the promotion process. As provost at Columbia I witnessed this displacement of institutional goals more than once. When it occurred, it was almost always in departments that were on the decline or that were mired in ideological disputes. The path to mediocrity is paved with these kinds of cases—where particularistic criteria dominate universalistic judgments. Nonetheless, today, the better the university, the less likely it is that faculty members will be valued simply because they are part of a kinship group. It would be misleading to say that the great universities didn't apply quality standards to tenure decisions in the early part of the twentieth century; however, they did operate more like local, small organizations, with power concentrated in the hands of presidents, trustees, and benefactors, with far less competition for stars, and with more loyalty and commitment to the institution than there is today. And at that time, discrimination against Jews, blacks, women, and new immigrants was much more prevalent than it is today.

2. Derek J. de Solla Price, *Little Science, Big Science* (New York: Columbia University Press, 1963). Many of the examples that I use here are discussed in Price's book.

3. Quoted in Solomon H. Snyder, "The Audacity Principle in Science," *Proceedings of the American Philosophical Society* 149, no. 2 (June 2005): 141.

4. Jonathan R. Cole and Stephen Cole, "The Ortega Hypothesis," *Science* 178 (October 27, 1972): 368–375.

5. Authors of papers who teach at American universities received 44 percent of the citations to published science and engineering articles in 2001. According to the *Science and Engineering Indicators*, "The U.S. literature is the most often cited in the world compared with other

regions. Over the past two decades, on average, the U.S. share of cited scientific research has been 35 percent greater than the U.S. share of the scientific literature" (http://www.nsf.gov/SEind08/). This is an important indicator of the quality of the work of U.S. scientists, because it takes into account the relatively larger size of the U.S. enterprise compared with that of other nations.

6. Roger L. Geiger, *Research and Relevant Knowledge: American Research Universities Since World War II* (New York: Oxford University Press, 1993), 217–219.

7. *Chronicle of Higher Education*, Almanac Issue, 2006–7, vol. 53, no. 1 (August 25, 2006): 20.

8. In 2006–2007, India sent the most (about 84,000), followed by China, South Korea, and Japan. Even Britain sent more than 8,000 Ph.D. students to the United States, and France sent almost 7,000.

9. Geiger, *Research and Relevant Knowledge*. Geiger provided these data and others on the growth of federal funding for academic research in the decades that followed the war. These data are easily obtained as well from various Internet sources.

10. Both the NSF and the NIH have benefited significantly from President Barack Obama's economic stimulus plan (American Recovery and Reinvestment Act of 2009). The NSF received $3 billion over two years; the NIH, $10 billion.

11. Richard R. Nelson, *The Sources of Economic Growth* (Cambridge: Harvard University Press, 1996), 206–224. Nelson notes the key roles of the Department of Defense, the Department of Energy, and NASA in their support of university-based research.

12. There are many other indicators of growth in universities, library holdings and expenditures over time being one. Today, these holdings include not only library books but also vast collections of government and other documents, rare books and manuscripts, scholarly and scientific journals, and an increasing array of accessible online digital materials. Harvard has by far the largest set of holdings of the research libraries—including more than 15.5 million volumes. It also subscribes to almost 99,000 serials. Staffed by almost 1,100 people, its libraries spent about $103 million in 2004–2005 on library holdings. No other center of learning of comparable size is as wealthy as Harvard, but expenditures on the storage and preservation of knowledge by other major universities have grown at an enormous rate over the past twenty-five years. Yale has more than 12 million volumes in its libraries; the University of Illinois at Urbana-Champaign and the University of California at Berkeley around 10 million each; Columbia more than 9 million; and the University of Michigan more than 8 million. These institutions are each spending between $50 million and $70 million annually on their libraries.

13. Richard C. Atkinson and William A. Blanpied, "Research Universities: Core of U.S. Science and Technology System," *Technology and Society* 20 (2008): 20–48.

Chapter 7: Finding a Smoother Pebble

1. Jonathan Cole, "Two Cultures Revisited," *The Bridge, National Academy of Engineering* 26, no. 3–4 (Fall/Winter 1996): 16–21. Reprinted in Albert H. Teich, Stephen D. Nelson, and Celia McEnaney, eds., *AAAS Science and Technology Policy Yearbook* (Washington, D.C.: Committee on Science, Engineering, and Public Policy, American Association for the Advancement of Science, 1997), 89–100.

2. Most experts now agree that science—at both universities and industrial laboratories— influences the advance of technology in at least two major ways: by expanding the body of theory, techniques, and data available to those employed in industrial research and development, thus increasing their problem-solving capabilities; and by directly opening up new technological possibilities, offering new possible solutions to old problems, and promoting new avenues of inquiry with technological possibilities. Discoveries in agriculture, biotechnology, and com-

puter science, for example, have had many direct applications in new technologies and products that have influenced our economic well-being.

3. *Science and Engineering Indicators 2006,* vol. 2, Table 3-9.

4. Http://www.stanford.edu/group/wellspring/. This website supplies data on companies founded by or affiliated with Stanford University alumni, faculty, and staff.

5. Http://www.stanford.edu/group/wellspring/economic.html. For the Silicon Valley 150, see http://www.mercurynews.com/business/ci_12091678?nclick_check=1.

6. BankBoston, *Engines of Economic Growth: The Economic Impact of Boston's Eight Research Universities on the Metropolitan Boston Area,* 1997. The eight universities are Harvard University, MIT, Boston University, Boston College, Brandeis University, Northeastern University, University of Massachusetts, and Tufts University.

7. *Engines of Economic Growth: The Economic Impact of Boston's Eight Research Universities on the Metropolitan Boston Area* (New York: Appleseed, 2003), 67. The full report is available at http://www.masscolleges.org/files/downloads/economicimpact/EconomicReport_Full%20 Report_FINAL.pdf. The 1997 and 2003 studies included the same eight universities.

8. *MIT: The Impact of Innovation,* A BankBoston Economics Department Special Report, 1997.

9. Other universities, such as Purdue University in Indiana, are beginning to measure their economic impact on their local environments. In 2004–2005, Purdue estimated that it had more than a $2.9 billion impact on the state of Indiana alone, while receiving $369 million from the state—which would mean it was producing roughly an 8 to 1 return on the state's investment.

10. Carey Goldberg, "Across the U.S., Universities Are Fueling High-Tech Economic Booms," *New York Times,* October 8, 1999, A-12.

11. For a limited list and links to politically oriented think tanks, see http://www.lib .umich.edu/govdocs/psthink.html.

12. The terms "science" and "technology" are often used loosely and interchangeably, and this can be confusing. Science and technology are closely related, but they are not the same thing. Science involves a body of knowledge that has accumulated over time through the process of scientific inquiry, as it generates new knowledge about the natural world—including knowledge in the physical and biological sciences as well as in the social and behavioral sciences. Technology, in its broadest sense, is the process by which we modify nature to meet our needs and wants. Some people think of technology in terms of gadgets and a variety of artifacts, but it also involves the processes that are employed to create and use artifacts. It includes the design process by which individuals or companies start with a set of criteria and constraints and work toward a solution of a problem that meets those conditions. See *Technically Speaking: Why All Americans Need to Know More About Technology* (Washington, D.C.: National Academies Press, Committee on Technological Literacy, 2002), 13. I was a member of this committee. Many achievements that are presented as triumphs of science are actually triumphs of technology, although they depend on prior scientific knowledge. For example, the successful landing of a man on the moon by the United States involved basic scientific knowledge, but it was more of a triumph of the technology of the machinery and the systems needed to launch a rocket, guide it, and land it on the moon and then return home than of basic scientific knowledge.

13. When referring to the individuals who have made discoveries, of necessity I have had to omit the hundreds of other individuals who were responsible for the growth of knowledge that led to these discoveries.

14. A different, and in some sense more systematic way of proceeding would have been to focus on the research papers or scientists receiving the most citations or references to their work. This method could be used as a point of departure for examining a set of discoveries, their creators, and the universities in which the work was done. I could have given statistical

measures of impact, cataloged the frequency with which various universities, within the United States or elsewhere, appeared in these lists, and then built stories around these cases. But this would have missed one of my central points. Not all of the discoveries that have a practical impact on our lives are among the greatest or most highly touted in a scientific or scholarly field, yet they may have a significant impact on our daily lives. Because I wanted to communicate *both* the breadth and depth of the discoveries created at our great universities, I consciously adopted a less systematic approach to generating my illustrations.

15. "The Nifty Fifty," http://www.nsf.gov/od/lpa/nsf50/nsfoutreach/htm/home.htm. The National Academy of Sciences produced over several years a set of essays called *Beyond Discovery: The Path from Research to Human Benefit* examining the origins of major medical and technological advances produced in the United States. The National Academy of Engineering produced a monograph entitled *A Century of Innovation* giving detailed descriptions of twenty great engineering achievements of the twentieth century, based upon nominations made by a consortium of twenty-nine engineering societies. On the Internet, one can visit hundreds of websites for universities where, often tucked away in a rather obscure location, it is possible to find descriptions of major research triumphs attributed to professors and scholars who held positions at those institutions.

Chapter 8: It Began with a Fly

1. Milislav Demerec in a 1951 Cold Spring Harbor Symposium on "Genes and Mutations," reflecting back on the state of genetics research a decade earlier. Quoted in an extremely informative biographical and analytic book by Evelyn Fox Keller, *A Feeling for the Organism: The Life and Work of Barbara McClintock* (New York: Owl Books, Henry Holt, 1983), 154.

2. Even the revolutionary discovery of the double helix model offers us an example of the role of serendipity in science and of the differences between what is found in brilliant scientific papers and what actually goes on in scientific laboratories during the process of discovery. The paper, in this case a truly elegant 900-word article in *Nature* on April 25, 1953 (pp. 737–738), entirely omits what sociologist of science Robert K. Merton described as the various "intuitive leaps, false starts, mistakes, loose ends, and *happy accidents* that actually cluttered up the inquiry." See Robert K. Merton's discussion of these elements, including serendipity, in this particularly famous discovery, in Robert K. Merton and Elinor Barber, *The Travels and Adventures of Serendipity* (Princeton, N.J.: Princeton University Press, 2004).

Watson and Crick were acutely aware of the difference between the reporting of science in professional journals and the true nature of everyday work. See James D. Watson's *The Double Helix: A Personal Account of the Discovery of the Structure of DNA* (New York: Atheneum, 1968), and Crick's own reminiscences, where he says that "the path" to "the discovery of the double helix" involved "misleading data, false ideas, [and] problems of interpersonal relationships" (quoted in Merton's "Afterword," in Merton and Barber, *Travels and Adventures*, 279). As Merton pointed out, Crick described the evolving discovery of the double helix in terms of serendipitous findings: "The key discovery was Jim's determination of the exact nature of the two base pairs (A with T, G with C). He did this not by logic but by serendipity. . . . In a sense Jim's discovery was luck, but then most discoveries have an element of luck in them. The more important point is that Jim was looking for something significant and immediately recognized the significance of the correct pairs when he hit upon them by chance—'chance favors the prepared mind'" (quoted from Francis Crick, *What Mad Pursuit: A Personal View of Scientific Discovery* [New York: Basic Books, 1988], 65–66).

3. The sources for many of these descriptions and quotations are the lists of discoveries sent to me by the provosts and presidents of the universities mentioned. In other cases I am paraphrasing or using the descriptive language that the universities have used on their websites, or

drawing from information sent to me by research scientists and scholars. Some other material comes from the citations for the Nobel Prize and other awards. The major funding foundations have also produced descriptions of discoveries resulting from work they have funded. I have relied heavily on their descriptions of these discoveries. In addition, some organizations have produced lists of discoveries produced at their member institutions, including the Association of American Universities (AAU). The AAU's list of discoveries has been valuable in helping me to construct my own set of notable discoveries. John Vaughn, executive vice president of the AAU, has been particularly helpful in supplying me with material on university-based discoveries.

4. Some of the major discoveries emerging from university research have involved what might be called "discoveries of techniques." These discoveries have often been essential for scientific and practical advances, although they are too often disparaged as being merely technical advances. New technologies such as recombinant DNA techniques have revolutionized fields, luring the best students in a field to universities where these new techniques have been discovered or perfected. These techniques open up possibilities for a host of new and important advances in science, and they are often among the most referenced or cited pieces of work in the scientific community—in part because those who use the technique must acknowledge its origins.

5. Http://www.cumc.columbia.edu/news/reporter/archives/repo_v7n4_0010.html. See also "Technology Transfer Works: 100 Cases from Research to Realization," *Reports from the Field*, 2006, www.betterworldproject.net, p. 52.

6. Ibid.

7. Kary Mullis developed PCR when he worked for Cetus and won a Nobel Prize for his contributions. Unlike the discovery of recombinant DNA, the initial discoveries involving PCR were not the result of a university-industry collaboration. The situation led to several intellectual property issues. PCR was invented with a specific purpose in mind, which was to facilitate the analysis of genes in biological samples and in minute quantities of blood, which was of particular value to forensics scientists.

8. The way this is done today seems almost simple. For a full description of the process, see http://www.madehow.com/Volume-7/Insulin.html.

9. Given our ability to genetically test people for many diseases for which there are no cures or effective treatments, how should physicians and others go about advising people who want to find out if they have the gene for a particular disease? This dilemma is a controversial one and creates significant social issues. Lawmakers, policy experts, ethicists, scientists, and social scientists are exploring these issues related to gene testing. On one hand, if a person tests positive for a disease, this may, in some cases, enable physicians to more closely monitor the individual for early onset or symptoms of the disease and to intervene earlier than might otherwise have been possible. On the other hand, there are some diseases, such as Huntington's, that are not yet treatable. What do people do with this knowledge if they can do nothing about it? Equally important is that in the future insurance companies could insist on genetic testing and deny policies to those with "prior conditions." A 1994 Institute of Medicine report suggested a set of guidelines for genetic screening, recommending extensive education and counseling of people receiving gene tests. Part of the Human Genome Project focused on supporting research on policies that would maximize the benefits of genetic testing while minimizing the potential for social, economic, and psychological harm for patients.

10. Increased research spending on cancer pales in comparison with the cost of the disease to our society. In 2000, the National Institutes of Health estimated that the overall cost for cancer was $180.2 billion. About a third of this total went for direct medical costs; another $15 billion for indirect morbidity costs (loss of worker productivity due to the illness); and more than $100 billion for indirect mortality costs (lost productivity due to early deaths). Here is

where Mary Lasker's statement about the cost of disease relative to the cost of research comes in.

11. The biographical material used here can be found at http://nobelprize.org/nobel_prizes/medicine/laureates/1966/press.html.

12. Http://nobelprize.org/nobel_prizes/medicine/laureates/1975/press.html.

13. Http://www.biomed-singapore.com/bms/sg/en_uk/index/career_centre/inspirations/year_2005/_professor_arnold1.html.

14. This account of Edward Taylor and Alimta relies on information found at http://www.princeton.edu/~paw/web_exclusives/plus/plus_112206alimta.html and http://www.hamilton.edu/news/more_news/display.cfm?ID=15017.

15. Http://www.princeton.edu/~paw/web_exclusives/plus/plus_112206alimta.html.

16. The Wellcome Trust has been one of the great supporters of basic biological research in England. Founded in 1936, it supports laboratory work in the United States and Great Britain. The industrial branch of the effort has become Glaxo Wellcome.

17. Http://www.essortment.com/all/uterinecancerp_ruxf.htm.

18. The "cloud chamber," which was used for detecting particles of ionizing radiation, was discovered more than a century ago, but when it morphed into the "bubble chamber" (invented by Donald Glaser in 1952) it became one of the most widely used and referenced discoveries in the physics literature.

19. Http://www.acm.org/crossroads/xrds13-1/leehood.html.

20. Sports medicine has led to many developments in advanced noninvasive surgical techniques and in the construction of artificial body parts.

21. Http://www.medterms.com/script/main/art.asp?articlekey=13864.

22. Http://www.discoveriesinmedicine.com/Bar-Cod/Blue-Baby-Operation.html.

23. Elga Wasserman, *The Door in the Dream: Conversations with Eminent Women in Science* (Washington, D.C.: Joseph Henry Press, 2002), 79–85.

24. National Academy of Sciences, "Beyond Discovery: The Hepatitis B Story," http://www.beyonddiscovery.org/content/view.article.asp?a=265. Baruch Blumberg's account of these discoveries was adapted for the National Academy of Sciences by science writer Margie Patlak. See also Barush S. Blumberg, *Hepatitis B: The Hunt for a Killer Virus* (Princeton, N.J.: Princeton University Press, 2002).

25. Http://nobelprize.org/nobel_prize/medicine/laureates/1976/blumberg-autobio.html. It turns out that a high proportion of liver cancer cases are linked to cases of hepatitis B. One study showed that carriers of the hepatitis B virus are a hundred times more likely to die of liver cancer than noncarriers. University and industrial research has led to the development of a vaccine based on the hepatitis B work that may prove highly efficacious in preventing liver cancer by preventing hepatitis B.

26. National Academy of Sciences, "Beyond Discovery: The Hepatitis B Story," http://www.beyonddiscovery.org/content/view.article.asp?a=265.

27. "Technology Transfer Works: 100 Cases from Research to Realization," *Reports from the Field*, 2006, www.betterworldproject.net, p. 32.

28. Starzl was not only a pioneer in organ transplantation but also one of the most prolific authors of scientific papers, producing on average one paper every 7.3 days, according to the Institute on Scientific Information.

29. Presidents' and provosts' responses to my survey.

30. Http://en.wikipedia.org/wiki/Embryonic_stem_cells.

31. Ibid.

32. Ibid.

33. Http://www.hhmi.org/research/investigators/hendrickson_bio.html.

34. Henry J. Kaiser Family Foundation, "HIV/AIDS: Policy Fact Sheet," April 2008.

35. R. H. Foote, "The History of Artificial Insemination: Selected Notes and Notables," *Journal of Animal Science* 80 (2002): 1–10.

36. Ibid.

37. Communications from presidents and provosts.

38. This description of E. O. Wilson and his contributions relies on the reading of his work and the controversies surrounding his work in the 1970s and on the description of his life and work on the E. O. Wilson Foundation website, http://www.eowilson.org/index.php?option=com_content+task=view+id=43+itemid=69, as well as on interviews with Wilson and on a lengthy profile of Wilson that appeared in *The Guardian*, February 17, 2001, http://www.guardian.co.uk/Archive/Article/0.4273.4137503.00.html. See also *Sociobiology: The New Synthesis* (Cambridge: Harvard University Press, 1975).

39. Ed Douglas, "Darwin's Natural Heir," *Guardian Unlimited*, Saturday, February 17, 2001, http://www.guardian.co.uk/Archive/Article/0,4273,4137503,00.html.

40. Http://www.eowilson.org/index.php?option=com_content&task=view&id=43&Itemid=69.

41. Ibid., n186.

42. Ibid.

43. Michael J. Novacek, "Lifetime Achievement: E.O. Wilson. From Ants to Sociobiology to Biodiversity—One of the Great Careers in 20th Century Science," http://www.cnn.com/SPECIALS/2001/americasbest/science.medicine/pro.eowilson.html.

Chapter 9: Buckyballs, Bar Codes, and the GPS

1. Over the past fifty years, sociologists, historians, and philosophers of science, as well as scientists themselves, have written extensively about scientific revolutions and the forces that produce advances in knowledge. For most of that half-century, the history of physics from the seventeenth to the twentieth century has been the principle focus of attention. Recently, interpreters of scientific and technological change have turned their attention more frequently to descriptions and analysis of the biological revolutions of the twentieth century and to engineering, with a special fascination with the growth of computer technology. While the seventeenth century remains a remarkable and important period for our understanding of modern science and the particular forces necessary for sustained scientific growth, little else can compare with the twentieth century, during which we have witnessed an unequalled explosion of knowledge and change in fundamental scientific thinking. As I've made clear, this is hardly limited to physics. You can't really understand twentieth-century America without an appreciation and firm grasp of how science and technology have influenced change. Yet the educational system, particularly in the United States, has failed miserably in communicating this understanding to an increasingly educated population. This is as true at the best universities as it is in our elementary schools. In addition to the sometimes wonderful biographies of scientists produced by journalists, and occasionally by the scientists themselves, there are accessible works for nonscientists to read if they want to have an understanding of these scientific revolutions. You would find, as I have, illuminating accounts of twentieth-century scientific revolutions in the works by Daniel Kevles, who writes with great analytic power and clarity about twentieth-century physics and biology; Gerald Holton, in his essays on these revolutions and the central themes and characters in play; Peter Galison, on laboratory science; and the more global and synthetic work of Charles Gillispie, who has written about the historical tension between objectivity and subjectivity.

2. The introductory section of this chapter relies on the work of the interpreters of science that I've mentioned above, among others. Former university presidents who also have written interestingly about the practical results of university research include James Duderstadt of the University of Michigan and Frank H. T. Rhodes of Cornell.

3. Here I rely on the important work by the historian of science Daniel Kelves, *The Physicists: The History of a Scientific Community in Modern America* (New York: Vintage Books, 1979), 84–90.

4. There are now many biographies of Einstein, but the work that has been most helpful to me has been that of the Harvard physicist and historian of science Gerald Holton. Peter Galison, another Harvard historian of science, has also written brilliantly on Einstein, as has Columbia historian Fritz Stern.

5. Http://www.aip.org/history/heisenberg/p01.htm. Werner Heisenberg, probably best known for the uncertainty principle, was the leader of Germany's nuclear fission research during World War II.

6. Http://nobelprize.org/nobel_prizes/physics/laureates/1938/fermi-bio.html.

7. It was extraordinary that the United States was willing to use the intelligence and scientific brilliance of these recent immigrants to propel the basic understanding of nuclear physics and chemistry forward—and to use their talent in a top secret military project—when so many of them had come from Germany or Austria just prior to the war.

8. Http://nobelprize.org/nobel_prizes/physics/laureates/1939/index.html.

9. Schawlow later married Townes's sister. Http://nobelprize.org/nobel_prizes/physics/laureates/1981/schawlow-autobio.html.

10. Physicists have a way with names, and Gell-Mann named these fundamental building blocks "quarks" in an allusion to James Joyce's *Finnegans Wake*, "Three quarks for Muster Mark." The nomenclature of science is extremely interesting. Physicists have tended to use metaphorical references as a way to characterize idea and theories. Biologists have an extremely cumbersome way of classifying discoveries, which makes it perhaps even more difficult for those unfamiliar with the technical language to follow. Here Gell-Mann uses literary references to describe his general theory and its components.

Gell-Mann's theory for organizing subatomic baryons and mesons into octets was part of a multiple discovery. Israeli physicist Yuval Ne'eman proposed a similar theory almost simultaneously. Both sets of discoveries led to the Eightfold Way, or quark model.

11. The Higgs boson was named after the English physicist Peter Higgs about forty years ago.

12. Http://nobelprize.org/nobel_prizes/physics/laureates/1969/gell-mann-bio.html.

13. Weak interactions occur for all fundamental particles except gluons and photons and involve the exchange or production of W or Z bosons. "There are a number of conservation laws that are valid for strong and electromagnetic interactions, but broken by weak processes. So, despite their slow rate and short range, weak interactions play a crucial role in the make-up of the world we observe" (http://www2.slac.stanford.edu/vvc/theory/weakinteract.html).

14. Among the fields typically found in engineering schools are applied mathematics, applied physics, electrical engineering, chemical engineering, bioengineering, aeronautical engineering, materials science, mechanical engineering, industrial engineering and operations research, civil engineering, earth and environmental engineering, and computer science.

15. Http://www.stanford.edu/home/welcome/research/laser.html. I received this information from the presidents' and provosts' response to my survey. Several of the great universities have particularly valuable websites for information about research discoveries and links to information focusing on their research in partnerships with industry. Two of the best can be found at the websites of Stanford University and MIT. My description of various aspects of the laser closely follows the information presented on these websites and the responses that I received from the presidents and provosts. There are now numerous histories of discoveries and technological applications of the laser that are easily accessible.

16. Ibid.

17. Http://www.eng.iastate.edu/explorer/topics/laser/Isruses.htm.

18. *Science* 304 (April 30, 2004): 679.

19. "The NSF's Nifty Fifty," http://www.nsf.gov/od/lpa/nsf50/nsfoutreach/htm/home.htm.

20. Radar had its theoretical origins in the work of Dr. A. Hoyt Taylor at the Naval Research Laboratory in Washington, D.C. in the 1920s. Robert Wilson-Watt in England demonstrated the first pulsed radio-wave system in 1935. The idea was clearly "in the air." The Russians and Dutch were developing systems of a similar kind, as were Americans. The Radiation Laboratory at MIT, more often referred to as the "Rad Lab," existed from 1940 through the end of 1945. President Roosevelt commissioned the National Defense Research Committee under MIT's president Karl T. Compton and Vannevar Bush. Other labs were set up at Columbia under I. I. Rabi and at Brooklyn Polytechnic Institute. Initially this project was a joint venture with the British, supported by private funding. Those who had spearheaded the project had given it a purposely deceptive name to suggest that it was about research in nuclear physics. About half of the radar used during the war was designed at the Rad Lab, including more than a hundred different radar systems. At its peak, the Rad Lab employed about 4,000 people in the United States and elsewhere. The work was secret and highly successful.

21. Http://en.wikipedia.org/wiki/Transistor#History.

22. Bardeen, Cooper, and Schrieffer received the Nobel Prize for this work in 1972—giving Bardeen his second Nobel Prize.

23. Communication from the provost and http://lane.stanford.edu/portals/history/linac.html.

24. Http://news-service.stanford.edu/news/2007/april18/med-accelerator-041807.html.

25. Http://www.fmri.org/fmri.htm.

26. Ibid.

27. Ibid.

28. Although this new set of techniques holds great promise, researchers recommend caution about relying on fMRI data. We need to gain a better understanding of the statistical and computational models used in fMRI data analysis. Neuroscientists working with fMRI report that our imaging techniques are still primitive compared to what will be needed to gain real understanding of the brain and its functioning, for example.

29. Although these diagnostic tools represent remarkable technological advances over older X-ray technology, it is less certain whether they actually lead to better medical outcomes in certain types of cases. For example, there is a heated debate within the medical community over the actual value of using CAT scans for early diagnosis of lung cancer. No one denies that CAT scans are far better than X-rays for detecting small numbers of cancerous or precancerous cells. What is debated is whether the technology is leading physicians to recommend unnecessary surgery or surgical procedures that have no relation to decreases in mortality rates. In short, the existence of technological breakthroughs does not ensure that the technology will be used in a way that actually improves public health.

30. A good summary of the scope of biomedical engineering can be found at the website of the Biomedical Engineering Society, http://www.bmes.org/careers.asp.

31. In fact, Fung has had several research careers. While at Caltech he published the seminal book on "the phenomenon of flutter, a dynamic instability of airplanes, spacecraft, and birds when their flight-speed exceeds certain critical value." The book became a bible for aeronautical engineering students who were interested in designing safe high-speed aircraft.

32. Http://embc.2006.njit.edu/bio/vanmow.php.

33. Http://en.wikipedia.org/wiki/Carl-Gustaf_Rossby.

34. A good deal of the material used here is drawn from personal knowledge of Lamont and from conversations with scores of Lamont scientists. A good introduction to Ewing can be found in two sources. One is a very informative interview with Frank Press, former presidential science adviser and head of the National Academy of Sciences, who worked as a student and colleague of Ewing. It is housed in the archives at Caltech. See http://oralhistories.library .caltech.edu/77. The other is Laurence Lippsett, "Maurice Ewing and the Lamont-Doherty Earth

Observatory," in Wm. Theodore de Bary, ed., with Jerry Kisslinger and Tom Mathewson, *Living Legacies at Columbia* (New York: Columbia University Press, 2006), 277–295. The quotation is on p. 282.

35. This account of the history and accomplishments of Woods Hole draws on the timeline produced by Woods Hole at http://www.whol.edu/page.do?pid=7503.

36. For one of the best and most accessible books on the geological revolutions surrounding Wegener's theory of continental drift and plate tectonics, see the work of Walter Sullivan, the preeminent science writer for many years at the *New York Times*. Walter Sullivan, *Continents in Motion: The New Earth Debate* (New York: McGraw Hill, 1974). A fourth edition was published by the American Institute of Physics Press in 1991.

37. Ibid., 4th ed.

38. Ibid.

39. The Vine-Matthews' paper, published in *Nature* in 1963 ("Magnetic Anomalies over Ocean Ridges"), supported the concept of seafloor spreading posited by Harry Hess. According to one account, "It had long been suspected, but not proven, that the earth's magnetic field has undergone a number of reversals in polarity in its long history. Vine and Matthews suggested that if ocean ridges were the sites of seafloor creation, and the earth's magnetic field does reverse, then new lava emerging would produce rock magnetized in the current magnetic field of the earth. Older rock would have an opposing polarity, depending on when it was created. By 1966, further studies confirmed the theory for all mid-ocean ridges. This evidence provided compelling support for the ideas of Wegener, and Hess, and resulted in a revolution in the earth sciences, in which the overlooked theory of continental drift was whole-heartedly adopted" (http://science.enotes.com/earth-science/vine-fred-j).

40. Http://vulcan.wr.usgs.gov/Glossary/PlateTectonics/description_plate_tectonics.html.

41. Mark Cane provided me with sources and information about this history.

42. Http://webcenter.ldeo.columbia.edu:81/people.nsf/0/50fe31c23436bb3c85256ef300647e48?OpenDocument.

43. Scripps actually developed the world's first experimental climate forecast center. Its development at Scripps goes back to earlier work by Walter Munk on wave forecasting that was used to support the Allied landings in North Africa and Normandy during World War II.

44. The original concept of a logarithmic scale came from Richter, and the important modification in the concept that established worldwide magnitudes came largely from Gutenberg. More the result of a collaboration of mutual respect and convenience than of friendship, the scale might well have been named the Gutenberg-Richter scale or the Richter-Gutenberg scale, but the honor went to Richter.

45. Http://www.ldeo.columbia.edu/~richards/.

46. Https://webcenter.ldeo.columbia.edu/people.nsf/571fc08d39383f1185256efc004fcb7e/ff261b314f40060c85256ef3006484c3?OpenDocument.

47. We'll encounter Hansen again in a later chapter. He openly protested efforts by members of the Bush administration to alter or truncate his scientific evidence that global warming is taking place and has been a leading figure in the climate-change debate, presenting evidence to Congress and the American people on several occasions.

48. Personal correspondence with Professor Mark Cane of Columbia University; also http://www.af-info.or.jp/eng/honor/hot/enrbro.html.

49. Http://www.beyonddiscovery.org/content/view.page.asp?I=92.

50. Ibid.

51. Cicerone carried out most of his research at the University of Michigan. In 1978, he moved to the Scripps Institution of Oceanography at the University of California at San Diego. From 1998 to 2005 he was chancellor of the University of California at Irvine, and he became president of the National Academy of Sciences in 2005.

52. National Research Council, *Funding a Revolution: Government Support for Computing Research* (Washington, D.C.: National Academy Press, 1999).

53. His device had three basic elements: a control, a memory, and a calculator for doing arithmetic operations. He called his first mechanical calculator, produced in 1936, the Z1; in 1939, he produced the Z2, the first fully functioning electromechanical computer. The Z3, which was the first electronic, fully programmable digital computer based on a binary floating-point number and switching system, was completed in 1941. Zuse's Z3, according to Horst Zuse, who wrote a biography of Konrad, "contained almost all of the features of a modern computer as defined by John von Neumann and his colleagues in 1946. The only exception was the ability to store the program in the memory together with the data. Konrad Zuse did not implement this feature in the Z3, because his 64-word memory was too small to support this mode of operation" (Horst Zuse, "The Life and Work of Konrad Zuse," Part 4, http://www.epemag.com/zuse).

54. Ibid.

55. Http://inventors.about.com/library/weekly/aa060298.htm.

56. Harriet Zuckerman and I interviewed Grace Hopper on June 29, 1981, as part of our NSF-sponsored project on women in science.

57. This was one of hundreds of lengthy taped interviews that I conducted with my Columbia colleague Harriet Zuckerman. We interviewed distinguished women scientists and a matched sample of men to compare the careers of men and women in science.

58. Http://www.sri.com/about/timeline/erma-micr.html.

59. Http://inventors.about.com/library/weekly/aa080498.htm.

60. For an extremely interesting interview with these Nobel laureates that includes a discussion on the shift over time from industrial-based to university-based research, see http://nobelprize.org/nobel_prizes/physics/laureates/2000/kroemer-interview.html.

61. Http://en.wikipedia.org/wiki/Photoshop#Early_history.

62. *The Search for Life: Can We Live Alone*, shown at American Museum of Natural History's Hayden Planetarium. See http://access.nsa.illinois.edu/Releases/02 Releases/03.07.02_San_Diego.html. For a brief description of the San Diego facility and its various uses, see http://portal.acm.org/citation.cf?id=62596.

63. Http://www.ncsa.illinois.edu.

64. Http://www.ncsa.illinois.edu/AboutUs/.

65. Http://www.nsf.gov/od/lpa/nsf50/nsfoutreach/htm/n50_z2/slct_shk.htm.

66. There are now many "histories" of the Internet. Here I rely largely on the work of David C. Mowery, one of America's best students of the interaction between government policies, firms, and research universities within the larger national system of innovation. Particularly useful is his essay, with Timothy Simcoe, "The Internet," in Benn Steil, David G. Victor, and Richard R. Nelson, eds., *Technological Innovation and Economic Performance* (Princeton, N.J.: Princeton University Press, 2002), 229–264.

67. See, for example, Andrew Donoghue, "AT&T: Internet to Hit Full Capacity by 2010," http://news.cnet.com/2100-1034_3-6237715.html.

68. Mowery and Simcoe, "The Internet," 231.

69. Ibid.

70. Ibid.

71. Ibid., 233.

72. Http://www.w3.0rg/People/Berners-Lee/Longer.html.

73. This does not mean that Google as a company will not be the leading search engine for the foreseeable future. Google may well develop its own extensions and innovations or purchase new search engine companies that have more advanced products.

74. Http://computer.howstuffworks.com/googleplex3.htm.

75. Of course, market capitalization is only one way of measuring a company's value, and it tends to be highly variable as stock prices fluctuate. For example, before the 2008 financial crisis, Google was trading at $533 per share (July 2008). In July 2009, its per share price was $442. This changed its market capitalization dramatically ($140 billion in July 2009).

76. My discussion of the activities of the MIT Media Laboratory draws heavily from its website, which is worth a look: http://www.media.mit.edu/research/.

77. Ibid.

78. Http://www.media.mit.edu/?page_id=22.

79. Http://www.media.mit.edu/research/highlights.

80. Http://www.azonano.com/applications.asp.

81. Http://inventors.about.com/library/weekly/aa091598.htm.

82. There continues to be huge inequalities in Internet usage. For example, 95 percent of households in 2007 with incomes of $150,000 or more had Internet access, and 90 percent had broadband connections. In contrast, only 50 percent of households with incomes between $25,000 and $35,000 have access, and only 405 of these had broadband connections. (Http://pewresearch.org/pubs/1254/home-broadband-adoption-2009.)

83. Http://www.stanford.edu/dept/news/pr/95/950613Arc5183.html.

Chapter 10: Nosce te Ipsum

1. Some effort has been made to identify those papers and books that are widely used and have had an impact. These estimates have been based upon quantitative metrics, such as citation counts or references to published work. The information scientist and entrepreneur Eugene Garfield, who was instrumental in developing citation indices as both a bibliographic tool and as a measure of impact and influence, produced, for example, many articles on "citation classics." He included articles on "the 100 articles most cited by social scientists" within some period of time, for example, or "the 100 books most cited" by members of the behavioral science disciplines. These have been useful additions to our knowledge of what makes for ideas and discoveries that have a significant impact within and beyond the profession.

2. Karl W. Deutsch, John Platt, and Dieter Senghaas, "Conditions Favoring Major Advances in Social Sciences," *Science* 171 (February 5, 1971): 450–459. The authors listed sixty-two such discoveries, identifying the authors or coauthors responsible for each core idea and noting the dates of the discoveries, where they were made, the type of support the scholars had received, and the number of years it took before the discoveries had an impact. They focused principally on discoveries made by European and American social scientists. Deutsch and his colleagues chose discoveries that had a significant impact and that either helped "people see something not perceived before" or enabled people to do "something that had not been done before."

3. European nations were producing more of the major advances until the nineteenth century, but it was the United States that took the lead in institutionalizing the social sciences as formal departments at universities and in creating disciplinary societies, particularly in the last quarter of the century. The University of Chicago and Columbia established social and behavioral science departments early on: Chicago had a disciplinary basis in sociology by 1892 (essentially at Chicago's inception) and Columbia in 1893. Émile Durkheim formed the first European department of sociology at Bordeaux in 1895, well before a social science curriculum arrived in Paris. In 1912, Durkheim renamed his chair in education at the Sorbonne as a chair in education and sociology. He had held the position since 1902.

4. One can turn to many sources for identifying substantive and methodological discoveries in the social and behavioral sciences. An excellent source for sociology is Craig Calhoun, ed., *Sociology in America: A History* (Chicago: University of Chicago Press, 2007).

There have been other efforts to catalog major advances in other disciplines, such as the famous *Handbook of Psychology* (New York: Wiley Interscience, 2003). More than forty years ago, Bernard Berelson and Gary A. Steiner developed an inventory of scientific findings in their book *Human Behavior* (New York: Harcourt, Brace, 1964). And one can always go to the discipline-specific *Annual Reviews* for articles on the most important new developments in the social and behavioral sciences. In short, a significant number of published sources try to distill the huge amount of literature being produced by social and behavioral scientists and to place it in a form that emphasizes what major authorities in these fields believe are the most important technological and methodological advances, findings, ideas, concepts, and theories.

5. Daniel Kahneman and Amos Tversky, "Choices, Values, and Frames," in Neil J. Smelser and Dean R. Gerstein, eds., *Behavioral and Social Science: Fifty Years of Discovery* (Washington, D.C.: National Academy Press, 1986), 153.

6. Robert K. Merton, "The Self-Fulfilling Prophecy" (SFP), in *Social Theory and Social Structure* (New York: Free Press, 1949; revised and expanded in 1957, 1968). Originally published in *The Antioch Review*, Summer 1948, 193–210.

7. Two books contain the results of these early voting studies: Paul F. Lazarsfeld, *The People's Choice*, 3d ed. (New York: Columbia University Press, 1988), and Bernard R. Berelson, Paul F. Lazarsfeld, and William N. McPhee, *Voting: A Study of Opinion Formation in a Presidential Election* (Chicago: University of Chicago Press, 1954).

8. Http://nobelprize.org/cgi-bin/print?from=%2Fnobel_prizes%2Feconomics%2Flaureates %2F2005%2Fpress.html. Jon Elster, a Norwegian-born social and political theorist, who has held positions at the University of Chicago and Columbia as well as at the Collège de France, has made fundamental contributions to rational choice theory and its limits, to political theory, to the study of technological change, and to the study of the role of emotion in decision-making. Elster has focused on the conditions under which people make rational choices, the mechanisms responsible for these choices, and the limits to rational choice as a social science theory. Game theorists and decision-making theories, such as those of Kahneman and Tversky, have influenced some of Elster's later works. Recognizing the difficulty of producing robust causal explanations, Elster turns our attention to identifying and understanding social mechanisms that may explain phenomena and how the existence of certain mechanisms will produce a set of social outcomes. Throughout much of his work he has been interested in issues of choice and how we affect or constrain choice.

9. Http://nobelprize.org/nobel_prizes/economics/laureates/2006/press.html.

10. Kahneman and Tversky's paper "Prospect Theory: An Analysis of Decisions Under Risk," in *Econometrica* 47 (March 1979), was the second most highly cited paper to appear in that prestigious economics journal.

11. In assessing the influence of Kahneman and Tversky, Nobel economist Kenneth Arrow said: "It is in the science of economics, however, in which Tversky's and Kahneman's ultimate influence is likely to be most lasting and profound. Most economic analysis presupposes the rationality of actors' decisions and the judgments and predictions upon which those decisions are based. Tversky and Kahneman challenged such presumptions. They demonstrated that very small risks are given disproportionate weight, that prospective losses and gains are not treated symmetrically, that the presence or absence of non-selected alternatives can reverse preference orderings, and that the manner in which options are semantically or mathematically 'framed' can exert undue influence on decision-makers. These violations of normative standards, in turn, are apt to distort private decisions and public policy alike." (Quoted from http://www.stanford .edu/dept/facultysenate/archive/1997_1998/reports/105949/106013.html.)

12. Richard Thaler, "Toward a Positive Theory of Consumer Choice," *Journal of Economic Behavior and Organization* 1 (1980): 39–60.

13. Cited in Jon Elster, *Explaining Social Behavior: More Nuts and Bolts for the Social Sciences* (Cambridge: Cambridge University Press, 2007), 223–224. As Elster noted, Kahneman and Tversky attribute this example to Richard Zeckhauser.

14. Ibid., 45.

15. Daniel Kahneman, Paul Slovic, and Amos Tversky, eds., *Judgment Under Uncertainty: Heuristics and Biases* (Cambridge: Cambridge University Press, 1982), 3.

16. Gary S. Becker, "Human Capital," *The Concise Encyclopedia of Economics*, http://www .econlib.org/library/enc/HumanCapital.html.

17. Private communication with James Heckman.

18. Paul F. Lazarsfeld, *The Academic Mind* (New York: Ayer, 1958), 264.

19. Mark Granovetter, "The Strength of Weak Ties: A Network Theory Revisited," *Sociological Theory* 1 (1983): 201–233. Quotation from pp. 201–202.

20. Dr. Leonard Wong, Thomas A. Kolditz, Raymond A. Millen, and Terrence M. Potter, "Why They Fight: Combat Motivation in the Iraq War," Strategic Studies Institute, U.S. Army War College, July 1, 2003.

21. The sociologist Herbert Hyman first coined the term "reference groups" in 1942. Much work in the social sciences has been done to deal with this social psychological idea in a systematic way. There remain many questions about the utility of the concept, since the specification of reference groups in different situations may vary greatly for the same individual.

22. Peter L. Bernstein, *Capital Ideas: The Improbable Origins of Modern Wall Street* (New York: Free Press, 1993), 113.

23. John B. Taylor, "Discretion Versus Policy Rules in Practice," Carnegie-Rochester Conference Series on Public Policy 39 (1993): 195–214; http://www.frbsf.org/education/activities/drecon/9803.html.

24. Several economist friends of mine helped develop this list of discoveries. I want to thank Robert Solow and James J. Heckman for their advice and counsel.

25. Http://experts.uchicago.edu/experts.php?id=84.

26. Http://www.innocenchproject.org/.

27. Http://www.law.uchicago.edu/socrates/coase.html. Coase's paper is "The Problem of Social Cost," in University of Chicago's *Journal of Law and Economics* 3 (1960): 1–44.

28. A major effort to create a series of "humanities indicators" was launched several years ago by the American Academy of Arts and Sciences. Those involved in this effort are attempting to produce for the humanities the type of compilation that the National Science Board produced for science and engineering in the influential series *Science and Engineering Indicators*. The first published set of humanities indicators appeared in 2009.

29. For an excellent account of Dewey's ideas within a broader social context, see Louis Menand, *The Metaphysical Club: A Story of Ideas in America: A Story of Ideas in America* (New York: Farrar, Strauss and Giroux, 2001).

30. The principles behind the idea of justice—that is, the "Original Position"—are formed behind what Rawls called "the veil of ignorance." The basic rules—the contract—are thus developed at a high level of abstraction, where those developing the rules, who are assumed to be equally rational, do so without knowing their own characteristics or social statuses. In other words, behind the veil of ignorance they do not know their own race, religion, ethnicity, or general endowments, such as intelligence or social class. Thus, in theory, when they derive the principles they will be more likely not to privilege anyone with particular characteristics. Since they will not find out whether they will be the beneficiaries of the rules until the contract is in place, they are likely to adopt rules that will not lead to inequalities on the basis of social characteristics. Rawls is not opposed to inequalities. From the Original Position, he derives Two Principles of Justice: The first "states that each person in a society is to have as much basic liberty as possible, as long as everyone is granted the same liberties." The second "states that while

social and economic inequalities can be just, they must be available to everyone equally (i.e., no one is to be on principle denied access to greater economic advantage) and such inequalities must be to the advantage of everyone. This means that economic inequalities are only justified when the least advantaged member of society is nonetheless better off than she would be under alternative arrangements" (John Rawls, *A Theory of Justice* [Cambridge: Harvard University Press, 1971]). These are ordered principles. Society cannot move to the second principle until it has satisfied the first principle of civil liberties.

31. I want to thank Columbia's highly distinguished Pierre Matisse Professor of Art History, David Freedberg, for providing me with the material used here.

32. There has been significant growth in the study of women's history over the past twenty years. Among the many leading scholars in the field are Natalie Zemon Davis, Nancy Chodorow, Carol Gilligan, Caroline Walker Bynum, Biddy Martin, Drew Gilpin Faust, Kathryn Kish Sklar, Gayatri Spivak, Mary Beth Norton, Joan W. Scott, Lynn Hunt, Joyce Appleby, Linda Kerber, and Margaret Rossiter. The field of African American studies has also burgeoned in the past two decades. Among the notable senior leaders in the field are: Henry Louis Gates, Jr., Anthony Appiah, William Julius Wilson, Lawrence Bobo, Cornel West, Patricia Williams, Kimberly Crenshaw, and Manning Marable.

33. Presidents' and provosts' list of discoveries and Paul Lehrman, "A Talk with John Chowning," February 1, 2005, http://mixonline.com/mag/audio_talk_john_chowning/.

34. And the humanists have been joined by other university-based public intellectuals, such as Brian Greene, a physicist working on string theory, who has now taken to educating a wider audience about the wonders of science. His book *The Elegant Universe* has sold hundreds of thousands of copies, as have the works of other scientists, such as Stephen Jay Gould, Steven Hawking, and Stephen Weinberg, who have gained the attention of the wider public. Political theorists such as Michael Walzer write extensively about issues of moral philosophy and political science, such as just and unjust wars, for the public. Economists such as Jeffrey Sachs are educating the world's population about the threats of global climate change and the need for attending to poverty throughout the world. Along with social class and distinctions based upon international power relations, the growth of literary studies that focus on gender, race, sexual orientation, and ethnic identities has been most pronounced.

Chapter 11: Academic Freedom and Free Inquiry

1. See *Sweezy v. New Hampshire*, 354 U.S. 234 (1957 at 250). Paul Sweezy was a well-known Marxist economist who taught at the University of New Hampshire. Also, in *Slochower v. Board of Education*, 350 U.S. 551 (1956), the Court found unconstitutional a New York statute that required the firing of city employees (including those in public colleges) who used their Fifth Amendment rights to avoid answering questions by a legislative committee.

2. While these examples are not proof, they will have to suffice, along with testimony from scientists and scholars, until we have more systematic evidence of the causal relationship between the existence of academic freedom and university distinction that I claim exists.

3. The foremost historian of Russian and Soviet science for the past half-century has been Loren Graham, who has held faculty positions at Columbia and Harvard. He has written many volumes on science and society in Russia, and these few paragraphs on Lysenko rely heavily upon his work. Among Graham's works worth consulting are *Science in Russia and the Soviet Union: A Short History* (New York: Cambridge University Press, 1993), Chap. 6; *Science and Philosophy in the Soviet Union* (New York: Knopf, 1972); *Between Science and Values* (New York: Columbia University Press, 1981), Chap. 8; *Science, Philosophy, and Human Behavior in the Soviet Union* (New York: Columbia University Press, 1987); and *Moscow Stories* (Bloomington: Indiana University Press, 2006).

4. In a major 1935 speech, Lysenko accused his critics, particularly the geneticists, of sabotage. He said: "A great deal of mortification has had to be endured in defending vernalization in all kinds of battles with so-called scientists. . . . The kolkhoz system [a form of Soviet collective farming] pulled it through . . . on the basis of the sole scientific methodology, the one and only scientific guiding principle, which Comrade Stalin teaches us daily." At this point Stalin was moved to jump from his seat shouting: "Bravo, Comrade Lysenko, bravo!" (Valery N. Soyfer, *Lysenko and the Tragedy of Soviet Science* [New Brunswick, N.J.: Rutgers University Press, 1994], 60–61). And when Stalin talked, Soviets listened.

5. Theodosius Dobzhansky, "N. I. Vavilov, A Martyr of Genetics: 1887–1942," in *Death of Science in Russia: The Fate of Genetics as Described in Pravda and Elsewhere* (Philadelphia: University of Pennsylvania Press, 1949), 80–89.

6. Loren Graham discusses this at some length in *Between Science and Values,* Chap. 8.

7. Geoffrey R. Stone, "Civil Liberties in Wartime," *Journal of Supreme Court History* 28, no. 3 (2003): 215–251. Quotation from p. 215.

8. To cite just a few recent books: Geoffrey Stone, *Perilous Times: Free Speech in Wartime from the Sedition Act of 1798 to the War on Terrorism* (New York: W. W. Norton, 2004); Cynthia Brown, ed., *Lost Liberties: Ashcroft and the Assault on Civil Liberties* (New York: New Press, 2003); Richard C. Leone and Greg Amig, Jr., eds., *Liberty Under Attack: Reclaiming Our Freedoms in an Age of Terror* (New York: PublicAffairs, 2007); Frederick A. O. Schwarz, Jr., and Aziz Z. Hug, *Unchecked and Unbalanced: Presidential Power in a Time of Terror* (New York: New Press, 2007); James L. Turk and Allan Manson, *Free Speech in Fearful Times: After 9/11 in Canada, the U.S., Australia, and Europe* (Toronto: James Lorimer, 2007); and Richard Posner, *Not a Suicide Pact: The Constitution in a Time of National Emergency* (Oxford: Oxford University Press, 2006).

9. Quoted in Ellen W. Schrecker, *No Ivory Tower: McCarthyism and the Universities* (New York: Oxford University Press, 1986), 19. Schrecker's book remains the best overall analysis and discussion of McCarthyism and the Cold War as they affected the academic community. An excellent but more limited analysis of the links between the intelligence community and university leaders during the McCarthy period, with a focus on the Ivy League universities, can be found in Sigmund Diamond, *Compromised Campus: The Collaboration of Universities with the Intelligence Community, 1945–1955* (New York: Oxford University Press, 1992).

10. "Alumni Roused by Nearing Case," *New York Times,* June 22, 1915, http://www.brocku.ca/MeadProject/NYT/NYT_1915_06_22.html.

11. As a fledgling organization that represented universities and professors, the leaders of the AAUP were notable in not supporting the speech of opponents to America's war effort.

12. Quoted in John A. Saltmarsh, *Scott Nearing: An Intellectual Biography* (Philadelphia: Temple University Press, 1991), 102.

13. As quoted in David Cole, *Enemy Aliens* (New York: New Press, 2003), 112.

14. There were enlightened leaders of universities in those early years—individuals who understood how critical academic freedom was to building great universities. Perhaps unsurprisingly, William Rainey Harper, the first president of the University of Chicago, understood this when, in 1892, he observed: "People must remember that, when, for any reason . . . the administration of their institution [a university] or the instruction in any one of its departments is changed by an influence from without, whenever effort is made to dislodge an officer or a professor because the political sentiment of the majority has undergone a change, at that moment the institution has ceased to be a university." Geoffrey Stone made me aware of this comment by Harper. See William Rainey Harper, *The Trend in Higher Education* (Chicago: University of Chicago Press, 1905), 8. See also http://www.archive.org/stream/trendinhigheredu00harprich/trendinhigheredu00harprich_djvu.txt.

15. Stone, *Perilous Times,* 236–237.

16. *Schenck v. United States,* 249 U.S. 47 (1919).

17. *Abrams v. United States,* 250 U.S. 616 (1919).

18. *Gitlow v. New York,* 268 U.S. 652 (1925).

19. After joining the Justice Department in 1917, Hoover worked for the department's Alien Enemy Bureau and then headed its Alien Radical division, "where he maintained lists of subversive foreigners and masterminded the first nationwide roundup of radicals" (Cole, *Enemy Aliens,* 116). At the "General Intelligence Division" within the Bureau of Investigation, Hoover was assigned to "gather and coordinate information relating to radical activities" (Stone *Perilous Times,* 223). He "created an elaborate card system including the names of more than 200,000 individuals suspected of radical activities, associations or beliefs" (ibid.).

20. Stone, *Perilous Times,* 221.

21. Ibid., 223.

22. In Charles Beard's letter of resignation from Columbia, he added: "I cannot find words to convey to you what it means to sever close ties of so many years standing. Above all do I regret to part from my colleagues. As I think of their scholarship and their world-wide reputation and compare them with the few obscure and willful trustees who now dominate the university and terrorize the young instructors, I cannot repress my astonishment that America, of all countries, has made the status of the professor lower than that of the manual laborer, who, through his union, has at least some voice in the terms and conditions of his employment. Holding his position literally by the day, the professor is liable to dismissal without a hearing, without the judgment of his colleagues who are his real peers." (Letter from Charles Beard to Nicholas Murray Butler on October 8, 1917, Charles Beard and Mary Ritter Beard papers, 1874–1976, DePauw University, Folder 1.)

23. The Palmer raids had a dramatic effect on membership in organizations that were considered by the government to be subversive, with membership plummeting in the early 1920s.

24. In 1940, the year the Smith Act was passed, New York state began its own efforts to purge schools of Communists. The infamous Rapp-Condert Committee investigated Communists in New York schools, and its inquiries led to the largest purge in the nation of teachers from the state and city colleges until the height of the McCarthy period.

25. See, for example, the excellent and most comprehensive discussion of the political repression of academic radicals from 1932 to 1942 in Schrecker, *No Ivory Tower,* 63–83. For a more general picture, see Robert Justin Goldstein, *Political Repression in Modern America from 1870 to the Present* (Cambridge: Schenkman, 1978); Diamond, *Compromised Campus,* Chaps. 7, 8, and 9.

26. Section 2385 of the act stated,

"Whoever knowingly or willfully advocates, abets, advises, or teaches the duty, necessity, desirability, or propriety of overthrowing or destroying the government of the United States[,] . . . whoever, with intent to cause the overthrow or destruction of any such government, prints, publishes, edits, issues, circulates, sells, distributes, or publicly displays any written or printed matter advocating, advising, or teaching the duty, necessity, desirability . . . of overthrowing or destroying any government of the United States by force or violence[,] . . . [w]hoever organizes or helps or attempts to organize any society, group, or assembly of persons who teach, advocate, or encourage the overthrow or destruction of any such governments by force or violence; or becomes or is a member of, or affiliates with, any such society, group, or assembly of persons, knowing the purposes thereof—Shall be fined under this title or imprisoned not more than twenty years, or both, and shall be ineligible for employment by the United States or any department or agency thereof, for the five years next following his conviction. (Now found in 18 *U.S. Code* §2385 [2000])."

27. Stone, *Perilous Times,* 395, notes that during the Cold War period, the Court handed down sixty decisions involving the First Amendment, compared with just six as a consequence

of World War I. For a penetrating discussion of *Dennis v. United States, 341 U.S. 494 (1951)*, as it relates to the evolution of theories of the First Amendment, and in particular the development of the thinking of Judge Learned Hand following the decision in *Masses Publishing Co. v. Patten*, 244 F. 535 (S.D.N.Y. 1917), and as a result of the evolving theory and use of the "clear and present danger" standard, see Stone, *Perilous Times*, Chap. 5.

28. *Dennis v. United States* (cited above) was the landmark defining case. In addition to *Dennis*, other decisions that Justice Douglas said "show the Court running with the hounds and joining the hue and cry against unpopular people" were *Adler v. Board of Education*, 342 U.S. 485, (1952), which upheld New York's Feinberg Law barring teachers who were members of the Communist Party; *Bailey v. Richardson*, 341 U.S. 918 (1951*)*; and *Barsky v. Board of Regents*, 347 U.S. 442 (1954). It was not until the mid-1950s that "the Court swerved its course and acted to protect the rights of those same people by limiting the thrust of the antisubversive program." See William O. Douglas, "Judicial Treatment of Nonconformists," in *The Court Years, 1939–1975: The Autobiography of William O. Douglas* (New York: Random House, 1980); and http://www.english.upenn.edu/~afilreis/50s/douglas-court-years.html. In *Dennis*, the Court affirmed the conviction of twelve members of the national board of the Communist Party who had been indicted under the Smith Act (18 U.S.C. 371) "for conspiring to advocate the duty and necessity of overthrowing the government of the United States by force and violence" (Stone, *Perilous Times*, 396).

29. Alan Brinkley, "The Politics of Anti-Communism," http://caho.columbia.edu/seminars/0712/web/sect_2/0712_S2_html.

30. Truman's Executive Order 9835 set up the program. The first Attorney General's List of Subversive Organization was published by the Truman administration in late 1947, which "was tantamount to public branding, without a hearing," wrote Stone: "Contributions to listed organizations quickly dried up, membership dwindled and available meeting places became scarce. The greatest impact of the Attorney General's list, however, was not on the organizations listed, but on the general willingness of Americans to express any dissent from the official orthodoxy" (Stone, *Perilous Times*, 344).

31. Schrecker, *No Ivory Tower*, 5.

32. The now famous Hollywood Ten were Alvah Bessie, Herbert Biberman, Lester Cole, Edward Dmytryk, Ring Lardner, Jr., John Howard Lawson, Albert Maltz, Samuel Ornitz, Adrian Scott, and Dalton Trumbo. For a brief description of the work of the Hollywood Ten, see http://www.lib.berkeley.edu/MRC/blacklist.html. Those ten were quickly dismissed from the hearing and subsequently charged, convicted, and sent to jail for contempt of Congress. Each served up to a year in prison. Shortly thereafter, the film industry, radio, and television began to produce blacklists to purge leftists from the entertainment industry. *Red Channels* was perhaps the most infamous blacklist. Because of its extensive use by advertisers who refused to sponsor shows that hired blacklisted actors, writers, or musicians, it effectively put these people out of work. The purging of actors, writers, directors, and producers from the entertainment industry was not limited to Hollywood. There were similar purges in New York, where blacklists were used to deny employment to any who had been "listed" in *Red Channels* or other blacklists as Communists, former Communists, or potentially subversive. *Red Channels: The Report of Communist Influence in Radio and Television* was published by the right-wing journal *Counterattack* in June 1950. It contained the names of 151 actors, writers, broadcast journalists, musicians, and others who allegedly had Communist ties. In its introduction, the tract says: "Several commercially sponsored dramatic series are used as sounding boards, particularly with reference to current issues in which the Party is critically interested: 'academic freedom,' 'civil rights,' 'peace,' the H-bomb, etc. . . . With radios in most American homes and with approximately 5 million TV sets in use, the Cominform and the Communist Party USA now rely more on radio and TV than on the press and motion pictures as 'belts' to transmit pro-Sovietism

to the American public." The advertising agencies used these blacklists like Bibles, referring to them and vetting individuals connected with radio, television, movies, or theater projects before agreeing to sponsor programs. For a full treatment of the Hollywood response to McCarthy, see Victor S. Navasky, *Naming Names* (New York: Viking Press, 1983).

33. Ellen Schrecker, "Political Tests for Professors: Academic Freedom During the McCarthy Years," paper presented at a fiftieth anniversary retrospective, Symposium on the California Loyalty Oath, University of California. See http://sunsite.Berkeley.edu/uchistory/archives_exhibits/loyaltyoaths/symposium/schrecker.html/.

34. As quoted in Schrecker, *No Ivory Tower,* 107, which includes an extended discussion of this case.

35. Ibid.

36. Ibid., 106.

37. The history of the state investigations and the loyalty oath debate are elaborated on in far greater detail in Ellen Schrecker's various works cited above.

38. Schrecker, *No Ivory Tower,* 110.

39. Diamond, *Compromised Campus,* 221–222.

40. Quoted in Eric Bentley, ed., *Thirty Years of Treason: Excerpts from Hearings Before the House Committee on Un-American Activities, 1938–1968* (New York: Viking Press, 1971), 611.

41. Robert M. MacIver, *Academic Freedom in Our Time* (New York: Columbia University Press, 1955), 149.

42. Quoted in Schrecker, *No Ivory Tower,* 111, from James Bryant Conant in the *Harvard Crimson,* June 23, 1949.

43. Quoted in James Hershberg, *James B. Conant: Harvard to Hiroshima and the Making of the Nuclear Age* (New York: Knopf, 1993), 606.

44. Diamond, *Compromised Campus,* 109.

45. Ibid., 3.

46. The Harvard policy was exemplified in Diamond's own FBI file: "From information provided the Boston Division by other individuals having Harvard Corporation appointments, it appears that Dean Bundy is insisting that former Communist Party members, who now have Harvard Corporation appointments, shall provide the Federal Bureau of Investigation with a full and complete account of their activities in the Communist Party and shall at the same time identify all individuals known to them as participants in activities of the Communist Party and its related front organizations" (Sigmund Diamond, *Compromised Campus,* 292). Diamond is quoting an FBI document, July 28, 1954, SAC [Special Agent in Charge] Boston to the director.

47. Bentley, *Thirty Years of Treason,* 568.

48. See Zechariah Chafee, Jr., *Free Speech in the United States* (Cambridge: Harvard University Press, 1941), 564–565. Chafee wrote in an introduction to Alan Barth's *The Loyalty of Free Men* (New York: Viking Press, 1951), xxxii, "Behind the dozens of sedition bills in Congress last session, behind teachers' oaths and compulsory flag salutes, is a desire to make our citizens loyal to their government. Loyalty is a beautiful idea, but you cannot create it by compulsion and force." Elsewhere, Chaffee said, "It is high time to stop this persistent probing of the patriotism of professors and schoolteachers. We teachers have a difficult job, and perhaps we are not doing it very successfully, but we shall surely do it worse when misguided people are constantly tearing us out of the ground to see whether we are growing straight or crooked. You can have perfectly sterilized minds in schools and universities, or you can have good teaching, but you can't have both." See Zechariah Chafee, Jr., *Free Speech in the United States* (Cambridge: Harvard University Press, 1941), xxxii.

49. See Robert M. MacIver, *Academic Freedom in Our Time* (New York: Columbia University Press, 1955). This study, which was authored by MacIver, had a curious history. It engaged

an executive committee and a panel of advisers, which included very distinguished members of the academy, including presidents of a number of prestigious colleges and universities. A. Whitney Griswold, president of Yale, was initially part of the advisory panel but dropped out because of lack of time. However, if one compares the outcome of the MacIver study and its recommendations with the AAU position statement that was authored by President Griswold, one sees two different worlds. The history of the Columbia project is discussed in Diamond, *Compromised Campus*.

50. Here even the MacIver committee allows for denial of appointments of members of the Communist Party: "The academic disqualifications of the Party communist are so serious that no injustice is committed if he is excluded from nomination or appointment" (Robert MacIver, *Academic Freedom in Our Time* [New York: Guardian Press, 1967], 192).

51. I have long known of the extraordinary career of Robert Hutchins as president and chancellor of the University of Chicago and how he built it into one of the nation's finest research universities, but I was not familiar with his testimony to the Broyles Commission or his other defenses of academic freedom until I read Stone's *Perilous Times*. I am grateful to Stone for this and for supplying me with the above text, which can also be found in his book.

52. For a more extended discussion of the overreaction to fear during the Cold War in the context of balancing perceived national security needs and civil liberties, as well as the evolution of thinking about the First Amendment, see Stone, *Perilous Times*, Chap. 5. Hutchins's statement is found in "The Great Investigation," published by the All-Campus Committee Opposing the Broyles Bills and the Broyles Investigation, University of Chicago, 1949, 2–4.

53. Ibid.

54. See Schrecker, *No Ivory Tower*, 112. Alan Barth said, "Where university officials have, like Chancellor Hutchins, courageously and toughly resisted political encroachment in their domain, they have managed so far to preserve academic freedom in the United States" (*The Loyalty of Free Men* [New York: Pocket Books, 1952], 237). It is difficult, of course, to estimate what the overall consequences of the Cold War were for American universities, since we can only speculate on what might have been different had McCarthyism and the academic purges not taken place. Such speculation can be found in some of the works that have been cited above, particularly in Ellen Schrecker's books and in the final chapter of Sigmund Diamond's *Compromised Campus*.

55. Paul F. Lazarsfeld and Wagner Thielens, Jr., *The Academic Mind: Social Scientists in a Time of Crisis* (New York: Free Press, 1955).

56. Samuel A. Stouffer, *Communism, Conformity, and Civil Liberties* (Gloucester, Mass.: Peter Smith, 1963). The data were collected for the study in 1954.

57. Ibid., 431.

58. New York Herald Tribune, December 24, 1947, as quoted in Stone, *Perilous Times*, who in turn found the reference in David Caute, *The Great Fear: The Anti-Communist Purge Under Truman and Eisenhower* (New York: Simon and Schuster, 1978), 26–27. Italics in original. Since Hutchins delivered his notable defenses of academic freedom and the idea of the university, there have been numerous other articulate defenders of academic freedom when it most needed defending. Perhaps it is not entirely surprising that some of the most articulate came, again, from the University of Chicago during the tumultuous days of student protests in the 1960s. In the face of public reaction to campus riots by students who were protesting the Vietnam War, and who were committed to the perfectibility of institutions through racial and gender equality, Edward H. Levi, president of the University of Chicago, held fast to the core notion of freedom from external political interference in his book *Point of View: Talks on Education* (Chicago: University of Chicago Press, 1969), 16–18. He defended the freedom of individuals to criticize and develop their own points of view, however annoying they might be to their colleagues or the outside world:

"The university has been a center of self-criticism for our society. . . . The university's role is not based upon a conception of neutrality or indifference to society's problems, but an approach to the problems through the only strength which a university is entitled to assert. It is a conservative role because it values cultures and ideas, and reaffirms the basic commitment to reason. It is revolutionary because of its compulsion to discover and to know. It is modest because it recognizes that the difficulties are great and the standards are demanding. . . . One does not direct the University of Chicago to the kinds of inquiry it should pursue, or the point of view its professors should have. I assume there has been no point in time when some professors' views were not irritating to some segment of the community. In a day when it is demanded by some groups that the university as an institution take an official position on social or political action, or close its campus to those whose presence carries an unacceptable symbol, this insistence upon freedom within the university may appear either as outmoded or as a test of whether the university really has meant what it has always said. I think we have shown, and I trust we will show, that we do mean this commitment to freedom—to inquiry, to know and to speak. For those who regret this conclusion, and believe a university can and should be captured as an instrument for directed social change in the society, there is perhaps this compensation: the world of learning is much too complicated to be directed in this way; the results would be disappointing in any event."

59. This was part of a statement composed by Joan W. Scott, a professor of social science at the Institute for Advanced Study, in Princeton, New Jersey, and former chair of the AAUP Professors' Committee A on Academic Freedom; Jeremy Adelman, chair of history at Princeton University; Steve Caton, director of the Center for Middle Eastern studies at Harvard University; Edmund Burke III, director of the Center for World History at the University of California at Santa Cruz; and me in October 2007.

60. I sat on more than seven hundred ad hoc committees considering tenure cases at Columbia while I was provost. These meetings are held in confidence and it is often difficult for those outside the committee hearing to understand why a candidate was turned down for tenure. I've overseen cases where the expectation for tenure was very high, yet the assessments suggested that the quality of work did not meet Columbia's standards for tenure. Few on the outside—and no candidate who was turned down—believed that the decisions were unbiased. In my judgment they were fair. Tenure reviews are a bit like black boxes: You may see what goes in and what comes out the other end, but you don't know what went on inside the black box. There may be cases where the decision is negative as a result of poor judgments of quality and potential, but where appropriate criteria were used, but there are undoubtedly just as many cases where people who probably did not deserve tenure on the basis of the quality of their work actually received it. In fact, the false positives (those who receive tenure but may not have deserved it) probably outnumber the false negatives.

61. Joseph Massad, "Intimidating Columbia University," *Al-Ahram Weekly Online*, http://weekly.ahram.org.eg/2004/715/op33.htm.

62. It is a well-known fact that Jewish academics, and Jewish Americans in general, are among the most liberal in the U.S. population. But their liberalism on so many issues has in recent decades confronted self-interest. Although a majority of Jewish professors have always supported progressive policies such as affirmative action, that has not always been the case among Jewish advocacy groups that have tried to influence educational policy. In the early days of efforts to diversify American university campuses, Jewish advocacy groups came out strongly against affirmative action for minorities, on the surface as a violation of meritocracy, but more probably because they saw the very high representation of their own minority group in student bodies and on university faculties at stake. Although these same organizations usually support such programs today, during the early political conflict over diversity and affirmative action they were very resistant to change. This was a source of tensions between the black and Jewish communities after decades of alliance on issues of civil rights.

63. Andrew Mytelka, "In Abrupt Reversal, Erwin Chemerinsky to Become Law School Dean at UC-Irvine," *Chronicle of Higher Education*, September 17, 2007.

64. Piper Fogg, "No Bounty for Reports of 'Bias' at UCLA," *Chronicle of Higher Education*, February 3, 2006.

65. Dan Frosch, "Court Upholds Dismissal of Colorado Professor," *New York Times*, July 8, 2009; Peter Schmidt, "Judge Rejects Ward Churchill's Plea for Reinstatement, Vacates Verdict in His Favor," *Chronicle of Higher Education*, July 8, 2009.

66. Karin Fischer, "Judge Overturns Florida's Ban on Academic Travel to Cuba," *Chronicle of Higher Education*, August 29, 2008.

67. The website for Students for Academic Freedom is at http://www.studentsforacademic freedom.org/. For the Student Bill of Rights, see the same website with the addition to the URL of: documents/1922/sbor.html.

68. The Columbia University Handbook in 2008, for example, said, "Academic freedom implies that all officers of instruction are entitled to freedom in the classroom in discussing their subjects; that they are entitled to freedom in research and in the publication of its results; and that they may not be penalized by the University for expression of opinion or associations in their private civic capacity; but they should bear in mind the special obligations arising from their position in the academic community," Appendix B, p. 184, or http://www.columbia .edu/cu/vpaa/handbook/appendixb.html.

69. This is not an easy thing to do, as Justice Oliver Wendell Holmes, Jr., reminded us in his memorable opinion in the 1919 Abrams case: "Persecution for the expressions of opinions seems to me perfectly logical. If you have no doubt of your premises or your power and want a certain result with all your heart you naturally express your wishes in law and sweep away all opposition" (*Abrams v. United States*, 250 U.S. 616 [1919]).

70. Akeel Bilgrami, private communication of an essay on academic freedom produced for a conference on the subject at the New School for Social Research, 2008.

71. This happens more often than scholars and scientists would like to admit. There is, however, a fine line between exclusion for good reasons and exclusion for poor reasons. The counterclaims or ideas may lack sufficient evidence to make them worthy of inclusion in the debate, or they may be truly premature, whereby there is not enough information for them to be fully understood or placed into a context allowing them to be reasonably discussed. Both of these are good reasons to exclude a subject. Creationism fits into the first category—there is not enough scientific evidence to make it worthy of debate and discussion as an alternative to Darwinian evolution.

72. I am omitting discussion here of a host of other possible constraints on academic freedom in research. I have not discussed the way other government regulations, such as those involving Institutional Review Boards, may needlessly limit free inquiry. Nor have I discussed the rise of the cadre of lawyers that are part of today's academic landscape and the role they play in limiting some dimensions of academic freedom.

73. Neil Gross (Harvard University) and Solon Simmons (George Mason University), "The Social and Political Views of American Professors," Working Paper, September 24, 2007. A version of this paper was delivered at the American Sociological Association Meetings in New York, August 2007.

74. Robert Post, "The Structure of Academic Freedom," in Beshara Doumani, ed., *Academic Freedom After September 11* (New York: Zone Books, 2006), 61–106. Quotation from p. 62.

75. In a report on the first global colloquium of university presidents held at Columbia University on January 18–19, 2005, a gathering of more than forty university leaders and professors defined the responsibility that societies grant universities throughout the world and the way in which academic freedom is essential for their adequate functioning. The organizer and general editor of the proceedings, Michael W. Doyle of Columbia, a professor of political science and

law, included the following statement, signed by sixteen university presidents from around the world who attended the colloquium, in the published proceedings:

"Modern societies now entrust universities with greater responsibilities than ever before. Universities are charged with preserving the knowledge of the past and transmitting it to the next generation; educating tomorrow's citizens, professionals, and leaders; and fostering the discovery of new knowledge that may either strengthen or challenge established ideas and norms— all with the aim of deepening human understanding and bettering the human condition. They also function as engines of economic development, foster technological and scientific innovation, stimulate creativity in the arts and literature, and address global problems such as poverty, disease, ethnopolitical conflict, and environmental degradation. . . . The activities of preserving, pursuing, disseminating, and creating knowledge and understanding requires societies to respect the autonomy of universities, of the scholars who research and teach in them, and of the students who come to them to prepare their lives as knowledgeable citizens and capable leaders. The autonomy of universities is the guarantor of academic freedom in the performance of scholars' professional duties. Academic freedom is therefore distinct from—and not a mere extension of—the freedoms of thought, conscience, opinion, assembly, and association promised to all human beings under Articles 18, 19, and 20 of the Universal Declaration of Human Rights and other international covenants."

76. Isaiah Berlin, "Two Concepts of Liberty" (1958), in *Four Essays on Liberty* (New York: Oxford University Press, 1969), 118–172. In the essay, Berlin distinguished "negative liberty" from "positive liberty," which is defined as freedom for a predefined end.

77. For an informative discussion of alternative bases on which one can justify academic freedom, see the debate between John Searle and Richard Rorty. An entrance into that debate can be found in Richard Rorty, "Does Academic Freedom Have Philosophical Presuppositions?" in Louis Menand, ed., *The Future of Academic Freedom* (Chicago: The University of Chicago Press, 1996), Chap. 2, and in John Searle, "Rationality and Realism: What's at Stake?" in Jonathan R. Cole, Elinor G. Barber, and Stephen R. Graubard, *The Research University in a Time of Discontent* (Baltimore: Johns Hopkins University Press, 1994), Chap. 3.

Chapter 12: The Enemy Is Us

1. Stanley Hoffmann, "America Goes Backward," *New York Review of Books*, June 12, 2003.

2. Uniting and Strengthening America by Providing Appropriate Tools Required to Intercept and Obstruct Terrorism Act of 2001, P.L. No. 107-56.

3. Stephen J. Schulhofer, "The Patriot Act and the Surveillance Society," in Richard C. Leone and Gregg Anrig, Jr., eds., *Liberty Under Attack: Reclaiming Our Freedoms in an Age of Terror* (New York: PublicAffairs, 2007), 119–141.

4. The Homeland Security Act of 2002, P.L. No. 107-296.

5. Ibid. The Lawyers Committee for Human Rights (LCHR) published a report entitled "Assessing the New Normal: Liberty and Security for the Post–September 11 United States," in 2003. It outlined with great clarity some of the provisions of the executive orders and legislation that created a new climate for the relationship between the government and the people in the post-9/11 era. I follow the LCHR report closely in the following paragraphs. Other sources that I have found particularly useful have been published by the American Civil Liberties Union (ACLU), the Cato Institute, and by newspapers, particularly the *New York Times* and the *Washington Post*. David Cole's essay, "The Course of Least Resistance: Repeating History in the War on Terrorism," in Cynthia Brown, ed., *Lost Liberties* (New York: New Press, 2003), 13–32, was also particularly useful. The act defines terrorism very broadly to include "acts dangerous to human life that are a violation of the criminal laws" if they "appear to be

intended . . . to influence the policy of a government by intimidation or coercion" and if they "occur primarily within the territorial jurisdiction of the United States." Under this broad definition, a person could easily be considered a "terrorist" if he or she, for example, contributed money to a charitable organization that then supported a group that was defined by the government as a terrorist organization or a government that supported terrorists.

6. Recall the language of the Fourth Amendment to the U.S. Constitution: "The right of the people to be secure in their persons, houses, papers, and effects, against unreasonable searches and seizures, shall not be violated, and no Warrants shall issue, but upon probable cause, supported by Oath or affirmation, and particularly describing the place to be searched, and the persons or things to be seized." An excellent essay on the provisions of the Patriot Act can be found in Nancy Chang, "How Democracy Dies: The War on Our Civil Liberties," in Cynthia Brown, ed., *Lost Liberties* (New York: New Press, 2003), 42.

7. LCHR, "Assessing the New Normal," 18–19.

8. The chief justice of the U.S. Supreme Court selects a set of district court judges to sit on the FISC.

9. Foreign Intelligence Surveillance Act (FISA). Italics added.

10. Between 2001 and 2002, there was a 31 percent increase in requests for FISA warrants, but only a 9 percent increase during the same period in standard federal criminal search warrants. According to the Lawyers Committee for Human Rights, "In addition, since September 11, the FBI has obtained 170 *emergency* FISA orders—searches that may be carried out on the sole authority of the attorney general for 72 hours before being reviewed by any court. This is more than triple the number employed in the prior 23-year history of the FISA statute" (quoted in LCHR, "Assessing the New Normal," x).

11. Chang, *Lost Liberties*, 44. Chang, among others, has pointed out that under what has become known as the "library records" provision, the Justice Department or federal law enforcement agencies do not have to demonstrate probable cause to get a court order. The library records provision actually applies to "any tangible things (including books, records, papers, documents, and other items)" (section 215 of the Patriot Act).

12. Chang, *Lost Liberties*, 45. The University of Illinois Library Research Center surveyed 906 public libraries in October 2002, a year after the passage of the Patriot Act, and found that since 9/11, federal and local law enforcement agencies had visited at least 545 of them to request information on patrons. Approximately 10 percent of those libraries reported that the visitors referred to Section 215 of the USA Patriot Act. The results of this survey are presented in Lauren Teffeau, Megan Mustafoff, and Leigh Estabrook, "Access to Information and the Freedom to Access: The Intersection of Public Libraries and the USA PATRIOT ACT," in Todd Loendorf and G. David Garson, *Patriotic Information Systems* (Hershey, Penn.: IGI, 2007). An ACLU Report, "Unpatriotic Acts," July 2003, 3, cites this survey and notes that 178 libraries in the sample of 906 had been visited by the FBI.

13. John Solomon and Barton Gellman, "Frequent Errors in FBI's Secret Records Requests: Audit Finds Possible Rule Violations," *Washington Post*, March 9, 2007, A01.

14. Diego Gambetta, "Of Truth and Terror," paper presented at Columbia University's 250th anniversary symposium, "Constitutions, Democracy and the Rule of Law," New York, October 16–17, 2003. Prepublication copy obtained from the author.

15. The federal government's national security policies have been impeding the free flow of scientific and technological information in other ways as well. For decades, the government has placed restrictions on the export of various goods, services, and technologies. These laws and regulations were designed to prevent the export of American technologies that could be used for military purposes by enemies of the United States; to help prevent the development and proliferation of weapons of mass destruction; and to advance U.S. foreign policy goals and protect the United States' economic position in the world. These are not major impediments to

scholarly exchanges at the moment, but the interpretation and enforcement of the policy by President Bush had university research contract officers, publishers of scientific information, and some scholars worried about whether the regulations could be used to impede the free flow of scientific research.

16. These concerns were expressed by the Association of American Universities, which represents sixty-two of the leading research universities in the United States and Canada, and the leaders of three other organizations representing universities and scientists, in a letter of October 15, 2003, to Secretary of Health and Human Services Tommy Thompson and Secretary of Agriculture Ann Veneman.

17. Martin Enserink and David Malakoff, "The Trials of Thomas Butler," *Science* 302 (December 19, 2003): 2054–2063. Quotation on p. 2054.

18. Kenneth Chang, "30 Plague Vials Put Career on Line," *New York Times*, October 19, 2003.

19. Enserink and Malakoff, "The Trials of Thomas Butler," 2062.

20. Chang, "30 Plague Vials."

21. Enserink and Malakoff, "The Trials of Thomas Butler," 2054. The president of the National Academy of Sciences, Bruce Alberts, and the president of the Institute of Medicine, Harvey V. Fineberg, in a letter to Attorney General John Ashcroft on August 15, 2003, noted that Butler was a decorated Vietnam War veteran and that he had "significantly contributed to our understanding of the kinds of communicable diseases that are currently of particular concern for the prevention of bioterrorism." Alberts and Fineberg went on to note the broader consequences of Butler's prosecution, saying: "We are particularly concerned about the impact that Dr. Butler's case may have on other scientists who may be discouraged from embarking upon or continuing crucial bioterrorism-related scientific research—thereby adversely affecting the nation's ability to fully utilize such research capabilities in preparing defenses against possible bioterrorist attacks." The New York Academy of Sciences castigated the Justice Department for "selective prosecution," for "piling on" extra charges, and for blowing "the whole episode out of proportion." Joseph Birman, a professor of physics at the City College of New York and chair of the New York Academy of Sciences' Committee on Human Rights, noted in the letter, "We find extremely troublesome the 'piling on' of 'Theft,' 'Embezzlement,' 'Fraud,' 'Smuggling,' and 'False Tax Return' charges." Birman asked Ashcroft in the letter "whether this highly unusual prosecution of Dr. Butler is, in truth, in the national interest or serves our national security." (John Dudley Miller, "More Support for Dr. Butler," *The Scientist*, September 22, 2003, www.the-scientist.com.)

22. Quoted in Chang, "30 Plague Vials."

23. Dr. Daniel Portnoy of the University of California at Berkeley destroyed his plague samples as well, saying, "The criteria for keeping them were particularly onerous. It would have required some fundamental changes of the running of the lab" (Paul Elias, "Scientists Say Post-9/11 Rules Hurting Research," Associated Press, September 11, 2003). Another researcher told Debora MacKenzie of the *New Scientist*, "If I am required to inventory every vial, even if it is in a locked freezer behind five layers of security, then be held criminally accountable for any mysterious disappearance when it is almost certainly only sloppy record keeping, then I'll work on Paramecium [a pond protist] and leave the select agents to someone else" (http://www.new-scientist.com/article/dn4345-us-crackdown-on-bioterror-is-backfiring.html?page=2). Dr. Donald Henderson, director of the Center for Civilian Biodefense Studies at Johns Hopkins University and the person who led the World Health Organization team credited with eradicating smallpox worldwide in the 1960s and 1970s, said that Butler's way of transporting his plague samples did not differ from accepted prior practice: "I carried a lot of smallpox around for a great many years. . . . They [the FBI] have lost all perspective in this" (quoted in John Dudley Miller, "Caught in Political Crosshairs," *The Scientist* 17, no. 18 [September 22, 2003], 50). Dr. William B. Greenough III, professor of medicine at Johns Hopkins University, and a

friend of Butler's, praised Butler for his Tanzania work, which suggested that two available antibiotics could be used effectively in treating plague, and concluded that putting Butler in jail would be "a rather bizarre and unusual approach to trying to protect the American public or anyone else" (Martin Enserink and David Malakoff, "The Trials of Thomas Butler," *Science* 302 [December 19, 2003]: 2054–2063). For a general website that collected many documents and accounts of the Butler case, see http://www.fas.org/butler/index.html.

24. Quoted in Debora MacKenzie, "US Crackdown on Bioterror Is Backfiring," November 5, 2003, http://www.newscientist.com/article/dn4345-us-crackdown-on-bioterror-is-backfiring.html.

25. Miller, "Caught in Political Crosshairs."

26. Kenneth Chang, "Scientist in Plague Case Is Sentenced to Two Years," *New York Times,* March 11, 2004. See also David Malakoff and Kerry Drennan, "Plague Scientist Gets 2 Years," *Science Online,* http://sciencenow.sciencemag.org/cgi/content/full/2004/310/2.

27. David Malakoff and Martin Enserink, "Butler Cleared on Most Biosecurity Charges, Convicted of Fraud," *Science* 302 (December 5, 2003): 1637.

28. In filing a suit against Attorney General Ashcroft and associates at the Department of Justice and the FBI, Thomas Connolly, Hatfill's attorney, said: "[Dr. Hatfill] had his home searched on national television—twice. He has been followed twenty-four hours a day, seven days a week, for months on end. He has been fired from his job, at the direction of the Department of Justice, and his future job prospects have been destroyed. . . . The Attorney General and his subordinates have taken Dr. Hatfill's life as he knew it; they have made him a prisoner in his own home. All this without any evidence linking Dr. Hatfill to the attacks and without bringing any formal charges against him. . . . Mr. Ashcroft publicly and repeatedly identified Dr. Hatfill as 'a person of interest' in the anthrax investigation. He used the phrase, which everyone understood as a euphemism for the person the government believes is responsible for the offense, to suggest to the public that real progress was being made in the case and that Dr. Hatfill was the culprit. . . . Having ruined Dr. Hatfill's reputation, DOJ went even further—they had him fired from his teaching job at Louisiana State University. Without producing any evidence against him, without officially naming him a suspect, and without giving him an opportunity to hear and respond to charges against him." (Quoted from "Statement of Thomas G. Connolly, Attorney for Dr. Steven J. Hatfill," August 26, 2003, upon the filing of a lawsuit on behalf of Dr. Hatfill against Attorney General John Ashcroft and other DOJ and FBI officials.)

29. Louisiana State University, Office of University Relations, "Chancellor Announces Decision to Terminate Steven J. Hatfill," September 3, 2002, 4:38 P.M.

30. *Steven J. Hatfill v. Attorney General John Ashcroft et al.*, in the United States District Court for the District of Columbia.

31. Quoted in Claudia Dreifus, "The Chilling of American Science: A Conversation with Robert C. Richardson," *New York Times,* July 6, 2004, D2.

32. Yudhijit Bhattochanjee, "Life Scientists Cautious About Dual Use Research, Study Finds," *Science* 323 (February 6, 2009).

33. The overregulation of U.S. laboratories designed to handle dangerous biological agents is another domain of federal oversight of biological research that is having unanticipated negative consequences in 2009. Laboratories with biosafety level ratings of 3 or 4 handle potentially lethal agents. There are several hundred BSL-3-rated labs in the United States and fewer than a dozen BSL-4 labs. Yet they are the labs that are conducting, or could be conducting, research at universities that might be able to find vaccines for deadly diseases. The labs, some of which I've toured, are built with at least as much security as Ft. Knox. Yet the politics surrounding the building and opening of these labs has become so pervasive that few scientists and universities are willing to get involved with the research. See Paul Baskin, "Universities

Seek 'Sensible' Balance in Federal Oversight of Toxins in Research," *Chronicle of Higher Education*, March 13, 2009.

34. "Experts Urge Exchange of Scientific Talent," *New York Times*, October 19, 2007.

35. Cornelia Dean, "Scientists Fear Visa Trouble Will Drive Foreign Students Away," *New York Times*, March, 3. 2009.

36. Ibid.

37. Ibid.

38. Http://abajournal.com/news/star_fl_student_free_still_to_be_deported/.

39. Http://socialistworker.org/2008/04/04/madison-deportations.

40. Http://www.studlife.com/news/1.846408.

41. Http://chronicle.com/news/index.php?id=6146&utm_sourc=pmt. News Blog, *Chronicle of Higher Education*, March 18, 2009.

42. Quoted in Jennifer Grogan, "Balancing Science and Security: The Dilemma of Dual Use Research," masters essay, Columbia School of Journalism, 2006, 6. Grogan had two sponsors of this essay: Nicholas Lemann, dean of the School of Journalism, and me.

43. National Security Decision Directive 189 (NSDD-189), issued September 21, 1985, contained "the national policy controlling the flow of science, technology and engineering information produced in federally funded fundamental research at colleges, universities, and laboratories." It stated that, "to the maximum extent possible, the products of fundamental research remain unrestricted," and said: "It is also the policy of this Administration that, where the national security requires control, the mechanism for control of information generated during federally funded fundamental research in science, technology and engineering at colleges, universities, and laboratories is classification." Fundamental research was defined in the directive as "basic and applied research in science and engineering, the results of which ordinarily are published and shared broadly within the scientific community, as distinguished from proprietary research and from industrial development, design, production, and product utilization, the results of which ordinarily are restricted for proprietary or national security reasons." "Classified project results are not published in open literature," the directive said. "Information is transferred only between those who obtain the required clearance. This applies even when the research is performed by scientists outside of government facilities." See http//www.fas.org/irp/offdocs/nsdd_189.htm.

44. Http://www.ombwatch.org/taxonomy/term/178.

45. It was also clear that there were internal disagreements within the White House over the wisdom of such a classification. Condoleezza Rice, who was national security adviser at the time and a former provost at Stanford, apparently opposed the policy outlined in a March 19, 2002, memo from President Bush's chief of staff, Andrew Card, to the heads of executive departments and agency heads. The memo said that sensitive information related to America's homeland security, but that might not meet the standard for "classified information," needed to be protected "from inappropriate disclosure." That information "should be carefully considered, on a case-by-case basis, together with the benefits that result from the open and efficient exchange of scientific, technical, and like information" (Memorandum for Departments and Agencies attached to Memorandum for the Heads of Executive Departments and Agencies from Andrew H. Card, Jr., The White House, March 19, 2002, available at http://www.fas.org/sgp/bush/wh031902.html).

The director of the Office of Science and Technology Policy, John Marburger, tried to clarify the administration's position when he reaffirmed in June 2003 that the 1985 policy on classification continued to be government policy, but the issue was not successfully resolved during the Bush presidency. In fact, as late as May 2008 the government continued to tweak the definition of what was now called Controlled Unclassified Information (CUI) to reduce ambiguity about what this classification covered (John Marburger, Director, Office of Science and Technology Policy, Executive Office of the President, in "Remarks" to the "Roundtable on

Scientific Communication and National Security," National Academy of Sciences, Washington, D.C., June 19, 2003).

In his remarks, Marburger made the distinction between classifications and restrictions placed on the support of students and scientists from certain countries, on the one hand, and prepublication review used in government grants and contracts, on the other. He was less clear when he said, "What is important here, in my opinion, is that the agencies sponsoring this type of work make their restrictions clear at the outset, so universities can decide whether or not they wish to perform the work. I do not regard any of the reported cases as intrusions into the scientific process, or impeding scientific progress."

46. Grogan, "Balancing Science and Security," 21.

47. As described and quoted in Willie Schatz, "Science Publishing Versus Security," *The Scientist,* January 13, 2003.

48. Grogan, "Balancing Science and Security," 14.

49. In a 2003 report by the National Academy of Sciences, named the "Fink Committee" report after its chair, Gerald R. Fink, professor of genetics at MIT, there are specific examples of research that could potentially have dual uses. The report cites a study by Australian scientists involving altering the mousepox genome that some thought could be "a blueprint or a roadmap for terrorists to engineer a more virulent strain of small pox that could overwhelm the human immune system in even well-vaccinated individuals." Several other detailed examples were also given in the report, which analyzes whether such results ought to be censored or reviewed for potential misuse by some panel of scientists and government officials (Committee on Research Standards and Practices to Prevent the Destructive Application of Biotechnology, National Research Council of the National Academies, *Biotechnology Research in an Age of Terrorism: Confronting the Dual Use Dilemma* [Washington, D.C.: National Academies Press, 2003], prepublication copy, p. 20, www.nap.edu). The report is one of the best documents for understanding the nature of the dilemma and the historical commitment to free and open communication, and indeed the necessity for science to maintain that commitment. The report is a model of a disinterested effort to maintain the integrity of scientific research while attending to the real possibilities of scientific information being misused for nefarious purposes.

50. Daniel J. Kevles, "Biotech's Big Chill," *Technology Review,* July 2003.

51. NRC Report, "Biotechnology Research in an Age of Terrorism," 3.

52. The Fink Committee's seven recommendations included:

- Educating the scientific community about the "nature of the dual use dilemma in biotechnology and their responsibilities to mitigate its risks."
- Creating a review process within the Department of Health and Human Services for seven classes of experiments ("experiments of concern").
- Relying on scientists and scientific journals to review publications for their potential national security risks.
- Creating a National Science Advisory Board for Biodefense (NSABB) consisting of scientists and national security experts to monitor, guide, and advise the scientific community about the review process.
- "Relying on the implementation of current [federal] legislation and regulation, with periodic review by the NSABB, to provide protection of biological materials and supervision of personnel working with these materials."
- Developing new channels of communication between the life sciences community and the national security and law enforcement communities to help mitigate the risks of bioterrorism.
- Developing international mechanisms "to develop and promote harmonized national, regional, and international measures that will provide a counterpart to the system we recommend for the United States."

Related efforts to demonstrate to the government that the scientific community was capable of policing itself were undertaken by the American Society of Microbiologists (ASM) and the editors of the major biological science journals, including the highly prestigious publication outlets of *Science, Nature, Cell,* and the *Proceedings of the National Academy of Sciences* (PNAS), which published a joint "Statement on Scientific Publication and Security" in January 2003. The statement is reproduced in the Academy Report at pp. 82–83 and is available at http://www.sciencemag.org/cgi/reprint299/5610/1149.pdf.

53. Richard Monastersky, "Scientists Urged to Screen Research to Avoid Aiding Terrorists," *Chronicle of Higher Education,* October 17, 2003, http://chronicle.com/weekly/v50/i08/08a02801.htm.

54. "Scientists Urged to Screen Research."

55. Grogan, "Balancing Science and Security," 33.

56. Ibid., 7.

57. Ibid., 29.

58. Kavita M. Berger and Alan J. Leshner, "New Rules for Biosecurity," *Science* 324 (May 29, 2009): 117.

59. Ibid.

60. Of course there is nothing quite comparable to the Library of Congress. Among the other great public libraries of the world are the New York Public Library, the Queen's Borough Public Library, the Cincinnati and Hamilton County Public Library, and the Chicago Public Library, as well as the Free Library of Philadelphia, the County of Los Angeles Library, the Boston Public Library, and the Brooklyn Public Library.

61. For example, scholars from all over the world come to use Columbia's Avery Library—one of the best collections for architecture and fine arts in the world. For a sense of the holdings of this unique collection, see http://www.columbia.edu/cu/lweb/indiv/avery/.

Great rare books collections, like the one held by Yale in its Beinecke Library, are resources for students and scholars around the world. For a sense of the holdings of one of the great rare books collections, see http://www.library.yale.edu/beinecke/.

62. American Library Association, "Privacy: An Interpretation of the Library Bill of Rights," http://www.ala.org/ala/oif/statementspols/statementsif/interpretations/privacy.htm.

63. In January 2003, the American Library Association (ALA) adopted a resolution opposing library surveillance: "The USA PATRIOT Act and other recently enacted laws, regulations, and guidelines increase the likelihood that the activities of library users, including their use of computers to browse the Web or access e-mail, may be under government surveillance without their knowledge or consent." The association "opposes any use of government power to suppress the free and open exchange of knowledge and information or to intimidate individuals exercising free inquiry."

64. Rene Sanchez, "Librarians Make Some Noise over Patriot Act," *Washington Post,* April 10, 2003, A20.

65. H.R. 1157, 108th Congress, 1st Session, March 6, 2003, http://www.fas.org/irp/congress/2003_cr/hr1157.html. A parallel bill, introduced by Senator Barbara Boxer in the Senate, was called the Library and Booksellers Protection Act, S. 1158. See http://www.fas.org/irp/congress/2003_cr/s1158.html. Senator Russ Feingold introduced a bill on July 21, 2003, called the Library, Bookseller, and Personal Records Privacy Act, S. 1507, that would amend Sections 215 and 505 of the Patriot Act and "would also require the FBI, when issuing National Security Letters under Section 505, to set forth information showing there is a factual, individualized suspicion that the information sought pertains to a suspected terrorist or spy when seeking such information from a library or bookseller." (Quoted from http://www.ala.org/Template.cfm?Section=issuesrelatedlinks&Template=/ContentManagement/ContentDisplay.cfm&ContentID=46741.)

66. Http://www.ala.org/ala/aboutala/offices/wo/woissues/civilliberties/theusapatriotact/usapatriotact.cfm#reauth.

67. Edwin Black, "Funding Hate," October 16, 2003, http://www.featuregroup.com/fgarchive/jta.org/jta.org1/index.html. The Jewish Telegraphic Agency website describes its mission and sources of funding, indicating that 60 percent of its revenues come from operations, including service fees paid by "client newspapers, national Jewish agencies and individual subscribers." "The remaining 40%," the site says, "comes from philanthropic sources. The largest of these are Jewish community federations in the United States and Canada, and contributions from the JTA Board of Directors." In short, although the JTA may present news of interest to the Jewish community, the point of view is clear.

68. Black said that his stories were based upon "a two-month investigation, involving interviews with dozens of individuals in seven countries, as well as a review of more than 9,000 pages of government and organizational documents." (Edwin Black, "Funding Hate," Part 1, "Ford Funded Durban Anti-Israeli Activists," October 16, 2003, http://www.featuregroup.com/fgarchive/jta.org/jta.org1/index.html.)

69. Black, "Funding Hate."

70. For example, more than $75,000 in grant funds was spent on first-class and business-class travel rather than coach and on "lavish hospitality," as well as on the purchase of "seven cars and trucks" for the "personal use of several former board members."

71. "Over the decades the foundation has made important contributions to higher education. We appreciate those contributions and hope that we can find a way to resolve our serious concerns about the new language specifying new conditions for grants that refers to 'violence, terrorism, bigotry, and the destruction of any state.'" The letter said, in part: "Our central concern is that the new condition attempts to regulate universities' behavior and speech beyond the scope of the grant—indeed, beyond the bounds of the universities. . . . We believe that the Foundation should not attempt to use its grants to regulate all other activities of our institutions." The provosts then concluded: "The proposed condition will create an unfortunate barrier to future cooperation between the Ford Foundation and universities that will be detrimental to both sides. We would welcome a conversation about how the Foundation can achieve the ends that have prompted the condition without imposing unacceptable restrictions on universities that transgress our highest values" (quoted from letters from the nine provosts to Susan Berresford, president of the Ford Foundation, and to Gordon Conway, president of the Rockefeller Foundation, April 27, 2004). The nine provosts signing the letters were Amy Gutmann, Princeton; Alan Brinkley, Columbia; John Etchemendy, Stanford; Steven Hyman, Harvard; Richard P. Saller, University of Chicago; Robert L. Barchi, University of Pennsylvania; Robert A. Brown, MIT; Susan Hockfield, Yale; and Carolyn A. Martin, Cornell.

72. Both Brinkley and Berresford are quoted in Daniel Golden, "Colleges Object to New Wording in Ford Grants," *Wall Street Journal Online*, WSJ.com, May 4, 2004.

73. Golden, "Colleges Object to New Wording," *WSJ.com.*

Chapter 13: "Political" Science

1. Union of Concerned Scientists (UCS), "Scientific Integrity in Policymaking: An Investigation into the Bush Administration's Misuse of Science," February 2004.

2. The office of Representative Henry A. Waxman, ranking minority member, House Committee on Government Reform, "Politics and Science in the Bush Administration," 2003. The general website for Representative Waxman, which includes other materials on abuses of scientific integrity, is http://www.house.gov/reform/min/politicsandscience/. The report can be found at http://www.house.gov/reform/min/politicsandscience/report.htm.

3. In April 2004 the Bush administration issued a report entitled "Bush Administration Science and Technology Accomplishments: Promoting Innovation for a Stronger, Safer America." This document is less of a policy position statement than a list of investments in R&D, efforts related to homeland security, and legislation supported by the administration to enhance "competitiveness" and create new jobs. A section of the report devoted to "improving the quality of life through discovery" lists several initiatives supported by the administration. Beyond such policy statements, which are often not of much value in themselves, there was little emphasis within the Bush administration on the value of knowledge creation to the future welfare of American society.

4. In response to the UCS report, Marburger said: "From all the evidence I can find, it certainly is not true that science is being manipulated by this administration to suit its policy. It's simply not the case" (*New York Times*, March 30, 2004, F1). Marburger issued a detailed response to the UCS report, "Statement of the Honorable John H. Marburger, III. On Scientific Integrity in the Bush Administration," on April 2, 2004. See http://stephenschneider.stanford .edu/Publications/PDF_Papers/ResponsetoCongressonUCSDocumentApril2004.pdf.

5. Rob Stein, "Researchers May Have Found Equivalent of Embryonic Stem Cells," *Washington Post*, July 24, 2009.

6. Http://stemcells.nih.gov/info/basics/basics5.asp; http://stemcells.nih.gov/info/basics/basics4.asp; and http://stemcells.nih.gov/info/basics/basics10.asp.

7. Peter Singer, *The President of Good and Evil: The Ethics of George W. Bush* (New York: Dutton, 2004), 35. An excellent earlier discussion of stem cell research and the attendant ethical issues can be found in Laura Shanner, "Embryonic Stem Cell Research: Canadian Policy and Ethical Considerations," University of Alberta, March 31, 2001. It is worth noting that the embryonic stem cells that are used for research are those derived from embryos at five to seven days of development (the blastocyst stage). These cells of the early embryo are "totipotent" for the first several divisions, "which means that each cell could give rise to an entire, functioning offspring." (Shanner, "Embryonic Stem Cell Research," 3–4.)

8. Letter from 58 Senators to President George W. Bush, June 4, 2004, available at http://www.genomenewsnetwork.org/articles/2004/06/08/stemcellpush.php.

9. President George W. Bush, remarks to the nation on stem cell research, August 9, 2001, http://www.whitehouse.gov/news/releases/2001/08/20010809-2.html.

10. Letter "signed by over 140 patient organizations, scientific societies, universities, and foundations sent to President Bush urging him to expand his current embryonic stem cell policy," from Coalition for the Advancement of Medical Research (CAMR) to President George W. Bush, June 2004, www.camradvocacy.org/fastaction/.

11. Although the nations mentioned here, and others, such as Canada, have adopted more liberal policies than the United States has, as of June 2004 there were many nations, including Spain, France, and Germany, whose policies on cloning, both in general and for therapeutic purposes, were as restrictive as those of the United States.

12. Poll sponsored by the Juvenile Diabetes Research Foundation, 2004.

13. Juvenile Diabetes Research Foundation, 2004.

14. Http://www.pollingreport.com/science.htm.

15. In May 2004, Britain opened the world's first national stem cell bank. Its mission is "to store, characterize and grow cells and distribute them to researchers around the world" ("Britain Opens World's First Stem-Cell Bank: Scientists Plan to Grow, Store and Distribute Cells for Research," Associated Press, May 19, 2004). Australia is also moving forward with the creation of a stem cell bank with the National Stem Cell Centre (NSCC). The NSCC is collaborating with a biotechnology company "to allow the development and distribution of new human embryonic stem . . . cell lines to scientists around the world" (Stem Cell Research Foundation, http://www.stemcellresearchfoundation.org).

16. Lynda Richardson, "Public Lives: The Slippery Intersection of Medicine and Politics," *New York Times*, July 27, 2004.

17. Singer, *President of Good and Evil*, 38.

18. Henry A. Waxman and Louise Slaughter, letter to President Bush, March 2, 2004. See http://oversight.house.gov/documents/20050622121359-08397.pdf.

19. Quoted from letter from Bettie Sue Masters, president of American Society for Biochemistry and Molecular Biology, to the Honorable George W. Bush, March 1, 2004.

20. One, Dr. Benjamin Carson, is a renowned pediatric neurosurgeon who performs surgery in very difficult cases at Johns Hopkins University. He is also a motivational speaker who once lamented, "We live in a nation where we can't talk about God in public" (http://findarticles.com/p/articles/mi_m1295/is_5_69/ai_n13819947/pg_4). A second, Dianna Schaub, a political scientist at Loyola College in Maryland, has talked publicly about the destruction of embryos as "the evil of the willful destruction of innocent human life" (http://www.lifenews.com/bio222.html). And in a book review, Professor Peter Lawler, professor of government at Berry College in Georgia, warned that if we did not soon "become clear as a nation that abortion is wrong," then women would be compelled to abort genetically defective babies (Chris Mooney, *The Republican War on Science* [New York: Basic Books, 2005], 318n203).

21. For a brilliant historical treatment of these conflicts, see Charles Gillispie, *The Edge of Objectivity* (Princeton, N.J.: Princeton University Press, 1996).

22. "Memorandum for the Heads of Executive Departments and Agencies," March 9, 2009, http://www.whitehouse.gov/the_press_office/Memorandum-for-the-Heads-of-Executive-Departments-and-Agencies-3-9-09/.

23. Http://www.sciencedebate2008.com/www/index.php?id=40.

24. UCS, "Scientific Integrity in Policymaking," 5.

25. Ibid., 6. The UCS pointed to efforts by the Bush administration to tamper with the integrity of scientific analysis when the White House tried to get a series of changes made in the EPA's draft report on the environment. The scientists listed the following examples as efforts to alter the report:

- The deletion of a temperature record covering 1,000 years in order to, according to the EPA memo, emphasize "a recent, limited analysis [which] supports the administration's favored message."
- The removal of any reference to the NAS review—requested by the White House itself—that confirmed that human activity was contributing to climate change.
- The insertion of a reference to a discredited study of temperature records funded in part by the American Petroleum Institute.
- The elimination of the summary statement—noncontroversial within the science community that studies climate change—saying that "climate change has global consequences for human health and the environment."

26. UCS, "Scientific Integrity in Policymaking," 7.

27. Ibid. Apparently, according to the British newspaper *The Observer* on February 22, 2004, the Bush administration ignored warnings from Defense Department experts about global climate change and its consequences. A group of eminent U.K. scientists visited the White House in 2004 to make its case for taking global warming seriously. Bob Watson, chief scientist for the World Bank, told *The Observer*, "Can Bush ignore the Pentagon? It's going [to] be hard to blow off this sort of document. It's hugely embarrassing. After all, Bush's single highest priority is national defense. The Pentagon is no wacko, liberal group, generally speaking it is conservative. If climate change is a threat to national security and the economy, then he has to act. There are two groups the Bush Administration tends to listen to, the oil lobby and the Pentagon."

28. Andrew C. Revkin, "Climate Expert Says NASA Tried to Silence Him," *New York Times*, January 29, 2006.

29. Mark Bowen, *Censoring Science: Inside the Political Attack on Dr. James Hansen and the Truth of Global Warming* (New York: Dutton, 2007), p. 28, advance copy version. For a highly readable account of the history of climate changes and the current dilemma, see Wallace S. Broeker and Robert Kunzig, *Fixing Climate: What Past Climate Changes Reveal About the Current Threat—And How to Conquer It* (New York: Hill and Wang, 2008).

30. Revkin, "Climate Expert."

31. Ibid.

32. Ibid.

33. Bowen, *Censoring Science*, 59–60.

34. Ibid., 165.

35. Andrew C. Revkin, "Lawmaker Condemns NASA over Scientist's Accusations of Censorship," *New York Times*, January 31, 2006.

36. UCS, "Scientific Integrity in Policymaking."

37. Ibid., 10–11.

38. Ibid., 11.

39. Institute of Medicine, *Unequal Treatment: Confronting Racial and Ethnic Disparities in Health Care*; "A Case Study in Politics and Science: Changes to the National Healthcare Disparities Report," prepared for Rep. Henry A. Waxman, ranking minority member, Committee on Government Reform, et al., United States House of Representatives, Special Investigations Division, January 2004, www.reform.house.gov/min. and www.politicsandscience.org.

40. "A Case Study in Politics and Science."

41. Letter to the National Institutes of Health (NIH) from Roland Foster, professional staff member, Subcommittee on Criminal Justice, Drug Policy and Human Resources, Committee on Government Reform, U.S. House of Representatives, 2003, quoted in March 13 memo forwarded to NIH Director Elias Zerhouni. In an April 11, 2003, memo to the NIH, Foster raised questions about another grant to UCSF to prevent HIV in gay men and asked for a list of HIV prevention studies. (Jocelyn Kaiser, "Studies of Gay Men, Prostitutes Come Under Scrutiny," *Science* 318 [April 2003], 403.)

42. Erica Goode, "Certain Words Can Trip Up AIDS Grants, Scientists Say," *New York Times*, April 18, 2003, http://www.nytimes.com/2003/04/18/national/18gran.html?ex=10516715333&ei=1&en=7e8bf09ad36db769. In fact, Sommers was right in suggesting that "traditionally" the process for funding medical research has been free from political interference, but there have periodically been episodes where members of Congress have questioned the rationale for particular research grants and even the fairness of the entire peer review system used by the federal agencies for awarding grants. One of the more notable episodes was the "Golden Fleece of the Month" awards handed out by Senator William Proxmire of Wisconsin. The distinction between his "awards" and the recent efforts is that Proxmire was focusing on what he believed was government waste of money, whereas the Bush administration was clearly opposing certain kinds of research for ideological and political reasons.

43. Jocelyn Kaiser, "Biomedical Politics: Sex Studies 'Properly Approved,'" *Science 300* (February 6, 2004): 741.

44. Letter from Henry A. Waxman to the Honorable Tommy G. Thompson, October 27, 2003, http://www.house.gov/reform/min/politicsandscience/.

45. Union of Concerned Scientists (UCS), Report of July 8, 2004 (reported by many news agencies). Here I have drawn on the reporting by Kenneth Chang, "Scientists Say White House Questioned Their Politics," *New York Times*, July 9, 2004. Other reports can be found in the *Washington Post*, the *Los Angeles Times*, and the *Boston Globe*, among many others.

46. Report issued by the Union of Concerned Scientists. See http://www.ucsusa.org/news/press_release.cfm?newsID=405.

47. Elizabeth Shogren, "Researchers Accuse Bush of Manipulating Science," *Los Angeles Times*, July 9, 2004, A11.

48. Ibid.

49. President of the National Academy of Sciences Bruce Alberts criticized the proposal because it "would prohibit most scientists who receive funding from a government agency from serving as peer reviewers, but would permit scientists employed or funded by industry to serve as reviewers (unless they had a direct financial interest in the issue under review)." (UCS, "Scientific Integrity in Policymaking," 17.)

50. Jocelyn Kaiser, "White House Softens Disputed Peer-Review Plan," *Science* 304 (April 23, 2004): 496–497.

51. Maggie Fox, "Bush Administration Distorts Science, Group Says," Reuters, February 18, 2004.

52. James Glanz, "At the Center of the Storm over Bush and Science," *New York Times*, March 30, 2004, F1.

53. UCS Report I, 28. See also "Politics and Science in the Bush Administration," Congressman Henry Waxman (D-CA), House of Representatives Committee on Oversight and Government Reform, 2003.

54. Tim Weiner, *The Legacy of Ashes: The History of the CIA* (New York: Doubleday, 2007).

55. Richard Shweder, of the University of Chicago, has written brilliantly on the clash between the belief in universal values and the moral imperative of American-style democracy, on the one hand, and alternative moral choices made by peoples in various parts of Asia and Africa, on the other. He used the Bush speech as a point of departure for raising larger questions about our tolerance of alternative values and views on morality. See Richard A. Shweder, "George W. Bush and the Missionary Position," *Daedalus* (Summer 2004): 26–36; Richard A. Shweder, *Why Do Men Barbecue? Recipes for Cultural Psychology* (Cambridge: Harvard University Press, 2003).

56. Will Youmans, "Campus Watch: The Vigilante Thought Police," *Counterpunch*, September 23, 2002.

57. Quoted in Alisa Solomon, "Targeting Middle East Studies, Zealots' 'Homeland Security' Creates Campus Insecurity," *The Village Voice*, February 25–March 2, 2004.

58. Martin Kramer, "Title VI in Congress: Not on Our Dime," http://www.geocities.com/martinkramerorg/2003_10_14.html.

59. Zachary Lockman, "Behind the Battles over US Middle East Studies," Middle East Report Online, January 2004.

60. Neil Gross and Solon Simmons, "The Social and Political Views of American Professors," paper presented at the American Sociological Association meetings, August 2007.

61. Lisa Anderson, "Scholarship, Policy, Debate and Conflict: Why We Study the Middle East and Why It Matters," 2003 MESA Presidential Address, *Middle East Studies Association Bulletin* 38, no. 1 (Summer 2004), preprint.

62. Ibid.

63. Http://www.insidehighered.com/news/2007/06/19/hea.

64. For a brilliant discussion of the clandestine role that the CIA played during the Cold War through its support (estimated at $200 million) of individuals and organizations, including foundations, that supported anticommunist efforts by prominent artists, writers, and intellectuals who worked in Europe to bring the "cultural" message of democracy to the people of Europe, see Frances Stonor Saunders, *Who Paid the Piper? The CIA and the Cultural Cold War* (London: Granta Books, 1999).

Chapter 14: Trouble in Paradise?

1. Organisation for Economic Co-operation and Development, Programme for International Student Assessment (PISA), http://www.pisa.oecd.org.

2. National Science Board, *Science and Engineering Indicators 2008*, vol. 1, Chap. 5, "Academic Research and Development," 5–38.

3. A fairly widespread belief among many Europeans, including European educators, is that the United States has exceptional research universities, but they are limited to the Ivy League plus other privates such as Stanford, Chicago, Caltech, and a small number of state universities. They believe that Europe as a whole would compare well to the United States in its number of top universities. This view betrays their lack of understanding of the size of the top tier of American research universities, which I believe would number around 100 to 125.

4. This set of problems with the French system of higher education is based on conversations with leading French educators and faculty members. On December 2, 2008, I had discussions with members of the Toulouse Economics Group, including Paul Seabright and Jean Tirole. In Paris, I learned more about the differences between the American and French systems through conversations with Jon Elster and Antoine Compagnon, among several others at the Collège de France.

5. Several factors contribute to this: One is that in many important fields, France is not where the current action is, and if you are truly brilliant and seek a major career you go where the action is. Second, French universities pay their professors very poorly compared with competing systems. Third, the prestige of the professoriate in France seems to have suffered in recent decades. French professors simply are not as highly respected as they once were, despite the relative stability of occupational prestige over time. Fourth, there seems to have been a significant neglect in France of the infrastructure that is necessary for world-class research, except in a very few major research institutes, such as the Pasteur Institute. If one walks through the corridors of the Sorbonne today, one is struck by the neglect of its physical structures.

6. My longtime colleague at Columbia, professor of French literature Antoine Compagnon, who now holds an appointment at the Collège de France, informed me that the heyday for the Sorbonne, when it actually was viewed as superior to the Collège de France, was at the turn of the twentieth century.

7. Diego Gambetta and Gloria Origgi, "'They Pretend to Pay and We Pretend to Work.' The Puzzling Connivance on Low Quality Outcomes," paper delivered at the Seminar of Investigations on Social Sciences and Political Studies: Legal, Moral, and Social Norms, Bogotá, Colombia, October 19–20, 2007. I refer here to the preprint I received from Diego Gambetta. See also http://gloriaoriggi.blogspot.com/2007/10/they-pretend-to-pay-and-we-pretend-to.html.

Whatever the struggles are that France faces in trying to reclaim its position in the top tier of great university systems, it would seem to face a far better state of affairs than Italy. The paper contained a damning analysis of why various actors in the Italian system connive to produce low-quality outcomes in the system of higher education. Gambetta, an Italian sociologist who works at Oxford University (his location is itself symptomatic of Italy's educational problems) and Origgi, his colleague, suggested that a normative system has evolved at Italian universities that will, in fact, not tolerate excellence. Furthermore, the system increasingly is built upon an implied compact between faculty members, administrators, and others who shape public opinion to produce low-quality outcomes that go unquestioned while pretending to be producing high-quality or world-class outcomes. The system of rewards and constraints reinforce this set of outcomes and drives the system toward mediocrity. Those who complain about the system are normatively sanctioned, if not directly, then on "the basis of oblique reasons and specious principles for nobody wants to acknowledge that LL [low-quality outcomes] was the preferred outcome" (p. 8).

Using an absolutely startling example to demonstrate this point, Gambetta and Origgi used the response to a revelation in print by Federico Varese (1996) that Stefano Zamagni, "a well-known Italian economist, had plagiarized verbatim several pages from [the American philosopher] Robert Novick." Varese "was privately criticized by several Italian colleagues who together evoked 9 norms or reasons that he would have violated by making the revelations. None of these include a justification of plagiarism per se" (pp. 8–9). Consider the list reproduced by Gambetta and Origgi, who provide examples that this is not an isolated case:

1. There is nothing original, everyone plagiarises [*sic*], so why bother? [journalist]
2. Whistle blowers are always worse than their targets. [sociologist]
3. What is the point of targeting Zamagni? They will never punish him anyway.
4. What's the point of blowing the whistle as *you* will pay the consequences? [family, friends]
5. The real author of the plagiarism is probably a student of Zamagni who wrote the paper for him. If you reveal the plagiarism the real victim will be his poor assistant. [economist] (This would, funnily enough, imply that Zamagni signed a paper he did not write, written by someone who also did not write it!)
6. He is a good "barone," much better than many others, so why target him? [economist]
7. Zamagni is a member of the left and you should not weaken the left during election times. [economist, various friends]
8. Zamagni shows good intellectual tastes as he plagiarizes very good authors, so he does not deserve to be attacked. [philosopher]
9. Given that many are guilty of plagiarism, targeting one in particular shows that the whistle blower is driven by base motives.

Italy faces many of the same structural problems as France (the system is underfunded, bloated with students who should not be at the universities, is too subject to government interference, has limited competition for excellence, and so forth), but if Gambetta and Origgi are even remotely accurate about the perversion of the normative structure and values in the Italian system, then it's hard to see a way out of a condition that borders on a corruption of fundamental academic values. Substantial excellence cannot be achieved within such a system and it will remain virtually impossible for Italy to prevent the continued migration of its most talented scholars and scientists to other nations. The Russian university system has also fallen on hard times. Limited budgets and crumbling infrastructure have not helped; nor has the level of corruption in the system. Perhaps more troubling has been the resistance to change among many university professors. It remains unclear whether the reforms proposed in 2008 will actually improve the best Russian universities. See Anna Nemtsova, "In Russia, University Reforms Meet with Faculty Resistance," *Chronicle of Higher Education*, April 10, 2009.

8. Aisha Labi, "France's Protestors Vow to Continue Fight Against Reform Efforts," *Chronicle of Higher Education*, July 27, 2008.

9. In France, the protests are extremely active. In February 2009 the universities were brought to their knees by actions taken by faculty unions and student groups. A spokesperson for the main union representing instructors said that the February protest had shut down about half of the teaching activities in France's eighty-three universities. Eventually some universities would close. See Aisha Labi, "Strikes Disrupt French Universities," *Chronicle of Higher Education*, February 2, 2009.

10. Of course, in the United States each state plays a critically important role in its state university system and is the source of a significant amount of support for the education of the students who attend those universities. But as I've noted, the proportion of the total operating budgets of these state universities that comes from the state is diminishing to the point where it represents only about 15 to 20 percent of many state university budgets.

11. Gretchen Vogel, "Max Planck Accused of Hobbling Universities," *Science* 319 (January 25, 2008): 396.

12. My observations here are based on my own limited work in China and on conversations with leaders of Chinese universities and Chinese students who graduated from American doctoral programs, including one of my own students who has studied the Chinese system of higher education and published on it.

13. It is also true that the Chinese system at the primary and secondary school levels, as well as at the university level, tends to be rigid and hierarchical. It has not fostered independent thought, but rather has honored the old Confucian system of the transfer of knowledge from older, highly respected masters to younger apprentices. This creates its own set of problems. Performance on standardized examinations is far more important for admissions to Chinese universities than it is in the United States, despite our cultural obsession with standardized examinations such as the Scholastic Aptitude Test (SAT). In China, the year prior to applying to university is described as "the black year" because young students believe their fate will be determined by their scores on the upcoming national examinations. And they are almost right.

14. Sharon LaFraniere, "China's College Entry Test Is an Obsession," *New York Times*, June 13, 2009.

15. Dr. Cong Cao, a former graduate student of mine, has written about the response of the Chinese government and the universities to the SARS scare, and I am grateful to him for sharing his thoughts with me about the system of higher education in China today.

16. To cite only one example: In 2009, He Weifang, an outspoken professor of law at the prestigious Peking University, was transferred to western China's Shihezi University because he had signed Charter '08, a critique of the Communist Party's political monopoly signed by 300 lawyers, scholars, and other elites. If they are not fired, critics of the party policies can find themselves transferred or denied promotions. See Henry Sanderson, "Peking Uni Transfers Outspoken Prof to West China," Associated Press, March 12, 2009. For the content of Charter '08, see Perry Link, trans., *New York Review of Books* 56, no. 1 (January 15, 2009).

17. Amar Bhidé, *The Venturesome Economy: How Innovation Sustains Prosperity and a More Connected World* (Princeton, N.J.: Princeton University Press, 2008), 1–30.

18. Ibid.

19. Ibid.

20. Ibid., 15.

21. Where I may depart from Bhidé's argument is in his acceptance of the role of the "free rider" in the acquisition of high-level knowledge. As I have argued, free-riding can be a problem because it allows others to set the intellectual agenda and scientific foci of attention, and these choices may not be consistent with the national interests or needs of the free-riding country.

22. Universities have over time had different investment strategies and policies, different spending policies, and different degrees of success at investing the liquid pieces of their endowment.

23. Nina Munk, "Rich Harvard, Poor Harvard," *Vanity Fair*, August 2009. Different research universities use different spending rules—that is, different ways of determining how much of the endowment should be used to meet operating expenses. Also, universities differ in the extent to which their endowments are restricted, with some being highly restricted, with different amounts earmarked for very specific purposes, and others being flexible, with a larger percentage that can be used for multiple purposes. Finally, endowments are often "counted" in different ways. Some universities include items that others do not, such as the value of some of their buildings. Inclusion of such numbers actually makes the sum available for spending lower than the strict application of the rule might suggest. Plainly, spending rules are intended not only to discipline universities to spend up to a certain percentage of their endowment values, but

also to save some of the cumulative returns for "rainy days." Thus, if a university earns a total return on its endowment in one year of 15 percent, it may only spend 5 percent, returning the rest to the corpus of the endowment and allowing it to appreciate over time. In fact, about 80 percent of the growth in the value of university endowments results from the appreciation of the corpus through investment.

24. As late as 1950, Harvard's endowment was $191 million. At the same time, Yale's was $125 million and Columbia's, beginning to fall noticeably behind, was at $82 million. In 1980, Harvard's reached about $1.6 billion; Yale's $431 million; Princeton's $345 million; and Columbia's $434 million. But the inequalities even among these "wealthy," top-tier universities have grown dramatically over the past twenty years. Harvard's endowment grew to $7 billion in 1995, to $19 billion in 2000, and seven years later, to almost $36 billion. In 1991, Harvard's endowment provided 17 percent of its operating budget; by 2001, that percentage had increased to 30 percent, and it has grown still further since then. Columbia's endowment in 1985 was just short of $1 billion. It grew to $2.2 billion in 1995, to $4.3 billion by 2000, and to about $7.2 billion by 2008. Meanwhile, the endowment for Princeton, a much smaller university, had grown to over $15.8 billion, while Yale's endowment surpassed $22 billion.

25. The great public universities, such as the University of California at Berkeley, the University of Michigan, and the University of Wisconsin, are becoming more like private institutions as state appropriations decline. Ann Arbor, for example, receives only about 10 percent of its total operating budget from state appropriations. They are growing more dependent on other revenue sources, including endowment growth and tuition income, but they find themselves at a relative disadvantage compared with the wealthiest private universities. In 2007, the University of Michigan had an endowment of about $7.1 billion, coming in third for state systems behind California and Texas—and had the potential to be far larger, considering the number of its alumni. So its endowment is roughly equal to Columbia's and Chicago's, but far smaller than Princeton's, Harvard's, and Yale's. Berkeley's is $2.3 billion, and Wisconsin's is only $1.3 billion.

26. There are many individual areas, and some clusters of disciplines, where other British universities, such as the London School of Economics, or Imperial College of the University of London, are arguably as good or better than Oxford and Cambridge, but the wealth differentials are so formidable that it makes competition with them extremely difficult.

27. The wealthiest of these institutions—many among the Ivy League schools plus a limited number of other private universities—have made it possible for students from families with incomes of less than $200,000 per year to attend without taking out student loans. This need-based financial aid has created substantial discount rates for those attending these schools. But commitments of this kind are difficult to rescind once students have entered college; they represent strong ideological commitments as well as large encumbrances on endowments and a university's general income—generally tuition income. Cutting back on the rate of expansion of research facilities is easier to accomplish at these places than cutting financial-aid packages—and it is precisely these cuts in the growth of facilities that have occurred at private institutions. The expansion of Harvard's research facilities at the new Alston campus in Cambridge, for example, has been slowed because of the reduced endowment payouts.

28. Josh Keller, "In California Budget Deal, Bad News for Colleges in 2010," *Chronicle of Higher Education*, July 21, 2009.

29. These figures, from the American Association of University Professors, do not include medical school professors. The salary differences are not compensated for by differences in the cost of living in the towns and cities where these universities are located.

30. The Internal Revenue Service requires universities to report annually on the five highest faculty and administrative salaries. These figures have revealed that some physicians at the affiliated medical schools have annual incomes well over $1 million. The question naturally

arises of whether the disparities in income within an institution promote discontent. In general, I believe they do not, particularly when the higher salaries are in schools such as business and medicine. The problem arises when the disparities are within schools, that is, when a few academic "stars" receive salaries that are much higher than those of other faculty members in the same department who are less renowned or who have not played "the academic marketplace." Many of the very large incomes come from clinical faculty members in a few departments who participate in physician practice plans. Those who are involved with certain surgical procedures, such as open-heart surgery or transplantation, tend to have far higher incomes than physicians in other specialties. What can elicit greater consternation among the faculty at exceptional universities is the public disclosure that the football or basketball coaches receive salaries higher than everyone else, despite the paucity of evidence that those coaches contribute more to the distinction of the university than others.

31. *Science*, May 15, 2009, 864, and *Chronicle of Higher Education*, June 9, 2009, http://chronicle.com/daily/2009/06/19650n.htm.

32. When students enter elite colleges and universities, academic careers are among those they are most likely to mention as being of interest. The number dwindles as students learn about attractive features of other occupations or receive grades that suggest they are not cut out for an academic career. See Stephen Cole and Elinor Barber, *Increasing Faculty Diversity: The Occupational Choices of High-Achieving Minority Students* (Cambridge: Harvard University Press, 2003).

33. These examples and quotations can be found in Marcia Angell, "Drug Companies and Doctors: A Story of Corruption," *New York Review of Books* 56, no. 1 (January 15, 2009). See Angell's article for more examples.

34. See also Reed Abelson, "Financial Ties Are Cited as Issue in Spine Study," *New York Times*, January 30, 2008; Duff Wilson, "Drug Maker Said to Pay Ghostwriters for Journal Articles," *New York Times*, December 12, 2008; Gardiner Harris and Janet Roberts, "Doctors' Ties to Drug Makers Are Put on Close View," *New York Times*, March 21, 2007; Benedict Cary, "Antidepressant Studies Unpublished," *New York Times*, January 17, 2008; Gardiner Harris and Benedict Cary, "Researchers Fail to Reveal Full Drug Pay," *New York Times*, June 8, 2008; Gardiner Harris, "Top Psychiatrist Didn't Report Drug Makers' Pay," *New York Times*, October 4, 2008; Jennifer Washburn, *University Inc: The Corporate Corruption of Higher Education* (New York: Basic Books, 2005); Katherine Mangan, "2 Academic Associations Urge the NIH to Increase Oversight of Research Conflicts," *Chronicle of Higher Education*, June 11, 2009.

35. Some presidents of universities spend a great deal of time educating trustees about the university's academic and research programs. We certainly gave frequent presentations to Columbia trustees on the academic affairs of the university. Robert Brown, the highly gifted president of Boston University, on whose board I sit, spends a great deal of time and energy "educating" the board about academic programs and strategic initiatives. Nevertheless, most trustees do not come even close to knowing as much about the universities they serve as they do about their own businesses. And yet, they govern these universities and select their leaders.

36. Here I follow the description of the case in David Bromwich, *Politics by Other Means: Higher Education and Group Thinking* (New Haven, Conn.: Yale University Press, 1994), 33–34.

37. Ibid., 45–50.

38. Derek Bok, "Reflections on Free Speech: An Open Letter to the Harvard Community," *Educational Record*, Winter 1985, 4, 6.

39. When we deal with the First Amendment in academic settings, we must remember that state and private universities are subject to very different constraints. Private universities are not regarded as "state actors," and consequently, constitutional constraints on free speech are not applicable to them in the legal sense. Public universities are subject to the same free-speech

doctrine that any citizen or legislative body must uphold. Thus we have few rulings on speech codes enacted at private universities. Of course, the moral or ethical dimensions of First Amendment doctrine for speech codes at private universities are a reasonable subject for discussion. I do not see the argument for distinguishing public and private universities as outweighing the value of applying First Amendment doctrine to private institutions. An example of the constraints placed on expression at a public institution can be seen in the policy on Discrimination and Discriminatory Harassment at the University of Michigan in 1989. It subjected people to discipline if, "in educational and academic centers, they engaged in: (1) Any behavior, verbal or physical, that stigmatizes or victimizes an individual on the basis of race, ethnicity, religion, sex, sexual orientation, creed, national origin, ancestry, age, marital status, handicap or Vietnam-era veteran status, and that a) involves an express or implied threat to an individual's academic efforts, employment, participation in University sponsored extra-curricular activities or personal safety; or b) has the purpose or reasonably foreseeable effect of interfering with an individual's academic efforts, employment, participation in University sponsored extra-curricular activities or person safety; or c) creates an intimidating, hostile, or demeaning environment for educational pursuits, employment or participation in University sponsored extra-curricular activities.'" See Kent Greenawalt, *Fighting Words: Individuals, Communities, and Liberties of Speech* (Princeton, N.J.: Princeton University Press, 1995), 72.

40. Ronald Dworkin, "A New Interpretation of Academic Freedom," in Louis Menand, ed., *The Future of Academic Freedom* (Chicago: University of Chicago Press, 1996), 196–197.

41. Henry Louis Gates Jr., "Critical Race Theory and Free Speech," in Louis Menand, ed., *The Future of Academic Freedom* (Chicago: University of Chicago Press, 1996), *146–155*. The example mentioned in the text is on p. 146.

42. Members of the committee have included Hannah Arendt, Saul Bellow, Allan Bloom, John Coetzee, Mircea Eliade, T. S. Eliot, François Furet, David Grene, Friederich Hayek, Leszek Kolakowski, Edward Levi, Paul Ricoeur, Charles Rosen, Harold Rosenberg, Edward Shils, Mark Strand, Karl J. Weintraub, and many others.

43. President Barack Obama, addressing members of the National Academy of Sciences, April 27, 2009.

44. Http://www.huffingtonpost.com/2009/08/01/obama-this-storm-will-pas_n_249268.html.

45. In his speech to a world audience in Cairo on June 4, 2009, Obama said, "All of us must recognize that education and innovation will be the currency of the twenty-first century. . . . On science and technology, we will launch a new fund to support technological development in Muslim-majority countries, and to help transfer ideas to the marketplace so they can create jobs."

46. Vivek Wadhwa, Anna Lee Saxenian, Richard Freeman, and Alex Salkever, *Losing the World's Best and Brightest: America's New Immigrant Entrepreneur*, Ewing Marion Kauffman Foundation, March 2009, Executive Summary.

47. Ibid., 3.

Index

AAAS. *See* American Association for the Advancement of Science

AAU. *See* Association of American Universities

AAUP. *See* American Association of University Professors

Abortion, 572n20

Aboul-Fadl, Tarek, 403

Abrams v. United States, 45, 49, 353, 557n17, 562n69

Academic Assistance Council, 79

Academic careers, interest in, 579n32

Academic community, vitality of, 68

Academic departments
  life cycle of, 67
  size of, 113

Academic disciplines, emergence of organized, 42–43

Academic discourse, goal of, 378

Academic dogmatism, 378–380

Academic freedom, 45–46, 63–64, 114, 555n2, 562n68, 562n70, 562–563n75, 563n77
  "balance," 354, 374, 444, 446
  Chinese university system and, 464, 465
  Cold War and, 349, 354–368
  defenses of, 49–50, 137, 346–347, 364–366, 385–386, 556n14, 560n51, 560n54
  government advisors and, 381
  Kirk and, 130
  peer review system and, 65
  in post-9/11 period, 350, 368–385
  pressure for ideological conformity and, 494–495
  structural relationships and, 383–384
  students and, 380

threats to, 47–52, 345–349, 351–368, 378–380, 562n72
  World War I and, 351–354

Academic literature, increase in, 176–178, 179–180

Academic mergers, 486–487

Academic Mind, The (Lazarsfeld and Thielens Jr.), 367

Academic societies, 526n68

Accelerators, 125, 251, 252, 261

ACLU. *See* American Civil Liberties Union

Adams, Henry C., 21

Adams, Herbert B., 21

Adams, John, 526n68

Addams, Jane, 336

Adelman, Jeremy, 561n59

Ad Hoc Committee to Defend the University, 369

Adler v. Board of Education, 558n28

Admissions process, 15, 26, 71, 72–73
  Chinese, 464
  French, 459–460

Adobe Systems, 283

Adorno, Theodor W., 81, 531n17

Advanced information technologies, 112–113

Adversary culture, 150, 538n5

Affirmative action, 561n62

Affluent Society, The (Galbraith), 317–318

African American Lives (television program), 341

African American studies, 555n32

Agassiz, Louis, 24

Agnew, Spiro T., 427

Agre, Peter, 396, 398

Agricultural programs, 29

Aiken, Howard, 278

Jonathan R. Cole is the former provost and dean of
faculty (1989–2003) of Columbia University and is
now the John Mitchell Mason Professor of the university. He is an elected member of the American Academy of Arts and Sciences, the American Philosophical
Society, and the Council on Foreign Relations.